ADOBE® COLDFUSION® 9
Getting Started

web application construction kit

VOLUME 2

Ben Forta and Raymond Camden

with Charlie Arehart, John C. Bland II, Ken Fricklas, Paul Hastings, Mike Nimer, Sarge Sargent, and Matt Tatam

Adobe ColdFusion 9 Web Application Construction Kit, Volume 2: Application Development

Ben Forta and Raymond Camden

with Charlie Arehart, John C. Bland II, Ken Fricklas, Paul Hastings, Mike Nimer, Sarge Sargent, and Matt Tatam

This Adobe Press book is published by Peachpit.
For information on Adobe Press books, contact:

Peachpit
1249 Eighth Street
Berkeley, CA 94710
510/524-2178
510/524-2221 (fax)

For the latest on Adobe Press books, go to www.adobepress.com
To report errors, please send a note to errata@peachpit.com
Peachpit is a division of Pearson Education

Series Editors: Rebecca Freed and Karen Reichstein
Editor: Judy Ziajka
Technical Reviewer: Brian Rinaldi
Production Editor: Tracey Croom
Compositor: Maureen Forys, Happenstance Type-O-Rama
Proofreader: Liz Welch
Indexer: Ron Strauss
Cover design: Charlene Charles-Will

ISBN 13: 978-0-321-67919-2
ISBN 10: 0-321-67919-9

Biographies

Ben Forta

Ben Forta is director of platform evangelism for Adobe Systems Incorporated and has more than two decades of experience in the computer software industry in product development, support, training, and marketing. Ben is the author of the best-selling ColdFusion book of all time, *Adobe ColdFusion Web Application Construction Kit*, as well as books on SQL, JavaServer Pages, Windows development, Regular Expressions, and more. More than half a million Ben Forta books have been printed in more than a dozen languages worldwide. Ben helped create the official Adobe ColdFusion training material, as well as the certification tests and study guides for those tests. He writes regular columns on ColdFusion and Internet development and spends a considerable amount of time lecturing and speaking on application development worldwide. Ben welcomes your email at ben@forta.com and invites you to visit his Web site at http://forta.com/ and his blog at http://forta.com/blog.

Ray Camden

Raymond Camden is a software consultant focusing on ColdFusion and RIA development. A longtime ColdFusion user, Raymond has worked on numerous ColdFusion books, including *Adobe ColdFusion Web Application Construction Kit*, and has contributed to the *Fusion Authority Quarterly Update* and the *ColdFusion Developers Journal*. He also presents at conferences and contributes to online webzines. He founded many community Web sites, including CFLib.org, ColdFusionPortal.org, and ColdFusionCookbook.org, and is the author of open source applications, including the popular BlogCFC (www.blogcfc.com) blogging application. Raymond is an Adobe Community Professional. He is the happily married proud father of three kids and is somewhat of a *Star Wars* nut. Raymond can be reached at his blog (www.coldfusionjedi.com) or via email at ray@camdenfamily.com.

Charlie Arehart

A veteran ColdFusion developer and troubleshooter since 1997 with more than 25 years in IT, Charlie Arehart is a longtime contributor to the ColdFusion community and a recognized Adobe Community Professional. As an independent consultant, he provides short-term troubleshooting and tuning assistance and training and mentoring for organizations of all sizes and ColdFusion experience levels (carehart.org/consulting). Besides running the 2000-member Online ColdFusion Meetup (coldfusionmeetup.com, an online CF user group), he hosts the UGTV repository of recorded presentations from hundreds of speakers (carehart.org/ugtv) and the CF411 site with more than 1000 tools and resources for ColdFusion developers (cf411.com). A certified Advanced ColdFusion Developer and an instructor for each version since ColdFusion 4, Charlie has spoken at each of the major ColdFusion conferences worldwide and is a contributor to all three volumes of *Adobe ColdFusion Web Application Construction Kit*.

John C. Bland II

John C. Bland II is founder of Katapult Media Inc. KM focuses on software and Web development with ColdFusion, the Adobe Flash platform, PHP, Java, the .NET platform, and Objective-C (iPhone and Mac OS X). At Katapult, John works diligently on FastKast, which continues to power numerous high-profile media players. John is also the CTO of UFrag.tv, where gamers go to broadcast. He is a contributor to the *Adobe ColdFusion Web Application Construction Kit* for ColdFusion 8 and 9 (Peachpit) as well as *Flex 4 in Action* (Manning). As an Adobe Community Professional, John continues give back to the community that helped mold him into the developer he is today. John blogs regularly on his blog, at www.johncblandii.com.

Paul Hastings

Paul Hastings, who after more than 20 years of IT work is now a perfectly fossilized geologist, is CTO at Sustainable GIS, a consulting firm specializing in geographic information systems (GIS) technology, ColdFusion Internet and intranet applications for the environment and natural resource markets, and of course, ColdFusion globalization. Paul is based in Bangkok, Thailand, but says that it's not nearly as exciting as it sounds. He can be reached at paul@sustainableGIS.com.

Mike Nimer

Mike Nimer is the director of engineering for nomee.com. Before joining nomee, Mike spent more than a decade building Web applications and the servers that run Web applications, as well as providing consulting and mentoring help for development teams around the world. Mike is a founding partner of Digital Primates IT Consulting Group, providing mentoring and development support on the Adobe RIA and ColdFusion platforms. Prior to founding Digital Primates, Mike was a member of the Adobe ColdFusion engineering team, where he was responsible for a number of key features, including PDF generation and the integration of Flex 1 and 2 with ColdFusion Server.

Matt Tatam

Matt Tatam has been developing and instructing in ColdFusion for more than 14 years. He has published articles and books on a number of Adobe technologies.

Acknowledgments

Ben Forta

Thanks to my co-authors, Ray Camden and Charlie Arehart, for their outstanding contributions. Although this book is affectionately known to thousands as "the Ben Forta book," it is, in truth, as much theirs as it is mine. An extra thank-you to Ray Camden for once again bravely accepting the role of lead co-author. Thanks to Brian Rinaldi for his thorough technical review. Thanks to Nancy Ruenzel and the crew at Peachpit for allowing me the creative freedom to build these books as I see fit. Thanks to Karen Reichstein and Rebecca Freed for bravely stepping in as series editors on this revision, and to Judy Ziajka for so ably shepherding this book through the publication process yet again. Thanks to the thousands of you who write to me with comments, suggestions, and criticism (thankfully not too much of the latter)—I do read each and every message (and even attempt to reply to them all, eventually), and all are appreciated. And last, but by no means least, a loving thank-you to my wife, Marcy, and our children for putting up with (and allowing) my often hectic work schedule. Their love and support make all that I do possible.

Raymond Camden

I'd like to thank Ben and Adobe Press for once again asking me to be a part of this incredible series. It is both an honor and a privilege! I'd also like to thank Adobe, specifically Adam Lehman and the engineers. Thanks for having me as part of the ColdFusion 9 beta process and allowing me to help shape the product I love. I promise I'll ask only half as many annoying questions for ColdFusion 10.

Charlie Arehart

First, I want to thank Ben for having me as a contributor to this series. With so many excellent authors among the current and past contributors, I really feel privileged. I also want to thank him for all his contributions to the community. Again, as with my fellow authors, I follow in the footsteps of giants. In that regard, I want to acknowledge the awesome ColdFusion community. I've so enjoyed being a part of it, as both beneficiary and contributor, since 1997. This book's for you.

John C. Bland II

I would like to thank my gorgeous wife, Season, for her continued support and love. You have been an amazing blessing in my life! Alex, you are the strongest eight-year-old I know. Through adversity you have stayed strong. I love you for that and am blessed you are my daughter. I also want to thank Ben, once again, for allowing me to be a part of a great book series. It humbles me each time. Adobe, thanks for providing a great product worth writing about! Lastly, I want to thank my family: Momma, Pac, Bubba, and Joe. You keep encouraging me in your own ways even though I keep catching the biggest and most fish, go figure. You all are major blessings in my life. To all of my nephews and nieces, aim higher than your mind can conceive, work extra hard, and one day you'll get there. I did.

Paul Hastings

I'd like to thank Ben Forta for the opportunity to once again work on this book as well to express my thanks to everybody on the ColdFusion team for doing such a fine job of building an excellent product.

Mike Nimer

I'd like to thank my wife, Angela, for being my own personal editor.

Dedications

Ben Forta

Dedicated to the ColdFusion community, a loyal and passionate group that I've been proud to call my friends for a decade and a half.

Ray Camden

As always, for my wife. Thank you, Jeanne, for your love and support.

Charlie Arehart

I'd like to dedicate this book to my wife of 10 years and the love of my life, Kim. I couldn't do all I do without your patience, support, and encouragement. Thank you, my love. God truly blessed me when He brought you into my life.

John C. Bland II

To my son, John III. You successfully stole my heart five years ago and continue to light up my life with laughter and love. Always be you and keep God first!

Paul Hastings

I would like to dedicate this book to my family: my wife, Mao, and our three children, Meow, Ning, and Joe, as well as my in-laws, Edwin and Pu, and their ever whirling-dervish daughter, Nadia.

Mike Nimer

For my wife, Angela, and son, Kayden.

Matt Tatam

To my family, who remind me daily what really matters in life.

CONTENTS AT A GLANCE

CONTENTS

IN THIS INTRODUCTION

Introduction

Who Should Use This Book

This book is written for anyone who wants to create cutting-edge Web-based applications.

If you are a Webmaster or Web page designer and want to create dynamic, data-driven Web pages, this book is for you. If you are an experienced database administrator who wants to take advantage of the Web to publish or collect data, this book is for you, too. If you are starting out creating your Web presence but know you want to serve more than just static information, this book will help get you there. If you have used ColdFusion before and want to learn what's new in ColdFusion 9, this book is also for you. Even if you are an experienced ColdFusion user, this book provides you with invaluable tips and tricks and also serves as the definitive ColdFusion developer's reference.

This book teaches you how to create real-world applications that solve real-world problems. Along the way, you acquire all the skills you need to design, implement, test, and roll out world-class applications.

How to Use This Book

This is the ninth edition of *ColdFusion Web Application Construction Kit*, and what started as a single volume a decade ago has had to grow to three volumes to adequately cover ColdFusion 9. The books are organized as follows:

- **Volume 1—*Adobe ColdFusion 9 Web Application Construction Kit, Volume 1: Getting Started (ISBN 0-321-66034-X)*** contains Chapters 1 through 21 and is targeted at beginning ColdFusion developers.
- **Volume 2—*Adobe ColdFusion 9 Web Application Construction Kit, Volume 2: Application Development (ISBN 0-321-67919-9)*** contains Chapters 22 through 45

and covers the ColdFusion features and language elements that are used by most ColdFusion developers most of the time. (Chapters 43, 44, and 45 are online.)

- **Volume 3—*Adobe ColdFusion 9 Web Application Construction Kit, Volume 3: Advanced Application Development (ISBN 0-321-67920-2)*** contains Chapters 46 through 71 and covers the more advanced ColdFusion functionality, including extensibility features, as well as security and management features that will be of interest primarily to those responsible for larger and more critical applications.

These books are designed to serve two different, but complementary, purposes.

First, as the books used by most ColdFusion developers, they are a complete tutorial covering everything you need to know to harness ColdFusion's power. As such, the books are divided into parts, or sections, and each section introduces new topics building on what has been discussed in prior sections. Ideally, you will work through these sections in order, starting with ColdFusion basics and then moving on to advanced topics. This is especially true for the first two books.

Second, the books are invaluable desktop references. The appendixes and accompanying Web site contain reference chapters that will be of use to you while developing ColdFusion applications. Those reference chapters are cross-referenced to the appropriate tutorial sections, so that step-by-step information is always readily available to you.

The following describes the contents of *Adobe ColdFusion 9 Web Application Construction Kit, Volume 2: Application Development*.

Part V: Creating Functions, Tags, and Components

Chapter 22, "Building User-Defined Functions," introduces the `<cffunction>` tag and explains how it can (and should) be used to extend the CFML language.

Chapter 23, "Creating Custom Tags," teaches you how to write your own tags to extend the CFML language—tags written in CFML itself.

Chapter 24, "Creating Advanced ColdFusion Components," continues exploring ColdFusion Components by introducing advanced topics, including persistence, encapsulation, and inheritance.

Part VI: ColdFusion Configuration and Performance

Chapter 25, "ColdFusion Server Configuration," revisits the ColdFusion Administrator, this time explaining every option and feature, while providing tips, tricks, and hints you can use to tweak your ColdFusion server.

Chapter 26, "Managing Threads," explains asynchronous development and how to use multithreaded processing to improve application performance.

Developers are always looking for ways to tweak their code, squeezing a bit more performance wherever possible. Chapter 27, "Improving Performance," provides tips, tricks, and techniques you can use to create applications that will always be snappy and responsive.

Part VII: Integrating with ColdFusion

Adobe PDF files are the standard for high-fidelity document distribution and online forms processing, and ColdFusion features extensive PDF integration, as explained in Chapter 28, "Working with PDF Files."

Chapter 29, "ColdFusion Image Processing," teaches you how to read, write, and manipulate image files using ColdFusion tags and functions.

Chapter 30, "Advanced ColdFusion-Powered Ajax," continues to explore Ajax user interface controls and concepts.

Chapter 31, "Integrating with Adobe Flex," introduces the basics of ColdFusion-powered Flex applications.

Chapter 32, "Integrating with Flash Data Services," discusses ColdFusion and Flash, exploring Flash Remoting, LiveCycle Data Services, Blaze DS, and more.

Chapter 33, "Building ColdFusion-Powered AIR Applications," teaches you how to use ColdFusion to build desktop applications, including applications that can be taken offline.

Chapter 34, "Creating Presentations," teaches you how to use ColdFusion to build dynamic Acrobat Connect presentations.

Chapter 35, "Full-Text Searching," introduces the Apache Solr search engine. Solr provides a mechanism that performs full-text searches of all types of data. The Solr engine is bundled with the ColdFusion Application Server, and the `<cfindex>` and `<cfsearch>` tags provide full access to Solr indexes from within your applications.

Chapter 36, "Event Scheduling," teaches you how to create tasks that run automatically and at timed intervals. You also learn how to dynamically generate static HTML pages using ColdFusion's scheduling technology.

Part VIII: Advanced ColdFusion Development

Chapter 37, "Using Stored Procedures," takes advanced SQL one step further by teaching you how to create stored procedures and how to integrate them into your ColdFusion applications.

Object Relational Mapping, or ORM, provides a powerful new way to build data-driven applications , with an emphasis on rapid development and simplified ongoing maintenance. Chapter 38, "Working with ORM," introduces this new ColdFusion 9 capability and explains how to fully use this powerful Hibernate-based technology.

Chapter 39, "Using Regular Expressions," introduces the powerful and flexible world of regular expression manipulation and processing. Regular expressions allow you to perform incredibly sophisticated and powerful string manipulations with simple one-line statements. ColdFusion supports the use of regular expressions in both find and replace functions.

Chapter 40, "ColdFusion Scripting," introduces the `<CFSCRIPT>` tag and language, which can be used to replace blocks of CFML code with a cleaner and more concise script-based syntax.

<CFSCRIPT> can also be used to create ColdFusion Components and user-defined functions, both of which are explained in this chapter, too.

Extensible Markup Language (XML) has become the most important means of exchanging and sharing data and services, and your ColdFusion applications can interact with XML data quite easily. Chapter 41, "Working with XML," explains what XML is and how to use it in your ColdFusion code.

Chapter 42, "Manipulating XML with XSLT and XPath," explains how to apply XSL transformations to XML data, as well as how to extract data from an XML document using XPath expressions.

The Internet is a global community, and multilingual and localized applications are becoming increasingly important. Chapter 43, "ColdFusion and Globalization" (online), explains how to build these applications in ColdFusion to attract an international audience.

Chapter 44, "Error Handling" (online), teaches you how to create applications that can both report errors and handle error conditions gracefully. You learn how to apply the <cftry> and <cfcatch> tags (and their supporting tags) and how to use these as part of a complete error-handling strategy.

Chapter 45, "Using the Debugger" (online), explores the ColdFusion Builder debugger and offers tips and tricks on how to best use this tool.

The Web Site

The book's accompanying Web site contains everything you need to start writing ColdFusion applications, including:

- Links to obtain ColdFusion 9
- Links to obtain Adobe ColdFusion Builder
- Source code and databases for all the examples in this book
- Electronic versions of some chapters
- An errata sheet, should one be required
- An online discussion forum

The book Web page is at `http://www.forta.com/books/0321679199/`.

And with that, turn the page and start reading. In no time, you'll be creating powerful applications powered by ColdFusion 9.

PART 5

Creating Functions, Tags, and Components

CHAPTER 22

Building User-Defined Functions

IN THIS CHAPTER

This chapter introduces you to the world of user-defined functions (UDFs). You can create your own functions to do just about anything you can think of. User-defined functions are easy to write and even easier to use. You use them just like ColdFusion's built-in functions.

Thinking About Extending CFML

Throughout this book, you have been learning how to use CFML's built-in tags and functions to produce dynamic Web pages. You have used tags like `<cfquery>` and `<cfoutput>` to display information stored in databases, and you have used functions like `uCase()` and `dateFormat()` to further tweak your work.

For the next few chapters, you will be exploring how to *extend* the CFML language by creating your own tags, functions, and components. Once you see how easy it is to do so, you will find that you can make your application code much more elegant and maintainable. It's a very exciting topic. It's even fun.

There are four basic ways in which you can extend ColdFusion:

- **User-Defined Functions.** As the name implies, UDFs are functions that you create yourself. If you feel that some function is missing from ColdFusion's list of built-in ones, or that a particular function would be especially handy for an application you're building, you can just make the function yourself. UDFs are what this chapter is all about.
- **Custom Tags.** UDFs let you make your own functions, but Custom Tags allow you to create your own CFML tags. For more information, see Chapter 23, "Creating Custom Tags."
- **ColdFusion Components (CFCs).** CFCs are conceptually similar to Custom Tags, but imply a more structured, object-oriented manner of programming. CFCs are also at the heart of ColdFusion's Flash and Web Services integration. See Chapter 24, "Creating Advanced ColdFusion Components," for details.

- **CFX Tags.** You can also write your own CFX tags. You can write the code to make the tag do its work in either Java or C++. For more information about writing CFX tags, see the ColdFusion 9 documentation.

NOTE

If you wish, you can also extend ColdFusion 9 by writing JSP tag libraries, COM/ActiveX controls, Java classes or JavaBeans, and more. The list above simply summarizes the extensibility methods specific to ColdFusion.

In this chapter, I will concentrate on the first option, user-defined functions. I recommend that you also read Chapters 23 and 24 so that you know the extensibility options available to you. In many cases, you can get a particular task done by creating a tag or a function, so it helps to have an understanding of both.

Functions Turn Input into Output

Think about the CFML functions you already know. Almost all of them accept at least one piece of information, do something with the information internally, and then return some kind of result. For instance, ColdFusion's `uCase()` function accepts one piece of information (a string), performs an action (converts it to uppercase), then returns a result.

So you can think of most functions as being like little engines, or mechanisms on an assembly line. Some functions accept more than one piece of information (more than one argument), but the point is still the same: almost all functions are about accepting input and creating some kind of corresponding output. A function's *arguments* provide the input, and its output is passed back as the function's *return value.*

As the designer of your own functions, you get to specify the input by declaring one or more arguments. You also get to pass back whatever return value you wish.

Building Your First UDF

As a ColdFusion developer for Orange Whip Studios, you often need to display movie titles. It's easy enough to write a `<cfquery>` tag that retrieves the title for a particular movie based on its ID, but that can get repetitive if you need to do it on many different pages. Also, you must keep the database's design in mind at all times, instead of just concentrating on the task at hand.

You find yourself wishing you had a function called `getFilmTitle()` that would return the title of whatever `FilmID` you passed to it. So, for example, if you wanted to display the title of film number 8, you could just use this:

```
<cfoutput>#getFilmTitle(8)#</cfoutput>
```

Well, it turns out that ColdFusion makes it remarkably easy to create this function. And you get to create it using the good old `<cfquery>` tag you already know and love. All you need to do is to surround the `<cfquery>` with a few extra tags!

Let's take a look at what it will take to put this new function into place.

NOTE

You can create UDFs using either tag notation or <cfscript>. Both provide the same functionality. This chapter uses tags just to keep things simple.

Basic Steps

To create a user-defined function, you follow four basic steps:

1. Start with a pair of <cffunction> tags. You will insert all the code needed to make the function do its work between the opening and closing <cffunction> tags.
2. Add a <cfargument> tag for each argument your function will be using as input. If you wish, you can specify some arguments as required and others as optional.
3. After the <cfargument> tags, add whatever CFML code is needed to make your function do its work. Feel free to use whatever tags and functions you want in this section.
4. The last step is to use the <cfreturn> tag to return the result of whatever computations or processing your function does. In other words, you use <cfreturn> to specify what your function's output should be.

I could now introduce the syntax and attributes for each of these new tags, but in this case it's easier if we just jump right in so you can see how the tags work together.

Here is the code needed to create the `getFilmTitle()` user-defined function:

```
<cffunction name="getFilmTitle">
 <cfargument name="filmID" type="numeric" required="Yes">

<!--- Get the film's title --->
 <cfquery name="getFilm" datasource="#datasource#"
 cachedwithin="#createTimespan(0,1,0,0)#">
SELECT MovieTitle FROM Films
 WHERE FilmID =
 <cfqueryparam cfsqltype="cf_sql_integer" value="#arguments.filmID#">
 </cfquery>

 <!--- Return the film's title --->
 <cfreturn getFilm.MovieTitle>
</cffunction>
```

As you can see, all three UDF-related tags are used here. First, a pair of <cffunction> tags surrounds the code for the whole function. Next, a <cfargument> tag at the top of the function defines what its input should be. Finally, a <cfreturn> tag at the end returns the function's output. Nearly all UDFs are constructed using this basic pattern.

Everything else between the <cffunction> tags is the actual CFML code that will be executed each time the function is invoked. In this simple example, the only processing that needs to occur to generate the function's output is a simple database query.

As you can see, a special `ARGUMENTS` scope will contain the value of each argument when the function is actually used. So, if the number `8` is passed to the function's `filmID` argument, then the value of the ARGUMENTS.filmID variable will be 8. In this case, ARGUMENTS.filmID dynamically creates the SQL that will retrieve the appropriate film title from the database. All that's left to do is to return the title as the function's output, using the <cfreturn> tag. It's that easy.

Using the Function

Once you've written a UDF, you can use it just like any other function. For instance, after the <cffunction> code shown above, you can use the function to display the title for a film, like this:

```
<cfoutput>#getFilmTitle(8)#</cfoutput>
```

When ColdFusion encounters the function, it will run the code between the corresponding <cffunction> tags. For the getFilmTitle() function, this means running the <cfquery> tag and returning the film title that gets retrieved from the database.

Of course, you can provide input to the function's arguments dynamically, as with any other function. For instance, if you have a form field named showFilmID, you could use code like the following to display the title corresponding to the ID number that the user provides on the form:

```
<cfoutput>#getFilmTitle(FORM.showFilmID)#</cfoutput>
```

You can also use UDFs in <cfset> tags or any other place where you would use a CFML expression. For instance, the following <cfset> tag would create a variable called myFilmInUpperCase, which is the uppercase version of the selected film's title:

```
<cfset myFilmInUpperCase = uCase(getFilmTitle(FORM.showFilmID))>
```

UDF Tag Syntax

Now that you've seen a simple example of how the code for a user-defined function is structured, let's take a closer look at the attributes supported by each of the tags involved: <cffunction>, <cfargument>, and <cfreturn>. Tables 22.1, 22.2, and 22.3 show the syntax supported by these three important tags.

Table 22.1 <cffunction> Tag Syntax

ATTRIBUTE	PURPOSE
name	The name of the new function. To actually use the function, you will call it using the name you provide here. The name needs to be a valid CFML identifier, which means it can contain only letters, numbers, and underscores, and its first character must be a letter.
returnType	Optional. You can use this attribute to indicate the type of information that the function will return, such as string, numeric, date, and so on. This attribute is optional, but it helps ensure your UDF runs correctly and should be used.
output	Optional. While most UDFs will simply return a value, a UDF can actually output data as well. This shouldn't be used very often, so in general you should set this value to False. Setting it to False also reduces the white space generated by a call to the UDF.

NOTE

The <cffunction> tag actually supports several more attributes, which are relevant only when the tag is used within the context of a ColdFusion Component. You will learn about the other <cffunction> attributes in Chapter 24.

Table 22.2 <cfargument> Tag Syntax

ATTRIBUTE	PURPOSE
`name`	The name of the argument. Within the function, a variable will be created in the `ARGUMENTS` scope that contains the value passed to the argument when the function is actually used.
`type`	Optional. The data type that should be supplied to the argument when the function is actually used. If you supply a `TYPE`, ColdFusion will display an error message if someone tries to use the function with the wrong kind of input.
`required`	Optional. Whether the argument is required for the function to be able to do its work. The default is `No` (i.e., not required).
`default`	Optional. For optional arguments (that is, when `required="No"`), this determines what the value of the argument should be if a value isn't passed to the function when it is actually used.

One of the neatest things about the UDF framework is how easy it is to create functions that have required arguments, optional arguments, or both:

- If a `<cfargument>` tag uses `required="Yes"`, the argument must be provided when the function is actually used. If the argument isn't provided at run time, ColdFusion will display an error message.
- If `required="No"` and a `default` attribute have been specified, the function can be called with or without the argument at run time. Go ahead and use the `ARGUMENTS` scope to refer to the value of the argument. If a value is provided when the function is actually used, that value will be what is present in the `ARGUMENTS` scope. If not, the `default` value will be what is in the `ARGUMENTS` scope.
- If `required="No"` and the `default` attribute has *not* been specified, the argument is still considered optional. If the function is called without the argument, there will be no corresponding value in the `ARGUMENTS` scope. You can use the `isDefined()` function to determine whether the argument was provided at run time. For instance, you would use `isDefined("ARGUMENTS.filmID")` within a function's code to determine if an optional `filmID` argument was provided.

You will see optional arguments at work in Listing 22.4 later in this chapter.

NOTE

By "run time," I just mean "at the time when the function is actually used." Programmers often use this term to refer to the actual moment of execution for a piece of code.

Table 22.3 <cfreturn> Tag Syntax

RETURN VALUE	PURPOSE
(any expression)	The <cfreturn> tag doesn't have any attributes per se. Instead, you place whatever string, number, date, variable, or other expression you want directly within the <cfreturn> tag.

For instance, if you wanted your function to always return the letter A, you would use

```
<cfreturn "A">
```

If you wanted your function to return the current time, you would use

```
<cfreturn timeFormat(now())>
```

You can use complex expressions as well, like this:

```
<cfreturn "The current time is: " & timeFormat(now())>
```

Using Local Variables

To get its work done, a UDF often needs to use <cfset> or other tags that create variables. Most of the time, you don't want these variables to be visible to pages that use the function.

Why Local Variables Are Important

Consider the getFilmTitle() function, which you have already seen. The code for this function runs a query named getFilm within the body of the function (that is, between the <cffunction> tags). That query returns only one column, MovieTitle. You probably don't want that query object to continue existing after the function is called. After all, what if someone already has a <cfquery> called getFilm that selects *all* columns from the Films table, then calls the UDF? That's right—after the UDF runs, the function's version of the getFilm query (which has only one column) will overwrite the one that the page created before calling the function, and any subsequent code that refers to getFilms probably won't work as expected.

NOTE

Developers often refer to this type of situation as a "variable collision" or a "namespace collision." Whatever the name, it's bad news, because it can lead to unpredictable or surprising results, especially if you are using a UDF that someone else wrote.

What you need is some way to tell ColdFusion that a particular variable should be visible only within the context of the <cffunction> block. Such a variable is called a *local variable.*

How to Declare a Local Variable

It's easy to create local variables in a UDF. One way is to *declare* the variable as a local variable, using the <cfset> tag and the var keyword, like this:

```
<cfset var myLocalVariable = "Hello">
```

The `var` keyword tells ColdFusion that the variable should cease to exist when the `<cffunction>` block ends, and that it shouldn't interfere with any other variables elsewhere that have the same name.

Here are some rules about local variables:

- You can declare as many local variables as you want. Just use a separate `<cfset>` for each one, using the `var` keyword each time.
- It isn't possible to declare a local variable without giving it a value. That is, `<cfset var myLocalVariable>` alone isn't valid. There has to be an equals sign (=) in there, with an initial value for the variable. You can always change the value later in the function's code, so just set the variable to an empty string if you're not ready to give it its real value yet.

To make the `getFilmTitle()` function work correctly so that the `getFilm` query object is discarded after the function does its work, you need to add a `<cfset>` tag at the top of the function body, declaring the `getFilm` variable as a local variable, like so:

```
<cffunction name="getFilmTitle">
 <cfargument name="filmID" type="numeric" required="Yes">

 <!--- This variable is for this function's use only --->
 <cfset var getFilm = "">

 <!--- Get the film's title --->
 <cfquery name="getFilm" datasource="#datasource#"
 cachedwithin="#createTimespan(0,1,0,0)#">
 SELECT MovieTitle FROM Films
 WHERE FilmID =
 <cfqueryparam cfsqltype="cf_sql_integer" value="#arguments.filmID#">
 </cfquery>

 <!--- Return the film's title --->
 <cfreturn getFilm.MovieTitle>
</cffunction>
```

Because the `<cfset>` uses the `var` keyword, ColdFusion now understands that it should discard the `getFilm` variable after the function executes, and that it shouldn't interfere with any variables elsewhere that have the same name.

NOTE

This `<cfset>` sets the `GetFilm` variable to an empty string. It doesn't matter what this initial value is, since the variable will be set to the results of `<cfquery>` on the next line. In other strongly typed languages, you might use an initial value of `null`, but CFML doesn't support the notion of a null value. Every variable always has some kind of value.

Another way to create a local variable is to explicitly use the `local` scope. The `local` scope represents all variables that exist only for the duration of the call to the UDF. The variable we created with the `var` keyword, `GetFilm`, automatically exists in that scope. We can skip the declaration and simply rename our variable to include the local scope. Here is a new version of the UDF using this syntax:

```
<cffunction name="getFilmTitle">
 <cfargument name="filmID" type="numeric" required="Yes">

<!--- Get the film's title --->
 <cfquery name="local.getFilm" datasource="ows" cachedwithin="#createTimespan(0,1,0,0
)#">
 SELECT MovieTitle FROM Films
 WHERE FilmID =
 <cfqueryparam cfsqltype="cf_sql_integer" value="#arguments.filmID#">
 </cfquery>

 <!--- Return the film's title --->
 <cfreturn local.getFilm.MovieTitle>
</cffunction>
```

Notice that I both renamed the query as `local.getFilm` and updated the `<cfreturn>` tag. So which "style" is better? The choice really is a matter of personal preference. The critical point to remember is that if you do not use the `var` keyword or specify the local scope, your variables will leak out of the UDF.

Where to Save Your UDFs

Now that you have seen what a completed `<cffunction>` block looks like, you may be wondering where exactly you are supposed to place it. The answer is simple: you can place your `<cffunction>` blocks anywhere you want, in any ColdFusion template. Your code can make use of the function anywhere after it encounters the `<cffunction>` block.

Creating and Using a UDF in the Same File

For instance, Listing 22.1 is a template that uses the `<cffunction>` block shown earlier to create the `getFilmTitle()` function, then uses the function to display a list of films (Figure 22.1).

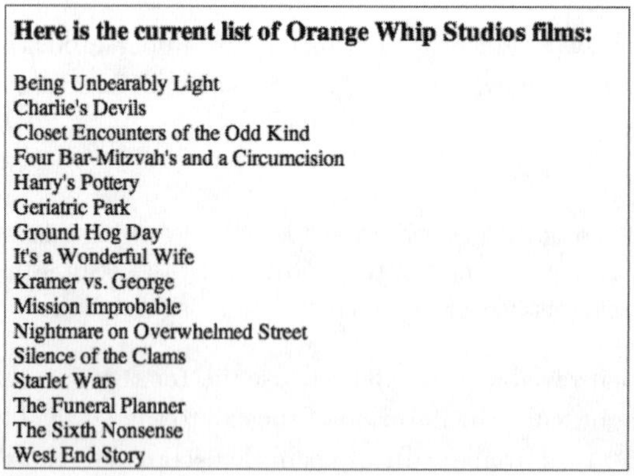

Figure 22.1

The `getFilmTitle()` function makes it easy to display film titles.

Here is the current list of Orange Whip Studios films:

Being Unbearably Light
Charlie's Devils
Closet Encounters of the Odd Kind
Four Bar-Mitzvah's and a Circumcision
Harry's Pottery
Geriatric Park
Ground Hog Day
It's a Wonderful Wife
Kramer vs. George
Mission Improbable
Nightmare on Overwhelmed Street
Silence of the Clams
Starlet Wars
The Funeral Planner
The Sixth Nonsense
West End Story

Listing 22.1 `FilmList.cfm`—Creating and Using a UDF

```
<!---
 Filename: FilmList.cfm
 Created by: Nate Weiss (NMW)
 Please Note Displays a list of films
--->

<!--- Function: getFilmTitle() --->
<!--- Returns the title of a film, based on FilmID --->
<cffunction name="getFilmTitle">
 <!--- One argument: FilmID --->
 <cfargument name="filmID" type="numeric" required="Yes">

 <!--- This variable is for this function's use only --->
 <cfset var getFilm = "">

 <!--- Get the film's title --->
 <cfquery name="getFilm" datasource="ows"
 cachedwithin="#createTimespan(0,1,0,0)#">
 SELECT MovieTitle FROM Films
WHERE FilmID =
 <cfqueryparam cfsqltype="cf_sql_integer" value="#arguments.filmID#">
 </cfquery>

 <!--- Return the film's title --->
 <cfreturn getFilm.MovieTitle>
</cffunction>

<!--- Get a list of all FilmIDs --->
<cfquery name="getFilms" datasource="ows">
 SELECT FilmID
 FROM Films
</cfquery>

<html>
<head><title>Film List</title></head>
<body>
 <h3>Here is the current list of Orange Whip Studios films:</h3>

 <!--- Now it is extremely easy to display a list of film links --->
 <cfoutput query="getFilms">
 #getFilmTitle(FilmID)#<br>
 </cfoutput>

</body>
</html>
```

Saving UDFs in Separate Files for Easy Reuse

In Listing 22.1, you saw how to create and use a user-defined function, all in the same ColdFusion template. While the function works just fine, it doesn't really make anything any easier. You wouldn't want to have to retype that function every time you wanted to display a movie's title.

Most of the time, you'll want to keep your UDFs in separate files to make them easy to reuse in your various ColdFusion pages. For instance, it would probably be a good idea to create a file named `FilmFunctions.cfm` that contains the `getFilmTitle()` function.

Later, as you create other film-related functions, you could put them in the same file. Once you have this file in place, you can simply include the file with a `<cfinclude>` tag to use the function it contains.

Listing 22.2 shows how to create such a file. As you can see, this is the same `<cffunction>` block shown in Listing 22.1; here it's simply dropped into its own template.

Listing 22.2 `FilmFunctions1.cfm`—Placing a UDF in a Separate File

```
<!---
 Filename: FilmFunctions1.cfm
 Created by: Nate Weiss (NMW)
 Purpose: Creates a library of user-defined functions
 related to films
--->

<!--- Function: GetFilmTitle() --->
<!--- Returns the title of a film, based on FilmID --->
<cffunction name="getFilmTitle">
 <!--- One argument: FilmID --->
 <cfargument name="filmID" type="numeric" required="Yes">

 <!--- This variable is for this function's use only --->
 <cfset var getFilm = "">

 <!--- Get the film's title --->
 <cfquery name="getFilm" datasource="ows"
 cachedwithin="#createTimespan(0,1,0,0)#">
 SELECT MovieTitle FROM Films
WHERE FilmID =
 <cfqueryparam cfsqltype="cf_sql_integer" value="#arguments.filmID#">
 </cfquery>

 <!--- Return the film's title --->
 <cfreturn getFilm.MovieTitle>
</cffunction>
```

Once you have a file like this in place, you just need to include the file via a simple `<cfinclude>` tag to be able to use the function(s) it contains. For instance, Listing 22.3 is a revised version of the Film List template from Listing 22.1. The results in the browser are exactly the same, but the code is much cleaner.

Listing 22.3 `FilmList2.cfm`—Using UDFs Stored in a Separate File

```
<!---
 Filename: FilmList2.cfm
 Created by: Nate Weiss (NMW)
 Purpose: Displays a list of films
--->

<!--- Include the set of film-related user-defined functions --->
```

Listing 22.3 (continued)

```
<cfinclude template="FilmFunctions1.cfm">

<!--- Get a list of all FilmIDs --->
<cfquery name="getFilms" datasource="ows">
 SELECT FilmID
 FROM Films
 ORDER BY MovieTitle
</cfquery>

<html>
<head><title>Film List</title></head>
<body>
 <h3>Here is the current list of Orange Whip Studios films:</h3>

 <!--- Now it is extremely easy to display a list of film links --->
 <cfoutput query="getFilms">
 #getFilmTitle(FilmID)#<br>
 </cfoutput>

</body>
</html>
```

Reusing Code Saves Time and Effort

The `<cfinclude>` tag at the top of Listing 22.3 allows you to use the `getFilmTitle()` function later in the same template. You could use this same `<cfinclude>` tag in any other templates that need to use the function.

In other words, once you have created a user-defined function, it is incredibly easy to reuse it wherever you need. This makes your work easier and more efficient. And if you ever have to make a correction in the `getFilmTitle()` function, you only need to do so in one place. This makes your project much easier to maintain over time.

Creating Libraries of Related UDFs

ColdFusion developers often refer to a file of conceptually related UDFs as a *UDF library*. Actually, there are no specific rules about what kinds of UDFs you can collect into a library, but it makes sense to group your UDFs into files according to some kind of common concept.

In fact, you have already seen a small UDF library: the `FilmFunctions1.cfm` file shown in Listing 22.2. It contains only one function, but you can still think of it as a library that you could expand to include other film-related functions in the future.

Designing the UDF Library

Let's say your team needs some more film-related functions added to the `FilmFunctions` library. Sounds like fun! You decide to create a new version of the library file, called `FilmFunctions2.cfm`. You sit down with the other members of your team, and come up with the list of functions shown in Table 22.4.

Table 22.4 Functions in the FilmFunctions UDF Library

FUNCTION	PURPOSE
getFilmsQuery()	This function returns a query object that contains information about films in the database. It supports one argument called filmID, which is optional. If the function is called without filmID, the function simply executes a <cfquery> that gets information about all films from the database and returns the query object. If a filmID is provided, however, the query object will only contain one row, corresponding to the specified film.
getFilmTitle()	This behaves in the same way as the getFilmTitle() function created in the first version of the library file. It takes one argument, filmID, which is the ID of the film to get the title for. Internally, this function can make use of the getFilmsQuery() function.
getFilmURL()	This function is similar to getFilmTitle(). It takes one argument, filmID. Instead of returning the film's title, however, it returns a standardized URL to a page called ShowFilm.cfm containing details about the film. The function includes the film's ID number in the URL so the ShowFilm.cfm template can display information about the correct film.
makeFilmPopupLink()	This function also accepts a filmID argument. It returns the HTML code needed to display a link for the selected film. When the link is clicked, a pop-up window appears with some basic information about the selected film. Internally, this function calls a general-purpose UDF function called JavaScriptPopupLink(), discussed later in this section.

Listing 22.4 shows the code for the new FilmFunctions2.cfm UDF library.

Listing 22.4 FilmFunctions2.cfm—A UDF Function Library

```
<!---
 Filename: FilmFunctions2.cfm
 Created by: Nate Weiss (NMW)
 Purpose: Creates a library of user-defined functions
 related to films
--->

<!--- Function: getFilmsQuery() --->
<!--- Returns a query object from the Films table in the database --->
<cffunction name="getFilmsQuery" returntype="query" output="false">
 <!--- Optional argument: FilmID --->
 <cfargument name="filmID" type="numeric" required="No">

 <!--- This variable is for this function's use only --->
 <cfset var filmsQuery = "">

 <!--- Query the database for information about all films --->
 <!--- The query is cached to improve performance --->
 <cfquery name="filmsQuery" datasource="ows"
  cachedwithin="#createTimespan(0,1,0,0)#">
 SELECT * FROM Films
  <!--- If a FilmID argument was provided, select that film only --->
```

Listing 22.4 (continued)

```
 <cfif isDefined("arguments.filmID")>
WHERE FilmID =
 <cfqueryparam cfsqltype="cf_sql_integer" value="#arguments.filmID#">
 <!--- Otherwise, get information for all films, in alphabetical order --->
 <cfelse>
 ORDER BY MovieTitle
 </cfif>
 </cfquery>

 <!--- Return the query --->
 <cfreturn filmsQuery>
</cffunction>

<!--- Function: getFilmTitle() --->
<!--- Returns the title of a film, based on FilmID --->
<cffunction name="getFilmTitle" returnType="string" output="false">
 <!--- One argument: FilmID --->
 <cfargument name="filmID" type="numeric" required="Yes">

 <!--- This variable is for this function's use only --->
 <cfset var getFilm = "">

 <!--- Get a query object of all films in the database --->
 <cfset getFilm = getFilmsQuery(arguments.filmID)>

 <!--- Return the film's title --->
 <cfreturn getFilm.MovieTitle>
</cffunction>

<!--- Function: getFilmURL() --->
<!--- Returns the URL to a film's detail page, based on FilmID --->
<cffunction name="getFilmURL" returnType="string" output="false">
 <!--- One argument: FilmID --->
 <cfargument name="filmID" type="numeric" required="Yes">

 <!--- Return the appropriate URL --->
 <cfreturn "ShowFilm.cfm?FilmID=#arguments.filmID#">
</cffunction>

<!--- Include another UDF function library --->
<!--- This one creates the JavaScriptPopupLink() function --->
<cfinclude template="SimpleJavaScriptFunctions.cfm">


<!--- Function: MakeFilmPopupLink() --->
<!--- Returns an HTML link for a film, based on FilmID --->
<cffunction name="MakeFilmPopupLink" returnType="string" output="false">
 <!--- One argument: FilmID --->
 <cfargument name="filmID" type="numeric" required="Yes">

 <!--- Return a link for the film --->
 <cfreturn javaScriptPopupLink(getFilmURL(ARGUMENTS.filmID),
 getFilmTitle(ARGUMENTS.FilmID))>
</cffunction>
```

Each of the `<cffunction>` blocks in Listing 22.4 is fairly simple. It's interesting to note here that UDFs can call other UDFs in the same file. They can even call functions in other files, as long as the `<cfinclude>` tag has been used to include the other files.

Let's take a closer look at each one of these new UDFs individually:

- For the `getFilmsQuery()`, note that the `<cfargument>` tag includes a `required="No"` attribute, which means the argument is optional. The first thing this function does is execute a `<cfquery>` tag to obtain film information from the database. Within the query, a simple `isDefined("ARGUMENTS.filmID")` test is used to find out whether the optional `filmID` argument has been provided when the function is actually used. If so, a `WHERE` clause is dynamically included in the SQL statement (so the query retrieves just the information about the specified film).
- The `getFilmTitle()` function has been reworked a bit, mainly to demonstrate that UDFs can call any other UDFs in the same file. Now, instead of using a `<cfquery>` tag within the body of the function, the new, convenient `getFilmsQuery()` function is used instead. Note that the `filmID` argument provided to `getFilmTitle()` is in turn passed to `getFilmsQuery()` internally, which means that the returned query contains data about the specified film only. It is then a simple matter to return the film's title using the `<cfreturn>` tag.
- The `getFilmURL()` function is the simplest of all the UDFs in this library. It just returns a URL that points to a template called `ShowFilm.cfm`, passing along the specified `filmID` as a URL parameter. The nice thing about this function is that it abstracts the idea of a film's Detail Page. If the URL that people should go to for more information about a film changes in the future, you can just edit the function in one place, rather than in multiple places throughout the application.
- The `makeFilmPopupLink()` function is interesting because it calls three functions internally. It uses both `getFilmURL()` and `getFilmTitle()` to get the URL and title of the specified film, respectively. It then passes the returned values to the `javaScriptPopupLink()` function, created in a separate UDF library file called `SimpleJavaScriptFunctions.cfm`. You will see the code for this function in a moment. For now, just take it on faith that the function returns the HTML and JavaScript code needed to create a link that opens a pop-up window.

Putting the UDF Library to Use

Listing 22.5 shows a new version of the Film List page (see Listings 22.1 and 22.3 for the previous versions). This version gets its work done with just a few lines of code, and it's more functional, too! Now, when the user clicks a film's title, a small pop-up window displays more information about that film (Figure 22.2).

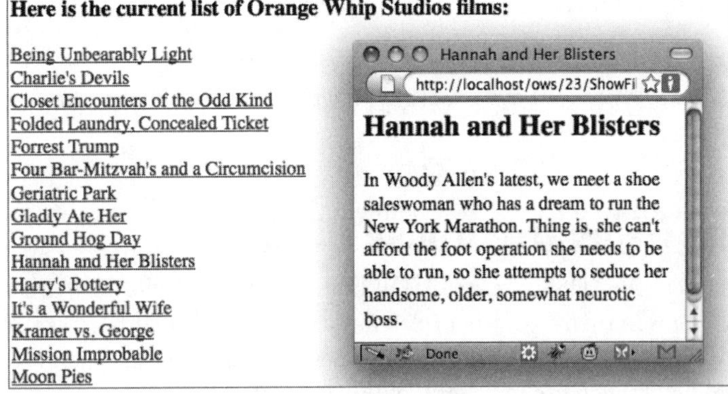

Figure 22.2

UDFs can encapsulate scripting, HTML, or other lower-level code.

Listing 22.5 `FilmList3.cfm`—Using Several UDFs Together

```
<!---
 Filename: FilmList3.cfm
 Created by: Nate Weiss (NMW)
 Purpose: Displays a list of films
--->

<!--- Include the set of film-related user-defined functions --->
<cfinclude template="FilmFunctions2.cfm">

<!--- Get a query object about films in database --->
<cfset getFilms = getFilmsQuery()>

<html>
<head><title>Film List</title></head>
<body>
 <h3>Here is the current list of Orange Whip Studios films:</h3>

 <!--- Now it is extremely easy to display a list of film links --->
 <cfoutput query="getFilms">
 #makeFilmPopupLink(getFilms.FilmID)#<br>
 </cfoutput>
</body>
</html>
```

First, a `<cfinclude>` tag is used to include the new library of film-related UDFs. That makes it possible to call the `getFilmsQuery()` function to get a query object full of information about the films in the company's database. The value returned by the function is assigned to the local `getFilms` variable. From that point on, the `getFilms` query object can be used just as if there was an actual `<cfquery name="getFilms">` tag on the page.

Now it just takes a simple call to `makeFilmPopupLink()` to create a pop-up–enabled link for each film in the `getFilms` query. Through the magic of the UDF framework, that one line of code looks up the movie's title, obtains the correct URL to display details about the film, and generates the JavaScript code needed to pop up the detail page in a small window. And it's all eminently reusable.

Don't user-defined functions rock?

Note

The file loaded by the pop-up window, `ShowFilm.cfm`, can be found on the Web site and downloaded with the rest of the book's code.

Creating General-Purpose UDFs

The functions in the `FilmFunctions` UDF library (refer to Table 22.4) are all related to the film concept, which is in turn somewhat related to the Films table in the `ows` database. As such, the library is really of interest only to the developers working on the Orange Whip Studios site. It's not going to be of much use to other ColdFusion developers.

It is, however, possible to create user-defined functions that have no ties to a particular application. You can think of such functions as *general-purpose functions*. They are useful for many different types of applications.

For instance, consider the `javaScriptPopupLink()` function used internally by the `FilmFunctions` library in Listing 22.4. That function isn't expecting any input that is specific to Orange Whip Studios or any other type of application. And its purpose—to create pop-up windows easily—might come in handy in any Web-based application.

Things to Consider

You don't need to do anything special to create a general-purpose function. Go ahead and use the same `<cffunction>`, `<cfargument>`, and `<cfreturn>` syntax you have already learned about. Just bear these things in mind as you go along.

Keep the list of arguments as short as possible. ColdFusion will let you create UDFs with many, many arguments, but such functions quickly become unwieldy. If you feel you need to have lots of arguments, consider creating a CFML Custom Tag instead, as discussed in the next chapter.

Keep code reuse in mind. If the problem at hand has both an application-specific aspect and a general-purpose aspect, try to isolate the two parts of the problems in two different functions. For instance, the problem of displaying a pop-up window about a film has an application-specific aspect (the film) and a general-purpose aspect (the pop-up window). By creating two different functions, you can reuse the pop-up aspect in situations that don't have anything to do with films.

In Chapters 23 and 24, you will learn how to create your own Custom Tags and Components (CFCs) as well as functions. Custom Tags are significantly more powerful and flexible than custom functions. Try to use UDFs for simple matters, especially quick retrieval and formatting. Use Custom Tags and Components for more involved processes, especially those you can think of as discrete actions rather than simple "massaging."

Writing the `SimpleJavaScriptFunctions` Library

As an example of a general-purpose UDF library, let's consider the `SimpleJavaScriptFunctions.cfm` library we used earlier, in Listing 22.4. Presently, this library contains only one function, `javaScriptPopupLink()`, which is responsible for creating a link that opens a pop-up window when clicked. This function supports six arguments, as listed in Table 22.5.

Table 22.5 `javaScriptPopupLink()` Function Syntax

ARGUMENT	DESCRIPTION
`linkURL`	Required. The URL for the page that should appear in the pop-up window when the user clicks the link.
`linkText`	Required. The text of the link—that is, the text the user will click to open the pop-up window. This text will also appear in the browser's status bar when the pointer hovers over the link.
`popupWidth`	Optional. The width of the pop-up window, in pixels. If this argument isn't provided, a default width of `300` is used.
`popupHeight`	Optional. The height of the pop-up window, in pixels. If this argument isn't provided, a default width of `200` is used.
`popupTop`	Optional. The vertical position of the pop-up window. If this argument isn't provided, a default value of `200` is used.
`popupLeft`	Optional. The horizontal position of the pop-up window. If this argument isn't provided, a default value of `300` is used.

NOTE

The `popupWidth`, `popupHeight`, `popupTop`, and `popupLeft` arguments correspond to the `width`, `height`, `top`, and `left` values supported by the JavaScript `window.open()` method. Consult a JavaScript reference for details

The function uses all these pieces of information to assemble the HTML code for an anchor element (that is, an `<a href>` tag) containing the appropriate JavaScript code to get the desired effect. The code is returned as the function's result (as a string).

Listing 22.6 is the ColdFusion code required to create `javaScriptPopupLink()`.

NOTE

The goal here isn't to teach you about JavaScript (that would take a whole book in itself), but rather to show you how you can distill something like JavaScript code and package it into a UDF for your ColdFusion pages. The nice thing about this kind of abstraction is that people can use the UDF without needing to understand the JavaScript code it generates.

Listing 22.6 `SimpleJavaScriptFunctions.cfm`—Creating a General-Purpose UDF

```
<!---
 Filename: SimpleJavaScriptFunctions.cfm
 Created by: Nate Weiss (NMW)
 Purpose: Creates a library of ColdFusion functions that
 encapsulate JavaScript ideas
--->
```

Listing 22.6 (continued)

```
<!--- Function: JavaScriptPopupLink() --->
<!--- Returns an HTML link that opens a pop-up window via JavaScript --->
<cffunction name="javaScriptPopupLink" returnType="string" output="false">
 <!--- One argument: FilmID --->
 <cfargument name="linkURL" type="string" required="Yes">
 <cfargument name="linkText" type="string" required="Yes">
 <cfargument name="popupWidth" type="numeric" default="300">
 <cfargument name="popupHeight" type="numeric" default="200">
 <cfargument name="popupTop" type="numeric" default="200">
 <cfargument name="popupLeft" type="numeric" default="300">

 <!--- These variables are for this function's use only --->
 <cfset var features = "">
 <cfset var linkCode = "">

 <!--- Window features get passed to JavaScript's window.open() command --->
 <cfset features = "width=#arguments.PopupWidth#,"
 & "height=#arguments.PopupHeight#,top=#ARGUMENTS.PopupTop#,"
 & "left=#arguments.PopupLeft#,scrollbars=yes">

 <!--- Create variable called LinkCode, which contains HTML / JavaScript --->
 <!--- needed to display a link that creates a pop-up window when clicked --->
 <cfsavecontent variable="linkCode">
 <cfoutput>
<a href="#arguments.linkURL#" onclick="popupWin = window.open('#arguments.linkURL#','
myPopup','#features#');  popupWin.focus(); return false;" >#arguments.LinkText#</a> </
cfoutput>
 </cfsavecontent>

 <!--- Return the completed link code --->
 <cfreturn linkCode>
</cffunction>
```

NOTE

This listing includes some JavaScript code, such as `window.open()`, `focus()`, `window.status`, and `return true`. These are very basic JavaScript concepts. If you aren't familiar with them, consult any reference or online guide.

As with the earlier UDF examples in this chapter, the first thing this code does is define the function's arguments with the `<cfargument>` tag. This is actually the first UDF example that accepts more than one argument. As you can see, you can add as many arguments as you like. Just don't get totally carried away, since functions with dozens of arguments will probably be somewhat harder to use.

Next, a variable called `features` is created; this is the list of "window features" that will be supplied to the JavaScript `window.open()` method. You can find out more about how to specify window features in a JavaScript reference guide, but the basic idea is that this describes the physical pop-up window, including its position and size. When the function executes, the value of `features` will be something like this (depending on the actual arguments used):

```
width=300,height=200,top=200,left=300,scrollbars=yes
```

The next block of code uses the `<cfsavecontent>` tag to create a variable named `linkCode`. ColdFusion will process and evaluate all the code between the opening and closing `<cfsavecontent>`

tags, then assign the final result to the `linkCode` variable. This makes it easier to create a variable that contains multiple lines, a variety of quotation marks, and so on. In this kind of situation, it's a lot easier than using the `<cfset>` tag. You can even use tags like `<cfloop>` within this type of block. That said, a `<cfset>` (or several `<cfset>` tags) would work equally well. The code might just be a bit harder to follow.

Within the `<cfsavecontent>` block, the basic idea is to generate a normal HTML `<a>` tag, with a normal `href` attribute. In addition to the `href` attribute, the `<a>` tag is also given `onclick`, `onmouseover`, and `onmouseout` attributes. These attributes contain JavaScript code that will execute when the user clicks the link, hovers over the link, and hovers away from the link, respectively.

NOTE

It is also necessary to use a pair of `<cfoutput>` tags here to force ColdFusion to evaluate the variables and expressions within this block. The final result (after all number signs (#), tags, and functions have been evaluated) is "captured" by `<cfsavecontent>` and placed into the `linkText` variable.

The result is the behavior shown earlier in Figure 22.2: when the user clicks the link, a pop-up window appears. If the user's browser doesn't support JavaScript, or if scripting has been disabled, the Film Details page simply appears in the main window (as a normal link would). You can use your browser's View Source option to examine the final HTML and JavaScript code that gets sent to the browser.

Sharing UDF Libraries with Others

Of course, you can download and use UDF function libraries that other people have written. Just save the `.cfm` file that contains the functions to an appropriate place on your server's drive, then include the file with `<cfinclude>`, just like the other examples in this chapter. You can also share your own general-purpose UDF libraries with others for fun or profit.

One great place to find or share user-defined functions is the Common Function Library Project, at `http://www.cflib.org`. `CFLib`, as the library is commonly known, currently has more than 1000 UDFs (Figure 22.3).

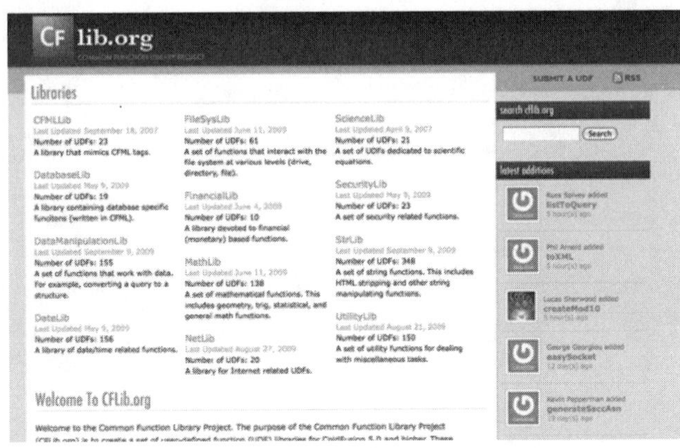

Figure 22.3

The Common Function Library Project's Web site is another great place to find user-defined functions.

CHAPTER 23

Creating Custom Tags

IN THIS CHAPTER

Easy, Powerful Extensibility

In Chapter 22, "Building User-Defined Functions," you learned how to create your own user-defined functions (UDFs). These are exciting because they allow you to add to the CFML language to better suit your needs. Once you have written a UDF, you can use it just like one of ColdFusion's own built-in functions. Extending ColdFusion's language lets you reuse your code in many different places. That makes your job easier and more productive—plus, it's fun!

Let's recap the four basic ways of extending ColdFusion:

- **User-Defined Functions.** If there is some function that you feel is missing from ColdFusion's list of built-in functions, or that would be handy for an application you're building, you can just make the function yourself.
- **Custom Tags.** While UDFs allow you to make your own functions, custom tags let you create your own CFML tags.
- **ColdFusion Components (CFCs).** Conceptually, CFCs are similar to custom tags, but imply a more structured, object-oriented manner of programming. CFCs are also at the heart of ColdFusion's Flash and Web Services integration.
- **CFX Tags.** It is also possible to write your own CFX tags in either Java or C++. For more information about writing CFX tags, see the ColdFusion documentation.

Introducing CFML Custom Tags

The UDF framework introduced in Chapter 22 is probably the easiest and most straightforward way to extend the language. That said, custom tags represent a more *flexible* way to extend ColdFusion is by creating your own tags. Like UDFs, custom tags let you add your own tags to the CFML language, for whatever purpose you want. Unlike UDFs, the custom tag framework has been around since ColdFusion 3.0, and has become a rich and mature part of the product. As of this writing, there are many more custom tags than UDFs. Custom tags excel at encapsulating concepts and processes and are the bedrock of many existing ColdFusion applications.

You can solve many problems using either framework. And you can write extensions in ColdFusion's native language, CFML, regardless of which framework you choose for a particular task. This means you already know most of what you need, and can get started right away.

The Basic Custom Tag Idea

The idea behind custom tags is simple: to enable ColdFusion developers like you to package chunks of ordinary CFML code into reusable modules. From that point on, you can refer to the modules by name, using ColdFusion's familiar tag-based syntax. You get to define attributes for your tags, just as for regular CFML tags. Your tags can run queries, generate HTML, and perform calculations. They have almost no special requirements or limitations.

Generally, custom tags are self-contained and goal-oriented. They take care of whatever processing is necessary to perform a particular task or set of related tasks. In short, custom tags can be many different things, depending on your needs.

Custom tags also promote modularity. In a modular approach, you package any process that is repeatable so that any part of your code can reuse it. Code reuse means less work for us—and that's *always* a good thing!

How to Use Custom Tags

It's sometimes said that lazy people make the best programmers because they tend to solve problems by taking advantage of proven, working solutions that are already in place. Lazy or not, it's often a great idea to reuse work others have done. Before you get started on a project or tackle a piece of code, see whether someone has already written a custom tag that does what you need. If so, you can just use it. It's almost like getting the entire ColdFusion developer community to help you write the code for your application.

How to "Install" a Custom Tag

A single ColdFusion template (`.cfm`) file represents each custom tag. Generally, the `.cfm` file and some type of documentation are placed together in a Zip file for easy downloading.

There isn't really any special installation step. All you have to do is place the custom tag template into the special `CustomTags` folder on your ColdFusion server.

To install a custom tag, follow these steps:

1. Find the custom tag you want and download the Zip file that contains the tag. If you have been given the `.cfm` file directly rather than compressed in a Zip file, go to step 3.

2. Open the Zip file and find the custom tag template (.cfm) file itself. The template's file name will be the name of the custom tag, without the cf_ prefix. So if you have downloaded a custom tag called <cf_PlaceOrder>, you should look for a file called PlaceOrder.cfm.
3. Place the custom tag template file into the CustomTags folder, located within the ColdFusion9 folder on your ColdFusion server.

That's it. The custom tag is now installed, and you can start using it in your code.

TIP

If you want to organize the custom tag templates you download (or write) into subfolders within the CustomTags folder, go ahead. As long as they are somewhere within the CustomTags folder, ColdFusion will find and use them in your applications.

NOTE

If you don't have access to the special CustomTags folder, or if you plan to use the custom tag in just one or two of your own templates, place the custom tag template into the folder where you plan to use it. See "Placing Custom Tags in the Current Directory," later in this chapter.

You can move the location of the special CustomTags folder, or create additional special custom tag folders. You can even specify your own custom tag folders for your application. See "Changing the Custom Tag Search Path," later in this chapter.

Some custom tags might require other tags or files to be present as well. The documentation that comes with the tag should point out what you need to know.

Using Custom Tags

After you install a custom tag by placing its template in the special CustomTags folder, it's ready for use in your code. To help you get your feet wet, this book's Web site includes a custom tag in the listings for this chapter. The custom tag, <cf_initcap>, allows you to provide text formatting that automatically capitalizes the first line of a paragraph, giving the text a fancy magazine-type look.

Using <cf_initcap>

CSS is a powerful tool for marking up your text. Along with adding pretty colors and other changes to your site, it can perform powerful text transformations. If your CSS (like mine) is a bit rusty, you can use the initcap custom tag to create the style sheet for you.

Listing 23.1 shows how you can use the <cf_initcap> custom tag on one of your pages.

Listing 23.1 UsingInitCap.cfm—Using the <cf_InitCap> Tag

```
<!---
 Filename: UsingInitCap.cfm
 Author: Raymond Camden
 Purpose: Demonstrates how to use a custom tag
--->

<cf_initcap>
```

Listing 23.1 (continued)

```
When in the Course of human events it becomes necessary for one people to
dissolve the political bands which have connected them with another and to
assume among the powers of the earth, the separate and equal station to
which the Laws of Nature and of Nature's God entitle them, a decent
respect to the opinions of mankind requires that they should declare the
causes which impel them to the separation.
</cf_initcap>
```

Don't worry about the code behind the `initcap` custom tag. The purpose of this listing is to show you how to use a custom tag in your code and give you a sense of what you can do with custom tags.

Changing the Custom Tag Search Path

As you have already learned, when you use a custom tag in one of your ColdFusion templates, the ColdFusion Application Server looks in the special `CustomTags` folder for the corresponding custom tag template. So when you use the `<cf_initcap>` custom tag in your own code, ColdFusion looks for the `initcap.cfm` file in the `c:\ColdFusion9\CustomTags` folder (assuming you are running ColdFusion on a Windows machine and that you accepted the default installation options).

If you want, you can change the location of the special `CustomTags` folder, or specify additional folders for ColdFusion to look in. Say you want to place the custom tags for the Orange Whip Studios project in a folder called `C:\OrangeWhip\CustomTags`, instead of `C:\ColdFusion9\CustomTags`. All you need to do is add the new folder to the custom tag search path. The custom tag search path is a list of folders ColdFusion looks through whenever you call a custom tag in one of your application templates. When you first install ColdFusion, only one folder is in the search path (the `CustomTags` folder within `ColdFusion9`).

After you add a new folder to the search path, you are free to place some custom tags in the new folder and others in the original `CustomTags` folder. Now, when you first refer to a custom tag in your own templates, the ColdFusion server first looks in the special `CustomTags` folder (and its subfolders) and then in your newly specified folder (and any of its subfolders).

NOTE

If all this path searching sounds like a lot of overhead for ColdFusion to incur, don't worry. Once ColdFusion successfully finds a custom tag template in the search paths you have configured, it remembers the template's location for all subsequent requests (until the server is restarted or until the server's template cache is exhausted). In other words, the custom tag search path is searched only once per custom tag per server restart, so there isn't much of a penalty for adding folders to the search path. Remember that if you test a custom tag and then move it, you will need to restart ColdFusion to have it "find" the custom tag again.

To add a folder to the custom tag search path, follow these steps:

1. Navigate to the Custom Tag Paths page of the ColdFusion Administrator (Extensions > Custom Tag Paths).

2. Specify the path and name of the folder you want to add to the custom tag search path. You can use the Browse Server button to avoid having to type the folder's path manually.
3. Click the Add Path button. The new folder appears in the list of custom tag paths.
4. Now you can place your custom tag templates in the folder you just added or in the original.

You can also remove folders from the custom tag search path using the Delete button. After you remove a folder from the search path, ColdFusion will no longer find custom tag templates in that folder.

NOTE

Throughout this chapter, you will find instructions to save files in the special `CustomTags` folder. Whenever I mention the `CustomTags` folder, you can also use any folders you have added to the custom tag search path.

Placing Custom Tags in the Current Directory

Sometimes placing custom tag templates in the special `CustomTags` folder isn't possible or convenient (see the section "How to 'Install' a Custom Tag," earlier in this chapter). For instance, if an Internet Service Provider is hosting your ColdFusion application, you might not have access to the ColdFusion Administrator or the `CustomTags` folder.

In such a situation, you can place the custom tag template (`InitCap.cfm`, for example) in the same folder as the template you want to use it in. When ColdFusion encounters the custom tag in your code, it first looks for the appropriate file in the current folder. (It doesn't automatically look in the parent folder or subfolders of the current folder.) If ColdFusion can't find the `.cfm` file for the custom tag in the current folder, it then looks in the special `CustomTags` folder (and its subfolders).

Placing the custom tag template in the current folder is a good idea when

- You don't have access to the special `CustomTags` folder.
- You are still developing and testing the custom tag. Just don't forget to restart ColdFusion so it can "find" it again if you subsequently move it to the `CustomTags` folder.
- You know you won't use the custom tag extensively, so you don't mind its being available only to code templates in the current folder.
- You want to simplify the distribution of your application and would rather not require that the custom tag template be dealt with separately.

These situations aside, it's smart to use the special `CustomTags` folder described earlier in this chapter. You will find all your custom tags in one place, and you won't have to maintain multiple copies of the same custom tag template (one for each folder in which you want to use the tag).

Specifying Locations with Application.cfc

Yet another option is to make use of a special THIS scope variable within your Application.cfc file. The this.customtagpaths setting can be either one or a list of directories. If you specify a list of directories here, ColdFusion will look in your specified folder (or folders) before using the folders specified in the ColdFusion Administrator. Here is a simple example:

```
<cfset this.customtagpaths = "/group/tags/">
```

This code tells ColdFusion first to look in the /group/tags folder when searching for a custom tag. If ColdFusion can't find the tag there, it will then check the paths specified at the server level.

NOTE

Another option for both calling and specifying the location of a custom tag is the <cfmodule> tag. This tag allows you to specify a relative path to a custom tag. In the past, this tag was especially useful for people who did not have access to the server's custom tag folder. However, with the addition of Application.cfc support for specification of custom tag folders, <cfmodule> is not really necessary any more. You should instead use this.customtagpaths and the "cf_" syntax to call custom tags.

Writing Custom Tags That Display Information

Now that you understand how to use existing custom tags, it's time to write your own. This section introduces you to the basic concepts involved in creating a custom tag. As you will soon see, it's an easy and productive way to write your code.

Writing Your First Custom Tag

It's traditional to illustrate a new language or technique with a "Hello, World" example. Listing 23.2 shows a custom tag that outputs a "Hello, World" message in the current Web page, formatted with ordinary HTML table syntax.

Save this listing as HelloWorld.cfm in either the special CustomTags folder or the folder you've been using as you follow along in this chapter.

Listing 23.2 HelloWorld.cfm—A Simple Custom Tag Template

```
<!---
 Filename: HelloWorld.cfm
 Author: Nate Weiss (NMW)
 Purpose: Creates the <CF_HelloWorld> custom tag example
--->

<div id="heading" style="font-weight:bold">
Hello, World, from Orange Whip Studios.
</div>
<div id="content" style="background-color: orange">
 Orange whip... two orange whips... three orange whips!
</div>
```

Now you can use the custom tag just by adding a `cf_` prefix to the tag's file name (without the `.cfm` part). This means you have just created a custom tag called `<cf_HelloWorld>`, which you can use in code as shown in Listing 23.3.

Listing 23.3 `UsingHelloWorld.cfm`—Testing the `<CF_HelloWorld>` Custom Tag

```
<!---
 Filename: UsingHelloWorld.cfm
 Author: Nate Weiss (NMW)
 Purpose: Shows how <CF_HelloWorld> can be used in a ColdFusion page
--->

 <!--- Display Hello World Message, via Custom Tag --->
 <cf_HelloWorld>
```

It's a start, but this custom tag isn't terribly exciting, since it will always output exactly the same thing. In fact, at this point, you could just replace the reference to the custom tag in Listing 23.3 with an ordinary `<cfinclude>` tag and the results would be the same:

```
<!--- Display Hello World Message, via Custom Tag --->
<cfinclude template="HelloWorld.cfm">
```

Things get a lot more interesting after you start making custom tags that accept attributes, just like ColdFusion's built-in tags.

Introducing the ATTRIBUTES Scope

To make your own custom tags really useful, you want them to accept tag attributes, just as normal CFML and HTML tags do. ColdFusion makes this very easy by defining a special `ATTRIBUTES` scope for use within your custom tag templates.

The `ATTRIBUTES` scope is a ColdFusion structure that is automatically populated with any attributes provided to the custom tag when it is actually used in code. For instance, if an attribute called `message` is provided to a tag, as in `<cf_HelloWorld message="Country and Western">`, then the special `ATTRIBUTES` scope will contain a `message` value, set to `Country and Western`. You could output this value to the page by referring to `#ATTRIBUTES.message#` between `<cfoutput>` tags within the custom tag template.

Outputting Attribute Values

Listing 23.4 shows another custom tag called `<cf_HelloWorldMessage>`, which is almost the same as `<cf_HelloWorld>` from Listing 23.2. The difference is the fact that this tag accepts an attribute called `message`, which gets displayed as part of the `"Hello, World"` message.

Listing 23.4 `HelloWorldMessage.cfm`—Defining Attributes for Your Custom Tags

```
<!---
 Filename: HelloWorldMessage.cfm
 Author: Nate Weiss (NMW)
 Purpose: Creates a custom tag that accepts attributes
--->
```

Listing 23.4 (continued)

```
<!--- Tag Attributes --->
<cfparam name="attributes.message" type="string">

<cfoutput>
<div id="heading" style="font-weight:bold">
Hello, World, from Orange Whip Studios.
</div>
<div id="content" style="background-color: orange">
 #attributes.message#<br>
</div>
</cfoutput>
```

The <cfparam> tag at the top of Listing 23.4 makes it clear that a `message` parameter is expected to be provided to the tag and that it is expected to be a string value. The <cfoutput> block near the end outputs the value of the `message` parameter provided to the tag. Listing 23.5 shows how to supply the `message` parameter that the tag now expects.

NOTE

To make this listing work, you must save the previous listing (Listing 23.4) as **`HelloWorldMessage.cfm`**, either in the same folder as Listing 23.5 or in the special **`CustomTags`** folder.

Listing 23.5 `UsingHelloWorldMessage.cfm`—Supplying Attributes to Your Custom Tags

```
<!---
 Filename: UsingHelloWorldMessage.cfm
 Author: Nate Weiss (NMW)
 Purpose: Shows how to use the <CF_HelloWorldMessage> custom tag
--->

 <!--- Display Hello World Message, via Custom Tag --->
 <cf_HelloWorldMessage
 message="We're getting the band back together!">
```

NOTE

Attribute names are not case sensitive. There is no way to determine whether a parameter was passed to a tag with code such as `Message="Hello"` or `MESSAGE="Hello"`. Of course, the case of each attribute's value is preserved, so there is a difference between `message="Hello"` and `message="HELLO"`.

Using <cfparam> to Declare Attributes

You don't have to include the <cfparam> tag in Listing 23.4. As long as the `message` attribute is actually provided when the tag is used, and as long as the parameter is a string value, the <cfparam> tag doesn't do anything. It only has an effect if the attribute is omitted (or provided with a value that can't be converted to a string), in which case it displays an error message.

However, I strongly suggest that you declare each of a custom tag's attributes with a <cfparam> tag at the top of the tag's template, for the following reasons:

- Always having your custom tag's attributes formally listed as <cfparam> tags at the top of your templates makes your custom tag code clearer and more self-documenting.

- Specifying the expected data type with <cfparam>'s `type` attribute acts as a convenient sanity check in case someone tries to use your tag in an unexpected way.
- If you declare all your tag's attributes using <cfparam> tags at the top of a tag's template, you know that the rest of the template will never run if the attributes aren't provided properly when the tag is actually used. This prevents problems or data inconsistencies that could arise from partially executed code.
- As discussed in the next section, you can easily make any of your tag's attributes optional by simply adding a `default` attribute for the corresponding <cfparam> tag.

Making Attributes Optional or Required

When you start working on a new custom tag, one of the most important things to consider is which attributes your new tag will take. You want to ensure that the attribute names are as clear, intuitive, and self-describing as possible.

Often, you will want to make certain attributes optional, so they can be omitted when the tag is actually used. That way, you can provide lots of attributes for your tags (and thus flexibility and customizability), without overburdening users of your tags with a lot of unnecessary typing if they just want a tag's normal behavior.

Using <cfparam> to Establish Default Values

The most straightforward way to declare an optional attribute for a custom tag is to provide a `default` attribute to the corresponding <cfparam> tag at the top of the tag's template.

Look at the version of the <cf_HelloWorldMessage> tag shown in Listing 23.6. This version is the same as the previous one (shown in Listing 23.4), except that it defines five new attributes: `topMessage`, `topColor`, `bottomColor`, `tableBorder`, and `tablePadding`. The values are given sensible default values using the `default` attribute.

Listing 23.6 `HelloWorldMessage2.cfm`—Making Certain Attributes Optional

```
<!---
 Filename: HelloWorldMessage2.cfm
 Author: Nate Weiss (NMW)
 Purpose: Creates a custom tag that accepts attributes
--->

<!--- Tag Attributes --->
<cfparam name="attributes.message" type="string">
<cfparam name="attributes.topMessage" type="string"
 default="Hello, World, from Orange Whip Studios.">
<cfparam name="attributes.topColor" type="string" default="yellow">
<cfparam name="attributes.bottomColor" type="string" default="orange">

<!--- Output message in HTML table format --->
<cfoutput>
<div id="heading" style="font-weight:bold;background-color: #attributes.topColor#">
#attributes.topMessage#
```

Listing 23.6 (continued)

```
<div id="content" style="background-color: #attributes.bottomColor#">
 #attributes.message#
 </div>
</cfoutput>
```

If the tag is explicitly provided with a `topColor` value when it is used, that value will be available as `attributes.topColor`. If not, the `default` attribute of the `<cfparam>` tag kicks in and provides the default value of `Yellow`. The same goes for the other new attributes: if values are supplied at run time, the supplied values are used; if not, the default values kick in.

NOTE

There's generally no harm in defining more attributes than you think people will need, as long as you supply default values for them. As a rule of thumb, try to provide attributes for just about every string or number your tag uses, rather than hard-coding them. This is what Listing 23.6 does.

Assuming you save Listing 23.6 as a custom tag template called `HelloWorldMessage.cfm`, you can now use any of the following in your application templates:

```
<cf_HelloWorldMessage
message="We're getting the band back together!">

<cf_HelloWorldMessage
topMessage="Message of the Day"
message="We're getting the band back together!">

<cf_HelloWorldMessage
message="We're getting the band back together!"
topColor="Beige"
bottomColor="##FFFFFF"
>
```

Using Functions to Test for Attributes

Instead of using the `<cfparam>` tag, you can use the `isDefined()` function to test for the existence of tag attributes. This is largely a matter of personal preference. For instance, instead of this:

```
<cfparam name="attributes.message" type="string">
```

you could use this:

```
<cfif not isDefined("attributes.message") >
 <cfabort showError="You must provide a Message attribute">
</cfif>
```

Or instead of this:

```
<cfparam name="attributes.topColor" type="string" default="Yellow">
```

you could use this:

```
<cfif not isDefined("attributes.topColor")>
 <cfset ATTRIBUTES.topColor="Yellow">
</cfif>
```

NOTE

Since the `attributes` scope is implemented as a ColdFusion structure, you can also use CFML's various structure functions to test for the existence of tag attributes. For instance, instead of `isDefined("attributes.topColor")`-shown in the previous code snippet-you could use `structKeyExists(attributes, "topColor")` to get the same effect.

NOTE

Because the special `ATTRIBUTES` scope exists only when a template is being called as a custom tag, you can use `isDefined("attributes")` if you want to be able to detect whether the template is being visited on its own or included via a regular `<cfinclude>` tag.

Local Variables in Custom Tags

So far, our custom tags have been rather simple. Not one of them created any variables. The last few tags used the `ATTRIBUTES` scope, but none of them actually created a variable. What happens when a custom tag creates a variable? ColdFusion creates a `VARIABLES` scope just for the custom tag itself. Any variable created without a scope or specifically in the variable's scope is unique to the custom tag.

This is an important aspect of ColdFusion's custom tag functionality. Whenever a custom tag is executed, it gets a private area in the server's memory to store its own variables. Unless you use a scope prefix (such as `ATTRIBUTES`, `APPLICATION`, or `SESSION`), all references to variables in the custom tag template refer only to this private area. The result is what some other programming languages call a namespace—an interim memory space for the tag to do its work, without regard to how it will affect the template in which it is used.

For instance, if you attempt to display the value of a variable created within a custom tag from the file that called it, you will get an error message saying that the variable doesn't exist—because the variable exists only within the custom tag's template. After the tag finishes its work, all its variables are discarded and are no longer available.

This is what enables custom tags to be so modular and independent. Because they don't affect the variables in the templates in which they run, they are free to create variables and run queries in any way they need to. All kinds of problems would arise if this weren't the case.

Remember these important points:

- Variables in custom tags are always local, unless you specify a special scope name (discussed shortly).
- Variables set before the tag is used aren't available within the custom tag itself.
- Similarly, variables set in the custom tag's template aren't available as normal variables in code that uses the tag.
- The `ATTRIBUTES` scope enables you to pass specific values into the tag.
- The special `CALLER` scope, which you will learn about shortly, lets you access or set specific variables in the calling template.

Custom Tags That Process Data

So far, we have concentrated on creating custom tags that display information. Many of the custom tags you will write are likely to be similar to it in that they will be in charge of wrapping up several display-related concepts (querying the database, including formatting, outputting the information, and so on).

However, you can also create custom tags that have different purposes in life: to process or gather information. This type of custom tag generally doesn't generate any HTML to be displayed on the current page. Instead, these tags perform some type of processing, often returning a calculated result to the calling template.

Introducing the CALLER Scope

ColdFusion defines two special variable scopes that come into play only when you're creating custom tags:

- The ATTRIBUTES scope—You have already learned about this scope, which passes specific information to a custom tag each time it is used.
- The CALLER scope—Gives a custom tag a way to set and use variables in the template in which you're using the tag (the calling template).

The special CALLER scope is easy to understand and use. Within a custom tag template, you prefix any variable name with CALLER (using struct notation) to access the corresponding variable in the calling template. Through the CALLER scope, you have full read-write access to all variables known to the calling template, meaning that you can set variables as well as access their current values. For instance, you can set variables in the calling template using an ordinary <cfset> tag.

Returning Variables to the Calling Template

Let's say you're writing a custom tag called <cf_PickFeaturedMovie>, which will choose a movie from the list of available films. In the calling template, you plan on using the tag like so:

```
<cf_PickFeaturedMovie>
```

Inside the custom tag template (PickFeaturedMovie.cfm), you could set a variable using a special caller prefix, such as this:

```
<cfset caller.featuredFilmID = 5>
```

This prefix would make featuredFilmID available in the calling template as a normal variable. For instance, this code snippet would call the custom tag and then output the value of the variable it returns:

```
<cf_PickFeaturedMovie>
<cfoutput>
 The featured Film ID is:
 #featuredFilmID#
</cfoutput>
```

Of course, using these snippets, the value of `featuredFilmID` would always be `5`, so the custom tag wouldn't be all that useful. Listing 23.7 shows how to expand the previous snippets into a useful version of the `<cf_PickFeaturedMovie>` custom tag. The purpose of the code is to select a single film's ID number in such a way that all films are rotated evenly on a per-session basis.

Listing 23.7 `PickFeaturedMovie.cfm`—Setting a Variable in the Calling Template

```
<!---
 Filename: PickFeaturedMovie.cfm
 Author: Nate Weiss (NMW)
 Purpose: Creates the <CF_PickFeaturedMovie> custom tag
--->

<!--- Tag Attributes --->
<!--- Use ""ows"" datasource by default --->
<cfparam name="attributes.dataSource" type="string" default="ows">

<cflock scope="session" type="exclusive" timeout="30">

  <!--- List of movies to show (list starts out empty) --->
  <cfparam name="session.movieList" type="string" default="">

  <!--- If this is the first time we're running this, --->
  <!--- Or we have run out of movies to rotate through --->
  <cfif session.movieList eq "">
    <!--- Get all current FilmIDs from the database. --->
    <cfquery name="getFilmIDs" datasource="#attributes.dataSource#">
    SELECT FilmID FROM Films
    ORDER BY MovieTitle
    </cfquery>

    <!--- Turn FilmIDs into a simple comma-separated list --->
    <cfset session.movieList = valueList(getFilmIDs.FilmID)>
  </cfif>

  <!--- Pick the first movie in the list to show right now --->
  <cfset thisMovieID = listFirst(session.movieList)>

  <!--- Re-save the list, as all movies *except* the first --->
  <cfset session.movieList = listRest(session.movieList)>
</cflock>

<!--- Return chosen movie to calling template --->
<cfset caller.featuredFilmID = thisMovieID>
```

The `<cfparam>` tag at the top of this custom tag template establishes a single optional attribute for the tag called `dataSource`, which will default to `ows` if not provided explicitly. We begin by using a `<cflock>` tag to ensure that the code here is thread-safe. Since we are reading and writing to a shared scope, it's important that we control how the code is accessed. We use `<cfparam>` to default the list of movies to an empty string. If the `session` variable already exists, this line will do nothing. If the `movieList` variable equals an empty string, it means we either just created the variable, or the list of movies has already been used. If this is the case, we run a query to grab all the film IDs. We then use the `valueList()` function to copy out the list of IDs from the query. The listFirst() function is used to get the first film ID from the list, and listRest() is used to remove the ID and resave the list to the session.movieList variable. Because the final <cfset> uses the special CALLER scope, the featured movie that the tag has chosen is available for the calling template to use normally.

Listing 23.8 shows how you can put this version of the <cf_PickFeaturedMovie> custom tag to use in actual code.

Listing 23.8 UsingPickFeaturedMovie1.cfm—Using a Variable Set by a Custom Tag

```
<!---
 Filename: UsingPickFeaturedMovie1.cfm
 Author: Nate Weiss (NMW)
 Purpose: Shows how <cf_PickFeaturedMovie> can be used in a ColdFusion page
--->

 <!--- Page Title and Text Message --->
 <h2>Movie Display Demonstration</h2>

 <!--- Pick rotating Featured Movie to show, via Custom Tag --->
 <cf_PickFeaturedMovie>

 <!--- Display Film info as "callout", via Custom Tag --->
 <cf_ShowMovieCallout
 filmID="#featuredFilmID#">
```

NOTE

The CALLER scope is for use only within custom tag templates. Don't use it in your ordinary ColdFusion templates. Doing so won't generate an error message, but it could produce unexpected results.

If you are calling a custom tag from within another custom tag, the CALLER scope of the innermost tag will refer to the local variables in the first custom tag template, not the variables in the top-level page template. To access the variables of the top-level template from the innermost tag, you must use caller.caller.VariableName instead of caller.VariableName. In some cases, this can be a pain; the REQUEST scope provides an effective solution.

First, the <cf_PickFeaturedMovie> custom tag from Listing 23.7 is called. As the custom tag executes, it selects the film ID it feels is appropriate and saves the value in the featuredFilmID variable in the calling template (which, in this case, is Listing 23.8). Next, the featured movie is actually displayed to the user, using the <cf_ShowMovieCallout> custom tag. This tag can be found in the Zip file containing all the chapter's code. It is a simple tag that displays details about a movie and can be read at your leisure as another example of what you can do with custom tags.

NOTE

These two custom tags (<cf_PickFeaturedMovie> and <cf_ShowMovieCallout>) each do something useful on their own and can be used together, as shown here. As you design custom tags for your applications, this type of synergy between tags is a nice goal to shoot for.

Of course, to make Listing 23.8 work, you need to enable session management by using an Application.cfc file. See Chapter 18, "Introducing the Web Application Framework," in *Adobe ColdFusion 9 Web Application Construction Kit, Volume 1: Getting Started*, for details. You will find a simple Application.cfc file for this in the Zip file that you download from the Web site.

NOTE

The more a custom tag relies on variables in the calling template, the less modular it becomes. So, although the `CALLER` scope gives you read-write access to variables in the calling template, you should use it mainly for setting new variables, rather than accessing the values of existing ones. If you find that you are accessing the values of many existing variables in the calling template, maybe you should just be writing a normal `<cfinclude>` style template rather than a custom tag, or maybe the values should be passed into the tag explicitly as attributes.

Variable Names as Tag Attributes

In the version of the `<cf_PickFeaturedMovie>` custom tag shown in Listing 23.7, the selected film ID is always returned to the calling template as a variable named `featuredFilmID`. Designing a custom tag to accept an additional `returnVariable` attribute allows a calling template to control the name of the variable modified by the custom tag template.

For instance, for the `<cf_PickFeaturedMovie>` custom tag, you might add an attribute called `returnVariable`, which allows the calling template to specify the variable in which to place the featured film's ID number.

To use the tag, change this line from Listing 23.8:

```
<!--- Pick rotating featured movie to show via custom tag --->
<cf_PickFeaturedMovie>
```

to this:

```
<!--- Pick rotating featured movie to show via custom tag --->
   <cf_PickFeaturedMovie
returnVariable="FeaturedFilmID">
```

This makes the custom tag less intrusive because it doesn't demand that any particular variable names be set aside for its use. If for whatever reason the developer coding the calling template wants the selected film to be known as `myFeaturedFilmID` or `showThisMovieID`, he or she can simply specify that name for the `returnVariable` attribute. The calling template is always in control.

NOTE

Also, code that uses the `<cf_PickFeaturedMovie>` tag will be a bit more self-documenting and easier to understand because it is now evident from where exactly the `FeaturedFilmID` variable is coming.

NOTE

If you think about it, a number of ColdFusion's own CFML tags use the same technique. The most obvious example is the `<cfquery>` tag's `name` attribute, which tells the tag which variable to store its results in. The `name` attributes of the `<cfdirectory>` and `<cfsearch>` tags are similar, as are the `OUTPUT` attribute for `<cfwddx>` and the `variable` attributes for `<cffile>` and `<cfsaveoutput>`.

Using `<cfparam>` with `type="variableName"`

You have already seen the `<cfparam>` tag used throughout this chapter to make it clear which attributes a custom tag expects and to ensure that the data type of each attribute is correct. When you want the calling template to accept a variable name as one of its attributes, you can set the `type` of the `<cfparam>` tag to `variableName`.

Therefore, the next version of the `<cf_PickFeaturedMovie>` custom tag will include the following lines:

```
<!--- Variable name to return selected FilmID as --->
<cfparam name="attributes.returnVariable" type="variableName">
```

When the `<cfparam>` tag is encountered, ColdFusion ensures that the actual value of the attribute is a legal variable name. If it's not, ColdFusion displays an error message stating that the variable name is illegal. This makes for a very simple sanity check. It ensures that the tag isn't being provided with something such as `returnValue="My Name"`, which likely would result in a much uglier error message later on because spaces aren't allowed in ColdFusion variable names.

NOTE

In ColdFusion, variable names must start with a letter, and the other characters can only be letters, numbers, and underscores. Any string that doesn't conform to these rules won't get past a `<cfparam>` of `type="variableName"`. What's nice is that if the rules for valid variable names changes in a future version of ColdFusion, you won't have to update your code.

Setting a Variable Dynamically

After you've added the `<cfparam>` tag shown previously to the `<cf_PickFeaturedMovie>` custom tag template, the template can refer to `ATTRIBUTES.returnVariable` to get the desired variable name. Now the final `<cfset>` variable in Listing 23.7 just needs to be changed so that it uses the dynamic variable name instead of the hard-coded variable name of `featuredFilmID`. Developers sometimes get confused about how exactly to do this.

Here's the line as it stands now, from Listing 23.7:

```
<!--- Return chosen movie to calling template --->
<cfset caller.featuredFilmID = thisMovieID>
```

People often try to use syntax similar to the following to somehow indicate that the value of `attributes.returnVariable` should be used to determine the name of the variable in the `CALLER` scope:

```
<!--- Return chosen movie to calling template --->
<cfset caller.#attributes.returnVariable# = thisMovieID>
```

Or they might use this:

```
<!--- Return chosen movie to calling template --->
<cfset #caller.##attributes.returnVariable### = thisMovieID>
```

These are not legal because ColdFusion doesn't understand that you want the value of `ATTRIBUTES.returnVariable` evaluated before `<cfset>` is actually performed. ColdFusion will just get exasperated, and display an error message.

Using Quoted <cfset> Syntax

ColdFusion provides a somewhat odd-looking solution to this problem. You simply surround the left side of the <cfset> expression, the part before the equals (=) sign, with quotation marks. This forces ColdFusion to first evaluate the variable name as a string before attempting to actually perform the variable setting. The resulting code looks a bit strange, but it works very well and is relatively easy to read.

So, this line from Listing 23.7:

```
<!--- Return chosen movie to calling template --->
<cfset caller.featuredFilmID = thisMovieID>
```

can be replaced with this:

```
<!--- Return chosen movie to calling template --->
<cfset "caller.#attributes.returnVariable#" = thisMovieID>
```

Since the custom tag was changed so little, we won't list it here. You can copy the complete template from the Zip file.

Listing 23.9 shows how to use this new version of the custom tag. This listing is nearly identical to Listing 23.8, except for the addition of the `returnVariable` attribute. Note how much clearer the cause and effect now are. In Listing 23.8, the `featuredFilmID` variable seemed to appear out of nowhere. Here, it's very clear where the `showThisMovieID` variable is coming from.

Listing 23.9 `UsingPickFeaturedMovie2.cfm`—Using the `returnVariable` Attribute

```
<!---
 Filename: UsingPickFeaturedMovie2.cfm
 Author: Nate Weiss (NMW)
 Purpose: Shows how <cf_PickFeaturedMovie2> can be used in a ColdFusion page
--->

<!--- Page Title and Text Message --->
<h2>Movie Display Demonstration</h2>

<!--- Pick rotating Featured Movie to show, via Custom Tag --->
<cf_PickFeaturedMovie2 returnVariable="showThisMovieID">

<!--- Display Film info as "callout", via Custom Tag --->
<cf_showMovieCallout filmID="#showThisMovieID#">
```

Using the setVariable() Function

Another way to solve this type of problem is with the `setVariable()` function. This function accepts two parameters. The first is a string specifying the name of a variable; the second is the value you want to store in the specified variable. (The function also returns the new value as its result, which isn't generally helpful in this situation.)

So, this example:

```
<!--- Return chosen movie to calling template --->
<cfset "caller.#attributes.returnVariable#" = thisMovieID>
```

could be replaced with this:

```
<!--- Return chosen movie to calling template --->
<cfset setVariable("caller.#attributes.returnVariable#", thisMovieID)>
```

Using `struct` Notation

One more way a custom tag can return information to the calling document is to simply treat the `CALLER` scope as a structure.

So, this example:

```
<!--- Return chosen movie to calling template --->
<cfset "caller.#attributes.returnVariable#" = thisMovieID>
```

could be replaced with this:

```
<!--- Return chosen movie to calling template --->
<cfset caller[attributes.returnVariable] = thisMovieID>
```

Either method—the quoted `<cfset>` syntax mentioned previously, the `SetVariable()` method shown, or `struct` notation—produces the same results. Use whichever method you prefer.

Additional Custom Tag Topics

So far, we have dealt with simple tags, and the rules we have learned work well enough for most uses, but ColdFusion also provides advanced features that can really enhance custom tags.

Passing Attributes with `attributeCollection`

ColdFusion reserves the `attributeCollection` attribute name for a special use: if a structure variable is passed to a custom tag as an attribute called `attributeCollection`, the values in the structure become part of the `ATTRIBUTES` scope inside the custom tag template.

That is, instead of doing this:

```
<!--- Display Hello World Message, via Custom Tag --->
<cf_HelloWorldMessage
 message="We're getting the band back together!"
 topColor="yellow"
 bottomColor="orange">
```

you could do this:

```
<!--- Set up attribute structure --->
<cfset attribs = structNew()>
<cfset attribs.message = "We're getting the band back together!"">
<cfset attribs.topColor = "yellow">
<cfset attribs.bottomColor = "orange">
<!--- Display Hello World Message, via Custom Tag --->
<cfmodule
 name="HelloWorldMessage"
 attributeCollection="#attribs#">
```

This is most useful in certain specialized situations, such as when you are calling a custom tag recursively (using the custom tag within the custom tag's own template, so that the tag calls itself repeatedly when used). You would be able to call a tag a second time within itself, passing the second tag the same attributes that were passed to the first, by specifying `attributeCollection="#attributes#"`.

Working with `<cfimport>`

The introduction of ColdFusion MX (the first Java-based version of ColdFusion, also known as ColdFusion 6) brought the capability to import a directory of CFML custom tags, by using the `<cfimport>` tag. If you are familiar with JavaServer Pages (JSP), you'll recognize that this method is similar to the method you use to import a JSP tag library (`taglib`). In fact, the `<cfimport>` tag does double duty: It also allows you to import JSP tag libraries for use in your ColdFusion page (JSP `taglib` importing is available in the Enterprise version only). Table 23.1 summarizes the `<cfimport>` tag and its attributes.

Table 23.1 Attributes of `<cfimport>`

ATTRIBUTE	REQUIRED	DEFAULT	DESCRIPTION
`taglib`	Yes	None	Directory containing CFML custom tags; can also point to a JSP tag library descriptor or JAR file.
`prefix`	Yes	None	Prefix for addressing imported CFML or JSP tags. To import without a prefix, pass an empty string (`""`).

As you can see from Table 23.1, you simply point the `taglib` attribute to a directory containing CFML custom tags and assign that directory to a tag prefix. Let's start with a directory named `mylib` under the `ows/23` directory. You set the `<cfimport>` tag's `taglib` attribute to `mylib`, and the `prefix` attribute to `lib`. You can call all the tags in the specified directory like this: `<lib:ThisTagName>`.

You would use this JSP (or XML) style of syntax only when accessing tags whose directory has been imported through `<cfimport>`. You call custom tags in other directories with the standard `<cf_ThisTagName>` syntax. If the `<cfimport>` tag's `prefix` attribute is passed an empty string, it results in HTML-style syntax with no `CF_` or JSP-style prefix (as in `<ThisTagName>`). The next code snippet shows this syntax.

NOTE

When using the `<cfimport>` tag, you must first ensure that the custom tag directory that you want to import–in this case, `mylib`–is located under one of the custom tag locations mentioned at the beginning of this section or is available via a relative path.

The ows/23/mylib directory contains a sample tag library that includes the IntelligentForm.cfm and IntelligentInput.cfm custom tags (covered in depth later in this chapter). You can call them using <cfimport>, like this:

```
<cfimport taglib="mylib" prefix="lib">

<lib:IntelligentForm formName="MyForm">
  <lib:IntelligentInput fieldName="SSN" size="12" maxLength="11"/>
  <lib:IntelligentInput fieldName="FirstName" size="22" maxLength="20"/>
  <lib:IntelligentInput fieldName="LastName" size="22" maxLength="20"/>
</lib:IntelligentForm>
```

You can also call these custom tags without using a tag prefix, like this:

```
<cfimport taglib="mylib" prefix="">

<IntelligentForm formName="MyForm">
  <IntelligentInput fieldName="SSN" size="12" maxLength="11"/>
  <IntelligentInput fieldName="FirstName" size="22" maxLength="20"/>
  <IntelligentInput fieldName="LastName" size="22" maxLength="20"/>
</IntelligentForm>
```

The use of <cfimport> gives you an advantage in large applications that use many custom tags from various sources. That's because you can isolate custom tags with identical names yet different logic into separate directories, import each directory using a different tag prefix, and call identically named tags without one tag occluding the other since you're effectively isolating each custom tag library in its own namespace. Although we do not have a listing that demonstrates <cfimport>, you can certainly build one that uses any of the custom tags discussed so far.

But before you go changing all your custom tag calls using <cfimport> syntax, be aware of these disadvantages:

- Because <cfimport> is a compile-time directive, you must place a call to <cfimport> on every page on which you intend to use <cfimport> syntax to call a custom tag.
- Because <cfimport> is processed at compile time, you cannot use any ColdFusion expressions as the values of attributes, which means that you must hard-code the value of taglib every time you call <cfimport>. This sometimes makes it difficult to migrate from development to staging and then to deployment—especially in shared hosting environments where a mapping name has already been assigned to another application.

Advanced Custom Tags

Now that you've been through this review of custom tag fundamentals, you're probably thinking, "So what's the big deal about custom tags, anyway? They seem like glorified cfinclude tags to me." And up to this point, you're right: simple custom tags are little more than separate templates of stand-alone code that can modify their behavior by changing the values of the attributes with which they are called.

Advanced custom tags, however, are to this day among the most powerful development tools in all of ColdFusion. You can build complete application subsystems of highly reusable code that adapt to the environments in which they are deployed. Well-written advanced custom tags can be instantly reused from application to application with little or no modification at all.

The remainder of this chapter provides an overview of the advanced features of custom tags, beginning with the most common form: paired custom tags.

Paired Custom Tags

All of the custom tags you've seen in the code listings are called *empty* custom tags because they do not span a region of content or code. *Paired* custom tags *do* span, or wrap, a region of content or code and act upon that region in some way. You deal with this concept every day; for example:

```
<b>The force is strong in this one.</b>
```

The HTML `Bold` element is a typical paired tag that acts on the span of content between its opening and closing tags. This may seem like baby steps to you, but the exact same process is applied to ColdFusion paired custom tags. In fact, the very first custom tag we demonstrated, `InitCap`, was an example of this.

Essentially, a paired tag of any kind always executes *twice*—once for the opening tag (Start mode) and once for the closing tag (End mode)—and performs a distinct operation in both Start mode and End mode. The HTML `Bold` tag, for example, in the opening tag establishes the beginning of the content to be modified; the closing tag establishes the end of that content and also instructs the browser to make the content bold. As you continue reading, keep in mind this concept of a paired tag executing twice and doing something different in each execution.

The Execution Cycle

A paired custom tag goes through three modes of execution, in order, when it is called:

- Start mode, which executes immediately after the opening tag and triggers the first execution of the paired custom tag
- Inactive mode, which is the idle period between the opening and closing tags
- End mode, which executes immediately after the closing tag and triggers the second execution of the paired custom tag

In a ColdFusion paired custom tag, the opening tag triggers the first execution, during which `ThisTag.ExecutionMode` is `"Start"`. `ThisTag` is a special scope that exists within custom tags and refers to specific properties of the custom tag, such as its current execution mode, whether the custom tag has an end tag (as a paired tag would), and more, as you'll see later in this chapter.

After the first execution of the paired custom tag, the tag goes into Inactive mode, during which time the contents in the body of the tag are accumulated into `ThisTag.GeneratedContent`. The closing tag then triggers the second execution of the paired custom tag, during which ThisTag.ExecutionMode is "End".

You separate Start mode logic from End mode logic using a simple If construct:

```
<cfif ThisTag.ExecutionMode EQ "Start">

<cfelse>

</cfif>
```

We test only for ThisTag.ExecutionMode EQ "Start" and assume that the <cfelse> clause refers to the End mode, even though there are two other execution modes besides Start. This is because Inactive mode isn't actually executed; it's an idle mode, during which the content is accumulated into ThisTag.GeneratedContent.

Like any other type of custom tag, a paired custom tag may take attributes that can be passed to the logic in the custom tag to modify its behavior. These attributes become part of the ATTRIBUTES scope just as they do in other types of custom tags. Because attributes are always passed in an opening tag, those attributes are "seen" by and can therefore be used by logic in the Start mode of the paired custom tag. Once an execution mode gains access to something, any other execution modes that follow will also have access; therefore, because the Start mode can access the attributes passed into the tag, so can the Inactive and End modes.

The Start mode may execute logic or output content, but it can neither see nor modify any content or code in the body of the paired tag. The Inactive mode is the first point at which the content in the body of the paired tag can be seen, but the only thing the Inactive mode can do with this content is accumulate it into a special variable. The End mode, which can see, access, and modify everything that happened in the execution modes before it, is therefore the most powerful execution mode, and as such it's often where the majority of paired custom tag logic is executed.

Confusion often exists about ColdFusion paired custom tags because of their added ability to programmatically modify the content in the span between the opening and closing tags, but you'll soon see how to visualize the process in a very simple way that eliminates confusion.

Let's look at a practical example of a paired custom tag that wraps a relatively large passage of content and outputs only a specified portion of that content formatted in a div container. We'll call the custom tag TruncateQuote, and it's called like this:

```
<cf_TruncateQuote numberOfCharacters="125">
Four score and seven years ago our fathers brought forth on this continent a new
nation, conceived in liberty and dedicated to the proposition that all men are
created equal. Now we are engaged in a great civil war, testing whether that nation
or any nation so conceived and so dedicated can long endure. We are met on a great
battlefield of that war. We have come to dedicate a portion of that field as a final
resting-place for those who here gave their lives that that nation might live. It is
altogether fitting and proper that we should do this.
</cf_TruncateQuote>
```

If you'd like to try this, type the preceding call to <cf_TruncateQuote> in a file named Test.cfm.

Listing 23.10 shows `cf_TruncateQuote`'s code. As long as you save this custom tag file within the same directory as the page that calls it (`Test.cfm`), you can run the calling page and see the results.

Listing 23.10 `TruncateQuote.cfm`—Implementing a Paired Tag

```
<!--- Author: Adam Phillip Churvis -- ProductivityEnhancement.com --->
<!--- Truncates and formats a body of text --->

<cfparam name="attributes.numberOfCharacters" type="numeric" default="300">

<cfif thisTag.executionMode EQ "Start">
  <div style="border: 1px solid Black; width:300px;">
<cfelse>
  ...
  </div>

  <cfset thisTag.generatedContent = left(thisTag.GeneratedContent,
    attributes.numberOfCharacters)>
</cfif>
```

The most confusing thing for most developers is why that ellipsis appears at the *end* of the truncated quote and not before, since it appears in order in the code. The answer lies in the way that content is accumulated during the Inactive mode and modified in the End mode.

The Concept of `GeneratedContent`

As mentioned earlier, during Inactive mode a paired custom tag accumulates the content that spans the range between the opening and closing tags in a special variable named `thisTag.GeneratedContent`. Since a paired custom tag has only two opportunities to run (once in Start mode and once in End mode), and since you can't yet see or modify `thisTag.GeneratedContent` in the Start mode, the only place you can modify `thisTag.GeneratedContent` is in the End mode. In the same way that the closing HTML `Bold` tag modifies the contents between it and the opening tag, so does ColdFusion by manipulating `thisTag.GeneratedContent` in the End mode.

But why does the ellipsis appear at the end? It's because of the way ColdFusion prepares and outputs the results of running a paired custom tag—sort of like preparing a sandwich in reverse (from the top down) and then serving it.

ColdFusion gathers into a buffer any content that is output during Start mode. Then, in Inactive mode, the content accumulated in `thisTag.GeneratedContent` is added to the buffer. Then, in End mode, any content that is output directly during the End mode is added to the buffer. Any manipulation of `thisTag.GeneratedContent` by the End mode is performed after this "sandwich" has been assembled in order. The completed package is then output from the buffer as a single chunk of content.

So even though the ellipsis appeared before the manipulation of `thisTag.GeneratedContent`, the ellipsis was directly output by the End mode, so it was placed after `thisTag.GeneratedContent`.

Custom Tags That May Be Called as Paired or Empty

You may sometimes need similar functionality that applies to an entire ColdFusion page, or to only a section of a page, but that behaves a little differently in each case. For example, you may want to create a custom tag that makes checking for authentication and authorization easy. So if you want to ensure that users attempting to access a ColdFusion page are both authenticated and authorized with the `ADMIN` role, you can call the custom tag as an empty (unpaired) tag at the top of the page, like this:

```
<cf_Auth roles="ADMIN">

<p>You won't see this page unless you're logged in and have been assigned the ADMIN
role.</p>
```

And if you want to prevent only a portion of a page from being displayed unless the user is both authenticated and authorized with the `ADMIN` role, you can call the custom tag as a paired tag, like this:

```
<cf_Auth roles="ADMIN">
  <p>You won't see this section unless you're logged in and have been assigned the
ADMIN role.</p>
</cf_Auth>

<p>You'll see this section no matter who you are, and you don't have to be logged
in, either.</p>
```

But you want the tag to react differently in each case. If it's called as an empty tag and the user isn't authorized, you want to redirect to a page that tells the user that he or she has insufficient privileges; on the other hand, if the tag is called as a paired tag under the same conditions, then you want anything in the body of the tag disregarded: both content and code. To determine whether a custom tag is called as an empty tag or a paired tag, you check the value of `ThisTag.HasEndTag`.

Using `thisTag.HasEndTag`

As mentioned earlier, the `ThisTag` scope contains a variable named `thisTag.HasEndTag` that describes whether or not a custom tag has a corresponding closing tag (that is, whether or not it is a paired tag). Here's how you would use `HasEndTag` in our scenario:

```
<!--- Check to see if the user is logged in --->
<cflogin>
  <cfif thisTag.HasEndTag>
    <!--- If this tag is called as a paired tag and the user is not logged in,
    exit the tag now to prevent execution of any code between the start and
    end tags. --->
    <cfexit method="ExitTag">
  <cfelse>
    <!--- If this tag is not called as a paired tag and the user is not logged
    in, redirect to the login form. --->
    <cflocation url="#application.urlRoot#/login/LoginForm.cfm" addtoken="No">
  </cfif>
</cflogin>
```

Although this code tests only the authentication portion of the security check, it gives you a clear idea of how you can create a custom tag that can adapt its behavior based on how it is called: either as an empty tag or as a paired tag.

Using `cfexit` to Control Custom Tag Processing Flow

Paired custom tags aren't relegated to only modifying content; they can also prevent code in the body of the paired tag from being executed, or they can control the flow of logic in such code. Let's see how this works.

Notice the `<cfexit method="ExitTag">` in the preceding code. It tells the flow of logic to ignore the remainder of the custom tag and continue immediately after the end tag. So if the user hasn't logged in yet, the `<cflogin>` section executes, and if the custom tag was called as a paired tag, it ignores the rest of the custom tag, its execution cycles, its output—everything. Any content wrapped with this custom tag will not be displayed, and any wrapped code will not be executed.

Keep this principle in mind as you review Listing 23.11, which is the completed `<cf_Auth>` custom tag.

Listing 23.11 `Auth.cfm`—Using `cfexit` to Control Custom Tag Processing Flow

```
<!--- Author: Adam Phillip Churvis -- ProductivityEnhancement.com --->
<!--- Ensures that user is authenticated and authorized --->

<cfparam name="attributes.roles" type="string" default="">

<cfif thisTag.executionMode EQ "Start">

  <!--- Check to see if the user is logged in --->
  <cflogin>
    <cfif thisTag.hasEndTag>
      <!--- If this tag is called as a paired tag and the user is not logged in,
      exit the tag now to prevent execution of any code between the start and
      end tags. --->
      <cfexit method="ExitTag">
    <cfelse>
      <!--- If this tag is not called as a paired tag and the user is not logged
      in, redirect to the login form. --->
      <cflocation url="#Application.urlRoot#/login/LoginForm.cfm" addtoken="No">
    </cfif>
  </cflogin>

  <!--- Check to see if the user must be a member of one or more roles --->
  <cfif len(trim(attributes.roles)) gt 0>
    <!--- We must now see if at least one of the user's roles match those in
    Attributes.roles --->

    <!--- Loop over the list of required roles --->
    <cfset inRole = FALSE>
    <cfif isUserInAnyRole(attributes.roles)>
            <cfset inRole = true>
    </cfif>
```

Listing 23.11 (continued)

```
      <!--- Check to see if the user may access content. --->
      <cfif not inRole>
        <cfif thisTag.hasEndTag>
          <!--- If this tag is called as a paired tag and the user cannot access
          content, exit the tag now to prevent execution of any code between the
          start and end tags. --->
          <cfexit method="ExitTag">
        <cfelse>
          <!--- If this tag is not called as a paired tag and the user cannot
          access content, redirect to the login form. --->
          <cflocation url="#application.urlRoot#/login/InsufficientPrivileges.cfm"
            addtoken="No">
        </cfif>
      </cfif>
    </cfif>

</cfif>
```

As shown in Table 23.2, `<cfexit>` has three possible methods: `ExitTag`, which exits the entire custom tag; `ExitTemplate`, which exits the current execution mode of the custom tag and continues with the next; and `Loop`, which exits the End mode and starts over again in the Inactive mode (most often used to repetitively execute nested child tags). If the body of the paired tag contains nested child tags, Inactive mode passes processing to the first such child tag.

Table 23.2 `<cfexit>` Method's Effect on Flow Control

METHOD	LOCATION	BEHAVIOR
`ExitTag`	Calling page	Terminate processing
	Start mode	Continue after end tag
	End mode	Continue after end tag
`ExitTemplate`	Calling page	Terminate processing
	Start mode	Jump down to Inactive mode
	End mode	Continue after end tag
`Loop`	Calling page	(Error)
	Start mode	(Error)
	End mode	Jump back into Inactive mode

Nested Custom Tags

Although not covered in this book, ColdFusion custom tags have yet another level of complexity: the ability to be nested. That sounds complex, but if you've ever worked with HTML tables, then you are already familiar with nesting. The `<tr>` tag lives within the `<table>` tags. The `<td>` tags live within the `<tr>` tags. This nesting allows developers to create tables of any form with any data. This works because the browser can understand the relationship between each parent and child and their tags.

ColdFusion's support for nesting is just as powerful. Tags can not only recognize when they are within other tags, but they can also communicate and share data. So, for example, child tags can help define how parent tags act, and vice versa.

While this nesting is not often used by developers, it can be a very powerful feature when you need it. For more information, see the ColdFusion documentation.

Where to Go from Here

If you've been thinking of ways to use custom tags in your own applications now that you know how to design them, start experimenting! And if you come up with a killer set of custom tags, make sure to share them with the ColdFusion community through your local ColdFusion user group, discussion lists, blogs, and any other sites frequented by ColdFusion developers. Everyone will be glad you did.

CHAPTER 24

Creating Advanced ColdFusion Components

IN THIS CHAPTER

Review of ColdFusion Components

An important part of ColdFusion is its ColdFusion Components (CFCs) framework. Think of the CFC framework as a special way to combine key concepts from custom tags and user-defined functions into *objects*. These objects might represent concepts (such as individual films or actors), or they might represent processes (such as searching, creating special files, or validating credit card numbers).

I covered the basics of ColdFusion Components in Chapter 11, "The Basics of Structured Development," in *Adobe ColdFusion 9 Web Application Construction Kit, Volume 1: Getting Started*, but I'll review them here.

About ColdFusion Components

You can think of CFCs as a structured, formalized variation on custom tags. The CFC framework gently forces developers to work in a more systematic way. If you choose to use the CFC framework for parts of your application, you will find yourself thinking about those aspects in a slightly more structured, better organized way. Because CFCs are more structured, the code is generally very easy to follow and troubleshoot. Think of the CFC framework as a way to write smart code, guiding you as a developer to adopt sensible practices.

But the most dramatic benefit is that the structured nature of CFCs makes it possible for ColdFusion to look into your CFC code and find the important elements, such as what functions you have included in the CFC and what each function's arguments are. This knowledge allows ColdFusion Builder to act as a kind of interpreter between your CFC and other types of applications, such as Dreamweaver, Flash, and Web Services. If you want them to, these components become part of a larger world of interconnected clients and servers, rather than only being a part of your ColdFusion code.

CFCs Can Be Called in Many Different Ways

This chapter and the previous one have been all about making it easier to reuse the code that you and other developers write. CFCs take the notion of code reuse to a whole new level, by making it easy to reuse your code not only within ColdFusion but in other types of applications as well. Components can be called directly in ColdFusion pages, but the functions in them can also be called directly from external URLs, like Web pages that return data instead of HTML. Because of this, CFCs both can provide functionality to ColdFusion pages similarly to custom tags and user-defined functions (UDFs) and can also be called directly from Flash, from Ajax code in Web browsers, and as Web Services from other applications not on the same machine as the CFCs.

In other words, if you like the idea of reusing code, you'll love the CFC framework even more than the UDF and custom tag frameworks.

CFCs Are Object-Oriented Tools

Depending on your background, you may be familiar with object-oriented programming (OOP). Whether you know OOP or not, CFCs give you the most important real-world benefits of object-oriented programming without getting too complicated—exactly what you would expect from ColdFusion.

Without getting too deeply into the specifics, you can think of object-oriented programming as a general programming philosophy. The philosophy basically says that most of the concepts in an application represent objects in the real world and should be treated as such. Some objects, like films or merchandise for sale, might be physical. Others, like expense records or individual merchandise orders, might be more conceptual but still easy to imagine as objects—or objectified, like many of Orange Whip Studios' better-looking actors.

ColdFusion's CFC framework is based on these object-oriented ideas:

- **Classes.** In traditional object-oriented programming, the notion of a class is extremely important. For our purposes, just think of an object class as a type of object, or a *thing*. For instance, Orange Whip Studios has made many films during its proud history. If you think of each individual film as an object, then it follows that you can consider the general notion of a film (as opposed to a particular film) as a class. CFCs themselves are the classes in ColdFusion.
- **Methods.** In the object-oriented world, each type of object (that is, each class) will have a few *methods*. Methods are functions that have been conceptually attached to a class. A method represents something an object can do. For instance, think about a car as an object. A car has to start, change gears, stop, accelerate, and so on. So, a corresponding object class called car might have methods named `Car.start()`, `Car.shift()`, `Car.avoidPedestrian()`, and so on.
- **Instances.** If there is a class of object called Film, then you also need a word to refer to each individual film the studio makes. In the OOP world, this is described as an *instance*. Each individual film is an instance of the class called Film. Each instance of an object

usually has some information associated with it, called its *instance data*. For example, Film A has its own title and stars. Film B and Film C have different titles and different stars.

- **Properties.** Most real-world objects have properties that make them unique, or at least distinguish them from other objects of the same type. For instance, a real-world car has properties such as its color, make, model, engine size, number of doors, license plate and vehicle identification numbers, and so on. At any given moment, it might have other properties such as whether it is currently running, who is currently driving it, and how much gas is in the tank. If you're talking about films, the properties might be the film's title, the director, how many screens it is currently shown on, or whether it is going to be released straight to video. Properties are just variables that belong to the object (class), and they are generally stored as instance data.
- **Inheritance.** In the real world, object have various types—cars are a type of motorized vehicle, which is a type of conveyance, while a bicycle is also a conveyance. ColdFusion's CFC framework allows you to define an order of inheritance, where you can have properties and methods that are shared between various kinds of objects share the high-level stuff and then implement more specific versions with custom features. In our car example, you'd have a conveyance that might define number of wheels. Bicycle, motor vehicles, and skateboards are all types (called *subclasses*) of conveyances. Cars are a subclass of motor vehicle (as are trucks), and electric cars are a subclass of cars. I'll talk about this in more detail later in the chapter.

The Two Types of Components

Most CFCs fall into two broad categories: *static* components and *instance-based* components.

Static Components

I'll use the term *static* to refer to any component where it doesn't make sense to create individual instances of the component. These contain methods (functions, remember?) but no data that hangs around after a function runs. Often you can think of such components as *services* that are constantly listening for and answering requests. For instance, if you were creating a film-searching component that made it easy to search the current list of films, you probably wouldn't need to create multiple copies of the film-searching component.

Static components are kind of like Santa Claus, the Wizard of Oz, or your father—only one of each exists. You just go to that one and make your request.

Instance-Based Components

Other components represent ideas where it is very important to create individual instances of a component. For instance, consider a CFC called `ShoppingCart`, which represents a user's shopping cart on your site. Many different shopping carts exist in the world at any given time (one for each user). Therefore, you need to create a fresh instance of the `ShoppingCart` CFC for each new Web visitor, or perhaps each new Web session. You would expect most of the CFC's methods to return different results for each instance, depending on the contents of each user's cart. Instance-based components contain properties as well as functions, which define the differences between each instance of the component and the other instances.

Simple CFCs

The best news about CFCs is that there is really very little to learn about them. For the most part, you just write functions in much the same way that you learned in the previous chapter.

When you want to use user-defined functions (UDFs) in general, you have to include the files that contain the functions on every page that runs them. Frequently you'll create a library file that contains just the functions you need—perhaps a file called `utilityfunctions.cfm` and include it on the page.

Simple static CFCs are just a different way to call these functions—one that doesn't require you to explicitly include them and instead lets you call them similarly to custom tags.

Structure of a CFC File

Each ColdFusion component is saved in its own file, with a `.cfc` extension. Except for one new tag, `<cfcomponent>`, everything in the file is ordinary CFML code. With the `.cfc` extension instead of `.cfm`, the ColdFusion server can easily detect which files represent CFC components.

Introducing the `<cfcomponent>` Tag

The `<cfcomponent>` tag doesn't have any required attributes, so in its simplest use, you can just wrap opening and closing `<cfcomponent>` tags around everything else your CFC file contains (mainly `<cffunction>` blocks). That said, you can use two optional attributes, `hint` and `displayName`, to make your CFC file more self-describing (see Table 24.1).

If you provide these optional attributes, ColdFusion and Dreamweaver can automatically show `hint` and `displayName` in various places to make life easier for you and the other developers who might be using the component.

Table 24.1 `<cfcomponent>` Tag Syntax

ATTRIBUTE	DESCRIPTION
`hint`	Optional. What your component does, in plain English (or whatever language you choose, of course). I recommend that you provide this attribute.
`displayName`	Optional. An alternative, friendlier phrasing of the component's name. Make the component's actual name (that is, the file name) as self-describing as possible, rather than relying on the `displayName` to make its purpose clear.
`output`	Optional. See `output` under `<cffunction>` below. Only affects any code not inside a `<cffunction>`.

NOTE

As you will soon see, the `<cffunction>` and `<cfargument>` tags also have `hint` and `displayName` attributes. Each aspect of a CFC that someone would need to know about to actually use it can be described more completely within the component code itself.

Using `<cffunction>` to Create Methods

The biggest part of a CFC is the ColdFusion code you write for each of the CFC's methods (functions). To create a component's methods, you use the `<cffunction>` tag the same way you learned in Chapter 23, "Creating Custom Tags." If the method has any required or optional arguments, you use the `<cfargument>` tag, again as shown in Chapter 23.

The `<cffunction>` and `<cfargument>` tags each take a few additional attributes that Chapter 23 didn't discuss because they are relevant only for CFCs. The most important new attributes are `hint` and `displayName`, which all the CFC-related tags have in common. Tables 24.2 and 24.3 summarize all `<cffunction>` and `<cfargument>` attributes.

Table 24.2 `<cffunction>` Syntax for CFC Methods

ATTRIBUTE	DESCRIPTION
`name`	Required. The name of the function (method), as discussed in Chapter 23.
`hint`	Optional. A description of the method.
`displayName`	Optional.
`returnType`	Optional.
`returnFormat`	Optional. The format in which the data should be returned when accessed remotely. By default, all data is returned in WDDX format, unless `returnType` is XML. You can specify WDDX, JSON (for JSON format, used by Ajax), or plain (for no formatting).
`access`	Optional. This attribute defines where your method can be used. See the "Implementing Security" section below for more information.
`roles`	Optional. A list of security roles or user groups that should be able to use the method. Again, see the "Implementing Security" section below for more information.
`output`	Optional. If `false`, acts like the entire function is within a `<cfsilent>` tag. If `true`, acts like the entire function is within a `<cfoutput>` tag. If not set, acts normal; variables being output must be in `<cfoutput>` tags.

NOTE

The valid data types you can provide for `returnType` are `any`, `array`, `binary`, `component`, `Boolean`, `date`, `guid`, `numeric`, `query`, `string`, `struct`, `uuid`, `variableName`, and `xml`. If the method isn't going to return a value at all, use `returnType="void"`. If the method is going to return an instance of another component, you can provide that component's name (the file name without the `.cfc`) as the `returnType` value.

Table 24.3 `<cfargument>` Syntax for CFC Method Arguments

ATTRIBUTE	SYNTAX
`name`	Required. The name of the argument.
`hint`	An explanation of the argument's purpose. Like the `HINT` attribute for `<cfcomponent>` and `<cffunction>`, this description will be visible in Dreamweaver to make life easier for you and other developers. It is also included in the automatic documentation that ColdFusion produces for your components.
`displayName`	Optional, friendly name.
`type`	Optional. The data type of the argument. You can use any of the values mentioned in the note below Table 24.2 except for `void`.
`required`	Optional. Whether the argument is required.
`default`	Optional. A default value for the argument, if `required="No"`.

NOTE

There is actually another CFC-related tag, called `<cfproperty>`. See the "Introspection and HINTs" section below.

`<cfcomponent>` and `<cffunction>` also have many other optional attributes that are discussed in the chapters on Web Services, ORM, and ActionScript.

CFCs as Groups of Functions

Let's look at a simple example of a CFC. Say you want to create a CFC called `FilmSearchCFC`, which provides a simplified way to search for films or print out the results. You like the idea of being able to reuse this component within your ColdFusion pages, instead of having to write queries over and over again. You'd also like to be able to flip a switch and have the component available to Flash Player or Web Services.

Listing 24.1 is a simple version of the `FilmSearchCFC`.

Listing 24.1 `FilmSearchCFC.cfc`—A Simple CFC

```
<!---
 Filename: FilmSearchCFC.cfc
 Author: Ken Fricklas (KF)
 Purpose: Creates FilmSearchCFC, a simple ColdFusion Component
--->

<!--- The <CFCOMPONENT> block defines the CFC --->
<!--- The filename of this file determines the CFC's name --->
<cfcomponent hint="Search and display films">

  <cffunction name="listFilms" returnType="query" output="false" access="remote"
hint="Search for a film, and return a query with the id and title of the matching
films.">
    <!--- Optional SearchString argument --->
    <cfargument name="searchString" required="no" default="" hint="movie title to
search for.  If not provided, returns all films.">

   <!--- var scoped variables --->
```

Listing 24.1 (continued)

```
        <cfset var getFilms = "">
        <!--- Run the query --->
        <cfquery name="getFilms" datasource="ows">
        SELECT FilmID, MovieTitle FROM Films
        <!--- If a search string has been specified --->
        <cfif ARGUMENTS.searchString neq "">
        WHERE (MovieTitle LIKE '%#ARGUMENTS.searchString#%'
        OR Summary LIKE '%#ARGUMENTS.searchString#%')
        </cfif>
        ORDER BY MovieTitle
        </cfquery>

        <!--- Return the query results --->
        <cfreturn getFilms>

    </cffunction>

    <cffunction name="printFilms" returnType="void" access="remote" hint="Search for a
  film, and display the results in an HTML table.">
        <cfargument name="searchString" required="no" default="" hint="Movie title to
  search for.  If not provided, returns all films.">
        <!--- call the local function getFilms with the argument searchString --->
        <cfset var qFilms = listFilms(arguments.searchString)>
        <table>
        <tr><th>ID</th><th>Title</th></tr>
        <cfoutput query="qFilms">
        <tr><td>#qFilms.FilmID#</td><td>#qFilms.MovieTitle#</td></tr>
        </cfoutput>
        </table>
        <!--- Return the query results --->
        <cfreturn>

    </cffunction>
  </cfcomponent>
```

NOTE

Earlier, I explained that there are two types of components: static components, which just provide functionality, and instance-based components, which provide functionality but also hold information. This CFC is an example of a static component. You will see how to create instance-based components shortly.

NOTE

The `access` attribute is set to `remote`, so this component can be called directly from a Web browser, as you'll see later in this chapter.

This version of the CFC has two methods: `listFilms()`, which queries the database for a listing of current films, and `printFilms()`, which prints them out as an HTML table. For `listFilms()`, the query object is returned as the method's return value (this is why `returnType="query"` is used in the method's `<cffunction>` tag).

The `listFilms()` method takes one optional argument called `searchString`. If the `searchString` argument is provided, a `WHERE` clause is added to the database query so that only films with titles or summaries containing the argument string are selected. If the `searchString` isn't provided, all films are retrieved from the database and returned by the new method.

`PrintFilms()` takes the same arguments but outputs the data as an HTML table. Since it does not return a value, it returns `void` as the return type.

As you can see, building a simple component isn't much different from creating a user-defined function. Now that you've created the component, let's take a look at how to use it in your ColdFusion code.

Using the CFC in ColdFusion Pages

Once you have completed your CFC file, there are two basic ways to use the new component's methods in your ColdFusion code:

- With the `<cfinvoke>` tag, as discussed next.
- Using the `new` keyword (new in ColdFusion 9) to create and initialize the object and calling its methods using function syntax, in the form `component.methodName()`. (You can also use the `<cfobject>` tag or the `createObject()` function, although these are less used since the introduction of the `new` keyword, which is simpler and does more.)

Calling Methods with `<cfinvoke>`

The most straightforward way to call a CFC method is with the `<cfinvoke>` tag. `<cfinvoke>` makes your CFC look a lot like a custom tag. To provide values to the method's arguments, as in the optional `searchString` argument in Listing 24.1, either you can add additional attributes to `<cfinvoke>` or you can nest a `<cfinvokeargument>` tag within the `<cfinvoke>` tag. Tables 24.4 and 24.5 show the attributes supported by `<cfinvoke>` and `<cfinvokeargument>`.

Table 24.4 `<cfinvoke>` Tag Syntax

ATTRIBUTE	DESCRIPTION
`component`	The name of the component, as a string (the name of the file in which you saved the component, without the `.cfc` extension) or a component instance.
`method`	The name of the method you want to use.
`returnVariable`	A variable name in which to store whatever value the method decides to return.
(method arguments)	In addition to the `component`, `method`, and `returnVariable` attributes, you can also provide values to the method's arguments by providing them as attributes. For instance, the `listFilms()` method from Listing 24.1 has an optional argument called `searchString`. To provide a value to this argument, you could use `searchString="Saints"` or `searchString="#FORM.keywords#"`. You can also provide arguments using the separate `<cfinvokeargument>` tag (see Table 24.5).
`argumentCollection`	Optional. This attribute lets you provide values for the method's arguments together in a single structure. It works the same way as the `attributeCollection` attribute of the `<cfmodule>` tag. This is great for passing all your arguments to another function, as you'll see in the section on inheritance.

NOTE

For the `component` attribute, you can use the component name alone (that is, the file without the `.cfc` extension) if the `.cfc` file is in the same folder as the file that is using the `<cfinvoke>` tag. You can also specify a `.cfc` file in another folder, using dot notation to specify the location of the folder relative to the Web server root, where the dots represent folder names. For instance, you could use the `FilmSearchCFC` component by specifying `component="ows.24.FilmSearchCFC"`. For more information, see the ColdFusion 9 documentation.

NOTE

You can also save `.cfc` files in the special `CustomTags` folder (or its subfolders) or in a mapped folder. Specify the path from the `customtag` root or from the mapping using the dot syntax above.

Table 24.5 `<cfinvokeargument>` Tag Syntax

ATTRIBUTE	DESCRIPTION
`name`	The name of the argument as specified in the arguments of the method
`value`	The value of the argument

Listing 24.2 shows how to use `<cfinvoke>` to call the `listFilms()` method of the `FilmSearchCFC` component created in Listing 24.1.

Listing 24.2 Using `FilmSearchCFC.cfm`—Invoking a Component Method

```
<!---
 Filename: UsingFilmSearchCFC.cfm
 Author: Nate Weiss (NMW)
 Purpose: Uses the FilmSearchCFC component to display a list of films
--->

<html>
<head><title>Film Search Example</title></head>
<body>

<!--- Invoke the ListFilms() method of the FilmSearchComponent --->
<cfparam name="FORM.keywords" default="ColdFusion">

<cfinvoke component="FilmSearchCFC" method="listFilms" searchString="#FORM.keywords#"
 returnVariable="FilmsQuery">

<!--- Now output the list of films --->
<cfoutput query="filmsQuery">
 #FilmsQuery.MovieTitle#<br>
</cfoutput>

</body>
</html>
```

First, the `<cfinvoke>` tag invokes the `listFilms()` method provided by the `FilmSearchCFC1` component. Note that the correct value to provide to `component` is the name of the component file name, but without the `.cfc` extension.

The returnVariable attribute has been set to FilmsQuery, which means that FilmsQuery will hold whatever value the method returns. The method in question, listFilms(), returns a query object as its return value. Therefore, after the <cfinvoke> tag executes, the rest of the example can refer to filmsQuery as if it were the results of a normal <cfquery> tag. Here, a simple <cfoutput> block outputs the title of each film.

We pass the argument searchString to the method, passing the keywords from the form (or in this case, from the <cfparam> tag).

The result is a simple list of film titles, as shown in Figure 24.1. Since ColdFusion was passed in as the searchString, only the single matching film is returned.

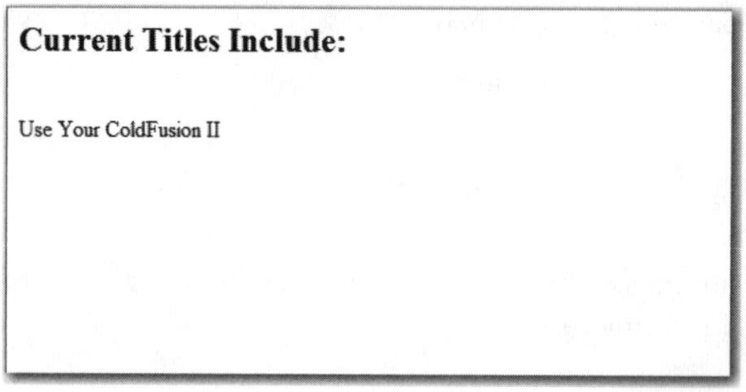

Figure 24.1

It's easy to execute a component's methods and use the results.

Current Titles Include:

Use Your ColdFusion II

NOTE

You can use the <cfinvokeargument> tag to supply the searchString argument (or any other argument), instead of providing the argument as an attribute of <cfinvoke>. This is useful when an argument is optional and may not always be passed in because of the program logic. This is an improvement over custom tag syntax, where you have to write extra code to accomplish this.

Creating an Instance of a CFC

In the previous listing, you saw how to use the <cfinvoke> tag to call a CFC method. Calling methods this way isn't much different from calling a custom tag with <cfmodule> or calling a UDF. It's also possible to create an instance of a CFC and then call the instance's methods. If the CFC doesn't track instance data (a shopping cart, say, or information about a particular film), there isn't much of a functional difference. It does, however, create a simpler syntax if you're going to invoke a lot of methods from a component, and you can also store the instance in a scope variable (application or session), as discussed later in this chapter.

To work with methods in this way, two steps are involved:

1. Create an instance of the CFC with the new keyword. You need to do this only once, since it is then in a variable that can be reused.

2. Call the method directly, using function syntax. (You can also use the <cfinvoke> tag, but instead of specifying the component by name, you pass the component instance variable directly to the component attribute.)

When using the new keyword, you simply set a variable to be a "new" copy of the CFC. You add parentheses to the end of the component name, as if it were a function. (You can also pass arguments to the component while creating it; I'll talk more about this in the section on initialization later in this chapter.) For example, to use this method in the code in Listing 24.2, you'd simply replace the <cfinvoke> tag with the following:

```
<!--- Create an instance of the CFC --->
<cfset cfcFilmSearch = new FilmSearchCFC()>

<!--- Invoke the ListFilms() method of the CFC instance --->
<cfset filmsQuery = cfcFilmSearcher.listFilms(searchString=variables.keywords)>
```

Just as in the previous example, filmsQuery would now contain the query returned by the listFilms() method.

If the component you are initializing isn't in the current path, you'd again use dot syntax; for example, if the code for FilmSearchCFC were in the path /ows/24/FilmSearchCFC, you would use this syntax:

```
<cfset cfcFilmSearch = new ows.24.FilmSearchCFC()>
```

You can see an example of this in action in Listing 24.3, below.

NOTE

It's good practice to name variables that contain CFCs in a way that's easily recognizable. In the examples below, I begin all CFC variables with cfc, for example cfcFilmSearch.

NOTE

You can also use the <cfimport> tag with the path attribute to import a directory of CFCs into the current namespace. This form of invocation will also execute the init() method if one is defined. <cfimport path="ows.24.*"> would allow you to use <cfset cfcFilmSearch = new FilmSearchCFC()> without specifying the path. This is similar to having a mapping in the ColdFusion Administrator, but one that's only valid for the current page. This can be great when you have multiple revisions of CFCs in different paths and are testing them.

Separating Logic from Presentation

As you can see, it's relatively easy to create a CFC and use its methods to display data, perhaps to create some sort of master-detail interface. The process is basically first to create the CFC and then to create a normal ColdFusion page to interact with each of the methods.

When used in this fashion, the CFC is a container for *logic* (such as extraction of information from a database), leaving the normal ColdFusion pages to deal only with *presentation* of information. Many developers find it's smart to keep a clean separation of logic and presentation while coding.

This is especially true in a team environment, where different people are working on the logic and the presentation. By keeping your interactions within databases and other logic packaged in CFCs, you can shield the people working on the presentation from the guts of your application. They can focus on making the presentation as attractive and functional as possible, without needing to know any CFML other than `<cfinvoke>` and `<cfoutput>`. And they can easily bring up the automatically generated documentation pages for each component to stay up to date on the methods each component provides.

Introspection and HINTs

If you access your component via a Web browser, it displays all the information you have provided in your component—methods, arguments, and any documentation you have provided in the `hint` arguments in a human-readable fashion. It also shows you the return types and argument types. This is known as *introspection*. This ability to see into the information in your component is also made available in logical form and is used by Flash, Web Services, ColdFusion Builder, and Dreamweaver to make the details of your component usable from within those environments.

Assuming you installed ColdFusion on your local machine and are saving this chapter's listings in the `ows/24` folder within your Web server's document root, the URL to access a component called `FilmSearchCFC` would be as follows:

```
http://localhost/ows/24/FilmSearchCFC.cfc
```

Figure 24.2 shows the data you see in a Web browser when you navigate to this URL.

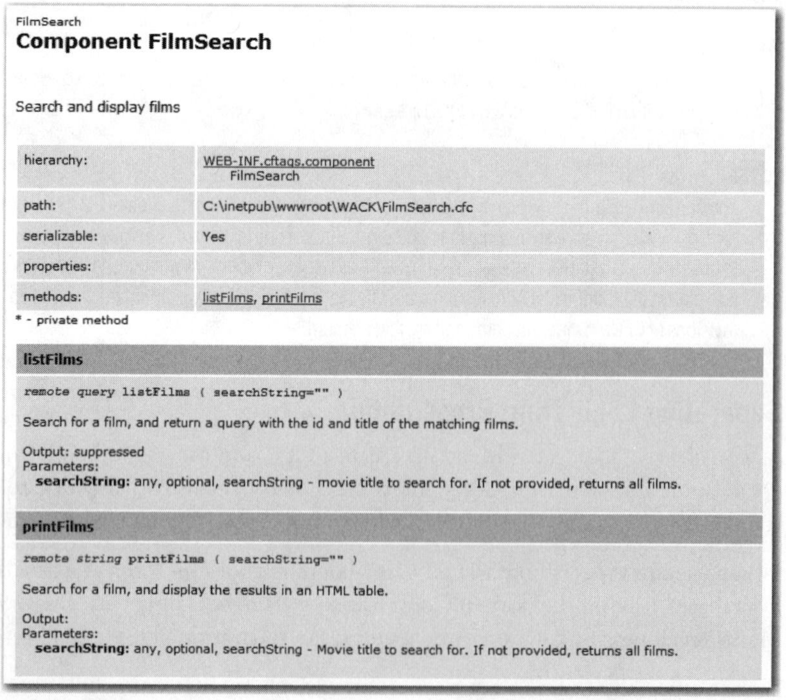

Figure 24.2

Introspection of ColdFusion component—an automatic reference page.

FilmSearch

Component FilmSearch

Search and display films

hierarchy:	WEB-INF.cftags.component FilmSearch
path:	C:\inetpub\wwwroot\WACK\FilmSearch.cfc
serializable:	Yes
properties:	
methods:	listFilms, printFilms

* - private method

listFilms

`remote query listFilms ( searchString="" )`

Search for a film, and return a query with the id and title of the matching films.

Output: suppressed
Parameters:
searchString: any, optional, searchString - movie title to search for. If not provided, returns all films.

printFilms

`remote string printFilms ( searchString="" )`

Search for a film, and display the results in an HTML table.

Output:
Parameters:
searchString: any, optional, searchString - Movie title to search for. If not provided, returns all films.

cfdump and the GetMetaData() Function

You can dump a component with `cfdump`. For example, you can dump `FilmSearchCFC` as shown here:

```
<cfobject component="FilmSearchCFC" name="cfcFilmRotation">
<cfdump var="#cfcFilmRotation#">
```

The result is shown in Figure 24.3.

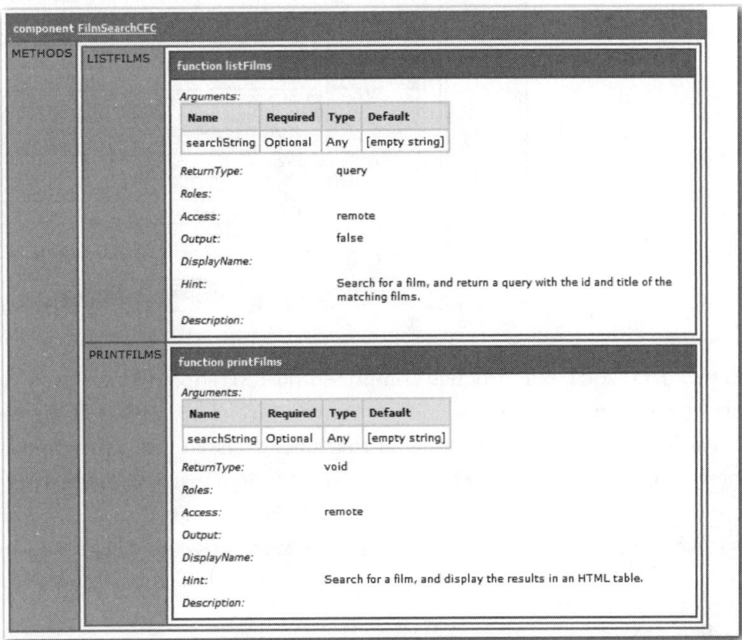

Figure 24.3

The result of `<cfdump>` on a component.

As you can see, the dump shows the component's methods and instance data. This data can be useful to your code. ColdFusion provides a means to programmatically examine an instance of a component to get this data: the `getMetaData()` function. The `getMetaData()` function returns a structure containing the same information that you can see in the HTML view of a component that `cfdump` provides.

There are two syntaxes for using the `getMetaData()` function. From outside of a component, pass the function a reference to the component object. Within a component, pass the function the component's own scope keyword `THIS`. So, for example, the code

```
<cfobject component="FilmSearchCFC" name="cfcFilmSearch">
<cfdump var="#getMetaData(cfcFilmSearch)#">
```

will produce a structure similar to that shown in Figure 24.4.

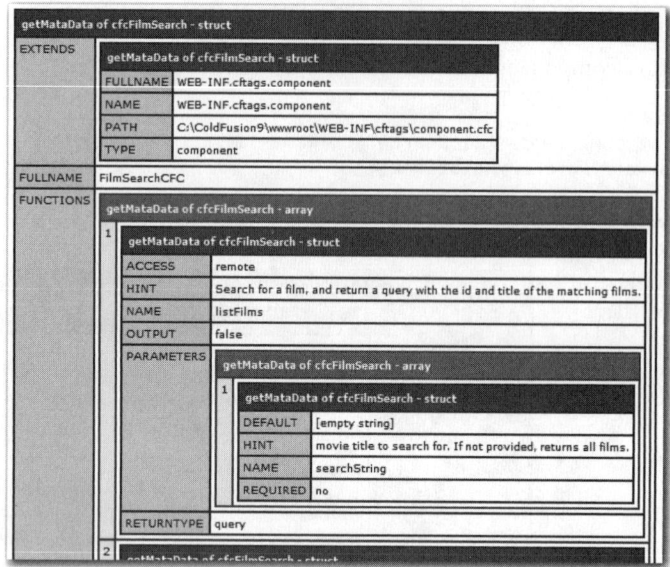

Figure 24.4
The result of the `getMetaData()` function.

With this data, you could produce component HTML documentation in whatever form you wish simply by accessing the information in the structure. This approach can be useful when you want to check the properties of a component that's been passed into a function or verify whether a method is implemented in it. This specification is demonstrated in Listing 24.3.

Listing 24.3 `getMetaData.cfm`—Display Data Using `getMetaData()`

```
<!---
  getMetaData.cfm
  Demonstrate use of getMetaData() function
--->
<!--- instantiate the FilmSearchCFC object into cfcFilmSearch --->
<cfset cfcFilmSearch = new FilmSearchCFC()>
<!--- now get the metadata, into the ourMetaData function --->
<cfset ourMetaData = getMetaData(cfcFilmSearch)>

<cfoutput>
<!--- Show the displayName and size; we could also show the hint,
  path, etc. --->
<h3>Welcome to the #ourMetaData. Name#!</h3>
Enjoy our #arrayLen(ourMetaData.functions)# functions:
<ul>
<!--- loop through and show each function's name and hint; could also show
   parameters array, etc. but let's keep it simple. --->
<cfloop index="thisFunction" from="1" to="#arrayLen(ourMetaData.functions)#">
<li>#ourMetaData.functions[thisFunction].Name# - #ourMetaData.
functions[thisFunction].Hint#</li>
</cfloop>
</ul>
</cfoutput>
```

Accessing a CFC via a URL

You have seen how to use CFC methods in your `.cfm` pages using the `<cfinvoke>` and `<cfobject>` tags. It's also possible to access methods directly with a Web browser.

NOTE

I recommend that you use CFCs by invoking their methods within a `.cfm` page (using `<cfinvoke>` or the `<cfscript>` method syntax), as you have seen already, rather than having browsers visit the CFC's methods directly. This keeps the separation of functionality and presentation clean. If you do decide to have your CFCs accessed directly via a URL, keep the parts of the code that output HTML in separate methods, as the example in this section does.

To use one of the component's methods, just add a URL parameter named `method` to the example in the previous section, where the value of the parameter is the name of the method you want to call. You can also pass any arguments on the URL. For instance, to use the method called `ProduceFilmListHTML`, passing the `searchString` value of `ColdFusion`, you would visit this URL with your browser:

```
http://localhost/ows/24/FilmSearchCFC.cfc?method=printFilms&searchString=ColdFusion
```

NOTE

It is possible to access a method via a URL only if the `<cffunction>` block that creates the method contains an `access="remote"` attribute. If you try to use the URL to access a method that has a different `access` level (including the default value `public`), ColdFusion will display an error message.

To provide values for multiple arguments, just provide the appropriate number of name-value pairs, always using the name of the argument on the left side of the equals (`=`) sign and the value of the argument on the right side of the equals sign.

NOTE

If the value of the argument might contain special characters such as spaces or slashes, you need to escape the value with ColdFusion's `URLEncodedFormat()` function. This is the case for any URL parameter, not just for CFCs. In fact, it's the case for any Web application environment, not just ColdFusion.

If you need to provide non-simple arguments such as arrays or structures, you can do so by creating a structure that contains all of your arguments (similar to creating a structure to pass to the `attributeCollection` attribute of the `<cfmodule>` tag), using the `<cfwddx>` tag to convert the structure to a WDDX packet and then passing the packet as a single URL parameter called `argumentCollection`. Or, if you are accessing the CFC via a form, you can provide such a packet as a form field named `argumentCollection`.

NOTE

In general, methods that generate HTML or other output with `<cfoutput>` should not also produce a return value. In other words, you generally shouldn't use `<cfoutput>` and `<cfreturn>` within the same method.

Getting Raw Data from a ColdFusion Component via a URL

The example I just used calls the `printFilms` method in the component, which returns the data in an HTML table. Formatted data isn't useful if you want to return your data to a program running on another machine or if you want to consume the data from within JavaScript running on a Web page. Fortunately, ColdFusion does something that makes these cases simple. Figure 24.5 shows the result of calling the `listFilms` method directly from a Web browser using this URL:

```
http://localhost/ows/24/FilmSearchCFC.cfc?method=listFilms&searchString=ColdFusion
```

Figure 24.5
A WDDX packet returned by running a component remotely.

Source of: http://localhost/ows/24/FilmSearchCFC.cfc?method=listFilms&searchString=ColdFusion - Mozilla Firefox
File Edit View Help


```
<wddxPacket version='1.0'><header/><data><recordset rowCount='1' fieldNames='FILMID,MOVIETITLE'
type='coldfusion.sql.QueryTable'><field name='FILMID'><number>19.0</number></field><field name='MOVIETITLE'>
<string>Use Your ColdFusion
II

</string></field></recordset></data></wddxPacket>
```


This is a WDDX packet, which is an XML representation of the data. This data can be consumed via JavaScript libraries, by a ColdFusion page, or by many other languages via a WDDX interpreter.

More often these days, however, you would like to return the data in JSON format, which is what Ajax Web applications most often consume. To return JSON, all you have to do is modify the definition of the function that is returning the data by setting the `returnFormat` attribute to JSON, as shown in the following example for the `listFilms` method:

```
<cffunction name="listFilms" returnType="query" output="false" access="remote"
hint="Search for a film, and return a query with the id and title of the matching
films." returnFormat="JSON">
```

The result is what you see in Figure 24.6—a JSON packet that is consumable by Ajax applications. Talk about making it easy!

Figure 24.6
The JSON response returned by component.

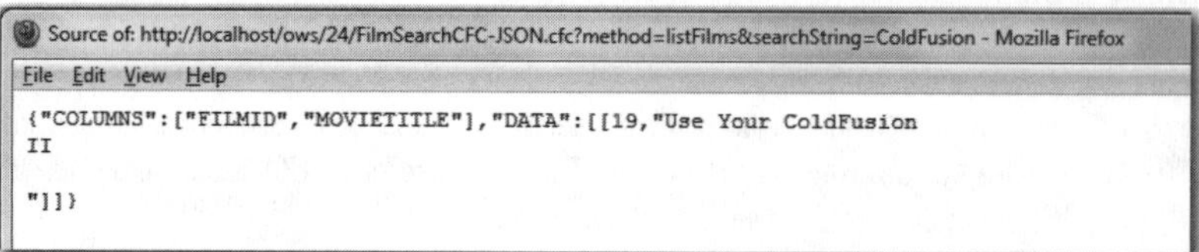

NOTE

Listing 24.1 contains one logic method and one presentation method. They are both included in the same CFC file. If you wanted, you could create a separate CFC for the presentation method. You would just use the `<cfinvoke>` tag within the presentation CFC to call the logic methods.

Accessing a CFC via a Form

It is also possible to access a method directly from a browser using a form. Conceptually, this is very similar to accessing a method via a URL, as discussed above in "Accessing a CFC via a URL." Just use the URL for the `.cfc` file as the form's action, along with the desired method name. Then add form fields for each argument that you want to pass to the method when the form is submitted. For example, the following snippet would create a simple search form, which, when submitted, would cause a list of matching films to appear:

```
<cfform action="FilmSearchCFC.cfc?method=PrintFilms">
 <input name="searchString">
 <input type="Submit" value="Search">
</cfform>
```

NOTE

Again, the method must use `access="remote"` in its `<cffunction>` tag. Otherwise, it can't be accessed directly over the Internet via a form or a URL.

Type Checking in Components

Methods in CFCs can return types through the use of the `returntype` attribute of `<cffunction>`. Consider this example:

```
<cffunction name="listFilms" returnType="query" output="false">
```

Here, the method must return a variable with a data type of `query`. Any other return type would cause an error. For example, it might make sense to return a value of the Boolean `false` because no valid query could be returned, but that would throw an error. Instead, you'd want to return an empty query or throw a custom error.

You can also specify data types in your arguments for methods. In any `<cfargument>`, you can specify the type that your method must return (just as with `<cfparam>`). This specification can prevent you from having to create a lot of custom error-handling code in your application to check the data types of arguments passed in, and it also helps in introspection. In addition, the `<cfproperty>` tag allows you to document variables and define their types for subsequent self-documentation (more on this in the next section).

NOTE

The data type attributes of `<cffunction>` and `<cfargument>` are required when creating Web Services (see Chapter 59, "Creating and Consuming Web Services," in *Adobe ColdFusion 9 Web Application Construction Kit, Volume 3: Advanced Application Development*, for more information).

Table 24.6 lists the allowed data types.

Table 24.6 Type Values Used for `returntype` (`<cffunction>`) and `type` (`<cfargument>`, `<cfproperty>`)

TYPE	DESCRIPTION
`Any`	Can be any type.
`Array`	ColdFusion array complex data type.
`Binary`	String of ones and zeros.
`Boolean`	Can be `1`, `0`, `true`, `false`, `yes`, or `no`.

Table 24.6 (continued)

TYPE	DESCRIPTION
`Date`	Any value that can be parsed into a date. Note that POP dates (see the `ParseDateTime()`function) and time zones are not accepted, but simple timestamps and ODBC-formatted dates and times are accepted.
`GUID`	The argument must be a UUID or GUID of the form `xxxxxxxx-xxxx-xxxx-xxxx-xxxxxxxxxxxx` where each `x` is a character representing a hexadecimal number (0–9, A–F).
`Numeric`	Integer or float.
`Query`	ColdFusion query result set.
`String`	ColdFusion string simple data type.
`Struct`	ColdFusion struct complex data type.
`UUID`	The argument must be a ColdFusion UUID of the form `xxxxxxxx-xxxx-xxxx-xxxxxxxxxxxxxxxx` where each `x` is a character representing a hexadecimal number (0–9, A–F).
`variableName`	A string formatted according to ColdFusion variable naming conventions (a letter, followed by any number of alphanumeric characters or underscores).
`Void`	Does not return a value.

If anything else is specified as a return type, ColdFusion processes it as returning a component for which properties have been defined. This technique allows components to define complex types for Web Services. Chapter 58, "Using Server-Side HTTP and FTP," in Volume 3, discusses this feature in depth. Typically, though, the standard data types will suffice.

Components That Hold Instance Data

The ColdFusion Components discussed so far in this chapter (the `FilmSearchCFC` and `FilmDataCFC` examples) have both been *static* components, meaning they don't hold any instance data. That is, although you can create an instance of a component with `<cfobject>` before using it, there really isn't any need to do so. One instance of a component isn't going to behave any differently from any other instance, so it's fine to simply call the CFC's methods directly.

If you create components that hold instance data, though, each instance of the component lives on its own and has its own memory in which to store information. If your component is about films, each instance might be an individual film, and the instance data might be the film's title, budget, gross receipts, or even critics' reviews. If your component is about shopping carts, each instance of the component would represent a separate user's shopping cart, and the instance data would be the cart's contents.

This section will explain how to create this type of component.

Introducing the THIS Scope

The CFC framework sets aside a special variable scope called THIS, which stands for *this instance* of a component. You can think of the word THIS as meaning "this film" or "this shopping cart" or "this object," depending on what you intend your component to represent.

The THIS Scope Represents an Instance

The THIS scope is similar in its function to the SESSION scope you learned about in Chapter 19, "Working with Sessions," in Volume 1, except that instead of being a place to store information that will be remembered for the duration of a user's session, THIS is a place to store information that will be remembered for as long as a particular instance of a component continues to exist.

As an example, consider a fictional CFC called ParrotCFC. The idea behind the component is that each instance of the component represents one parrot. Each instance of the component needs to have a name, an age, a gender, a wingspan, a favorite word or cracker, and so on. This kind of information is exactly what the THIS scope was designed for. Your CFC code just needs to set variables in the THIS scope (perhaps THIS.favoriteWord or THIS.wingSpan) to remember these values. ColdFusion will keep each component's variables separate.

Steps in the THIS Process

Here are the steps involved:

1. Create the CFC file. Within the file, use the THIS scope as the component's personal memory space, keeping in mind that each instance of the component (that is, each parrot) will get its own copy of the THIS scope for its own use.
2. In your ColdFusion pages, create an instance of the CFC with new before you use any of the component's methods. If you want the instance to live longer than the current page request, you can place the instance in the SESSION or APPLICATION scope.
3. Now go ahead and use the instance's methods with the <cfinvoke> tag as you learned in previous examples. Make sure that you specify the instance (that is, the individual parrot) as the component attribute of the <cfinvoke> tag, rather than as the name of the CFC. Alternatively, call the methods using function syntax.

In this scenario, each individual instance of the ParrotCFC has a life of its own. The <cfobject> tag is what makes a particular parrot come to life. The THIS scope automatically maintains the parrot's characteristics.

Extending the metaphor, if the parrot is the pet of one of your Web users, you can make the parrot follow the user around by having it live in the user's SESSION scope. Or if the parrot doesn't belong to a particular person but instead belongs to your application as a whole (perhaps the parrot is your site's mascot), you could have it live in the APPLICATION scope. Or you might have a bunch of parrots that are looking for owners. You could keep these parrots (each one an instance of the ParrotCFC component) in an array in the APPLICATION scope. When a user wants to take one of the parrots home as a pet, you could move the parrot out of the array and into the SESSION scope.

Okay, that's enough about parrots. The idea here is to think of a CFC as an independent thing or object with its own properties. You store individual instances of the object in the `APPLICATION` or `SESSION` scope if you want it to remain in memory for a period of time, or just leave it in the normal scope if you need the instance to live only for the current page request.

NOTE

By definition, a component that doesn't refer to the `THIS` scope at all in its methods doesn't need to be instantiated with `<cfobject>` before calling its methods and can therefore be considered a static component. Any component that does use the `THIS` scope internally probably needs to be instantiated to function properly.

Instance Data CFC Example

Let's look at a simple example of a CFC that holds instance data. The component is called `FilmRotationCFC`, and its purpose is to keep track of a featured film.

Designing `FilmRotationCFC`

To demonstrate the use of multiple methods within an instantiated component, the `FilmRotationCFC` component will contain the methods listed in Table 24.7.

Table 24.7 Methods Provided by `FilmRotationCFC`

METHOD	DESCRIPTION
`currentFilmID()`	Returns the ID number of the currently featured film. Because this method uses `access="Private"`, it can only be used internally within the `FilmRotationCFC`.
`isFilmNeedingRotation()`	Returns `TRUE` if the current film has been featured for more than the amount of time specified as the rotation interval (5 seconds by default). Returns `FALSE` if the current film should be left as is for now. This is a private method that can only be used internally.
`rotateFilm()`	Rotates the currently featured film if it has been featured for more than the amount of time specified as the rotation interval (5 seconds by default). Internally, this method calls `isFilmNeedingRotation()` to find out if the current film has expired. If so, it sets the current film to be the next film in the rotation.
`getCurrentFilmID()`	Rotates the current movie (if appropriate) and then returns the currently featured film. Internally, this function calls `rotateFilm()` and then returns the value of `currentFilmID()`. This is a public method.
`getCurrentFilmData()`	Returns the title, summary, and other information about the currently featured film. Internally, this function calls `getCurrentFilmID()` and then returns the information provided by the `GetFilmData()` method of the `FilmDataCFC2` component. This method is included mainly to show how to call one component's methods from another component.
`randomizedFilmList()`	Returns a list of all `FilmID` numbers in the `ows` database, in random order. Internally, this uses the `listRandomize()` method to perform the randomization.

Table 24.7 (continued)

METHOD	DESCRIPTION
`listRandomize(list)`	Accepts any comma-separated list and returns a new list with the same items in it, but in a random order. Because this method uses `access="Private"`, it can only be used internally within the `FilmRotationCFC`. This method really doesn't have anything to do with this CFC in particular; you could reuse it in any situation where you wanted to randomize a list of items.

TIP

In this CFC, I am adopting a convention of starting all public method names with the word `Get`. You might want to consider using naming conventions such as this when creating your own component methods.

It is conventional in many programming languages to start the name of any function that returns a Boolean value with the word `Is`. You might want to consider doing the same in your own CFCs.

Building `FilmRotationCFC`

Listing 24.4 shows the code for the `FilmRotationCFC` component. Because this component includes a number of methods, this code listing is a bit long. Don't worry. The code for each of the individual methods is quite short.

Listing 24.4 `FilmRotationCFC.cfc`—Building a CFC That Maintains Instance Data

```
<!---
 Filename: FilmRotationCFC.cfc
 Author: Nate Weiss (NMW)
 Purpose: Creates FilmRotationCFC, a ColdFusion Component
--->

<cfcomponent output="false" hint="Provide Randomized Film List Functions">
  <cfproperty name="currentListPos" hint="current position in list" type="numeric"
required="no" default="1">
  <cfproperty name="filmList" hint="randomized list of films" type="string">
  <cfproperty name="rotationInterval" hint="how often the film rotates, in seconds"
type="numeric" required="no" default="5">
  <cfproperty name="currentUntil" hint="when does this film expire, and the next in
the list becomes current" type="date">

  <!--- *** begin initialization code *** --->
  <cfset THIS.filmList = randomizedFilmList()>
  <cfset THIS.currentListPos = 1>
  <cfset THIS.rotationInterval = 5>
  <cfset THIS.currentUntil = dateAdd("s", THIS.rotationInterval, now())>


  <!--- *** end initialization code *** --->
  <!--- Private function: RandomizedFilmList() --->
  <cffunction name="randomizedFilmList" returnType="string" access="private"
  output="false"
  hint="For internal use. Returns a list of all Film IDs, in random order.">
```

Listing 24.4 (continued)

```
    <!--- This variable is for this function's use only --->
    <cfset var getFilmIDs = "">

    <!--- Retrieve list of current films from database --->
    <cfquery name="getFilmIDs" datasource="ows"
    cachedwithin="#CreateTimeSpan(0,1,0,0)#">
    SELECT FilmID FROM Films
    ORDER BY MovieTitle
    </cfquery>

    <!--- Return the list of films, in random order --->
    <cfreturn listRandomize(valueList(getFilmIDs.FilmID))>
  </cffunction>

  <!--- Private utility function: ListRandomize() --->
  <cffunction name="listRandomize" returnType="string"
  output="false"
  hint="Randomizes the order of the items in any comma-separated list.">

    <!--- List argument --->
    <cfargument name="list" type="string" required="Yes"
    hint="The string that you want to randomize.">

    <!--- These variables are for this function's use only --->
    <cfset var result = "">
    <cfset var randPos = "">

    <!--- While there are items left in the original list... --->
    <cfloop condition="listLen(ARGUMENTS.list) gt 0">
      <!--- Select a list position at random --->
      <cfset randPos = randRange(1, listLen(ARGUMENTS.list))>
      <!--- Add the item at the selected position to the Result list --->
      <cfset result = listAppend(result, listGetAt(ARGUMENTS.list, randPos))>
      <!--- Remove the item from selected position of the original list --->
      <cfset ARGUMENTS.list = listDeleteAt(ARGUMENTS.list, randPos)>
    </cfloop>

    <!--- Return the reordered list --->
    <cfreturn result>
  </cffunction>

  <!--- Private method: IsFilmNeedingRotation() --->
  <cffunction name="isFilmNeedingRotation" access="private" returnType="boolean"
  output="false"
  hint="For internal use. Returns TRUE if the film should be rotated now.">

    <!--- Compare the current time to the THIS.CurrentUntil time --->
    <!--- If the film is still current, DateCompare() will return 1 --->
    <cfset var dateComparison = dateCompare(THIS.currentUntil, now())>

    <!--- Return TRUE if the film is still current, FALSE otherwise --->
    <cfreturn dateComparison neq 1>
  </cffunction>

  <!--- RotateFilm() method --->
  <cffunction name="rotateFilm" access="private" returnType="void" output="false"
```

Listing 24.4 (CONTINUED)

```
hint="For internal use. Advances the current movie.">

  <!--- If the film needs to be rotated at this time... --->
  <cfif isFilmNeedingRotation()>
    <!--- Advance the instance-level THIS.CurrentListPos value by one --->
    <cfset THIS.currentListPos = THIS.currentListPos + 1>

    <!--- If THIS.CurrentListPos is now more than the number of films, --->
    <!--- Start over again at the beginning (the first film) --->
    <cfif THIS.currentListPos gt listLen(THIS.FilmList)>
      <cfset THIS.currentListPos = 1>
    </cfif>

    <!--- Set the time that the next rotation will be due --->
    <cfset THIS.currentUntil = dateAdd("s", THIS.rotationInterval, now())>
  </cfif>
</cffunction>

<!--- Private method: CurrentFilmID() --->
<cffunction name="currentFilmID" access="private" returnType="numeric"
output="false"
hint="For internal use. Returns the ID of the current film in rotation.">

  <!--- Return the FilmID from the current row of the GetFilmIDs query --->
  <cfreturn listGetAt(THIS.filmList, THIS.currentListPos)>
</cffunction>

<!--- Public method: GetCurrentFilmID() --->
<cffunction name="getCurrentFilmID" access="public" returnType="numeric"
output="false"
hint="Returns the ID number of the currently 'featured' film.">
  <!--- First, rotate the current film --->
  <cfset rotateFilm()>

  <!--- Return the ID of the current film --->
  <cfreturn currentFilmID()>
</cffunction>

<!--- Public method: GetCurrentFilmData() --->
<cffunction name="getCurrentFilmData" access="remote" returnType="struct"
output="false"
hint="Returns structured data about the currently 'featured' film.">

  <!--- This variable is local just to this function --->
  <cfset var currentFilmData = "">

  <!--- Invoke the GetCurrentFilmID() method (in separate component) --->
  <!--- Returns a structure with film's title, summary, actors, etc. --->
  <cfinvoke component="FilmDataCFC2" method="getFilmData"
  filmID="#getCurrentFilmID()#" returnVariable="currentFilmData">

  <!--- Return the structure --->
  <cfreturn currentFilmData>
</cffunction>

</cfcomponent>
```

The most important thing to note and understand about this CFC is the purpose of the first few `<cfset>` tags at the top of Listing 24.4. Because these lines sit directly within the body of the `<cfcomponent>` tag, outside any `<cffunction>` blocks, they are considered *initialization code* that will be executed whenever a new instance of the component is created. Notice that each of these `<cfset>` tags creates variables in the special `THIS` scope, which means they are assigned to each instance of the component separately. Typically, all that happens in a CFC's initialization code is that it sets instance data in the `THIS` scope.

NOTE

It's important to understand that these lines don't execute each time one of the instance's methods is called. They execute only when a new instance of the component is brought to life with the `<cfobject>` tag.

The `<cfset>` tags at the top of the listing create these instance variables:

- `THIS.filmList` is a list of all current films, in the order in which the component should show them. The component's `randomizedFilmList()` method creates the sequence. This order will be different for each instance of the CFC.
- `THIS.currentListPos` is the current position in the randomized list of films. The initial value is `1`, which means that the first film in the randomized list will be considered the featured film.
- `THIS.rotationInterval` is the number of seconds that a film should be considered featured before the component features the next film. Right now, the interval is 5 seconds.
- `THIS.currentUntil` is the time at which the current film should be considered expired. At that point, the CFC will select the next film in the randomized list of films. When the component is first instantiated, this variable is set to 5 seconds in the future.

Let's take a quick look at the `<cffunction>` blocks in Listing 24.4.

The `randomizedFilmList()` method will always be the first one to be called, since it is used in the initialization code block. This method simply retrieves a record set of film IDs from the database. Then it turns the film IDs into a comma-separated list with ColdFusion's `valueList()` function and passes the list to the CFC's `listRandomize()` method. The resulting list (which is a list of films in random order) is returned as the method's return value.

The `listRandomize()` method uses a combination of ColdFusion's list functions to randomize the list supplied to the `list` argument. The basic idea is to pluck items at random from the original list, adding them to the end of a new list called `result`. When there are no more items in the original list, the `result` variable is returned as the method's return value.

The `currentFilmID()` method simply returns the `FilmID` in the current position of the CFC's randomized list of films. As long as `THIS.currentListPos` is set to `1`, this method returns the first film's ID.

The `isFilmNeedingRotation()` method uses `dateCompare()` to compare `THIS.currentUntil` to the current time. If the time has passed, this method returns `TRUE` to indicate that the current film is ready for rotation.

The `rotateFilm()` method is interesting because it actually makes changes to the variables in the `THIS` scope first created in the initialization code block. First, it uses `isFilmNeedingRotation()` to see whether the current film has been featured for more than 5 seconds already. If so, it advances the `This.currentListPos` value by 1. If the new `currentListPos` value is greater than the length of the list of films, that means all films in the sequence have been featured, so the position is set back to `1`. Lastly, the method uses ColdFusion's `dateAdd()` function to set the `THIS.currentUntil` variable to 5 seconds in the future.

The `getCurrentFilmID()` method ties all the concepts together. Whenever this method is used, the `rotateFilm()` method is called (which will advance the current film to the next item in the sequence if the current one has expired). It then calls `currentFilmID()` to return the current film's ID.

Storing CFCs in the APPLICATION Scope

Now that the `FilmRotationCFC` component is in place, it's quite simple to put it to use. Listing 24.5 shows one way of using the component.

Listing 24.5 `UsingFilmRotationCFCa.cfm`—Instantiating a CFC at the Application Level

```
<!---
 Filename: UsingFilmRotationCFCa.cfm
 Author: Nate Weiss (NMW)
 Purpose: Demonstrates storage of CFC instances in shared memory scopes
--->

<html>
<head>
 <title>Using FilmRotationCFC</title>
</head>

<body>

<!--- If an instance of the FilmRotatorCFC component hasn't been created --->
<!--- yet, create a fresh instance and store it in the APPLICATION scope --->
<cfif not isDefined("APPLICATION.filmRotator")>
 <cfset APPLICATION.FilmRotator = new FilmRotationCFC()>
</cfif>

<!--- Invoke the GetCurrentFilmID() method of the FilmRotator CFC object --->
<cfset featuredFilmID = Application.filmRotator.getCurrentFilmID()>

<p>The callout at the right side of this page shows the currently featured film.
The featured film changes every five seconds.
Just reload the page to see the next film in the sequence.
The sequence will not change until the ColdFusion server is restarted.</p>

<!--- Show the current film in a callout, via custom tag --->
<cf_ShowMovieCallout
 filmID="#featuredFilmID#">

</body>
</html>
```

The idea here is to keep an instance of `FilmRotationCFC` in the `APPLICATION.filmRotator` variable. Keeping it in the `APPLICATION` scope means that the same instance will be kept in the server's memory until the ColdFusion server is restarted. All sessions that visit the page will share the instance.

First, a simple `isDefined()` test sees if the CFC instance called `APPLICATION.filmRotator` already exists. If not, the instance is created with the `<cfobject>` tag. So, after this `<cfif>` block, the instance is guaranteed to exist. Keep in mind that the CFC's initialization code block is executed when the instance is first created.

NOTE

If you wanted the CFC instance to be available to all pages in the application, you could move the `<cfif>` block in Listing 24.5 to your `Application.cfc` file.

Displaying the currently featured film is simply a matter of calling the `getCurrentFilmID()` method and passing it to the `<cf_ShowMovieCallout>` custom tag. When a browser visits this listing, the currently featured movie is displayed. If you reload the page repeatedly, you will see that the featured movie changes every 5 seconds. If you wait long enough, you will see the sequence of films repeat itself. The sequence will continue to repeat until the ColdFusion server is restarted, at which point a new sequence of films will be selected at random.

Storing CFCs in the `SESSION` Scope

One of the neat things about CFCs is their independence. You will note that the code for the `RotateFilmCFC` component doesn't contain a single reference to the `APPLICATION` scope. In fact, it doesn't refer to any of ColdFusion's built-in scopes at all, except for the `THIS` scope.

This means it's possible to create some instances of the CFC that are kept in the `APPLICATION` scope, and others that are kept in the `SESSION` scope. All the instances will work properly and will maintain their own versions of the variables in the `THIS` scope.

To see this in action, go back to Listing 24.5 and change the code so that the CFC instance is kept in the `SESSION` scope instead of the `APPLICATION` scope. Now each Web session will be given its own `FilmRotator` object, stored as a session variable. You can see how this looks in Listing 24.6 (in the upcoming section "Modifying Properties from a ColdFusion Page").

To see the difference in behavior, open the revised listing in two different browsers (say, Firefox and Internet Explorer 8), and experiment with reloading the page. You will find that the films are featured on independent cycles and that each session sees the films in a different order. If you view the page on different computers, you will see that each machine also has its own private, randomized sequence of featured films.

Instance Data as Properties

As I've explained, the code for the `FilmRotationCFC` component uses the `THIS` scope to store certain variables for its own use. You can think of these variables as *properties* of each component instance, because they are the items that make a particular instance special, giving it its individuality, its life.

Sometimes you will want to display or change the value of one of these properties from a normal ColdFusion page. ColdFusion makes it very easy to access an instance's properties. Basically, you can access any variable in a CFC's `THIS` scope as a property of the instance itself.

Modifying Properties from a ColdFusion Page

If you have a CFC instance called `SESSION.myFilmRotator` and you want to display the current value of the `currentUntil` property (that is, the value of the variable that is called `THIS.currentUntil` within the CFC code), you can do so with the following in a normal `.cfm` page:

```
<cfoutput>
 #timeFormat(SESSION.myFilmRotator.currentUntil)#
</cfoutput>
```

To change the value of the `rotationInterval` property (referred to as `THIS.rotationInterval` in the `FilmRotationCFC.cfc` file) to 10 seconds instead of the usual 5 seconds, you could use this line:

```
<cfset SESSION.myFilmRotator.rotationInterval = 10>
```

After you changed the `rotationInterval` for the `SESSION.FilmRotator` instance, then that session's films would rotate every 10 seconds instead of every 5 seconds. Listing 24.6 shows how all this would look in a ColdFusion page.

Listing 24.6 `UsingFilmRotationCFCb.cfm`—Interacting with a CFC's Properties

```
<!---
 Filename: UsingFilmRotationCFCc.cfm
 Author: Nate Weiss (NMW)
 Purpose: Demonstrates storage of CFC instances in shared memory scopes
--->

<html>
<head>
 <title>Using FilmRotationCFC</title>
</head>

<body>

<!--- If an instance of the FilmRotatorCFC component hasn't been created --->
<!--- yet, create a fresh instance and store it in the SESSION scope --->
<cfif not isDefined("SESSION.myFilmRotator")>
 <cfset SESSION.myFilmRotator = new FilmRotationCFC()>

 <!--- Rotate films every ten seconds --->
 <cfset SESSION.myFilmRotator.rotationInterval = 10>
</cfif>

<!--- Display message --->
<cfoutput>
 <p>
 The callout at the right side of this page shows the currently featured film.
 Featured films rotate every #SESSION.myFilmRotator.rotationInterval# seconds.
 Just reload the page to see the next film in the sequence.
 The sequence will not change until the web session ends.</p>
 The next film rotation will occur at:
```

Listing 24.6 (continued)

```
 #timeFormat(SESSION.myFilmRotator.currentUntil, "h:mm:ss tt")#
</cfoutput>

<!--- Show the current film in a callout, via custom tag --->
<cf_ShowMovieCallout filmID="#SESSION.myFilmRotator.getCurrentFilmID()#">

</body>
</html>
```

NOTE

You can experiment with changing the `RotationInterval` property to different values. Keep in mind that the code in the `<cfif>` block will execute only once per session, so you may need to restart ColdFusion to see a change. If you are using J2EE Session Variables, you can just close and reopen your browser. Or you could move the `<cfset>` line outside the `<cfif>` block.

What all this means is that the CFC's methods can access an instantiated CFC's properties internally via the `THIS` scope, and your ColdFusion pages can access them via the instance object variable itself. As you learned in the introduction to this topic, CFCs can be thought of as containers for data and functionality, like many objects in the real world. You know how to access the data (properties) as well as the functionality (methods).

Documenting Properties with `<cfproperty>`

As you learned earlier, you can easily view a CFC's methods in the Component tree in the Dreamweaver's Application panel. You can also view them in the automatically generated reference page that ColdFusion produces if you visit a CFC's URL with your browser. Since a CFC's properties are also important, it would be nice if there was an easy way to view them too.

ColdFusion provides a tag called `<cfproperty>` that lets you provide information about each variable in the `this` scope that you want to document as an official property of a component. The `<cfproperty>` tags must be placed at the top of the CFC file, just within the `<cfcomponent>` tag, before any initialization code.

Another function that `<cfproperty>` provides for you is the ability to do type checking on your properties (this is new in ColdFusion 9). Using the attributes `validate` and `validateparams`, you can specify the data types that are allowed for your components' properties, and if something tries to set them to an invalid value, ColdFusion will throw an error.

Table 24.8 shows the syntax for the `<cfproperty>` tag.

Table 24.8 `<cfproperty>` Tag Syntax

ATTRIBUTE	DESCRIPTION
`name`	The name of the property. This should match the name of the variable in the `THIS` scope that is used within the component's methods.
`type`	The data type of the property, such as `numeric`, `string`, or `query`.
`required`	Whether the property is required (documentation only).

Table 24.8 (continued)

ATTRIBUTE	DESCRIPTION
`default`	The initial value of the property (documentation only).
`hint`	An explanation of what the property does or represents.
`displayName`	An alternate name for the property.
`validate`	Data type for the parameter. See the "Implicit Getters and Setters" section below.
`validateparams`	Parameters required for the validation type, such as `if`, `range`, `max`, and so on. See the "Implicit Getters and Setters" section below.

You'll notice in Listing 24.6 that I've documented all the properties with `<cfproperty>`, for example:

```
<cfproperty
 name="RotationInterval"
 type="numeric"
 required="No"
 default="5"
 hint="The number of seconds between film rotations.">
```

NOTE

Remember that `<cfproperty>` doesn't actively create a property in this version of ColdFusion. Just because you add the `<cfproperty>` tag to document the `THIS.rotationInterval` property doesn't mean that you can remove the `<cfset>` tag that actually creates the variable and gives it its initial value.

CFCs and the VARIABLES Scope

The `THIS` scope isn't the only way to persist data within a CFC. Each CFC also has a `VARIABLES` scope. This scope acts just like the `VARIABLES` scope within a simple CFM page. Like the `THIS` scope, each method in the CFC can read and write to the scope. However, unlike the `THIS` scope, you can't display or modify the value outside the CFC.

Some people consider this a good thing. Look at the code in Listing 24.6. One line sets the CFC's `rotationInterval` variable. What happens if the code sets it to a value of "ten" instead of the number "10"? The next time this page, or any other, runs the `getCurrentFilmID` method, the code will blow up because the property is no longer a number. The whole point of encapsulation is to prevent problems like this. How can you prevent this?

Keeping Your Properties Clean: Getters and Setters

To make sure your properties are the right type, in the right range, and so on, you generally don't want to allow your users to directly access the properties of your CFCs. To prevent this, for each property of your CFC, build two methods—one to get the current value and another to set its value. This allows you to check and make sure the value being set is valid, as well as massage any data on the way out so code that's getting a property's value gets it in a way that's useful. For example, instead of directly accessing the `rotationInterval` value of the CFC, the CFC itself could define a setRotationInterval method. Any CFM that needs to set this value would simply use the method. If an invalid value is passed in, the component can throw an error or simply ignore it.

It's considered good programming practice to always name the getters and setters getProperty() and setProperty(). For example, for the currentUntil property, you would name them getCurrentUntil() and setCurrentUntil().

Listing 24.7 shows an excerpt from the FilmRotationCFC that contains a typical getter and setter for the rotationInterval property.

Listing 24.7 FilmRotationCFCb.cfc—Film Rotation with Getters and Setters (Excerpt)

```
<!--- getter method for rotationInterval --->
<cffunction name="getrotationInterval" returntype="numeric" hint="getter for
rotationInterval property">
  <cfreturn this.currentUntil>
</cffunction>

<!--- setter method for rotationInterval --->
<cffunction name="setrotationInterval" returntype="void" hint="setter for
rotationInterval property">
  <cfargument name="newValue" required="yes" type="numeric" hint="new value for
rotationInterval property">
  <cfif isNumeric(arguments.newValue)>
    <cfset this.currentUntil = arguments.newValue>
  <cfelse>
    <cfthrow type="application" message="Invalid value for setrotationInterval: must
be numeric">
  </cfif>
  <cfreturn>
</cffunction>
```

Implicit Getters and Setters

Since all getter and setter methods generally do is validate the data being set, most of these methods wind up looking almost exactly the same. Because of this, the folks who designed the ColdFusion 9 language added a feature to components that lets ColdFusion provide this functionality without you actually having to write the functions.

All you need to do to add getter and setter functions to all your properties is add a single attribute to the <cfcomponent> tag: accessors="true". For example, in FilmRotationCFC.cfc, you'd simply change the first line to read as follows:

```
<cfcomponent output="false" hint="Provide Randomized Film List Functions"
             accessors="true">
```

Without any additional work, you can now call getters and setters for any of the properties you have defined with <cfproperty> tags. getFilmList, setFilmList, getCurrentListPos, setCurrentListPos, and so on, are all now available.

In addition, you can now use the validate and validateparams attributes of <cfproperty> to automatically create the validation code for your properties. To effectively create the setrotationInterval validation in Listing 24.7, you'd just change your <cfproperty> tag to this:

```
<cfproperty name="rotationInterval" hint="how often the film rotates, in seconds"
type="numeric" validate="numeric">
```

NOTE

If you explicitly define getters and setters for some of your properties, ColdFusion won't override them if you have accessors=true. Also, If you don't want certain properties to have a getter or setter, for those individual properties you can add a "getter=no" or "setter=no" attribute to the <cfproperty> tag, and ColdFusion won't create them.

Initializing Components

Most of the time, when you create a component, you'll want it to be independent of the application that is calling it. For example, you wouldn't want to hard-code the value of the data source into a component, because it would be different between one application using it and another. However, the component isn't usable until it "knows" what its data source is and probably some other initialization values. Therefore, most components require some sort of initialization to work.

The typical thing to do with a component is create a special method called init that is called when starting up the component; it returns a reference to the component itself. ColdFusion 9 supports this behavior with the new keyword by automatically calling the init method with whatever arguments are passed to the component when it is invoked.

Listing 24.8 contains an excerpt of the init method from the updated version of the FilmRotationCFC that contains the init function. Note that the code outside the methods has been moved to the init method, and the <cfquery> tag in the randomizedFilmList method now uses the local variable variables.dsn instead of the hard-coded value for the data source.

Listing 24.8 Updated FilmRotationCFCc.cfc with init Method

```
<!---
 Filename: FilmRotationCFCc.cfc
 Author: Nate Weiss (NMW)
 Purpose: Creates FilmRotationCFC, a ColdFusion Component
--->
<cfcomponent output="false">
  <cfproperty name="currentListPos" hint="current position in list" type="numeric">
  <cfproperty name="filmList" hint="randomized list of films" type="string">
  <cfproperty name="rotationInterval" hint="how often the film rotates, in seconds"
type="numeric">
  <cfproperty name="currentUntil" hint="when does this film expire, and the next in
the list becomes current" type="date">
  <!--- *** begin initialization code *** --->
  <!--- init method --->
  <cffunction name="init" returntype="component" hint="initialization">
    <cfargument name="datasource" required="yes" type="string">
    <cfargument name="rotationInterval" required="no" default="5" type="numeric">
    <cfset variables.dsn = arguments.datasource>
    <cfset THIS.rotationInterval = arguments.rotationInterval>
    <cfset THIS.filmList = randomizedFilmList()>
```

Listing 24.8 (continued)

```
    <cfset THIS.currentListPos = 1>
    <cfset THIS.currentUntil = dateAdd("s", THIS.rotationInterval, now())>
  </cffunction>
  <!--- *** end initialization code *** --->
  <!--- Private function: RandomizedFilmList() --->
  <cffunction name="randomizedFilmList" returnType="string" access="private"
  output="false"
  hint="For internal use. Returns a list of all Film IDs, in random order.">

    <!--- This variable is for this function's use only --->
    <cfset var getFilmIDs = "">

    <!--- Retrieve list of current films from database --->
    <cfquery name="getFilmIDs" datasource="#variables.dsn#"
    cachedwithin="#CreateTimeSpan(0,1,0,0)#">
    SELECT FilmID FROM Films
    ORDER BY MovieTitle
    </cfquery>

    <!--- Return the list of films, in random order --->
    <cfreturn listRandomize(valueList(getFilmIDs.FilmID))>
  </cffunction>
```

To call this new method, you change the line in Listing 24.5 that creates the component variable to pass in the required arguments, as shown here:

```
<cfset APPLICATION.FilmRotatorc = new FilmRotationCFCc(datasource="ows",
rotationInterval="#variables.rotInterval#")>
```

NOTE

It's standard practice to use the initialization method `init`, but ColdFusion allows you to override that value by passing the argument `initmethod=<methodname>`.

CFCs, Shared Scopes, and Locking

In Chapter 18, "Introducing the Web Application Framework," in Volume 1, you learned that it's important to beware of *race conditions*. A race condition is any type of situation where strange, inconsistent behavior might arise if multiple page requests try to change the values of the same variables at the same time. Race conditions aren't specific to ColdFusion development; all Web developers should bear them in mind. See Chapter 18 for more information about this important topic.

Since the past few examples have encouraged you to consider storing instances of your CFCs in the `APPLICATION` or `SESSION` scope, you may be wondering whether there is the possibility of logical race conditions occurring in your code and whether you should use the `<cflock>` tag or some other means to protect against them if necessary.

The basic answer is that packaging your code in a CFC doesn't make it more or less susceptible to race conditions. If the nature of the information you are accessing within a CFC's methods is such that it shouldn't be altered or accessed by two different page requests at the same time, you most likely should use the <cflock> tag to make sure one page request waits for the other before continuing.

Direct Access to Shared Scopes from CFC Methods

If your CFC code is creating or accessing variables in the APPLICATION or SESSION scope directly (that is, if the words APPLICATION or SESSION appear in the body of your CFC's <cffunction> blocks), place <cflock> tags around those portions of the code. The <cflock> tags should appear inside the <cffunction> blocks, not around them. Additionally, you should probably place <cflock> tags around any initialization code (that is, within <cfcomponent> but outside any <cffunction> blocks) that refers to APPLICATION or SESSION. In either case, you would probably use scope="SESSION" or scope="APPLICATION" as appropriate; alternatively, you could use <cflock>'s NAME attribute as explained in Chapter 18 if you wanted finer-grained control over your locks.

Also, ask yourself why you're even using the APPLICATION or SESSION scope in your CFC code. Is it really necessary? If the idea is to persist information, why not simply store the CFC itself in one of the persistent scopes? This will be helpful if you decide that the information needs to be specific to the SESSION and not to the APPLICATION. If you never directly referenced any scope in your CFC code but instead simply stored the CFC in one of the scopes, "moving" the CFC then becomes a simple matter.

Locking Access to the THIS Scope

The FilmRotationCFC example in this chapter (Listing 24.4) doesn't manipulate variables in the APPLICATION or SESSION scope; instead, the CFC is designed so that entire instances of the CFC can be stored in the APPLICATION or SESSION scope (or the SERVER scope, for that matter) as the application's needs change over time. This is accomplished by only using variables in the THIS scope, rather than referring directly to SESSION or APPLICATION, within the CFC's methods.

You may wonder how to approach locking in such a situation. I recommend that you create a unique lock name for each component when each instance is first instantiated. You can easily accomplish this with ColdFusion's CreateUUID() function. For instance, you could use a line like this in the component's initialization code, within the body of the <cfcomponent> tag:

```
<cfset THIS.lockName = CreateUUID()>
```

The THIS.lockName variable (or property, if you prefer) is now guaranteed to be unique for each instance of the CFC, regardless of whether the component is stored in the APPLICATION or SERVER scope. You can use this value as the name of a <cflock> tag within any of the CFC's methods. For instance, if you were working with a CFC called ShoppingCartCFC and creating a new method called addItemToCart(), you could structure it according to this basic outline:

```
<cffunction name="addItemToCart">
 <cflock name="#THIS.lockName#" type="Exclusive" timeout="10">
 <!--- Changes to sensitive data in THIS scope goes here --->
 </cflock>
</cffunction>
```

For more information on the `<cflock>` tag, especially when to use `type="Exclusive"` or `type="ReadOnly"`, see the “Using Locks to Protect Against Race Conditions” section in Chapter 18.

Working with Inheritance

Frequently it is useful to have components that implement similar functionality in different ways. For example, you might have a `circle` component and a `square` component. Each has a `draw` method: The `circle` component draws a circle on the screen, and the `square` component draws a square. Each also has independent properties. For example, the circle has `circumference`, and the square has `length`. The two components also have a lot in common: They each have `perimeter` and `area`. The `square` and `circle` components are special cases of a shape; they have everything a shape has, plus more. Thus, it would make sense to create a single `parent` component called `shape` that has the information that is common to all types of shapes and then to have `child` components that inherit this information and also add their own. Thus, `square`, as a child of `shape`, would have all the things that `shape` has plus `length`, and it would implement its own variation of `draw`.

Just as you can use the word *my* to refer to a CFC’s `THIS` scope (“*my* ID is 123 and *my* first name is Fred…”), in *inheritance*, you can think of the words *is a*. A square *is a* shape. An actor *is a* person. A cat *is a* mammal. In these cases, `actor`, `square`, and `cat` are children of `person`, `shape`, and `mammal`. Some parents can exist by themselves; there can be a person who is not an actor. Some other parents, though, are abstract; `shape` can’t draw itself without knowing what shape it is. Rather, the parent is intended as more of a handy template upon which more specific things can be based.

In a movie studio application, actors and directors are both types of people, with some properties that are common and some that are unique. So, for types of `people`, you could create a component to represent a `person` and have each of these variants inherit from it.

Listing 24.9 shows the basic `person` component. It has a first name and last name (stored in the `THIS` scope) and has one function that “shows” the person by outputting the first and last names.

Listing 24.9 `person.cfc`—The Basic `person` Component

```
<!---
 Filename: Person.cfc
 Author: Ken Fricklas (KF)
 Purpose: Basic Person CFC
--->
<cfcomponent hint="Parent Component - Person">

<cfparam name="THIS.firstName" default="John">
<cfparam name="THIS.lastName" default="Doe">

<cffunction name="showPerson" output="true" hint="showPerson in person.cfc" >
  <B>#THIS.firstName# #THIS.lastName#</B>
</cffunction>

</cfcomponent>
```

A component inherits from a parent component with the EXTENDS attribute of the <cfcomponent> tag. The value of the attribute is the name of the component upon which the new component should be based. Thus, a director component could consist of nothing more than Listing 24.10.

Listing 24.10 director.cfc—The director Component

```
<!---
 Filename: Director.cfc
 Author: Ken Fricklas (KF)
 Purpose: A Minimal Inherited CFC
--->
<cfcomponent displayName="Movie Director" extends="person">
</cfcomponent>
```

Now, the director is an exact copy of the person component and has inherited all the properties and methods of its parent. A CFML page, then, could create an instance of the director and invoke the methods of the person component as though they were part of the director component (Listing 24.11).

Listing 24.11 showDirector.cfm—Display the Director

```
<!---
 Filename: showDirector.cfm
 Author: Ken Fricklas (KF)
 Purpose: Show the director
--->
<cfset cfcDirector = new Director()>
<cfoutput>#cfcDirector.showPerson()#</cfoutput>
```

NOTE

In fact, every component inherits from a root component called WEB-INF.cftags.component. This component is the mother of all components. In its default case, it is simply an empty file without any functions or properties, but you can implement custom logging, debugging, and other behavior by modifying this root component.

Overriding Properties and Methods

Just because the parent does something doesn't mean that the child is stuck with it. The component can override parts of the parent component. If you want the director component to set the firstName and lastName properties to different values than those of the person component, you simply add code that redefines the values. The director, because it's the one being invoked, will take precedence. So, the director component is now coded like this:

```
<cfcomponent displayName="Movie Director" extends="person">
  <cfset THIS.firstName = "Jim">
  <cfset THIS.lastName = "Jarofmush">
</cfcomponent>
```

When invoked from the CFML page, this component now will output "Jim Jarofmush" instead of "John Doe." The THIS scope assignments made in a child override those of its parent. Likewise, adding a showPerson function to the director component will override the showPerson function from the parent:

```
<cffunction name="showPerson" output="true" hint="showPerson in director.cfc">
  <B>A swell director named #THIS.firstName# #THIS.lastName#</B>
</cffunction>
```

Using the SUPER Scope

What if a child component needs to use the functionality in a method in its parent, but it has redefined that method already? In the director component, you could call the parent showPerson method, but you want to add your own information to it. You do this with the special scope SUPER. SUPER acts similarly to THIS, but instead of referring to a property or method in the current component, it refers to the property or method in the component's parent. You could redefine showPerson in the director component as shown in Listing 24.12.

Listing 24.12 Final director.cfc

```
<!---
 Filename: director.cfc
 Author: Ken Fricklas (KF)
 Purpose: Demonstrates use of super and property overrides
--->
<cfcomponent displayName="Movie Director" extends="person">
  <cfset THIS.firstName = "Jim">
  <cfset THIS.lastName = "Jarofmush">
  <cffunction name="showPerson" output="true" hint="showPerson in director.cfc">
    <B>A swell director - #super.showPerson()#</B>
  </cffunction>
</cfcomponent>
```

This code calls the showPerson method in the person component.

NOTE

In addition to the child being able to invoke functions that are really part of the parent component (and overriding them, if desired), the parent can call functions that are part of the child by referencing them in the instance's THIS scope. This technique can be useful when multiple components are descendants of the same parent but require slightly different methods.

Must you use inheritance in your ColdFusion applications? Certainly not. But it can be very useful in ways similar to other code-reuse techniques. Components can be built-in "branches," as in a family tree with chains of ancestral parent components, each providing base functionality to their children.

Component packages can help with this type of organization, too, to make applications more easily maintainable. In that case, the extends="..." attribute uses the same package path syntax as a <cfinvoke> tag. For example, to inherit from a component called person in the package myApp.components, the <cfcomponent> tag would be coded like this:

```
<cfcomponent extends="myApp.components.person">
```

NOTE

Inheritance can also be more than one level deep. Just as `actor` is a special case of `person`, `comedian` is a special case of `actor`. `comedian` could extend `actor`, which extends `person`. Then `comedian` would inherit methods and properties from `actor`, which inherits from person. `Super()` can also be chained; `super.super.showPerson()` is a valid construct, if you wanted to run the `showPerson()` from `person` directly from `comedian` and bypass an override method in `actor`.

Defining Interfaces

When designing components, it's frequently useful to define a template for anyone passing components to general functions. For example, you might create a function that takes as an argument an instance of a cast or crew member of a movie, calls a method named `getResume` to get a copy of the crew member's résumé as a query, and calls another method named `showPersonHTML` to show the crew member's name and information in an HTML display.

When requesting several implementations of this function to implement different types of cast members, actors, directors, producers, and so on, you might want these components to each do everything differently—you don't want them to inherit from a common parent, but they all have to implement a minimum set of functionality to meet the requirements of the system.

The definition of functions without actual implementation is a special type of component definition called an *interface*. An interface is basically a contract between a component and a system. You define an interface in a file with an extension of `.cfc`, but instead of enclosing the component with `<cfcomponent?` tags, you use a tag called `<cfinterface>`. Any component that implements the interface must contain all the methods defined in it, or the system will display an error.

Listing 24.13 contains an interface for the component just described.

Listing 24.13 `iCastCrew.cfc`—An Interface

```
<cfinterface hint="cast or crewmember interface">
   <cffunction name="getResume" access="public" returntype="query" hint="return
resume as query">
   </cffunction>
   <cffunction name="showPersonHTML" access="public" returntype="string" hint="show
person information as HTML">
      <cfargument name="detail" type="boolean" required="no" default="true"
hint="show detailed information">
   </cffunction>
</cfinterface>
```

Introspection and inheritance (via the `extends` attribute of `<cfinterface>`) can be used with interfaces the same way as with components.

NOTE

Interfaces are typically given names that start with a lowercase *i*–for example, `iComponent.cfc`–to distinguish them from other components.

To make sure that a component implements an interface, you use the `implements` keyword in the `<cfcomponent>` tag; for example, to make the director an implementation of `iCastCrew`, you would change the first line to this:

```
<cfcomponent displayName="Movie Director" extends="person" implements="iCastCrew">
```

If you ran this code, you would get the error shown in Figure 24.7, since the `director` component is missing some of the functions defined in the interface.

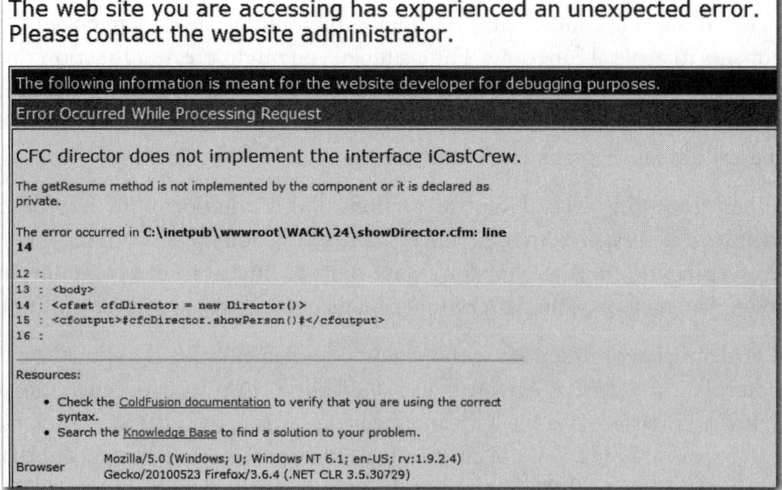

Figure 24.7

Error results from a failed implementation of an interface.

Implementing Security

ColdFusion provides two ways to secure the functionality that you encapsulate in a ColdFusion component: roles-based authorization and access control. Chapter 52, "Understanding Security," in Volume 3, discusses application user authentication and authorization, which allows the assignment of roles to your application's users. This roles-based security can also be applied to the functions in a CFC. The second technique, access control, was used in the preceding chapter in every `<cffunction>` tag as the attribute `access="..."`.

Implementing Access Control

The `access` attribute of the `<cffunction>` tag basically answers the question, "Who can use this function?" The attribute has four options: `private`, `package`, `public` (the default), and `remote`. These four options represent, in that order, the degree of openness of the function.

The `access` options range from a narrow group of potential consumers to a very broad audience. The consumers allowed by each option are as follows:

- **Private.** Only other functions within the same CFC can invoke the function. This is great to hide the details of how your component is implemented and to keep sneaky developers from writing code based on parts of your component that may not stay the same in future revisions. Note that private functions are inherited like any other methods.

- **Package.** Only components in the same package can invoke the function. This is just like `private`, except if you have implemented a system made up of multiple related CFCs, they can all use the methods declared `package`.
- **Public.** Any CFML template or CFC on the same server can invoke the function. This is the default.
- **Remote.** Any CFML template or CFC on the same server can invoke the function, as can programs running through the Web server. For example, Flash, Web Services, and methods can be invoked directly from a Web browser, as shown in the examples earlier in the chapter.

Implementing Role-Based Security in CFCs

In some applications, you'll want to control access to a component's functions based on who is using your application. This will be most common in traditional, HTML-based user interface applications, but it may also be true of Adobe Flash applications. Role-based security is not, however, a common approach to securing access to Web Services, since a Web Services client is a *program* and not an *individual.*

To see this technique in action, let's go back to the `director` component that was created earlier in this chapter—the one that retrieves information about all actors. Part of the Orange Whip Studios Web application allows studio executives to review the salaries of the stars—how much should the studio expect to fork over for their next box-office smash? Of course, this information is not exactly something that they want just anybody seeing.

First you need to create the basic security framework for this part of the application, with the security tags in ColdFusion: `<cflogin>`, `<cfloginuser>`, and `<cflogout>`. (I discuss this process in detail in Chapter 21, "Securing Your Applications," in Volume 1.)

For the purposes of this exercise, you can test by running the `<cfloginuser>` tag with the role you want to test with:

```
<cfloginuser name="Test" password="dummy" roles="Producers">
```

Any roles for the logged-in user will be the roles that correspond to those listed in the component function—more on this after you create the function in Listing 24.14.

The function will be simple: It takes an actor ID as an argument, queries that actor's salary history, and returns a record set. Notice, though, that the `roles` attribute in the `<cffunction>` tag has a comma-delimited list of values. Only users who have authenticated and been assigned one or more of those roles will be allowed to invoke the method.

Listing 24.14 `actor.cfc`—The Salary Method

```
<!---
 Filename: actor.cfc
 Author: Ken Fricklas (KF)
 Purpose: Demonstrates roles
--->
<cfcomponent name="actor" extends="person">
<cffunction name="init" returntype="component">
  <cfargument name="datasource" required="yes" type="string">
  <cfset variables.dsn = arguments.datasource>
  <cfreturn this>
</cffunction>
<cffunction name="getActorSalary" returnType="query" roles="Producers, Executives">
  <cfargument name="actorID" type="numeric" required="true"
    displayName="Actor ID" hint="The ID of the Actor">
  <cfquery name="salaries" dataSource="#variables.dsn#">
    SELECT Actors.ActorID, Actors.NameFirst, Actors.NameLast,
      FilmsActors.Salary, Films.MovieTitle
    FROM Films
    INNER JOIN (Actors INNER JOIN FilmsActors
     ON Actors.ActorID = FilmsActors.ActorID)
       ON Films.FilmID = FilmsActors.FilmID
    WHERE Actors.ActorID = #Arguments.actorID#
  </cfquery>
  <cfreturn salaries>
</cffunction>
</cfcomponent>
```

The roles assigned to this function are producers and executives—they don't want any prying eyes finding this sensitive data. All you need now, then, is a page to invoke the component—something simple, as in Listing 24.15.

Listing 24.15 `showSalary.cfm`—Show Salary Page

```
<!---
 Filename: showSalary.cfm
 Author: Ken Fricklas (KF)
 Purpose: Demonstrate CFC roles
--->
<!--- Make sure they are logged in. Change roles to "User" to see what happens if
they don't have sufficient access. --->
<cfloginuser name="Test" password="dummy" roles="Producers">
<!--- Invoke actors component.  getActorSalary method will fail unless
  they have sufficient access. --->
<cfset cfcActor = new actor(datasource="ows")>
<cfset salaryHistory = cfcActor.getActorSalary(17)>
<h1>Salaries of our stars...</h1>
<cfoutput>
<H2>
#salaryHistory.NameFirst# #salaryHistory.NameLast#</H2>
<cfloop query="salaryHistory">
  #MovieTitle# - #dollarFormat(Salary)#<BR>
</cfloop>
</cfoutput>
```

ColdFusion now has all it needs to control the access to the component. When the `salaryHistory` method is invoked, since there are values specified in the `roles` attribute, a comparison is automatically made between the values in the `roles` attribute of the `<cffunction>` tag and those in the `roles` attributes that were set in the `<cfloginuser>` tag. If the user is not logged in, this function will fail.

A match will allow the function to be executed as usual; a failure will cause ColdFusion to throw the error "The Current user is not authorized to invoke this method."

NOTE

> As noted, an unauthorized attempt to execute a secured function causes ColdFusion to throw an error. Consequently, you should put a `<cftry>` around any code that invokes secured functions.

This is not the only way to secure component functionality, of course. You could use the `isUserInRole()` function to check a user's group permissions before even invoking the function, or you could use Web server security for securing the CFML files themselves. The role-based security in CFCs is, however, a good option, particularly if you are already using the ColdFusion authentication/authorization framework in an application.

Using the `OnMissingMethod` Method

It would be nice if all the CFCs that we write could handle their own errors. Starting in ColdFusion 8, any component can have a special method named `OnMissingMethod` that will run whenever code attempts to run a method that hasn't been defined in it. You can use this method to serve several purposes:

- Implement custom error handling. The `OnMissingMethod` method can be especially useful when methods in different child classes might be called, even though they are not implemented in a particular component. For example, you could use `OnMissingMethod` to handle a call to `getActorSalary` made to a `director` component.
- Run different code for several methods in a common place. If the same code can take the place of several methods, `OnMissingMethod` can provide a way to run the common code from a single point. This approach is not recommended, however; it's more straightforward to define all the methods separately and call the common code from each.
- Act as a proxy that calls another object or component that will actually implement the function. For example, you could create a component that is empty except for `onMissingMethod` that takes any method passed to it and calls a Web Service on another machine that consumes the method name and its arguments and returns a value. This approach is a good way to implement a flexible, distributed system.

The `onMissingMethod` function takes exactly two arguments, which contain the name of the method that was being called and a structure with the arguments that were passed to it. For example, here is a simple `onMissingMethod` method:

```
<cffunction name="onMissingMethod">
  <cfargument name="missingMethodName" type="string">
```

```
  <cfargument name="missingMethodNameArguments" type="struct">
    Hey! You called <cfoutput>#arguments.missingMethodName#</cfoutput> and I haven't
got one!
</cffunction>
```

NOTE

Since `onMissingMethod` always returns successfully, if you can't handle an error in this method, you should throw a new error.

Distributed CFCs and Serialization

I've already discussed storing CFCs in the session scope. One problem with storing CFCs in this way is that when more than one server is in use, each server has its own session variables; if a user moves to another server during the course of a visit to your site, the session data can be lost. One way to solve this problem is to create "sticky" sessions, which requires special software or hardware—but what if the Web server goes down?

Many Java application servers that ColdFusion runs on can support distributed sessions. Basically, what the servers do is "serialize" the data in the session scope, which means that a server writes the data in a flat form (turns it into a string, in the same way that `CFWDDX` does) and passes it to all other servers in the cluster that might process the new request. No matter which server is used, it has a copy of the session data.

Before ColdFusion 8, components could not be serialized, so they would not be passed between machines as part of the session. As of ColdFusion 8, however, components can be serialized and distributed.

NOTE

In Java parlance, this means that ColdFusion now supports the Java serializable interface. You can read more about this at `http://java.sun.com/developer/technicalArticles/Programming/serialization/`.

In addition, you can directly call the Java's `java.io.ObjectOutputStream` API to write objects to a file.

Listing 24.16 shows some sample code that checks to see whether a CFC exists in the session scope. If the CFC isn't found in the session, the code checks to see whether a serialized copy of the component exists in a file and loads that. Finally, if the CFC is neither in the session nor on the disk, the CFC is instantiated and written out as a new serialized copy.

Listing 24.16 `serialize.cfm`—Serializing a CFC

```
<!---
  FileName: serialize.cfm
  Author: Ken Fricklas (KF)
  Purpose: Implement a distributed, serialized system
--->
<cfapplication sessionmanagement="yes" name="serialdemo">
<cfif not isdefined("session.cfcDirector")>
   <!--- check to see if we've got a copy --->
```

Listing 24.16 (continued)

```
        <cftry>
           <cfset fileIn = CreateObject("java", "java.io.FileInputStream")>
             <cfset fileIn.init(expandpath("./serialized_director.txt"))>
             <cfset objIn = CreateObject("java", "java.io.ObjectInputStream")>
             <cfset objIn.init(fileIn)>
             <cfset session.cfcDirector = objIn.readObject()>
             Read!
            <cfcatch>
                <!--- no copy to load, create it --->
                <cfset session.cfcDirector = createObject("component", "director")>
                <!--- save it --->
                <cfset fileOut = CreateObject("java", "java.io.FileOutputStream")>
                <cfset fileOut.init(expandpath("./serialized_director.txt"))>
                <cfset objOut = CreateObject("java", "java.io.ObjectOutputStream")>
                <cfset objOut.init(fileOut)>
                <cfset objOut.writeObject(session.cfcDirector)>
                Written!
            </cfcatch>
        </cftry>
    </cfif>
    <cfoutput>
       #session.cfcDirector.showPerson()#
    </cfoutput>
```

NOTE

ColdFusion 9 adds a new attribute, `serializable`, to the `<cfcomponent>` tag. If this is set `false`, only the component will be serialized, and any local variables (in the variables or `THIS` scope of the component) will not be written, giving you a "clean" copy. This can be used to pass program logic from one machine to another, such as serializing a component, passing it via an HTTP request, and reassembling it on the far side and running the logic there on another copy of ColdFusion.

PART 6

ColdFusion Configuration and Performance

CHAPTER 25
ColdFusion Server Configuration

IN THIS CHAPTER

The ColdFusion Administrator

The ColdFusion Administrator is a Web-based console that gives you an easy way to adjust how ColdFusion behaves. Adobe provides this simple, straightforward Administrator so that we developers don't have to fiddle around with configuration files to get ColdFusion to behave the way we need it to.

Because the Administrator is Web-based, you can use it to monitor and configure your ColdFusion server from nearly anywhere, armed with nothing more than a browser and a password.

The primary functions of the ColdFusion Administrator are

- Tweaking and monitoring the server's performance
- Configuring ColdFusion's external resources, such as databases, full-text search collections, and mail servers
- Installing extensions to the CFML language, in the form of CFX tags, event gateways, and more
- Administrative tasks, such as backing up applications, reviewing log files, and securing portions of the server

This chapter will walk you through each part of the ColdFusion Administrator, explaining important settings and making recommendations along the way. Let's begin.

The Administrator Home Page

Log in to the Administrator as was explained in Chapter 2, "Accessing the ColdFusion Administrator," in *Adobe ColdFusion 9 Web Application Construction Kit, Volume 1: Getting Started.*

Once you log in, the Administrator's home page appears. The Administrator is designed much like many other Web application interfaces, with a toolbar along the top and a navigation column along the left-hand side. This home page contains links to various online resources related to ColdFusion and the CFML developer community.

One really important—and often overlooked—screen is the System Information screen (there is a link at the top right of the page; look for a blue circle containing a white letter `i`). This screen has three primary uses:

- **Serial number change.** You can enter a new serial number, perhaps to upgrade the Developer Edition to a commercial edition, or upgrade ColdFusion Standard to ColdFusion Enterprise. You can accomplish this without performing a reinstallation and without restarting the server.
- **System information.** You can view a detailed list of system settings, including ColdFusion information (version, edition, serial number, and more), and Java settings (JVM details, class path, and more).
- **Update file.** You can update the server through the use of an update file.

TIP

If you get confused at any time during your visit to the ColdFusion Administrator, the Help link at the top-right corner of the screen will provide you with context-sensitive help about whatever Administrator page you happen to be on.

Server Settings

Let's begin our page-by-page tour of the ColdFusion Administrator with the Server Settings section, which makes up the first part of the left navigation column. The pages in this section pertain mostly to tweaking the server's performance. Aside from the Data Sources page in the next section, this is the most important portion of the ColdFusion Administrator, and the part you will probably become most familiar with.

The Settings Page

The Settings page contains various options related to tweaking the server's performance and responsiveness to page requests from your users. It also contains options for controlling what happens when errors occur.

Timeout Requests After (Seconds)

If you want to make sure that ColdFusion spends no more than 20 or 30 seconds working on a particular page request, go ahead and check the Timeout Requests After checkbox, and provide the appropriate value for the number of seconds. If a page takes longer than the number of seconds you specify, the page will simply halt and display an error message.

I strongly suggest that you enable this option, and set it to a relatively low number to start off with, perhaps 20 or 30. A long-running page can be terminated, so the server can move on to other page requests that should be easier for it to generate quickly.

You can override the request timeout you provide for this setting on a page-by-page basis. Just use the `<cfsetting>` tag, specifying the maximum number of seconds that you would like the page to be allowed to execute as the `requesttimeout` attribute. For instance, if you wanted a particular page to run for up to five minutes (perhaps it performs a large file transfer operation with `<cfftp>`), you would use the following code, near the top of the page:

```
<!--- Allow this page to execute for up to five minutes --->
<cfsetting
 requesttimeout="300">
```

Keep in mind, however, that a long-running page could block other pages from executing. You might, therefore, want to use the `<cflock>` tag to make sure that only one instance of the long-running page is able to execute at the same time. You would use the `<cflock>` attribute with a `name` attribute that was unique to that particular ColdFusion file, like this:

```
<cftry>
 <cflock
 name="MyLongRunningFTPTransferPage"
 type="EXCLUSIVE"
 timeout="30">
<!--- Allow this page to execute for up to five minutes --->
 <cfsetting
 requesttimeout="300">
 <!---  ...long running code would go here... --->
 </cflock>
 <!--- If the lock can't be obtained, display a message and stop --->
 <cfcatch type="Lock">
 Sorry, but another user is currently using this page. Please try again in a few
minutes.
 <cfabort>
 </cfcatch>
</cftry>
```

Alternatively, you could use a `name` value that was the same for all long-running pages; this would ensure that only one of the long-running pages was allowed to execute at one time.

➜ For more information about `<cflock>`, see Chapter 18, "Introducing the Web Application Framework," in Volume 1.

NOTE

Of course, you can customize the look of the error message that appears if a page takes longer than the number of seconds you specify. See the Sitewide Error Handler setting, later in this section, and the discussion of the `<CFERROR>` tag in Chapter 18.

Enable per-App Settings

Settings defined in the ColdFusion Administrator apply to all applications running on the server. ColdFusion allows specific settings to be overridden at the application level. For example, the Custom Tags folder is shared by all applications. If two applications create custom tags with the same name, there is a real risk that the wrong tag will be invoked inadvertently. The capability to define a different Custom Tag folder for each application (overriding the default location that is specified) solves this problem.

Per-application settings are not defined in the ColdFusion Administrator. Rather, they are defined programmatically in the application's `Application.cfc` file.

➜ `Application.cfc` was introduced in Chapter 18.

To enable support for per-application settings, check the Enable per App Settings box (this is enabled by default).

Use UUID for `cftoken`

As you learned in Chapter 19, "Working with Sessions," in Volume 1, ColdFusion uses values called `CFID` and `CFTOKEN` to identify each browser machine. The `CFTOKEN` value is used as a kind of password that allows users to be connected to their client variables on the server. In addition, this value is used (in concert with the notion of a session timeout) to connect users with their session variables on the server.

I recommend that you go ahead and enable this option unless you have an existing application that uses the `CFTOKEN` internally in some manner and depends on it being a number.

TIP

If you need to be able to generate unique identifiers for your own use within your application, you can use the `CreateUUID()` function.

Enable HTTP Status Codes

This setting allows ColdFusion to return true HTTP status codes in the header of its response if an unexpected error occurs. For instance, if a user requests a ColdFusion page that doesn't exist on the server, ColdFusion will be able to return a true error message (HTTP status code number `404`) that other machines can understand to mean "not found." If this option is unchecked, ColdFusion would simply display a page that contained a message saying the page could not be found (not so helpful for proxy servers, search engines, or machines trying to access Web Services on your server).

Similarly, if ColdFusion needs to report an error message, the HTTP status code of the server's response will be set to `500` if this option is checked. If left unchecked, the error message is displayed, but the status code remains set to the normal HTTP status code, `200`, which means that other automated systems on the network can't really tell that anything has gone wrong.

As a general rule, never keep this option checked on development servers. If desired, keep it checked (it is enabled by default) on production servers only.

Enable Whitespace Management

When enabled, this option makes sure that extraneous white space (such as the various hard returns, spaces, and tabs that you use to indent your ColdFusion code) is removed from any generated HTML code before it's sent back to browsers.

I recommend that this option be enabled (it is enabled by default) in nearly all cases. There are a few special situations in which you would not want white space to be removed (for instance, if you are using `<pre>` blocks in your pages), but you can always turn off the white-space management on a case-by-case basis with the `<cfprocessingdirective>` tag.

➜ For more information about white-space management, see Chapter 27, "Improving Performance."

Disable CFC Type Check

Arguments for ColdFusion Components methods (and user-defined functions) are validated by ColdFusion. This means that if the argument expects a specific data type to be passed to it, ColdFusion checks that the correct type was indeed passed.

Arguments can accept lots of types, including ColdFusion Components. By default, when an argument accepts a ColdFusion Component, ColdFusion checks that the component passed is of the right type. This check can be time consuming (milliseconds, but still slower than other argument type checks). To improve performance, you can disable CFC type checking.

NOTE

This option is meant for production servers only. On development (and testing) servers, you'll want to know if you are passing the wrong type of CFC as an argument.

➜ See Chapter 22, "Building User-Defined Functions," and Chapter 24, "Creating Advanced ColdFusion Components," for more information about UDFs and CFCs.

Disable Access to Internal ColdFusion Java Components

ColdFusion features internal Java objects that can be used to perform all sorts of server administration. Indeed, the ColdFusion Administrator itself (and the Administrator APIs) use these Java objects extensively.

Because ColdFusion code can invoke Java objects, these internal objects can also be invoked and used. On shared servers, this can be a potential security problem, so you can block access to ColdFusion's internal Java components if needed.

➜ See Chapter 68, "Extending ColdFusion with Java," in *Adobe ColdFusion 9 Web Application Construction Kit, Volume 3: Advanced Application Development*, for more information about ColdFusion Java integration.

TIP

As a rule, check this box on servers where you do not control all code and applications, and leave it unchecked if the server is all yours.

Prefix Serialized JSON With

JSON is an XML data format used in Ajax applications and by ColdFusion's Ajax controls. Web Services that return data in JSON format could contain JavaScript code and could therefore be compromised to allow JavaScript cross-site scripting attacks. Check this box to prefix potentially harmful strings to prevent them from executing.

→ See Chapter 15, "Beyond HTML Forms: ColdFusion-Powered Ajax," in Volume 1, and Chapter 30, "Advanced ColdFusion-Powered Ajax," to learn about ColdFusion and Ajax integration.

Enable in-Memory File System

A virtual file system (VFS) has been added to ColdFusion 9. It is a RAM-based file system that can be manipulated similarly to the local file system, but because it is in memory, it has better performance and execution time. Any file and directory operations and manipulations performed in ColdFusion can be performed with the VFS: that is, you can create runtime CFCs and CFMs in RAM and execute them, and any tag that uses a local disk file as input and output can also use a VFS file as the same input and output. There is also the option to set a memory limit for the in-memory VSS.

NOTE

The `ram:///` file system is available systemwide. To limit access to the VFS from other applications, you can use sandbox security.

Watch Configuration Files for Changes

ColdFusion configuration settings are stored in external XML files. These files are typically never modified directly; they are updated as needed by ColdFusion itself (when changes are made using the ColdFusion Administrator or the Administrator API). If changes are made to the files directly, these changes will not be seen by ColdFusion until the server has been restarted.

However, if needed, ColdFusion can watch its own configuration files and reload their contents (the settings) if file changes have occurred. If this capability is needed, check this option.

TIP

If you are using ColdFusion on IBM WebSphere using network deployment, this option should be enabled (checked).

Enable Global Script Protection

Check this box to have ColdFusion check `URL`, `FORM`, `CGI`, and `COOKIE` variables for potential cross-site scripting attacks.

→ This option is explained in Chapter 21, "Securing Your Applications," in Volume 1.

Default `ScriptSrc` Directory

The `<cfform>` tags (introduced in Chapters 12, "ColdFusion Forms," and 14, "Using Forms to Add or Change Data," in Volume 1) use JavaScript files that are installed in a folder named `/CFIDE/scripts` under the ColdFusion root. If this location must be changed (for example, to lock down the entire `CFIDE` directory structure), you should provide the new path in this field.

Allow Extra Attributes in Attribute Collection

ColdFusion tags can pass nonstandard attributes in the attribute collection structure.

Google Maps API Key

A valid `googleMap` API key is required to use ColdFusion's built-in `googleMaps` capabilities in your application. You can specify this key in this ColdFusion Administrator section, which is available globally, per server instance, or define it in your code before you use this functionality.

The `CFMAP` key can be defined at three levels, or scopes. Thus, the accessibility of the key depends on where you have defined it.

- Server scope: Shared for all applications running within the server instance.
- Application scope: Available from within the application scope.
- Template scope: Accessible only within that template.

NOTE

Both the component with the `OnServerStart()` method and the `Application.cfc` and `Application.cfm` lookup order sections of this page are self-explanatory.

Missing Template Handler

You can create a ColdFusion page that will be executed and displayed whenever a user requests a ColdFusion page that doesn't actually exist on the server. This page will take the place of the default Not Found message that would ordinarily appear. The missing template handler can contain whatever ColdFusion code you like. Just specify its location here, in the ColdFusion Administrator. Be sure to include the complete file path to the file (including the `c:` or whatever is appropriate), not just its name.

Site-wide Error Handler

You can also create a ColdFusion page that will be executed and displayed whenever an uncaught error (exception) is displayed. This page will take the place of the standard error message that would ordinarily appear. Again, just specify its location here, in the ColdFusion Administrator. Be sure to include the complete file path to the file (including the `c:` or whatever is appropriate), not just its name.

➜ You can still specify customized error handling pages on a page-by-page or application-by-application basis with the `<cferror>` tag, as explained in Chapter 44, "Error Handling," online.

Maximum Size of Post Data

One type of server attack overloads the server by making it process requests with massive amounts of data attached. This type of attack uses `POST` submission, and so ColdFusion can be instructed to ignore (and terminate) any requests with `POST` data greater than a specified size. To implement this option, specify a size.

Request Throttle Threshold

ColdFusion can throttle (forcefully slow down) incoming requests if needed. However, really small requests (those with a small *payload*) can be allowed through regardless of the throttle state. To allow small requests to be processed, specify the maximum allowed size (the default is a maximum of 4 MB).

Request Throttle Memory

To throttle requests, specify the maximum amount of memory allocated for the throttle. If not enough total memory is available, ColdFusion queues requests until enough memory is free (the default is 200 MB).

The Request Tuning Page

The Request Tuning page is used to manage and control how ColdFusion handles the processing of concurrent requests.

Maximum Number of Simultaneous Template Requests

ColdFusion is fast and efficient, but it obviously can't handle an unlimited amount of page requests at once. At some point, any server will become overwhelmed if it tries to serve too many users at once. This setting allows you to tweak your server's performance by adjusting the maximum number of page requests that it can process at the same time.

NOTE

If you change this setting, you need to restart the ColdFusion Application Server to make the changes take effect.

Because this setting can have a big impact on an application's performance, it would be nice if there were a hard-and-fast rule that you could use to determine the best value to provide. Unfortunately, there is no such rule. The more powerful your hardware—a greater amount of RAM, faster processors, quicker hard drives, and faster network connections to your databases—the more requests it can handle at one time.

Therefore, depending on your hardware specifications, reducing the number of requests allows ColdFusion to devote its resources to a small number of tasks, thus executing all tasks more quickly. If you think your server can handle more requests, try your ColdFusion applications with the increased setting under load in a staging environment.

Here are some rules of thumb:

- Start with a value of 10, which is a pretty reasonable starting point.

- If your server has more than one processor, or if your server is extremely powerful in other ways, increase the number of simultaneous requests per processor. If the server is starting to show its age, decrease the number.
- If pages take more than a second or two in development, you may wish to consider reducing this number.
- To assist fast pages not being blocked by slow pages you should probably increase the number of simultaneous requests. In addition, you could use the `<cflock>` tag to make sure that a large number of the slow pages aren't allowed to execute all at once. For instance, you could place a `<cflock>` tag with `name="VerySlowProcess"` and `type="Exclusive"` attributes around code that you know will be time consuming or generally hard on the server. See Chapter 18 for more information about locking.
- If your application uses shared variables, especially `APPLICATION` variables, in such a way that you often need to request an exclusive lock to protect against race conditions, you will probably want to decrease the number of simultaneous requests (so that fewer locks actually block one another at runtime). See Chapter 18 for more information about race conditions.

TIP

There is another important approach that you can use to manage different applications and requests with differing loads and response times. ColdFusion Enterprise allows you to install multiple copies (instances) of ColdFusion on a single machine, and each instance can have its own settings optimized for its own use.

Maximum Number of Simultaneous Flash Remoting Requests

Most inbound requests to ColdFusion originate from Web browsers, but ColdFusion also accepts requests from Flash (and Flex) applications via Flash Remoting. Thus, it is possible (if your site has lots of Flash applications) that Web browser requests may be queued waiting for Flash Remoting requests to complete.

ColdFusion allows you to specify how many requests to allow for Flash Remoting.

Maximum Number of Simultaneous Web Service Requests

ColdFusion requests can also be Web Services (SOAP) requests. As with Flash Remoting requests, ColdFusion allows Web Services requests to be restricted.

TIP

If your site exposes many public-facing Web Services, you may want to increase this number to match the Maximum Number of Simultaneous Template Requests value.

➜ See Chapter 59, "Creating and Consuming Web Services," in Volume 3, to learn how to create and publish Web Services.

Maximum Number of Simultaneous CFC Function Requests

ColdFusion Components are usually invoked directly (from within other ColdFusion files and templates). CFCs can also be invoked via Flash Remoting and Web Services, and as already seen, this type of access can be capped if needed. ColdFusion Components can also be invoked via direct HTTP request. To cap this type of access, set the maximum here.

NOTE

This setting does not affect CFC invocations from within local CFML code.

Maximum Number of Running JRun Threads

When ColdFusion runs using the integrated JRun server, it must share the total available threads with JRun. In addition to the threads that ColdFusion needs for processing, the underlying JRun requires threads itself. Thus, this value should always be greater than the sum of the previous four values (20 higher is a good starting point).

Maximum Number of Queued JRun Threads

The underlying JRun server can accept Java and J2EE requests in addition to ColdFusion requests (which are processed by ColdFusion running within JRun). JRun queues requests until they can be processed (by their destination, wherever it is), and that queue size is specified here.

Maximum Number of Simultaneous Report Threads

ColdFusion has an integrated reporting engine (used by `<CFREPORT>`). As report processing can be very resource intensive (especially the concurrent processing of very large reports), there is a risk that ColdFusion will be so busy creating reports that all other requests suffer from poor performance.

Thus, ColdFusion allows you to specify the maximum number of threads that can be allocated to report generation. Any requests greater than the specified maximum will be queued until they can be processed.

TIP

Unless your application generates reports continuously, set this value to a value far lower than the total number of available requests.

➜ See Chapter 16, "Graphing, Printing, and Reporting," in Volume 1, to learn about ColdFusion reporting.

Maximum Number of Threads Available for `CFTHREAD`

ColdFusion requests are single threaded, but, using `<cfthread>`, ColdFusion applications can spawn additional threads to perform asynchronous processing. Although this feature can boost performance tremendously, it also introduces a risk that so many threads will be spawned that total system performance suffers.

Thus, ColdFusion allows you to specify the maximum number of threads that can be allocated for spawned thread processing. Any requests greater than the specified maximum will be queued until they can be processed.

➜ See Chapter 26, "Managing Threads," to learn how to use threading and the `<cfthread>` tag.

Timeout Requests Waiting in Queue After *n* Seconds

If ColdFusion is busy processing as many requests as have been specified, any additional inbound requests will be queued until there is a free thread to process them. In theory, requests can be queued indefinitely, but in practice, you'll probably want to timeout the requests and display a custom error message.

The maximum request queue time can be specified in this option.

NOTE

This value should never be less than the Request Timeout value (the first option on the Settings page, discussed previously in this chapter).

Request Queue Timeout Page

If queued requests time out, users will see a generic 500 message in their browser. To provide a custom error page, specify the path to a static HTML file (relative to the Web root) here.

CAUTION

Do not use a `.cfm` page as the custom error page. If pages are timing out in the queue, you don't want to queue another page to display an error message!

The Caching Page

The word *cache* is a general term that refers to the use of a temporary area of a computer's memory or disk drive to store information that can be time-consuming to retrieve or calculate normally. The idea is to perform the action or calculation once, store it in the cache, and then use the information in the cache (the *cached version*) for subsequent requests, rather than performing the action or calculation over and over again. There always needs to be some limit placed on the amount of information in the cache; otherwise the size of the cache would become unwieldy and inefficient.

The Caching page of the ColdFusion Administrator is used to control the cache that ColdFusion uses to cache your ColdFusion code files, and the database cache that ColdFusion uses whenever you use the `cachedwithin` or `cachedafter` attributes in a `<cfquery>` tag.

NOTE

Don't confuse the caching options on this page of the Administrator with the `<cfcache>` tag, which is for caching functions, caching page fragments, or caching individual pages. For details about `<cfcache>`, see Chapter 27, "Improving Performance."

Maximum Number of Cached Templates

ColdFusion converts your ColdFusion templates to compiled Java classes in the background. Whenever someone visits one of your ColdFusion pages, ColdFusion checks to see if the page has been converted to a Java class, and whether the Java class is up to date (that is, whether the `.cfm` file has been changed since the Java class was compiled). The same goes for any included pages, custom tags, and components. Certain aspects of this decision-making process, as well as the compiled Java classes themselves, are cached in memory to improve performance.

This setting lets you tweak the size of this template cache to improve performance. Ideally, you would want the cache to be big enough to hold all your templates.

NOTE

Remember, a template is just another name for a ColdFusion page. Any `.cfm` or `.cfc` file is a template.

Trusted Cache

Normally, when a user requests one of your ColdFusion pages, the server needs to check to see if the `.cfm` file has been changed since the last time the page was executed. If so, it recompiles the `.cfm` file into an updated version of the corresponding Java class; if not, the existing version of the Java class can be used. The same goes for any included files, custom tags, or ColdFusion components. It doesn't take much time for the server to check whether each file has changed, but even that little bit of time is for naught if you know that your ColdFusion files won't be changing over time.

Checking this option tells ColdFusion not to bother checking whether each ColdFusion file has changed. This can improve performance quite a bit, especially if the server is receiving a lot of page requests.

TIP

In general, you should enable this option on your production servers, since the files would not normally be changing often. Leave it unchecked on your development servers.

Cache Template in Request

If the Cache Template in Request option is not checked, every time a template is accessed (within the same request), it is inspected to see whether there are any changes. If this option is checked, then the template is inspected only the first time it is accessed within the request.

Component Cache

When the Component Cache option is checked, the components path is cached and not resolved again.

Save Class Files

The class files generated by ColdFusion `.cfm` source code may be cached in server memory or written to disk. To save class files to disk, check this option. This can improve performance on high-volume sites.

TIP

Don't enable this option on your development servers.

Cache Web Server Paths

ColdFusion can cache the paths to files and how these paths map to URLs to improve performance. Check this option to cache paths, but never check this option if you host multiple Web sites on the same server (as this could cause paths to get mixed up resulting in the wrong pages being served).

Maximum Number of Cached Queries

As you learned in Chapter 27, you can use the `cachedwithin` or `cachedafter` attributes of the `<cfquery>` tag to reuse query results so they don't have to be retrieved from the database with each and every page request. Of course, it's not possible for the server to cache an unlimited number of query result sets in memory; there's only so much memory to go around.

By default, ColdFusion will allow up to 100 cached result sets to reside in its memory; when the 101st query needs to be cached, the query that was cached first will be removed from the cache. Increasing the number will allow more cached result sets to remain in memory at once; decreasing the number will reduce the amount of RAM that the cached queries will use up.

Like some of the options discussed earlier (particularly the number of simultaneous requests), this setting is a matter of balance, and there is no hard and fast rule about what the best value is.

In general, if you use cached queries extensively in your code, and you find that your server still has plenty of available RAM after your applications have been running for a while, you can increase the value. On the other hand, if you find that your server tends to run out of available RAM, you should try decreasing this value.

TIP

The ColdFusion System Monitor can be used to determine which queries are being cached and whether the cache is being used effectively.

➜ Chapter 47, "Monitoring System Performance," in Volume 3, explains how to use the System Monitor.

The Client Variables Page

In Chapter 19, you learned about the `CLIENT` variable scope, which allows you to create variables that become associated with a particular Web browser. You can use `CLIENT` variables to create pages that show personalized information or that otherwise maintain state between each user's visits and page requests.

Choosing a Client Variable Storage Mechanism

In general, the idea behind `CLIENT` variables is to store the actual variables on the server, so that the burden (and responsibility) for remembering the values isn't placed on each browser machine.

There are two methods for storing values on the server: in a database, or in the registry. (For Windows servers, *registry* refers to the Windows Registry, which is a special information store that is built into the operating system; for other servers, *registry* refers to a special text file that Adobe ships with ColdFusion.) Because the values are stored on the server side, the total size of all the accumulated client variables can become quite large over time. Either the database or the registry will have to become large enough to store the total size of all client variables for all users.

You can also choose to have your client variables stored as a cookie on the browser machine. This takes care of the problem of your servers having to store every client variable for every user, but has some significant trade-offs. Conceptually, you are trusting the browser to store the values for you (dependent on its local settings). Adobe recommends that you only use the default registry option for development, and that you create a database storage mechanism for your staging or production machines (even if it's just a lowly Access database). You can set the database to be the default storage mechanism (as discussed in the next section) so that your code doesn't have to change as you move your applications out of development.

NOTE

The primary reason to use `CLIENT` variables is to share this information across multiple servers. As this can also be accomplished using `SESSION` variables, there is rarely a need to use `CLIENT` variables anymore.

On this page, you also can select a data source to add as a client store.

Choosing the Default Storage Mechanism

To choose the default storage mechanism used for client variables, make the appropriate selection under the heading Select Default Storage Mechanism for Client Sessions; then click Apply.

NOTE

You can override this setting on an application-by-application basis by specifying a `clientstorage` attribute in your `<cfapplication>` tag. For details, see Chapter 19.

Purge Interval

`CLIENT` variables persist over time, and are purged (deleted) at a predetermined interval. The default interval is 1 hour 7 minutes, and this can be changed if needed.

The Memory Variables Page

In Chapter 18, you learned about application variables, which allow you to maintain counters, flags, and other variables on an application-wide basis. In Chapter 19, you learned about session variables, which provide a way to track variables for your users on a per-session basis.

This page of the Administrator allows you to change how these variables are tracked, and for how long. Either type of variable can be disabled by unchecking the Enable Application Variables or Enable Session Variables checkbox.

Use J2EE Session Variables

ColdFusion can manage session variables, or it can rely on the underlying J2EE server to perform this task. To have the J2EE server manage the session, check this box.

TIP

There are significant advantages to using J2EE session variables; ideally, this checkbox should be checked.

NOTE

If you have existing applications that explicitly use `CFID` and `CFTOKEN` values, don't check this box without updating that code.

Enable Application Variables

To enable the use of application variables, check this box (checked by default).

NOTE

As a rule, this box should always be checked.

Enable Session Variables

If any applications on your server will need to use session variables, check this box (it is checked by default).

NOTE

As a rule, this box should always be checked.

Maximum Timeout

You can adjust the Maximum Timeout value for each type of variable, which gives you a way to make sure that no individual `<cfapplication>` tag specifies a `sessiontimeout` or `applicationtimeout` value that is unreasonably long. If the `<cfapplication>` tag specifies a timeout value that exceeds the maximum value you supply here, the maximum value is used instead.

Default Timeout

You can also edit the Default Timeout value for each type of variable by typing in the desired number of days, minutes, hours, and seconds. This default value will be used whenever you don't specify a `sessiontimeout` or `applicationtimeout` attribute in your `<cfapplication>` tags. For instance, you can set a longer timeout session timeout if users are complaining that their session variables disappear while they're filling out long forms or making complex decisions. You can use a shorter timeout if you suspect that too much memory is being used to store your session variables.

The Mappings Page

The Mappings Page is used to define path mappings, aliases that are used in CFML code to refer to specific folders.

By default two mappings are created (`cfide` and `gateway`) and these should not be removed. To add your own mappings, enter the alias and path in the form displayed, and click Add.

NOTE

If Enable Per App Settings (on the Settings page) is checked, you can define mappings for specific applications in `Application.cfc`.

The Mail Page

In Chapter 20, "Interacting with Email," in Volume 1, you learned to create ColdFusion pages that send dynamic, personalized email messages with the `<cfmail>` tag. ColdFusion can also send automatically generated reports to server administrators in case of problems, as you will learn in the section "The System Probes Page," later in this chapter. Use the Mail Server page to establish an SMTP email server connection for ColdFusion to use for these purposes.

NOTE

If you are using the ColdFusion Developer Edition, some of the options listed for this page may not be available.

Mail Server

Enter either the Internet domain name or the IP address for your company's outgoing mail server (also known as an SMTP server) in the Mail Server text box.

NOTE

Username (if your SMTP server requires that you log in, enter the username here) and Password (if your SMTP server requires that you log in, enter the password here) are self-explanatory.

Sign

The Sign option enables ColdFusion to digitally sign its mail.

Keystore

The Keystore option specifies the location of the keystore containing the certificate and private key. The Java keystore (JKS) and pkcs12 keystore are supported.

NOTE

The Keystore Password option is self-explanatory.

Keystore Alias

The first entry in the keystore is used as an alias unless this option is not blank.

Verify Mail Server Connection

When defining your mail server, check this box to have ColdFusion Administrator attempt to connect to the mail server to verify the connection.

Server Port

Enter your email server's port number. This is almost always 25, so you can usually leave the port number alone.

Backup Mail Servers

If you have access to backup SMTP servers (which can be used if the primary SMTP server is unavailable), list these here.

NOTE

If you select Maintain Connection to Mail Server, the connection cannot be severed by the ColdFusion server.

Connection Timeout

This setting lets you specify the number of seconds ColdFusion should wait for a response from the email server. In general, the default value of 60 seconds is sensible. If your mail server is far away or available only via a slow network connection, you may need to increase this value.

Enable SSL Socket Connections to Mail Server

Select this checkbox to enable SSL encryption on the connections to the mail server.

NOTE

For you to use this option, your mail server must support SSL encryption.

Enable TLS Connection to Mail Server

Select this checkbox to enable transport level security (TLS) on the connection to the mail server.

NOTE

For you to use this option, your mail server must support SSL encryption.

Spool Interval

This setting lets you specify the number of seconds ColdFusion waits before checking to see if new email messages are waiting to be sent out. You can decrease this value if it's critical that your messages be sent out very soon after they are created; you can increase the value to conserve server resources. Note this value is ignored whenever you use the `spoolenable="No"` attribute in your `<cfmail>` tags.

Mail Delivery Threads

You can specify the maximum number of threads that the ColdFusion mail spooler can use. The higher this number, the greater the number of messages that will be deliverable at any given time.

NOTE

Before raising this value, make sure that your mail server supports multiple concurrent connections from the same client.

Spool Mail Messages for Delivery

Mail is spooled by ColdFusion and then delivered by the spooler. Messages can be spooled to disk or to memory.

As a general rule, messages should be spooled to disk. While spooling to memory can be faster, it does increase memory load and also prevents delivery of mail after a system failure.

Maximum Number of Messages Spooled to Memory

Disk spooling of messages will occur after the ColdFusion server reaches the threshold specified here.

View Undelivered Mail

This option opens a window that allows the deletion and respooling of undelivered mail.

Error Log Severity

Mail delivered by ColdFusion can be logged for future analysis. The logs are saved in the `/ColdFusion9/Log` folder and can be viewed using the log viewer pages within the ColdFusion Administrator (see the section "The Log Files Page" later in this chapter). You can specify the log level here.

Log All Messages Sent by ColdFusion

To aid in troubleshooting, ColdFusion can log all messages (including all contents) if needed (this option is not enabled by default).

CAUTION

Do not leave this option checked for extended periods of time, as saving all messages can consume vast amounts of disk space.

Mail Charset Setting

To change the default character set used in generated email messages, specify the value here.

NOTE

UTF-8 is the default and generally the preferred option for this setting.

The Charting Page

In Chapter 16, you learned how to use the ColdFusion `<cfchart>` tag to create dynamic charts and graphs that create visual representations of your application's data. ColdFusion automatically caches charts for later use. Conceptually, the chart cache is the charting equivalent of the query caching feature you learned about in Chapter 27. Its purpose is to improve performance by automatically reusing the results of a `<cfchart>` tag if all of its data and attributes are the same, rather than having to re-render each chart for every page request.

The Charting page of the ColdFusion Administrator contains a number of options that you can use to tweak the way the chart cache behaves.

Cache Type

You can set this to Disk Cache (the default value) or Memory Cache. The Memory Cache setting will perform better under high load, but will require more of the server's memory to do so. The Disk Cache setting may not perform quite as quickly, but it won't have much of an impact on the server's RAM. We recommend leaving this value alone unless you are specifically experiencing performance problems with `<cfchart>` under heavy load.

Maximum Number of Cached Images

You can increase this number to allow ColdFusion to store more charts in its cache, thereby improving performance if your application is serving up lots of different charts. If you are using the Memory Cache option, keep in mind that this will cause even more of the server's memory to be used for chart caching.

Maximum Number of Charting Threads

The maximum number of `<cfchart>` tags that you want ColdFusion to be willing to process at the same moment in time. Under high load, a higher number here may improve responsiveness for individual chart requests, but it will put more overall strain on your server.

Disk Cache Location

If you are using the Disk Cache option, you may adjust this value, which is the location where ColdFusion stores charts for later reuse.

The Font Management Page

Fonts are used by the ColdFusion printing and reporting features. When generating printed output, ColdFusion must know what fonts are available, what output type they support, and whether to embed fonts in generated output.

The Font Management page lists available fonts and allows you to specify a folder containing additional fonts to be installed.

➜ See Chapter 16 to learn about ColdFusion printing and reporting.

The Document Page

This page enables you to edit the OpenOffice configuration. The configuration lets you specify the location of OpenOffice and whether it can be configured remotely. For further information about using OpenOffice, see Chapter 67, "Integrating with Microsoft Office," in Volume 3.

The Java and JVM Page

ColdFusion runs on top of the Java platform. Your ColdFusion pages are translated into Java classes, and those classes are executed within the context of a Java Virtual Machine (JVM). The Java and JVM page of the Administrator allows you to adjust which JVM is used to execute your pages. You can also make other JVM-related adjustments, such as the amount of memory that the JVM is allowed to use while executing your pages.

NOTE

This page is only available when using ColdFusion with the integrated J2EE server. If ColdFusion is installed on a J2EE server, use the server management tools to define these settings.

Java Virtual Machine Path

In theory, ColdFusion should be able to use any up-to-date JVM. To use an alternate JVM, install it, change the Java Virtual Machine Path setting in the ColdFusion Administrator, and then restart the ColdFusion Application Server.

NOTE

Before using a different JVM on your production servers, you should definitely test your applications with that same JVM on some kind of development, staging, or beta-testing server. You should also see whether the JVM is officially supported by Adobe.

NOTE

You can always find out which JVM ColdFusion is running under by clicking the System Information link at the top of the ColdFusion Administrator.

Minimum JVM Heap Size

This setting allows you to provide an initial amount of your server's memory that the JVM should claim when ColdFusion is started. By default, this setting is left blank, which means that the JVM will make its own decisions about how much memory it should claim at startup. If your server encounters a lot of traffic, the JVM will generally need to claim more memory. You may be able to save the JVM some time by telling it to claim a larger amount of memory at start-up. In general, this could make the whole start-up process (which includes the initial processing of your pages) more efficient.

If you provide a value for this setting, it's strongly recommended that you specify a size of at least 32 MB.

Maximum JVM Heap Size

In a default ColdFusion installation, the JVM is instructed to use no more than 512 MB of memory for the ColdFusion runtime and your ColdFusion pages. If your server has considerably more than 512 MB of RAM installed, you may want to allow the JVM to use more of it, which would generally improve performance. Simply specify the maximum amount of memory that you wish the JVM (and thus the ColdFusion server, and thus your ColdFusion pages) to be able to use, in megabytes.

NOTE

Don't set this value to anything lower than 32 MB, because ColdFusion probably won't be able to start with less than that amount of memory.

ColdFusion Class Path

If your applications use any external Java objects that in turn refer to other Java classes (that is, any Java classes that aren't provided by the JVM itself), you can tell ColdFusion where to find the class files by adjusting the Class Path setting in the ColdFusion Administrator. By *Java objects*, I mean any Java classes that you are accessing via `<cfobject>` or `CreateObject()`, any servlets or JSP tag libraries that you are using via `<cfimport>`, CFX tags that have been written in Java, and so on.

In general, you will either be specifying the path to a directory or the path to a Java Archive (`.jar`) file. If you need to specify multiple directories or archives, separate them with commas.

NOTE

If you're familiar with invoking Java on the command line, this Administrator setting is equivalent to the `-classpath` or `-cp` option.

JVM Arguments

If you want any additional arguments to be passed to the JVM when the ColdFusion server is started, you can specify them here. Separate multiple arguments with spaces. Presumably, you would provide such arguments if they were required by an external Java object that you wanted to use, or if the argument was suggested by the JVM vendor to improve performance or stability. The exact purpose and effect of the arguments will depend on the JVM and classes you are using.

Settings Summary

The Settings Summary page provides a quick overview of all ColdFusion Administrator settings. Detailed information about all data sources, CFX tags, mappings, Verity full-text archives, and nearly all other settings discussed in this chapter are displayed. Most of the information from the Version Information page is included in the report as well. You can print this page to get a hard-copy record of all ColdFusion settings on the server.

Data and Services

The Data and Services section of the ColdFusion Administrator contains pages that let you create, edit, and delete data sources and Verity full-text search collections. You can also create aliases for Web Services.

The Data Sources Page

The Data Sources page provides tools to manage the list of data sources available to ColdFusion. Any data source listed here can be used as the `data source` attribute of a `<cfquery>` (or `<cfinsert>`, `<cfupdate>`, `<cfgridupdate>`, or `<cfstoredproc>`) tag.

To define a new data source, specify the name, select the data source type from the drop-down list, click the Add button, and then specify the database specific options as requested.

The Data Sources page is also used to verify that data sources are working. Click the Verify All Connections button to verify all data sources, or click the green check button for a specific data source to validate it alone.

The ColdFusion Collections Page

ColdFusion features an integrated Verity/Solr full-text search engine. CFML includes three tags related to Verity/Solr: `<cfsearh>`, `<cfindex>`, and `<cfcollection>`. All three tags have a `collection` attribute, which refers to what Verity/Solr calls a *collection*. A collection is to Verity/Solr as data sources are to databases: it's a name that you can use to refer to or search a particular set of data.

➜ See Chapter 35, "Full-Text Searching," to learn about ColdFusion's integrated full-text search engine.

Add New Verity Collections

To create a collection, simply provide a name for the new collection and click the Create Collection button. By default, the new collection will be created in the `/verity/collections` folder under the ColdFusion root; if you want the collection files to be kept somewhere else, you can specify the location in the Path field.

Verity Collections

To delete a collection, click the Delete Collection icon for the collection in the Connected Local Connections list.

TIP

You can also create and delete collections programmatically with the `<cfcollection>` tag, rather than using the ColdFusion Administrator. For details, see Chapter 35.

Next to each listed collection are four buttons (from left to right):

- **Index Collection** re-indexes a collection.

- **Optimize Collection** performs optimization on the collection to improve performance (this is generally used for collections that are being constantly updated).
- **Purge Collection** empties a collection.
- **Delete Collection** deletes a collection completely.

The Verity K2 Server Page

Verity support is provided by the Verity K2 engine, which must be running for you to use any Verity functionality (Verity can also be installed on a separate host). By default, ColdFusion uses a local K2 server, but an alternate server can be specified in this screen if required. Settings such as the name, path, and language and whether to enable the collection can be edited here.

NOTE

Verity isn't supported on all platforms.

The Solr Server Page

ColdFusion now supports Solr. Solr is based on, and extends, the Apache Lucene Java search library. Apache Lucene is a free open source project. From this screen, you can configure the Solr server's host name and home directory and the option to migrate from Verity to Solr. For more information about searching, see Chapter 35.

Migrate Verity Collections

As just mentioned, ColdFusion 9 introduced Solr as an alternative for full-text search support. If you have existing Verity collections, you can use the Migrate Verity Collections option to migrate them for use with Solr. For more information about searching, see Chapter 35.

The Web Services Page

ColdFusion allows you to use (*consume*) Web Services via the `<cfinvoke>` or `<cfobject>` tag, or via the `CreateObject()` function. You can use the Web Services page to create aliases for the Web Services that you plan to use. You can then use the alias name instead of providing the full URL for the Web Service in every `<cfinvoke>` tag. If the Web Service requires a username and password, they can be associated with the alias as well, which means that the username and password don't have to appear in your ColdFusion code at all.

To create an alias for a Web Service, enter the alias in the Web Service Name field. Provide the URL for the service's WSDL description in the WDSL URL field (if the service requires a username and password, enter them as well), then click the Add Web Service button. The new alias will appear in the Active ColdFusion Services list at the bottom of the page. You can now use the alias name as the `Webservice` attribute for `<cfinvoke>`, `<cfobject>`, or `CreateObject()` where you would normally need to provide the complete WSDL URL. Another common use for this page is to clear the cached version of Web Services that have been automatically registered.

The Flex Integration Page

ColdFusion can be used as a powerful backend for Flash and Flex applications, as well as for applications powered by LiveCycle Data Services.

➜ See Chapters 31, "Integrating with Adobe Flex," and 33, "Building ColdFusion-Powered AIR Applications," to learn about ColdFusion and Adobe AIR and Flex integration.

Enable Flash Remoting support

To allow ColdFusion Components to be accessed via Flash Remoting, check this box.

Enable Remote Adobe LiveCycle Data Management Access

ColdFusion features an integrated Adobe LiveCycle Data Services server (if that option was selected during installation). Usually this integrated server will be sufficient for ColdFusion integration. However, if you need to connect ColdFusion to an external (or remote) LiveCycle Data Services server, check this box (and specify the server identity).

NOTE

Server Identity specifies the ColdFusion server on which Flex data management support is enabled.

Enable RMI over SSL for Data Management

RMI is used for communication between ColdFusion and external LiveCycle Data Services servers. To secure this connection, check this box and provide the key information as required.

Select IP Addresses Where LiveCycle Data Services Are Running

To secure communication between ColdFusion and external LiveCycle Data Services servers, you can specify the IP addresses of those servers allowed to connect to ColdFusion. If any IP addresses are specified, any connections not listed will be refused.

Debugging and Logging

The Debugging and Logging section of the ColdFusion Administrator provides a set of tools that can help you understand what your applications are doing, where and when any performance bottlenecks are occurring, and whether any error messages are occurring without your knowledge. There is also a rich set of debugging options that make it easier to troubleshoot errors while coding. In short, this section is all about making it easier for you to identify and avoid problems, both during and after the development process.

The Debug Output Settings Page

The Debugging Settings page allows you to customize what exactly appears in the debugging output. This page also lets you monitor the ColdFusion server externally, via the command line or the System Monitor in Windows.

➜ See Chapter 17, "Debugging and Troubleshooting," in Volume 1, to learn about ColdFusion debugging options.

Enable Robust Exception Information

ColdFusion error messages provide lots of useful information about your server and code to help you diagnose problems. Unfortunately, this information may also be useful to hackers trying to gain unauthorized access to your server. As such, this option should be enabled on development machines but not on production servers.

Enable AJAX Debug Log Window

To enable the pop-up Ajax debug window, check this box.

➜ See Chapter 30 to learn about Ajax debugging.

Enable Request Debugging Output

Check this option to enable debugging output. Information about variables, queries, execution times, and more will begin appearing at the bottom of each page processed by ColdFusion. You can customize what information is included in the debugging output.

NOTE

This option appends content to the generated page, so it should not be used when generating XML output. It can be disabled using `cfsetting`.

TIP

Even when this option is enabled, you can make sure that only the appropriate people (presumably yourself and the other developers on your team) see the debugging output by restricting the output by IP address. This is discussed shortly, in the Debugging IP Addresses page.

Custom Debugging Output

You can customize exactly what is included in the debugging output and how it's displayed with the options in this section.

Enable Performance Monitoring

If you're using ColdFusion with Windows, you can monitor the ColdFusion server with the standard Performance Monitor application that comes with Windows. This is the same application that you use to monitor internal Windows processes such as memory management and CPU use, or other Microsoft applications such as IIS or SQL Server.

Check this option to tell ColdFusion to make information available to the Performance Monitor. When enabled, the Performance Object called ColdFusion Server will be available for display and monitoring within the Performance Monitor.

To monitor performance with the Performance Monitor, follow these steps:

1. Make sure the Enable Debugging option is checked, since it affects all options on this page of the Administrator.
2. Make sure the Enable Performance Monitoring option is checked.
3. Launch the Windows Performance Monitor (choose Start > Run > Perfmon) and select ColdFusion from the Performance Object list as the process to monitor. Select All Counters or add individual counters from the list.

The Performance Monitor will show a live graph of the various counters available, such as the number of database interactions per second, the average page execution time, and the number of currently executing page requests. If you wish, you can also add counters from other Performance Objects, such as the IIS object (to monitor the IIS Web server) or the Processor object (to monitor the CPU itself). Use the Help icon on the Performance Monitor toolbar for more information.

Enable `CFSTAT`

For non-Windows servers, you can use the `CFSTAT` command-line utility to take the place of the Performance Monitor. It doesn't show up as a nice graph, but it displays the same information.

To use `CFSTAT`, follow these steps:

1. Make sure the Enable Debugging option is checked, since it affects all options on this page of the Administrator.
2. Make sure the Enable `CFSTAT` option is checked.
3. Do whatever is appropriate for the operating system you're using to execute the `cfstat` executable in the `/bin` folder (under the ColdFusion root). It's helpful to add a command-line switch of `1`, so that the statistics will be updated once per second.

The Debugging IP Addresses Page

While ColdFusion's debugging output is certainly helpful to you as a developer, you probably don't want your users or beta testers to see it. You may also want to get rid of it from time to time while you work, to see what your pages will look like without it.

Rather than having to turn the debugging output on or off for the entire server at once, ColdFusion allows you to turn it on only for specific IP addresses. This allows you to selectively decide who receives the debugging information. To add an IP address, go to the Debugging IP Addresses page, type it in the IP Address field, and click Add. To remove an IP address, select it from the list and click Remove Selected.

TIP

To add your own IP address with one click, you can just click the Add Current button.

The Debugger Settings Page

ColdFusion provides an Eclipse-based interactive debugger. To use the debugger, you must enable support on this page.

Allow Line Debugging

To turn on Eclipse debugging support, check this box.

NOTE

Checking this setting requires restarting the ColdFusion Server.

Debugger Port

The ColdFusion debugger communicates with ColdFusion on a designated port. By default, this is port 5005, but any port value can be used if needed.

NOTE

Do not use the same port that is used by ColdFusion or your Web server.

TIP

If you are debugging against a remote server, make sure that your firewall allows communication via the specified port.

Maximum Simultaneous Debugging Sessions

ColdFusion allows multiple concurrent debugging sessions. Specify the maximum number of sessions needed here.

TIP

Don't set this number higher than necessary, and if you are the only developer using a local server, set it to `1`.

The Logging Settings Page

ColdFusion keeps detailed log files that can be extremely helpful for monitoring or debugging an application. This page controls how ColdFusion maintains the log files, and allows you to turn on some additional log files that aren't kept by default.

Log Directory

By default, ColdFusion stores all log files in the `/logs` folder (beneath the ColdFusion root). You can use this option to change the location of the log files.

Maximum File Size

When log files get very large, they can become unwieldy and hard to read. Use this option to set the maximum amount of information to keep in each log file. The default value is 5000 KB. When a log file exceeds this size, its contents are copied into a *log archive* file. Log archives are the same as the original log files, except that they are given an extension of `.1`, `.2`, and so on, instead of `.log`.

Maximum Number of Archives

A new archive file will be created each time the log file reaches 5000 KB (or whatever you specify). If you don't want an indefinite number of these archive files hanging around forever, you can tell ColdFusion to only maintain a certain number of archives for each log file. By default, a limit of ten archives is used. If, when the actual log file reaches 5000 KB, there are already ten archives present (perhaps `application.1` through `application.10`), the oldest archive file is deleted.

Log Slow Pages

If you enable this option, a special entry in the `server.log` file will be made for any ColdFusion pages that take longer than the specified number of seconds to execute. You can use this information to identify bottlenecks in your application. (On some operating systems, you may also have an option to use OS logging features.)

Log All CORBA Calls

In you happen to be using CORBA objects in your application, enable this option to have ColdFusion log all CORBA interactions to the `server.log` file.

Enable Logging for Scheduled Tasks

If you are using ColdFusion's built-in task scheduler (see "The Scheduled Tasks Page" section in a moment and Chapter 36, "Event Scheduling"), you can enable this option to have all scheduler-related actions logged to a special log file called `scheduler.log`.

The Log Files Page

The Log Files page allows you to view and manage all of the log files on your server. Each `.log` file in the `/log` folder (or whatever log file location you have specified) is listed. For each log, icons are provided for viewing, downloading archiving, or deleting the log. When viewing a log, you can click the Launch Filter button to launch the Log Viewer filter window.

The Scheduled Tasks Page

ColdFusion has a built-in task scheduler, which allows you to create ColdFusion pages that run every few minutes or hours, or that execute at a certain time of day. Such pages are usually used to do things like sending mail, indexing collections, deleting temporary files that are no longer needed, and other administrative tasks.

➜ For more information about scheduling tasks, see Chapter 36.

TIP

You can also schedule tasks programmatically with the `<cfschedule>` tag, instead of using the ColdFusion Administrator.

The System Probes Page

The System Probes page allows you to set up *probes* that check to see whether a particular page is executing normally. If not, ColdFusion can send you an email message so that you are among the very first to know when problems occur.

The System Probes page lists all currently defined probes. Icons are provided to edit or delete each probe. There is also a Disable/Enable icon for each probe, which you can use to temporarily turn a probe on or off. Finally, you can use the Run Probe icon to run a probe immediately, rather than waiting for it to run at its normally scheduled time or interval.

Define New Probe

To create a new probe, click the Define New Probe button. The Add/Edit System Probe page appears. This is discussed in further detail in Chapter 47.

System Probe Options

At the bottom of the System Probes page, you will find a number of options to control the way ColdFusion handles notification when a probe finds a problem:

- **Notification Email Recipients.** Provide a list of email addresses that ColdFusion should use when sending out a notification that a probe has found a problem. Everyone you specify here will receive a notification about every failed probe.
- **E-mail.** Specify a valid email address that ColdFusion's notification messages should use as their *from* field.
- **`Probe.cfm` URL.** Internally, the probe mechanism needs to be able to execute the `Probe.cfm` template in the `CFIDE` folder within your Web server root. If for some reason you need to move the template or place it on a different virtual server, edit the URL accordingly.
- **`Probe.cfm` Username and Password.** If you have used your Web server software to secure access to the `Probe.cfm` file with a username and password, enter that username and password here.

The Code Analyzer Page

While every effort is made to ensure backwards compatibility with prior versions of ColdFusion, it's always best to check your code before upgrading your server. The Code Analyzer page can help you identify most of the potential compatibility issues ahead of time, before you even try to run your application under ColdFusion.

To run the analyzer, specify the location of the application files you would like to test in the Directory to Analyze field, then click Run Analyzer. If you click the Advanced Options button, you will be able to tell ColdFusion which files to inspect (the default is all `.cfm` files), which incompatibilities to check for (the default is to check for all incompatibilities), which language elements to check, whether to display only serious problems (the Warn or the Info option), and more.

The License Scanner Page

Every non-Developer Edition of ColdFusion must be licensed. To help the system administrator, the License Scanner page can scan your local network and report the ColdFusion servers present and their license numbers.

NOTE

The License Scanner checks the local subnet only, and does not report information to any external locations. This is purely a local reporting option for system administrators.

Server Monitoring

The Server Monitoring section has a single page, which provides access to the ColdFusion Server Monitor.

➜ To learn about the ColdFusion Server Monitor, see Chapter 47.

The Server Monitor Page

The ColdFusion Server Monitor is a Flex application (requiring Flash Player 9 or higher).

Launch Server Monitor

This option launches the Server Monitor in a separate window. The Server Monitor is used to monitor a single server only, as well as to define system alerts.

Launch Multiserver Monitor

This option launches a dashboard page that can be used to monitor as many ColdFusion servers as needed, both local and remote. Each server must be registered, and a valid server login must be provided. The dashboard will then display the health of each server, and it will provide easy access to the Server Monitor for each of the listed servers.

Server Manager

The Server Manager client allows you to monitor and manage multiple servers. With the Server Manager client, you can manage servers in groups as well as individuals. The following tasks are some of the most common with which the Server Manager client can assist:

- Clear the template cache.
- Apply the settings from one ColdFusion server to another ColdFusion server or servers (data sources, mappings, scheduled tasks, mail, charts, logging, and so on).

- Apply a hotfix.
- Restart a ColdFusion server.
- Compare whether there are any differences in the configuration settings of two server instances.

NOTE

Server Manager is not supported on previous ColdFusion servers. Only ColdFusion 9 servers can be managed using Server Manager.

You must register the ColdFusion server with its host name and IP address, port number, context root (for J2EE servers), username, and password, and a name that will identify it.

NOTE

Each instance in a cluster must be registered individually.

NOTE

You must have Adobe AIR installed to run the Server Manager client.

Extensions

ColdFusion supports several extensibility options, including writing CFX tags with Java or C++, by using CORBA objects, and more. The Extensions section of the Administrator allows you to manage certain options related to extensibility.

The Java Applets Page

You can use the Java Applets page to create aliases for client-side Java applets that you use often throughout your applications. These aliases let you add the applets to individual pages with simpler, more manageable code. Once the alias has been created, you include the actual applet in your pages with the `<cfapplet>` tag.

The CFX Tags Page

It's possible to create new tags for ColdFusion that are written with Java or C++, rather than CFML; these are called CFX tags. CFX tags are usually created to add some kind of capability that is intrinsically easier or more sensible to implement with Java or C++ than with ColdFusion code. For instance, if you already have C++ code available that completes a particular task, why translate it into the corresponding ColdFusion code when you can just create a CFX tag that leverages the existing C++ code?

Before a CFX tag can be used in your ColdFusion pages, it must be registered using the ColdFusion Administrator. The first thing you will need to know is whether the CFX tag in question was written with Java or C++. If you have been given a `.class` file (or files), the CFX was written with Java. If it has a `.dll` extension, it was created with C++.

NOTE

Until you know how a CFX tag behaves on your system, and until you can be sure of its safety and reliability, it is best to uncheck the Keep Library Loaded option.

The Custom Tag Paths Page

The default location for custom tags is the `/CustomTags` folder directory beneath the ColdFusion root.

To add a new custom tag path, enter the location in the New Path field and click Add Path. Once the path has been created, you can then place custom tag files within the folder you specified, and they will be found automatically, as if they were placed in the default folder.

To edit or delete an existing tag path, use the icons provided for each entry in the Current Custom Tag Paths list.

NOTE

If Enable Per App Settings (on the Settings page) is checked, you can define custom tag locations for specific applications in `Application.cfc`.

The CORBA Connectors Page

If you plan to invoke CORBA objects or services within your ColdFusion pages, you need to set up a CORBA connector for the ORB you plan to use to broker your requests. ColdFusion ships with support for Borland's VisiBroker product. If you need support for a different ORB vendor's product, you will need to contact Adobe.

Assuming you intend to use the VisiBroker support rather than some other ORB, you need to add a connector for VisiBroker by following these steps:

1. Click the Register CORBA Connector button on the CORBA Connectors page of the Administrator. The Edit CORBA Connector page appears.
2. In the ORB Name field, enter a descriptive name for the connector, such as `visibroker`.
3. In the ORB Class Name field, enter `coldfusion.runtime.corba.VisibrokerConnector`.
4. Leave the `Classpath` field blank.
5. In the ORB Property File field, enter the path to the `vbjorb.properties` file in ColdFusion's `lib` folder. For a default Windows installation, the correct path would be `C:ColdFusion9libvbjorb.properties`.
6. Click Submit to create the connector.
7. Edit the `SVCnameroot` property in the `vbjorb.properties` file appropriately so that ColdFusion is able to find the root.

In addition, you will need to provide the appropriate value to the `SVCnameroot` property in the `vbjorb.properties` file. You will also need to make sure that the `vbjorb.jar` file is present (this file is distributed with VisiBroker) and that the path to `vbjorb.jar` is part of ColdFusion's Java class path setting (see the section "The Java and JVM Page" earlier in this chapter).

Event Gateways

Event gateways are the means by which ColdFusion connects to external systems (to generate messages as well as to respond to inbound requests). This section is used to define and manage event gateways and their settings.

→ Event gateways are covered in detail in Chapter 70, "Working with Gateways," in Volume 3.

The Settings Page

The Setting page is used to enable or disable event gateway processing, and to define gateway settings.

Enable ColdFusion Event Gateway Services

The gateway engine must be enabled to perform any gateway processing, and can be turned off to reduce overhead if gateways aren't being used.

Event Gateway Processing Threads

By default, 10 threads are allocated for gateway processing. If you have a large number of active gateways, or very heavy gateway load, you should increase this number. Higher numbers will improve gateway performance but will also increase server resource use.

NOTE

The defaults and values are lower in the ColdFusion Developer Edition.

Maximum Number of Events to Queue

The maximum number of events to be queued is set to 25,000 by default. When this number is reached, no additional events will be placed in the processing queue.

SMS Test Server

ColdFusion includes an SMS test server that can be used to simulate the SMS world so as to build SMS applications. The SMS test server can be started and stopped as needed.

→ The SMS Gateway is covered in detail in Chapter 71, "Integrating with SMS and IM," in Volume 3.

The Gateway Types Page

Gateways are written in Java, and must be registered on the server before they can be instantiated. Gateway Type management is performed in this page.

To add a gateway, provide a name, a description, and the location of the Java `.class` file. Then click the Add button.

To edit or delete defined gateways, use the icons to the left of the Configured Gateway Type list.

The Gateway Instances Page

Gateway instances are defined in this page. One or more instances of any gateway type may be defined.

To add a gateway instance, provide a unique ID (name), select a type, provide the path to the CFC file that should process gateway requests, specify an optional configuration file, and select a startup mode. Then click the Add Gateway Instance button.

To edit or delete defined gateways, or to start and stop gateway instances, use the icons to the left of the Configured Gateway Instances list.

Security

ColdFusion provides a number of security-related features. Some of these features let you add login and role-based security mechanisms to your own applications. The options in the Security portion of the ColdFusion Administrator, in contrast, are about securing the server itself so that only the proper people have the ability to administer ColdFusion. You can also lock down various parts of the server (tags, files, data sources, and so on) so that each application only has the right to use its own files and data.

NOTE

Your Web server software also provides its own security measures. You should become familiar with them as well.

The Administrator Page

The ColdFusion Administrator enables the configuration and management of the ColdFusion server. Therefore, the ColdFusion Administrator should generally be password protected to prevent unauthorized access.

ColdFusion Administrator Authentication

To support a single administration login and password, select the first option. To support multiple administrators, each possibly with a different level of access, select the second option. To allow access without a password, select the third option.

CAUTION

Use of the third option is not recommended.

Root Administrator Password

Use this option to change the primary ColdFusion Administrator password.

The RDS Password Page

RDS is used to provide development time access to ColdFusion data sources, files, reporting building, and more. Because RDS can expose sensitive files and data, it should always be secured.

NOTE

RDS should never be installed on production servers.

RDS Authentication

To support a single RDS login and password, select the first option. To support multiple RDS logins, each possibly tied to a different sandbox, select the second option. To allow access without a password, select the third option.

CAUTION

Use of the third option is not recommended.

RDS Single Password

Use this option to change the primary RDS password.

The Sandbox Security Page

ColdFusion includes a feature called *sandbox security*. This feature is mostly aimed at Internet service providers or people running large enterprise-wide servers, where a server may have many different ColdFusion applications written by many different developers. In such a situation, there needs to be some way to keep one set of developers from accessing the data sources that are being used by another set of developers. Similarly, there needs to be some way to keep one application from being able to use `<cffile>` or `<cfdirectory>` to read or destroy files that are important to another application.

NOTE

This topic requires a dedicated chapter. Chapter 55, "Creating Server Sandboxes," in Volume 3, explains in detail how to implement sandbox security.

The User Manager Page

As seen previously, both the ColdFusion Administrator and RDS support single-password logins and multiple logins. To use the latter, you define users using this page.

Click the Add User button to add a user and then define the username, password, and permissions for this user.

→ For more information, see Chapter 53, "Securing the ColdFusion Administrator," in Volume 3.

NOTE

Allowed IP Addresses gives permission to access services from specific client IP addresses.

Packaging and Deployment

ColdFusion applications are collections of files that can easily be copied and moved between servers. But moving individual files is a highly error-prone exercise, and so ColdFusion provides more manageable ways to distribute and deploy applications.

The ColdFusion Archives Page

At any point during your application's development, you can use the ColdFusion Administrator to create a *ColdFusion archive* of your application. ColdFusion archives are files that can contain all the files needed to run your application, such as your ColdFusion (`.cfm`) pages, image files, XML files, desktop database files, Flash movies, and any other files that your application depends on.

But ColdFusion archives can include more than just your application files; they can also include any Administrator settings that your application depends on. In other words, the idea behind the ColdFusion archive feature is to give you a way to create a single file that contains everything needed to make your application work. It's a great way to back up your work.

ColdFusion archives are also about deployment. Once you have created an archive for your application, you can copy the single archive file to another ColdFusion server. Your application can then be installed in one step. All of your application's files will be unpacked from the archive and placed in the appropriate places on the server, and all of the required configuration changes (such as setting up data sources and mappings) will be made automatically. ColdFusion archives are created and used from within the ColdFusion Archives page.

Procedures for creating an archive, displaying the current archive definition list, and deploying an archive are discussed in more detail in Chapter 51, "Deploying Applications," in Volume 3.

The J2EE Archives Page

Java applications deployed on J2EE servers are usually deployed as EAR or WAR files. As ColdFusion itself is a Java application, it can be installed as an EAR or a WAR, as can applications you create. J2EE archive packaging is managed from the J2EE Archives page. For more information, see Chapter 51.

Add New Archive

To create a new deployment archive, enter an archive name and click the Add button to display the Add/Edit J2EE Archive screen. You will be prompted for the location of your application, the location to store the created archive, the destination serial number, as well as the ColdFusion features to include in the deployment package. Once you have specified these values, click Submit to create the deployment package.

Configured Archives

Packages may be modified and deleted as needed. Package deployment is performed using your J2EE server management tools.

CHAPTER 26

Managing Threads

IN THIS CHAPTER

ColdFusion event gateways can be used to perform asynchronous programming. Asynchronous coding allows requests to run concurrently yet independently of each other. The asynchronous CFML gateway allows developers to run code parallel to the user request. The template requested in the browser can issue multiple calls to the gateway. The code running in the gateway is completely autonomous, meaning that it runs in its own thread, consumes its own resources, and does not depend on the parent request thread. The parent thread continues execution without waiting for CFML gateway requests to be complete. This approach allows multiple tasks to finish simultaneously in contrast to the sequential execution of traditional procedural programming.

TIP

The terms parent thread, parent request, and page-level thread are all synonyms for the ColdFusion template or page requested in the client browser.

The problem with the CFML gateway is that it provides limited feedback and interaction with the page-level thread. The CFML gateway sends messages to CFC methods and provides a status message only to the page-level thread. Although it can access shared scoped variables (such as `Server`, `Application`, and `Session`), CFML gateway requests run in a thread pool separate from the page-level thread, so they cannot share the `REQUEST` scope or provide output to the user. ColdFusion 8 provided a better solution, with ColdFusion threads.

ColdFusion threads are also autonomous and allow asynchronous, simultaneous code execution. They are created with the `<cfthread>` tag. Like the CFML gateway, the `<cfthread>` tag is called in the request or page thread, and it creates additional threads that run independent of the page thread. However, ColdFusion threads can provide output to and interact with the page thread. ColdFusion threads can also process synchronously, by suspending execution of the page thread until the thread execution finishes. Table 26.1 summarizes the differences between the CFML gateway and ColdFusion threads.

Table 26.1 CFML Gateway Compared to ColdFusion Threads

CFML GATEWAY	COLDFUSION THREADS
Initialized by `sendGatewayMessage()` call to a gateway CFC.	Initialized with `cfthread`.
`SendGatewayMessage()` returns status value to page thread.	Thread scope containing metadata variables accessible by page thread.
Data passed by `CFEvent` scope.	Data passed by `ATTRIBUTES` scope.
Can access shared scopes but not `REQUEST` scope.	Can access all scopes.
Strict autonomous execution; page thread continues processing without waiting for gateway thread completion.	Flexible autonomous execution; can suspend page thread until thread completion.
Provides asynchronous processing.	Provides synchronous and asynchronous processing.
Thread runs in event gateway thread pool.	Thread runs in separate thread request pool.
Limited interaction with other gateway requests.	Threads can interact with and join each other.
Nesting allowed.	Nesting allowed, but child thread generation is unsupported.
Cannot set priority.	Can set thread priority.
Cannot suspend execution.	Can suspend thread execution.
Does not provide user feedback.	Can provide output to page-level thread.
Difficult to debug.	Provides `Error` metadata variable containing error information.

Using the `<cfthread>` Tag

The `<cfthread>` tag manages ColdFusion threads. Developers use `<cfthread>` to

- Start thread execution
- Suspend thread execution
- Stop thread execution
- Join threads to each other or the page-level request

Only a page-level request can generate threads with `<cfthread>`—child threads are not supported. You can pass thread-specific attributes to the `<cfthread>` tag. Code inside the `<cfthread>` body executes in a separate thread pool. The thread pool limit is set in the ColdFusion Administrator; any threads created beyond this limit are queued. Table 26.2 lists the `<cfthread>` attributes and descriptions.

TIP

Only `<cfthread>` calls with `action="run"` can have a tag body. All other actions must not have tag bodies and must use a slash (/) to end the tag or must use `</cftrhead>` immediately after the opening tag.

NOTE

ColdFusion supports nested `<cfthread>` calls, but only the outermost `<cfthread>` can specify `action="run"`. Generation of child threads is currently not supported.

Table 26.2 `<cfthread>` Attributes

ATTRIBUTE	DESCRIPTION	APPLIES TO	REQUIRED
`action`	Action to perform; options are `join`, `run` (default), `sleep`, and `terminate`.	All	No
`duration`	Number of milliseconds to suspend processing.	`sleep`	Yes
`name`	Name of the thread receiving the action	`join`, `run`, `terminate`	Yes if action is `join` or `terminate`
`priority`	Run-level priority for the thread. Options are `HIGH`, `LOW`, and `NORMAL` (default).	`run`	No
`timeout`	Number of milliseconds (default = 0) that the page-level thread waits for running threads or threads being joined to complete before continuing processing.	`join`	No

Scripting the `<cfthread>` tag

ColdFusion 9 extended the tag support in CFScript. As part of this language enhancement, CFScript now provides the `thread` statement as the script equivalent of `<cfthread>`. The thread statement requires only the `<cfthread>` `name` attribute. The `<cfthread>` `action` and `priority` parameters are optional.

The `action` attribute is optional for the `thread` statement because the statement can only create new threads. ColdFusion 9 provides two new function equivalents for joining and ending threads: `threadJoin` and `threadTerminate`, respectively. Table 26.3 lists the `threadJoin` function parameters. The `threadTerminate` function accepts only the `threadName` parameter: the name of the thread to end. You will find details on the CFScript language enhancements in Chapter 40, "ColdFusion Scripting."

Table 26.3 `threadJoin` Parameters

PARAMETER	DESCRIPTION	OPTIONAL
`threadName`	The name of the thread to join to the current thread. Specify a comma-separated list to join multiple threads	Yes
`timeout`	The number of milliseconds to suspend processing	Yes

Starting Threads

Call `<cfthread>` with the `action` attribute set to `run` to start a new thread. Name the thread with the `name` attribute to provide a control handle for interaction with the page-level thread or other threads. Use the `priority` attribute to specify a runtime processing priority level for individual threads. Valid values are `NORMAL`, `HIGH`, and `LOW`. The page-level thread continues processing while the thread is running, unless it is suspended with the `sleep` function or by the joining of threads.

NOTE

You may want to suspend the page thread to allow `<cfthread>`-generated threads to finish and return output for the page thread. Since threads process non-sequentially in a separate queue from the parent request, they typically do not affect the total page execution time. However, suspending the page-level thread to allow spawned threads to finish increases the total page execution time by the value of the sleep function, thus increasing the risk of eclipsing the configured request timeout. To prevent this, use the `cfsetting` tag and set the `requestTimeout` attribute equal to or greater than the total value of all the coded sleep functions, including any inside the `cfthread` body.

Here is the tag syntax:

```
<cfthread name="thread name" [action="run" [, priority="NORMAL|HIGH|LOW" [,
attributes]]]>
   Code to execute
</cfthread>
```

Here is the script syntax:

```
<cfscript>
    Thread name="thread name" [[action="run"] [priority="NORMAL|HIGH|LOW"]
[attributes]] {
            Code in thread body
    }
</cfscript>
```

TIP

ColdFusion provides more processing time to higher-priority threads. Since page-level code always has a priority of `NORMAL`, you can provide more processing time to your threads by running them at a higher priority than the page-level code.

TIP

User-defined attributes can be specified.

Suspending Threads

Occasionally you may want one or more threads to pause or suspend execution while another thread begins and then continue execution simultaneous to that thread. For example, you may start `ThreadA`, but it may depend on data generated in `ThreadB`, so you need to suspend `ThreadA` until `ThreadB` provides the necessary data. To suspend a thread, either call the `sleep` function within the `<cfthread>` body or provide the `sleep` value to the `<cfthread> action` attribute.

TIP

The `cfthread sleep` action and the `sleep` function are equivalent. Essentially, they both call `java.lang.Thread.sleep(n)`.

Here is the tag syntax:

```
<cfthread action="sleep" duration= "milliseconds" />
```

Here is the script syntax:

```
<cfscript>
   Thread name="thread name" {
      sleep(milliseconds);
   }
</cfscript>
```

Ending Threads

Specify `terminate` for the `<cfthread>` `action` attribute or use the `terminateThread()` function to end running or suspended threads. Remember that threads run in their own execution pools; there is no request timeout value applicable to threads, so they can potentially run forever. For example, the following code creates an infinite loop:

```
<cfloop condition="1">
  <cfset sleep(10000) />
</cfloop>
```

This code performs a continuous loop over a 10-second `sleep` call. If you run this code in a regular template with a timeout request enabled, ColdFusion will kill the page after it reaches the timeout limit. However, if you call this code inside `<cfthread>`, the page-level request will end, but the loop will continue in the thread. Use `<cfthread>` with `action="terminate"` and the `name` attribute set to the thread name to kill this runaway thread.

Here is the tag syntax:

```
<cfthread name="thread name" action="terminate" />
```

Here is the script syntax:

```
<cfscript>
   threadTerminate(threadName);
</cfscript>
```

Joining Threads

Normally threads run independently of each other and the page-level thread. Sometimes, though, you may need co-dependent threads, where one thread depends on the completion of one or more threads before it can continue processing. Other times you may need synchronization with the page-level thread, to display thread-generated output for example.

Specify `join` for the `<cfthread>` `action` attribute or the `threadJoin()` function to join threads. Joining threads effectively suspends the execution of the thread creating the join as it waits for the join operation to finish. Provide the name of the threads to be joined in the `name` attribute (or `threadName` parameter). You can join multiple threads using a comma-separated list. Omit the `name` attribute to have the thread join the page thread. Use the `timeout` attribute to specify the amount of time a request waits for the thread join operation to finish.

NOTE

The default `timeout` value is 0, which tells the request to wait indefinitely for thread join to complete. If the current thread is the page-level thread, then the page request continues to wait for the thread join to complete. If you have hung or long-running threads, this will cause the page-level thread to execute beyond the configured request timeout in the ColdFusion Administrator.

Here is the tag syntax:

```
<cfthread action="join name="thread name [, thread name]… " [,
timeout="milliseconds"] />
```

Here is the script syntax:

```
<cfsript>
   threadJoin([[thread name][,timeout]]);
</cfscript>
```

Accessing Thread Data

ColdFusion threads have access to all ColdFusion scopes. Threads perform processing simultaneously, but they share access to data, so it is paramount that shared data access be protected to ensure integrity. ColdFusion threads also have their own scopes for managing data internally. They provide metadata variables containing thread-specific data for processing at the page level.

Thread Scopes

ColdFusion threads have three scopes:

- `THREAD-LOCAL` scope
- `ATTRIBUTES` scope
- `THREAD` scope

In addition, a special `CFTHREAD` scope is available to the page-level request.

THREAD-LOCAL Scope

`THREAD-LOCAL` scope is a private scope containing variables available only to the current thread. Variables in this scope exist only for the life of the thread. They cannot be accessed by other threads or the page-level thread. Create variables in the thread-local scope by defining them in the `<cfthread>` body without a prefix:

```
<cfset counter = 1 />
```

TIP

You can also define thread-local variables using the `var` keyword: for example, `<cfset var counter = 1 />`. However, such variable definitions must occur immediately after the `<cfthread>` tag.

ATTRIBUTES Scope

The ATTRIBUTES scope contains any user-defined attributes specified for the <cfthread> tag (or CFScript thread operation) individually or with the attributesCollection attribute. ColdFusion makes a deep copy of variables passed as attributes, making the variable values independent of values in other threads, including the page thread. Variables in the thread's ATTRIBUTE scope exist only for the life of the thread and are available only to the current thread. This restriction provides thread safety because other threads cannot access attribute data. Because the attributes are thread safe, threads can have the same attribute names, which is useful when you are dynamically defining threads in a loop:

```
<cfparam name="URL.numOfThreads" default="5" type="integer" />
<cfloop index="i" from="1" to="#URL.numOfThreads#">
  <cfthread name="thread#i#" action="run" loopCtr="#i#">
    <cfset counter = ATTRIBUTES.loopCtr />
  </cfthread>
</cfloop>
```

This code block shows the loopCtr passed as an attribute to <cfthread> and accessed in the thread body with the ATTRIBUTES keyword prefix. ColdFusion makes a deep copy of variables before passing data to the <cfthread> attribute, which ensures that the values manipulated inside the <cfthread> body are independent of the original values. For example, this approach protects CFC instances passed to the thread; any manipulation of the CFC instance inside the thread does not affect the external CFC instances, and vice versa.

TIP

In general, use proper locking with <cflock> to prevent race conditions and deadlocks in all your CFML. Here is a good rule of thumb: If you are not sure it's thread-safe, lock it.

THREAD Scope

The THREAD scope contains thread-specific variables and metadata about the thread. Variables in the THREAD scope are available to the current thread and external threads. Only the current thread can write to this scope. All external threads in the page request (including the page-level thread) have read-only access. THREAD scope variables exist while the page and any threads in that page are still running. You create variables in the THREAD scope by prefixing them with either the thread name or the THREAD keyword:

```
<cfset THREAD.message = THREAD.name & " is initialized..." />
```

Use the thread's name to access THREAD scope data in external threads:

```
<cfset dataFromThreadA = THREADA.data />
```

NOTE

Be aware that variables in the THREAD scope can persist beyond the current page request if any threads generated in that request continue to run after the page request finishes.

TIP

THREAD scope data is available only to the current page request. If you need cross-request thread access, store the thread data in a shared scope (SERVER, APPLICATION, or SESSION), database, or file.

CFTHREAD Scope

The special CFTHREAD sub-scope of ColdFusion's REQUEST scope contains the THREAD scope variables and metadata for all threads generated in the current page request. CFTHREAD exists for the entire page request or the life of the last running thread, whichever is longer. CFTHREAD is a ColdFusion structure whose keys are the thread names. Use the CFTHREAD keyword and the thread name to access data:

```
<cfoutput>#CFTHREAD.threadName.data#</cfoutput>
```

Since you can also use the thread name to access thread data, there are only a few instances where you might actually need to call CFTHREAD:

- When accessing dynamically named threads
- When threads have the same name as a VARIABLES scoped variable

TIP

Remember that CFTHREAD belongs to the page request, so all threads in the current request can access it.

Thread Metadata

The THREAD scope contains several thread-specific variables. This metadata is available for every ColdFusion thread. Access the metadata as you would other THREAD scope variables by using either the thread name or CFTHREAD.threadName as a prefix. Thread metadata is also available for the duration of the page request or while a thread is running, whichever time is longer. This approach allows access to thread variables and metadata after the thread has finished processing. Table 26.4 lists the <cfthread> metadata variables.

Table 26.4 <cfthread> Metadata Variables

VARIABLE	DESCRIPTION
elapsedTime	Total processor time spent running the thread.
error	ColdFusion structure containing errors that occur during thread execution.
name	The name of the thread; corresponds to the <cfthread> name attribute.
output	Displays thread-generated output in page-level code.
priority	Thread processing priority as specified in the <cfthread> priority attribute; valid values are HIGH, LOW, and NORMAL.
starttime	The time thread processing began.
status	The current status of the thread.

TIP

If you dump the THREAD scope, the error metadata variable may be missing. It is present in the THREAD scope only if an error occurred during thread processing.

Other ColdFusion Scopes

ColdFusion threads have access to all ColdFusion scopes. All threads created in the same template (.cfm, .cfc, and so on) share the same variables and THIS scope. All the threads created in any templates within a single page request share the same FORM, URL, REQUEST, CGI, COOKIE, SESSION, APPLICATION, SERVER, and CLIENT scopes. Let's examine this point:

1. The user makes a request to index.cfm.
2. Index.cfm creates threads A, B, and C (ThreadA, ThreadB, and ThreadC) and then invokes the getFeeds method of component rss.cfc.
3. The getFeeds method creates threads D, E, and F.

   Threads A, B, and C share the same variables and THIS scope; threads D, E, and F share separate variables and THIS scope.

   Threads A through F share the same FORM, URL, REQUEST, CGI, COOKIE, SESSION, APPLICATION, SERVER, and CLIENT scopes.

Threads share ColdFusion scopes, so you need to protect simultaneous access to these variables with <cflock> and the appropriate scope attribute value. Threads have concurrent access to the variables and REQUEST scope of the page-level request, so use the new REQUEST scope lock to provide thread safety. Use name locks when accessing other shared resources such as FTP connections.

Good coding practices call for scoping of all variables. ColdFusion checks for un-scoped variables inside the thread body in the following order:

1. FUNCTION-LOCAL (for functions created within the thread)
2. THREAD-LOCAL
3. ATTRIBUTES
4. VARIABLES
5. THREAD or CFTHREAD

Listing 26.1 shows the basic idea of <cfthread>. Threads.cfm uses a URL parameter (numOfThreads) to dynamically spawn threads inside <cfloop>. It creates variables in the THREAD-LOCAL and THREAD scopes. The loopCtr attribute determines which threads are suspended. The special CFTHREAD scope provides access to thread-specific and metadata variables (Figure 26.1).

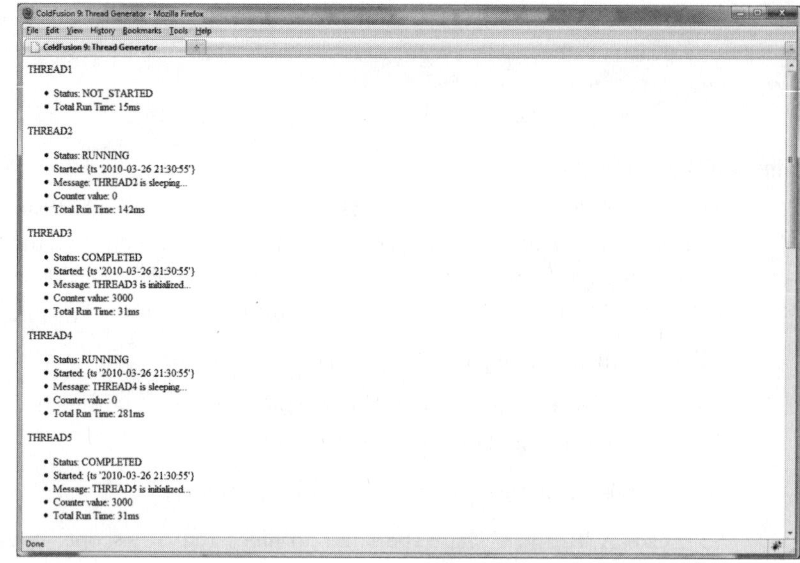

Figure 26.1 Dynamically generating threads and displaying their metadata.

Listing 26.1 `threads.cfm`—`<cfthread>` Example

```
<cfsilent>
<!---####
  File name: threads.cfm
  Description: Demonstrates <cfthread>.
  Assumptions: None
  Author name and e-mail: Sarge (sarge@sargeway.com) www.sargeway.com/blog/
  Date Created: September 11, 2007
####--->
<cfparam name="URL.numOfThreads" default="5" type="integer" />
<cfloop index="i" from="1" to="#URL.numOfThreads#">
  <cfthread name="thread#i#" action="run" loopCtr="#i#">
    <!---#### Initialize Thread-local scope variable. ####--->
    <cfset counter = 0 />

    <!---#### Initialize Thread scope variables.  --->
    <cfset THREAD.ctr = 0 />
    <cfset THREAD.message = THREAD.name & " is initialized..." />

    <!---#### Suspend all even numbered threads for 1/2 second. ####--->
    <cfif NOT ATTRIBUTES.loopCtr % 2>
       <cfset THREAD.message = THREAD.name & " is sleeping..." />
       <cfthread action="sleep" duration="500" />
    </cfif>
    <!---#### Update thread-level variable as loop counter. ####--->
    <cfloop index="j" from="1" to="3000">
      <cfset counter = j />
    </cfloop>
    <cfset THREAD.ctr = counter />
  </cfthread>
</cfloop>
```

Listing 26.1 (continued)

```
<!---#### Suspend page-level processing to allow threads to process. ####--->
<cfset sleep(5) />
</cfsilent>
<html>
  <head><title>ColdFusion 9: Thread Generator</title></head>
  <body>
<cfoutput>
  <cfloop index="k" from="1" to="#structCount(cfthread)#">
    <cfsilent>
<!---#### Create a deep copy of the CFTHREAD scope to handle thread variables. ####-
--->
      <cfset VARIABLES.demoThread = duplicate(cfthread["thread"&k]) />
    </cfsilent>
    <p>#VARIABLES.demoThread.name#
    <ul id="threadList" type="disc">
      <li>Status: #VARIABLES.demoThread.status#</li>
      <cfif VARIABLES.demoThread.status neq "NOT_STARTED">
        <li>Started: #VARIABLES.demoThread.starttime#</li>
        <li>Message: #VARIABLES.demoThread.message#</li>
        <li>Counter value: #VARIABLES.demoThread.ctr#</li>
      </cfif>
      <li>Total Run Time: #VARIABLES.demoThread.elapsedTime#ms</li>
    </ul><cfflush />
  </cfloop>
</cfoutput>
</body>
</html>
```

Using the Thread Status

Every ColdFusion thread has a status. ColdFusion records the thread's status in the `THREAD` scope's `status` metadata variable. The page-level and other threads can use the status to determine the processing state of a thread and take appropriate actions. For example, if the page-level thread requires data from a spawned thread, it can check the thread's status to see if the thread has finished before attempting to join the thread. Table 26.5 lists the `status` variable values.

Table 26.5 `status` Metadata Variable Values

VALUE	DESCRIPTION
`NOT_STARTED`	The thread has been queued.
`RUNNING`	The thread is being processed.
`TERMINATED`	Thread processing has stopped running because of one of the following actions: • The thread is terminated by a `<cfthread>` tag that specifies a `action="terminate"` or `threadTerminate` function call. • A `<cfabort>`, `<cfexit>`, `<cfrethrow>`, `<cfthrow>`, or `throw` function is called in the thread body. • An exception occurred in the thread that caused the thread to terminate. • An administrator issued a kill instruction from the ColdFusion Server Monitor or Server Monitoring API.

Table 26.5 (continued)

VALUE	DESCRIPTION
`COMPLETED`	The thread ended normally.
`WAITING`	Thread execution is suspended by a `<cfthread>` tag with `action="join"` (or `threadJoin` function), and the thread is waiting for the joining thread or threads to finish processing.

Displaying Thread Output

ColdFusion threads can generate output, but they do not have access to the output buffer. ColdFusion restricts access to the output buffer to the page-level request to prevent conflicts. So how do you return thread-generated output to the page-level request?

ColdFusion stores thread-generated output in the `THREAD` scope's `output` metadata variable. The `output` variable contains all output including HTML and plaintext, generated text inside `<cfoutput>` tags, and `<cfdump>` content. The page-level request can access thread-generated output by calling `threadName.output`.

TIP

ColdFusion stores the generated text of `<cfdump>` or `writeDump()` in the `output` variable. Use `<cfoutput>` to display the color-coded `<cfdump>` contents–for example, `<cfoutput>#threadName.output#</cfoutput>`. Calling `<cfdump var="#threadName.output#">` simply displays the generated text.

Note the following important thread output considerations:

- ColdFusion populates the `output` metadata variable only when the thread process ends.
- All tags and tag attributes that create output inside the thread body must generate plaintext or HTML.
- You can use `<cfdocument>`, `<cfimage>`, `<cfpresentation>`, and `<cfreport>` only if you redirect their output to disk (a file or directory).

Monitoring and Administering Threads

ColdFusion thread management is ultimately the developer's job. Developers must responsibly spawn ColdFusion threads with thread safety and unresponsiveness in mind. Use proper locking techniques for shared scope access. Provide reasonable timeouts to prevent runaway threads. Use good error handling techniques to capture thread exceptions.

Handling Thread Exceptions

Errors in ColdFusion threads do not affect page-level requests. As with the CFML gateway, ColdFusion will not return an exception to the page request. Unhandled thread-level exceptions will terminate thread processing and populate the `THREAD` scope's `error` metadata variable with the exception object (Figure 26.2). External threads can access this variable and determine a resulting course of action.

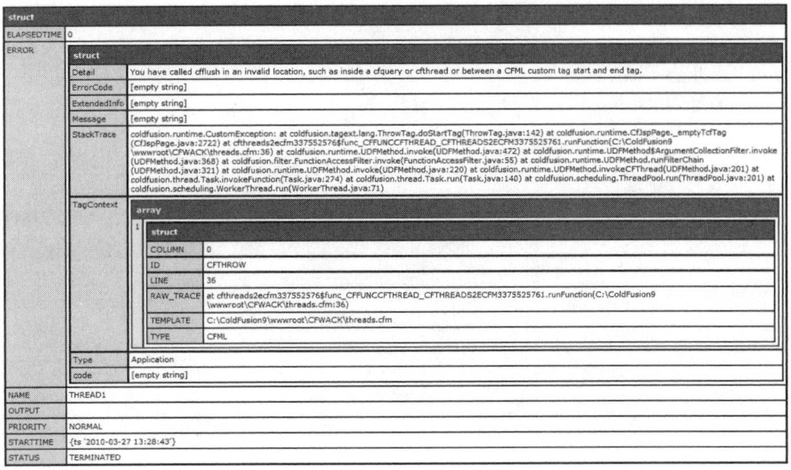

struct			
ELAPSEDTIME	0		
ERROR	struct		
	Detail	You have called cflush in an invalid location, such as inside a cfquery or cfthread or between a CFML custom tag start and end tag.	
	ErrorCode	[empty string]	
	ExtendedInfo	[empty string]	
	Message	[empty string]	
	StackTrace	coldfusion.runtime.CustomException: at coldfusion.tagext.lang.ThrowTag.doStartTag(ThrowTag.java:142) at coldfusion.runtime.CfJspPage._emptyTcfTag (CfJspPage.java:2722) at cfthreads2ecfm337552576$func_CFFUNCCFTHREAD_CFTHREADS2ECFM3375525761.runFunction(C:\ColdFusion9 \wwwroot\CFWACK\threads.cfm:36) at coldfusion.runtime.UDFMethod.invoke(UDFMethod.java:472) at coldfusion.runtime.UDFMethod$ArgumentCollectionFilter.invoke (UDFMethod.java:368) at coldfusion.filter.FunctionAccessFilter.invoke(FunctionAccessFilter.java:55) at coldfusion.runtime.UDFMethod.runFilterChain (UDFMethod.java:321) at coldfusion.runtime.UDFMethod.invoke(UDFMethod.java:220) at coldfusion.runtime.UDFMethod.invokeCFThread(UDFMethod.java:201) at coldfusion.thread.Task.invokeFunction(Task.java:274) at coldfusion.thread.Task.run(Task.java:140) at coldfusion.scheduling.ThreadPool.run(ThreadPool.java:201) at coldfusion.scheduling.WorkerThread.run(WorkerThread.java:71)	
	TagContext	array	
		1 struct	
		COLUMN	0
		ID	CFTHROW
		LINE	36
		RAW_TRACE	at cfthreads2ecfm337552576$func_CFFUNCCFTHREAD_CFTHREADS2ECFM3375525761.runFunction(C:\ColdFusion9 \wwwroot\CFWACK\threads.cfm:36)
		TEMPLATE	C:\ColdFusion9\wwwroot\CFWACK\threads.cfm
		TYPE	CFML
	Type	Application	
	code	[empty string]	
NAME	THREAD1		
OUTPUT			
PRIORITY	NORMAL		
STARTTIME	{ts '2010-03-27 13:28:43'}		
STATUS	TERMINATED		

Figure 26.2

Use `<cfthrow>` to populate the `THREAD` scope's `Error` metadata variable.

NOTE

You must join the thread to the page thread to display the `THREAD.ERROR` metadata variable.

Threads cannot use page- or application-level error handling. Recall that threads do not have access to the output buffer, so you cannot use `<cferror>` or the `onError` application event handler for thread-level exceptions. Use the following techniques to handle thread-level exceptions:

- Trap errors within the thread body by using `<cftry>` or `<cfcatch>` or their CFScript equivalents. When catching thread errors with the try-catch paradigm, ColdFusion creates the `Thread.Error` variable and sets `Thread.Status` to `TERMINATED`. The `CFCATCH` data is displayed in the `Thread.Error` variable.
- Use `<cfabort>`, `<cfrethrow>`, `<cfthrow>`, or the `throw()` to immediately terminate thread processing, populate the `Thread.Error` variable, and set the `Thread.Status` variable to `TERMINATED`.
- Use the `threadName.Error` metadata variable to handle thread errors outside the thread. You can extend your application error logic by combining `threadName.Error` with `threadName.Status`.

The `watcher.cfm` template in Listing 26.2 provides an example of the handling of thread exceptions and other concepts discussed in this chapter. The code accepts a `URL.timeout` parameter to control page-level suspension: for example, `http://localhost:8500/ows/26/watcher.cfm?timeout=5000&ctr=10`. A browser request to `watcher.cfm` will create a dynamically named thread whose body includes the `runaway.cfm` template within a try-catch block. `Runaway.cfm` contains an infinite loop and increments a `REQUEST` scope variable, shared by all the templates and threads in the request. The page-level thread pauses processing as it waits to joins the spawned thread. If the spawned thread exceeds the timeout value, the page-level thread terminates the child thread and displays the available `THREAD` scope metadata, including output and error values. If an error occurs anywhere during processing, ColdFusion terminates the child thread and displays error messages (Figure 26.3).

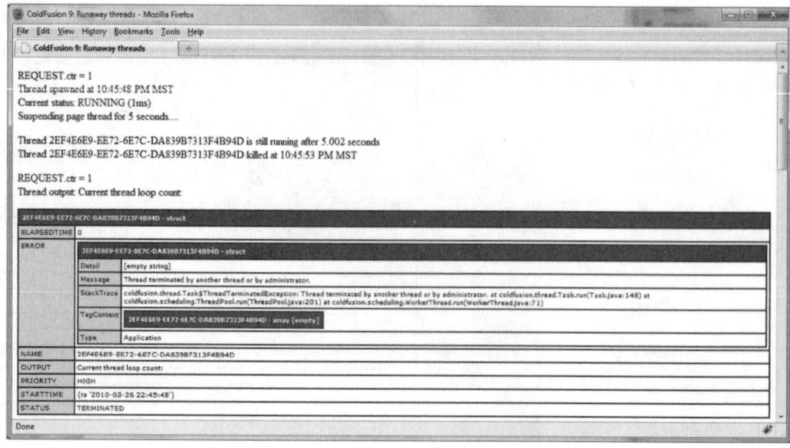

Figure 26.3

Terminating threads and handling thread-level exceptions in a page thread.

Listing 26.2 `watcher.cfm`—Error Handling Example

```
<cftry>
<cfsilent>
<!---####
  File name: watcher.cfm
  Description: Demonstrates joining and terminating threads, as well as exception
handling.
  Assumptions: Timeout requests disabled or set higher than URL.timeout value.
  Usage: http://localhost:8500/ows/26/watcher.cfm?timeout=5000&ctr=5
  Author name and e-mail: Sarge (sarge@sargeway.com) www.sargeway.com/blog/
  Date Created: September 11, 2007
  Updated: March 19, 2010
####--->
<cfparam name="URL.timeout" default="10000" type="integer" />
<cfparam name="REQUEST.ctr" default="0" type="integer" />

<!---#### Dynamic name value ####--->
<cfset variables.dynThreadName = createUUID() />

<!---#### Create dynamically named threads to prevent deadlocks ####--->
<cfthread name="#dynThreadName#" action="run" priority="high">
  <cftry>
    Current thread loop count:
    <cfinclude template="runaway.cfm" />

    <!---#### Demonstrate thread and included template share Request scope. ####--->
    <cfset Thread.ctr = Request.ctr>
    <cfoutput>#Thread.ctr#</cfoutput>
    <cfcatch type="any">
      <!---#### Throw thread-specific exception to page-thread for handling. ####
      <cfthrow message="#cfcatch.Message#" detail="#cfcatch.Detail#" />--->
    </cfcatch>
  </cftry>
</cfthread>
```

Listing 26.2 (continued)

```
<!---#### Create a pointer to dynamic thread in the CFTHREAD scope to
    handle thread variables. ####--->
<cflock name="#variables.dynThreadName#" type="readonly" throwontimeout="yes"
timeout="5">
  <cfset Variables.demoThread = CFTHREAD[variables.dynThreadName] />
</cflock>
</cfsilent>

<!DOCTYPE html PUBLIC "-//W3C//DTD XHTML 1.0 Transitional//EN" "http://www.w3.org/TR/
xhtml1/DTD/xhtml1-transitional.dtd">
<html xmlns="http://www.w3.org/1999/xhtml">
<head>
  <meta http-equiv="Content-Type" content="text/html; charset=utf-8" />
  <title>ColdFusion 9: Runaway threads</title>
</head>

<body><!---#### Display available Request variable and Thread scope metadata. ####--
->
<cfoutput><p>REQUEST.ctr = #Request.ctr#<br />
  Thread  spawned at #timeFormat(Variables.demoThread.starttime, "full")#<br />
  Current status: #Variables.demoThread.status# (#Variables.demoThread.
elapsedTime#ms)<br />
  Suspending page thread for #URL.timeout/1000# seconds....</p>
</cfoutput>
<cfflush>

<!---#### Suspend page-level thread until timeout is reached. ####--->
<cfthread action="join" name="#Variables.demoThread.name#" timeout="#URL.timeout#" />

<!---#### Kill thread if it runs beyond the timeout. ####--->
<cfif FindNoCase("RUNNING", Variables.demoThread.status)>
  <cfoutput>Thread #Variables.demoThread.name# is still running after #Variables.
demoThread.elapsedTime/1000# seconds<br /></cfoutput><cfflush>
  <cflock name="runaway_killer" type="EXCLUSIVE" throwontimeout="yes" timeout="5">
    <cfthread action="terminate" name="#Variables.demoThread.name#" />
    <!---#### Log the killed thread. ####--->
    <cflog application="yes" date="yes" file="threads" time="yes" thread="yes"
text="#variables.dynThreadName# terminated!" />
  </cflock>
  <cfoutput>Thread #Variables.demoThread.name# killed at #timeFormat(now(),
"full")#<br /></cfoutput>
</cfif>

<!---#### Check value of Request variable. ####--->
<p><cfoutput>REQUEST.ctr = #Request.ctr#</cfoutput><cfflush>
 <!---#### Display available Thread output. ####--->
<cfif len(trim(Variables.demoThread.output))><cfoutput><br />Thread output:
#Variables.demoThread.output#</cfoutput></cfif></p>
 <!---#### Dump the Thread scope ####--->
<cfdump label="#Variables.demoThread.name#" var="#Variables.demoThread#">
</body>
</html>

<cfcatch type="any">
  <!---#### Determine if the CFTHREAD scope is populated. ####--->
  <cfif structCount(CFTHREAD)>
```

Listing 26.2 (continued)

```
    <!---#### Kill spawned thread in event of any page-level exception. ####--->
      <cflock name="runaway_killer" type="EXCLUSIVE"  throwontimeout="yes" timeout="5">
        <cfthread name="#dynThreadName#" action="terminate" />
        <!---#### Dump the Thread scope Error data. ####--->
        <cfdump var="#cfthread[variables.dynThreadName].Error#">
        <!---#### Log the killed thread. ####--->
      </cflock>
      <cflog application="yes" date="yes" file="threads" time="yes" thread="yes"
text="#variables.dynThreadName# terminated!" />
    </cfif>
    <cfdump var="#cfcatch#">
  </cfcatch>
  </cftry>
```

Administrator Tools

The ColdFusion Administrator and Server Monitor provide tools for controlling and viewing information about threads. The Maximum Number of Threads Available for CFTHREAD setting in the Tag Limit Settings section of the ColdFusion Administrator Server Settings > Request Tuning page specifies a limit for the number of concurrently running `<cfthread>`-generated threads. Any threads created by `<cfthread>` beyond this limit are queued. The default value is 10.

TIP

Ten is also the default value for ColdFusion 9 Standard Edition. You may be able to increase this number in the ColdFusion Administrator, but the Standard Edition allows only two concurrent ColdFusion threads and will queue the remaining threads.

The ColdFusion 9 Server Monitor provides several views for monitoring ColdFusion threads. You will find details on the ColdFusion Server Monitor in Chapter 47, "Monitoring System Performance," in *Adobe ColdFusion 9 Web Application Construction Kit, Volume 3: Advanced Application Development*.

- Statistics > Request Statistics section
  - Active ColdFusion threads—Lists all currently active threads launched by `<cfthread>`.
  - Report view—Lists the thread name, the template path that spawned the thread, the execution time, and the Java thread name. It also provides the method to terminate individual threads manually.
  - Detail view—Displays the CFML and Java stack traces for the thread selected in the Report view.

TIP

You can also double-click a thread to invoke the Detail view.

  - Chart view—Displays the processing time for running and queued ColdFusion threads.

  - Slowest ColdFusion threads—Lists the slowest-running ColdFusion threads. Double-click a thread to view thread statistics including response times, request sizes, expanded template paths, and CFML stack traces.
- Statistics > Memory Usage section
  - ColdFusion threads by memory usage—Lists the ColdFusion threads that are consuming more memory than the configured number of kilobytes. Double-click a thread to see memory details, including variable names, values, and sizes (in bytes).

TIP

Memory tracking must be started to be able to track `<cfthread>` memory usage.

NOTE

At the time of publication, the ColdFusion Server Monitor alerts do not monitor ColdFusion threads. If any `<cfthread>`-generated threads run beyond the page request that spawned them, the only way to kill them is to either manually use the Server Monitor Active ColdFusion Threads page or code your own ColdFusion thread monitor using the Server Monitoring component that is part of the Administrator API (see Chapter 57, "Using the Administrator API," in Volume 3).

Best Practices

The following are best-practice techniques for generating and controlling ColdFusion threads. Add these to your coding methodology to ensure better performance and thread safeness.

- Do not overuse ColdFusion threads; performance gains may be realized by leveraging the ColdFusion CFML gateway for some tasks.
- Keep thread names unique.
- Always specify a timeout when joining threads. Specify a `timeout` value that is less than the ColdFusion Administrator Timeout Request setting when joining threads to the page-level request.
- Properly scope all variables inside the thread body. Remember that unscoped variables default to the `THREAD-LOCAL` scope and are not accessible outside the thread.
- Use the thread's name to access `THREAD` scope variables. Use `CFTHREAD` when accessing dynamically named threads.
- Use `<cflock>` to prevent potential deadlocks and race conditions between threads. Use the proper scope locks when threads access shared server resources: `SERVER`-, `APPLICATION`-, or `SESSION`-scoped variables. Use a `REQUEST` scope lock when threads modify variables or `REQUEST`-scoped variables. Use named locks when threads access shared resources such as Microsoft Exchange Server or FTP connections.
- Use the `cfthread output` metadata variable in page-level code to display thread-generated text.

- Use `<cfabort>`, `<cfrethrow>`, `<cfthrow>`, or `throw()` to send thread-level exceptions to the page-level code and properly set the `threadName.Error` and `threadName.Status` metadata variables.
- Use the `theadName.Error` metadata variable to handle thread-specific exceptions in external threads.
- Use `<cflog>`, `<cftrace>`, or their CFScript equivalents to help track threads.
- Use the ColdFusion Administrator's Maximum Number of Threads Available for `CFTHREAD` setting to control the pool size for concurrently running ColdFusion threads.
- Use the ColdFusion Server Monitor or the Server Monitor API to monitor and terminate hung threads.

CHAPTER 27

Improving Performance

IN THIS CHAPTER

Options in the ColdFusion Administrator

This chapter discusses a number of ways to improve the performance of your ColdFusion templates, some of which are a bit involved. Before getting into the specific solutions, you should be aware of a number of server-wide options provided by the ColdFusion Administrator that can affect the overall performance of your applications.

The Administrator options most likely to directly affect performance are

- **Maximum Number of Simultaneous Template Requests.** This option is found on the Server Settings > Request Tuning page of the Administrator. The best value for your application will depend on how heavily it is used and how much processing is done per page request.
- **Maximum Number of Simultaneous Flash Remoting, Web Service, and CFC Function Requests.** Also found under Server Settings > Request Tuning, these three options allow you to control the number of remote requests to CFCs, whether they be Flash Remoting, Web service, or direct CFC calls. As with the previous setting, the best values will vary.
- **Maximum Number of Cached Templates.** Ideally, this option on the Caching page should be set to a number greater than (or at least close to) the number of ColdFusion templates that get used on a regular basis.
- **Trusted Cache.** This option on the Caching page should be enabled for best performance, but only when your application has moved into a production mode (after you have completely finished writing your code). When you turn on this option, any changes to your files will *not* be reflected until you clear the cache.
- **Maintain Connections.** This option for each of your data sources should be enabled for best performance. When configuring or editing a data source, click the Show Advanced Settings button to configure this option.

- **Limit Connections.** In general, if you choose Maintain Connections (above), this option (found in the same location) should also be enabled for each of your data sources, and you should provide a sensible number for the Restrict Connections To field next to the Limit Connections checkbox. As a rough guide, consider starting with a value that is approximately the same as the number you provided for Maximum Number of Simultaneous Requests, above.

➜ See Chapter 25, "ColdFusion Server Configuration," for details on each of these options.

Improving Query Performance with Caching

Nearly all ColdFusion applications have a database at their heart, and most ColdFusion templates contain at least one `<cfquery>` or other database interaction. In fact, depending on the type of application you are building, your ColdFusion templates might be solely about getting information in and out of a database. In such a situation, ColdFusion is basically behaving as database middleware, sitting between your database and your Web server.

Because database access is such an integral part of ColdFusion development, the server provides a number of features relevant to the performance of your database queries. This section helps you understand which options are available and how to make the most of them.

In particular, we will discuss the following:

- Query caching, which cuts down on the amount of interaction between your database and ColdFusion. This can improve performance dramatically.
- Helping ColdFusion deal with larger query results via the `blockfactor` attribute.

Understanding Query Caching

To improve performance, ColdFusion provides a wonderful feature called *query caching*. Basically, query caching allows ColdFusion to keep frequently used query results in its internal memory, rather than retrieving the results from the database over and over again.

You tell ColdFusion to cache a query by adding a `cachedWithin` or `cachedAfter` attribute to the `<cfquery>` tag. If one of your templates is visited often and contains a query that won't return different results each time it runs, you can usually give the page an instant performance boost by simply using one of these two special attributes. Table 27.1 explains what each of the attributes does.

Table 27.1 `<cfquery>` Attributes Relevant for Query Caching

ATTRIBUTE	PURPOSE
`cachedWithin`	Optional. Tells ColdFusion to cache the query results for a period of time, which you can specify in days, hours, minutes, or seconds. You specify the time period using the `createTimeSpan()` function.

Table 27.1 (continued)

ATTRIBUTE	PURPOSE
`cachedAfter`	Optional. Tells ColdFusion to cache the query results based on a particular date and time. This attribute is generally less useful in real-world applications than `cachedWithin`. If you know that your database will be updated at a certain moment in time, perhaps after some type of external batch process, you can specify that date and time (as a ColdFusion date value) here.

Query caching is really easy to use. Say you use the following query in one of your ColdFusion templates:

```
<cfquery name="GetFilms" datasource="ows">
 SELECT FilmID, MovieTitle FROM Films
</cfquery>
```

Assuming that the data in the `Films` table doesn't change very often, it would probably be sufficient to only query the database occasionally, rather than with every page request. For instance, you might decide that the database really only needs to be checked for new or changed data every 15 minutes. Within each 15-minute period, the data from a previous query can just be reused. To get this effect, simply add a `cachedWithin` attribute that uses `createTimeSpan()` to specify a 15-minute interval, like this:

```
<cfquery name="getFilms" datasource="ows"
 cachedWithin="#createTimeSpan(0,0,15,0)#">
 SELECT FilmID, MovieTitle FROM Films
</cfquery>
```

That's all you have to do. The first time the query runs, ColdFusion interacts with the database normally and retrieves the film records. But instead of discarding the records when the page request is finished—as it would do normally—ColdFusion stores the query results in the server's RAM. The next time the template is visited, ColdFusion uses the records in its memory instead of contacting the database again. It continues to do so for 15 minutes after the first query ran (or until the ColdFusion server is restarted). The next time the template is visited, the original records are flushed from the server's RAM and replaced with new records, retrieved afresh from the database.

There's more. Queries aren't cached on a per-page basis. They are cached on a server-wide basis. If two `<cfquery>` tags on two different pages specify exactly the same SQL code, `datasource`, `name`, `dbtype`, `username`, and `password`, they will share the same cache. That is, the first time either page is accessed, the database is contacted and the records are retrieved. Then, for the next 15 minutes (or whatever interval you specify), a visit to either page will use the cached copy of the query results.

NOTE

The SQL statements in the two `<cfquery>` tags must be exactly the same, including any white space such as tabs, indenting, and spaces. If they aren't the same, the two queries will be cached independently.

Clearly, if a query is at all time-consuming, the performance benefits can be tremendous. Every template that uses the cached query will be sped up. Plus, if the database and ColdFusion are on different machines, using query caching will likely cut down dramatically on network traffic. This tends to improve performance as well, depending on how your local network is configured.

NOTE

A possible disadvantage to caching a query is that changes to the actual data in the database won't show up in the cached version of the query, because the database isn't actually being contacted. Any new records (or updates or deletes) will show up only after the cache interval has expired. For details and solutions, see "Refreshing Cached Queries Programmatically" later in this chapter.

Using Cached Queries

One obvious situation in which ColdFusion's query caching feature can be of great benefit is when you're building a next-n type of record-browsing interface.

Listing 27.1 is a simple example of such a situation. It creates a page browser for all the movies in the Orange Whip Studios database. With the query cached, ColdFusion won't have to go to the database each time the user views a new page.

Listing 27.1 `NextNCached.cfm`—Adding the `cachedWithin` Attribute to Speed Up Record Browsing

```
<!---
 Filename: NextNCached.cfm
 Created by: Nate Weiss (NMW)
 Purpose: Displays Next N record-navigation interface
 Please Note Includes NextNIncludeBackNext.cfm and NextNIncludePageLinks.cfm
--->

<!--- Retrieve expense records from database --->
<cfquery name="getExp"
 cachedWithin="#createTimeSpan(0,0,15,0)#">
SELECT
 f.FilmID, f.MovieTitle,
 e.Description, e.ExpenseAmount, e.ExpenseDate
 FROM
 Expenses e INNER JOIN Films f
 ON e.FilmID = f.FilmID
 ORDER BY
 e.ExpenseDate DESC
</cfquery>

<!--- Number of rows to display per Next/Back page --->
<cfset rowsPerPage = 10>
<!--- What row to start at? Assume first by default --->
<cfparam name="url.startRow" default="1" type="numeric">
<!--- Allow for Show All parameter in the URL --->
<cfparam name="url.showAll" type="boolean" default="No">

<!--- We know the total number of rows from query --->
<cfset totalRows = getExp.recordCount>

<!--- Show all on page if ShowAll passed in URL --->
<cfif url.showAll>
 <cfset rowsPerPage = totalRows>
</cfif>

<!--- Last row is 10 rows past the starting row, or --->
<!--- total number of query rows, whichever is less --->
<cfset endRow = min(url.startRow + rowsPerPage - 1, totalRows)>
```

Listing 27.1 (continued)

```
<!--- Next button goes to 1 past current end row --->
<cfset startRowNext = endRow + 1>
<!--- Back button goes back N rows from start row --->
<cfset startRowBack = url.startRow - rowsPerPage>

<!--- Page Title --->
<html>
<head><title>Expense Browser</title></head>
<body>
<cfoutput><h2>#application.companyName# Expense Report</h2></cfoutput>

<!--- Simple style sheet for formatting --->
<style>
 TH { font-family:sans-serif;font-size:smaller;
 background:navy;color:white}
 TD { font-family:sans-serif;font-size:smaller}
 TD.DataA { background:silver;color:black}
 TD.DataB { background:lightgrey;color:black}
</style>

<table width="600" border="0" cellspacing="0" cellpadding="1">
 <!--- Row at top of table, above column headers --->
 <tr>
 <td width="500" colspan="3">
 <!--- Message about which rows are being displayed --->
 <cfoutput>
 Displaying <b>#url.startRow#</b> to <b>#endRow#</b>
 of <b>#totalRows#</b> Records<br>
 </cfoutput>
 </td>
 <td width="100" align="right">
 <cfif not url.showAll>
 <!--- Provide Next/Back links --->
 <cfinclude template="NextNIncludeBackNext.cfm">
 </cfif>
 </td>
 </tr>

 <!--- Row for column headers --->
 <tr>
 <th width="100">Date</th>
 <th width="250">Film</th>
 <th width="150">Expense</th>
 <th width="100">Amount</th>
 </tr>

 <!--- For each query row that should be shown now --->
 <cfloop query="getExp" startRow="#url.startRow#" endrow="#endRow#">
 <!--- Use class "DataA" or "DataB" for alternate rows --->
 <cfset class = getExp.currentRow mod 2 eq 0?"DataA":"DataB">

 <cfoutput>
 <tr valign="baseline">
 <td class="#class#" width="100">#lsDateFormat(expenseDate)#</td>
 <td class="#class#" width="250">#movieTitle#</td>
<td class="#class#" width="150"><i>#description#</i></td>
```

Listing 27.1 (continued)

```
<td class="#class#" width="100">#lsCurrencyFormat(expenseAmount)#</td>
</tr>
</cfoutput>
</cfloop>

<!--- Row at bottom of table, after rows of data --->
<tr>
<td width="500" colspan="3">
<cfif not url.showAll and totalRows gt rowsPerPage>
<!--- Shortcut links for "Pages" of search results --->
Page <cfinclude template="NextNIncludePageLinks.cfm">
<!--- Show All link --->
<cfoutput>
<a href="#cgi.script_name#?&showAll=Yes">Show All</a>
</cfoutput>
</cfif>
</td>
<td width="100" align="right">
<cfif NOT url.showAll>
<!--- Provide Next/Back links --->
<cfinclude template="NextNIncludeBackNext.cfm">
</cfif>
</td>
</tr>
</table>

</body>
</html>
```

If you want, you can watch which queries ColdFusion is actually caching by turning on the Database Activity option in the Debug Output Settings page of the ColdFusion Administrator. Whenever a query is returned from the cache, the execution time will be reported as `0ms`, accompanied by the words `Cached Query`, as shown in Figure 27.1. When the cache timeout expires, you will see the execution time reappear, in milliseconds, as it does normally.

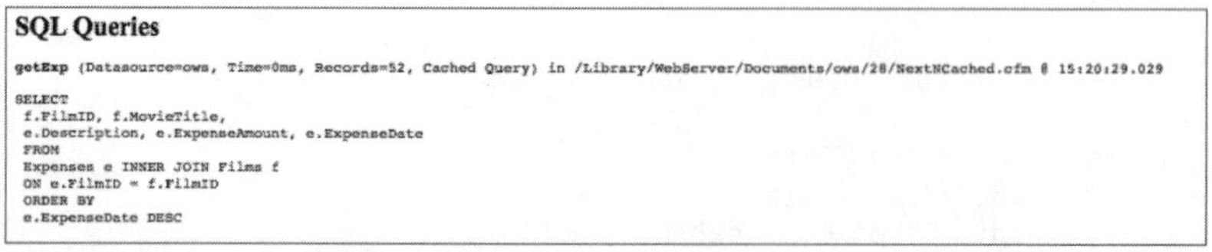

SQL Queries

```
getExp (Datasource=ows, Time=0ms, Records=52, Cached Query) in /Library/WebServer/Documents/ows/28/NextNCached.cfm @ 15:20:29.029

SELECT
 f.FilmID, f.MovieTitle,
 e.Description, e.ExpenseAmount, e.ExpenseDate
 FROM
 Expenses e INNER JOIN Films f
 ON e.FilmID = f.FilmID
 ORDER BY
 e.ExpenseDate DESC
```

Figure 27.1

Cached queries are fetched directly from ColdFusion's internal memory, which can greatly improve performance.

NOTE

Before you try this file in your browser, copy the `Application.cfc`, `NextNIncludeBackNext.cfm`, and `NextN-IncludePageLinks.cfm` files from the book Web site.

Refreshing Cached Queries Programmatically

Query caching is most often used for queries that don't change often over time, or in situations where it is acceptable for your application to show information that might be slightly out of date. However, you might run into situations in which you want a query cached for several hours at a time (because the underlying data hardly ever changes), but where it is very important for any changes that *do* get made to the database to be reflected right away.

Flushing a Specific Cached Query After an Update

ColdFusion doesn't provide a specific attribute for flushing a particular cached query, but you can achieve the same effect by including a `<cfquery>` tag with a negative `cachedWithin` value right after a relevant change is made to the database. This will force ColdFusion to contact the database and fetch the updated records. From that point on, the updated version of the query results will be what is shared with other pages that use the same query.

NOTE

Of course, this technique is not effective if the database is being updated via some application other than ColdFusion. Your ColdFusion application needs to be aware of when to discard a cached version of a query.

For instance, let's say you are using the following cached query in your code:

```
<cfquery name="getFilms" datasource="ows"
 cachedWithin="#createTimeSpan(0,3,0,0)#">
 SELECT * FROM Films
</cfquery>
```

Left to its own devices, this query's cache will only be refreshed every three hours. Now say that some other page updates one of the film records, perhaps using a `<cfupdate>` tag, like so:

```
<cfupdate datasource="ows" tablename="Films">
```

Again, left to its own devices, the `SELECT` query will continue to show the cached records until the three-hour timeout expires. Only then will the changes that the `<cfupdate>` made be fetched from the database. However, you could force the updated records into the cache by placing the following query right after the `<cfupdate>`:

```
<cfquery name="getFilms" datasource="ows"
 cachedWithin="#CreateTimeSpan(0,0,0,-1)#">
 SELECT * FROM Films
</cfquery>
```

Now, when the first `SELECT` query is next executed, it will read the updated records from the cache. Your application will always show the most current version of the records, even though it is usually reading the records from the query cache.

NOTE

The SQL statements in the two `<cfquery>` tags (the one that uses the `cachedWithin` of three hours and the one that uses the negative `cachedWithin` value) must be exactly the same, including indenting and other white space. The `name` and `datasource` attributes must also be identical, as well as any `dbtype`, `username`, and `password` attributes you might be providing. If not, ColdFusion will consider the queries separate for caching purposes, which means that the second query won't have the desired effect of refreshing the first.

Flushing All Cached Queries

As you just saw, you can use a negative value for a specific query's `cachedWithin` attribute to make sure a particular query gets removed from the query cache. This method is simple and straightforward, but you may also find that there are situations in which you would like to discard *all* cached query records. One way to do this is to simply restart the ColdFusion application server.

You can also refresh all cached queries programmatically, using the `<cfobjectcache>` tag. At this time, `<cfobjectcache>` takes one attribute, action, which must always be set to Clear. When ColdFusion encounters this tag in your code, all cached queries are discarded. The next time a `<cfquery>` tag is encountered for the first time, it will re-contact the database and retrieve the current data from your tables.

Here is how the tag would look in your code:

```
<!--- Discard all cached queries --->
<cfobjectcache
 action="Clear">
```

Limiting the Number of Cached Queries

To ensure that your cached queries don't take up crippling amounts of the server's RAM, ColdFusion imposes a server-wide limit on the number of queries that can be cached at any given time. By default, the limit is set to 100 cached queries. If a new `<cfquery>` tag that uses `cachedWithin` or `cachedAfter` is encountered after 100 queries are already in the cache, the oldest query is dropped from the cache and replaced with the new query.

NOTE

You can increase this limit by editing the Maximum Number of Cached Queries field in the Caching page of the ColdFusion Administrator. Keep in mind that the final SQL code determines how a query is cached.

Controlling the Number of Records Fetched at Once

Normally, ColdFusion retrieves each record from your database individually. That said, if you know a query will return more than a few records, you can speed up ColdFusion a bit by giving it a hint about how many records are likely to be returned. To do so, provide a `blockFactor` attribute in your `<cfquery>` tags. In using `blockFactor`, make a reasonable guess as to how many records the query might return.

Don't provide a `blockFactor` value that is more than the number of records the query returns. If you do, your database driver will tell ColdFusion that the specified `blockFactor` is invalid, and ColdFusion will try again—this time repeatedly subtracting 1 from the value you supplied until `blockFactor` no longer exceeds the total number of records. This could slow down your query. Unfortunately, ColdFusion can't determine the appropriate `blockFactor` automatically.

For instance, if you know that the `Films` table will contain 25 or more records for the foreseeable future, you should provide a `blockFactor` value of `25`, like this:

```
<cfquery name="getFilms" datasource="ows" blockFactor="25">
 SELECT * FROM Films
</cfquery>
```

The larger the number of records involved, the more effect `blockFactor` is likely to have on overall query performance. Don't obsess about getting `blockFactor` exactly right. Just think of it as a way to let ColdFusion know whether to expect a large number of records or just one or two. At the very least, consider providing a `blockFactor="100"` attribute for all queries that will return hundreds or thousands of records.

NOTE

If you are using stored procedures, it's worth noting that the `<cfstoredproc>` tag also supports the `blockFactor` attribute. See Chapter 37, "Working with Stored Procedures," for details.

NOTE

Currently, the maximum value that `blockFactor` allows is `100`. If a query might return hundreds or thousands of records, you should still go ahead and set `blockFactor="100"`. Because ColdFusion will be retrieving the records in 100-record chunks, this can often improve performance rather dramatically.

Caching Page Output

You already have learned that ColdFusion allows you to cache query results. It also provides a page-caching feature, which enables you to cache either the complete HTML page that each of your templates generates or a portion of it. Similar to query caching, ColdFusion's page-caching feature is designed to improve your Web pages' overall performance.

The idea is simple. If you have certain ColdFusion templates that are time-consuming or get hit often, you can tell ColdFusion to cache them for a specified period of time. This can have a huge effect on overall application performance. The caching can take place on the browser machine, on the server machine, or on both. Let's begin by taking a look at how the `<cfcache>` tag can cache an entire page.

Introducing the `<cfcache>` Tag

If you want ColdFusion to cache an entire page, place the `<cfcache>` tag at the top of the template, before any other CFML or HTML tags. The most important attribute for the `<cfcache>` tag is the `action` attribute, which tells ColdFusion whether you want the page cached on the client machine, on the ColdFusion server machine, or on both.

Client-Side Page Caching

The `<cfcache>` tag can provide two types of caching: client-side page caching and server-side page caching. Both are of great benefit. Let's look first at client-side page caching, which is of particular relevance when you're putting together personalized pages that might take some time to display. Then we will look at server-side page caching, which is most useful for putting together nonpersonalized pages that get hit very often.

Finally, we will see how to use client-side and server-side page caching together, usually the best option.

Background

All modern Web browsers provide some type of internal page-caching mechanism. As you use your Web browser to visit sites, it makes local copies of the HTML for each page, along with local copies of any images or other media files the pages contain. If you go back to that same page later, the browser will show you the local copies of the files, rather than refetching them from the Web server. Your browser also provides settings you can use to control where the cached files are kept and how large the collection of all cached files can get. If it weren't for your browser's cache, most casual Web browsing would be much slower than it is.

Normally, the browser just relies on these settings to determine whether to display a page from its local cache or to recontact the Web server. If you haven't adjusted any of these settings, your own browser is probably set to use the cached copy of a page until you close the browser. When you reopen the browser and visit that same page, the browser recontacts the Web server and fetches the page afresh.

Gaining More Control

The `<cfcache>` tag gives you programmatic control over when the browser should use its local, cached copy to display a page to the user. You use the `timeSpan` attribute to tell ColdFusion how old the browser's cached version of the page can be before ColdFusion should refetch it from the server. If the browser fetched its local copy of the page after the date you specify, it uses the local copy to show the page to the user. If not, it visits the template normally.

For instance, if you wanted the browser to use its local copy of a page for six hours at a time, you would include the following at the top of your ColdFusion template:

```
<!--- Let browser use a cached version of --->
<!--- this page, from up to six hours ago --->
<cfcache
 action="ClientCache"
 timeSpan="0.25">
```

The first time a user visits the page, ColdFusion processes the template normally and sends the generated page back to the browser. The browser then stores the page in its local cache. The next time the user visits the same page, the browser quickly contacts the server, providing the server with the exact date and time that the page was visited the first time (that is, the date and time the local copy was saved). If the browser tells the server that its local copy is not older than the date specified in `timeSpan`, the server then tells the browser to show the local copy to the user and immediately stops processing the rest of the template. Otherwise, ColdFusion tells the browser that the local copy is now out of date, processes the rest of your code normally, and returns the newly generated version to the browser, where it can be cached locally for the next six hours (or whatever interval you specify).

What It Means

By using `<cfcache>`, you can keep the amount of interaction between the browser and server to a minimum. Yes, the browser will contact the Web server, and ColdFusion will begin executing your template code. But as soon as ColdFusion encounters the `<cfcache>` tag—which should be at the top of your CFML code—ColdFusion will often be able to tell the browser to just use its local copy of the page. This is a fast operation because only the initial handshake between browser and server is necessary to determine whether the local copy can be used.

This improves performance in three important ways:

- The browser can display the template more quickly. This is because it can just use the local copy instead of waiting for your template code to generate the template and refetch it over the Internet. The longer the page and the more time-consuming your CFML code is, the greater the benefit.
- It cuts the amount of work ColdFusion needs to do. As long as the browser's local copy is still valid, ColdFusion can stop processing your template as soon as it encounters the `<cfcache>` tag. This frees ColdFusion to complete its next task more quickly, which benefits all your users. The more often the same users revisit your pages, the greater the benefit.
- By reducing the number of times complete pages must be sent back to browsers, traffic on your local network is kept to a minimum. This makes better use of your network bandwidth. Again, the more often the same users revisit your pages, the greater the benefit.

Server-Side Page Caching

You can also use the `<cfcache>` tag to enable ColdFusion's server-side page caching mechanism. Like client-side caching, this method takes advantage of a previously generated version of your template code. However, server-side caching doesn't use the cached copy of the page that might be on the browser machine. Instead, it looks for a cached copy of the page that ColdFusion stores on the server's drive.

Enabling Server-Side Caching

To enable server-side caching for one of your templates, place a `<cfcache>` tag at the top of the template before your other CFML and HTML tags. The tag supports many optional attributes that are relevant for using `<cfcache>` to do server-side caching. Most of the time, you can just specify `action="ServerCache"` and whatever time span you desire.

For instance, you could place the following snippet at the top of any of your ColdFusion templates. It tells ColdFusion that your template code only needs to execute once every 30 minutes at most:

```
<!--- Let browser use a cached version of --->
<!--- this page, from up to six hours ago --->
<cfcache
 action="ServerCache"
 timeSpan="#createTimeSpan(0, 0, 30, 0)#">
```

The first time the template is accessed, ColdFusion processes your code as it would normally do. But before it sends the generated page back to the browser, it also saves the page in the server's RAM. The next time the page is accessed, ColdFusion simply sends back the static version from RAM, without executing any code that appears after the `<cfcache>` tag. ColdFusion will continue to send this static version back to all visitors until 30 minutes have passed. After the 30 minutes have elapsed, the next page request re-executes your template normally.

For most situations, that's all you have to do. Your visitors will immediately begin to see improved performance. The more often your pages are hit and the longer your template code takes to execute, the larger the benefit.

Listing 27.2 is a simple example that demonstrates this effect. The template uses the `timeFormat()` function to output the current time. At the top of the template, the `<cfcache>` tag allows the page to be cached for 30 seconds at a time. Try visiting this page repeatedly in your browser.

Listing 27.2 `ServerSideCache.cfm`—Testing the Server-Side Cache Mechanism

```
<!---
 Filename: ServerSideCache.cfm
 Author: Nate Weiss (NMW)
 Purpose: Demonstrates use of server-side caching
--->

<!--- Cache this template for 30 seconds at a time --->
<cfcache
 action="ServerCache"
 timespan="#createTimeSpan(0, 0, 0, 30)#">

<!--- Display the current time --->
 This page was generated at:
 <cfoutput>#timeFormat(now(), "h:mm:ss tt")#</cfoutput>
```

The first time you visit this template, it displays the current time. For the next 30 seconds, subsequent page accesses will continue to show that same time, which proves that your template code is not re-executing. Regardless of whether you access the page using another browser or from another machine, click the browser's Reload or Refresh button, or close and reopen the browser, you will continue to see the original time message until the 30 seconds have elapsed. Then the next page request will once again reflect the current time, which will be used for the next 30 seconds.

NOTE

Remember, if you are using `<cfcache>` for server-side caching (that is, with an `action` of `Cache` or `ServerCache`), the page won't be regenerated for each user. In particular, you should make sure that the page doesn't depend on any variables kept in the `CLIENT`, `COOKIE`, or `SESSION` scopes because the generated page will be shared with other users, without checking that their `CLIENT`, `COOKIE`, or `SESSION` variables are the same. So in general, you shouldn't cache personalized pages using server-side caching. For personalized pages, enable client-side caching with `action="ClientCache"` instead.

ColdFusion-Optimized Caching

So far, you have learned about client-side page caching (that is, using `<cfcache>` with `action="ClientCache"`) and server-side page caching (`action="ServerCache"`).

As noted earlier (in Table 27.1), you can use both types of caching together by specifying `action="Cache"`. For each page request, ColdFusion will first determine whether the browser has an appropriate version of the page in its local cache. If not, ColdFusion determines whether it has an appropriate version of the page in its own server-side cache. Only if there isn't an appropriate version in either cache will your template code re-execute.

The result is greatly enhanced performance in most situations.

Caching Pages That Use URL Parameters

ColdFusion maintains a separate cached version of your page for each combination of URL parameters with which it gets accessed. Each version expires on its own schedule, based on the `timeSpan` parameter you provide. In other words, you don't need to do anything special to employ server-side caching with pages that use URL parameters to pass ID numbers or any other information.

ColdFusion doesn't cache the result of a form submission, regardless of whether the target page contains a `<cfcache>` tag, so `<cfcache>` is disabled whenever the `CGI.request_method` variable is set to `POST`.

NOTE

Remember, if you are using `<cfcache>` for server-side caching, the page won't be regenerated for each user, so server-side caching shouldn't be used for pages that are personalized in any way. The only type of caching that is safe for personalized pages is client-side caching (`action="ClientCache"`). See the important caution in the previous section.

Flushing the Page Cache

Earlier in this chapter, you learned about query caching and how to make a cached query refresh when the data in the underlying database tables change. You have the same option for server-side page caching, via the `flush` action provided by the `<cfcache>` tag. You can also delete ColdFusion's cache files manually.

Using `action="flush"`

To flush a page from the cache before it would time out on its own, simply use the `<cfcache>` tag with `action="flush"`.

If one of your templates makes some type of change that your application should reflect immediately, even in pages that would otherwise still be cached, you could use the following line to delete all cached pages in the current directory. You would place this code in the change template, right after the `<cfquery>` or whatever else is making the actual changes:

```
<!--- Flush the server-side page cache --->
<cfcache
 action="flush">
```

If you don't need to expire all cached pages from the directory, you can provide an `expireURL` attribute. For instance, suppose you are using server-side caching to cache a template called `ShowMovie.cfm`, and that movie accepts a URL parameter called `FilmID`. After some kind of update to the `Films` table, you might want to flush the `ShowMovie.cfm` template from the cache, but only for the appropriate `FilmID`. To do so, you might use code like the following:

```
<!--- Flush the server-side page cache --->
<cfcache
 action="flush"
 expireURL="ShowMovie.cfm?FilmID=#form.FilmID#">
```

Or to flush the cache for all versions of the `ShowMovie.cfm` template (regardless of URL parameters), leaving all other cached pages in the directory alone, you would use something like this:

```
<!--- Flush the server-side page cache --->
<cfcache
 action="flush"
 expireURL="ShowMovie.cfm?*">
```

Caching Page Fragments

The <cfcache> tag makes caching entire pages easy, but it tends to be a blunt instrument. If you want to cache only a portion of your page, what can you do? Instead of just putting one <cfcache> tag on top of your templates, you can place two of them around the portion of your page that you want cached. Listing 27.3 demonstrates a simple example of this.

Listing 27.3 PartialPageCache.cfm—Caching a Page Fragment

```
<!---
 Filename: PartialPageCache.cfm
 Author: Raymond Camden (RKC)
 Purpose: Demonstrates use of partial page caching
--->

<cfoutput>
<p>
This number will always change: #randRange(1,10000)#
</p>
</cfoutput>

<cfcache>
    <cfoutput>
    <p>
    This number will be cached: #randRange(1,100000)#
    </p>
    </cfoutput>
</cfcache>
```

This page contains two random numbers. However, notice that the second random number is wrapped with the <cfcache> tag. If you view this page in your browser and reload it, the top number will change every time, whereas the bottom number is static since it is being cached.

This is an incredibly powerful technique. If your site contains user-specific information, perhaps a username in the header, you can still make use of the <cfcache> tag for the portions of the page that are not user specific.

Another useful option, available only when you are using <cfcache> to wrap a page fragment, is the stripWhiteSpace argument. If true, ColdFusion will do its best to strip unnecessary white space from the cached fragment. This option is off by default; to enable it, simply add stripWhiteSpace="true" to the <cfcache> tag. White space is not so much an issue now that most of us aren't using dial-up modems, but it doesn't hurt to give some thought to it. This topic is discussed in depth later in this chapter.

Caching Data

So far, our examples of caching with <cfcache> have focused on the cache of text: either the full text of a page or the textual portion of a page fragment. What if you want to cache data? Imagine that your Web site makes use of a Web service that returns news data. This Web service may provide important information but be slow to respond. What if you could store the results data from that Web service so you don't have to hit the Web service? The <cfcache> tag enables you to do that.

In a nutshell, data-based caching is a simple matter of put and get. You ask the cache to get you something from the cache. If it doesn't return the data, then either the data hasn't been cached or the cache has expired. You can then simply store the information in the cache. Listing 27.4 shows a simple example of this.

Listing 27.4 DataCache1.cfm—Testing the Data Cache Mechanism

```
<!---
 Filename: DataCache1.cfm
 Author: Raymond Camden (RKC)
 Purpose: Demonstrates use of partial page caching
--->

<cfcache action="get" id="films" name="films">

<cfif isNull(films)>

    <cfset sleep(2000)>

    <cfquery name="films" datasource="ows">
    SELECT FilmID, MovieTitle FROM Films
    </cfquery>

    <cfcache action="put" id="films" value="#films#">

</cfif>

<cfoutput query="films">
#movietitle#<br/>
</cfoutput>
```

We begin the listing by using the get action of <cfcache> to retrieve data stored with the ID "films". If the data exists in the cache, it will be stored in a variable named films as specified by the name attribute. There is no need for the ID to match the name value, but as it makes sense here where they both use the same value. If the data doesn't exist, then films won't actually exist. We can use the isNull() function, introduced in ColdFusion 9, to check whether the variable was created. (The isDefined() function could be used as well.)

If films doesn't exist, we run a simple query to retrieve the film data. This is the same query we ran earlier in the chapter to demonstrate query caching. Notice the sleep() command. This is added simply to make the caching take a bit longer than normal. When you run the template in your browser, you will definitely notice the improvement. The last operation in the <cfif> code block puts the data into the cache. Note that the ID here should match the one we checked earlier.

Finally, we output the query. Whether it was fetched from the cache or generated and stored, this query will always work.

You may be asking yourself where this data is cached, It's obviously in RAM, but where exactly? When storing data via <cfcache> (and the caching functions we will discuss soon), ColdFusion stores the data in a *per-application* bucket of RAM. Just as the APPLICATION scope is specific per ColdFusion application, any cached data is application specific. Therefore, if you use a generic ID like "data", it will not conflict with other applications using the same ID for cached data.

Using the Caching Functions

The <cfcache> tag provides a simple way to handle caching, both for pages and data, but some people prefer to use functions instead of tags. ColdFusion 9 introduces a set of new functions to work with caching.

Listing 27.5 demonstrates the caching functions in use.

Listing 27.5 CacheFunctions1.cfm—Cache Functions Example

```
<!---
 Filename: CacheFunctions1.cfm
 Author: Raymond Camden (RKC)
 Purpose: Demonstrates use of cache functions
--->

<cfset films = cacheGet("films")>

<cfif isNull(films)>

    <cfset sleep(2000)>

    <cfquery name="films" datasource="ows">
    SELECT FilmID, MovieTitle FROM Films
    </cfquery>

    <cfset cachePut("films",films)>

</cfif>

<cfoutput query="films">
#movietitle#<br/>
</cfoutput>
```

Look familiar? It should. This listing uses the exact same logic as the previous listing. Check whether "films" exists in the cache, and if it doesn't, run the query and stuff the data into the cache. We've swapped out the <cfcache> tags with the cacheGet() and cachePut() functions. Which is better? The one you prefer to use!

Now let's look at a slightly more realistic example in Listing 27.6.

Listing 27.6 CacheFunctions2.cfm—Caching an RSS Feed

```
<!---
 Filename: CacheFunctions2.cfm
 Author: Raymond Camden (RKC)
 Purpose: Demonstrates use of cache functions
--->

<cfif isDefined("url.clear")>
    <cfset cacheRemove("feed")>
</cfif>

<cfset articles = cacheGet("feed")>

<cfif isNull(articles)>
    <cfset feedUrl = "http://feeds.feedburner.com/RaymondCamdensColdfusionBlog">
```

Listing 27.6 (continued)

```
    <cffeed source="#feedUrl#" query="articles">
    <cfset cachePut("feed", articles, createTimeSpan(0,0,30,0))>
</cfif>

<cfoutput query="articles">
    <a href="#rsslink#">#title#</a><br/>
</cfoutput>
```

Listing 27.6 begins with a little trick. If a URL variable, `clear`, is passed to the template, the `cacheRemove()` function will be used to remove our cached data. This allows us to quickly refresh the cache manually whenever we want. After that, we perform a quick check to see whether a cached ID `"feed"` exists. If it doesn't, we use the `<cffeed>` tag to grab Raymond Camden's RSS feed and convert it into a query. That query is then passed to the cache. Finally, we simply output the query. The first time you run this template, it should take a second or two. This lag represents the network call to the RSS feed. After the template has been stored in cache, however, the next request will run immediately. You can re-create the cache by adding `?clear=1` to the URL.

Inspecting the Cache

Working with a cache is more than just putting and getting. How do you measure the effectiveness of your cache? Are you caching something that is barely used? Are you caching something that is used *a lot* more than you think? In both of the previous examples, if you can determine how your cached data is being used, you can adjust what you cache and how exactly you store it in the cache. So, for example, a cached item that is used quite heavily may be a candidate for a longer cache. Of course, business rules also come into play here. Your customers may demand fresher content. At the end of the day, you have to balance both your technical requirements and recommendations for your cache with what your customers expect in terms of performance and data. ColdFusion provides a nice way to examine how well your cache is working. Listing 27.7 shows an example.

Listing 27.7 `CacheInspector.cfm`—Returning Metadata About the Cache

```
<!---
 Filename: CacheInspector.cfm
 Author: Raymond Camden (RKC)
 Purpose: Demonstrates cacheGetMetadata
--->

<cfset ids = cacheGetAllIds()>

<cfloop index="id" array="#ids#">

<cfoutput>
    <p>
    id: #id#</br>
    <cfset meta = cacheGetMetadata(id)>
    <cfdump var="#meta#">
    </p>
    </cfoutput>


</cfloop>
```

Listing 27.7 begins with the `cacheGetAllIds()` function. As you can probably guess, this will return a list of all the items in your cache. This list is returned as an array of ID values. After we have that array, we loop over each, display the ID, and dump the result of `cacheGetMetadata()`. This is a struct that returns `cache_hitcount`, `cache_miscount`, `createdtime`, `hitcount`, `idletime`, `lasthit`, `lastupdated`, `size`, and `timespan` values. Each of these values will tell you something about the cached data. The `hitcount` value, for example, provides a great way to compare cached items to see which ones are actually being used.

Digging Even Deeper

If all of this caching stuff sounds pretty powerful, it is, but if comic books have taught us anything, it's that with great power comes great responsibility. Caching is *not* to be used as a Band-Aid. Every time you "fix" a slow piece of code with a cache, you are giving up on trying to really fix the problem, and eating up a bit more RAM on your server. As you begin to increasingly use ColdFusion's caching, you may want to learn a bit more about how it operates.

ColdFusion's caching system makes use of an open source project called Ehcache (http://ehcache.org/). This is a Java project that is shipped with ColdFusion (and provides support much as ColdFusion's ORM support comes from Hibernate). Ehcache is an extremely powerful caching system that enables even greater control over ColdFusion caching. ColdFusion provides both the `cacheGetProperties()` and `cacheSetProperties()` functions, which return low-level information about the cache. The `cacheGetProperties()` function can return information about either the template or object cache. (The object cache is simply the *data* cache.) This information includes details about the low-level persistence of the cache, how large the cache can grow, and how items are forcibly removed from the cache. In most use cases, you won't have to worry about these settings at all, nor will you have to consider modifying them with `cacheSetProperties()`. However, the option is there if you need it.

TIP

Read up on Ehcache for more information. For an excellent series about caching in ColdFusion 9 and Ehcache, see Rob Brooks-Bilson's blog series at http://bit.ly/robcache.

Controlling White Space

One of the side effects of CFML's tag-based nature is the fact that white-space characters (such as tabs, spaces, and return characters) that you use to indent your CFML code are usually passed on to the browser as part of the final generated page. In certain cases, this white space can considerably inflate the size of the generated HTML content, and this in turn can hurt performance. ColdFusion provides several options for dealing with these extraneous white-space characters.

NOTE

ColdFusion's ability to automatically control white space is better than ever. You will find that in most cases, you can just enable the automatic Whitespace Management feature (discussed in a moment) and never think about white-space issues again. Nonetheless, it is worthwhile to discuss the other options available to you, just in case.

Understanding the Issue

In a ColdFusion template, you use CFML and HTML tags together. The processing instructions for the server are intermingled with what you actually want to generate. That is, there is no formal separation between the code and the content parts of your template. Most other Web scripting environments separate code from content, generally forcing you to put the HTML code you want to generate into some type of `Write()` function or special block delimited by characters such as `<%` and `%>` (depending on the language).

The fact that you get to use CFML tags right in the body of your document is a big part of what makes ColdFusion development so powerful, but it has a disadvantage. Often ColdFusion can't easily determine which white-space characters in a template just indent the code for clarity and which should actually be sent to the browser as part of the final, generated page. When ColdFusion can't make the distinction, it errs on the side of caution and includes the white space in the final content.

Automatic White-Space Control

The good news is that ColdFusion already does a lot to eliminate excess white space from your generated pages. ColdFusion includes an automatic white-space elimination feature, enabled by default. As long as you haven't disabled this feature, it's already pulling much white space out of your documents for you, before the generated page is sent to the browser.

Enabling White-Space Suppression

On the Settings page of ColdFusion Administrator, you'll see an option called Enable Whitespace Management. When this is enabled, portions of your template that contain only CFML tags will have the white space removed from them before the page is returned to the browser. Basically, ColdFusion looks at the template, finds the areas that contain only CFML tags, removes any white space (extra spaces, tabs, indents, new lines, or hard returns) from those areas, and then processes the template.

It's easy to see this in action. To do so, follow these steps:

1. Visit the `NextNCached.cfm` template (refer to Listing 27.1) via your Web browser.
2. Use the browser's View Source option to see the final HTML code that the template generated. Leave the source code's window open.
3. On the Settings page of ColdFusion Administrator, uncheck (or check) the Enable Whitespace Management option and submit the changes.
4. Visit the `NextNCached.cfm` template and view the source code again.

If you compare the two versions of the page source, you will see that the second (or first) version has a lot more blank lines and other white space in it. In particular, it has a lot more space at the very top, consisting of all the white space that surrounds the comments and various `<cfquery>`, `<cfparam>`, and `<cfset>` tags at the top of Listing 27.1. The first version of the page source has eliminated that white space from the top of the document.

There are very few situations in which this automatic suppression of white space would be undesirable. In general, you should leave the Enable Whitespace Management option enabled in ColdFusion Administrator.

Controlling White-Space Suppression Programmatically

You can turn off ColdFusion's automatic white-space suppression feature for specific parts of your document. Such situations are rare because HTML usually ignores white space, so there is generally no need to preserve it.

However, in a few situations you wouldn't want ColdFusion to remove white space for you. For instance, a few rarely used HTML tags like `<pre>` and `<xmp>` do consider white space significant. If you are using either of these tags in a Web document, ColdFusion's white-space suppression might eliminate the very space you are trying to display between the `<pre>` or `<xmp>` tags. You might run into the same problem when composing an email message programmatically using the `<cfmail>` tag (see Chapter 20, "Interacting with Email," in *Adobe ColdFusion 9 Web Application Construction Kit Volume 1: Getting Started*).

In this case, you can use the `suppressWhitespace="No"` attribute of the `<cfcfprocessingDirective>` tag to disable the automatic suppression of white space. Place the tag around the block of code that is sensitive to white-space characters, like so:

```
<cfprocessingDirective suppressWhitespace="No">
 <pre>
 ...code that is sensitive to white space here...
 </pre>
</cfprocessingDirective>
```

Suppressing White-Space Output with `<cfsilent>`

Unfortunately, ColdFusion can't always correctly identify which parts of your code consist only of CFML tags and should therefore have white space automatically removed. This is most often the case with code loops created by `<cfloop>` and `<cfoutput>`.

If you find that a particular portion of code generates a lot of unexpected white space, you can add the `<cfsilent>` tag, which suppresses all output (even actual text and HTML tags). The `<cfsilent>` tag takes no attributes. Simply wrap it around any code blocks that might generate extraneous white space when executed, such as `<cfloop>` or `<cfoutput>` loops that perform calculations but don't generate any output that the browser needs to receive.

NOTE

The `<cfsilent>` tag doesn't just suppress white-space output. It suppresses all output, even output you would generally want to send to the browser (such as HTML code and text).

Suppressing Specific White Space with `<cfsetting>`

For situations in which ColdFusion's automatic suppression isn't suppressing all the white space in your generated pages (for instance, the first `<cfloop>` snippet in the previous section), but where `<cfsilent>` is too drastic, you can use the `<cfsetting>` tag to suppress output in a more selective manner.

The <cfsetting> tag takes a few optional attributes, but the only one relevant to this discussion is the enableCFOutputOnly attribute. When this attribute is set to Yes, it suppresses all output (similar to how the <cfsilent> tag works), except for <cfoutput> blocks. Any HTML code or text that should be sent to the browser must be between <cfoutput> tags, even if the code doesn't include any ColdFusion variables or expressions. This is different from ColdFusion's normal behavior, where it assumes that it can send any non-CFML text or code to the browser.

So if you find that a section of code is generating a lot of white space, but you can't easily use <cfsilent> because your code must be able to generate *some* output, then you should place a <cfsetting> tag with enableCFOutputOnly="Yes" just above the section of code, and a <cfsetting> tag with enableCFOutputOnly="No" just below the section. Within the section of code, make sure <cfoutput> tags surround any item (even plain text) that you want to include in the final, generated version of the page. This gives you complete control over all generated white space and other characters.

NOTE

Note that when you use <cfsetting> to control white space, it acts like a "stack." What do we mean by that? If you have two or more <cfsetting> tags, both of which turn on enableCFOutputOnly, you can imagine that ColdFusion has an internal value of 2 for suppressing white space. This means you would need to turn off the setting twice in order to return to the default behavior. The upshot? Be sure to always switch this setting off after turning it on, even if it is at the end of the page.

PART 7

Integrating with ColdFusion

CHAPTER 28

Working with PDF Files

IN THIS CHAPTER

ColdFusion 7 added `cfdocument format="pdf"` and started a long conversation with what was then Macromedia regarding better PDF integration. After the Adobe and Macromedia merger, the ColdFusion community clamored for more PDF support in ColdFusion, and Adobe answered in ColdFusion 8. With ColdFusion 9, Adobe builds on the success of ColdFusion 8 PDF support and puts more control in your hands.

ColdFusion provides so much PDF support that all of the features could fill a small book. Here, we will focus on the main features, which you can build on to add more features in your own applications. To round out the chapter, a real-world application implements many of the features discussed throughout.

NOTE

Visit Adobe.com for more information about Portable Document Format (PDF): `http://www.adobe.com/products/acrobat/adobepdf.html`.

Using `cfpdf`

ColdFusion 9 boasts powerful integration and an easy-to-use API for working with PDF files. Most of the functionality found in Adobe Acrobat is available in ColdFusion 9. This section discusses how to manipulate and manage PDF files using the `<cfpdf>` tag.

NOTE

You can use `cfdocument` to create PDF files using HTML and CFML, and you can also save the output as a PDF file. See Chapter 16, "Graphing, Printing, and Reporting," in *Adobe ColdFusion 9 Web Application Construction Kit, Volume 1: Getting Started*, for more about `cfdocument`.

Creating PDF Files

Creating PDF files in ColdFusion is simple. The example in Listing 28.1 shows `cfdocument` wrapped around basic HTML content to create an in-memory PDF and the `PDF` variable then passed to `cfpdf` as the source parameter.

Listing 28.1 `create.cfm`—Creating a PDF File

```
<!--- Create a custom in-memory pdf --->
<cfdocument name="cover" format="PDF">
       <h1>PDF created from <i>cfdocument</i></h1>
       <h3><cfoutput>#DateFormat(now(),"mm/dd/yyyy")#</cfoutput></h3>
</cfdocument>

<!--- Write the PDF to disk --->
<cfpdf action="write" source="cover" overwrite="yes"
       destination="pdfs/create.pdf" />
```

Running this page does not yield any browser output, but the file is created in the `/pdfs` folder as expected. Even though `cover` is a variable, the `source` attribute expects a string value. The `overwrite` attribute tells ColdFusion to overwrite the `destination` PDF file if it exists. ColdFusion throws an error if the destination exists and the `overwrite` attribute is false. Wrap the call in `cftry/catch` if you don't use `overwrite` and want to catch the error.

There is nothing special here, but don't leave just yet. It doesn't get any tougher, but there is a lot more to discuss. Listing 28.2 builds on Listing 28.1, adding a few steps. The extra steps add metadata to the saved PDF file.

Listing 28.2 `create-meta.cfm`—Creating a PDF File and Adding Metadata

```
<!--- Create a custom in-memory pdf --->
<cfdocument name="cover" format="PDF">
  <h1>PDF created from <i>cfdocument</i></h1>
  <h3><cfoutput>#DateFormat(now(),"mm/dd/yyyy")#</cfoutput></h3>
</cfdocument>

<!--- Write the PDF to disk --->
<cfpdf action="write" source="cover" overwrite="yes"
       destination="pdfs/create-meta.pdf" />

<!--- Create and populate the metadata struct --->
<cfset meta = StructNew() />
<cfset meta.Author = "John C. Bland II" />
<cfset meta.Title = "Adobe Derby" />
<cfset meta.Subject = "Adobe Derby Official Rules" />
<cfset meta.Keywords = "Adobe, Adobe Derby, Rules" />
<!--- Set the PDF info --->
<cfpdf action="setinfo" source="pdfs/create-meta.pdf" info="#meta#" />

<!--- Read the PDF info --->
<cfpdf name="info" action="getinfo" source="pdfs/create-meta.pdf" />

<!--- Dump PDF info to the screen --->
<cfdump var="#info#" />
```

The first nine lines are the same as Listing 28.1, only changing the `destination` PDF name. The lines following actually deal with the addition of the metadata. Notice first that the `meta` struct contains values for `Author`, `Title`, `Subject`, and `Keywords` followed by another `cfpdf` tag using the `setinfo` action. This code successfully sets the metadata of a PDF file, as evident in Figure 28.1, which shows `cfdump` results of the `info` variable. The dump shows the PDF information, settings, and metadata. In the "Using DDX" section later in the chapter, you will see how to specify the PDF settings. Those settings are not affected by the values in the `meta` struct. In other words, specifying `meta.HideMenubar` will not affect this setting.

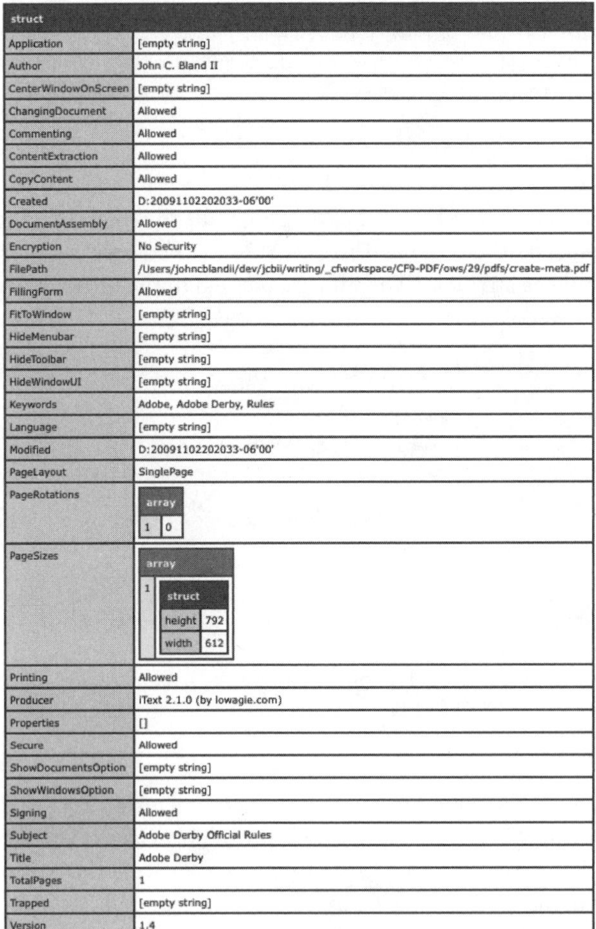

struct	
Application	[empty string]
Author	John C. Bland II
CenterWindowOnScreen	[empty string]
ChangingDocument	Allowed
Commenting	Allowed
ContentExtraction	Allowed
CopyContent	Allowed
Created	D:20091102202033-06'00'
DocumentAssembly	Allowed
Encryption	No Security
FilePath	/Users/johncblandii/dev/jcbii/writing/_cfworkspace/CF9-PDF/ows/29/pdfs/create-meta.pdf
FillingForm	Allowed
FitToWindow	[empty string]
HideMenubar	[empty string]
HideToolbar	[empty string]
HideWindowUI	[empty string]
Keywords	Adobe, Adobe Derby, Rules
Language	[empty string]
Modified	D:20091102202033-06'00'
PageLayout	SinglePage
PageRotations	array: 1 → 0
PageSizes	array: 1 → struct: height 792, width 612
Printing	Allowed
Producer	iText 2.1.0 (by lowagie.com)
Properties	[]
Secure	Allowed
ShowDocumentsOption	[empty string]
ShowWindowsOption	[empty string]
Signing	Allowed
Subject	Adobe Derby Official Rules
Title	Adobe Derby
TotalPages	1
Trapped	[empty string]
Version	1.4

Figure 28.1

Dump of data obtained from `action="getinfo"`.

Reading PDF Files

You've seen how to grab PDF metadata information and dump it to the screen. Listing 28.3 shows how to read the body of a PDF file and then dump the contents in the same way.

Listing 28.3 `read.cfm`—Reading a PDF File

```
<!--- Read the PDF file --->
<cfpdf name="doc" action="read" source="pdfs/create-meta.pdf" />
<!--- Dump PDF contents --->
<cfdump var="#doc#" />
```

This code is almost the same as that used in Listing 28.2 with one slight change: `action="read"`. We now have an in-memory PDF file. This PDF file can be manipulated in different ways by referencing the variable name.

NOTE

When the variable of an in-memory PDF file is used in `cfdump`, the resulting struct is very similar to the `cfdump` from `action="getinfo"` except that you cannot access the values in the struct from an in-memory PDF file like you can from a `getinfo` call. Calling `cfdump` on the in-memory PDF file produces an internal call to `getinfo`.

Merging PDF Files

There are several ways to merge PDF files. Merging pulls the source files together into one PDF file and saves them in a destination file. Listing 28.4 shows how we can merge two PDF files into one using the `source` attribute. The files are merged in the order they exist in the comma-separated `source` list.

Listing 28.4 `merge.cfm`—Merging PDF Files with `source attribute`

```
<cfpdf action="merge" overwrite="yes"
       source="samples/title.pdf, samples/page.pdf"
                    destination="pdfs/titlepagemerge.pdf" />
```

Alternatively we can use `cfpdfparam` tags within the `cfpdf` tag to specify the source files, as shown in Listing 28.5.

Listing 28.5 `merge-params.cfm`—Merging PDF Files with `cfpdfparam`

```
<cfpdf action="merge" overwrite="yes"
       destination="pdfs/titlepagemerge2.pdf">
   <cfpdfparam source="samples/title.pdf" />
   <cfpdfparam source="samples/page.pdf" />
</cfpdf>
```

Both approaches achieve the same result; be sure to note that the order of `cfpdfparam` define the page order, as in Listing 28.4. The `cfpdfparam` approach provides the most capability of the three merge approaches. You can use the `password` attribute to provide the user or owner password and the `pages` attribute to merge only specific pages from the source PDF file.

There is also another way to merge PDF files: by directory. The `directory` attribute tells ColdFusion to take all PDF files from the directory and merge them into the destination PDF file.

Listing 28.6 shows how to merge an entire directory of PDF files into one PDF file.

Listing 28.6 `merge-directory.cfm`—`<cfpdf>` with the `directory` Attribute

```
<cfpdf action="merge" overwrite="yes" order="name" ascending="yes"
       stoponerror="yes" directory="samples/pdfsToMerge"
       destination="pdfs/titlepagemerge3.pdf" />
```

Notice the additional attributes in this example: `order`, `ascending` and `stoponerror`. The `order` parameter can be assigned a value of either `name` or `time`. Ordering by `name` sorts the files alphabetically by file name, and ordering by `time` sorts the files chronologically. You can assign `ascending` the value `yes` or `no` to control the ordering direction. Play with the options to achieve your desired order of input for the destination PDF file.

The other attribute from Listing 28.6 is `stoponerror`. When you use the `directory` attribute, ColdFusion throws an error if the directory contains a non-PDF file and the `stoponerror` attribute is set to `yes`. The default attribute value is `no`. This attribute is valid only when the `directory` attribute is used. ColdFusion doesn't simply check for a PDF extension to make sure the file is a PDF file. When `stoponerror` is `no`, ColdFusion filters the files only if they are not PDF files, using the handy `isPDFFile()` function. You can put this feature to the test by renaming a PDF file with an obscure extension. Listing 28.6 will still work.

These are not the only ways to merge PDF files. In the "Using DDX" section, we will revisit merging using Document Description XML (DDX).

Using the `pages` Attribute

ColdFusion also allows you to remove pages from a PDF file. Before we look at how to delete pages, we will explore the `pages` attribute and how we can apply it to many actions, including page deletion.

If you have ever used Adobe Acrobat to print or delete pages, the `pages` attribute in ColdFusion will feel familiar. The `pages` attribute has a lot of options. You can specify specific pages and ranges of pages. For example, the specification `pages="1, 9-20, 23, 25"` applies to pages 1, 9 through 20, 23, and 25. You can mix single pages (1, 23, and 25) with a range of pages (9 through 20) without a problem.

The `pages` attribute is highly useful. It can be used with the following actions: `addWatermark`, `deletePages`, `merge`, `removeWatermark`, `optimize`, `extracttext`, `extractimage`, `addheader`, `addfooter`, `removeheaderfooter`, and `transform`. It is optional for all of these actions except `deletePages`. When `pages` is used with `removeWatermark`, it refers only to the type of watermark.

ColdFusion also handles incorrect pages. If you pass a page number higher than the total number of pages, the invalid pages are ignored. ColdFusion also ignores duplicate page numbers: for example, `pages="1, 2, 3, 2, 1, 3, 2, 1"`. Here, ColdFusion will act on pages 1, 2, and 3, as expected, and then ignore all of the duplicates. To demonstrate the `pages` attribute, we will explore how to delete pages from a PDF file.

Deleting Pages

To delete pages, you use the `deletePages` action. The following snippet shows how you can delete pages from a PDF file:

```
<cfpdf action="deletepages" overwrite="yes" source="samples/comps.pdf"
       destination="pdfs/comps-page1.pdf" pages="2-3" />
```

The `pages` attribute, which is required, marks pages 2 and 3 for deletion. Once the pages are deleted, the new PDF file is saved as `pdfs/comps-pdf1.pdf`. If a `destination` is not provided, the `deletepages` action will delete the pages from the source PDF file and overwrite the file, so be sure to specify a `destination` if you do not want the action to overwrite the `source file`.

Creating Thumbnails

ColdFusion 9 gives developers some new goodies for generating PDF file thumbnails. There are a lot of new settings available, but we'll discuss just a few here. Creating thumbnails doesn't take much code if you don't mind letting ColdFusion use the defaults for a few settings. Here is the bare minimum code needed to create thumbnails:

```
<cfpdf action="thumbnail" source="samples/comps.pdf" />
```

By default, ColdFusion creates a folder named `thumbnails` in the same directory that contains the CFM template running the code. For example, suppose that you run the preceding snippet from `/thumbs.cfm`. Since there is not a target directory set, ColdFusion will create `/thumbnails` if it does not exist. If `/thumbnails` is not the directory you want to use, you can control the target folder by using the `destination` attribute, like so:

```
<cfpdf action="thumbnail" source="pdfs/comps.pdf" destination="images/thumbs"
overwrite="yes" />
```

NOTE

Unless you use the `overwrite` attribute, running this code with the thumbnails already in the destination folder will result in an error.

The default naming convention for the created thumbnails is `{pdf name or imageprefix attribute}_page_{page number}.{image extension}`. For example, the PDF file we used was named `comps.pdf`, and it has three pages. Generating PDF thumbnails using the preceding snippet created the following images: `comps_page_1.jpg`, `comps_page_2.jpg`, and `comps_page_3.jpg`. Maybe your PDF file has a nondescript name, or you want to separate thumbnails in custom folders and use a common naming convention across every PDF file processed for thumbnails (for example, `pdf_page_#.pdf`), which rules out using the default naming convention. In this instance, you could add a prefix to replace the PDF file name in the naming convention. In this example, the resulting file names are `v1_page_1.jpg`, `v1_page_2.jpg`, and `v1_page_3.jpg`.

```
<cfpdf action="thumbnail" source="pdfs/Comps.pdf" destination="images/thumbs"
overwrite="yes" imageprefix="v1" />
```

NOTE

By default, every page is processed and a thumbnail is created. Use the `pages` attribute if you need to generate thumbnails for only specific pages in your PDF file.

The images are now created, and we can now look at them in the browser using a little more Cold-Fusion, as shown in Listing 28.7.

Listing 28.7 `thumbnails.cfm`—Creating and Displaying Thumbnail Images

```
<!--- Create the thumbnails --->
<cfpdf action="thumbnail" overwrite="yes" imageprefix="v1"
      source="samples/comps.pdf" destination="images/thumbs" />

<!--- Read the thumbnails directory --->
<cfdirectory name="thumbs" directory="#ExpandPath('images/thumbs')#" />

<!--- Output the images to the browser --->
<cfoutput query="thumbs">
#currentRow#)       # name#<br />
<img src="images/thumbs/#name#" align="top" />
<br />
<hr />
</cfoutput>
```

Listing 28.7 is the same code as in previous snippets plus some new stuff. We added the use of `cfdirectory` to read the images and generic HTML in a query output using `cfoutput`. Since the `format` (JPEG, TIFF, or PNG) attribute was not set, the images were created as JPEG files. In using `cfdirectory`, we could filter the files and pull only the images, but for this simple example, this wasn't necessary. Figure 28.2 shows the final output.

We kept the thumbnail generation pretty simple, but as mentioned earlier, you have a lot available to you. Let's look at a few other attributes now.

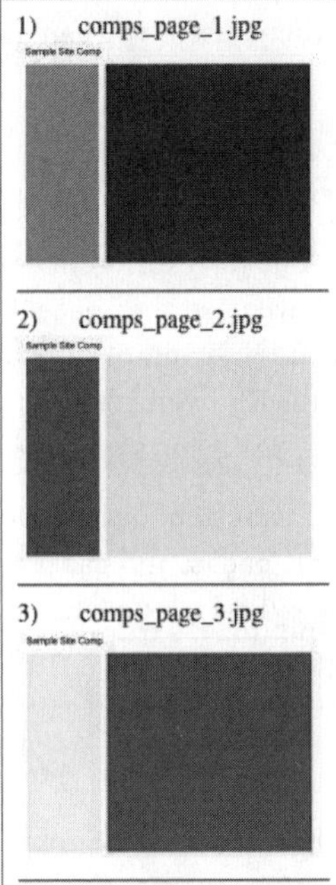

Figure 28.2
The final thumbnail output.

The `scale` attribute is available to control the resulting size of the created thumbnails. All thumbnails are created at 25 percent of the original size by default. Figure 28.2 shows thumbnails at 200 × 150 pixels (25 percent of 800 × 600, the original size). This setting is great unless you want to generate thumbnails for a page of size 1920 × 1200 pixels; then your thumbnails are 480 × 300 pixels, which could take up more page space than desired. In that case, you can use the brand-new `maxScale` attribute to control the maximum scale percentage of the thumbnails.

Thumbnails are created with high quality by default, but you can create a low-quality thumbnail by using the `resolution` attribute, which accepts `high` or `low` as its value. ColdFusion 9 adds a `hires` (Boolean) attribute, which extracts high-resolution images, giving you more control over the output quality.

Remember that JPEG isn't the only format you can use. You can also output TIFF and PNG images. When using the PNG image format, you can make the generated thumbnails respect transparency by using the `transparent` attribute, which takes a value of `yes` or `no` (`no` is the default value). Transparency is not available in the JPEG and TIFF formats. TIFF output allows the images to be compressed using `compresstiffs`.

If you need to create PDF thumbnails, spend a little time looking into the various options for thumbnail generation. You have a lot of control in your hands, but sometimes page thumbnails may not be your need. Maybe you need all of the images pulled from the PDF file. Can we do that? I'm glad you asked. Let's take a look at how to extract images.

Extracting Images

You can extract thumbnail images to display flat image representations of the page. ColdFusion allows you to pull all of the images from a PDF file and store them just as you can do with thumbnails.

The following snippet shows how to use the `extractimage` action:

```
<cfpdf action="extractimage" source="samples/cfkit_en.pdf"
       destination="images/pdfimages" overwrite="yes" />
```

This snippet is pretty much a replica of Listing 28.7. The only difference is the action and the absence of a prefix specification, although you could have used the `imagePrefix` attribute. The `cfkit_en.pdf` file, which is the ColdFusion Evangelism Kit, contains lots of images; look at the files in the `images/pdfimages` folder, and you will see images from `cfimage-0.jpg` all the way to `cfimage-224.jpg`. Sift through the images, and you will see all sorts of graphics from the PDF file.

You do have not all of the functionality of the `thumbnail` action, but on top of the preceding snippet, you can provide the following: `format`, `imagePrefix`, `pages`, and `password`.

We can now read, write, delete, and get thumbnails and images from PDF files. We can also add watermarks, as we'll discuss next.

Creating Watermarks

Watermarks are useful in any document type and are great for versioning. For instance, a visitor could upload a first draft of a résumé, book chapter, or any type of document, and you can add a visual version indicator within the created PDF file. With the watermark actions (see Listing 28.8), you now can easily add and remove watermarks.

Listing 28.8 `watermark.cfm`—Adding a Watermark

```
<!--- Adds a watermark using an image --->
<cfpdf action="addwatermark" overwrite="yes" foreground="yes"
       destination="pdfs/comps-image-watermark.pdf"
       source="samples/comps.pdf" image="samples/watermark.png" />
```

Here we used an actual image path, but the `image` attribute could be an in-memory image created with `cfimage` (see Chapter 29, "ColdFusion Image Processing"). To add a watermark from an image, we used the aptly named `image` attribute and the `addwatermark` action. By default, the watermark has an opacity of 3 out of 10—the lower the opacity, the lighter the watermark. Depending on the document needs, you may not want the watermark on top of the content. In this case, you can place the watermark in the foreground or the background using the `foreground` attribute (Boolean). Be mindful of your content, though. If your PDF file has images, they could cover the watermark so that you never see it.

Instead of using an image as a watermark, you can use the first page of another PDF file. To do this, you use the `copyFrom` attribute instead of the `image` attribute:

```
<!--- Adds a watermark using a pdf --->
<cfpdf action="addwatermark" source="samples/comps.pdf"
       destination="pdfs/comps-pdf-watermark.pdf"
       copyFrom="samples/watermark.pdf" overwrite="yes" opacity="10"
       foreground="yes" rotation="45" position="375,-275" />
```

The watermark source PDF file (`samples/watermark.pdf`) is a PDF file created from Microsoft Word. The document simply has the words "PDF WATERMARK" in it. Nothing special is done in the document other than setting the font size. When you use this document as a watermark, the result is a watermark at the top of the page, but the watermark doesn't have to stay there; you can control the location with the `position` attribute and the rotation with the `rotation` attribute, as shown in Listing 28.9.

Listing 28.9 `watermark-pdf.cfm`—Adding a Watermark from a PDF File


```
<!--- Adds a watermark using a pdf --->
<cfpdf action="addwatermark" source="samples/comps.pdf"
       destination="pdfs/comps-pdf-watermark.pdf"
       copyFrom="samples/watermark.pdf" overwrite="yes" opacity="10"
       foreground="yes" rotation="45" position="375,-275" />
```


Here the `position`, `rotation`, and `opacity` attributes are set. For clarity, this example uses an opacity of 10, which is full opacity; available values are 0 to 10. The rotation is 45 degrees. You have access to all 360 degrees of rotation, so use the value that works best for your watermark source (see Figure 28.3).

Positioning is based on x and y positioning of the fourth dimension (lower right) in the Cartesian coordinate system (`http://en.wikipedia.org/wiki/Cartesian_coordinate_system`). This means that the top-left corner of the page is (0, 0) and the bottom-right corner is (*page width, page height*). This is one of those attributes you'll need to play with to see what works best for your watermark needs.

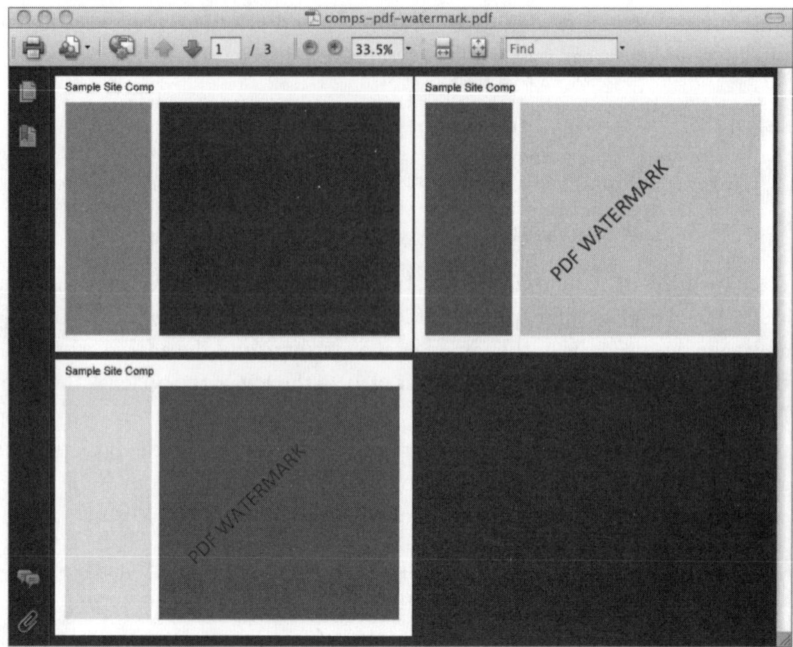

Figure 28.3

The original source for `pdfs/watermark.pdf`.

TIP

Positioning a watermark can be tricky if you are not familiar with the Cartesian coordinate system. To counteract the need to learn it, you can position the text in your Word document before exporting to a PDF file. Later in the chapter, in the section "Using DDX," we will cover another way to set a text-based watermark.

Removing a watermark is as easy as adding one, as you can see in Listing 28.10.

Listing 28.10 `watermark-remove.cfm`—Removing a Watermark

```
<!-- Removes watermark -->
<cfpdf action="removewatermark"
       source="pdfs/comps-image-watermark.pdf"
       destination="pdfs/comps-image-watermark-removed.pdf" />
```

This syntax should look familiar. We're taking the initial PDF file created in Listing 28.8 (`source="pdfs/comps-image-watermark.pdf"`) and creating a new one (`destination="pdfs/comps-image-watermark-removed.pdf"`).

NOTE

Not all watermarks can be removed. All PDF files created using the ColdFusion Developer and Trial Editions have a permanent watermark that cannot be removed (by ColdFusion or Acrobat).

Extracting Text

After developers worked with PDF files in ColdFusion 8, many people noticed and complained about the inability to extract text without using DDX (which we explore later in the chapter).

ColdFusion 9 adds a new action to extract PDF text, which you can save in a file, or you can perform any number of actions on the XML output.

We're going to use the ColdFusion Evangelism Kit PDF file (`http://www.adobe.com/products/coldfusion/evangelism_kit/`) since it contains a fair amount of text. Our first example, Listing 28.11, shows how to output the text to the browser using normal ColdFusion constructs.

Listing 28.11 `extract-text.cfm`—Extract and Display Text from a PDF File

```
<!--- Extract the text from the PDF --->
<cfpdf name="textxml" action="extracttext"
       source="samples/cfkit_en.pdf" />
<!--- Traverse the text XML and pull the pages --->
<cfset xml = XmlSearch(textxml, "/DocText/TextPerPage/Page") />
<cfoutput>
  <!--- Loop over the pages and output the content --->
  <cfloop array="#xml#" index="row">
    <strong>Page #row.xmlattributes.pageNumber#</strong>)
    #row#<br /><br />
  </cfloop>
</cfoutput>
```

The first line of code from Listing 28.11 uses the action `extracttext`, targets `samples/cfkit_en.pdf`, and saves the result to the `textxml` variable. At this point, if you dump the `textxml` variable, you will see an array of XML objects.

The next thing we want to do is traverse the XML object so that we have only the page objects. To do this, we use XPath and the `XmlSearch` function.

The extracted XML uses the following structure:

```
<DocText>
  <TextPerPage>
    <Page pageNumber="1">Some Text</Page>
    <Page pageNumber="2">More Text</Page>
  </TextPerPage>
</DocText>
```

To get to all of the `Page` nodes, ColdFusion allows us to use an XPath expression: `XmlSearch(text, "/DocText/TextPerPage/Page")`. This expression "walks" the XML object and returns all `Page` nodes in the `TextPerPage` node within the `DocText` node. We're not going to go deep into XML in ColdFusion here, but you will learn more about XML in Chapter 41, "Working with XML."

The result from the XPath search returns an array of XML objects consisting of the `Page` nodes in the XML. At this point, we're ready to output the text to the screen.

Since we have an array, we can use `cfloop` to iterate over the array and set our output however we want. In this case, we want the output format to look like this:

```
Page #) Some Text

Page #) More Text
```

To achieve this, we access the page number from the `Page` XML object's `xmlattributes` struct: `row.xmlattributes.pageNumber`. The text from the XML object is displayed by row. Throw in a few line breaks and boldface the page number, and we have the expected display (see Figure 28.4).

Figure 28.4

Display results of extracted text.

Page 1) ADOB E ® COLDFUSIO N ® Rapidly build , deploy , and maintain robust Internet applications

Page 2) " ColdFusion adoption has accelerated since we introduced support for Flex , Ajax , and PDF with ColdFusion 8 . The increased integration with everything from Adobe AIR applications to enterprise - based Adobe LiveCycle ES software enables companies to meet critical business needs quickly , while ColdFusion Builder provides developers with an enhanced workflow between ColdFusion and the Adobe Flash Platform for RIA development . " David Wadhwani , General Manager and Vice President of the Platform Business Unit at Adobe

Page 3) Adobe ColdFusion 3 ADOB E COLDFUSIO N THRIVING 12,000 + companies (20 % increase since 2007) 778,000 developers * 1,089,000 applications 350 + user groups 10,000 downloads per month * EDC 2008 Global Developer Population and Demographics Report

Page 4) 4 Adobe ColdFusion ADOB E COLDFUSIO N WIDE ADOPTION Customers To see who is using ColdFusion , visit www.adobe.com / products / coldfusion / customers / . Manufacturing Boeing Casio USA Caterpillar Honeywell Logitech Qualcomm Scott's Corporation Xerox Retail Allied Office Products Crayola eBags FAO Schwarz Foot Locker Hasbro Moen New Era Cap Company Pottery Barn Simon & Schuster The Limited Under Armour Government City of Davis , California County of San Diego , Department of Child Support Services Department of Homeland Security DISA / NSA Environmental Protection Agency European Commission Federal Reserve Bank NASA Goddard Space Flight Center State of New York United States Senate Healthcare Blue Cross Blue Shield Eli Lilly Mayo Clinic Mayo Health Systems Roche Pharmaceuticals Sloan - Kettering IT Amkor Technology Cisco eBay eMCSaatchi Intuit McAfee / Foundstone Siemens Symantec 192 . com Telecommunications AT & T British Telecom Cingular Wireless Sprint Verizon Travel and leisure Aspen Skiing Company Chicago Bears Dallas Stars iHotelier International Speedway Corporation MySwitzerland.com New York Giants One World Alliance PGA of America Rugby Football Union Sandals United States Olympic Committee Automotive BMW USA GlobalSpec.com Goodyear Jaguar Australia Michelin Education East

Note that the text from the PDF files will not follow the exact format from the PDF document. Looking at the output in Figure 28.4, you can see that the text isn't formatted as perfectly as the PDF document. The text is a flat pull of all the text on the page, and no formatting is preserved. This text is still useful, though. It can be indexed and searched, saved to a database, saved to a file, and so on.

We're jumping ahead of the curve just a bit by looking at file writing, but Listing 28.12 shows simple file writing in ColdFusion. The first line of code is the same as Listing 28.11. The second line takes the content and writes it to `data/cfkit_en.xml`. Remember that the output is XML, so the file is saved as a legitimate XML file. Reading a flat XML file should always be faster than reading a PDF file potentially containing graphics, form elements, `.swf` files, and so on. This approach is a useful way to archive PDF text for quick searching and access later.

Listing 28.12 `extract-text-save.cfm`—Extracting and Saving Text from a PDF File

```
<!--- Extract the text from the PDF --->
<cfpdf name="textxml" action="extracttext"
        source="samples/cfkit_en.pdf" />
<!--- Save the text output to a file --->
<cffile action="write" file="#ExpandPath('data/cfkit_en.xml')#"
         output="#textxml#" />
```

Optimizing PDFs

PDFs, as with many file types, can gain a little bloat every now and then. For many reasons, you may want users to download a custom uploaded or generated PDF file, but your clients may have Internet speed comparable to snail mail. ColdFusion 9 provides new ways to optimize PDF files by removing certain elements and reducing the quality with the `optimize` action.

ColdFusion 9 adds eight new attributes to the `<cfpdf />` tag for the new `optimize` action, as shown in Table 28.1 (source: `http://help.adobe.com/en_US/ColdFusion/9.0/CFMLRef/`).

Table 28.1 `cfpdf` Optimization Attributes

ATTRIBUTE	DESCRIPTION
`noattachments`	Remove all file attachments
`nobookmarks`	Remove bookmarks from PDF document
`nocomments`	Remove comments from PDF document
`nofonts`	Remove font styling
`nojavascript`	Remove all document-level JavaScript actions
`nolinks`	Remove external cross-references
`nometadata`	Remove document information and metadata
`nothumbnails`	Remove embedded page thumbnails
`noattachments`	Remove all file attachments
`nobookmarks`	Remove bookmarks from PDF document
`nocomments`	Remove comments from PDF document
`nofonts`	Remove font styling

These optimizations are considered lossy since they remove elements or data from the PDF file. Lossless optimization, with Limpel-Ziv-Welch (LZW) and Flate encoding, does not remove elements or data from the PDF file and therefore maintains image quality.

Not all streams in your PDF files are encoded. By using the `encodeAll` attribute and the `write` action, you can encode all streams, whether previously encoded or not. The encoding of all the streams will not differ from stream to stream, so all nonencoded streams will get a Flate encoding. Listing 28.13 shows examples of lossless optimization and lossy optimization. Note that this is purely an example to show all of the features in use. In a real-world scenario, you might mix and match the attributes and actions.

Listing 28.13 `optimize.cfm`—Optimizing a PDF

```
<!--- Optimize the PDF using lossy optimization --->
<cfpdf action="optimize" overwrite="yes"
      nofonts="true" nometadata="true" nolinks="true"
      noattachments="true" nobookmarks="true" nocomments="true"
                     nojavascripts="true" nothumbnails="true"
      source="samples/cfkit_en.pdf" destination="pdfs/cfkit_en_1.pdf"/>
```

Listing 28.13 (continued)

```
<!--- Encode all non-encoded streams --->
<cfpdf action="write" overwrite="yes" encodeall="true"
       saveoption="linear"
       source="samples/cfkit_en.pdf" destination="pdfs/cfkit_en_2.pdf"/>
```

Listing 28.13 shows two different optimizations. The first shows the `optimize` action with all of the available attributes; refer to Table 28.1 for the meaning of each attribute. The second optimization shows the use of the `encodeAll` attribute. Both optimizations use the same PDF file, but each saves it to a separate file so we can compare the differences.

Notice that there is another attribute in the second optimization: `saveoption`. A `linear saveoption` specification saves the file for faster Web display. The `linear` specification will remove PDF form interactivity and electronic signatures, but you can keep electronic signatures by using `incremental saveoption`.

ColdFusion also allows you to specify an optimization algorithm when using the `optimize` action. The `algo` attribute is used to downsample images using one of three algorithms: `bicubic`, `bilinear`, or `nearest_neighbour`. See Table 28.2 for details on each algorithm.

Table 28.2 Algorithm for the `algo` Attribute

ALGORITHM	DESCRIPTION
`nearest_neighbor`	Applies the nearest-neighbor method of interpolation. Image quality is lower than with the other interpolation methods, but processing is fastest (default).
`bicubic`	Applies the bicubic method of interpolation. Generally, the quality of image is highest with this method, and processing is slowest.
`bilinear`	Applies the bilinear method of interpolation. The quality of the image is less pixelated than the default, but processing is slower.

Each line in Listing 28.14 optimizes `pdf101.pdf` using each of the algorithms and saves a respective file name.

Listing 28.14 `optimize-algos.cfm`—Downsampling PDF Images

```
<!--- Optimize the PDF using Nearest_Neighbour algorithm --->
<cfpdf action="optimize" overwrite="yes" algo="Nearest_Neighbour"
       source="samples/pdf101.pdf"
       destination="pdfs/pdf101_nearest.pdf"/>

<!--- Optimize the PDF using Bicubic algorithm --->
<cfpdf action="optimize" overwrite="yes" algo="Bicubic"
       source="samples/pdf101.pdf"
       destination="pdfs/pdf101_bicubic.pdf"/>

<!--- Optimize the PDF using Bilinear algorithm --->
<cfpdf action="optimize" overwrite="yes" algo="Bilinear"
       source="samples/pdf101.pdf"
       destination="pdfs/pdf101_bilinear.pdf"/>
```

Use these optimization options to improve your PDF footprint, provide faster PDF file viewing for your users, or simply clean your PDF files of superfluous functionality. Whatever your goal, ColdFusion 9 gives you a solid set of PDF optimization features.

Creating PDF Portfolios

PDF portfolios are essentially PDF Zip files. A portfolio allows you to take multiple files of different file types, embed them in a PDF portfolio, and distribute one file instead of a group of files and the intended PDF content. What's even sweeter is that ColdFusion 9 lets you create these portfolios with ease!

Listing 28.15 shows how to merge files of different types into a portfolio. The code is similar to Listing 28.5. In fact, it is 99 percent the same, differing only in the `cfpdfparam` source files. The difference is in the `package` attribute, which tells ColdFusion to create a PDF package instead of merging all of the files into one PDF file. If the `package` attribute is left off and you attempt to merge a non-PDF file, ColdFusion will let you know with an "Invalid Document" error.

Listing 28.15 `portfolio.cfm`—Creating PDF Portfolios

```
<!--- Create a PDF portfolio --->
<cfpdf action="merge" package="yes" overwrite="yes"
       destination="pdfs/portfolio.pdf">
  <cfpdfparam source="samples/MonthlyTimesheet.doc" />
       <cfpdfparam source="samples/watermark.docx" />
       <cfpdfparam source="samples/Sample.html" />
       <cfpdfparam source="samples/title.pdf" />
       <cfpdfparam source="samples/cfkit_en.pdf" />
</cfpdf>
```

PDF portfolios are easy to create and provide more functionality than merged PDF documents. A merged PDF document becomes a single PDF file, so removing a whole PDF document requires removing each individual page. This isn't difficult, but with a portfolio you can remove files without affecting the remaining files. Adobe Acrobat and Acrobat Reader also allow you to preview the document, where possible, without opening the file in the native application, as seen in Figure 28.5 on the next page.

For more information about PDF portfolios, you can read the Adobe Acrobat documentation here: `http://help.adobe.com/en_US/Acrobat/9.0/Standard/WSA2872EA8-9756-4a8c-9F20-8E93D59D91CE.html`.

Manipulating Headers and Footers

ColdFusion 8 provided powerful PDF functionality with minimal code, but manipulation of headers and footers was not as simple. You could do it, but many people complained about the complexity. Adobe responded.

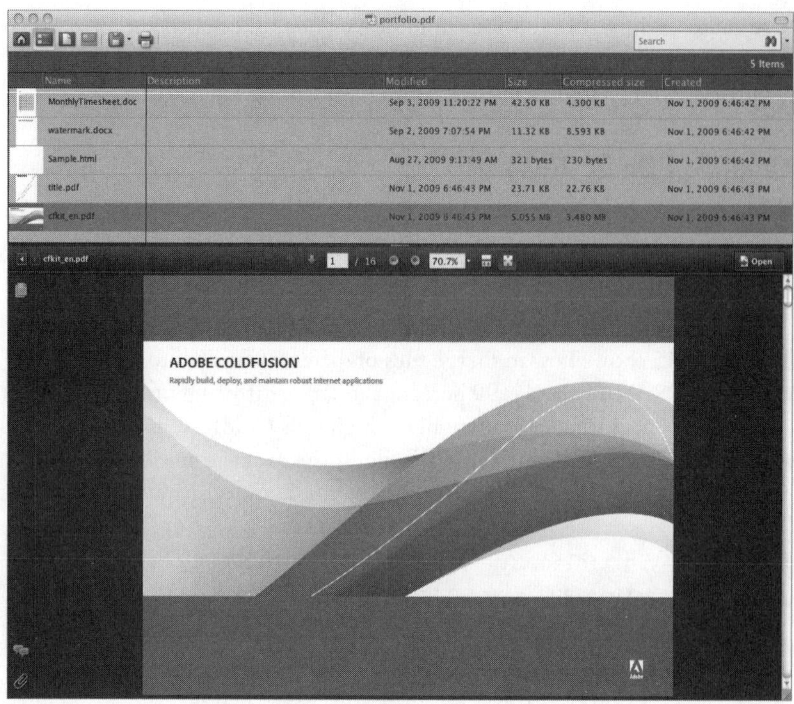

Figure 28.5
PDF portfolio in Acrobat Reader 9.

Listing 28.16 adds custom headers and footers on different pages to the source PDF file.

Listing 28.16 `headerfooter-add.cfm`—Adding Headers and Footers to Multiple Pages

```
<!--- Create a formatted date for display in header --->
<cfset today = DateFormat(now(), "long") />
<!--- Add a header to page 1 --->
<cfpdf action="addheader" overwrite="yes" text="Comps" pages="1"
       source="samples/comps.pdf"
                      destination="pdfs/comps-headfoot.pdf" />
<!--- Add a header to all pages --->
<cfpdf action="addheader" overwrite="yes" text="last edited #today#"
       align="right" showonprint="false"
       source="pdfs/comps-headfoot.pdf" />
<!--- Add a footer to the bottom left --->
<cfpdf action="addfooter" overwrite="yes" align="left"
       text="Page _PAGENUMBER of _LASTPAGENUMBER"
       source="pdfs/comps-headfoot.pdf" />
<!--- Add an image to footer on the bottom right --->
<cfpdf action="addfooter" overwrite="yes" align="right"
       image="samples/adobe-lq.png"
       source="pdfs/comps-headfoot.pdf" />
```

Adding headers and footers, as shown in Listing 28.16, is far easier now than it was previously. Line 1 creates a simple date variable, which we will add to one of the headers. The first `cfpdf` call uses the new `addheader` action and sets a few attributes. The `addheader` action has the following relevant attribute options: `align`, `image`, `isBase64`, `leftmargin`, `numberformat`, `opacity`, `rightmargin`, and `showonprint`.

The first header added uses the default value for the `align` attribute, so that it is centered and consists of a simple string; then it saves the output to a new PDF file. The second header shows static text plus the `today` variable created on line 1; it is aligned on the right and is turned off for printing, using `showonprint="false"`. Notice that two separate `cfpdf` calls are needed, because you may want different headers aligned in different positions (left, center, or right). The second `addheader` action targets the destination from the first `addheader` action, so we are editing the same PDF file instead of adding a header to the original PDF file.

After the headers are in place, we add two footers. In the first `addfooter` call, we set the footer at the bottom left and use dynamic values in the `text` attribute. The `text` attribute has four dynamic options: `_LASTPAGELABEL`, `_LASTPAGENUMBER`, `_PAGELABEL`, and `_PAGENUMBER`. The values refer to the current page being processed or the last page of the PDF document. Use these dynamic values as you like, as shown in the first `addfooter` call, in which we create a footer that reads `Page # of #`.

The last `addfooter` call aligns an image at the bottom right. Yes, an image. You can simply set the `image` attribute to a valid path to an image. The `isBase64` attribute allows you to use ColdFusion image functionality, similar to the `addWatermark` action. Figure 28.6 shows all of the pages with the headers and footers in place.

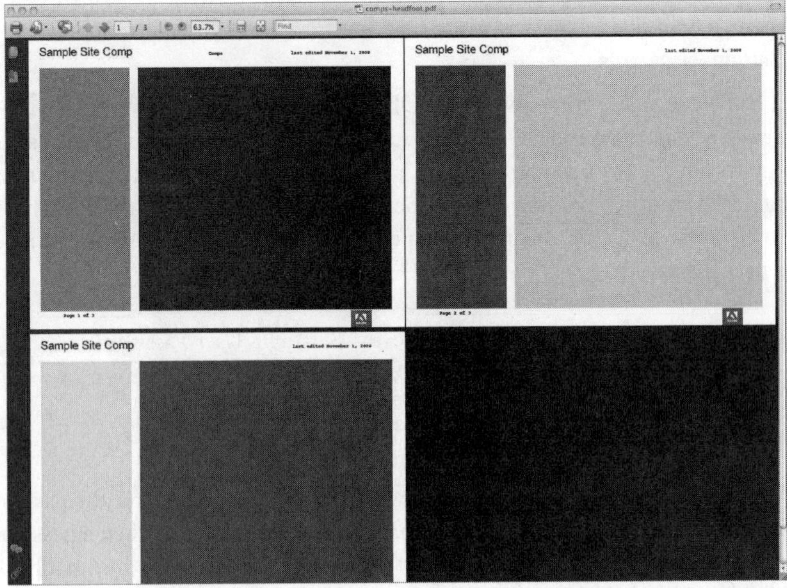

Figure 28.6

Comps PDF file with custom headers and footers.

Remember how earlier we used two separate `addheader` calls to add two different headers in different positions? What happens if we don't specify separate positions? If you do not specify a position, or if you specify the same position in both calls, the result is overlapping headers. In this case, we're in control of all headers and footers, but what if you aren't in control? Maybe you need to make sure your header is the only header in the document. In this case, you can remove the headers and footers and then add your own, as desired, as shown in Listing 28.17.

Listing 28.17 `headfoot-remove.cfm`—Removing Headers and Footers

```
<!--- Remove headers and footers --->
<cfpdf action="removeheaderfooter" overwrite="yes"
       source="pdfs/comps-headfoot.pdf"
       destination="pdfs/comps-headfoot-removed.pdf" />
```

Notice there isn't a different action for removing headers versus footers. The `removeheaderfooter` action takes care of all of the headers and footers in the document unless you use the `pages` attribute. After running Listing 28.17, the `pdfs/comps-headfoot.pdf` file, created in Listing 28.16, has all headers and footers removed; then a new file (`pdfs/comps-headfoot-removed.pdf`) is saved that, ultimately looks just like `samples/comps.pdf` since the only differences were the changes made in Listing 28.16.

Protecting PDF Files with Passwords, Permissions, and Encryption

Protecting PDF files is important for many scenarios, and multiple levels of protection are needed. ColdFusion answers the call with 4 levels of encryption and 10 levels of permissions, plus user and owner password support. Here, we will look at the different types of passwords, owner permissions, and encryption.

Setting Passwords

The base level of protection for a PDF file is a password. There are two types of passwords: `newownerpassword` and `newuserpassword`. To set either password type, use the `protect` action with the specific password type attribute, a requirement for `protect`. Setting `newuserpassword` requires a user to enter the password upon opening the PDF file. After the PDF file is opened in Acrobat, or a similar program, the user can openly edit the PDF file. Listing 28.18 demonstrates how to set a user password.

Listing 28.18 `protect-userpassword.cfm`—Setting a User Password

```
<!--- Protects the pdf with a user password --->
<cfpdf action="protect" source="samples/comps.pdf"
       destination="pdfs/comps-protected-user.pdf"
       newuserpassword="test" overwrite="yes" />
```

When this PDF file is opened, a password prompt appears. After the password is typed, the user will be able to edit the PDF file in whatever way you allow. When a password is set, with `new ownerpassword`, you have a solid set of permissions to control editing. The `permissions` attribute, which is required when setting `newownerpassword`, allows the options, or combinations of them, listed in Table 28.3 (source: `http://help.adobe.com/en_US/ColdFusion/9.0`). The best part of these options, as with most ColdFusion attributes, is their clarity. For instance, you can safely assume that if `AllowPrinting` is set to true, printing is allowed. If you do not explicitly set the permission for an option, the option is not allowed.

Table 28.3 `Permissions` Options

PERMISSION	DESCRIPTION
`All`	There are no restrictions on the PDF document.
`AllowAssembly`	Users can add the PDF document to a merged document.
`AllowCopy`	Users can copy text, images, and other file content. This setting is required to generate thumbnail images with the `thumbnail` action.
`AllowDegradedPrinting`	Users can print the document at low resolution (150 dpi).
`AllowFillIn`	Users can enter data into PDF form fields. Users can sign PDF forms electronically.
`AllowModifyAnnotations`	Users can add or change comments in the PDF document.
`AllowModifyContents`	Users can change the file content. Users can add the PDF document to a merged document.
`AllowPrinting`	Users can print the document at high resolution (print-production quality). This setting is required for use with the `cfprint` tag.
`AllowScreenReaders`	Users can extract content from the PDF document.
`AllowSecure`	Users can sign the PDF document (with an electronic signature).
`None`	Users can only view the document.

The goal in Listing 28.19 is to protect a PDF file with an owner password of `test` and to remove all permissions by setting the `permissions` attribute to `none`.

Listing 28.19 `protect-ownerpassword.cfm`—Setting an Owner Password and Removing Permissions

```
<!--- Protects the pdf with an owner password --->
<cfpdf action="protect" source="samples/comps.pdf" overwrite="yes"
       destination="pdfs/comps-protected-owner.pdf"
       newownerpassword="test" permissions="none" />
```

Figure 28.7 on the next page shows the Adobe Reader 9 Security settings window.

Alternately, changing the `permissions` attribute to `all` will remove all restrictions. Listing 28.20 uses the same code as in the previous example but with a few permissions set to demonstrate the use of multiple permissions.

Listing 28.20 `protect-ownerpassword-permissions.cfm`—Setting Permissions

```
<!--- Adds owner password and sets permissions --->
<cfpdf action="protect" overwrite="yes" source="samples/comps.pdf"
       destination="pdfs/comps-ownerpassword-permissions.pdf"
       newownerpassword="test" permissions="allowdegradedprinting,
                     allowmodifycontents, allowscreenreaders" />
```

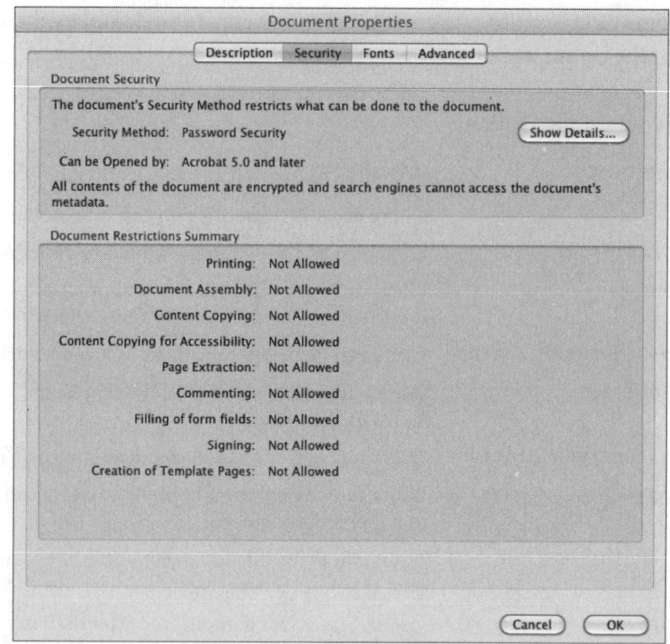

Figure 28.7
Adobe Reader 9 Security settings dialog box.

The previous listing allows the user to modify the contents, allows screen readers, and sets lower-quality printing. The `allowdegradedprinting` and `allowprinting` options allow printing. The difference is in the quality of the print: `allowprinting` has no restrictions on print quality, whereas `allowdegradedprinting` sets a maximum of 150 dpi for printing.

After permissions are set, they apply not only in Acrobat but also in ColdFusion. For PDF files with user passwords, the user must supply the password in the `password` attribute to read or manipulate the PDF file:

```
<cfpdf action="read" source="pdf source path" password="mypassword" name="mypdf">
```

The same goes for certain PDF manipulations that are protected by owner permissions. The `password` attribute works for both owner and user passwords.

Your PDF files now have restrictions preventing user manipulation by either a simple password or by specific manipulation permissions. You can add PDF encryption to further protect your PDF files.

Adding Encryption

The available encryption algorithms are based on version compatibility. They are listed in Table 28.4 from the most secure to the least secure (source: `http://help.adobe.com/en_US/ColdFusion/9.0/CFMLRef/`).

Table 28.4 Encryption Algorithms

ENCRYPTION	ADOBE ACROBAT COMPATIBILITY	ALLOWS USERS TO ENCRYPT
AES_128	7.0 and later	All document contents
		All document contents except for the metadata
		Only file attachments
RC4_128M	6.0 and later	All document contents
		All document contents except for the metadata
RC4_128	5.0 and later	Document contents, but not the document metadata
RC4_40	3.0 and later	The lowest encryption level

Encrypting a PDF file goes hand in hand with setting passwords; `newuserpassword` or `newownerpassword` is required, along with `action="protect"` and `source` attributes, as shown in Listing 28.21.

Listing 28.21 `protect-userpassword-encrypted.cfm`—Encrypting a PDF File

```
<!--- Protects the PDF with a user password and AES encryption --->
<cfpdf action="protect" overwrite="yes" encrypt="aes_128"
       newuserpassword="test" source="samples/comps.pdf"
       destination="pdfs/comps-userpassword-encrypted.pdf" />
```

Listing 28.21 uses the same `comps.pdf` file, sets the user password to *`test`*, and encrypts the PDF file with AES_128. In Acrobat Reader, go to the Document Properties, Security tab and click Show Details (see Figure 28.8) to see the encryption information.

Figure 28.8

Document Security pop-up window showing permissions and encryption.

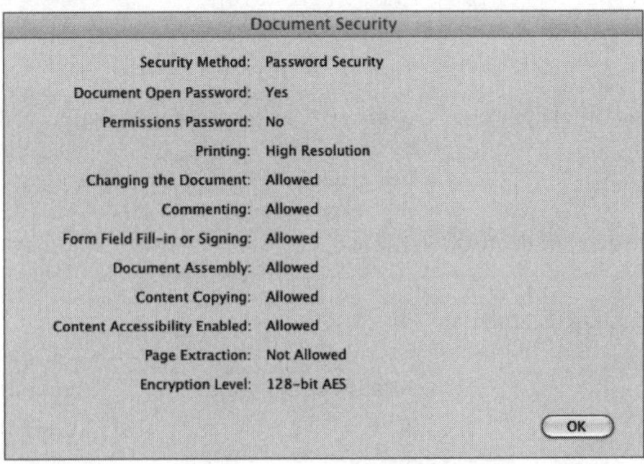

Play around with the different encryption techniques. Refer to Table 28.4 to ensure that you're targeting the proper version of Adobe Acrobat.

NOTE

The metadata in a PDF file is used in Internet searches. When the document is encrypted, the metadata is no longer available to search engines. You also have to make sure that the encryption you choose works in the targeted Acrobat version.

Using DDX

We have created, manipulated, and protected PDF files quickly and easily with `cfpdf`. Throughout the first part of the chapter, DDX was mentioned as another tool for handling specific PDF tasks. Most of what we have done so far is available through DDX.

Document Description XML, or DDX, is an XML-based syntax for constructing PDF files. You can create actual DDX files or use `cfsavecontent` to construct DDX on the fly. ColdFusion 9 does not provide support for the entire DDX language, but the available subset is still very useful and impressive. Table 28.5 lists only the available tags. We won't cover every tag in full here; for more information, read the LiveCycle DDX Reference (`http://livedocs.adobe.com/livecycle/es/sdkHelp/programmer/sdkHelp/ddxRefMain.163.1.html`).

Table 28.5 Available DDX Elements

`About`	`Author`	`Background`
`Center`	`DatePattern`	`DDX`
`DocumentInformation`	`DocumentText`	`Footer`
`Header`	`InitialViewProfile`	`Keyword`
`Keywords`	`Left`	`MasterPassword`
`Metadata`	`NoBookmarks`	`OpenPassword`
`PageLabel`	`Password`	`PasswordAccessProfile`
`PasswordEncryptionProfile`	`PDF (see Note)`	`PDFGroup`
`Permissions`	`Right`	`StyledText`
`StyleProfile`	`Subject`	`TableOfContents`
`TableOfContentsEntryPattern`	`TableOfContentsPagePattern`	`Title`
`Watermark`		

Table 28.6 shows the restricted DDX elements.

Table 28.6 Restricted DDX Elements

`ArtBox`	`AttachmentAppearance`	`Bookmarks`
`BlankPage`	`BleedBox`	`Comments`
`Description`	`FileAttachments`	`FilenameEncoding`
`LinkAlias`	`Links`	`NoBackgrounds`
`NoComments`	`NoFileAttchments`	`NoFooters`

Table 28.6 (continued)

NoForms	NoHeaders	NoLinks
NoPageLabels	NoThumbnails	NoWatermarks
NoXFA	PageMargins	PageSize
PageRotation	PageOverlay	PageUnderlay
PDFsFromBookmarks	Transform	TrimBox

DDX provides a way to separate the manipulation "instructions" for PDF documents into separate files. We will explore several DDX examples, but keep in mind that the possibilities are vast.

Creating a Simple DDX Processing Application

To test the various DDX options, we'll use a simple form that shows the available DDX files in a drop-down list, allowing the user to select a script to process. All examples use the same PDF files, so all we need to do is switch DDX files and look at the results. Before we cover DDX syntax, let's explore the code for the simple application built to test DDX files (Listing 28.22).

The `/ddx` directory is read, and the values populate a `cfselect` form element. When the form is submitted, a PDF file will be written with the same name as the selected DDX file, minus the `.ddx` extension. Simply create a new DDX file, save it as `/ddx/filename.ddx`, reload the application, and test away!

Listing 28.22 `ddxform.cfm`—DDX Processing Application

```
<!--- Check for the form field "ddxfile" --->
<cfif structKeyExists(form, "ddxfile")>
   <!--- verify the file is valid DDX --->
   <cfif isDDX(ExpandPath("ddx/#form.ddxfile#"))>
      <!--- Construct input files struct --->
      <cfset input = StructNew() />
      <cfset input.TitlePage = "samples/title.pdf" />
      <cfset input.SamplePage = "samples/page.pdf"/>
      <cfset input.Comps = "samples/comps.pdf" />

      <!--- Construct output files struct --->
      <cfset output = StructNew() />
                     <!--- Set the Output1 filename --->
      <cfset output.Output1 = "pdfs/"&Replace(form.ddxfile,".ddx",
                                                ".pdf") />

      <!--- Process DDX --->
      <cfpdf name="myBook" action="processddx" inputfiles="#input#"
             outputfiles="#output#" ddxfile="ddx/#form.ddxfile#" />

      <!--- Output result --->
      <cfoutput>
         <strong>DDX instruction processing: #myBook.Output1#</strong>
                                <hr />
      </cfoutput>
   <cfelse>
```

Listing 28.22 (CONTINUED)

```
        <!--- Invalid DDX --->
        <cfoutput>
        <strong>ddx/#form.ddxfile# is not a valid DDX file.</strong>
        </cfoutput>
    </cfif>
</cfif>

<!--- Filter the /ddx directory for all ddx files --->
<cfdirectory name="ddxDirectory" action="list" filter="*.ddx"
            directory="#ExpandPath('ddx')#" />

<!--- Create a form for processing DDX;
        preservedata for ease of testing --->
<cfform name="DDXSelector" preservedata="yes">
  Select a DDX File: <cfselect name="ddxfile" query="ddxDirectory"
                        required="yes" display="name" value="name" />
  <br />
  <cfinput name="submitButton" type="submit" value="Submit" />
</cfform>
```

The testing application is ready to roll. We can look at some DDX examples and start learning more about DDX.

Adding a Table of Contents

You add a table of contents (toc) with the TableOfContents element inside a PDF, PDFGroup, or StyleProfile element. Listing 28.23 merges multiple PDF files and adds a simple table of contents.

Listing 28.23 ddx/toc-simple.ddx—Simple DDX with Table of Contents

```
<?xml version="1.0" encoding="UTF-8"?>
<DDX xmlns="http://ns.adobe.com/DDX/1.0/"
    xmlns:xsi="http://www.w3.org/2001/XMLSchema-instance"
    xsi:schemaLocation="http://ns.adobe.com/DDX/1.0/ coldfusion_ddx.xsd">
  <PDF result="Output1">
     <PDF source="TitlePage"/>
     <TableOfContents/>
     <PDF source="SamplePage"/>
     <PDF source="Comps" />
  </PDF>
</DDX>
```

The PDF element has the result attribute set to Output1. This setting is equivalent to the destination attribute for cfpdf. If you look at our application's source, you'll see Output1 used in two places: in the output struct used in the cfpdf tag, and in the result output. Also notice the source attributes used in the internal PDF elements are used in the input struct. The names of both of these attributes are completely up to you. Instead of using TitlePage, SamplePage, and Comps, you could name them Doc1, Doc2, and Doc3, for instance. Running this DDX file through our application creates a table of contents for all PDF pages with bookmarks (Figure 28.9).

NOTE

The file extension .ddx is not required. Initially the files were named with an .xml extension. The files can be edited in any text editor.

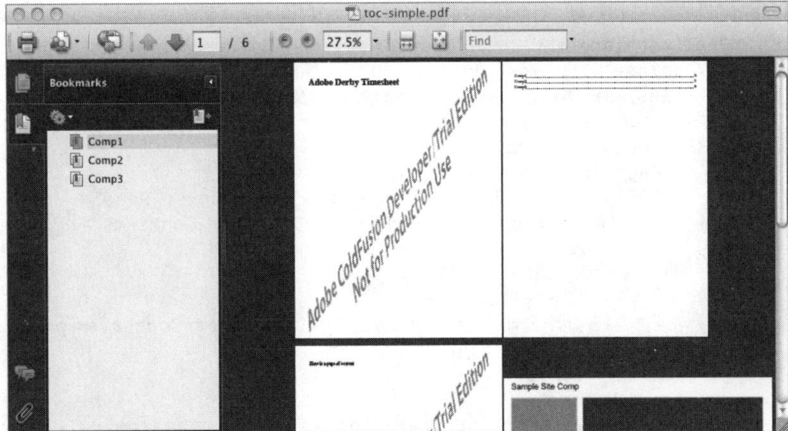

Figure 28.9
Simple table of contents.

The Bookmarks view is expanded in Figure 28.9, and it shows all the bookmarked pages with the exception of the table of contents. The bookmark name is the same as that of the original PDF file. The comps PDF file has three pages (Comp1, Comp2, and Comp3), and they flow one after another rather than being grouped. We can group the included PDF files into a single bookmark folder by using the `bookmarkTitle` attribute, as demonstrated in Listing 28.24.

NOTE

The `includeInTOC` attribute defaults to `true`, but it applies only when the `bookmarkTitle` attribute is used.

Listing 28.24 `ddx/toc-simple-titles.ddx`—DDX with `bookmarkTitle` Attribute

```
<?xml version="1.0" encoding="UTF-8"?>
<DDX xmlns="http://ns.adobe.com/DDX/1.0/"
    xmlns:xsi="http://www.w3.org/2001/XMLSchema-instance"
    xsi:schemaLocation="http://ns.adobe.com/DDX/1.0/ coldfusion_ddx.xsd">
   <PDF result="Output1">
      <PDF source="TitlePage" bookmarkTitle="Cover Page"/>
      <TableOfContents bookmarkTitle="Table of Contents" />
      <PDF source="SamplePage" bookmarkTitle="Sample Page" />
      <PDF source="Comps" bookmarkTitle="Site Designs" />
   </PDF>
</DDX>
```

The sample PDF files are only one level deep, but you can embed multiple levels of bookmarks in a PDF file, and you can control the number of levels by using the `maxBookmarkLevel` attribute on the `TableOfContents` element.

A great feature of the generated table of contents is the creation of live links applied to the page names. The `createLiveLinks` attribute, from the `TableOfContents` element, defaults to `true`. Set it to `false`, and the table of contents will be pure text, with no links.

We can also customize the look of the table of contents page by adding a few elements to the DDX, as shown in Listing 28.25.

Listing 28.25 `ddx/toc-simple-title-custom.ddx`—DDX with Table of Contents Customization

```
<?xml version="1.0" encoding="UTF-8"?>
<DDX xmlns="http://ns.adobe.com/DDX/1.0/"
   xmlns:xsi="http://www.w3.org/2001/XMLSchema-instance"
   xsi:schemaLocation="http://ns.adobe.com/DDX/1.0/ coldfusion_ddx.xsd">
  <PDF result="Output1">
     <PageLabel format="Decimal"/>
     <PDF source="TitlePage" bookmarkTitle="Cover Page"/>
     <TableOfContents bookmarkTitle="Table of Contents">
        <Header>
           <Center>
              <StyledText>
                 <p font="Arial,18pt">Table of Contents</p>
              </StyledText>
           </Center>
        </Header>
       <TableOfContentsEntryPattern>
          <StyledText>
             <p font="Arial,10pt">
               <_BookmarkTitle/>
               <leader leader-pattern="solid" />
               Page <_BookmarkPageCitation/>
             </p>
          </StyledText>
       </TableOfContentsEntryPattern>
    </TableOfContents>
    <PDF source="SamplePage" bookmarkTitle="Sample Page" />
    <PDF source="Comps" bookmarkTitle="Site Designs" />
  </PDF>
</DDX>
```

We introduce a few new elements in Listing 28.25: `TableOfContentsEntryPattern`, `StyledText`, and `Header`. The `Header` element will be covered in more detail later, but as you can see, it is very straightforward and, yes, it adds a header to the generated table of contents page. To style each individual line of the table of contents, we use the `TableOfContentsEntryPattern` element with `StyledText`. In this DDX, we changed the dotted line to solid with the `leader` element and added the word `Page` before each page number. You can build on these few DDX examples to generate your own style of table of contents.

Adding Headers and Footers

As we saw in the `cfpdf` section, headers and footers can now be added in the `cfpdf` tag. You may sometimes need more advanced techniques, though, and this is where DDX shines. The `Header` and `Footer` elements both have the same structure, as follows:

```
<Header or Footer …>
  <Left or Center or Right>
     <StyledText or PDF source>
        ...
     </StyledText or PDF source>
     <TargetLocale … />
  </Left or Center or Right>
</Header or Footer>
```

In Listing 28.26, we throw in `PDFGroup` as well so that the header and footer are applied to the grouped PDF files.

Listing 28.26 `ddx/toc-simple-titles-custom-styled-header-footer.ddx`—Using DDX with `PDFGroup`

```
<?xml version="1.0" encoding="UTF-8"?>
<DDX xmlns="http://ns.adobe.com/DDX/1.0/"
    xmlns:xsi="http://www.w3.org/2001/XMLSchema-instance"
    xsi:schemaLocation="http://ns.adobe.com/DDX/1.0/ coldfusion_ddx.xsd">
   <PDF result="Output1">
      <PageLabel format="Decimal"/>
      <PDF source="TitlePage" bookmarkTitle="Cover Page"/>
      <TableOfContents bookmarkTitle="Table of Contents">
         <Header>
            <Center>
               <StyledText>
                  <p font="Arial,18pt">Table of Contents</p>
               </StyledText>
            </Center>
         </Header>
         <TableOfContentsEntryPattern>
            <StyledText>
               <p font="Arial,10pt">
                  <_BookmarkTitle/>
                  <leader leader-pattern="solid" />
                  Page <_BookmarkPageCitation/>
               </p>
            </StyledText>
         </TableOfContentsEntryPattern>
      </TableOfContents>
      <PDFGroup>
         <Header>
            <Center>
               <StyledText>
                  <p font="Arial,18pt">My Header</p>
               </StyledText>
            </Center>
         </Header>
         <Footer>
            <Center>
               <StyledText>
                  <p font="Arial,18pt">My Footer</p>
               </StyledText>
            </Center>
         </Footer>
         <PDF source="SamplePage" bookmarkTitle="Sample Page" />
         <PDF source="Comps" bookmarkTitle="Site Designs" />
      </PDFGroup>
   </PDF>
</DDX>
```

Remember that DDX is XML, so the hierarchy of the elements controls the way the elements are applied. The `Header` and `Footer` elements used in the `TableOfContents` element have no effect on the `PDF` elements in the `PDFGroup` element. The `Header` and `Footer` elements have a direct relationship to the sibling elements—for example, putting the `Header` element in the initial `<PDF result="Output1">`

element would cause all pages to have the specified header (see Figure 28.10). We can also see alignment in action, with the `Center` element, and styling, in Listing 28.26. More details on `StyledText` are coming shortly, in the section "Using Style Profiles," but as you can see, we can control the font and font size.

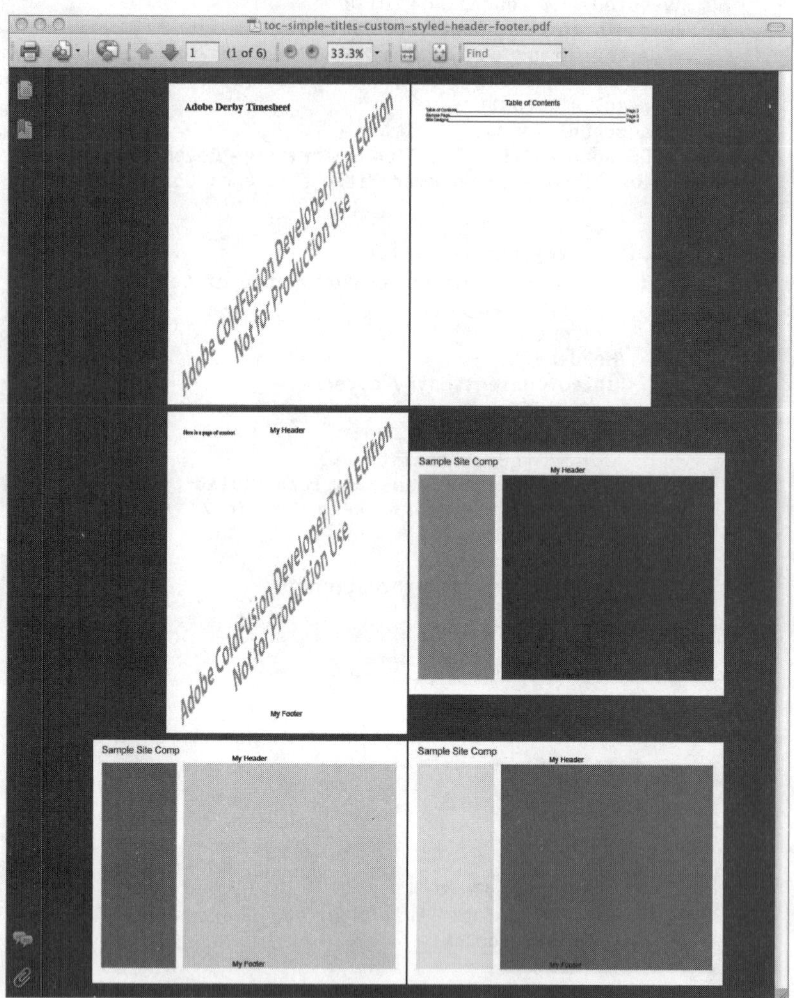

Figure 28.10

The `PDFGroup` header and footer; pages 1 and 2 do not have the same header and footer.

Headers and footers are as simple in DDX as they are in `cfpdf`. The approach is different, but most of the DDX is just as simple and powerful.

Adding Watermarks

You saw how to add different types of watermarks earlier in the chapter using `cfpdf`. Through DDX, you can also add easily styled watermarks using the `Watermark` element. The `Watermark` element allows you to set scale, horizontal and vertical offsets based on horizontal and vertical anchors, opacity, text, and so on. The use of a PDF file as a watermark is still an option as well. To save space, the example in Listing 28.27, based on the previous DDX example, shows only the `Watermark` element and the parent element (see the source file for the full script).

Listing 28.27 `ddx/toc-simple-titles-custom-styled-header-footer-watermark.ddx`

```
<?xml version="1.0" encoding="UTF-8"?>
<DDX xmlns="http://ns.adobe.com/DDX/1.0/"
     xmlns:xsi="http://www.w3.org/2001/XMLSchema-instance"
     xsi:schemaLocation="http://ns.adobe.com/DDX/1.0/ coldfusion_ddx.xsd">
   <PDF result="Output1">
      <Watermark opacity="25%" rotation="30" fitToPage="true">
         <StyledText>
            <p>My Watermark</p>
         </StyledText>
      </Watermark>
      ... the remaining source ...
   </PDF>
</DDX>
```

This simple example added the text "My Watermark" to all pages at 25 percent opacity, rotated 30 degrees, and sized to properly fit the page—how easy is that! The `Watermark` element also allows you to place the watermark on alternate pages or on odd or even pages only and to control whether the watermark appears in printed documents, on the screen, or both.

In a few examples, you have seen how to style individual text elements. In addition to styling each individual text element, you can create and apply style profiles with DDX.

Using Style Profiles

You can use `StyleProfile` elements to create a named profile for referencing using the `styleReference` attribute on the following elements: `Background`, `Footer`, `Header`, `Watermark`, and `TableOfContents`. You can think of this profile as an internal CSS declaration: you create the style and then reference it by name.

Building on our current PDF example, suppose that you need to watermark and add a specific footer on the image pages in `comps.pdf` and on page 1 of the PDF file but not the rest of the document. With page 1 and the rest of the `PDF` elements separated by the `TableOfContents` element, you can use `StyleProfile` with your DDX.

Listing 28.28 follows previous examples but is changed quite a bit. We no longer use `PDFGroup`, and the main `Watermark` element has been removed.

Listing 28.28 `ddx/toc-simple-titles-custom-styled-header-footer-watermark-styleprofiles.ddx`

```
<?xml version="1.0" encoding="UTF-8"?>
<DDX xmlns="http://ns.adobe.com/DDX/1.0/"
     xmlns:xsi="http://www.w3.org/2001/XMLSchema-instance"
     xsi:schemaLocation="http://ns.adobe.com/DDX/1.0/ coldfusion_ddx.xsd">
```

Listing 28.28 (continued)

```
    <PDF result="Output1">
        <PageLabel format="Decimal"/>
        <PDF source="TitlePage" bookmarkTitle="Cover Page">
            <Watermark styleReference="MyWatermark" />
        </PDF>
        <TableOfContents bookmarkTitle="Table of Contents">
            <Header>
                <Center>
                    <StyledText>
                        <p font="Arial,18pt">Table of Contents</p>
                    </StyledText>
                </Center>
            </Header>
            <TableOfContentsEntryPattern>
                <StyledText>
                    <p font="Arial,10pt">
                        <_BookmarkTitle/>
                        <leader leader-pattern="solid" />
                        Page <_BookmarkPageCitation/>
                    </p>
                </StyledText>
            </TableOfContentsEntryPattern>
        </TableOfContents>
        <PDF source="SamplePage" bookmarkTitle="Sample Page" />
        <PDF source="Comps" bookmarkTitle="Site Designs">
            <Footer styleReference="CompsFooter" />
            <Watermark styleReference="MyWatermark" />
        </PDF>
    </PDF>
    <StyleProfile name="CompsFooter">
        <Footer>
            <Left>
                <StyledText>
                    <p font="Arial,10pt">
                        Page <_PageNumber/> / <_LastPageNumber/>
                    </p>
                </StyledText>
            </Left>
            <Right>
                <StyledText>
                    <p font="Arial,10pt">Last Modified: <_Modified/></p>
                </StyledText>
            </Right>
        </Footer>
    </StyleProfile>
    <StyleProfile name="MyWatermark">
        <Watermark opacity="25%" rotation="30" fitToPage="true">
            <StyledText>
                <p>Copyright My Company</p>
            </StyledText>
        </Watermark>
    </StyleProfile>
</DDX>
```

You can view the `StyleProfile` elements as groups of style information. For the `PDF` element with `source="Comps"`, we have two subelements and both use a `styleReference` attribute; one style sets up a footer, and the other controls the watermark. The initial `PDF` element, `TitlePage`, also uses the same watermark style profile.

What we have done is watermarked our cover page and every page included from the `Comps` source PDF file. The table of contents and `SamplePage` source do not use the either `StyleProfile`, so the source pages are not affected.

`StyleProfile` elements allow you to create custom styles for the PDF document. They help you begin to develop a much more dynamic, cleanly styled DDX document, by separating the design from the layout.

Extracting PDF Text

DDX also provides a quick and easy way to index PDF text. Instead of using the `PDF` element as the main `Output1 result`, we use another element: `DocumentText`. This element requests information about the words that appear in the specified source documents. The DDX, in Listing 28.29, is quite simple. We'll strip away all previous DDX examples and just use the same source documents.

Listing 28.29 `ddx/extractingtext.ddx`—DDX Using `DocumentText`

```
<?xml version="1.0" encoding="UTF-8"?>
<DDX xmlns="http://ns.adobe.com/DDX/1.0/"
    xmlns:xsi="http://www.w3.org/2001/XMLSchema-instance"
    xsi:schemaLocation="http://ns.adobe.com/DDX/1.0/ coldfusion_ddx.xsd">
   <DocumentText result="Output1">
      <PDF source="TitlePage" />
      <PDF source="SamplePage"/>
      <PDF source="Comps" bookmarkTitle="Site Designs" />
   </DocumentText>
</DDX>
```

A change had to be made to the sample application in order to output an XML file instead of a PDF file. Listing 28.30 shows the final source with the changes highlighted.

Listing 28.30 `ProcessDDX.cfm`—DDX Test Application

```
<!--- Check for the form field "ddxfile" --->
<cfif structKeyExists(form, "ddxfile")>
   <!--- verify the file is valid DDX --->
   <cfif isDDX(ExpandPath("ddx/#form.ddxfile#"))>
      <!--- Construct input files struct --->
      <cfset input = StructNew() />
      <cfset input.TitlePage = "samples/title.pdf" />
      <cfset input.SamplePage = "samples/page.pdf"/>
      <cfset input.Comps = "samples/comps.pdf" />

                    <!--- Determine the output folder path --->
                    <cfset folder = "pdfs" />
                    <cfif form.outputtype NEQ "pdf">
                     <cfset folder = "data" />
                    </cfif>
```

Listing 28.30 (CONTINUED)

```
        <!--- Construct output files struct --->
        <cfset output = StructNew() />
        <cfset output.Output1 = folder&"/"
                                    & Replace(form.ddxfile, ".ddx", "."&form.outputtype) />

        <!--- Process DDX --->
                       <cfpdf name="myBook" action="processddx" inputfiles="#input#"
              outputfiles="#output#" ddxfile="ddx/#form.ddxfile#" />

        <!--- Output result --->
        <cfoutput>
           <strong>DDX instruction processing: #myBook.Output1#</strong>
        </cfoutput>
                       <!--- If the output is successful and type is xml, read and
                             display the file contents --->
        <cfif form.outputtype EQ "xml" AND myBook.Output1 EQ "successful">
                          <br />
           <cffile variable="xmloutput"
                   file="#ExpandPath(output.Output1)#"
                   action="read" charset="utf-8" />
           <cfoutput>#XMLFormat(xmloutput)#</cfoutput>
                               <hr />
        </cfif>
     <cfelse>
        <!--- Invalid DDX --->
        <cfoutput>
           <strong>ddx/#form.ddxfile# is not a valid DDX file</strong>
        </cfoutput>
     </cfif>
  </cfif>

  <!--- Filter the /ddx directory for all ddx files --->
  <cfdirectory name="ddxDirectory" action="list" filter="*.ddx"
              directory="#ExpandPath('ddx')#" />

  <!--- Create a form for processing DDX;
          preservedata for ease of testing --->
  <cfform name="DDXSelector" preservedata="yes">
    Select a DDX File: <cfselect name="ddxfile" query="ddxDirectory"
                    required="yes" display="name" value="name" />
    <br />
     Output type:
     <cfselect name="outputtype">
        <option value="pdf">pdf</option>
        <option value="xml">xml</option>
     </cfselect>
          <br />
     <cfinput name="submitButton" type="submit" value="Submit" />
  </cfform>
```

Processing DDX with `DocumentText` does not output a PDF file—it outputs XML—so the changes here basically check the selected `outputtype` and either read the generated XML file and then display the contents or operate as our previous examples did and just show a success message.

The following XML shows the result of running the `DocumentText` DDX:

```
<?xml version="1.0" encoding="UTF-8"?>
<DocText xmlns="http://ns.adobe.com/DDX/DocText/1.0/">
<TextPerPage>
<Page pageNumber="1">Adobe Derby Timesheet</Page>
<Page pageNumber="2">Here is a page of content</Page>
</TextPerPage>
</DocText>
```

This XML can be parsed, searched, stored, and so on to fit your needs. Compare the previous result snippet to the output from Listing 28.11, where `cfpdf` was used to extract text, and you will notice the same output format.

Controlling the Initial View

Have you ever opened a PDF file only to find that it doesn't start on page 1 or that it is zoomed to some weird percentage? With DDX, you can control the initial view of the PDF file when it is opened.

Listing 28.31 changes the initial view of `samples/comps.pdf` to adjust it to our liking.

Listing 28.31 `ddx/initialview.ddx`—Setting the Initial PDF View

```
<?xml version="1.0" encoding="UTF-8"?>
<DDX xmlns="http://ns.adobe.com/DDX/1.0/"
   xmlns:xsi="http://www.w3.org/2001/XMLSchema-instance"
   xsi:schemaLocation="http://ns.adobe.com/DDX/1.0/ coldfusion_ddx.xsd">
       <PDF result="Output1" initialView="globalView">
              <PDF source="TitlePage" />
              <PDF source="SamplePage"/>
              <PDF source="Comps" />
       </PDF>
       <InitialViewProfile name="globalView" pageLayout="Continuous"
                           show="PagesPanel" windowOptions="CenterOnScreen"
                           magnification="50%" />
</DDX>
```

The `InitialViewProfile` element is given a name, the same as `StyleProfile`, and referenced in the output `PDF` element. In the event that there are multiple view changes, you can create multiple initial view profiles and reference them accordingly. In this case, we're setting the page layout to `Continuous`, showing the pages panel, centering the viewing application (Adobe Reader 9) on the screen, and reducing the magnification to 50 percent. Figure 28.11 on the next page shows the result of processing the DDX in Listing 28.31.

Wow—what power! DDX opens the floodgates to dynamic PDF customizations. The best next step is to play with the settings to see what suits your needs. Remember to bookmark the DDX reference for ease of access.

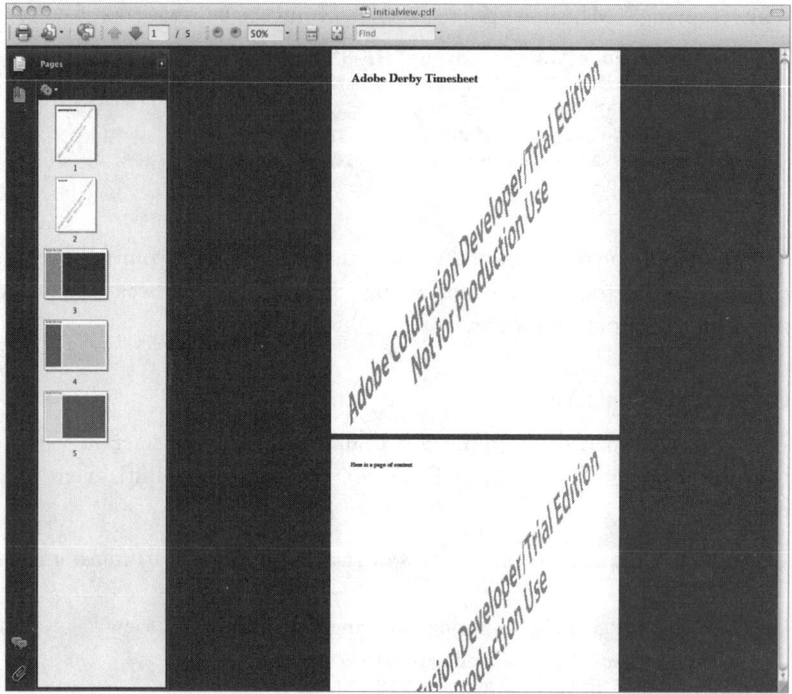

Figure 28.11

Results from `InitialViewProfile`.

Working with PDF Forms

The PDFs we've been using are all flat, with no interactivity. ColdFusion wouldn't be complete without the ability to manage and manipulate PDF forms.

Just about every Web site has an HTML form of some sort to collect user information, sign up users for a newsletter, and so on. PDF forms aren't much different from HTML forms. They elicit information from the user, and upon submission or saving, the information is transmitted to a Web page for processing. ColdFusion now has the capability to manage PDF form submissions as well as manipulate the content.

Unlike HTML forms, not all PDF forms are the same, beyond the internal form elements. A PDF form created with Adobe Acrobat is different from one created with Adobe LiveCycle Designer. We will explore the differences between the two types of forms as well as the different types of form submissions: HTTP and PDF.

Populating PDF Forms

You can populate PDF forms in several ways: with `cfpdfsubform`, `inline xml`, and `external xml`. The PDF form we are using (Listing 28.32) is a sample timesheet PDF form from Adobe LiveCycle Designer CS3 (Figure 28.12), which uses a more hierarchical PDF structure than Adobe Acrobat, which uses a flat structure.

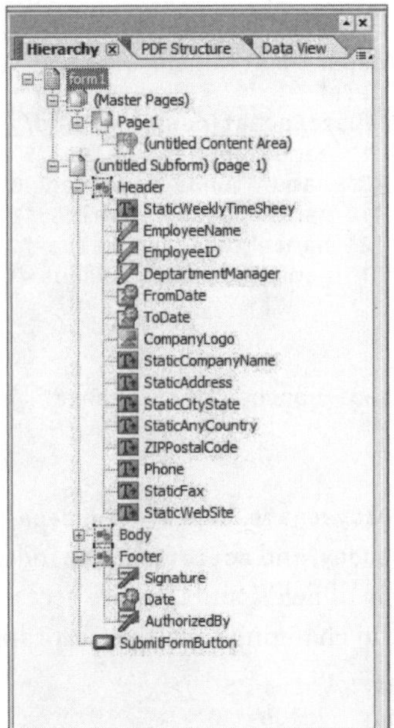

Figure 28.12
Hierarchy tab in LiveCycle Designer.

To populate the form, you need to know the names of the form fields you're populating. If you're using Acrobat, you can export the form data to XML by choosing Forms > Manage Form Data > Export Data, or you can choose Forms > Edit in Designer to open the PDF form in Adobe LiveCycle Designer. The simple and geek way is to write code to view the fields. Listing 28.32 reads the PDF form and dumps the results to the browser. The code is very similar to that we have used for reading PDF files, except in this case we use `cfpdfform` instead of `cfpdf`. The attributes are the same, though.

Listing 28.32 `pdfform-read.cfm`—Sample Timesheet PDF Form

```
<!--- Loads a pdf into result var --->
<cfpdfform result="result" action="read"
        source="samples/Adobe Derby Timesheet.pdf" />
<!--- Dumps the pdf form contents --->
<cfdump var="#result#" />
```

To populate the form, we'll use `cfpdfsubform`, which specifies our PDF form's structure in CFML (Listing 28.33). The parameters used in `cfpdfsubform` follow the same structure as the form dump seen in Listing 28.24.

Listing 28.33 `pdfform-populate.cfm`—Populating a PDF Form

```
<!--- Populate form data --->
<cfpdfform name="timesheet" action="populate"
        source="samples/Adobe Derby Timesheet.pdf">
     <cfpdfsubform name="form1">
          <cfpdfformparam name="employeename" value="John C. Bland II" />
          <cfpdfformparam name="employeeid" value="32" />
```

Listing 28.33 (continued)

```
                <cfpdfformparam name="departmentmanager" value="Ben Forta" />
                <cfpdfformparam name="date"
                                value="#DateFormat(now(), 'mm/dd/yyyy')#" />
                <cfpdfformparam index="1" name="monday" value="5" />
                <cfpdfformparam index="2" name="monday" value="10" />
                <cfpdfformparam index="1" name="tuesday" value="7" />
                <cfpdfformparam index="2" name="tuesday" value="18" />
                <cfpdfformparam index="1" name="activity" value="CF 9" />
        </cfpdfsubform>
</cfpdfform>
<!--- Reads the pdf into result var --->
<cfpdfform result="result" action="read" source="#timesheet#" />
<!--- Dumps the pdf form contents --->
<cfdump var="#result#" />
```

Here we specify a few regular form fields (`employeename`, `employeeid`, `departmentmanager`, and `date`) and a few index-based fields (`Monday`, `Tuesday`, and `activity`). The index-based fields are merely fields with the same name, like an array of fields, and they are accessed like an array, keeping the name the same, updating the index, and changing the value accordingly:

```
<cfpdfformparam index="1" name="monday" value="5" />
<cfpdfformparam index="2" name="monday" value="10" />
```

This code sets the `monday` box of index 1, in this case row 1, to the value 5, and index 2, or row 2, to the value 10. The `index` attribute is required only if you want to set a specific `index` value. Otherwise, for an index-based field, the default `index` value, 1, is used.

```
<!--- index defaults to 1 --->
<cfpdfformparam name="monday" value="5" />
```

NOTE

Specification of an `index` value is not based on position in the code. You can specify index 2 before index 1, for instance.

NOTE

The `monday` field expects a number. If anything else is passed in, the field defaults to `0.0`.

`cfpdfsubform` has an index property and serves the same purpose. For PDF forms with multiple subforms, you can use the `index` attribute to access a specific subform. In our example, we specified the exact name of the subform since only one subform is available.

Running Listing 28.33 loads the same timesheet into the `result` variable using `cfpdfform action="read"` and dumps the results to the browser using `cfdump`. Look at the dump, and you will see the same dump as in Listing 28.24, but with the prepopulated values displayed in place of empty fields.

You can also populate a PDF form using XML. The structure of a PDF form populated with XML is quite different from that of a form populated with `cfpdfsubform`. A PDF form created in Adobe LiveCycle Designer uses XML Forms Architecture (XFA), whereas one created in Adobe Acrobat uses XML Forms Data Format (XFDF). Our sample PDF form was created with LiveCycle. The XML in Listing 28.34 populates the PDF form with the same information as in our previous `cfpdfsubform` example.

Listing 28.34 `pdfform-data.xml`—XML PDF Form Data

```
<?xml version="1.0" encoding="UTF-8"?>
<form1>
        <EmployeeName>John C. Bland II</EmployeeName>
        <EmployeeID>32</EmployeeID>
        <DepartmentManager>Ben Forta</DepartmentManager>
        <Date>08/27/2009</Date>
        <Monday>5</Monday>
        <Monday>10</Monday>
        <Tuesday>7</Tuesday>
        <Tuesday>18</Tuesday>
        <Activity>CF 9</Activity>
</form1>
```

TIP

Instead of writing the entire structure and worrying about which format to use, export the form data in Adobe Acrobat (choose Forms > Manage Form Data > Export Data). You can also use Ray Camden's `toXML` component (see `http://www.coldfusionjedi.com/projects/toxml/`) to convert the `result` struct from a PDF file to XML.

To populate a PDF form via XML, you can use the following code:

```
<!--- Populate form data from XML --->
<cfpdfform action="populate"
            source="pdfs/Adobe Derby Timesheet.pdf"
            xmldata="data/pdfform-data.xml" />
```

In addition to an external XML file, you can use `cfsavecontent` to create inline XML to populate the form, as shown in Listing 28.35.

Listing 28.35 `pdfform-populate-xml.cfm`—Populating a PDF Form with Inline XML

```
<!--- Save XML info to a variable --->
<cfsavecontent variable="pdfxml">
<form1>
  <EmployeeName>John C. Bland II</EmployeeName>
  <EmployeeID>32</EmployeeID>
  <DepartmentManager>Ben Forta</DepartmentManager>
  <Date>08/27/2009</Date>
  <Monday>5</Monday>
  <Monday>10</Monday>
  <Tuesday>7</Tuesday>
  <Tuesday>18</Tuesday>
  <Activity>CF 9</Activity>
</form1>
</cfsavecontent>

<!--- Populate form data from XML and show in browser --->
<cfpdfform name="timesheet" action="populate" xmldata="#pdfxml#"
            source="samples/Adobe Derby Timesheet.pdf" />
<!--- Reads the pdf into result var --->
<cfpdfform result="result" action="read" source="#timesheet#" />
<!--- Dumps the pdf form contents --->
<cfdump var="#result#" />
```

TIP

Use `overwriteData="yes"` to overwrite prefilled form values.

TIP

Use the `destination` attribute to save the populated PDF form to a new PDF file instead of displaying the PDF file in the browser.

Whether you use `cfpdfsubform` or `xml`, inline or external, the result is the same. What happens to the result isn't always the same, though. In the preceding examples, we have dumped the result to the browser, but in a real scenario, using `cfdump` probably won't help you keep your job or get that promotion you want. ColdFusion allows us to not only prepopulate the form, but also to save that data in a new PDF file or in an XML Data Package (XDP) file.

An XDP file is a PDF file represented in XML. You can open the XDP file in Adobe Acrobat just like a PDF file, and the populated content will appear as well. Listing 28.36 shows the same populated code, but instead of using `cfdump`, we will save the output in a new XDP file using `action="populate"` and add a destination to `cfpdfform`.

Listing 28.36 `pdfform-populate-save-xdp.cfm`—Populating and Saving an XDP File

```
<!--- Populate form data --->
<cfpdfform name="timesheet" action="populate" overwrite="yes"
          source="samples/Adobe Derby Timesheet.pdf">
       <cfpdfsubform name="form1">
              <cfpdfformparam name="employeename" value="John C. Bland II" />
              <cfpdfformparam name="employeeid" value="32" />
              <cfpdfformparam name="departmentmanager" value="Ben Forta" />
              <cfpdfformparam name="date"
                              value="#DateFormat(now(), 'mm/dd/yyyy')#" />
              <cfpdfformparam index="1" name="monday" value="5" />
              <cfpdfformparam index="2" name="monday" value="10" />
              <cfpdfformparam index="1" name="tuesday" value="7" />
              <cfpdfformparam index="2" name="tuesday" value="18" />
              <cfpdfformparam index="1" name="activity" value="CF 9" />
       </cfpdfsubform>
</cfpdfform>
<!--- Save populated pdf to XDP file --->
<cfpdfform action="populate" overwrite="yes" source="#timesheet#"
          destination="pdfs/timesheet-populated.xdp" />
```

NOTE

Open the XDP file in a text editor to see the underlying XML content.

TIP

Use XDP files sparingly. The file size differences between a PDF and an XDP file are notable.

The XDP file is now ready for viewing or insertion into the LiveCycle Designer workflow. Saving the PDF file as an XDP file is not your only option, though. In many cases, you may want to email or archive the PDF file. To do so, you need to add a slight tweak to Listing 28.36:

```
<!--- Save populated pdf to PDF file --->
<cfpdfform action="populate" overwrite="yes" source="#timesheet#"
          destination="pdfs/timesheet-populated.pdf" />
```

TIP

If your plan is to email or archive the PDF file and are not using the form aspect, flatten the PDF file using `action="write"` and `flatten="yes"` to remove the form functionality.

Unless you look really closely, the code change isn't easily noticed. The only difference is that the resulting file-name extension is `.pdf` instead of `.xdp`. ColdFusion yet again makes easy even easier.

Submitting PDF Forms

There are two types of form submissions: HTTP and PDF. ColdFusion allows you to manage both submission types, but they are slightly different. For the examples here, the sample timesheet PDF form has been copied and saved as two separate PDF forms: one for each submission type.

NOTE

The PDF files point directly to a development server. Open the file in LiveCycle Designer to change the submission URL.

Handling HTTP Submissions

A PDF form created in LiveCycle submits using `HTTP Post`. To access the submitted information, you treat it almost like a regular HTML form submission. The only difference is that the submitted values are in the hierarchy of the PDF form. To demonstrate, Listing 28.37 uses the previous code for populating the PDF form with XML.

Listing 28.37 `pdfform-http-post.cfm`—Submitting a PDF Form via HTTP

```
<!--- Check if the form1 property exists in the form struct --->
<cfif StructKeyExists(form, "form1")>
   <!--- Dump the contents of the form submission --->
   <cfdump var="#form#" />
<cfelse>
   <!--- Prepopulate form data and show in the browser --->
   <cfpdfform action="populate"
              source="samples/Adobe Derby Timesheet - HTTP Post.pdf"
              xmldata="data/pdfform-data.xml" />
</cfif>
```

If the variable `form.form1` exists, we dump the contents of `form`; otherwise, we load the PDF file in the browser. After the PDF file is loaded in the browser, the page is done processing and merely waits for the PDF form to be submitted, or it is presented for downloading, pending the operating system or browser. Once the form is submitted, the values are dumped to the browser; the dumped form values are shown in Figure 28.13 on the next page.

If you look at the PDF form in LiveCycle Designer, the PDF form is set up with `Header`, `Footer`, and `Body` elements within the `Subform` element, which is in the main `form1` element. This is the same structure seen when the form is read and dumped to the browser as in Listing 28.37. The form results can go to a database, be archived to the server as seen previously, or used in many other actions, just as with a normal HTTP post.

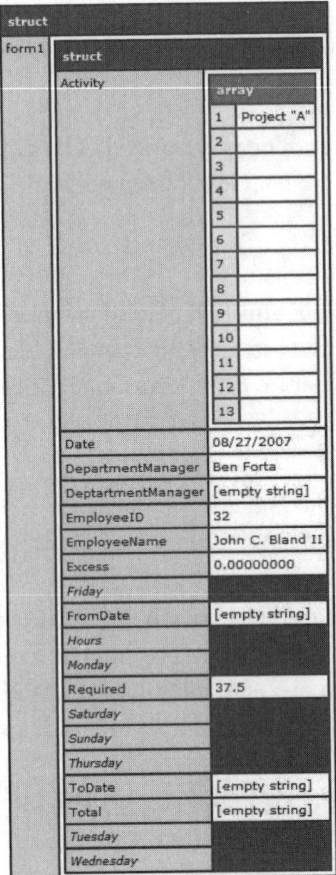

Figure 28.13

A ColdFusion dump of a LiveCycle PDF post submission.

But, as noted earlier, there is also another submission type, which we will now explore.

Handling PDF Submissions

A PDF form created in Acrobat does not fill the `FORM` scope, as shown previously. Instead, the `PDF` scope is filled with a binary `content` variable. You cannot access the data in `PDF.content` until you read it. This requirement does add one more step, but it is painless. Listing 28.38 shows how to handle an Acrobat form submission.

Listing 28.38 `pdfform-pdf-post.cfm`—Submitting a PDF Form via PDF

```
<!--- Check if the PDF scope exists --->
<cfif isDefined("PDF")>
   <!--- Read the PDF contents into a variable --->
   <cfpdfform action="read" source="#PDF.content#" result="timesheet" />
   <!--- Dump the contents of the PDF variable --->
   <cfdump var="#timesheet#" />
<cfelse>
   <!--- Prepopulate form data and display --->
   <cfpdfform action="populate"
              source="samples/Adobe Derby Timesheet - PDF Post.pdf"
              xmldata="data/pdfform-data.xml" />
</cfif>
```

NOTE

Mac users loading the PDF file in Preview mode will not see the populated PDF form. To display the content, open the PDF file in Acrobat or Acrobat Reader.

We follow the same steps as for the HTTP post, but we check for the `PDF` scope, read the `PDF.content` variable, and then dump the result of the read operation (Figure 28.14).

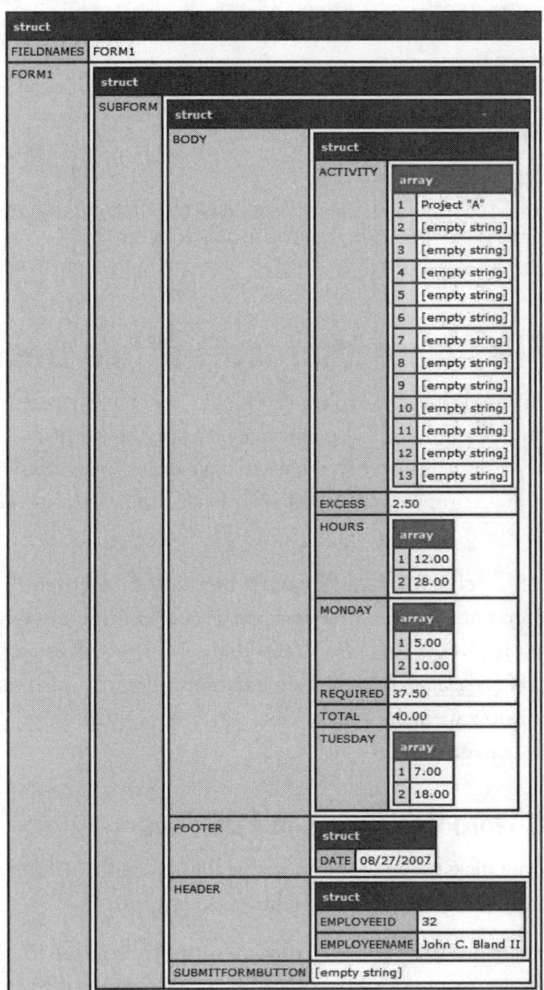

Figure 28.14
A ColdFusion dump of an HTTP post submission; several nodes are closed to save space.

As you can see, this dump doesn't follow the exact PDF form structure but is a flat hierarchy. For both submission types, multiple form fields with the same name are submitted as an array. To access the values, you use normal ColdFusion array syntax.

Both submission types ultimately result in normal ColdFusion coding to handle the results, and regardless of the submission type, you are well equipped to process the data.

Embedding PDF Forms

Using `cfdocument` (for a refresher, see Chapter 16), you can embed a PDF form into a static PDF file. Only one `cfpdfform` tag can be included in a `cfdocument` tag, and the `cfpdfform` tag should be a child of `cfdocument`, not of `cfdocumentsection` or any other `cfdocument` child node.

NOTE

The `cfdocument format` value must be `PDF`;, `flashpaper` conversion isn't possible.

```
<cfdocument format="pdf">
   <cfdocumentsection>
      PDF Form examples...
   </cfdocumentsection>

   <cfpdfform action="populate"
              source="pdfs/Adobe Derby Timesheet - PDF Post.pdf"
              xmldata="xml/PopulatingPDFs-LiveCycle.xml" />
</cfdocument>
```

Creating PDF Files from Microsoft Office Documents

At this point, you are definitely the cool kid on the block. You have learned the differences in managing and manipulating PDF files, but so far everything has been short, simple code blocks, with no real meat. There is a lot of power in what we have done so far. It all comes together in the employee management application we will build after learning how to convert Microsoft Office documents.

As seen in the first part of the chapter, ColdFusion 9 boasts solid PDF integration. It also provides PDF conversion from Microsoft Word and Microsoft PowerPoint documents. In Chapter 67, "Integrating with Microsoft Office," in *Adobe ColdFusion 9 Web Application Construction Kit, Volume 3: Advanced Application Development*, you will learn more about ColdFusion and Microsoft Office integration, but for now we will explore the conversion options and then build an application to include document conversion.

Converting Microsoft Word Documents to PDF Files

You may be expecting some massive conversion script that loads a PDF file and calls some wild, nondescript methods, but one tag and three attributes do the job.

Listing 28.39 uses the `cfdocument` tag and specifies an output file name to `pdfs/MonthlyTimesheet.pdf`. The only thing needed to convert a Microsoft Office document is to set the `srcfile` attribute to the location of the document.

Listing 28.39 `office-convert.cfm`—Converting a Microsoft Word File to PDF

```
<!--- Convert Doc file to PDF and save it --->
<cfdocument format="pdf" filename="pdfs/MonthlyTimesheet.pdf"
            srcfile="#ExpandPath('samples\MonthlyTimesheet.doc')#" />
```

Let's put what we've learned so far to work with a simple résumé manager application.

Creating the Résumé Manager Application

There is a ton of functionality we could add to this application, but we're going to focus on the use of PDF files in a ColdFusion application. This application uses a timesheet form, which flows well within the application.

Here, we'll focus on the implementation of the PDF functionality rather than the application structure (Listing 28.40).

Listing 28.40 resume-manager.cfm—Creating the Résumé File Uploads Management Application

```
<!--- Query the database for contacts --->
<cfquery name="contacts" datasource="ows">
  SELECT * FROM app.contacts
</cfquery>

<!--- Table display of current contact information --->
<table width="100%">
  <!--- Table headers --->
  <tr style="font-weight:bold;">
        <td>Resume</td>
        <td>Name</td>
        <td>Address</td>
        <td>State</td>
        <td>Zip</td>
        <td>Country</td>
        <td>Phone</td>
       </tr>
       <!--- Output contacts in table --->
  <cfoutput query="contacts">
        <!--- Determine if the current contact (row) has a saved resume --->
        <cfset hasResume = isPDFFile("pdfs/contacts/"&contactid&".pdf") />
        <tr>
          <td>
           <cfif hasResume>
            <!--- the resume exists, display links to open --->
                      <a href="pdfs/contacts/#contactid#.doc">Word</a> |
                      <a href="pdfs/contacts/#contactid#.pdf">PDF</a>
                     <cfelse>
                      <!--- the resume doesn't exist, display the upload form --->
                      <cfform name="form#contactid#" action="resume-file-upload.cfm"
                              enctype="multipart/form-data">
                        <input type="hidden" name="contact" value="#contactid#" />
                        <input type="file" name="resume" size="10" />
                             <input type="submit" value="Upload" />
                      </cfform>
                     </cfif>
               </td>
               <td><a href="mailto:#email#">#firstname# #lastname#</a></td>
               <td>#address#</td>
               <td>
                <cfif len(trim(state)) EQ 0>
        <!--- show a filler for empty states --->
```

Listing 28.40 (continued)

```
        --
                     <cfelse>
        <!--- state isn't empty, display state --->
        #state#
                     </cfif>
               </td>
               <td>#zip#</td>
               <td>#country#</td>
               <td>#phone#</td>
        </tr>
  </cfoutput>
</table>
```

Listing 28.40 creates a simple display showing the contacts from the OWS database with a separate column for either an upload form or links to the Microsoft Word and Adobe PDF documents, seen in Figure 28.15. Each line is commented so we won't examine the code line by line. Listing 28.41 shows the form processing page, which gets back to our focus: document conversion. Typically, this functionality would be separate from the HTML (view), but we're focusing on functionality, not application design, in this example.

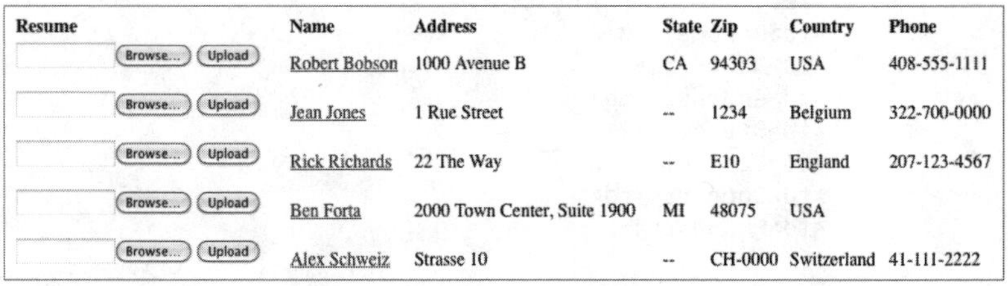

Figure 28.15

Résumé manager contact list.

Resume	Name	Address	State	Zip	Country	Phone
Browse... Upload	Robert Bobson	1000 Avenue B	CA	94303	USA	408-555-1111
Browse... Upload	Jean Jones	1 Rue Street	--	1234	Belgium	322-700-0000
Browse... Upload	Rick Richards	22 The Way	--	E10	England	207-123-4567
Browse... Upload	Ben Forta	2000 Town Center, Suite 1900	MI	48075	USA	
Browse... Upload	Alex Schweiz	Strasse 10	--	CH-0000	Switzerland	41-111-2222

Listing 28.41 `resume-file-upload.cfm`—Managing Resume File Uploads

```
<!--- Check for the form.resume property to manage uploads --->
<cfif StructKeyExists(form, "resume")>
  <!--- Save the uploaded file --->
  <cffile action="upload" nameconflict="overwrite" filefield="resume"
               accept="application/msword"
               destination="#expandPath('pdfs/contacts/')#" />
  <!--- Variables holding filename info --->
       <cfset path = cffile.ServerDirectory & "/" />
       <cfset ext = "." & cffile.ClientFileExt />
  <cfset source = path & cffile.ClientFileName & ext />
       <cfset dest = path & form.contact />
       <!--- Rename the uploaded file to a contact-specific name --->
       <cffile action="rename" source="#source#" destination="#dest##ext#" />
       <!--- Convert uploaded file to PDF and save it --->
       <cfdocument format="pdf" overwrite="yes" filename="#dest#.pdf"
                srcfile="#dest##ext#" />
       <!--- Redirect to manager --->
       <cflocation url="resume-manager.cfm" />
</cfif>

<!--- Show simple text if a file isn't uploaded (direct page load) --->
No file selected. <a href="resume-manager.cfm">&laquo; Back</a>
```

The uploaded form from Listing 28.40 submits to Listing 28.41. If the `form.resume` property exists, the uploaded Word document is saved in the `pdfs/contacts` folder and renamed with the format `{contact id}.ext`, where `.ext` is the file extension. Now all of this is normal ColdFusion code. The next line, after the file rename, converts the source file to a PDF file and saves it in the same location: `pdfs/contacts`. Once this process is complete, we simply redirect to the `resume-manager.cfm` page to display the list again.

Document conversion has lots of applications, and it's easy to implement. ColdFusion again takes a formerly difficult or tedious task and makes it a breeze!

CHAPTER 29

ColdFusion Image Processing

IN THIS CHAPTER

One often repeated request of ColdFusion developers prior to version 8 was the capability to manipulate images directly in ColdFusion. Adobe has listened to ColdFusion's developer community and has given developers, with just a few lines of code, the ability to dynamically resize images, inspect image metadata, and much more. ColdFusion lets developers remove much of the drudgery of working with images in applications and even allows developers to create new types of graphically rich applications. So without further ado, let's jump into ColdFusion's new image processing capabilities.

Introducing <cfimage>

Probably at some point, every ColdFusion developer has had to create an application or Web site that uses multiple sizes of the same image, such as in a thumbnail gallery that links to larger, high-resolution images. This scenario often requires tedious editing of images to make smaller, thumbnail sizes of the full-scale image.

ColdFusion lets you create such multiple versions simply by using the new `<CFIMAGE>` tag. Instead of walking through the incredible number of new image functions and attributes, let's first look at a few examples. For this exercise, you can use any image you want, but we will use the image of a scorpion found at Wikipedia under the GNU free license. You can find that image at `http://upload.wikimedia.org/wikipedia/commons/9/93/Black_scorpion.jpg` and also with the code samples for this book.

NOTE

Image processing and `<cfimage>` is a huge topic. With more than 18 attributes for `<cfimage>` and 50 image manipulation functions, there is just not enough space to cover every possible function and use of `<cfimage>` here. So for this chapter, we will focus on the most common and important points and suggest that you review the full power of `<cfimage>` and image processing functions at Adobe's LiveDocs site: `http://help.adobe.com/en_US/ColdFusion/9.0/CFMLRef/index.html`.

The image (and code samples) should all be saved in a chapter named 29 under your ows folder created for earlier chapters. Listing 29.1 is our first example of working with images in ColdFusion.

Listing 29.1 `resizeimage.cfm`—Image Resizing Example

```
<cfimage
    action = "resize"
    height = "25%"
    source = "#ExpandPath( './Black_scorpion.jpg' )#"
    width = "25%"
    destination = "#ExpandPath( './NewBlack_scorpion.jpg' )#"
    overwrite = "true"
    >

<table width="200" border="1">
  <tr>
    <td><img src="Black_scorpion.jpg"></td>
    <td><img src="NewBlack_scorpion.jpg"></td>
  </tr>
  <tr>
    <td><div align="center">Old Image</div></td>
    <td><div align="center">New Image</div></td>
  </tr>
</table>
```

If you run this code and look in the same directory in which you put `Black_scoprion.jpg`, you should see a new file called `NewBlack_scorpion.jpg`, and if you look at it you will see that it is 25 percent smaller than the original. You should see something like Figure 29.1 if you compare the images side by side.

Figure 29.1
Black scorpion image resized to 25 percent of its previous size.

So with one simple tag, we are able to consume an image, resize it to 25 percent of its height, and then write out the new image to the file system. If we look at the code syntax for `<cfimage>` more closely for resizing, it has this general form:

```
<cfimage
    action = "resize"
```

```
    height = "number of pixels|percent%"
    source = "absolute pathname|pathname relative to the web root|URL|#cfimage
variable#"
    width = "number of pixels|percent%"
    destination = "absolute pathname|pathname relative to the web root"
    isBase64 = "yes|no"
    name = "cfimage variable"
    overwrite = "yes|no">
```

As you can see, the attributes for the tag are pretty self-explanatory, with the four attributes `destination`, `isBase64`, `name`, and `overwrite` being optional. Several of the `<cfimage>` tag's attributes have multiple options, allowing a wide variety of uses. For example, you can get the scorpion image directly from the URL by changing the source in Listing 29.1 from

```
source = "#ExpandPath( './Black_scorpion.jpg' )#"
```

to

```
source = "http://upload.wikimedia.org/wikipedia/commons/9/93/Black_scorpion.jpg"
```

If you run the code, you will see that `<cfimage>` has retrieved the image from the Web, resized the image, and written it to the file system again. Adobe's development team has added an incredible amount of functionality, which shows in the `<cfimage>` tag's 18 attributes.

TIP

`<cfimage>` and ColdFusion image manipulation functions are mostly extensions or wrappers around Java classes and methods found in `java.awt`, `java.image`, and the Java Advanced Image API, which can be accessed directly from ColdFusion. If you run into a situation where ColdFusion cannot do something you need, you should explore ColdFusion's tight integration with Java, which is covered in Chapter 68, "Extending ColdFusion with Java," in *Adobe ColdFusion 9 Web Application Construction Kit, Volume 3: Advanced Application Development*.

Manipulating Images with `<cfimage>`

Now that you have seen those attributes, let's put them to use by creating a more involved series of examples. We'll create a simple application that will let us upload or retrieve an image from a URL, display information about that image, resize the image, and more.

Resizing an Image

We will start by making a simple Web page that will allow us to view everyone in the contacts table of the OWS database, upload images for each person, and automatically create thumbnails. Listing 29.2 contains the first part of this application.

Listing 29.2 `image_upload_example.cfm`—Image Upload Example

```
<cfset imageDirPath = ExpandPath("user_photos")>

<cfquery name="get_users" datasource="ows">
    SELECT *
    FROM Contacts
    ORDER BY lastname, firstname
```

Listing 29.2 (continued)

```
</cfquery>


<cfif isDefined("form.fileToUpload") and form.fileToUpload neq "">
    <cfset userPhotoPath = "#imageDirPath#/user_#form.contactid#.jpg">
    <cfset userThumbPath = "#imageDirPath#/user_#form.contactid#_thumb.jpg">

    <cfif not directoryExists(imageDirPath)>
       <cfdirectory action="create" directory="#imageDirPath#">
    </cfif>

    <!--- Accept the file upload --->
    <cffile
    action="upload"
    destination="#getTempDirectory()#"
    fileField="fileToUpload"
    nameConflict="overwrite">

    <!--- Get info about the photo --->
    <cfimage
    action="info"
    source="#cffile.serverDirectory#/#cffile.serverFile#"
    structName="uploadedFileInfo">

    <cfif uploadedFileInfo.width lt 100
    or uploadedFileInfo.height lt 100
    or uploadedFileInfo.width gt 1000
    or uploadedFileInfo.height gt 1000>
        <cfthrow message="Please provide an image between 100 and 1000 pixels tall
and wide.">
    </cfif>

    <!--- Convert the photo --->
    <cfimage
    action="convert"
    source="#cffile.serverDirectory#/#cffile.serverFile#"
    destination="#userPhotoPath#"
    overwrite="true">

    <!--- Resize the photo to create a thumbnail --->
    <cfimage
    action="resize"
    width="100"
    height="100"
    source="#userPhotoPath#"
    destination="#userThumbPath#"
    overwrite="true">

</cfif>

<cfinclude template="upload_form.cfm">
<cfinclude template="user_list.cfm">
```

Note the two templates included with `<cfinclude>`. The first is the form for uploading files and goes in the same place as Listing 29.2. To create the upload form, make a new file called `upload_form.cfm` as shown in Listing 29.3.

Listing 29.3 `upload_form.cfm`—Upload Form

```
<hr>
<form action="" method="post" enctype="multipart/form-data">
Provide new image for:

<!--- DROPDOWN LIST OF USERS --->
<select name="contactid">
<cfoutput query="get_users">
<option value="#contactid#">#firstname# #lastname#</option>
</cfoutput>
</select>

<!--- FILE UPLOAD UI --->
<input type="file" name="fileToUpload">

<!--- SUBMIT BUTTON --->
<button type="submit">Upload</button>
</form>
<hr>
```

Listing 29.4 will display a list of users and their associated images.

NOTE

This listing uses `default.jpg`, which can be copied from the Zip file containing all the code files.

Listing 29.4 `user_list.cfm`—User List UI

```
<cfoutput>
<table>
    <cfloop query="get_users">
    <tr>
    <td>
    <cfif fileExists(ExpandPath("user_photos") & '/user_#contactid#_thumb.jpg')>
    <a href="user_photos/user_#contactid#.jpg"><img src="user_photos/
user_#contactid#_thumb.jpg" border="0"></a>
    <cfelse>
    <img src="default.jpg" border="0">
    </cfif>
    </td>
    <td><h3>#firstname# #lastname#</h3></td>
    </tr>
</cfloop>
</table>
</cfoutput>
```

Assuming that you have placed these files in your `webroot/ows/29` directory, you should be able to see the application by going to `http://localhost/ows/29/upload_image_example.cfm`, and you should see something like Figure 29.2. By selecting a name from the resulting drop-down list, you can select a person, such as Ben Forta, and assign an image to that person.

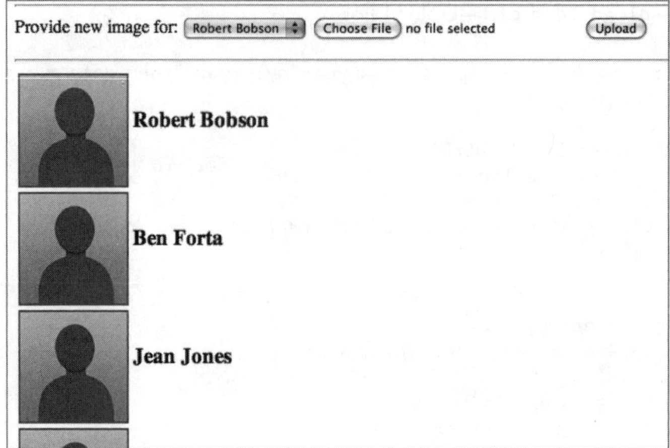

Figure 29.2

Sample output showing what you should see what you view the image management application in your browser.

When you assign an image to a person who does not yet have an image, the template first uploads the image to a specific directory and then uses the `<cfimage>` tag to get information about the image, such as its size. To get information from for an image using `<cfimage>`, use this format:

```
<cfimage
   action = "info"
   source = "absolute pathname|pathname relative to the web root|URL|#cfimage
variable#"
   structname="">
```

The `info` action lets you retrieve valuable information about an image, including the color model, height, width, and source, all written to a structure. Here, all we are interested in is the width and height, but depending on the scenario you may be interested in other information about the image.

Once you have the image information you need, you can have all images saved to your system in one format, such as the JPEG format. So the next thing you do in the code is use `<cfimage>` to convert files from other formats to JPEG by using this syntax:

```
<cfimage
   action = "convert"
   source = "absolute pathname|pathname relative to the web root|URL|#cfimage
variable#"
   destination = "absolute pathname|pathname relative to the web root"
   overwrite="true|false">
```

NOTE

There are a number of practical reasons for standardizing on one image format, from ease of support to security.

Here, you simply write

```
<cfimage
   action="convert"
   source="#cffile.serverDirectory#/#cffile.serverFile#"
   destination="#userPhotoPath#"
   overwrite="true">
```

The `<cfimage>` tag will now convert supported file formats from one format to the destination format (JPEG, GIF, TIFF, PNG, or BMP). Simply setting the destination without the `action="convert"` but being explicit improves code readability as well because some image conversions (such as conversion to a ColdFusion image variable) require that the action be set to `"convert"`. You can test your code by adding a `.gif` or other image extension to one of names in the list. When you upload the image and check the `user_photos` directory, you should see that the image has been converted to JPEG.

NOTE

Image processing in ColdFusion is usually very fast but, depending on what actions you perform and how often, image processing can impose significant overhead on your server. Some ways around this are to work with small or lower-quality images or use asynchronous processes and ColdFusion gateways to perform batch operations on your images. For more about gateways and asynchronous processes, see Chapter 70, "Working with Gateways," in Volume 3.

Adding Borders

Now that we have made sure that all our images are a certain size and are of the same type, we can finally generate the thumbnail. You have to create a simple template that allows you to add images for people in a database, validate the uploaded image information, convert the images to other image file formats, and autogenerate thumbnails of a specific size—all with only about 50 lines of code. But let's do some more. Suppose that you are now asked to add more features to the photos in the gallery, including a border for the images, the person's name on the image, and a simple watermark.

We'll start with the border. To do this, use this syntax:

```
<cfimage
   action="border"
   source="absolute pathname|pathname relative to the web root|URL|#cfimage
variable#"
   destination="absolute pathname|pathname relative to the web    root|URL|#cfimage
variable#"
   thickness="in pixels"
   color ="supported colors"
   overwrite="true">
```

To change the code to add a border, change the lines

```
<!--- Convert the photo --->
<cfimage
   action="convert"
   source="#cffile.serverDirectory#/#cffile.serverFile#"
   destination="#userPhotoPath#"
   overwrite="true">
```

to

```
<!--- Convert the photo and write it to a variable--->

<cfimage
   action="convert"
   source="#cffile.serverDirectory#/#cffile.serverFile#"
```

```
    destination="#userPhotoPath#"
    name="tempImage"
    overwrite="true">

<!--- add a black border with a thickness of 5 pixels around the image --->
<cfimage
    source="#tempImage#"
    action="border"
    thickness="5"
    color="black"
    destination="#userPhotoPath#"
    overwrite="true">
```

Now if you try uploading a new image or even the same image for Ben Forta, you should see a border generated around the image. If you look at the code, you also see that we are doing something a little different in the `<cfimage>` tag used to convert the images: We are using the tag `name` attribute, which allows us to create or store the image not as a file on the file system but as an object that is stored as a ColdFusion variable, allowing us to pass it to the next `<cfimage>` tag as the source to which the tag applies a border. The `name` attribute allows you to save most `<CFIMAGE>` operations output to a ColdFusion variable, which is useful for many purposes, such as performing operations on an image before you write the file system.

Controlling JPEG Quality and Drawing Text

The next thing we need to do is add the person's full name to each image. To do this, you will use the image manipulation function `ImageDrawText()`. This function is one of the 50 image functions now in ColdFusion. The `ImageDrawText()` function simply draws a text string on an image with X-Y coordinates, starting in the upper-right corner of the image (the Y axis is inverted from a normal Cartesian coordinate system). The `ImageDrawText()` function uses this format:

```
ImageDrawText(name, str, x, y [, attributeCollection])
```

Tables 29.1 and 29.2 list the attributes and elements of this function.

Table 29.1 `ImageDrawText` Attributes

ATTRIBUTE	DESCRIPTION
`name`	The name of the ColdFusion image that you will draw on; it is required.
`str`	The text string you wish to draw on the image; it is required.
`x`	Starting point for the string on the horizontal axis in pixels; required. The origin is the upper-left corner of the image.
`y`	Starting point for the string on the vertical axis in pixels; required. The origin is the upper-left-corner of the image.
`attributeCollection`	A structure of text attributes; optional.

Table 29.2 `ImageDrawText` Elements

ELEMENT	DESCRIPTION
`font`	Font for your text. This is an optional element, and if it is left out, ColdFusion will switch to the system default.
`size`	Font point size; optional.
`style`	Style supports bold, italic, bold italic, and plain.
`strikeThrough`	Optional element. If set to Yes, a line will be drawn through each character.
`underline`	Optional parameter. If set to Yes, will underline the drawn text.

To use `ImageDrawText()` in our code, you will need to rewrite the code as in Listing 29.5.

Listing 29.5 `image_upload_example_text.cfm`—Image Upload with Text

```
<cfset imageDirPath = ExpandPath("user_photos")>

<cfquery name="get_users" datasource="ows">
   SELECT *
   FROM Contacts
   ORDER BY lastname, firstname
</cfquery>


<cfif isDefined("form.fileToUpload") and form.fileToUpload neq "">
   <cfset userPhotoPath = "#imageDirPath#/user_#form.contactid#.jpg">
   <cfset userThumbPath = "#imageDirPath#/user_#form.contactid#_thumb.jpg">

   <cfif not directoryExists(imageDirPath)>
      <cfdirectory action="create" directory="#imageDirPath#">
   </cfif>

   <!--- Accept the file upload --->
   <cffile action="upload" destination="#getTempDirectory()#"
   fileField="fileToUpload" nameConflict="overwrite">

   <!--- Get info about the photo --->
   <cfimage action="info"
   source="#cffile.serverDirectory#/#cffile.serverFile#"
   structName="uploadedFileInfo">

   <cfif uploadedFileInfo.width lt 100 or uploadedFileInfo.height lt 100
   or uploadedFileInfo.width gt 1000
   or uploadedFileInfo.height gt 1000>
     <cfthrow
     message="Please provide an image between 100 and 1000 pixels tall and wide.">
   </cfif>

   <!--- Convert the photo and write it to a variable--->
   <cfimage action="convert"
   source="#cffile.serverDirectory#/#cffile.serverFile#"
   destination="#userPhotoPath#"
   name="tempImage" overwrite="true">
```

Listing 29.5 (continued)

```
        <!--- add a black border with a thickness of 5 pixels around the image --->
        <cfimage source="#tempImage#" action="border"
        thickness="5" color="black" destination="#userPhotoPath#"
        overwrite="true">

        <cfquery name="get_user" datasource="ows">
        SELECT *
        FROM Contacts
        Where  CONTACTID =
        <cfqueryparam cfsqltype="cf_sql_integer" value="#form.contactid#">
        </cfquery>

        <!--- Resize the photo to create a thumbnail --->
        <cfimage action="resize" width="100" height="100"
        source="#userPhotoPath#" destination="#form.contactid#_thumb.jpg"
        name="tempThumbImage" overwrite="true">


        <!---  Draw text --->
        <!--- Set the text attributes. --->
        <cfset attr = StructNew()>
        <cfset attr.underline = "yes">
        <cfset attr.size = 10>
        <cfset attr.style = "bold">
        <cfset ImageSetDrawingColor(tempThumbImage,"black")>

        <cfset ImageDrawText(tempThumbImage,
        "#trim(get_user.firstname)# #trim(get_user.lastname)#",5, 90, attr)>

        <!--- Write out image to the file system --->
        <cfimage  source="#tempThumbImage#"  action="write"
        destination="#userThumbPath#" overwrite="true">

    </cfif>

    <cfinclude template="upload_form.cfm">
    <cfinclude template="user_list.cfm">
```

As you can see in Listing 29.5, we have changed the code to add the individuals' first and last names to the thumbnail by using this code:

```
<!---  Draw text --->
<!--- Set the text attributes. --->
   <cfset attr = StructNew()>
   <cfset attr.underline = "yes">
   <cfset attr.size = 10>
   <cfset attr.style = "bold">
   <cfset ImageSetDrawingColor(tempThumbImage,"black")>

   <cfset ImageDrawText(tempThumbImage, "#trim(get_user.firstname)# #trim(get_user.
lastname)#",5, 90, attr)>
```

We first create a simple structure called `attr` to hold the attributes for the text we want to draw. We then use `ImageDrawText` to draw the text on the image, which is held in the `tempThumbImage` variable, and later in the code we use `<cfimage>` once again to write the image to the file system.

This is another good example showing why you may want to use ColdFusion variables to hold images as you apply multiple manipulations to them for writing them to their final destination.

Adding a Watermark

Now all we need to do is add a watermark to our images. For this example we are going to add a copyright image to the images. We are going to use the image `copyright.gif`, which can be found in the Zip file for the sample code for this chapter.

ColdFusion allows you to add watermarks to existing images by pasting one image on top of another using the image function `ImagePaste()`. The image that will be the watermark—in our case, `copyright.gif`—will be made transparent by using the image function `ImageSetDrawingTransparency()`.

To generate the watermark, all you need to do is add this code right after line 41 in Listing 29.5, where we use the `<cfimage>` tag to convert the images to JPEG format:

```
<!--- create a watermark from an existing image. --->
<cfimage source="copyright.gif" name="myImage2">

   <cfset ImageSetDrawingTransparency(tempImage,50)>
   <!--- Paste myImage2 on myImage at the coordinates (0,0). --->
   <cfset ImagePaste(tempImage,myImage2,0,0)>
```

As you can see, we first create a ColdFusion image from `copyright.gif`. We then use `ImageSetDrawingTransparency()` to make the image 50 percent transparent. The function simply takes a ColdFusion image and then a percent value between 1 and 100 (decimal values are okay) to define the amount of transparency. Once we have made the image transparent, we can paste the copyright image on the main image in the upper-right corner. Your results should resemble Figure 29.3.

Figure 29.3

You can use the `imageSetDrawingTransparency()` function to add copyright information to an image.

Once again, with a few lines of ColdFusion code we have accomplished something that would be difficult and complex in another programming language.

Adding a CAPTCHA Test

Our simple template now supports a large number of image functions. Now let's add some security to our simple application to make sure that Web robots don't add images to our simple user gallery.

A common problem these days on the Internet is spammers who create bots, or programs that look for Web sites where users are allowed to post comments, links, suggestions, or photos and then these scripts automatically post links to advertisements, distasteful Web sites, or images of items for sale. Often these scripts are smart enough to circumvent simple security solutions such as login names, email addresses, and other tests to confirm the user. One way to defeat these scripts is to create a Completely Automated Public Turing test to tell Computers and Humans Apart, or CAPTCHA test. One of the most common CAPTCHA tests on the Web requires the user to type the letters or characters in a distorted image. We'll add this simple CAPTCHA test to our code, so the user has to pass the test before uploading an image.

To create a CAPTCHA test, we once again use `<cfimage>`, but this time we are going to use the `action` attribute and set it to CAPTCHA. Here is the basic syntax for `<cfimage>` to create a CAPTCHA:

```
<cfimage
   action="captcha"
   fontsize="fontsize"
   text="#captchaText#"
   difficulty="difficut"
   fonts="fonts"
   width="width"
   height="height">
```

Table 29.3 lists the attributes for `<cfimage>`, assuming the CAPTCHA action.

Table 29.3 `<cfimage>` CAPTCHA Attributes

ATTRIBUTE	DESCRIPTION
`fontsize`	The font size in points.
`text`	A text string that will be used to generate the CAPTCHA characters.
`difficulty`	Set to `low`, `medium`, or `high` to govern how obfuscated the generated text in the image is.
`fonts`	Can be a list of JVM-supported fonts. You should define at least one font since the default is all supported fonts, which may result in human-unreadable CAPTCHAs.
`width`	Must be larger than the `fontSize` value times the number of characters in the text; otherwise, ColdFusion may throw an error.
`height`	Height of the CAPTCHA image.
`size`	Font point size; optional.

To use the CAPTCHA in our simple application, we need to change the UI a bit, so we are going to rewrite Listing 29.3. To get the form to look like Figure 29.4, we need to add some code to the upload form as shown in Listing 29.6, where we introduce some new UI elements as well as the CAPTCHA test.

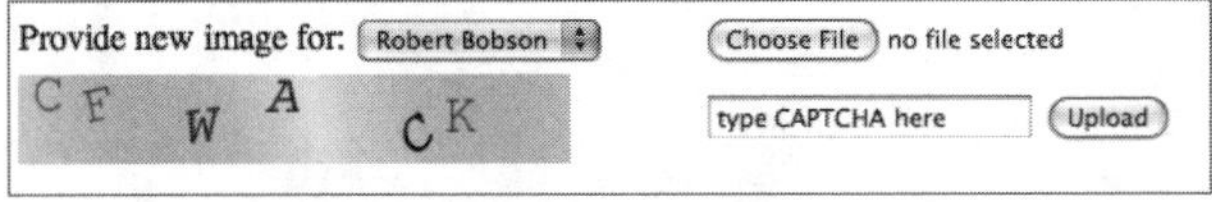

Figure 29.4
Example of the CAPTCHA output on the screen.

Listing 29.6 `upload_form2.cfm`—Upload Form

```
<hr>
<form action="" method="post" enctype="multipart/form-data">
    <table width="597" border="0">
      <tr>
        <td>Provide new image for:
          <!--- DROPDOWN LIST OF USERS --->
          <select name="contactid">
            <cfoutput query="get_users">
              <option value="#contactid#">#firstname# #lastname#</option>
            </cfoutput>
          </select></td>
        <td><input type="file" name="fileToUpload" /></td>
      </tr>
      <tr><!--- CFIMAGE being used to create a CAPTCHA image --->
        <td>
            <cfimage action="captcha" fontsize="25"
        text="#captchaText#" difficulty="low"
            fonts="Arial,Courier New,Courier"
        width="250" height="40"/>
            </td>
        <td>
          <label>
        <input name="captchaTextField" value="type CAPTCHA here" type="text"
id="captchaTextField" size="20" />
        </label>
          <!--- SUBMIT BUTTON --->
          <button type="submit">Upload</button></td>
      </tr>
    </table>

</form>
<hr>
```

We need to make some changes to the main template to add logic for the simple CAPTCHA test. You can see these changes in Listing 29.7.

Listing 29.7 `image_upload_example_captcha.cfm`—Image Upload with CAPTCHA Test

```
<cfset imageDirPath = ExpandPath("user_photos")>
<!--- This is our default captcha text--->
<!--- In real life you would want to use a random Text generator --->
```

Listing 29.7 (continued)

```
<cfset captchaText = "CFWACK"/>
<!--- Form param for the captcha entered text --->
<cfparam name="FORM.captchaTextField" default=""/>
<!--- get the list of users from the DB --->
<cfquery name="get_users" datasource="ows">
    SELECT *
    FROM Contacts
    ORDER BY lastname, firstname
</cfquery>

<cfif isDefined("form.fileToUpload") and form.fileToUpload neq "">

    <cfif not directoryExists(imageDirPath)>
        <cfdirectory action="create" directory="#imageDirPath#">
    </cfif>

    <!--- Check if the user is human --->
    <cfif captchaText eq TRIM(FORM.captchaTextField)>
        <cfset isHuman = true />
    <cfelse>
        <cfset isHuman = false/>
    </cfif>

    <!--- If the user passes as human then move on to handle the file upload --->
    <cfif isHuman eq true>

    <cfset userPhotoPath = "#imageDirPath#/user_#form.contactid#.jpg">
    <cfset userThumbPath = "#imageDirPath#/user_#form.contactid#_thumb.jpg">

    <!--- Accept the file upload --->
    <cffile action="upload" destination="#getTempDirectory()#"
    fileField="fileToUpload" nameConflict="overwrite" />

    <!--- Get info about the photo --->
    <cfimage action="info"
    source="#cffile.serverDirectory#/#cffile.serverFile#"
    structName="uploadedFileInfo">

    <cfif uploadedFileInfo.width lt 100
    or uploadedFileInfo.height lt 100
    or uploadedFileInfo.width gt 1000
    or uploadedFileInfo.height gt 1000>
     <cfthrow
     message="Please provide an image between 100 and 1000 pixels tall and wide.">
    </cfif>

    <!--- Convert the photo and write it to a variable--->
    <cfimage action="convert"
    source="#cffile.serverDirectory#/#cffile.serverFile#"
    destination="#userPhotoPath#" name="tempImage"
    overwrite="true"/>

    <!--- create a watermark from an existing image. --->
    <cfimage source="copyright.gif" name="myImage2"/>

    <cfset ImageSetDrawingTransparency(tempImage,50)>
```

Listing 29.7 (continued)

```
        <!--- Paste myImage2 on myImage at the coordinates (0,0). --->
        <cfset ImagePaste(tempImage,myImage2,0,0)>
        <!--- Write the result to a file. --->

        <!--- add a black border with a thickness of 5 pixels around the image --->
        <cfimage source="#tempImage#" action="border"
        thickness="5" color="black" destination="#userPhotoPath#"
        overwrite="true"/>

        <cfquery name="get_user" datasource="ows">
        SELECT *
        FROM Contacts
        Where  CONTACTID =
        <cfqueryparam cfsqltype="cf_sql_integer" value="#form.contactid#">
        </cfquery>

        <!--- Resize the photo to create a thumbnail --->
        <cfimage action="resize" width="100" height="100"
        source="#userPhotoPath#" destination="#form.contactid#_thumb.jpg"
        name="tempThumbImage" overwrite="true"/>

        <!---  Draw text --->
        <!--- Set the text attributes. --->
        <cfset attr = StructNew()>
        <cfset attr.underline = "yes">
        <cfset attr.size = 10>
        <cfset attr.style = "bold">
        <cfset ImageSetDrawingColor(tempThumbImage,"black")>
        <cfset ImageDrawText(tempThumbImage,
        "#trim(get_user.firstname)# #trim(get_user.lastname)#",5, 90, attr)>

        <!--- Write out image to the file system --->
        <cfimage source="#tempThumbImage#" action="write"
        destination="#userThumbPath#" overwrite="true"/>

        <cfelse>
            <!--- Refresh Page --->
            <cflocation url="#CGI.SCRIPT_NAME#" addtoken="false"/>
        </cfif>
    </cfif>

    <cfinclude template="upload_form2.cfm">
    <cfinclude template="user_list.cfm">
```

Now if you run the new code in your browser, you should have to pass the CAPTCHA test before you can upload your images.

Exploring Other ColdFusion Image Manipulation Techniques

We have explored some of the more common uses of `<cfimage>`. Now let's look at some of the other powerful image manipulation options available in `<CFIMAGE>`. For all of these examples, we will be using our Ben Forta JPEG file (available via the Zip file download from the book's Web site).

We will start by seeing how to flip or invert an image, using the code in Listing 29.8.

Listing 29.8 `flip.cfm`—Image Flip

```
<cfset filename = expandPath("benfortalarge.jpg")>

<cfimage
   action="read"
   name="myimage"
  source="#filename#">

<cfset imageFlip(myimage, "vertical")>

<cfimage
  action="writeToBrowser"
  source="#myimage#">
```

As you can see, we are introducing two new elements here. The first is the image manipulation function: `ImageFlip()`. This function uses this syntax:

```
imageFlip(name [, transpose])
```

It takes two parameters: the name of the ColdFusion image to be flipped and the transposition value, which can be vertical, horizontal, diagonal, antidiagonal, or degrees of rotation clockwise (90, 180, or 270 degrees only). If you do not select a transposition parameter, ColdFusion defaults to vertical.

The other new item you see here is the `<cfimage>` action `writeToBrowser()`. The `writeToBrowser()` element for the `action` attribute tells ColdFusion to push the image directly to the Web browser without first writing it to a variable or the file system. There are many reasons why you may want to not save an image before you display it.

Now let's try rotating an image.

Rotating is just as simple as flipping an image. It makes use of another image manipulation function, called `imageRotate()`, which has this syntax:

```
ImageRotate(name,[ x, y,] angle[, interpolation])
```

`ImageRotate()` has five attributes, listed in Table 29.4.

Table 29.4 `ImageRotate` Attributes

ATTRIBUTE	DESCRIPTION
`name`	The required ColdFusion image.
`x`	An optional parameter for the horizontal axis coordinate relative to the upper-left corner of the image. The default is the center of the image.
`y`	An optional parameter for the vertical axis coordinate relative to the upper-left corner of the image. The default is the center of the image.
`angle`	Required rotational angle in degrees.

Table 29.4 (continued)

Attribute	Description
`interpolation`	Optional interpolation type: • `nearest` This is the default method. It uses the nearest-neighbor method. Image quality is lower than with other types, but it is the fastest setting. • `bilinear` Uses the bilinear method, where image quality is less pixelated than nearest, but processing is slower. • `bicubic` Applies the bicubic method of interpolation. Generally, the quality of the image is high, but processing is slow.

NOTE

Nearest-neighbor, bilinear, and bicubic interpolation are all mathematical methods for constructing new data points from a discrete set of known points. To learn more about the interpolation techniques, view the Wolfram Mathworld articles on each method at `http://mathworld.wolfram.com/`.

To rotate the Ben Forta image, we'll use the same code as before but replace `imageFlip()` with `ImageRotate()`, like this:

```
<cfset imageRotate(myimage, "90")>
```

You can even turn the color JPEG into a grayscale image, with the `imageGrayscale()` function:

```
<cfset imageGrayscale(myimage)>
```

Or you can invert the pixel values on the image with the `ImageNegative()` function, like this:

```
<cfset imageNegative(myimage)>
```

The Zip file contains examples of all of the preceding functions. You can use some of the 50 other image manipulation functions to blur, transpose, and sharpen the image, and more. `<CFIMAGE>` and ColdFusion's associated image processing functions are too numerous and varied to cover in depth in this chapter, but by this time you should have a strong understanding of how `<CFIMAGE>` and image functions work. Almost any image manipulation or action you want to perform can be done in ColdFusion. All that is left now is for you to imagine and create.

Creating and Drawing Images with ColdFusion

So far, we have looked at methods and ways you can manipulate images in ColdFusion, but with ColdFusion you can actually create images from scratch and even draw your own images. Among the image processing functions, ColdFusion has a number of basic drawing functions that allow you to draw basic lines, arcs, and shapes. For example, to create the drawing in Figure 29.5, you first draw a rectangle and then rotate it some number of times, as in Listing 29.9.

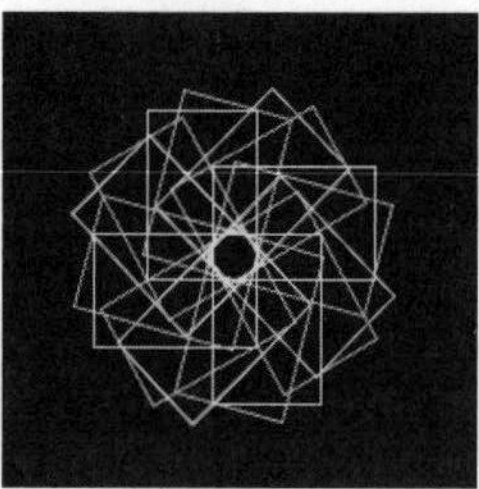

Figure 29.5

Geometric flower created by rotating the axis on which the square is drawn.

Listing 29.9 `flower.cfm`—Flower Image

```
<!--- Create a 400x400-pixel image. --->
<cfset myImage=imageNew("",400,400)>

<cfset imageSetDrawingColor(myImage,"yellow")>

<!--- Turn on antialiasing to improve image quality. --->
<cfset imageSetAntialiasing(myImage)/>

<!--- Translate the origin to (100,100). --->
<cfset imageTranslateDrawingAxis(myImage,200,200)/>

<!--- draw a rectangle and keep rotating the axis to make flower --->
<cfset i = 15/>
<cfloop condition="i LESS THAN OR EQUAL TO 360">
    <cfset imageRotateDrawingAxis(myImage,i,10,10)>
    <cfset i += 15/>
    <!--- Draw a rectangle at the offset location. --->
    <cfset imageDrawRect(myImage,0,0,50,75)>
</cfloop>

<!--- Display the image in a browser. --->
<cfimage source="#myImage#" action="writeToBrowser">
```

In Listing 29.9, the first thing you will notice is the use of the function `imageNew()`, which has this syntax:

```
imageNew([source, width, height, imageType, canvasColor])
```

Table 29.5 explains its attributes.

Table 29.5 `ImageNew` Attributes

ATTRIBUTE	DESCRIPTION
`source`	Valid ColdFusion image source; optional.
`width`	Width of the image in pixels; valid only when source is not defined.
`height`	Height of image in pixels; valid only when source is not defined.
`imageType`	Type of ColdFusion image to create, which can be `rgb`, `argb`, or `grayscale`. You can use this attribute only when `source` is not specified.

Table 29.5 (continued)

ATTRIBUTE	DESCRIPTION
canvasColor	Optional; color value of the image canvas: • Hexadecimal value of RGB color. • String value of color; default is "black". • List of three numbers for R, G, and B values. Each value must be in the range 0–255.

Next we will use the imageSetDrawingColor() function, which has this syntax:

```
imageSetDrawingColor(name, color)
```

The name attribute is simply a valid ColdFusion image, and color is a valid ColdFusion color, such as yellow or ##FFFFFF. This function sets the color of our drawing.

We can then use the function imageSetAntialising() to make the generated image look smoother and less blocky. It has this syntax:

```
imageSetAntialiasing(name [, antialias])
```

Here, name is a ColdFusion image, and antialias is Yes or No.

The next function we will use is imageTranslateDrawingAxis(), which has this syntax:

```
imageTranslateDrawingAxis(name, x, y)
```

It takes three parameters: name, which identifies your ColdFusion image, and X and Y coordinates to reset the origin point. In Listing 29.9, we set the origin to **200,200**, which is the center of the new image on which we plan to draw.

Next we'll use a conditional loop, where we increment by 15 degrees until we have traveled 360 degrees, and for each increment we will rotate the axis also by 15 degrees, using imageRotate DrawingAxis(), which has this syntax:

```
imageRotateDrawingAxis(name, angle [, x, y])
```

Here, name identifies a valid ColdFusion image, and angle is an angle in degrees; an optional set of X-Y coordinates allows you to further offset the drawing axis. For this example, we will offset the axis 10 pixels on both the X and Y axes, which will create the illusion of an open center in the drawing.

Finally, we will draw a rectangle using the function imageDrawRect(), which has this syntax:

```
imageDrawRect(name, x, y, width, height [, fill])
```

imageDrawRect() has six parameters: name is a ColdFusion image, x and y are coordinates to start drawing from, width is the width in pixels, height is the height in pixels, and fill is an optional parameter that, if set to Yes, will fill the rectangle with the color we set earlier.

As you can see, it is pretty easy to programmatically create drawings using shapes. You can create similar programmatic drawings using `imageDrawLine()`, which has this syntax:

```
imageDrawLine(name, x1, y1, x2, y2)
```

The parameters are `name`, which identifies a valid ColdFusion image, and then two sets of X and Y coordinates, which the line will be drawn between. You can programmatically draw lines just as you can shapes. For an example, look at Listing 29.10.

Listing 29.10 `drawlines.cfm`—Draw Lines

```
<!--- Create the image variable --->
<cfset myImage = imageNew("",400,300) />
<!--- Set the drawing color to yellow. --->
<cfset imageSetDrawingColor(myImage,"yellow") />
<!--- Turn on antialiasing to improve image quality. --->
<cfset imageSetAntialiasing(myImage,"on") />
<cfset i=10>
<cfloop condition="i LESS THAN OR EQUAL TO 300">
   <cfset i += 10>
   <cfset x1 = 300-i>
   <cfset x2 = 290>
   <cfset y1 = 290>
   <cfset y2 = i>
   <cfset imageDrawLine(myImage, x1, y1, x2, y2)>

</cfloop>
<!--- Draw the text --->
<cfset stAtrCollection = structNew() />
<cfset stAtrCollection.size = 25 />
<cfset stAtrCollection.style = "bold" />
<cfset imageDrawText(myImage,"Cool Line Drawing",20,20,stAtrCollection) />
<!--- Display the image in a browser. --->
<cfimage action="writeToBrowser" source="#myImage#" />
```

In this example, we again loop over some simple code, which draws a series of lines that creates an image as in Figure 29.6.

Figure 29.6

Using the ColdFusion `imageDrawLine()` function to create a simple mesh surface.

Drawing and creating images in ColdFusion is straightforward and simple, but we have hardly scratched the surface. ColdFusion functions also support various forms of arcs, curves, circles, and other drawing controls. Using these along with ColdFusion's other image processing functions, you should be able to fulfill your custom imagery needs.

In Summary

Image processing in ColdFusion is a deep topic. For almost any need you can think up, from drawing and creating images programmatically to rotating, resizing, copying, converting, and more, ColdFusion has a function. In this chapter, you saw how simple it is to create a photo gallery that automatically resizes and converts images while simultaneously adding borders, watermarks, and text to them. You also learned how to create your own images and draw shapes and lines programmatically.

By exposing and simplifying the underlying Java image processing classes and methods, the ColdFusion team has allowed ColdFusion developers to perform, in a single line, operations that can be very difficult in plain Java.

CHAPTER 30

Advanced ColdFusion-Powered Ajax

IN THIS CHAPTER

This chapter continues the discussion of Asynchronous JavaScript and XML—Ajax—begun in Chapter 15, "Beyond HTML Forms: ColdFusion-Powered Ajax," in *Abode ColdFusion 9 Web Application Construction Kit Volume 1: Getting Started*. In the previous chapter, you learned the basics of working with Ajax and ColdFusion. In this chapter, we will go deeper and discuss Ajax-based layout controls, more binding options, JavaScript, and security options for your ColdFusion-based Ajax Web sites.

Ajax-Based Layout Controls

ColdFusion has many layout controls that can greatly enhance the look of your application. Some controls help lay out your page, whereas others act as widgets or containers for other content. Let's start with the `cflayout` and `cflayoutarea` tags.

As you can probably guess, the `cflayout` tag is concerned with layout. It will allow you to define a layout for a Web page. This layout can contain a left-hand panel, or a top panel, or both, or maybe even a bottom and right panel as well. It can also be used to create tabbed containers, a very handy way to split up complex forms into simpler sections. The type of layout used is based on the `type` attribute. The `cflayout` tag allows you to set up four different types of layouts.

There are certain restrictions on what can be placed inside a `cflayout` tag. In general, within `<cflayout>` tags you can use only non-output-generating tags. This includes the `cflayoutarea` tag we will introduce shortly as well as tags like `cfloop`. You will put your HTML and other output inside `cflayoutarea` tags. Let's look at a simple example. Listing 30.1 demonstrates a border layout with a left-hand panel.

Listing 30.1 `layout1.cfm`—Basic Layout

```
<!---
Name:        layout1.cfm
Author:      Raymond Camden (ray@camdenfamily.com)
Description: Basic layout
```

Listing 30.1 (continued)

```
--->

<cflayout type="border">

    <cflayoutarea position="left" size="250">
    <p>
    Menu 1
    </p>
    <p>
    Menu 2
    </p>
    <p>
    Menu 3
    </p>
    </cflayoutarea>

    <cflayoutarea position="center">
    <p>
    This is the main body of the page.
    </p>
    </cflayoutarea>

</cflayout>
```

Listing 30.1 begins and ends with a `cflayout` tag using `type="border"`. Inside are two `cflayoutarea` tags. The `cflayoutarea` tag is used to define an area within the `cflayout`. For border layouts, it defines a positioned panel. For the first tag, we set a position of left. This sets the content in the left side of the page. A width of 250 is set for this area. The next area has a center position. Notice that no width is set. This will let the area expand as big as the browser will allow it. Figure 30.1 shows the result.

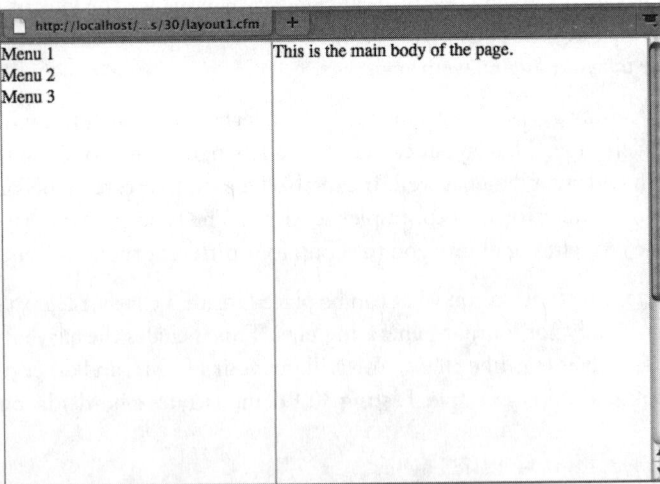

Figure 30.1
Simple `cflayout` example.

The bordered cflayout layout can have five different sections: left, right, top, bottom, and center. Which you use is up to you and your particular design needs. Listing 30.2 demonstrates a layout with all five in use.

Listing 30.2 layout2.cfm—All Layout Positions

```
<!---
Name:        layout2.cfm
Author:      Raymond Camden (ray@camdenfamily.com)
Description: Basic layout
--->

<cflayout type="border">

    <cflayoutarea position="left">
    <p>
    LEFT
    </p>
    </cflayoutarea>

    <cflayoutarea position="right">
    <p>
    RIGHT
    </p>
    </cflayoutarea>

    <cflayoutarea position="top">
    <p>
    TOP
    </p>
    </cflayoutarea>

    <cflayoutarea position="bottom">
    <p>
    BOTTOM
    </p>
    </cflayoutarea>

    <cflayoutarea position="center">
    <p>
    CENTER
    </p>
    </cflayoutarea>

</cflayout>
```

Listing 30.2 isn't much different from 30.1. This time, however, all five positions of the cflayoutarea tag are used. Within each cflayoutarea tag the name of the position is printed. Figure 30.2 shows how this lays out in the browser. So far we've used the layout tags simply to position and partition areas of the page. You can also add interactivity to these partitions. Each area, except the center area, can be allowed to resize, collapse, or even go away.

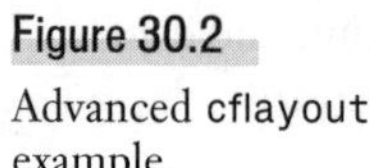

Figure 30.2

Advanced cflayout example.

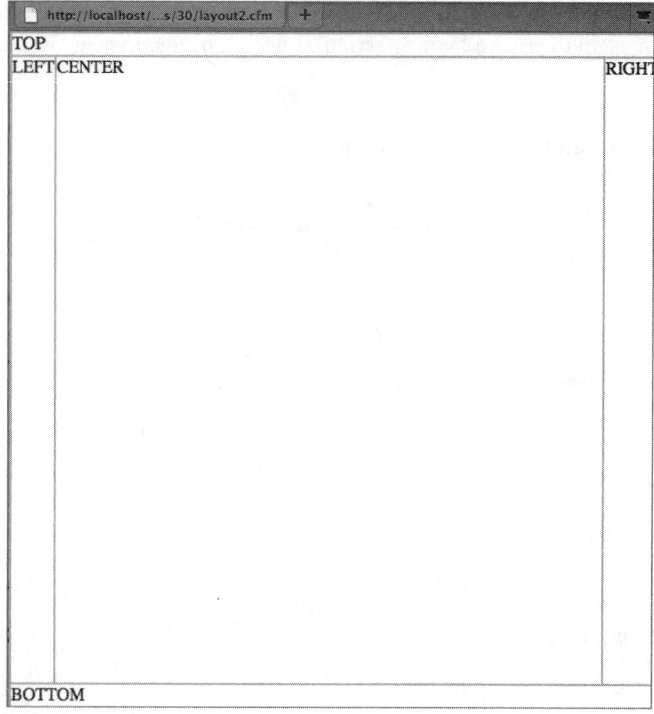

Listing 30.3 demonstrates some of these attributes in action.

Listing 30.3 layout3.cfm—<cflayoutarea> Options

```
<!---
Name:        layout3.cfm
Author:      Raymond Camden (ray@camdenfamily.com)
Description: Basic layout
--->

<cflayout type="border">

    <cflayoutarea position="left" align="center"
            size="400" collapsible="true" title="Menu">
    <p>
    Menu 1
    </p>
    <p>
    Menu 2
    </p>
    <p>
    Menu 3
    </p>
    </cflayoutarea>

    <cflayoutarea position="right" collapsible="true">
    <p>
```

Listing 30.3 (continued)

```
        This area can be collapsed.
        </p>
        </cflayoutarea>

        <cflayoutarea position="top" size="100"
                      splitter="true" minsize="50">
        <p>
        This area can be resized, but has a minsize of 50
        </p>
        </cflayoutarea>

        <cflayoutarea position="center">
        <p>
        CENTER
        </p>
        </cflayoutarea>

    </cflayout>
```

This example has a lot going on, so let's cover it area by area. The left area is now collapsible and has a title of "Menu." The right area is also set to be collapsible. The top area can be resized with the splitter, but a minimum size was set to ensure it doesn't get too small. Figure 30.3 shows the result of this page.

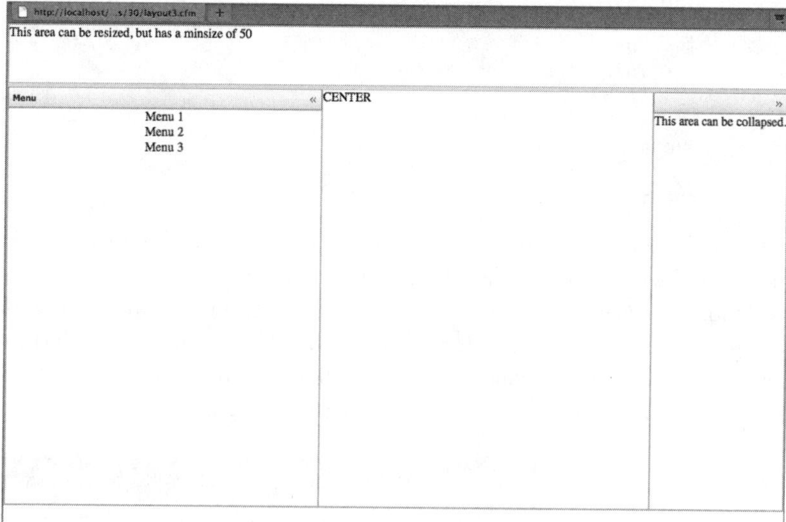

Figure 30.3

A cflayout example with different options.

Working with Tabs

One basic usability tip is to not overwhelm your user with too much text. A page full of text or form controls is sure to cause the user to either give up halfway in frustration or to simply leave your site. Tabs are a way to exert some control over this problem. Imagine the fairly standard checkout process. Normally this is a multi-page process asking the user for shipping, billing, and credit card information. Instead of forcing the user to work through three pages of forms, tabs could be employed to provide the information in a nicely segmented, easy-to-work with manner. Listing 30.4 demonstrates a simple tabbed example.

Listing 30.4 `tab1.cfm`—Tab Layout

```
<!---
Name:        tab1.cfm
Author:      Raymond Camden (ray@camdenfamily.com)
Description: Basic tabs
--->

<cflayout type="tab" tabheight="200">

    <cflayoutarea title="Tab One">
    <p>
    This is the first tab.
    </>
    <form>
    Name: <input type="text" name="name"><br />
    Email: <input type="text" name="email"><br />
    <input type="submit">
    </form>
    </cflayoutarea>

    <cflayoutarea title="Tab Two">
        <cfloop index="x" from="1" to="10">
        <p>
        This is the second tab.
        </p>
        </cfloop>
    </cflayoutarea>

</cflayout>
```

As with the earlier examples, we begin by wrapping our content with the `cflayout` tag. This time, however, the type is set to `tab`. When using this type, each `cflayoutarea` tag pair inside represents one tab. The `cflayout` tag allows for a `tabheight` attribute when you're working with tabs. As you can guess, this sets the height for the total tabbed area. The first tab has a simple paragraph of text and a basic form. The second tab contains 10 paragraphs of text generated by a simple `cfloop` tag. Figure 30.4 shows this layout with the first tab selected.

Figure 30.4

Tab-based layout.

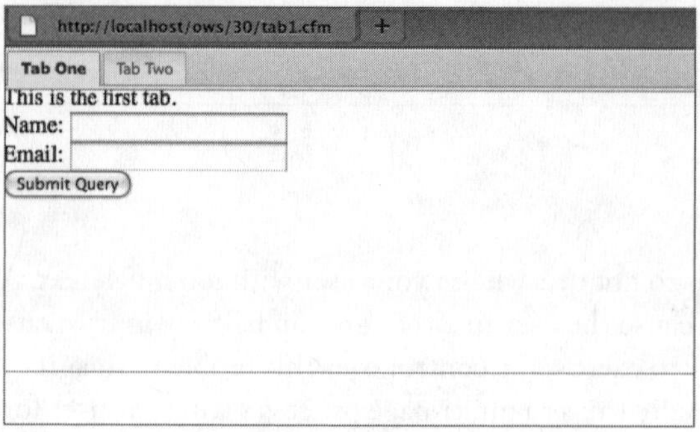

Pay particular attention to the content in the second tab. Note that while the content was bigger than the tab, ColdFusion automatically placed a scrollbar for the content. This behavior can be controlled with the `overflow` attribute. Valid values are `auto` (show scrollbars when needed), `hidden` (the additional content will not be visible), `scroll` (always show scrollbars), and `visible` (content will leak outside the layout area).

As with the border type, the tabs have options that let you add interactivity and other default behavior. Listing 30.5 demonstrates tabs with various options applied to them.

Listing 30.5 `tabs2.cfm`—Tab Layout with Optional Settings

```
<!---
Name:        tab2.cfm
Author:      Raymond Camden (ray@camdenfamily.com)
Description: Basic tabs
--->

<cflayout type="tab" tabheight="200">

    <cflayoutarea title="Tab One">
    <p>
    This is the first tab.
    </>
    <form>
    Name: <input type="text" name="name"><br />
    Email: <input type="text" name="email"><br />
    <input type="submit">
    </form>
    </cflayoutarea>

    <cflayoutarea title="Tab Two" selected="true">
        <cfloop index="x" from="1" to="10">
        <p>
        This is the second tab.
        </p>
        </cfloop>
    </cflayoutarea>

    <cflayoutarea title="Tab Three" disabled="true">
        <p>
        This tab content won't be shown.
        </p>
    </cflayoutarea>

</cflayout>
```

This listing is just slightly more advanced than the previous one. First we set the second tab as selected. The next change is the addition of a third tab. This one is disabled, though, and cannot be selected by the user. (You will see that this can be changed via the JavaScript API later in the chapter.)

Working with Accordions

The accordion panel is very similar to the tab layouts described previously. In fact, switching from a tab-based layout to an accordion-based layout is simple: just change the `<cflayout>` type attribute from tag to accordion. Listing 30.6 is a modified version of tab1.cfm. The type has been changed (along with some of the text). The tabheight attribute was removed since it isn't valid for accordion layouts.

Listing 30.6 accordion1.cfm—Accordion Example

```
<!---
Name:        accordion1.cfm
Author:      Raymond Camden (ray@camdenfamily.com)
Description: Basic accordion
--->

<cflayout type="accordion">

  <cflayoutarea title="Panel One">
  <p>
  This is the first panel.
  </>
  <form>
  Name: <input type="text" name="name"><br />
  Email: <input type="text" name="email"><br />
  <input type="submit">
  </form>
  </cflayoutarea>

  <cflayoutarea title="Panel Two">
    <cfloop index="x" from="1" to="10">
    <p>
    This is the second panel.
    </p>
    </cfloop>
  </cflayoutarea>

</cflayout>
```

Pretty simple, right? Figure 30.5 shows how the accordion panel will be rendered.

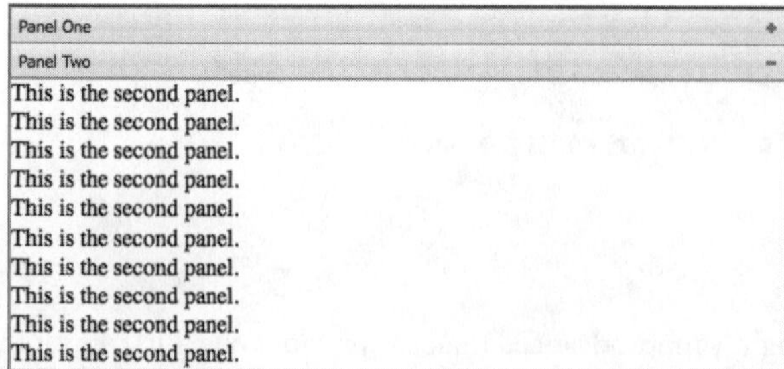

Figure 30.5
Accordion panel.

Working with Pods

We've covered border and tabbed layouts; now it is time to work with basic containers or widgets. The next set of controls are used to hold simple "blocks" of information. The simplest of these tags is the <cfpod> tag. The <cfpod> tag creates a small block on a Web page. This block may have an optional title as well. Listing 30.7 demonstrates a simple pod.

Listing 30.7 pod1.cfm—Simple Pod

```
<!---
Name:        pod1.cfm
Author:      Raymond Camden (ray@camdenfamily.com)
Description: Basic pod
--->

<cfpod title="Pods rule the world..." width="300"
       height="200">
<p>
This is the content of the pod. Groovy content
will go in here.
</p>
</cfpod>
```

As you can see, this is a fairly simple code listing. The cfpod tag wraps the content and a title, width, and height are provided to customize the pod. Figure 30.6 shows how the pod renders in the browser.

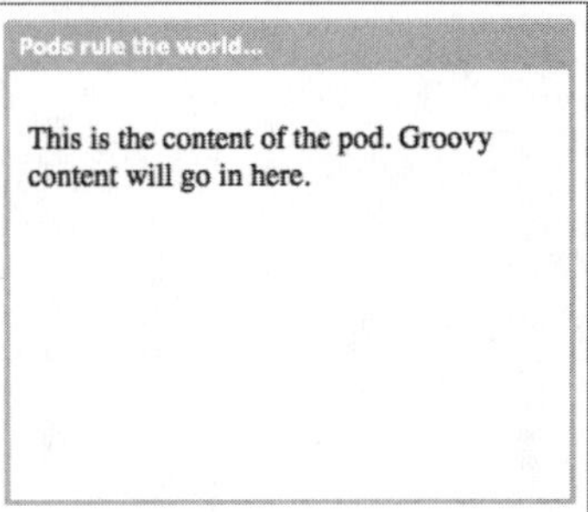

Figure 30.6
A simple pod.

Working with Windows

No, we don't mean the Windows from Redmond, nor do we mean pop-up windows. The next control we will discuss is the <cfwindow> tag. This creates a UI element that looks like a new window, but is instead generated within the same main browser window. Like "real" pop-up windows, the window can be position, moved, resized, or even set as modal so that the user must interact with the window instead of the content beneath. Windows created by the <cfwindow> tag have many options, just like the tabs and border layouts.

Now let's look at a simple example of <cfwindow> in action. Listing 30.8 demonstrates <cfwindow>.

Listing 30.8 window1.cfm—Simple Window

```
<!---
Name:        window1.cfm
Author:      Raymond Camden (ray@camdenfamily.com)
```

Listing 30.8 (continued)

```
Description: Basic window
--->

<p>
This is content on the main page.
</p>

<cfwindow title="Logon Window" center="true" width="300"
          height="300" modal="true" initShow="true">
<p>
This is the content inside the window.
</p>
</cfwindow>
```

In the previous listing a window is created using the `<cfwindow>` tag. The height and width are set to 300 each and the window is centered and set as modal. Remember that "modal" simply means it will be on top of any other content on the rest of the page. The last attribute, `initShow="true"`, forces the window to show up when the page is displayed. Figure 30.7 shows the browser with the window displayed.

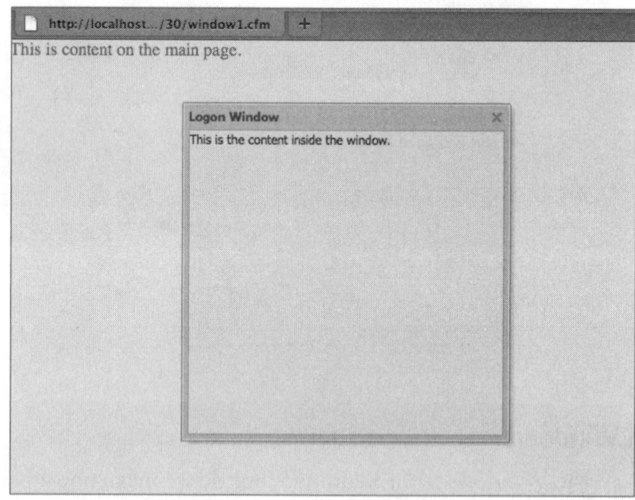

Figure 30.7

A `<cfwindow>` display. Notice how the rest of the page is dimmed due to the modal mode.

Normally you will not display a window immediately with the rest of the page. This is where the JavaScript API comes in. Commands to show, hide, and create windows will be discussed later in the chapter.

Working with Menus

All of the previous tags have dealt with layout or "containers," items that contain other bits of HTML. Now we will discuss a few tags that simply generate a display of some sort. The first will be the `<cfmenu>` tag. As you can probably guess, the `<cfmenu>` tag creates dynamic, expandable menus, a feature that is pretty common on most sites. The tag supports both vertical and horizontal menus and allows for any level of nesting. (But for your user's sake, I wouldn't go more than two or three levels deep.) The `<cfmenu>` tag creates the menu as a whole, but the pieces of the menu (the labels and URLs) are made with the `<cfmenuitem>` tag. The `<cfmenuitem>` tag also allows for dividers to help visually separate different sections of a menu. Let's take a look at a simple example in Listing 30.9.

Listing 30.9 `menu1.cfm`—Horizontal Menu

```
<!---
Name:        menu1.cfm
Author:      Raymond Camden (ray@camdenfamily.com)
Description: Horizontal menu
--->

<cfmenu type="horizontal" bgcolor="##b6fa5d">
    <cfmenuitem display="Adobe"
                href="http://www.adobe.com" />
    <cfmenuitem display="Microsoft"
                href="http://www.microsoft.com" />
    <cfmenuitem display="CNN"
                href="http://www.cnn.com" />
    <cfmenuitem display="Raymond Camden's Blog"
                href="http://www.coldfusionjedi.com" />
</cfmenu>
```

Listing 30.9 begins by defining a horizontal menu. We also set a lovely puke green background color for the menu. (Most of the Ajax controls discussed already have numerous styling options that will be discussed later.) Inside of the menu are four `cfmenuitem` child tags. Each tag defines a display (what you see in the browser) and an `<href>` tag. Note that each `cfmenuitem` tag is self closed (that's the `/` at the end). This isn't done for stylistic reasons but out of necessity. Every `cfmenuitem` must have a closing tag as well. This all comes together to create the display in Figure 30.8.

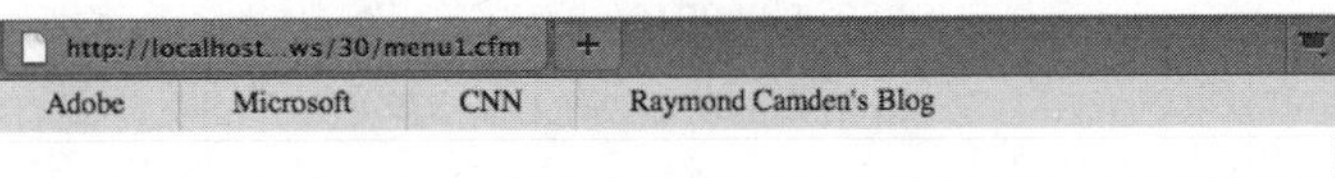

Figure 30.8
Menu with four items.

Most menus wont be a simple list of links but rather a complex set of sections and subsections. To create submenus, all you need to do is nest `cfmenuitem` tags under existing `cfmenuitem` tags. Listing 30.10 demonstrates a more realistic menu.

Listing 30.10 `menu2.cfm`—Advanced Horizontal Menu

```
<!---
Name:        menu2.cfm
Author:      Raymond Camden (ray@camdenfamily.com)
Description: Horizontal menu
--->

<cfmenu type="horizontal" bgcolor="##fffba0"
        selectedItemColor="##e7d844">

    <cfmenuitem display="Products">
        <cfmenuitem display="Books"
```

Listing 30.10 (continued)

```
                href="products/books.cfm" />
        <cfmenuitem display="Music"
                href="products/music.cfm" />
        <cfmenuitem display="Movies"
                href="products/movies.cfm" />
        <cfmenuitem display="Video Games"
                href="products/vidgames.cfm" />
        <cfmenuitem display="Weapons of Mass Destruction"
                href="products/womd.cfm" />
    </cfmenuitem>

    <cfmenuitem display="Services">
        <cfmenuitem display="Car Washing"
                href="services/car.cfm" />
        <cfmenuitem display="Car Tuning"
                href="services/tuneup.cfm" />
        <cfmenuitem display="Starship Construction"
                href="services/starship.cfm" />
    </cfmenuitem>

    <cfmenuitem display="Our People">
        <cfmenuitem display="Entertainment">
            <cfmenuitem display="Abba Jones"
                    href="people/aj.cfm" />
            <cfmenuitem display="Jacob Camden"
                    href="people/jc.cfm" />
        </cfmenuitem>

        <cfmenuitem divider />

        <cfmenuitem display="Finances">
            <cfmenuitem display="Jeanne Camden"
                    href="people/jc2.cfm" />
            <cfmenuitem display="Charlie Griefer"
                    href="people/sd.cfm" />
        </cfmenuitem>

        <cfmenuitem divider />

        <cfmenuitem display="Security">
            <cfmenuitem display="Alfonse Albertorinia"
                    href="people/aa.cfm" />
            <cfmenuitem display="Lynn Camden"
                    href="people/lc.cfm" />
            <cfmenuitem display="Noah Camden"
                    href="people/nc.cfm" />
        </cfmenuitem>
    </cfmenuitem>
</cfmenu>
```

This menu is significantly bigger than the previous example, but it will help if you approach the code from an outwards-in direction. Remember that menus must be wrapped in the `cfmenu` tag, so the outer portion of the file contains a beginning and end `cfmenu` tag. Inside are three sections of `cfmenuitem` tag pairs. They are named Products, Services, and Our People. Notice that these items do not have an `<href>` tag. They simply serve as section titles. Inside Products and Services are a simple set of `cfmenuitem` tags. Our People is more complex, though. It has sections: Entertainment, Finances, and Security. To help differentiate these sections, the `cfmenuitem` divider tag is used. This simply lays down a divider between menu items. Note that none of the URLs used in this listing actually work. Figure 30.9 shows this menu in action.

Figure 30.9

Menu with multiple sections and children.

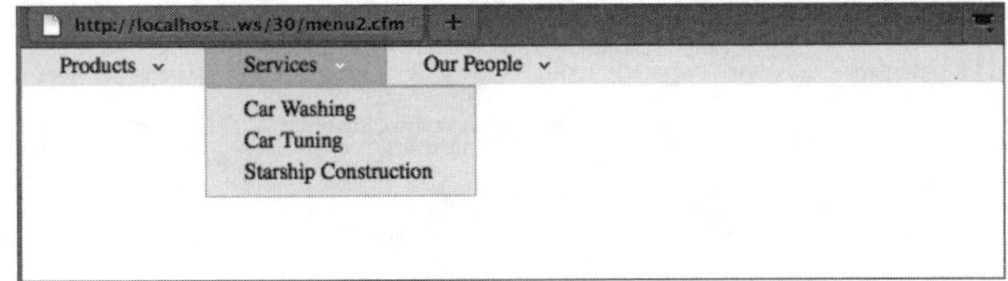

Adding Tooltips

You may not know it by the name *tooltip*, but many applications use tooltips and you probably encounter them within most applications. A tooltip is a piece of text that appears if you pause your mouse over a particular item on the application. They are most often used for graphical items. So a trash can icon may pop up text that says "Remove Delete Items" if you hover your mouse over it. ColdFusion adds the ability to add tooltips with the `<cftooltip>` tag. You can create a simple tooltip by just wrapping a piece of content (text, graphic, form element, anything) and supplying the text attribute. Listing 30.11 demonstrates this.

Listing 30.11 `tooltip1.cfm`—Tooltips in Action

```
<!---
Name:        tooltip1.cfm
Author:      Raymond Camden (ray@camdenfamily.com)
Description: Basic tooltip
--->

<form>

<cftooltip tooltip="This will delete the record forever!">
<input type="button" value="delete">
</cftooltip>

<cfsavecontent variable="archivetext">
This will archive the data so that it can be<br />
restored later. This will <b>not</b> delete<br />
the record.
</cfsavecontent>

<cftooltip tooltip="#archivetext#">
<input type="button" value="archive">
</cftooltip>

</form>
```

In Listing 30.11, a simple form with two buttons has tooltips applied to them. The first tooltip is provided in line with the tag. The second tooltip's text is created within a pair of `cfsavecontent` tags. Either method is fine, but the second tooltip has additional text and HTML, creating the text outside of the `<cftooltip>` tag makes it easier to read. Also notice that HTML is just fine and dandy in a tooltip. You can even include images! Figure 30.10 demonstrates the tooltips in action.

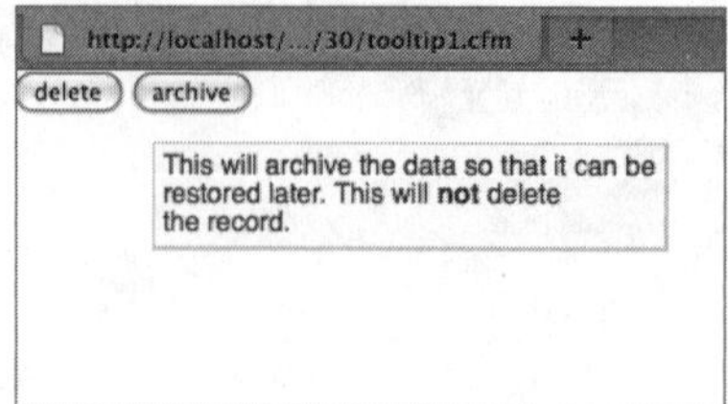

Figure 30.10
The `<cftooltip>` tag makes it easy to add helpful text to your Web applications.

The `<cftooltip>` tag gives you control over how quickly the tooltip appears, disappears, and when it goes away on its own. You can also specify an external URL for the tooltip using the `sourceForToolTip` attribute.

Working with Trees

Yet another widget ColdFusion provides out of the box is the tree. Trees are UI interfaces based on "nodes" (branches) that can be opened to reveal more nodes (leaves) underneath. Previous version of ColdFusion had a Java applet and Flash form of the tree, but ColdFusion now has a completely HTML form of the control. The tree itself can be populated directly or via Ajax-style calls to the server. This section will discuss static trees and later in the chapter we will cover dynamically loading data for all of ColdFusion's Ajax-based controls.

To build a ColdFusion HTML tree, you will work with the `<cftree>` and `<cftreeitem>` tags. Listing 30.12 demonstrates a simple, hard-coded static HTML tree.

Listing 30.12 `tree1.cfm`—HTML-Based Tree

```
<!---
Name:        tree1.cfm
Author:      Raymond Camden (ray@camdenfamily.com)
Description: Basic tree
--->

<cfform name="main">
<cftree format="html" name="mytree">
    <cftreeitem display="Products" value="products"
                expand="false">
        <cftreeitem display="ColdFusion" value="cf"
                    parent="products" >
        <cftreeitem display="Dreamweaver" value="dw"
                    parent="products" >
        <cftreeitem display="Flash" value="flash"
                    parent="products" >
```

Listing 30.12 (continued)

```
        <cftreeitem display="Other" value="other"
                    expand="false">
        <cftreeitem display="Alpha" value="alpha"
                    parent="other" >
</cftree>

</cfform>
```

First and foremost, the `<cftree>` tag is a part of the overall `<cfform>` framework. Therefore the listing begins and ends with `<cfform>` tags. The `<cftree>` tag uses a format value of `HTML` and a name of `mytree`. Six `<cftreeitem>` tags are stored inside the `<cftree>` pair. Each item has a label (display) and a value. Some of the tags, though, specify parents. This places the items under parent nodes (think branches) so that they can be expanded and collapsed. Figure 30.11 demonstrates how this tree renders in the browser.

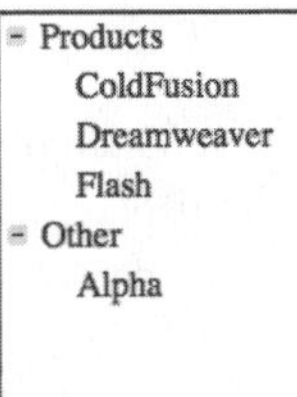

Figure 30.11

A simple `<cftree>` tag adds a dynamic tree control to a form.

As stated above, later in the chapter we will discuss how to tie the values of the tree to CFCs and other server-side data.

Working with Message Boxes

ColdFusion 9 adds many new UI widgets, including the message box. The message box acts much like a JavaScript confirmation and prompt window in that it creates a widget that includes a message and allows the user to accept or cancel an option. As with the JavaScript prompt widget, you can also ask the user to enter specific information. Full details of the arguments available for this tag are beyond the scope of this book, but note that the message box is very customizable. You can specify which buttons to show, what text to use, positioning values, and other formatting options. Listing 30.13 presents an example of the three types of message boxes: for alerts, confirmations, and prompts.

Listing 30.13 `messagebox.cfm`—Message Box Examples

```
<!---
Name:        messagebox.cfm
Author:      Raymond Camden (ray@camdenfamily.com)
Description: Basic messagebox examples.
--->

<cfmessagebox name="mb1" type="alert" title="Danger!"
message="This operation will result in the end of the world!">
```

Listing 30.13 (continued)

```
<cfmessagebox name="mb2" type="confirm" title="Are you sure?"
message="This requires smarts - and - um - not too sure about you.">

<cfmessagebox name="mb3" type="prompt" title="Desired Username"
message="Enter your desired username." callbackhandler="getPrompt">

<input type="button" onclick="ColdFusion.MessageBox.show('mb1')"
       value="Show Alert"><br/>
<input type="button" onclick="ColdFusion.MessageBox.show('mb2')"
       value="Show Confirm"><br/>
<input type="button" onclick="ColdFusion.MessageBox.show('mb3')"
       value="Show Prompt">

<script>
var getPrompt = function(btn,message){
alert("You entered: "+message);
}
</script>
```

The template begins with the three separate `<cfmessagebox>` tags. Much like the `<cfwindow>` tag, each of these tags simply creates the UI item but doesn't actually display the item. We've added three buttons so that we can use the ColdFusion JavaScript functions to display the message boxes. The third message box supports a call to a callback handler. This is a fancy way of saying, "After the user clicks the button, run this function." We can put whatever we want in the handler, but for now we simply get the value from the prompt. Figure 30.12 shows the prompt message box in action.

Figure 30.12 The prompt message box.

Handling Multiple File Uploads

One of the new UI controls added in ColdFusion 9 is the multiple-file uploader. This control is created with the `<cffileupload>` tag. It creates a simple Flash-based list in which users can add any number of files to a list of items to be uploaded. Users can even change their minds and remove items before the upload begins. This control solves the problem of how to make one simple form work with any number of file uploads. By default, the `<cffileupload>` control allows users to select any number of files, but you can put a limit on both the total number of files and the total size of the files that can be uploaded. Listing 30.14 demonstrates one example of this control.

Listing 30.14 `multifile.cfm`—Multiple-File Uploader

```
<!---
Name:        multifile.cfm
Author:      Raymond Camden (ray@camdenfamily.com)
```

Listing 30.14 (continued)

```
Description: Multi-file uploader control.
--->

<form action="multifile.cfm" method="post">
<cffileupload name="files" maxfileselect="5" url="multiupload.cfm">
</form>
```

There isn't much to this file. We have a form tag, the `<cffileupload>` tag, and a closing form tag. The multifile control uses the optional `maxfileselect` attribute to limit the number of files to five. Most important, notice the `url` attribute. When you use the multifile uploader, it creates a kind of mini form within your form, which can, as in Listing 30.14, submit to a file totally different from that used by the rest of the form. The next listing will show how you can handle the uploads, but first look at Figure 30.13 to see how the control is rendered.

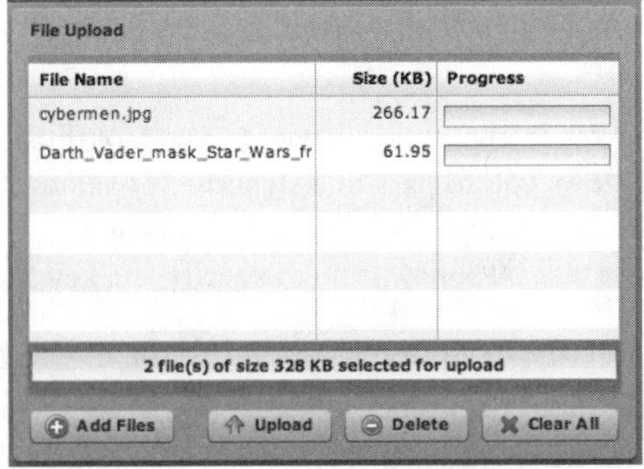

Figure 30.13

The multifile uploader control (with a few files selected).

As mentioned, the multifile uploader will send file data to the script specified in the `url` argument. Handling the file upload is simple: you use the same `<cffile>` tag you've used before. Listing 30.15 demonstrates the new `uploadAll` support.

Listing 30.15 `multiupload.cfm`—Handling Multiple File Uploads

```
<!---
Name:        multiupload.cfm
Author:      Raymond Camden (ray@camdenfamily.com)
Description: Handle multiple uploads.
--->

<cffile action="uploadAll" destination="#getTempDirectory()#" />
<cflog file="ows"
    text="Uploaded #cffile.serverdirectory#/#cffile.serverfile#">
```

Listing 30.15 shouldn't look too different from other file upload processors, but note that we use `uploadAll` instead of `upload` for the action. This tells the `<cffile>` tag to look for any and all files sent to the script. There is no need to specify a particular form field. (And yes: this approach will also work with non-multiple-file uploaders. If you have a form with just a few hard-coded file form fields, you can process them all at once with `uploadAll`.) In this script, we simply copy the files to the temporary directory as we don't actually need them. A `<cflog>` tag is used to log each upload.

Working with Maps

One of the cooler additions in ColdFusion 9 is the `<cfmap>` tag. As you can probably guess, this tag allows developers to embed maps on a Web page. The `<cfmap>` tag wraps up the Google Map service and therefore requires you to get a Google Map API key. Don't worry—it's free. Open your browser to `http://code.google.com/apis/maps/signup.html` and enter your URL. And in case you're wondering, yes, you can enter `http://127.0.0.1` for local server use. After you've received the map key, you can install it for use on your server in several ways.

- The ColdFusion Administrator Settings page contains a new setting, for the Google Map API key. Entering a value here defines a default key for the entire server. This method provides the easiest and quickest way to set the value.
- The `Application.cfc` file (described in Chapter 18, "Introducing the Web Application Framework," in Volume 1) defines multiple `THIS` scope variables that define an application's behavior. You can now specify `this.googlemapkey` to specify a key value for the application.
- You can also specify the key in the `<cfajaximport>` tag. ColdFusion 9 adds a new attribute, `params`, that allows you to pass in a structure of values. Currently, the only use of this attribute is for maps. For example, you would use `<cfajaximport params="#{googlemapkey="Map API Key"}#">` to specify the key for a particular page.

For now, simply paste your key into the ColdFusion Administrator and be sure to click the Submit Changes button to save the change.

Now that the requirements that must be met to display a map, let's look at a simple example in Listing 30.16.

Listing 30.16 `map1.cfm`—Displaying a Map

```
<!---
Name:        map1.cfm
Author:      Raymond Camden (ray@camdenfamily.com)
Description: Basic map examples.
--->

<h2>The Jedi</h2>

<cfmap centeraddress="403 Robinhood Circle, Lafayette, LA" />

<h2>The Jedi - Closer</h2>

<cfmap centeraddress="403 Robinhood Circle, Lafayette, LA"
       zoomlevel="9" type="terrain" />

<h2>The Jedi - Too Close</h2>

<cfmap centeraddress="403 Robinhood Circle, Lafayette, LA"
    zoomlevel="17" type="satellite" title="Home, Sweet, Home"
    hideborder="false" />
```

Listing 30.16 demonstrates three different maps. Each uses the same `centeraddress` value. Remember that `<cfmap>` also supports the use of longitude and latitude for placement. Each map slightly tweaks the display. ColdFusion offers a lot of options for customizing the map display.

Markers are another cool mapping feature. ColdFusion 9 has a `<cfmapitem>` tag that can be used to add markers to a map. You can add any number of markers you want to a map.

Listing 30.17 presents a simple example of the `<cfmapitem>` tag.

Listing 30.17 `map2.cfm`—Displaying a Map

```
<!---
Name:        map2.cfm
Author:      Raymond Camden (ray@camdenfamily.com)
Description: Map item example.
--->

<cfmap centeraddress="403 Robinhood Circle, Lafayette, LA"
       zoomlevel="13">

    <cfmapitem address="Pinhook Road, Lafayette, LA"
               tip="Pinhook Road"
               markerwindowcontent="Busy during lunch...">
    <cfmapitem address="Johnston Street, Lafayette, LA"
               tip="Johnston"
               markerwindowcontent="Visit the comic book store!">

</cfmap>
```

Listing 30.17 demonstrates the addition of two static map items to the map. For each map item, a tooltip and a marker window content value are used. The tooltip (specified with the `tip` attribute) appears when you mouse over the item. The marker window content (specified with the `markerwindowcontent` attribute) appears when you click the item.

Playing Videos

If YouTube is to be believed, watching videos is a popular pastime for people on the Internet. With the `<cfmediaplayer>` tag, ColdFusion 9 makes displaying videos on your site even easier. This tag creates a simple video player that works with any FLV-encoded video. (You can use this tag with MPEG-3 and MPEG-4 files if Adobe Flash Media Server is used to host the content.) You can specify multiple attributes to help control the display of the player as well as specify JavaScript functions to run during the video playback. Listing 30.18 presents a simple example of this new feature.

Listing 30.18 `video1.cfm`—Displaying Videos

```
<!---
Name:        video1.cfm
Author:      Raymond Camden (ray@camdenfamily.com)
Description: Media Player example.
--->

<cfmediaplayer autoplay="false"
               fullscreencontrol="true"
               source="sample.flv">
```

Pretty simple, right? This tag by itself will create the Flash embedding, the JavaScript, and anything else necessary to display the video on the screen. The user simply needs to click Play. A full JavaScript API is provided to allow you to start, stop, control the volume, and perform other operations.

Displaying a Progress Bar

While it would be nice if everything in our Web application were lightning fast, sometimes processes that we do not control take a lot longer to run than users may like. Sometimes a long process will cause a user to reload the page, which just fires off the slow process again. Other times a user will simply click Stop on the browser, leave the site, and never return again. When you don't have control over a slow process, it may be beneficial to create a progress bar. A progress bar gives the user a visual cue that something is happening and that progress, even if it is slow, is being made toward some goal. ColdFusion 9 adds a new `<cfprogressbar>` tag, which allows you to create a simple progress bar. This progress bar can use a static duration, which is useful when you are sure (for the most part) that a process takes a specific amount of time: for instance, 60 seconds. You can also create a progress bar that uses Ajax to check the status of a process and report a precise completion value. Look at a simple example in Listing 30.19.

Listing 30.19 `progress1.cfm`—Displaying a Progress Bar

```
<!---
Name:        progress1.cfm
Author:      Raymond Camden (ray@camdenfamily.com)
Description: Simple, static progress bar
--->

<html>
<head>
<script>
function startIt() {
    ColdFusion.ProgressBar.start('mybar');
}

function showDone() {
    ColdFusion.MessageBox.create('mymb','alert','Progress Done','All Done!');
    ColdFusion.MessageBox.show('mymb');
}
</script>
</head>

<body>
<h2>Stand by - this will take a while...</h2>

</body>
</html>

<!--- Duration is in milliseconds. --->
<!--- So do some simple math to make it easier. --->
<cfset dur = 5 * 1000>
<cfprogressbar name="mybar" duration="#dur#" oncomplete="showDone">

<cfset ajaxOnLoad("startIt")>
<cfajaximport tags="cfmessagebox">
```

This example is complex, so we'll carefully examine each part. The progress bar, much like `<cfwindow>` discussed earlier, will not actually start doing anything until you tell it to. Therefore, you have to use the JavaScript API (which will be covered in more detail later) to actually start the bar. The function, `startIt()`, handles this process. Notice that the `ColdFusion.ProgressBar.start()` function takes the name of a progress bar. This is the same name used later in the file in the `<cfprogressbar>` tag itself.

Another option is to run code when the progress bar has completed filling. The function `showDone()` was created to handle this approach. It also makes use of the ColdFusion JavaScript API. This time the API is used to dynamically create and display a message box.

Finally, note the two lines at the end of the file. The `ajaxOnLoad()` function and the `<cfajaximport>` tag are both discussed in detail later in the chapter. For now, just note that they run the `startIt()` function when the page loads and let ColdFusion know that message box support is needed.

This progress bar uses a static duration of 5 seconds. Later in the chapter, you will see how a bound progress bar can track a real process.

Dynamically Populating Ajax Controls

So far all of the controls covered in the chapter have had static (or predefined) values. For example, `<cfpod>` in Listing 30.6 showed the content of the pod stored directly inside the tag. Each control can be populated via an Ajax request instead. What this means is that the initial page loads in the browser and then the content of the control is loaded afterward. Let's look at the pod example as a way to move to Ajax-populated data. In order to populate the pod like this, you simply supply the `source` attribute. Consider Listing 30.20.

Listing 30.20 `pod2.cfm`—Ajax-Loaded Pod

```
<!---
Name:        pod2.cfm
Author:      Raymond Camden (ray@camdenfamily.com)
Description: Ajax populated pod
--->

<cfpod title="Pods with Ajax content" width="300"
       height="200" source="content1.cfm" />
```

The major change here compared to Listing 30.6 is the removal of all text from inside the `<cfpod>` tag pair. Next a `source` attribute was added to the tag. When loaded in the browser, ColdFusion's Ajax code will load the contents of `podcontent.cfm` into the pod. The contents of `podcontent.cfm` are displayed in Listing 30.21.

Listing 30.21 `content1.cfm`—Content for Pod

```
<!---
Name:        content1.cfm
Author:      Raymond Camden (ray@camdenfamily.com)
Description: Pod content
```

Listing 30.21 (continued)

```
--->

<cfoutput>
<p>
This is the content.<br />
Here is a random number: #randRange(1,100)#
</p>
</cfoutput>
```

Listing 30.21 simply provides the content for the pod in Listing 30.20. A bit of randomness is used so that on multiple reloads, the content is slightly different every time. As you can see, however, no JavaScript code was necessary at all. While JavaScript code was certainly generated by ColdFusion, as a developer you don't have to know a line of JavaScript in order to generate this Ajax-based code. One final note about the `source` attribute, and for any remote source you use with ColdFusion's controls—the source must point to a local URL. This is not a ColdFusion limitation. The browser will not load data from a remote source as a security precaution. Let's look at another example, this time using `<cfwindow>`. Listing 30.22 demonstrates how the `source` attribute can be added there as well.

Listing 30.22 `window2.cfm`—Ajax-Loaded Window

```
<!---
Name:        window2.cfm
Author:      Raymond Camden (ray@camdenfamily.com)
Description: Ajax-loaded window
--->

<p>
This is content on the main page.
</p>

<cfwindow title="Logon Window" center="true" width="300"
          height="300" modal="true" initShow="true"
          source="content1.cfm" />
```

As before, the main change here was to remove the text inside the opening and closing `<cfwindow>` tag and provide a `source` attribute. We used the same content used with the pod example. Let's look at yet another example. Listing 30.23 takes the earlier tabs example and mixes and matches Ajax-loaded content with static content.

Listing 30.23 `tab3.cfm`—Ajax-Loaded Tabs

```
<!---
Name:        tab3.cfm
Author:      Raymond Camden (ray@camdenfamily.com)
Description: Tabs with ajax magic
--->

<cflayout type="tab" tabheight="200">

    <cflayoutarea title="Tab One">
    <p>
```

Listing 30.23 (continued)

```
        This is the first tab.
        </>
        <form>
        Name: <input type="text" name="name"><br />
        Email: <input type="text" name="email"><br />
        <input type="submit">
        </form>
        </cflayoutarea>

        <cflayoutarea title="Tab Two" selected="true"
                      source="content1.cfm" />

        <cflayoutarea title="Tab Three"
                      source="content1.cfm"
                      refreshOnActivate="true" />

    </cflayout>
```

Listing 30.23 is a modified version of Listing 30.5. The second and third tabs no longer have content inside. Instead both point to `content1.cfm` for their source. Notice, though, that the third tab has `refreshOnActivate`. By default, ColdFusion will load remote content only once. By using `refreshOnActive="true"`, the tab will reload each time the tab is activated. With the random content used in `content1.cfm`, you can see a new number each time the tab is loaded. Now let's look at yet another example, this time working with `<cftooltip>` (Listing 30.24).

Listing 30.24 `tooltip2.cfm`—Ajax-Loaded Tooltips

```
<!---
Name:        tooltip2.cfm
Author:      Raymond Camden (ray@camdenfamily.com)
Description: tooltip ajax example
--->

<cfloop index="x" from="1" to="5">

<cftooltip sourceForTooltip="tooltipcontent.cfm?id=#x#">
<cfoutput>
<p>
This is paragraph #x#. Mouse over the paragraph to geet
interesting information about it.
</p>
</cfoutput>
</cftooltip>

</cfloop>
```

Listing 30.24 uses a simple loop to create five paragraphs of text. Each paragraph is wrapped by a `cftooltip` tag. Unlike the previous examples, instead of using a `source` attribute, a `sourceForTooltip` attribute is used instead. While it is named differently, it acts the same as the `source` attribute. Listing 30.25 shows the contents of the file loaded by the tooltip.

Listing 30.25 `tooltipcontent.cfm`—Content for Tooltip

```
<cfparam name="url.id" default="1">

<cfoutput>
<h2>Help for #url.id#</h2>
<p>
This is the dynamic help for paragraph #url.id#.
</p>
</cfoutput>
```

The tooltip content in Listing 30.25 isn't very complex. Since the tooltips in Listing 30.24 passed along an ID, this value is used in Listing 30.25. While this value is just displayed, you could imagine the content being loaded from the database instead. Figure 30.14 shows the display of the tooltip in the browser.

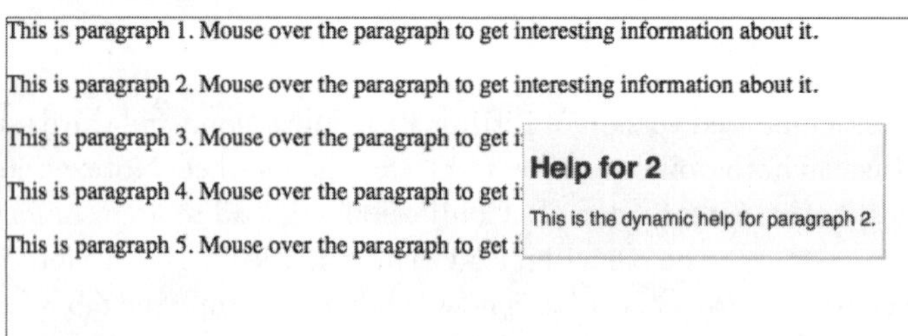

Figure 30.14

Dynamic tooltips that change with the content.

Using Bindings to Load Content

The previous examples all used the `source` (or similar) attribute to load content for the controls. But as you learned in Chapter 15, ColdFusion controls can also be bound to remote data sources as well. In general, bindings can be made to

- ColdFusion Components
- JavaScript Functions
- URLs (for example, `content1.cfm`)
- Other controls on the page

Bindings that point to external resources are typically specified with their type and location within one attribute. So for example, to bind a control to `content1.cfm`, you would use

```
bind="url:content1.cfm"
```

To link to a ColdFusion Component, the format would be

```
bind="cfc:someCFC.someMethod()"
```

To connect a control directly to a JavaScript function, the syntax would be

```
bind="javaScript:javascriptFunction()"
```

To introduce this concept we will look at a new ColdFusion UI control, the `<cfdiv>` tag. The `<cfdiv>` tag creates a simple div, or block, on a page. This div is typically loaded with other content. Listing 30.26 demonstrates a simple example of `<cfdiv>`.

Listing 30.26 `div1.cfm`—`<cfdiv>` Example

```
<!---
Name:        div1.cfm
Author:      Raymond Camden (ray@camdenfamily.com)
Description: cfdiv example
--->

<cfdiv bind="url:content1.cfm" />
```

This template is extremely short, but if you haven't figured it out yet, most of the examples are relatively simple and that just speaks to the power of ColdFusion. The `<cfdiv>` tag in Listing 30.16 has one attribute, `bind`. Again this should be familiar to you from Chapter 18. The bind points to `content1.cfm`, the file we've used for a few sources now. When loaded in the browser you see the same content you've seen before. Nice and powerful, but not terribly exciting yet. What if we modified it to be a bit more dynamic? ColdFusion bindings can include pointers to form fields and other UI elements. Listing 30.27 demonstrates an Ajax-based search form.

Listing 30.27 `search1.cfm`—Ajax-Based Search

```
<!---
Name:        search1.cfm
Author:      Raymond Camden (ray@camdenfamily.com)
Description: Dynamic search example
--->

<form>
Search: <input type="text" name="search">
<input type="button" value="Search">
</form>

<cfdiv bind="url:movieresults.cfm?search={search}" />
```

Listing 30.27 has a very simple form. Notice there is no action or method for the form tag. Also note there is no submit button—just a simple button. The last line is a `<cfdiv>` tag using a bind that points to a URL: `movieresults.cfm`. Notice that it passes a value in the query string, search. The token `{search}` refers to the text input field named search. This is all it takes to bind the `<div>` element to the form field. When the field changes, ColdFusion will automatically load the URL, with the value of the form field, into the div. Listing 30.28 shows the contents of `movieresults.cfm`.

Listing 30.28 `movieresults.cfm`—Search Results

```
<!---
Name:        movieresults.cfm
Author:      Raymond Camden (ray@camdenfamily.com)
Description: Dynamic search example
--->
<cfparam name="url.search" default="">
```

Listing 30.28 (continued)

```
<cfinvoke component="movies" method="searchMovies"
          search="#url.search#" returnVariable="results">

<table border="1">
    <tr>
        <td>Title</td><td>Summary</td>
    </tr>
    <cfoutput query="results">
    <tr>
        <td>#movietitle#</td>
        <td>#summary#</td>
    </tr>
    </cfoutput>
</table>
```

This template is rather simple. It takes a URL parameter and passes it to a CFC, which performs a search against the Orange Whip Studios movie database. The results are then output in a simple table.

NOTE

For this code sample to work, you must copy `Application.cfc` and `movies.cfc` from the CD into the current folder.

While this listing is slick, you may notice that the results do not change until you click somewhere on the page, or on the button. By default, bindings to form fields will look for a change event. If you are familiar with JavaScript, this is the `onChange` event. You can change the event that ColdFusion listens to by using the `@` symbol and the event name, minus the "`on`" portion. You could change the bind in Listing 30.27 to this:

```
<cfdiv bind="url:movieresults.cfm?search={search@keypress}" />
```

This will fire off the Ajax request as soon as you start typing, providing a filter-as-you-type interface to the search engine. You can find this version as `search2.cfm` on the book's Website.

Loading Content with `AjaxLink`

If you play with loading content within one of ColdFusion's UI elements like the window or pod, you may notice something odd. Links will not load inside the element. Instead it will completely overwrite the current document. If you want a link inside a pod, for example, to load inside the pod, you must use the `AjaxLink` function. Listing 30.29 demonstrates this function in action.

Listing 30.29 `ajaxlink1.cfm`—`AjaxLink()` Example

```
<!---
Name:        ajaxlink1.cfm
Author:      Raymond Camden (ray@camdenfamily.com)
Description: Ajax link example
--->

<cfpod title="Links">
```

Listing 30.29 (continued)

```
<a href="content1.cfm">Without AjaxLink</a><br />

<cfoutput>
<a href="#ajaxLink('content1.cfm')#">With AjaxLink</a>
</cfoutput>

</cfpod>
```

This template contains a pod with two links. The first link is a simple link. The second link uses the `ajaxLink` function to wrap the URL. If the first URL is clicked, the entire page is reloaded with the contents of `content1.cfm`. If the second link is clicked, however, the pod's content will reload with `content1.cfm`.

Working with the JavaScript API

Most of the Ajax controls discussed so far have both server-side options as well as an API that lets you work with them on the client side too. So for example, it is possible to set a default selected tab using the `<cflayoutarea>` tag. But what if you wanted to change the selected tab with JavaScript? ColdFusion provides a set of APIs that allow for many operations like this, including manipulating windows, updating tabs, as well as getting access to the lower-level objects that make up the UI elements. A complete list of the available JavaScript APIs is available in the ColdFusion documentation, but here are some of the actions possible with the API:

- Create Windows (like those made with `<cfwindow>`)
- Load another URL into a UI element
- Disable, enable, and select tabs
- Submit forms
- Sort, refresh grids
- Shrink or expand layout areas
- Send debug message (this will be covered later in the chapter)

Listing 30.30 demonstrates an example of this API in action.

Listing 30.30 `jstabs.cfm`—JavaScript API Example

```
<!---
Name:        jstabs.cfm
Author:      Raymond Camden (ray@camdenfamily.com)
Description: JS API Example
--->

<cflayout type="tab" tabheight="200" name="tabs">

    <cflayoutarea title="Tab One" name="tab1">
    <p>
    This is the first tab.
```

Listing 30.30 (continued)

```
        </p>
        </cflayoutarea>

        <cflayoutarea title="Tab Two" name="tab2">
        <p>
        This is the second tab.
        </p>
        </cflayoutarea>

    </cflayout>

    <p>
    <a href = ""
    onClick="ColdFusion.Layout.selectTab('tabs','tab1');
    return false;">select tab 1</a> /
    <a href = ""
    onClick="ColdFusion.Layout.selectTab('tabs','tab2');
    return false;">select tab 2</a>
    </p>

    <p>
    <a href = ""
    onClick="ColdFusion.Layout.enableTab('tabs','tab2');
    return false;">enable tab2</a> /
    <a href = ""
    onClick="ColdFusion.Layout.disableTab('tabs','tab2');
    return false;">disable tab2</a>
```

Listing 30.30 begins with a simple tab layout. Unlike the earlier tab examples, in this one we specifically named both the main layout and each tab. This wasn't required earlier, but will be necessary for the JavaScript API to work with the tabs. After the tabs, the first paragraph of links use the JavaScript API function `ColdFusion.Layout.selectTab`. As you can guess, this will select a tab. The function's first parameter is the name of the layout area. The second parameter is the name of the tab. The next paragraph demonstrates two different API functions, `ColdFusion.Layout.enableTab` and `ColdFusion.Layout.disableTab`. Again the result of this is pretty obvious. If you click on the disable tab link, the second tab will become grayed out and will not be selectable. This even blocks the `selectTab` function.

Now let's look at a second example. You learned earlier about the `AjaxLink` function. It helps ensure content is loaded within a UI element like a pod or window. There is a similar feature within the API. Listing 30.31 demonstrates this.

Listing 30.31 `navigate.cfm`—Navigate Example

```
<!---
Name:        navigate.cfm
Author:      Raymond Camden (ray@camdenfamily.com)
Description: Navigate example
--->

<cfpod title="Load Stuff" name="mypod" />

<a href="" onClick=
```

Listing 30.31 (continued)

```
"ColdFusion.navigate('content1.cfm','mypod');
return false">Load Content1</a>

<a href="" onClick=
"ColdFusion.navigate('content2.cfm','mypod');
return false">Load Content2</a>
```

The listing begins with a simple pod. Notice no content is defined inside the pod. Below the pod are two links. Both make use of `ColdFusion.navigate`. This function will load the contents of a URL into a UI element. In this example, the first link loads `content1.cfm` into the pod while the second example loads `content2.cfm`. (This file is available as an electronic download.)

Working with <CFAjaxProxy>

Ajax is all about connecting the front end (your browser) to the back end (ColdFusion). The closer the connection, the greater integration you can have between the two. ColdFusion 8 introduced a new tag that makes the connection between your JavaScript and ColdFusion code as close as possible. The `<cfajaxproxy>` tag has two main abilities. The first is to create a JavaScript proxy to a ColdFusion Component. The second is to easily bind a CFC, JavaScript function, or URL to a form element. Let's focus on the first feature.

In order for ColdFusion to create a proxy to a CFC, you must first ensure the CFC is under the Web root, and you have to use remote methods. Listing 30.32 is a simple CFC that will be used for our examples.

Listing 30.32 `proxytest.cfm`—`AjaxProxy` Component

```
<cfcomponent>

<cffunction name="sayHello" access="remote"
            returnType="string" output="false">
  <cfargument name="name" type="string" required="true"
              default="Nameless">

  <cfreturn "Hello, #arguments.name#">
</cffunction>


</cfcomponent>
```

This is a rather simple component with a grand total of one method, `sayHello`. Note that it is marked remote. This will be important for the JavaScript code coming in the next example (Listing 30.33).

Listing 30.33 `ajaxproxy1.cfm`—`AjaxProxy` Example

```
<!---
Name:        ajaxproxy1.cfm
Author:      Raymond Camden (ray@camdenfamily.com)
Description: AjaxProxy example
```

Listing 30.33 (continued)

```
--->

<cfajaxproxy cfc="proxytest" jsclassname="proxytest">

<script>
var myProxy = new proxytest();

function runProxy() {
  var name = document.getElementById("name").value;
  var result = myProxy.sayHello(name);
  alert(result);
}
</script>

<form>
<input type="text" id="name">
<input type="button" onclick="runProxy()"
       value="Run Proxy">
</form>
```

Listing 30.33 begins with the `<cfajaxproxy>` tag. The `cfc` attribute points to the CFC created in Listing 30.32. The `jsclassname` attribute uses the same name for simplicity's sake. At this point we now have a JavaScript class that we can instantiate and use. The script block shows an example of this. The first line creates an instance of the class. The variable is named `myProxy`. At this point, the `myProxy` variable can be considered a proxy to the CFC. Any remote method can be called by invoking the function within the JavaScript variable. The form at the bottom of the page contains a simple text field and a button that invokes the `runProxy` function. This function gets the name value from the field and then passes it to the `sayHello` method. This is the same method defined in Listing 30.32. The result is then alerted.

By default, calls to the CFC are synchronous. This means that JavaScript will make the call to the CFC and wait for it to respond. This isn't always desirable, especially if the call to the CFC could be slow. The browser would be essentially locked waiting for the response. Luckily this is behavior you can tweak along with a whole set of other options as well.

Let's look at an example that uses a few of these functions. Listing 30.34 is a new version of the CFC used in Listing 30.32.

Listing 30.34 `proxytest2.cfc`—Second `ProxyTest` CFC

```
<cfcomponent>

<cffunction name="sayHello" access="remote"
                     returnType="string" output="false">
    <cfargument name="name" type="string" required="true"
                           default="">
    <cfif arguments.name is "paris">
            <cfthrow message="Paris is NOT a valid name!">
    </cfif>
    <cfset sleep(1000)>
    <cfreturn "Hello, #arguments.name#">
</cffunction>
</cfcomponent>
```

This CFC is exactly like the earlier version except for two important changes. If the name value is `paris`, an exception will be thrown. Otherwise, the CFC will pause for 1000 milliseconds using the `sleep` function and then return a string. Now consider Listing 30.35, a modified version of Listing 30.33.

Listing 30.35 `ajaxproxy2.cfm`—Second `AjaxProxy` CFC

```
<!---
Name:        ajaxproxy2.cfm
Author:      Raymond Camden (ray@camdenfamily.com)
Description: AjaxProxy example
--->

<cfajaxproxy cfc="proxytest2" jsclassname="proxytest">

<script>
var myProxy = new proxytest();
myProxy.setErrorHandler(handleError);
myProxy.setCallbackHandler(handleResult);


function handleResult(result) {
    alert(result);
}

function handleError(code,msg) {
    alert('Status Code: '+code+'\n'+'Message: '+msg);
}

function runProxy() {
    var name = document.getElementById("name").value;
    var result = myProxy.sayHello(name);
}
</script>

<form>
<input type="text" id="name">
<input type="button" onclick="runProxy()"
       value="Run Proxy">
</form>
```

Again let's try to focus on how this differs from the earlier version. The first change is that `<cfajaxproxy>` points to `proxytest2` instead of `proxytest`. Next notice that within the script block, both an error handler and a callback handler are set. These will both set the proxy to be asynchronous. The error handler is a function named `handlerError`. By default a status code and message is passed to the method, so all the listing does is alert these values.

The callback handler, `handleResult`, simply alerts the result. Since this is a string, we should see what we saw in the earlier version. Open `ajaxproxy2.cfm` in your browser and enter a name. Notice that it takes a second for the result to return, but the page doesn't lock up. Then enter the name, `Paris`. The error handler function will alert the message that was used in Listing 30.34.

AjaxProxy as a Binding

As mentioned in the beginning of this section, <cfajaxproxy> could also be used as a binding. In this form, the tag creates a connection between a form or UI element (like a <cftree>) and a binding. The binding can be to either a CFC, URL, or JavaScript function. You can use this as a simpler way to communicate with the server. Listing 30.36 demonstrates the tag being used in this fashion.

Listing 30.36 ajaxproxy3.cfm—AjaxProxy as a Binding

```
<!---
Name:        ajaxproxy3.cfm
Author:      Raymond Camden (ray@camdenfamily.com)
Description: AjaxProxy example
--->

<cfajaxproxy
        bind="cfc:proxytest2.sayHello({name@keyup})"
        onError="handleError"
        onSuccess="handleResult">

<script>
function handleResult(result) {
    document.getElementById("result").innerHTML = result;
}

function handleError(code,msg) {
    alert('Status Code: '+code+'\n'+'Message: '+msg);
}
</script>

<form>
<input type="text" id="name">
</form>

<div id="result" />
```

This example begins with the <cfajaxproxy> tag. Instead of defining a JavaScript class name and CFC, a binding is used. The binding is to the proxytest2.cfc from Listing 30.34. The value from the form field is used in the binding as well the as keyup event. The onError and onSuccess attributes are used to define which functions to run when an error occurs or when the binding is successful. Inside the script block, the error function, handleError, is the same as in the previous listing. The handleResult function is slightly different. Instead of using alerts, the innerHTML value of a <div> element is updated with the result. This is quite a bit less annoying than JavaScript alerts.

Working with JSON

JSON, or JavaScript Object Notation, is a way to represent data in string format. In this manner it is a lot like XML or WDDX, but JSON has a few advantages over XML. First, it can be quite a bit slimmer than XML. If you think about it, smaller data equals quicker data transfers between the server and the browser, and that's definitely a good thing. Second, JSON also acts as a literal representation of JavaScript data. That means to convert JSON into "real" data, the browser just needs to evaluate it. ColdFusion uses JSON for its communication between the various bits of Ajax plumbing, and for the most part, you don't even have to worry about it. But if you want to get under the hood and play with JSON yourself, there are a few functions you should be aware of.

First is the `isJSON` function. As you can imagine, this will check if a string represents valid JSON data.

Next is the `SerializeJSON` and `DeserializeJSON` functions. The former will convert ColdFusion data into JSON and the latter will translate JSON back into ColdFusion data. Let's look at a simple example (Listing 30.37).

Listing 30.37 `json1.cfm`—JSON Examples

```
<!---
Name:        json1.cfm
Author:      Raymond Camden (ray@camdenfamily.com)
Description: JSON example
--->

<cfset string = "Jeanne,Jacob,Lynn,Noah">
<cfset array = ["Darth","Fetch","Nick","HDTV","Dharma"]>
<cfset struct = {name="Raymond",cool=true,age=34}>

<cfquery name="query" maxrows="4">
  select filmid, movietitle, summary
  from     films
  order by movietitle asc
</cfquery>

<cfset json_string = serializeJSON(string)>
<cfset json_array = serializeJSON(array)>
<cfset json_struct = serializeJSON(struct)>
<cfset json_query = serializeJSON(query)>

<cfif isJSON(json_string)>
  <p>
  Yes, json_string is a JSON string.
  </p>
</cfif>

<cfoutput>
<p>
json_string=#json_string#
</p>
<p>
json_array=#json_array#
</p>
<p>
json_struct=#json_struct#
</p>
<p>
json_query=#json_query#
</p>
</cfoutput>
```

Listing 30.37 (continued)

```
<cfset rString = deserializeJSON(json_string)>
<cfset rArray = deserializeJSON(json_array)>
<cfset rStruct = deserializeJSON(json_struct)>
<cfset rQuery = deserializeJSON(json_query)>

<cfdump var="#rString#">
<cfdump var="#rArray#">
<cfdump var="#rStruct#">
<cfdump var="#rQuery#">
```

This is a rather large template, but all in all not much is happening. First the template creates a set of variables, including a string, an array, a structure, and a query. These are all then serialized to JSON using the `serializeJSON` function. Next we test one of them, `json_string`, to see if it is a valid JSON string. All could have been checked, but only one is necessary to get the point across. Next all the variables are deserialized using `deserializeJSON`. Finally they are all dumped to the browser. If you run this template, you will notice something odd. The query, when serialized and deserialized, becomes a structure, not a query!

Why did this happen? If you think about it, a ColdFusion query doesn't translate to a native JavaScript variable. When the query was turned into JSON, it becomes an object with properties that represent the columns and rows of data. When translated back into ColdFusion, the closest representation of an object is a structure. The `deserializeJSON` function allows for a second argument, `strictMapping`. It is true by default and enforces a strict conversion of data—hence the structure. If set to false, though, the function will see if the JSON string could represent a query. If it does, then a query is created. Therefore you can change the line

```
<cfset rQuery = deserializeJSON(json_query)>
```

to

```
<cfset rQuery = deserializeJSON(json_query,false)>
```

to get a valid ColdFusion query back.

Another place that ColdFusion supports JSON is within the JavaScript API. ColdFusion 9 adds both `ColdFusion.JSON.decode` and `ColdFusion.JSON.encode` functions. These allow you to work with JSON within your own JavaScript code in a ColdFusion application.

Special Considerations with ColdFusion Ajax Applications

Working with Ajax applications requires some special handling at times. While ColdFusion goes out of its way to make this as easy as possible, there are some things that require a bit of extra work. The following section details a few special things you should be aware of.

Importing JavaScript Ajax Libraries

When you use one of the new ColdFusion Ajax-related tags, the server will automatically import any JavaScript libraries needed for the code to work. But what if ColdFusion doesn't know that you are using a particular tag? Consider Listing 30.38.

Listing 30.38 `ajaximport1.cfm`—Ajax Import Example

```
<!---
Name:        ajaximport1.cfm
Author:      Raymond Camden (ray@camdenfamily.com)
Description: AjaxImport Test
--->

<cfpod source="tooltip2.cfm" title="cfajax import demo" />
```

This template has one line—a `<cfpod>` tag that points to one of the earlier `<cftooltip>` examples. If you run this in your browser, though, you will get a bunch of JavaScript errors. Figure 30.15 demonstrates an example of this.

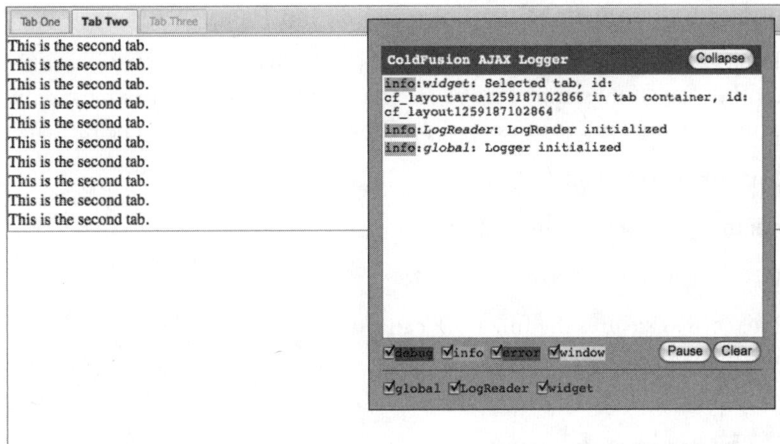

Figure 30.15

The browser throws a number of errors—why?

Luckily the error is pretty clear. It tells you that the imports for `<cftooltip>` are missing. It even tells you what to use: `<cfajaximport>`. As mentioned above, ColdFusion looks at the code to determine what JavaScript to load, but in Listing 30.38, the only tag *directly* on the page is `<cfpod>`. The pod ends up loading a page that uses `<cftooltip>`, but ColdFusion didn't know this. Luckily the `<cfajaximport>` tag makes this easy, as demonstrated in Listing 30.39.

Listing 30.39 `ajaximport2.cfm`—Ajax Import Example

```
<!---
Name:        ajaximport2.cfm
Author:      Raymond Camden (ray@camdenfamily.com)
Description: AjaxImport Test
--->
<cfajaximport tags="cftooltip">

<cfpod source="tooltip2.cfm" title="cfajax import demo" />
```

The only difference between Listings 30.39 and 30.38 is the addition of the `<cfajaximport>` tag. Since we know that `tooltip2.cfm` will need the tooltip JavaScript code, we specify `tags="cftooltip"`.

If `<cfwindow>` was used as well, this could be used: `tags="cftooltip,cfwindow"`. The `<cfajaximport>` tag also allows you to specify alternate JavaScript and CSS locations as well.

Running Functions on Page Load

Another common task is running a set of JavaScript code when the page loads. While this is normally a pretty simple task, with a page made up of multiple Ajax-loaded items, it becomes more difficult to know when a page is really done. ColdFusion provides the `AjaxOnLoad` function. With this function, you simply specify the name of the function to be run and ColdFusion will run it when the page is done. Here's an example: `<cfset ajaxOnLoad("setup")>`.

Defining JavaScript Functions in Loaded Pages

This is a simple tip but it's important. If you are writing code for a page that will be included by another page (for example, the source for a pod or window), you must define JavaScript in a particular format. Instead of using the normal "function name" type format:

```
function doIt() { alert('Hi'); }
```

you must instead use this format:

```
doIt = function() { alert('Hi'); }
```

This format ensures the functions can run properly when used inside containers such as the pod or window.

Debugging Ajax

Debugging with ColdFusion can be relatively simple, especially with the use of the Eclipse-based debugger in ColdFusion. Debugging Ajax applications can be trickier, however, especially when you have to worry about both server-side and client-side code. Luckily ColdFusion ships with an Ajax debugger to aid your development. To begin, you must first enable debug support for Ajax applications. In your ColdFusion Administrator, select the Enable Ajax Debug Log Window option on the Debug Output Settings page.

Ajax debugging follows the same IP restrictions as normal debugging, so ensure that your IP is listed on the Debugging IP Addresses page. Next you have to enable debugging for the request. Visit any page that makes use of Ajax tags and add `?cfdebug` to the URL. Figure 30.16 shows the earlier tabs demo with `?cfdebug` added to the URL. Notice the window at the upper right of the page.

Without your doing anything at all, the window reveals a lot of information. You can see HTTP requests and other messages as the page is displayed. If you click the tabs multiple times, you will see additional messages as well. Along with messages that are automatically added to the window, you can use JavaScript to add your own messages.

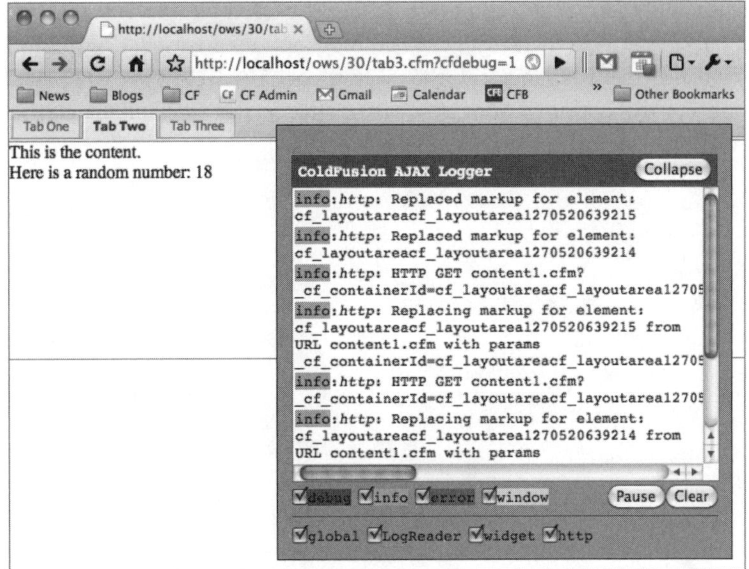

Figure 30.16 The Ajax Debug window.

Security Options

Ajax applications are not any more secure or insecure simply because they are Ajax. In fact, with Ajax being the "Hot New Thing" for Web 2.0, it is safe to assume that hackers will turn quite a bit of attention to Ajax applications as a new way to attack Web sites. ColdFusion has two main ways to deal with potential Ajax security risks.

The first deals with JSON prefixes. A JSON prefix is simply a string that is placed in front of a JSON string. Since JSON is evaluated by the browser, this prefix essentially breaks the application. But if the client-side code is aware of the prefix, it can remove the prefix before working with the data. There are a few ways you can add a JSON prefix to your code. First is a global option in the ColdFusion Administrator: Prefix serialized JSON with. This creates a default of `//`, but that can be changed. The second way to add a prefix is with `Application.cfc` variables. Two variables may be added to the `THIS` scope in an `Application.cfc` file: `THIS.secureJSON` tells ColdFusion to add a prefix to JSON strings. `THIS.secureJSONPrefix` lets you specify a prefix. The last way to add a prefix is at the method level. When you add `secureJSON="true"` to a CFC method, its JSON results will automatically be prefixed. (You cannot specify a prefix this way, though.) The best thing about this feature is that once you've enabled it, ColdFusion automatically updates all client-side code. You don't have to do a thing to remove the prefix from the code.

The second option is a bit more subtle. Imagine you have a CFC method that is only meant to be called via Ajax, or a CFM page also only meant to be used from Ajax. How can you ensure someone won't open that page or call that CFC in a non-Ajax request? You have two options. For the CFC method, simply add `verifyClient="true"`. For the CFM file, just add a call to the new `verifyClient` function: `<cfset verifyClient()>`. When these options are used, ColdFusion will pass a special token when it makes the Ajax request. If the token is not passed, then the CFC method or CFM file will not respond. For this option to work, you must enable session or client management. This option should be used for any sensitive request.

CHAPTER 31

Integrating with Adobe Flex

IN THIS CHAPTER

Traditionally, Web application development has been a matter of generating HTML from a server application language, giving you the powerful yet dangerous capability to intermix your server logic with the generated HTML. In the beginning, this is what made ColdFusion such a powerful option: execute a query, generate a table, execute another query, generate some more HTML, and so on. This made sense in the limited world of HTML; however, with new presentation technologies like Flex, presentation and business logic now have a clear division, with very specific bridges between the two. This type of design is commonly referred to as services-oriented architecture (SOA).

The clear division within a Flex application allows you to design and build your application along a more traditional client-server model. It also allows you to pass a lot of the work back to the client, so everything does not need to be done on the server: for instance, sorting and filtering are both great examples of work left on the client.

As you develop and build your ColdFusion applications with Flex, you will find that most of the ColdFusion code you write is accessed through a few specific CFC files (services) that are exposed to the Flex application and the rest of the world as a well-defined access to your application.

Understanding the Relationship Between ColdFusion and Flex

When Flex was created, the ColdFusion team made it a goal to make ColdFusion the easiest language you can use to build Flex applications.

Between ColdFusion 7 and 8, Adobe divided the Flex Data Server into two offerings: an open source server called BlazeDS, and LiveCycle Data Services, an enterprise server that adds more functionality on top of BlazeDS.

ColdFusion 9 has continued in this direction, adding two new features for Flex developers to ColdFusion: ColdFusion as a Service and offline AIR support.

ColdFusion services let you invoke a number of ColdFusion tags from directly inside ColdFusion, bringing the power of ColdFusion directly to MXML. These tags are `CFCHART`, `CFDOCUMENT`, `CFIMAGE`, `CFMAIL`, `CFPOP`, and `CFPDF`.

Offline AIR support allows you to build an AIR application that can work either offline or online. This AIR library does this by managing the data and any changes to the data so that when you go back online after using the application offline, the data is synchronized with the data on the server (in your database). See Chapter 33, "Building ColdFusion-Powered AIR Applications," for more information about building offline AIR applications with ColdFusion.

The primary way for a Flex application to talk to a ColdFusion server is through the embedded BlazeDS Server. You can think of BlazeDS Server as providing the plumbing layer for data between your client application (Flash) and the server-side code (ColdFusion). For instance, the BlazeDS Server does not have the capability to talk directly to a database. You still write the code to talk to the database in your language of choice, be it a CFC or even a Java class, but CFCs are easier to use.

With the BlazeDS Server, there are two primary ways to connect to the ColdFusion server:

- Remote Procedure Call (RPC)
  - REST
  - Web Services
  - Flash Remoting
- Messaging

The most commonly method of connecting is through RPC services. RPC services are the calls to the server that use the request-and-response model: send a request, and return a response with the data. RPC has three options. The first option is REST, which sends a regular HTTP call with URL parameters but returns XML. The second option is Web Services, which sends a SOAP-encoded XML packet with the request parameters to the server and returns XML (XML both ways). The third option is Flash Remoting, a protocol that sends binary AMF data back and forth over HTTP. With ColdFusion and Flex, Flash Remoting is the most common form of communication. Even ASP and PHP—really any language through which a Flex application will try to connect—should use Flash Remoting if it is available.

NOTE

Technically, you can invoke ColdFusion through REST requests and Web Services, but if Flash Remoting is an option, why do so? Flash Remoting is faster and easier to use. Leave REST and Web Services to the other languages that can't use Flash Remoting.

A key advantage of the AMF protocol is that because it's binary, the request size is smaller than for a plain text request, and you can send actual objects in the request and response data packets. You don't need to convert the objects to some simple string format, such as XML or JSON, and then back to an object on the server. This approach results in a noticeable performance advantage since you don't have the serialization and deserialization layers on the client side and again on the server side. And the binary protocol is compressed so you use less bandwidth.

The other server option is to connect ColdFusion to an instance of LiveCycle Data Services (LCDS). When you do this, you are able to use everything BlazeDS has plus a new feature called Data Management Services. Data Management manages your data with a few simple methods and adds the capability for your application to stay synchronized between clients with conflict resolution, which we will discuss in more detail later in this chapter.

So what connection option should you use? Here are some guidelines for determining when to use each option:

- Flash Remoting
  - All users have their own data sets, so you don't need to worry about conflicts between users.
  - Your application works with the request-and-response model: for instance, the user clicks a button, so go to the server, get new data, and return.
- Publish and Subscribe
  - You need to send real-time notification of changes to many clients.
  - You want to be able to push system messages to clients at any time.
- LCDS Data Management
  - You have multiple users sharing and editing the same data.
  - You are working with very large result sets and want to return only a subset of data at a time with the paging feature.

This covers the different technology options, but what about the differences between products: specifically, BlazeDS and LCDS? The main difference between these two products is the different options for the three types of connections mentioned earlier. LCDS is built on top of BlazeDS, so everything BlazeDS can do, LCDS can do too. However, LCDS adds more, better-performing options.

For Publish and Subscribe messaging, in BlazeDS your only option is HTTP polling. This means that the client will connect to the server on a timer: for example, maybe every 10 seconds, asking for new alerts. In addition, the number of connections to a server is limited by the Web server (IIS or Apache). This may be fine for a lot of applications. However, if you need real-time messaging, then you need to use LCDS.

With LCDS you have two more options. The first is the Real-Time Messaging Protocol (RTMP), which was originally developed for Flash Media Server. With RTMP, all your clients have a full-time connection to the server, so messages are sent to the clients immediately. This is the fastest option available.

The second option is LCDS nonblocking I/O (NIO) polling. If a slight delay in HTTP polling is okay but limitations on the number of connections to a server is an issue, NIO polling can help. NIO allows a server to handle thousands more connections to a server than HTTP polling. This means you can buy a lot fewer servers to serve the same number of clients.

The next difference between LCDS and BlazeDS is the LCDS Data Management. This feature allows you to build applications that have multiple users viewing and editing the same data. Read the "Data Management" section later in this chapter for more details.

In Chapter 32, "Integrating with Flash Data Services," we will first build an application with Flash Remoting and then change it to use LCDS Data Management. You will see that the differences between a Flash Remoting application and a Data Management application are very small, and that both are easy to create with ColdFusion.

ColdFusion-Powered Flex

Traditionally, ColdFusion and HTML were intermixed; there are even a number of tags in ColdFusion that generate HTML directly. When you want to change the HTML, you go through ColdFusion and reexecute the CFML page. However, when you are building a Flex application, the two are completely separate, with a small direct connection between the two.

Inside the Flex application, you will do everything client-side until you need to get or save new data, and then you call the ColdFusion server and execute a remote CFC method. On the server, you create only a set of services—basically one or more CFC files with all of the individual methods that your application will need to execute. Remember there are lots of small requests in a Flex-ColdFusion application. This is the services layer of a SOA. The nice side effect of building your application this way is that now you have a clean, well-defined services layer to the business side of your application. You can expose the same service to other developers in your company or in the world, and you know that the core of the application has already been built and tested, or you can use these same services next time you want to rewrite the front-end of the application. You don't need to start over and rewrite the application from scratch (the database doesn't change, so why should the code that accesses the database?).

When comparing a Flex application to HTML, think of an HTML page with lots of DHTML layers, with different sections being visible or hidden at any one time, and instead of the page being reloaded, everything is done with Ajax calls back to the ColdFusion server. Flex works the same way, except you don't have to build your whole application in one HTML page, and you have a lot more data-access options than with an Ajax application (AMF, messaging, data management, and so on).

No More Request and Response

The hardest part of learning how to build rich Internet applications for traditional Web developers—and I mean all Web developers using ColdFusion, ASP, PHP, and so on—is getting the idea of building for a page-reload (request and response) architecture out of their heads and starting to think of applications in an event-driven way.

Typical Web applications work like this: You click a link (request), and the page reloads (response); you click another link (request), and a new page is loaded (response). Get this out of your head and forget about this concept of clicking a link and reloading a page. Now you're working on only the part of the application that you are interested in. It sounds simple, but by far this concept is the hardest thing for people to give up.

A useful point to keep in mind is that HTML uses events too, though only on form controls. Therefore, you are probably familiar with programming a little JavaScript call when a `<select>` list changes, but making this sort of approach the core of the way that the application functions and changes is more challenging. But really, you can just think of Flex events in the same way as HTML events, except that in Flex everything—not just the form controls—has events that you can use.

Asynchronous Requests and Callbacks

The concept of asynchronous requests is at the core of data access in Flex, meaning that when you do call the server, Flex doesn't wait for a response. It doesn't matter if that call comes back 10 milliseconds later or 10 minutes later—Flex doesn't wait. Instead, when the server finally does return data, an ActionScript (AS) function that you wrote is called, and inside this function you can do what you need to with the result.

In a way, this approach is great because the Flash client doesn't wait for the response. This is why the Flex application doesn't stop and freeze while some long-running query is being executed. The user can still move the mouse, see a progress bar running, click other screens, and so on—kind of like when you run batch jobs and then go to lunch. However, programming with asynchronous requests can be tricky when you need to execute instructions in sequence and you can't easily execute one item until the previous item is done.

Session Scope

When building a Flex or AIR application, note that the session scope is used differently in these applications than in a regular CFML application. In a regular CFML application, there is a need to save information as a user goes from page to page. This can be done with cookies or with the SESSION scope, and as users request new pages, you can access this SESSION scope to get data.

However, when you are building a Flex application, the whole application is loaded and in memory. It's like the application is it's own session scope. If you need to access data between screens, you can easily reference the other screens to get the data, or more commonly data is referenced from a central location where you store data (the "model" in MVC architecture). So on the client, you won't use the ColdFusion SESSION scope or cookies.

Does this mean you no longer need the ColdFusion SESSION scope? No, you still need it for server data. However, you will probably use it a lot less. When you have a Flex application, all of the interaction with the server is through the CFC methods (SOA layer) that you have made. Because these methods are usually small and exact, rarely will you need to store data between the methods calls for any given user. They use the arguments you pass in to figure out what to do to return the correct data. One case in which you may need the SESSION scope is when you want to store login credentials.

If you do need the SESSION scope, that's okay. It will work exactly the same as it does with CFML pages. Flex talks to the server by handing the HTTP request back to the user's browser and letting the browser manage the request, and by this means, all of the cookies that ColdFusion reads and sets are still stored in the user's browser, and ColdFusion can tell the difference between Flex applications.

TIP

You can use a sniffer program, such as Service Capture, on the Flash Builder 4 network monitor to see the Flash Remoting requests, and when you do you will see your cookies passed in every request.

Data Translation

ColdFusion-powered Flash and Flex applications usually need to move data back and forth between ColdFusion on the server and the Flash Player on the client. Even though data, and how it is represented, differs between ColdFusion and Flash, the process is still remarkably easy.

Returning Simple Objects

A great advantage of using ColdFusion with Flex is that this combination is 100 percent supported: you can return any ColdFusion data to Flex and back again. However, you need to understand a few details.

Queries

There is not a matching `Query` type in Flex. However, at the core, a query is just an array of structs, one for each row, so when you send a ColdFusion `Query` object to Flex, it will be converted to a Flex `ArrayCollection` object type. However, when you send the `ArrayCollection` object back to ColdFusion, it is not converted back to a `Query` object. Instead, it becomes a regular array in ColdFusion.

Why? First, `ArrayCollection` is a wrapper around an array, adding support for sorting, filtering, and cursors, but at the core, it's an array. Second, you can create an `ArrayCollection` object out of any data, not just simple values, so converting it back to a `Query` object may not always work or be the right conversion. Converting it to an array is the safest option.

Dates

Dates are transferred over AMF in UTC format. That means that every proper date object has time zone information relative to GMT. This also means the dates as you see them are automatically converted to local time as the dates are transferred.

For instance, if you create a date on a server on which the OS is set to Eastern Standard Time and send it to a Flash client running in California, the hour portion of the date/time will be shifted back three hours to compensate for the change in time zones. The same is true the other direction too: if you create a date in a Flash application in Pacific Standard Time and send it to a server hosted in Eastern Standard Time, the time will be shifted ahead three hours accordingly.

This is not a problem if your application can treat dates as relative: for instance, if you are outputting dates in simple format, such as "created: 2 minutes ago." If all of the dates are relative to each other, you can just let Flash and ColdFusion translate dates this way.

However, if you need to make sure that every user, anywhere in the world, sees the dates with the same time, usually the server's time, you have two options:

- If you know the UTC offset of the server, you can add or remove the offset between the client's time zone and the servers. This is a great place for `get` and `set` methods. Be sure to account for daylight savings time, when the time zones may shift an hour.
- Pass dates back and forth as strings, without the GMT offset. This approach is relatively easy to implement in ColdFusion, since everything is already a string.

Returning Value Objects

One of the main advantages to using Flash Remoting instead of Web Services or XML REST service is support for value objects. A value object, also called a data-transfer object (DTO), is a pattern for passing class and CFC instances between languages. For instance, suppose that you have a `Product` CFC on the server side and all of the logic needed to create new instances, update existing instances, or return an instance of `Product`. If you are working with a `Product` object on the server, you likely will want to work with the same `Product` objects in your Flex application and not deal with the XML needed to transfer the objects back and forth and the logic needed to re-create the `Product` object.

After the proper linking is in place, when a ColdFusion CFC is returned, it will arrive in the result method as an AS `Product` class. The same is true the other way: If your CFC requires a CFC `Product` instance as an argument, you can create a new AS `Product` class and pass it as an argument to your CFC method (when you invoke the CFC with the `<mx:RemoteObject>` tag); it will automatically be converted to a `Product` CFC when it gets to ColdFusion.

You need to do a few things to set up this linking correctly. Once they are done, you won't need to worry about this again.

First, you must make sure that the property names—spelling, including case—and data types match exactly. The tricky part is that ColdFusion is typeless (everything is a string) and case insensitive, and ActionScript 3 (AS3) in Flex is strongly typed and case sensitive—not conducive to one-to-one mapping. To ensure a strong linkage without any chance that ColdFusion will guess wrong while it tries to perform the translation, use the `cfproperty` tag in your ColdFusion CFC. Until now, `cfproperty` was used only for documentation, but with Flash Remoting, the `cfproperty` tag is also your contract with Flash. ColdFusion will use the case of the `name` attribute and will convert the data, if possible, to the type of data defined by the `type` attribute:

```
<cfproperty name="ACTORID" type="numeric" default="0">
<cfproperty name="NAMEFIRST" type="string" default="">
```

The second task you need to do is define the path and name of the CFC with the `alias` attribute of the `cfcomponent` tag. ColdFusion provides a number of options for finding a CFC: in the same directory, under the Web root, under a `CFMAPPING` folder, or in your custom tags folder. The problem is that ColdFusion will use the path to the location of the CFC to define the alias of your CFC.

You might get lucky and link Flash and ColdFusion with the right paths; however, it's easy to break this link—all it takes is the addition of a new virtual directory or a new `CFMAPPING` definition, and ColdFusion suddenly finds the same CFC from a new direction and changes the metadata alias for the CFC.

To lock the path so the link can never suddenly change on you, define an alias for your ColdFusion Component and set this `alias` attribute to the exact same path you use in a `CFOBJECT()` or `CREATE-OBJECT()` call when you invoke the CFC.

Listing 31.1 shows a sample CFC with the `alias` and `cfproperty` tags defined.

Listing 31.1 `actors.cfc`

```
<cfcomponent output="false"
          alias="ows.35.example4.components.ACTORS">
   <cfproperty name="ACTORID" type="numeric" default="0">
   <cfproperty name="NAMEFIRST" type="string" default="">
   <cfproperty name="NAMELAST" type="string" default="">
   <cfproperty name="AGE" type="numeric" default="0">
   <cfproperty name="NAMEFIRSTREAL" type="string" default="">
   <cfproperty name="NAMELASTREAL" type="string" default="">
   <cfproperty name="AGEREAL" type="numeric" default="0">
   <cfproperty name="ISEGOMANIAC" type="numeric" default="0">
   <cfproperty name="ISTOTALBABE" type="numeric" default="0">
   <cfproperty name="GENDER" type="string" default="">

   <cfscript>
   // set the default values,
   // notice that the case of the property doesn't matter
   this.actorid = 0;
   this.nameFirst = "";
   this.nameLast = "";
   this.age = 0;
   this.nameFirstRead = "";
   this.nameLastReal = "";
   this.ageReal = 0;
   this.isEgoManiac = 0;
   this.isTotalBase = 0;
   this.gender = "";
   </cfscript>

</cfcomponent>
```

Now to link from the Flex side, you need to perform the same two tasks but a little differently. First, define the properties with the matching data type and case of the `CFPROPERTY` tags:

```
public var ACTORID:Number = 0;
public var NAMEFIRST:String = "";
```

Next, map the same `alias` attribute in the AS class, using the AS3 metadata tag `RemoteClass`. Note that the string in the `alias` attribute must be exactly the same as the alias in the CFC (including the case), and the alias must be a valid path that the CFC can use to invoke the CFC.

```
[RemoteClass(alias="ows.35.example3.components.ACTORS")]
```

Listing 31.2 shows the complete AS class that matches Listing 31.1.

Listing 31.2 `Actors.as`

```
package model.beans
{
   [RemoteClass(alias="ows.35.example3.components.ACTORS")]
   [Managed]
   public class Actors
   {
      public var ACTORID:Number = 0;
      public var NAMEFIRST:String = "";
      public var NAMELAST:String = "";
      public var AGE:Number = 0;
      public var NAMEFIRSTREAL:String = "";
      public var NAMELASTREAL:String = "";
      public var AGEREAL:Number = 0;
      public var ISEGOMANIAC:Number = 0;
      public var ISTOTALBABE:Number = 0;
      public var GENDER:String = "";
   }
}
```

With this link set up, you can now work in straight OOP and pass objects back and forth instead of first creating generic structs and queries of the data. In this approach, the properties are transferred back and forth, and new objects are created in the process. However, only public properties are transferred back and forth. Methods are not transferred.

TIP

Flash will link only if AS code that it knows is used, and it won't know about the AS class unless you reference it in your code as a data type for a variable or use it in a cast. So if you set up everything but your CFC isn't converted to the right AS class, add a `temp` variable so the compiler will make sure to include your AS class. This approach guarantees that the class is available at runtime. It doesn't matter where you put this variable as long as it's in the source code somewhere: `var _t1:Actors`.

Adobe Flash Player and the Flex server work together to make this translation between server and client transparent to you for ColdFusion CFC and Java classes only. For all other languages, a translation layer needs to be written—another reason why ColdFusion provides the easiest way to build the back-end of Flex applications.

ColdFusion Data Wizards

Most of this chapter is devoted to helping you learn and understand the code required to connect your ColdFusion server to a Flex client application. However, before we get into the nitty-gritty of code, we'll look at another option that is available to you.

Adobe has added a number of data-centric wizards (DCWs) in the latest version of Flash Builder. One of them is for applications that need to connect to ColdFusion.

This chapter won't provide step-by-step directions for using these wizards; this information can be found in the IDE documentation. You can find these wizards on the Data menu in Flash Builder.

There are four wizards:

- Connect to ColdFusion: This wizard generates the ActionScript code that links a Flex client to your CFC service. It can also generate a sample service to help you quickly prototype the code.
- Bind to Data: This wizard lets you quickly bind UI elements to the results of calls to services (created in the first wizard).
- Generate Form: This wizard generates a data-entry form based on the data types required by your service.
- Generate Details View: Like the form wizard, this wizard creates a detailed view to display the data returned by your service.

Calling the Server (RPC)

When you need to call the server with a RPC request (REST, Web Services, or AMF), three Flex tags are available: REST uses `<mx:HTTPService>`, Web Services uses `<mx:WebService>`, and AMF uses `<mx:RemoteObject>`.

These three tag are all similar in that they send asynchronous requests to the server and they return a result or fault event when they are complete. Since AMF is the most common and preferred means of communicating with Flex, we'll use that as our example.

```
<mx:RemoteObject>
```

Communication between Flex and ColdFusion uses the `<mx:RemoteObject>` tag in Flex. This tag manages the asynchronous calls to the ColdFusion server and the mapping of each call to the correct result and fault methods. Think of this tag as like `CFOBJECT` in Flex. With this tag, you can invoke any CFC on the ColdFusion server from inside your Flex application.

The key properties that you need to know to use the `<mx:RemoteObject>` tag are:

- ID: This is the ID you will use to reference this `remoteObject` object and to invoke the methods.
- `destination="ColdFusion"`: By default, ColdFusion ships with the default destination `"ColdFusion"` preconfigured in the Flex server configuration files. However, if you want

multiple destinations with different configurations, you can configure these. See the ColdFusion documentation for more information.

- `source="ows.components…"`: This is the fully qualified path to the CFC you want to invoke. This is the same dot path you would use inside a `CFOBJECT` tag in a regular CFM page.
- `mx:Method` child tags: Since every request to a server is asynchronous, two callback methods need to be defined for every server call. The first method is the result handler. This is the method that will be called when the server finally returns data from your server call. The second call (optional, but always recommended) is a fault handler; if the server throws an error, then this fault method will be invoked instead. By creating a child tag for each server call, you can define different result and fault methods for every server call.

Here is a sample of an `<mx:RemoteObject>` tag with two server calls defined:

```
<mx:RemoteObject
    id="cfService"
    destination="ColdFusion"
    source="ows.components…">

    <mx:Method name="getAll" result="getAllResultHandler"
fault="getAllFaultHandler"/>

    <mx:Method name="save" result="saveResultHandler" fault="saveFaultHandler" />

</mx:RemoteObject>
```

Result and Fault Handlers

As mentioned earlier, every server call is an asynchronous request with two possible methods that can be invoked. The result method is called when the request works, and the fault method is called when there is an error.

Flex data is usually passed inside events, and this is true with the result and fault methods.

When Flex invokes your result method, it passes in a `ResultEvent` instance. Inside this event is a `result` property that holds the data returned from the server. For instance, this result method will trace the data returned from the server:

```
public function getAllResultHandler(event:ResultEvent):void
{
    trace( event.result );
}
```

Likewise, when the fault event is invoked, a `FaultEvent` object is used. This event wraps the exception thrown by the server inside a `fault` property:

```
public function getAllFaultHandler( event:FaultEvent ):void
{
    trace( event.fault.faultString );
}
```

Invoking a CFC Method

Now that you have defined the `<mx:RemoteObject>` tag, the link to your CFC, and the methods that will process the result or any errors, it's time to call your CFC on the server.

Flex has made this very easy. Using the ID of your remote object, all you need to do is reference the CFC method you want to call as if it were a local method.

For instance, suppose you define an `<mx:RemoteObject>` tag with the ID `"movieService"`:

```
<mx:RemoteObject
    id="movieService"
    destination="ColdFusion"
    source="ows.components..."/>
```

Now you call the `getAll` method of the CFC, like this:

```
var token:AsyncToken = movieService.getAll();
```

Notice that the result is not the data returned from your CFC but instead an object of type `AsyncToken`. The result will always be an `AsyncToken` object.

AsyncToken

Since all requests to a server are asynchronous, you are not able to wait for a reply. Instead, replies are handled in the result function. However, sometimes you need to keep track of a piece of data both before the call to the server and when the result is back.

For instance, suppose you have five items of the same type and you are looping over them, calling `save()` for each item. Now you've called `save()` five individual times, and your result method has been called five times: once for each result. But you want to update the original item with the new ID returned from the server. This is what `AsyncToken` is for.

After you call the server, Flex returns a new token. This token is a dynamic class, which allows you to add new properties on the fly. Flex guarantees that this same token with your new properties will be passed to the result handler for each call.

In this example, we create a new film in Flex and call `save()` on the server. Then we update our local copy with the ID assigned by the database and returned from the server.

```
var film:Film = new Film();
film.title = "History of ColdFusion";
film.staring = "Ben Forta, Tim Buntel";

var token:AsyncToken = movieService.getAll();
token.localFilmInstance = film;
```

Now in the result handler method, we can get this local `film` instance and set the ID property:

```
public function saveFilmResultHandler( event:ResultEvent ):void
{
    var localFilm:Film = event.token.localFilmInstance;
    var newID = event.result.Id;

    localFilm.Id = newId;
}
```

ColdFusion Flex Services

New in ColdFusion 9 are a number of ActionScript and MXML proxy classes that allow you to invoke a few specific ColdFusion tags directly from your Flex application. The proxy classes are CFCHART, CFDOCUMENT, CFIMAGE, CFMAIL, CFPOP, and CFPDF. Imagine creating PDFs from inside your Flash applications!

To use these new classes, you need to configure some security settings so that only the Flash applications you create can ask your server to use its processing power.

First, you need to create a user for your application.

1. In ColdFusion Administrator, choose User Manager. Create a new user and give the user permission for each of the proxy classes you are going to use in your Flash application.
2. The next step is to configure your Flash application with your security setting. You do this with the ActionScript class called Config. With this Config class, you define the username and password of the user you defined in the ColdFusion Administrator as well as the IP and port address of the Web server that is serving the .swf file.

```
<cf:Config
    id="cfConf"
    serviceUserName="maxUser"
    servicePassword="maxUser"
    cfServer="localhost"
cfPort="8300" />
```

Here is an example showing the use of the CFMAIL tag from inside your Flash application. As you can see in this example, the Flash version of Mail and the CFMail tag have the same properties. However, there is one difference: the Flash version won't run automatically; you need to call the execute() method when you are ready to run the tag and send the email.

```
<mx:Script>
<![CDATA[
    import mx.rpc.events.FaultEvent;
    import mx.controls.Alert;
    import mx.managers.PopUpManager;

    [Bindable]
    public var emailMsg:String;

    public function sendReminder():void
    {
        // create message text
        emailMsg = "Everyone forgets their password now and then. Click here to
reset your password.\n" +
                    "http://localhost:8300/resetpassword.cfm?email=" +toEmail.text;

        cfMailService.execute();

    }
]]>
</mx:Script>
```

```
<cf:Mail id="cfMailService"
     server="localhost"
     to="{toEmail.text}"
     replyTo="{toEmail.text}"
     subject="Password Reminder"
     content="{emailMsg}"
     from="mikenimer@yahoo.com"
     type="text" charset="utf-8" mailerId="CF" priority="1"
     timeout="60" useTLS="true" wrapText="5"
     result="handleResult(event)"
     fault="handleError(event)"
     />
```

Data Messaging

The BlazeDS Server data messaging functionality provides your application with true push. Unlike RPC, with which you need to request data to get data, data messaging allows you to send a message from a client to other clients through the BlazeDS Server or directly from the server to the client without the client's needing to periodically check for data.

For example, if you have a dashboard application used by the executives of your company to see the company sales figures in real time, you can use RPC and a timer to have all the dashboards check for new data every 30 seconds. As you can imagine, this is a lot of overhead and excess network traffic for nothing. However, if you use the data messaging feature, your application can send a single message to all of the connected clients when a new sale is recorded in the database, thus using network bandwidth only when something happens. With the cool Flex Charting components, the dashboard charts could be animating and changing in real time automatically. Imagine showing that application to your boss (make sure you ask for a raise when you do it).

The Flex data messaging functionality is modeled on other messaging frameworks, such as JMS in Java, using much of the same terminology and architecture. If you are familiar with these other languages, you will find Flex data messaging similar. Since Flex is a plumbing layer written on Java, you can even connect Flex to other messaging frameworks, JMS, or ColdFusion event gateways.

Like Flash Remoting, data messaging uses the AMF binary protocol to talk to the server. However, it doesn't use, by default, the HTTP protocol that Flash Remoting uses. Instead, the data messaging functionality uses the Real-Time Messaging Protocol (RTMP). RTMP was originally developed for the Flash Media Server (originally called the Flash Communications Server) to provide audio, video, and data streaming. Unlike TCP/IP, which was designed for short bursts of traffic, RTMP was designed and optimized for thousands of concurrent connections.

Messaging in Flex

When creating a Flex application that uses messaging, you need to understand two concepts: publishing and subscribing. Flex has a different MXML tag for each. Under the covers, these two tags share the same connection to the server, but dividing the connection into two tags allows you to create different handlers for pushing and receiving messages.

The first tag, `mx:Publisher`, is used to send messages to the server. The second tag, `mx:Consumer`, is used to receive messages from the server.

Messaging in ColdFusion

Using the event gateway technology in ColdFusion, you can send messages from other CFML applications (`.cfm` pages). and receive messages to parse on the ColdFusion server.

After you have created an instance of the `DataMessagingGateway` type in the ColdFusion Administrator, you can send messages to your Flash clients from a CFM page using the `sendGatewayMessage()` method.

```
<cfset flexMesssage = StructNew()>

<cfset messageObject = structNew()>
<cfset messageObject.message = "This is the message I want to send back">
<cfset messageObject.type = "Information">
<cfset flexMesssage.body = messageObject>

<cfset flexMesssage.Destination = "ColdFusionMessagingGateway">
<cfset ret = SendGatewayMessage("ows31 ", flexMesssage)>
<p>Message has been sent!</p>
```

Suppose you have a Flash reporting dashboard application that shows charts of the daily sales figures. You could keep requesting new data from the server, or you can use messaging to send a message from your CFML e-commerce application for each transaction. All of the clients running the Flash dashboard will get the messages and be able to update their charts on the fly, without having to reload all the data.

Data Management

The third part of the LCDS Server data layer is the Flex Data Management service functionality. Data Management provides your application with two key pieces of functionality: data synchronization and conflict resolution. Data Management is built as a layer on top of the push functionality provided by the Flex data messaging—which is how the data messaging keeps the data set synchronized between clients.

Data synchronization allows you to link many clients to the same set of data (query result set, array, and so on), and when one person changes the data, all of the other clients will see the change immediately—well, as immediately as their bandwidth allows. This functionality can be clustered and scaled for a large number of connected clients.

Conflict resolution works in conjunction with the data synchronization and provides you with a client-side answer to the problem of what happens when two people try to edit and save the same data. See Chapter 32 for an example of conflict handling.

Imagine this: One user opens a record and changes the phone number but then gets distracted and doesn't save the record (but the record is still open in the application). At the same time, another user opens the same record and edits the same phone number and saves it. Now the second user has his or her changes saved to the database, but the first client is out of sync. Flex Data Management service comes to the rescue: the first user will get an alert saying that data—the phone number—is out of sync and allowing the user to either override this data with the new data from the second user or override the second user's changes with his or her own modifications. As you can imagine, this is a much better experience for the user than having a form submitted to the server, having a version ID or time stamp checked in the database, and then receiving an error message, making the user start over.

The LCDS Server does have the capability to fall back to HTTP for data messaging, but under the covers, all it is doing is adding a timer and periodically checking for new messages. This process is not especially efficient, but it is guaranteed to work on all networks. RTMP requires two new ports to be open on the client's firewall. Luckily, the LCDS Server allows you to configure both protocols at the same time, so users who can use RTMP will, and users who have it blocked can default to HTTP. HTTP doesn't offer as great an experience, but it is still good. The Flex SESSION scope on the server keeps track of messages waiting to be delivered to the client the next time the client asks for messages.

Where is the SESSION scope? This is a common question for new Flex developers. You've just spent the last 10 years figuring out different ways to pass variables from page to page so you can remember a user: cookies, a server-side variable tied to a cookie, and URL variables. However, with Flex, the application is the session. In Flex, you load one application, and as long as that application is running, it maintains state. You don't need to pass variables when you switch screens.

But this doesn't mean that your server-side code can't share a session with the client. A cool side effect of the way that Flash works is that Flash actually uses the browser's HTTP engine when a call is made back to the server. This means that all of the cookies and browser information gets passed back and forth whenever you call the server. So if you set a cookie with `<CFCOOKIE>` every time you make a Flash Remoting request from Flex to the ColdFusion server, that same cookie is sent back each time. The CFC doesn't know if it's a CFM page or a Flash movie, and it can maintain state exactly the same way.

ColdFusion and Flex Configuration Settings

You have a number of options when you set up ColdFusion and Flex, and no approach is necessarily better than another. You can merge everything into one server or divide the servers and configure them separately.

What makes this flexibility possible is the remote structure of a Flex application. With standard CFM pages, the server did all the work, and it needed access to everything. However, with Flex, a lot of the application is running on the client's computer, and all the interaction with the server occurs as individual HTTP requests. Just as with a request to get the HTML, in a Flex application you have an individual request for every query, so there are lots of little requests instead of one big request.

ColdFusion Administrator Settings

The ColdFusion Administrator has a new page dedicated to the integration of ColdFusion and Flex. However, most of these settings matter only if you have ColdFusion and Flex installed separately. If ColdFusion and Flex are installed together with the ColdFusion installer, only the first setting affects you.

- Enable Flash Remoting Support: This setting turns on or off the ability to invoke ColdFusion CFCs with Flash Remoting. This is a security setting. If you are using CFCs with Flash Remoting and being careful about how you build your CFCs and which CFCs you put in your Web root, then you need this capability turned on. However, you can use this setting to shut down this access so no one can build a Flash movie to call code on your server.
- Enable Remote Adobe LiveCycle Data Management Access: This is another on/off switch, but in this case you might choose to disable this feature for performance and resource reasons instead of security reasons. Turning off this option tells ColdFusion not to load the libraries it needs into memory and not to listen for RMI requests.
- Enable RMI over SSL for Data Management: This setting allows you to configure the keystore for the SSL connection between servers. This setting is useful if you have ColdFusion and Flex installed on different servers and are working with sensitive data.
- Select IP Addresses Where LiveCycle Data Services Are Running: If you have enabled remote Data Management service access, this setting will let you lock this access down to a specific IP address as an additional security precaution.

services-config.xml

Every application has a special configuration file you need to know about: the WEB-INF/flex/services-config.xml file. This little file is the key to the whole system. This file tells the Flex server which CFC or Java classes to load for the different types of requests, the URL to use to access everything, security settings, level of logging, and so on.

NOTE

This file is used by both the Flash Builder IDE and the Flex server. Flash Builder uses the files to get the URL of the Flex server for the services you want to call. The Flex server uses the file for everything else.

In general, ColdFusion ships with Flex configured and ready to go, and you may never need to edit this file. However, if you do, you need to understand destinations and channels.

Destinations

You use destinations to define the different services you want to invoke. By design, you would create a new destination for every CFC you want to invoke; this is what the Java developers have to do. However, ColdFusion has another option: you can define the source as a wildcard (*). This wildcard tells Flex that you will be setting the source in your MXML code. A nice feature is that you can start by defining the path to the CFC in your MXML file, and if you need to change it (if you're moving to a quality assurance server), you can override what is in your MXML file at the `<destination>` level.

You can also set for each destination a list of channels that your Flex client should try to use to connect to ColdFusion.

Channels

In the Flex server, channels define the behaviors of connections and the protocol that is used. For instance, you might have one channel for regular HTTP and another for HTTPS. These channels can also define the way that clients connect to the server: Do they make simple requests (HTTP), make lots of requests checking for new data (polling), or connect to the server and leave the connection open (RTMP)?

When you define the channels for a destination, you can define more than one, allowing for failover at the client level. For instance, you might want to tell clients to start by trying to connect to the server with RTMP, giving users real-time push. However, it is common for users to have RTMP blocked by their firewall, so you may want to define a second channel that users can try if RTMP fails: a polling channel. This channel will continue to send HTTP requests to the server, getting all of the messages that are waiting. This option isn't as good as RTMP, but it's close, and it is better than no connection at all.

Here is an example of a messaging destination, that starts by trying to connect with RTMP and then fails over to a polling channel:

```
<destination>
<channels>
<channel ref="cf-rtmp"/>
<channel ref="cf-polling-amf"/>
</channels>
</destination>
```

Channel Properties

You can define a number of properties at the channel level that can make development easier for you. Table 31.1 summarizes these properties.

Table 31.1 Flex Channel Properties

PROPERTY	SETTING	DESCRIPTION
`Access`	`use-mapping`	This setting tells ColdFusion to use the ColdFusion mappings, set in the ColdFusion Administrator to find the CFC.
`Access`	`method-access-level`	By default, ColdFusion allows only applications from a remote location (any Flash application) to invoke CFC methods defined with an access level of `remote`. However, this is the same setting that allows Web Services to connect. You can set the access level to `public` if you want to let only Flash connect to the CFC, and not allow Web Services to invoke the method.

Table 31.1 (continued)

PROPERTY	SETTING	DESCRIPTION
`use-accessors`	`use-implicit-accessors`	This setting tells ColdFusion to use the `get` and `set` methods for all of the properties if they are defined. However, if you aren't using `get` and `set` methods, turning this setting off can speed up the creation of CFCs.
`use-structs`	x	ColdFusion can map a ColdFusion struct of names and values to a ActionScript object instead of mapping a CFC to an ActionScript class. You might want to use a struct for performance. To stop this behavior if Flex is converting structs that you don't want to convert, set this property to false to disable this translation.
`property-case`	`force-cfc-lowercase`	Since ColdFusion is case insensitive and Flex is case sensitive, these three properties can make development a lot easier. These tell ColdFusion to force specific data type properties to lowercase, allowing you to always code for lowercase in your Flex application.
`property-case`	`force-query-lowercase`	
`property-case`	`force-struct-lowercase`	

Debugging

As with any programming language, you can't do much if you don't have a way to debug your code. There are at least three ways to debug your Flex application, two of which require a separate application. You can use console logging output, a packet sniffer, and the new ColdFusion Debugging plug-in in Flash Builder.

The first step in debugging a Flex application is to figure out if the client and the server are talking to each other. If you can see traffic going in to ColdFusion but not back out, the problem is on the ColdFusion side. If you see the request go to ColdFusion and then back out, the problem is on the Flex side. With this knowledge, you can focus your debugging.

Console Output

When developing your Flex application, run ColdFusion from a command prompt in a console window instead of running ColdFusion as a service. Watching the traffic going in and out can be very useful—so much so that you may want to always start your ColdFusion and Flex servers from a command prompt during development.

To see the Flex, traffic, you need to change the Flex logging level to `Debug`. This setting is configured in `WEB-INF/flexservices-config.xml`.

```
<logging>
   <target class="flex.messaging.log.ConsoleTarget" level="Debug">
      <properties>
         <prefix>[Flex] </prefix>
         <includeDate>false</includeDate>
         <includeTime>false</includeTime>
         <includeLevel>false</includeLevel>
         <includeCategory>false</includeCategory>
      </properties>
      <filters>
         <pattern>Endpoint.*</pattern>
         <pattern>Service.*</pattern>
         <pattern>Configuration</pattern>
         <pattern>Message.*</pattern>
      </filters>
   </target>
</logging>
```

You can make a number of tweaks to the logging settings. If you are curious, check the Flex documentation for descriptions of these settings. However, the default settings in most situations work fine.

ColdFusion has startup scripts located in the `%install location%bin` folder. These are the exact same scripts that ColdFusion uses when it starts ColdFusion as a service. In the command window, this script is named `cfstart.bat`.

1. Open a command window (if using Windows choose Start > Run and type `cmd`).
2. Browse to your ColdFusion installation directory and run the ColdFusion start script.

   When you run ColdFusion and Flex from a command window, you will see a lot of output from Flex, but most of the time, you should look for messages that start with one of these two strings (`request` = incoming and `response` = outgoing):

   ```
   [Flex] Deserializing AMF/HTTP request
   [Flex] Serializing AMF/HTTP response
   ```

Here is a sample request going into Flex. Most of the properties listed here are internal Flex properties; however, there are three that will matter to you: `source` will tell you what CFC is being invoked, `operation` will tell you the method name, and `body` will tell you the method arguments, if any, being passed in.

```
[Flex] Deserializing AMF/HTTP request
Version: 3
  (Message #0 targetURI=null, responseURI=/6)
    (Array #0)
      [0] = (Typed Object #0 'flex.messaging.messages.RemotingMessage')
        source = "ows.35.example2.components.exampleService"
        operation = "getData"
        messageId = "17D2C76D-C1A8-98E1-58EB-0EEF673F54ED"
        body = (Array #1)
        timeToLive = 0
```

```
clientId = "F87123ED-040A-3CF2-321C-FA19C732C6AE"
headers = (Object #2)
  DSEndpoint = "my-cfamf"
destination = "ColdFusion"
timestamp = 0
```

Here is a sample response coming out of ColdFusion and back to Flex. This example returns a query of two rows. As you can see, a query is returned as a `flex.messaging.io.ArrayCollection` data type, which is an array of objects.

```
[Flex] Serializing AMF/HTTP response
Version: 3
  (Message #0 targetURI=/6/onResult, responseURI=)
    (Typed Object #0 'flex.messaging.messages.AcknowledgeMessage')
      timestamp = 1.185661549358E12
      headers = (Object #1)
      body = (Externalizable Object #2 'flex.messaging.io.ArrayCollection')
        (Array #3)
          [0] = (Object #4)
            AGE = 56
            NAMEFIRST = "Sean"
            NAMELAST = "Conway"
            ACTORID = 1
          [1] = (Object #5)
            AGE = 45
            NAMEFIRST = "Harry5"
            NAMELAST = "Floyd4"
            ACTORID = 2
      correlationId = "17D2C76D-C1A8-98E1-58EB-0EEF673F54ED"
      messageId = "F876ABBB-4E08-C3CA-1E34-0198DBB06D47"
      timeToLive = 0.0
      clientId = "F87123ED-040A-3CF2-321C-FA19C732C6AE"
      destination = null
```

By using the console output for debugging, you can easily home in on a problem while debugging. If you see data going in and out of ColdFusion, then you know the problem is on the Flex side. If you see data going in but nothing coming out, or error messages in the console, then you know the problem is on the ColdFusion side. Also, the use of the console will help you handle simple case-sensitivity issues. For instance, if you created your bindings with lowercase column names and nothing is showing up but you do see data coming in and out of ColdFusion, then you can use this console output to confirm the case of the column name binding variables in your Flex application. You should always be mindful of case sensitivity because it's very easy to flip the case of a property in memory without affecting your ColdFusion code.

TIP

For Windows users, make sure that you increase the command window screen buffer size so you can scroll back up and see the debugging data.

Flash Builder and ColdFusion Line Debuggers

Another option for debugging is a line-by-line debugger. For the client side, you can use Flash Builder to start your application in debugging mode and insert a breakpoint in your result method to see what is being sent back from ColdFusion.

For the server side, you can use ColdFusion Builder. By running the plug-in inside Flash Builder, you can connect to a running instance of ColdFusion and insert a breakpoint in the CFC that is invoked with Flash Remoting to see what is being passed to ColdFusion.

If you have enough RAM, you can run both the Flex application and ColdFusion in debug mode, debugging both sides of the application at the same time.

Network Monitors

If you cannot run your ColdFusion server from a command line—for instance, if you are working on a remote development server—then you will need to use a separate program called a network monitor. Luckily, there are a number of different programs available that understand the AMF protocol, and one is built into the new Flash Builder 4 IDE.

CHAPTER 32

Integrating with Flash Data Services

IN THIS CHAPTER

Configuring Flash Builder for Flash Remoting

Every new Flex project you create requires you to use the New Flex Project wizard. When you run the wizard, you will be presented with a ColdFusion-specific project type: ColdFusion Flash Remoting Service. Choose this project type, and all of the compiler arguments will be set up for you automatically. Then click Next to move on.

NOTE

If you use the Basic wizard type, you'll need to define the `-services` compiler argument yourself or use the runtime configuration described at the end of this chapter. Many people prefer to use the Basic option so that they have full control.

Next, you need to provide three pieces of information: the root folder, root URL, and context root. By default, with the stand-alone version of ColdFusion, the context root is /. If you installed ColdFusion with the Multiserver option, you will also need to point to the location of the ColdFusion WAR file.

These fields allow Flash Builder to find `services-config.xml` and know how to launch the application when you run it from Flash Builder. This is the only step that is unique to the ColdFusion project wizard. The other screens are the same for all three types of new projects.

- Root Folder: This is Web root folder in your ColdFusion installation, the same folder that contains the `WEB-INF` folder.
- Root URL: This is the URL you use to browse the folder where Flex outputs the compiled movie. Usually this is a folder called `bin` under your project root, but if you moved the default `bin` folder or your project is in a subfolder or virtual directory, make sure that this path reflects this.
- Context Root: The stand-alone installation and the default J2EE installation use `/` as the context root. If you are running ColdFusion in a J2EE configuration, the root may be different.

On the next screen of the wizard, you define the name of the project and the location of your development folder: where you want the files to be created. The default location is a folder under the Eclipse workspace folder, but rarely will this be the same folder in which you do your development. Instead, it will usually be a folder under your Web root; for instance, with IIS it might be a folder under `/INETPUB/wwwroot/`.

On the final wizard screen, you can leave the defaults; however, it's considered a best practice to create a `/src` folder for your Flex files. This way, the system folders (`.settings` and `html-templates`), the compiled files, and the source files for the project are cleanly separated.

Configuring the Flash Builder `-services` Compiler Argument

The `services-config.xml` file contains the URLs that the client needs to use to call Flex, and the Flex server loads this file for its configuration settings, but how does the `.swf` file on the client's machine know this information? This information is provided automatically when the Flash movie is compiled. Using the `-services` compiler argument, Flash Builder loads and parses the `services-config.xml` file and pulls that `<endpoint>` value out of the XML file for the destinations you are using. Then when the Flex application needs to call the server, the movie already knows the URL to use.

To specify this setting in Flash Builder, right-click your open Flex project, choose Properties from the menu, and go to the Flex Compiler screen. This screen has a text input field labeled Additional Compiler Arguments. There, add this line:

```
-services "<path to your services-config.xml>"
```

NOTE

If you do development on a remote server, you can point Flash Builder to a local copy of `services-config.xml`. You don't have to use the exact same file; it just needs to have the same XML elements.

FlashBuilder 4 contains a new option, Flex Server, in the project properties (right-click the project). Choose Flex Server from the menu. In this panel, you can choose ColdFusion from the drop-down list and validate the settings. This process will set up the services argument correctly for your installation.

Flash Remoting Application

Our first application simply calls ColdFusion and displays the results of a query. You can think of this as the Flex version of the use of `CFQuery` and `CFOUTPUT` in an HTML page.

NOTE

This example appears in the `example1/src/example1.mxml` file.

After creating the new Flash Builder project, we will create a new folder for ColdFusion components, `components`, so your folder structure should look like this:

```
project
   bin
   components
   html-templates
   src
```

NOTE

You'll notice when you compile this project that it will also copy the `components` folder into the `bin` folder, even though the code is not technically Flex code. This is a good thing, since you will be able to deploy just the `bin` folder when you are done with development.

When starting a new Flex project, you first should define the services that the UI will access, so the first piece of code we will write is the ColdFusion component that our Flex project will access.

In the new `components` folder, create a new file named `Example1Service.cfc` containing the code in Listing 32.1.

Listing 32.1 `ExampleService.cfc`

```
<cfcomponent alias="ows.32.example1.components.exampleService">
   <cffunction name="getData" access="remote" returnType="query">
      <cfset var qData="">

      <cfquery name="qData" datasource="ows">
      select ACTORID, NAMEFIRST, NAMELAST, AGE
      from APP.ACTORS
      </cfquery>

      <cfreturn qData/>
   </cffunction>
</cfcomponent>
```

As you can see, this CFC has one remote method with a simple query that returns the ID, age, and name of each of the actors in the database. There is nothing special about this method, nothing Flex specific; this CFC method could be called from any CFM page.

The next step in writing our application is to modify the MXML application that was created when the Flex project was created. To get our Flex application to talk to ColdFusion and to display the results of our query, we need three pieces: the remote object definition, the button to load the data, and the data grid to display the data.

First, we'll define the link between Flex and ColdFusion. To do this, we use the `<mx:RemoteObject>` tag, which defines a link between Flex and your CFC and allows Flex to call CFC methods via methods on the `RemoteObject` tag.

Flex determines the URL to invoke based on the destination attribute and how it is configured in the `WEB-INF/flex/services-config.xml` file. By default, ColdFusion ships with the default destination `ColdFusion` already configured. This destination is configured to allow you to call any CFC that is defined in the source attribute on the `RemoteObject` tag.

The source attribute of the `RemoteObject` tag is the path to CFC, just as when you call a CFC with `CFOBJECT`. However, don't forget that this source value must point to a ColdFusion component under the Web root.

```
<fx:Declarations>
<s:RemoteObject id="ro"
                destination="ColdFusion"
                source="ows.32.example1.exampleService"/>
</fx:Declarations>
```

TIP

To test your CFC path, take this source value and replace the period (`.`) with a slash (`/`) in your browser and make sure that you can browse the CFC. For example, in the browser the source value would be `http://localhost:8500/ows/32/example1/exampleService.cfc`.

Next, define a button that will call the CFC and load the data. This button has a click event, just like the HTML `onClick` event. When the button is clicked, this event calls the CFC method `getData()` by going through the `RemoteObject` tag.

```
<s:Button label="Load Actors"
          click="ro.getData()"/>
```

TIP

If you want this feature loaded automatically when the application starts, you can use the Flex `creationComplete` event on the application instead of the button:

```
<s:Application
      xmlns:fx="http://ns.adobe.com/mxml/2009"
      xmlns:s="library://ns.adobe.com/flex/spark"
   xmlns:mx="library://ns.adobe.com/flex/mx"
   initialize="ro.getData();">
      <s:layout>
         <s:VerticalLayout/>
   </s:layout>
```

This is the Flex equivalent of the HTML `<body onLoad="">` event.

Next, we'll define `<mx:DataGrid>` to output our results.

When we create the grid, Flex can automatically define the columns based on the columns in the query, but this method does not allow any control of formatting or header text, so we will add child tags for each of the columns.

The `<mx:DataGrid>` grid is populated by passing in an array of objects that maps from ColdFusion as an array of structs: one struct for each row in our query.

NOTE

ColdFusion automatically performs this conversion from a query to an array of structs for you.

For the data grid to display the query returned from a ColdFusion CFC, we need to set the value of the `dataProvider` property on the Flex data grid to equal the results of our CFC method.

The `RemoteObject` tag has a special property we can use to create this binding: `lastResult`. Since Flex requests are asynchronous and multiple requests could be returned at different times in a different order, this `lastResult` property will always be the returned value from the last request sent, not the last response received. The format is remote object ID > CFC method name > `lastResult`.

```
<mx:DataGrid width="100%"
             height="100%"
             dataProvider="{ro.getData.lastResult}">
   <mx:columns>
```

```
      <mx:DataGridColumn dataField="ACTORID" headerText="id" width="50"/>
      <mx:DataGridColumn dataField="AGE" headerText="age" width="50"/>
      <mx:DataGridColumn dataField="NAMEFIRST" headerText="First Name"/>
      <mx:DataGridColumn dataField="NAMELAST" headerText="Last Name"/>
   </mx:columns>
</mx:DataGrid>
```

When you are done, the final MXML file should look like Listing 32.2.

Listing 32.2 `Example1.mxml`

```
<?xml version="1.0" encoding="utf-8"?>
<s:Application
   xmlns:fx="http://ns.adobe.com/mxml/2009"
   xmlns:s="library://ns.adobe.com/flex/spark"
   xmlns:mx="library://ns.adobe.com/flex/mx" >
   <s:layout>
      <s:VerticalLayout/>
   </s:layout>

   <fx:Declarations>
      <!-- define a connection to our CFC -->
      <s:RemoteObject
         id="ro"
         destination="ColdFusion"
         fault="cfFaultHandler(event)"
         source="ows.32.example1.components.exampleService"/>
   </fx:Declarations>

   <fx:Script>
      <![CDATA[
         import mx.controls.Alert;
         import mx.rpc.events.FaultEvent;

         public function cfFaultHandler(event:FaultEvent):void
         {
            Alert.show(event.fault.message, "error");
         }
      ]]>
   </fx:Script>

   <s:Group width="100%" height="100%">
      <s:layout>
         <s:VerticalLayout/>
      </s:layout>

      <!--   using the RemoteObject we defined we'll call our CFC method   -->
      <s:Button
         label="Load Actors"
         click="ro.getData()"/>

      <!-- Display the query that is returned from our CFC -->

      <mx:DataGrid
         width="100%"
         height="100%"
         dataProvider="{ro.getData.lastResult}">
```

Listing 32.2 (continued)

```
            <mx:columns>
               <mx:DataGridColumn dataField="ACTORID" headerText="id" width="50"/>
               <mx:DataGridColumn dataField="AGE" headerText="age" width="50"/>
               <mx:DataGridColumn dataField="NAMEFIRST" headerText="First Name"/>
               <mx:DataGridColumn dataField="NAMELAST" headerText="Last Name"/>
            </mx:columns>
         </mx:DataGrid>
      </s:Group>

   </s:Application>
```

Adding Best-Practice Improvements to the Data Grid

The preceding application was very simple. There are a few modifications we can make to our application that don't directly change the functionality but are considered best practices.

To see these modifications, look at the `example1/src/example1a.mxml` file.

The first change will be the way we define the `RemoteObject` tag. The `RemoteObject` tag allows you to specifically define each CFC method and the `result` and `fault` methods that should be called when a value is returned.

By default, Flex calls any method that you define in your code; however, the results and errors of all of the methods will share the same `result` and `fault` errors. This approach isn't desirable when you are trying to make multiple calls to your server with the different results—trying to put all of this logic into one method can very quickly become problematic.

To solve this problem, we can use a child tag of the `<mx:RemoteObject>` tag: `<mx:method>`. The `<mx:method>` tag allows you to define a different `result` and `fault` method for each ColdFusion method.

```
<mx:RemoteObject id="ro"
                 destination="ColdFusion"
                 source="ows.32.example1.components.exampleService">
   <mx:method name="getData"
              result="doGetDataResult(event)"
              fault="doErrorHandler(event)"/>
</mx:RemoteObject>
```

Instead of binding our grid to `lastResult`, we will bind `DataGrid` to a local property, which is set in the result handler of our method.

In `RemoteObject`, we define a result handler, with the result event as an argument:

```
result="doGetDataResult(event)"
```

Then in the `doGetaDataResult(event)` method, we set a local property:

```
private var qResults:ArrayCollection;
private function doGetDataResult(event:ResultEvent):void
{
   this.qResults = event.result as ArrayCollection;
}
```

Then we update the binding in `DataGrid` to this new local property:

```
<mx:DataGrid width="100%"
             height="100%"
             dataProvider="{this.qResults}">
   <mx:columns>
      <mx:DataGridColumn dataField="ACTORID" headerText="id" width="50"/>
      <mx:DataGridColumn dataField="AGE" headerText="age" width="50"/>
      <mx:DataGridColumn dataField="NAMEFIRST" headerText="First Name"/>
      <mx:DataGridColumn dataField="NAMELAST" headerText="Last Name"/>
   </mx:columns>
</mx:DataGrid>
```

Adding an Edit Form to the Data Grid

Displaying data is not enough. You need to be able to modify it, too. In this next example, we will add a pop-up edit form to the preceding application, allowing you to view and edit all the rows in your database.

To see this example, look at the `example2/src/example2.mxml` file.

We will also add logic to the data grid that will call our method to launch a pop-up window with our edit form when a user double-clicks a row in the data grid.

NOTE

In Flex, a pop-up window is not another browser instance; it's just another box floating over the movie that looks like a pop-up window.

TIP

The `doubleClick` event is the only event for `DataGrid` that requires a second property, `doubleClickEnabled`, to turn on the `doubleClick` event.

```
<mx:DataGrid width="100%"
             height="100%"
             dataProvider="{this.qResults}"
             doubleClickEnabled="true"
             doubleClick="doEditActor(event)">
   <mx:columns>
      <mx:DataGridColumn dataField="ACTORID" headerText="id" width="50"/>
      <mx:DataGridColumn dataField="AGE" headerText="age" width="50"/>
      <mx:DataGridColumn dataField="NAMEFIRST" headerText="First Name"/>
      <mx:DataGridColumn dataField="NAMELAST" headerText="Last Name"/>
   </mx:columns>
</mx:DataGrid>
```

Next, we will add a new function, `doEditActor (event)`, to handle the `DoubleClick` event. This function will use the Flex `PopUpManager` class to open a new component over the application.

```
private function doEditActor(event:Event):void
{
   // Create a new UI component.
   var popup:EditActor = new EditActor();
   popup.width = 300;
   popup.height = 400;
```

```
        // Set the actor property so the new form
        // knows which actor to edit.
        popup.actor = event.currentTarget.selectedItem;

        PopUpManager.addPopUp( popup, this, true );
        PopUpManager.centerPopUp(popup);
    }
```

Next, we'll create a new component (Listing 32.3), which will be our edit form pop-up. This component takes an `actor` object, which was the item selected in `DataGrid`. This component also handles the call back to the server to save the object, with its own `<mx:RemoteObject>` tag. This keeps the component self-contained and easy to modify if required.

Listing 32.3 `EditActor.mxml`

```
<?xml version="1.0" encoding="utf-8"?>
<mx:TitleWindow
   title="Edit Form"
   showCloseButton="true"
   close="PopUpManager.removePopUp(this);"
   xmlns:fx="http://ns.adobe.com/mxml/2009"
   xmlns:s="library://ns.adobe.com/flex/spark"
   xmlns:mx="library://ns.adobe.com/flex/mx" >

   <fx:Declarations>
      <!--define a connection to our CFC-->
      <mx:RemoteObject
         id="ro"
         destination="ColdFusion"
         source="ows.32.example2.components.exampleService">
         <mx:method name="save" result="doSaveResultHandler(event)"
                    fault="doSaveFaultHandler(event)"/>
      </mx:RemoteObject>
   </fx:Declarations>

   <fx:Script>
      <![CDATA[
         import mx.controls.Alert;
         import mx.rpc.events.FaultEvent;
         import mx.rpc.events.ResultEvent;
         import mx.managers.PopUpManager;
         import mx.utils.StringUtil;

         [Bindable]
         public var actor:Object;

         private function doSave():void
         {
            ro.save(this.actor, null);
         }

         private function doSaveResultHandler(event:ResultEvent):void
         {
            this.actor = event.result;
            dispatchEvent( new Event("closeWin") )
            // save successful, close this popup.
```

Listing 32.3 (continued)

```
            PopUpManager.removePopUp(this);
        }

        private function doSaveFaultHandler(event:FaultEvent):void
        {
            // save didn't work, Show alert
            Alert.show("Error saving actor", "Error");
        }
    ]]>
  </fx:Script>

  <mx:Form width="100%">
    <mx:FormItem label="First Name">
      <s:TextInput
        id="firstName"
        width="100"
        text="{StringUtil.trim(this.actor.NAMEFIRST)}"
        change="this.actor.NAMEFIRST = event.currentTarget.text" />
    </mx:FormItem>
    <mx:FormItem label="Last Name">
      <s:TextInput
        id="lastName"
        width="100"
        text="{StringUtil.trim(this.actor.NAMELAST)}"
        change="this.actor.NAMELAST = event.currentTarget.text" />
    </mx:FormItem>
    <mx:FormItem label="Age">
      <s:TextInput
        id="age"
        width="100"
        text="{StringUtil.trim(this.actor.AGE)}"
        change="this.actor.AGE = event.currentTarget.text" />
    </mx:FormItem>
    <mx:FormItem>
      <s:Button
        label="Save"
        click="doSave()" />
    </mx:FormItem>
  </mx:Form>

</mx:TitleWindow>
```

TIP

A component can be more than a single MXML file, so in more complex components you may have multiple MXML files, ActionScript files, item renderers, events, commands, and so on. Thus, for good code maintainability, I recommend creating a new folder within a common `/components` folder–one for each component of your application–and then building your application with these components, like blocks stacked together.

Data Management Application

We will now modify the preceding example to use the LCDS Data Management Services to create a result set synchronized between clients. When this application is working, you will be able to open it in multiple browsers or on other servers, and when one client changes the code, all the other clients will see that change instantly.

NOTE

BlazeDS ships with ColdFusion by default. To use LCDS with ColdFusion, you will need to follow the documentation in LCDS to set ColdFusion to start LCDS instead of BlazeDS.

The key difference between this example and the Flash Remoting example is that things happen automatically with Data Management. With Flash Remoting, you needed to code both the request and response handlers. You don't have to choose one approach or the other, however. In a large application, you likely will access some data through a synchronized result set and other data with simple one-off calls with Flash Remoting or with Web Services.

WARNING

You can't use data messaging and Flash Remoting on the same object; if you use data messaging to get the object, all changes have to go through data messaging, or the object will get out of sync between clients.

NOTE

This example appears in the `example3/src/example3.mxml` file.

Configuring the ColdFusion Data Push Destination

A data push destination is made of two elements: the ID of the ColdFusion Flex event gateway and the protocols for talking to ColdFusion. In this example, we define two channels. This tells Flex to first try the real-time RTMP protocol, in LCDS, and if that fails, to fall back to a built-in HTTP polling code.

```
<destination id="ColdFusion_example4">
   <adapter ref="cfgateway" />
   <properties>
      <gatewayid>ows35_example4</gatewayid>
   </properties>

   <!-- You should use the ColdFusion specific channels -->
   <channels>
<channel ref="cf-rtmp"/>
<channel ref="cf-polling-amf"/>
   </channels>
</destination>
```

Channels

To configure a new channel or protocol that can access a Flex server, use the `<channel-definition>` XML element. Here is the default ColdFusion channel:

```
<channel-definition id="my-cfamf"
                    class="mx.messaging.channels.AMFChannel">
<endpoint uri=http://{server.name}:{server.port}
            {context.root}/flex2gateway/"
         class="flex.messaging.endpoints.AMFEndpoint"/>
<properties>
```

```
<polling-enabled>false</polling-enabled>
<serialization>
   <instantiate-types>false</instantiate-types>
</serialization>
</properties>
</channel-definition>
```

The important part of this XML is the `<endpoint>` tag. This defines the URL that the client uses to connect to Flex on the ColdFusion server. The sample includes three variables in the URL; however, you can easily hard-code the URL, too:

```
<endpoint uri="http://www.myserver.com:8500/flex2gateway/"
          class="flex.messaging.endpoints.AMFEndpoint"/>
```

These different endpoint URLs in the channel are what let a Flex application talk to a ColdFusion server for CFCs and a Flex server for Java classes in the same application.

TIP

If your application is having difficulty connecting to a ColdFusion server, make sure that the `endpoint` path and the port are correct.

Assembler CFC

One server-side piece that is required to build a Data Management application is the assembler CFC. This CFC works like a gateway service for the Flex client and has four key functions:

- `fill`: This function returns an array populated with an array of CFC instances.
- `get`: This function returns a single CFC instance, based on the primary key ID.
- `sync`: This function is a smart method that can determine whether an object needs to be created or updated, usually by checking the primary key property of the object to see whether it has a value.
- `count`: This function is similar to the `fill()` method except that it returns a count instead of the full result set or array of CFC objects.

With these four functions, Flex can load objects, create new objects, and update existing objects. Flex decides when to invoke these methods for you based on actions and events in Flex application.

You can build the assembler CFC in either of two ways. The first, and easiest, way is to run the Create CFC wizard from the RDS plug-in that ships with Flash Builder. The second way is to write your own code, since every assembler is going to be custom to your application, database, and CFC. Let's go through the logic of what you need to write in your assembler CFC instead of looking at the actual code:

```
<cfcomponent output="false">
   <cffunction name="count" output="no"
              returntype="Numeric" access="remote">
      <!-- These are the same param attributes that you would pass to the fill()
method.-->
     <cfargument name="param" type="string" required="no">
```

```
        <!-- 1. Run a query to get all of the items that match the parameters that are
passed in. -->

        <!-- 2. Return the #query.recordCount# variable. -->
    </cffunction>

    <cffunction name="fill" output="no"
                returntype="ACTORS[]" access="remote">
        <!-- The parameters passed to the param attribute are defined by the client
application.
        These are usually the search parameters needed for a result set. -->
        <cfargument name="param" type="string" required="no">

        <!-- 1. Run a query to get all of the items that match the parameters that are
passed in. -->

        <!-- 2. Loop over the results and create a CFC for each item in the result set.
-->

        <!-- 3. Add each new CFC to an array. -->

        <!-- Return the new array full of CFC. -->
    </cffunction>

    <cffunction name="get" output="no"
                returnType="ACTORS" access="remote">
        <cfargument name="obj" type="struct" required="yes">
        <!-- 1. Pull the primary key out of the obj argument. -->

        <!-- 2. Query the database for the item matching the ID. -->

        <!-- 3. Create a CFC instance for it. -->

        <!-- 4. Return the CFC.-->
    </cffunction>

    <cffunction name="sync" output="no"
                returnType="array" access="remote">
        <cfargument name="changes" type="array" required="yes">
        <!-- 1. Loop over the array of CFC instances. -->

        <!-- 2. Check the primary key property of each CFC. If it's empty insert a new
row in the database -->
        <!-- and update the item with the new ID from the database insert.-->
        <!-- If it's not empty, update the database instead.-->

        <!-- 3. Return the array with the updated objects.-->
    </cffunction>
</cfcomponent>
```

Synchronizing the Data Grid

Currently, the Flash Remoting application we've built works fine for one user. However, if more than one user is looking at the same data, the users won't be able to see each other's changes without reloading the data. We can change that.

This example takes the Flash Remoting application we've already built and uses LCDS Data Management to create a synchronized `<mx:DataGrid>`, grid, so that when the application makes changes in one client, all the other clients will automatically see the changes immediately after.

The next step is to configure the Flex server for our new assembler CFC. With a Flash Remoting application, we can define a reference to our CFC in the code directly. However, with a data messaging application, we need to configure a reference to our assembler CFC in the Flex `services-config.xml` file.

All of these files are located in the `%flex server%WEB-INFflex` folder.

1. Add this destination to the `data-management-config.xml` file:

```
<destination id="ColdFusion_Example3">
   <adapter ref="coldfusion-dao"/>
   <channels>
      <channel ref="cf-dataservice-rtmp"/>
      <channel ref="cf-polling-amf"/>
   </channels>
   <properties>
      <component>ows.35.example2.components.ActorsAssembler</component>
     <scope>application</scope>
      <metadata>
         <identity property="ACTORID"/>
      </metadata>
   </properties>
</destination>
```

2. Add this `adapter-destination` code to the same file, if it is not already defined.

```
<adapter-definition id="coldfusion-dao"
class="coldfusion.flex.CFDataServicesAdapter"/>
```

3. Add these channels to `services-config.xml`:

```
<!--  ColdFusion specific RTMP channel -->
<channel-definition id="cf-dataservice-rtmp"
                    class="mx.messaging.channels.RTMPChannel">
   <endpoint uri="rtmp://{server.name}:2048"
             class="flex.messaging.endpoints.RTMPEndpoint"/>
   <properties>
      <idle-timeout-minutes>20</idle-timeout-minutes>
      <serialization>
         <!-- This must be turned off for any CF channel -->
         <instantiate-types>false</instantiate-types>
      </serialization>
   </properties>
</channel-definition>

<!-- ColdFusion specific HTTP channel -->
<channel-definition id="cf-polling-amf"
                    class="mx.messaging.channels.AMFChannel">
   <endpoint uri=http://{server.name}:{server.port}/
                 {context.root}/messagebroker/cfamfpolling
             class="flex.messaging.endpoints.AMFEndpoint"/>
   <properties>
      <serialization>
```

```
            <!-- This must be turned off for any CF channel -->
            <instantiate-types>false</instantiate-types>
        </serialization>
        <polling-enabled>true</polling-enabled>
        <polling-interval-seconds>8</polling-interval-seconds>
    </properties>
</channel-definition>
```

4. Restart your Flex server.

In our Flex code, we need to remove the `<mx:RemoteObject>` tag that we added in the previous examples in this chapter and replace it with the `<mx:DataService>` tag. In the `<mx:DataService>` tag, you will need to set the destination to the same destination you defined in the `data-management-config.xml` file. This destination has the path to the CFC relative from the Web root.

```
<mx:DataService id="ds"
                autoCommit="false"
                autoMerge="true"
                destination="ColdFusion_Example3"/>
```

NOTE

To use LCDS data messaging and the `<mx:DataService>` tag, you need to add the `WEB-INF/flex/libs/fds.swc` library to your Flex project build path.

The next change is a call to the CFC. In the earlier example, we called the `ro.getData()` method in our button click event. However, for data services you don't execute methods directly. Instead, you can call one of the predefined methods of the `<mx:DataService>` tag. Flex knows how to map these components to the assembler CFC methods. The first call to ColdFusion needs to be to the `fill()` method with an empty `arrayCollection` object. Flex will take this empty object and fill it with the array of CFCs returned from the CFC `fill()` method. This behavior allows you to bind to the `arrayCollection` variable before the results are returned, but note that Flex's binding mechanism will handle the results correctly when they are returned.

```
<mx:Button label="Load Actors"
          click="ds.fill(results)"/>
```

Next, we'll add a binding to the `results` variable:

```
<mx:DataGrid width="100%"
             height="100%"
             dataProvider="{this.results}">
```

At this point, if you run the application you should see `<mx:DataGrid>` populate with the results of your `fill()` method: all of the actors in the database.

The next step in our application development is to add the capability to edit these objects and see them synchronize across clients. Since our application is based on our earlier example, we already have the double-click code to open a pop-up edit form; however, we do need to change it a little. In our earlier example, we needed to call a save method to do the work. With data messaging, we don't call the server. Instead, we tell the data source to commit the changes, and the data messaging tag takes over.

First remove the `<mx:RemoteObject>` tag in the `/editActor/EditActor/EditActor.mxml` file.

Now add a new property that is a reference to our `<mx:DataService>` tag instance:

```
public var dataService:DataService;
```

Next, in the `example3.mxml` file, set the `dataService` property for when we open the pop-up window:

```
private function doEditActor(event:Event):void
{
   var popup:EditActor = new EditActor();
   popup.actor = Actors(event.currentTarget.selectedItem);
   popup.dataService = this.ds;
   popup.width = 350;
   popup.height = 300;

   PopUpManager.addPopUp( popup, this, true );
   PopUpManager.centerPopUp(popup);
}
```

Now that the pop-up window has a reference to the `dataService` property, it's easy to save the changes. We already have a `doSave()` function in this component: where we used to call the server in the earlier example. Now we just need to call the `commit()` function on the `dataService` property:

```
private function doSave():void
{
   dataService.commit();
   PopUpManager.removePopUp(this);
}
```

To see the data synchronization in action, open two or more browsers and try editing the information for an actor. When you save your changes, you will immediately see the same changes in all the open browsers.

NOTE

Flex also gives you another way to achieve this synchronization. Currently, we are explicitly deciding when to save data. However, Flex supports a function called `autoCommit`. With `autoCommit` enabled, any change you make to the data will automatically be implemented in real time. To see this function in action, remove the `dataServices` property and the `dataService.commit()` code in `EditActor.mxml`. In the file `example3.mxml`, change the `autoCommit` property of the `<mx:DataService>` tag to true.

```
<mx:DataService id="ds"
                autoCommit="true"
                autoMerge="true"
                destination="ColdFusion_Example3"/>
```

TIP

One other change you can try is to make the data grid in `example3.mxml` editable too. As you edit the data in the grid, the changes will also be saved and synchronized among all of the clients.

Adding Conflict Resolution to the Form

Now we have a synchronized data set, which is great. But what if two people edit the same item at the same time? In previous applications, there was really only one way to handle this: Before you inserted or updated the data in the database table, you needed to compare a date stamp or a version number on the server to make sure that the file hadn't changed since you pulled the record for editing. If it had, you threw an exception back to the client—not the best user experience. Luckily, Flex is smarter than this.

Flex data messaging can detect a conflict between one or more users' versions of the data and tell the users before they try to save the data.

Flex alerts the client applications with a special conflict event. In this event, you have access to the old data and the new data, allowing you to decide how to handle the event. You might not even tell the user there is a conflict and just overwrite the change with the new modifications automatically. For instance, maybe the user is a manager and always overwrites other users' changes.

You can also build a nice UI alert to show the user that the data has changed and let the user decide whether to overwrite his or her changes with the new changes or overwrite the other changes.

In `example3a.mxml`, we add a conflict handler with a UI that prompts the user for the right action.

To add a conflict handler, the first step is to add an event listener to the `<mx:DataService>` tag for the conflict event. When this `DataConflictEvent` event is triggered, it has a special `conflict` property. With this `conflict` object, Flex returns four elements: an array of the property names that were changed, the original object, your version of the object, and the modified object from the server.

```
<mx:DataService id="ds"
                autoCommit="false"
                autoMerge="true"
                destination="ColdFusion_Example3"
                conflict="dsConflictHandler(event)"  />
```

After you catch and handle this event, you can either decide which version to keep—the original or the server version—or you can make this decision automatically or by prompting the user for a decision. After the decision has been made, you will need to call one of two methods on the `DataService` object:

- `.acceptServer()`: Updates your version to match the server version.
- `.acceptClient()`: Replaces the server version with your version.

Messaging Application

The third type of communication between Flex and ColdFusion uses publish and subscribe functionality, which allows Flex clients to receive messages (as strings) from the ColdFusion server or from other Flex clients, such as a chat application. You can also use this functionality to make ColdFusion and other Flex clients listen to messages being broadcast from the client.

You might notice that data push and data messaging seem very similar to each other. They both automatically send messages between the server and the clients and from client to client. In fact, data messaging is built on top of the data messaging functionality.

A message can also be a trigger for your application to get more data. Consider the example of an executive dashboard that displays sales data in real time. Traditionally, your application would set up a timer and every 30 seconds or so ask the server if there is anything new. However, this approach can eat up a lot of bandwidth unnecessarily if nothing has changed. With the capability to subscribe to messages, every time you insert a new sale into the database, you can also send an event to all connected clients telling them to reload the data for the dashboard (charts) or send the updated data with the message and have the listener add it to the data provider directly.

In this next example, we are going to create a regular ColdFusion CFML page with a form to allow a system administrator to send a message, such as an emergency reboot of the server, to all users who are currently connected.

NOTE

This example appears in the `example4/src/example4.mxml` file.

Configuring the ColdFusion Data Messaging Destination

ColdFusion 9 ships with a default event gateway type, called `DataServicesMessaging`, that adds support for Flex messaging. With this gateway type, you don't need to define a configuration file. In addition, ColdFusion will automatically map the incoming messages to the right destinations. based on the `destination` property of the event message.

Creating an Event Gateway

We need to create and register a new ColdFusion event gateway. Since this example is only listening for events, this will be the easiest CFC you've ever written, shown in Listing 32.4.

Listing 32.4 `MessagingEventGateway.cfc`

```
<cfcomponent>
</cfcomponent>
```

Yes, this is an empty CFC. To use an event gateway, we need to create an instance that is linked to a CFC. Since the CFC is going to process only outgoing messages, we don't need to write any functions to process the incoming events from the Flex clients.

To register the new gateway instance, go to the ColdFusion Administrator, choose Event Gateways > Gateway Instances, and create a new gateway instance with the following settings:

- Gateway ID: `ColdFusionGateway`
- Gateway type: `DataServicesMessaging`
- CFC path: The absolute path to the CFC you created
- Startup mode: `auto`

➜ For more information on creating, configuring and using the event gateways, see Chapter 70, "Working with Gateways," in *Adobe ColdFusion 9 Web Application Construction Kit, Volume 3: Advanced Application Development.*

The next step is to create our ColdFusion page and form to send the message. This CFML page has a `CFFORM` tag with a simple form handler. In the form handler, we will create a data struct to send through our event gateway. The two key items to include in this message struct are the body (the data to send) and the name of the destination defined in the `services-config.xml` file.

Notice that in the `body` variable, we are creating another struct to send to Flex instead of a string. You can send any ColdFusion data type in the body (strings, dates, structs, arrays, CFC instances, and so on). In this example, shown in Listing 32.5, we are sending the two form fields: `type` and `message` in the message body.

Listing 32.5 `sendSystemMessage.cfm`

```
<cfif isDefined("form.submit")>
    <cfset messageObject = structNew()>
    <cfset messageObject.message = form.message>
    <cfset messageObject.type = form.msgType>

    <cfset flexMessage = StructNew()>
    <cfset flexMessage.body = messageObject>
    <cfset flexMessage.Destination = "ColdFusionGateway">
    <cfset ret = SendGatewayMessage("ows32_example4", flexMessage)>
    <p>Message has been sent!</p>
</cfif>

<cfform>
    <b>Type:</b><br/>
    <cfinput type="radio" name="msgType" value="Information" checked="true">
Information<br/>
    <cfinput type="radio" name="msgType" value="Warning"> Warning <br/>
    <cfinput type="radio" name="msgType" value="Error"> Error <br/>
    <b>Message</b><br/>
    <cftextarea id="message" name="message" rows="6" cols="50"/><br/>
    <cfinput type="submit" name="submit" value="Send Message">
</cfform>
```

Now we need to modify our Flex application. We'll build on the first example in this chapter; however, you can add this modification to any of the other examples in this chapter.

First we'll add the `<mx:Consumer>` tag to our application and link it to our `ColdFusion_example4` destination, defined in `services-config.xml`. We also need to give the tag an ID to reference later and register a function that will be called whenever a message is received.

```
<!--
Create a listener for ColdFusion messages
-->
<mx:Consumer id="consumer"
             destination="ColdFusionGateway"
             message="doMessageReceivedHandler(event)"/>
```

Next we need to create the `doMessageReceivedHandler` function. To keep this example simple, our new function will just display an alert with the message.

```
private function doMessageReceivedHandler(event:MessageEvent):void
{
   Alert.show(event.message.body.message, event.message.body.type);
}
```

Finally, we need to start the consumer. To do this, we will use the `creationComplete` event of the application to have the consumer subscribe itself to the server. When it does, the Flex application starts listening for events.

```
<mx:Application xmlns:mx="http://www.adobe.com/2006/mxml"
                creationComplete="consumer.subscribe()"
                layout="vertical" >
```

Conclusion

So as you can see from these examples, there are a number of different ways to build your Flash applications with ColdFusion: Flash Remoting, data management, and messaging. And this is just the beginning. You can also mix and match some of these options. For example, you can use Flash Remoting and messaging together in the same application to keep the application up to date as the database changes. For instance, a reporting dashboard application could use this application to keep the charts up to date.

All of these examples did have one thing in common, though: they work only while a user is online. One of the biggest reasons for building Adobe AIR applications, instead of Flex applications, is that you need applications that can work offline. In the next chapter, you will see how to build offline AIR applications with ColdFusion.

CHAPTER 33

Building ColdFusion-Powered AIR Applications

IN THIS CHAPTER

Creating AIR Clients for ColdFusion Applications

One of the main reasons to build an AIR application instead of a standard Web application is to be able to use your application offline. However, building support to load data, save data, and synchronize data for an offline application can take a large amount of code.

First you need to build a way to save the data you load from the server when you are online. All of your server calls will also need to know if the user is offline or online so as to determine whether to load and save the data from a local cache or from the server. You will also need code to save any items that you edit to the local cache and server. Finally, you need a way to synchronize changes that occurred on the client or server while the user was offline.

As you can imagine, this can take some time to code. And you will find that you will rewrite this same code again and again as you build increasing numbers of AIR applications.

ColdFusion 9 has a new feature specifically for building offline AIR applications: the ColdFusion Data Persistence Library. This new feature in ColdFusion keeps track of the objects you use locally and synchronizes them with the server, alleviating the pain of building all of the logic just mentioned.

This chapter uses the same master detail application that was used in Chapter 32, "Integrating with Flash Data Services," and applies the ColdFusion 9 AIR libraries for data persistence and synchronization.

Comparison with LCDS Data Management

Before we begin building an application with AIR, let's look at how this feature differs from the Data Management Services feature of LiveCycle Data Services (LCDS), which was built to solve many of the same problems as AIR. As discussed in the previous two chapters, the LCDS Data Management feature can also be used to synchronize data with Flash applications. The LCDS data management and ColdFusion AIR libraries are both options for synchronizing data between the client and the server. However, the two have some differences that you need to understand to decide which tool you should use for a job.

- AIR is built into ColdFusion; LCDS Data Management requires the Enterprise LCDS Server.
- LCDS can also work with Flex applications and AIR applications. The ColdFusion AIR libraries work only inside AIR applications.
- Conflict resolution is handled differently. LCDS Data Management works by using a combination of remote objects and messaging. Using the messaging options of LCDS, changes to an object are pushed to all of the other clients, and each client then decides whether a conflict exists between the local version and the version being pushed in and can throw a conflict event back to the user. The ColdFusion data persistence library uses the server to determine whether a conflict exists when the object is being saved. If a conflict exists, ColdFusion returns a conflict object to the client instead of saving the object in the database. Then the user can fix the data and try again.
- Objects are stored locally in different ways. LCDS stores objects as binary objects in the SQLite database, for AIR, or as Flash cookies, for Web applications. However, ColdFusion will build and maintain a relational table structure in the SQLite database that is embedded in AIR, allowing you to query the objects in the local database directly when you need to build additional features with the objects. For instance, if you want to add a local search feature to your application, in LCDS you would need to load all of the objects and loop over them. With the ColdFusion data persistence database, you can just run a simple query against the database to get the data you need.

Configuring the Flash Builder Project

Before you can start writing code that uses the ColdFusion Data Persistence Library, you need to link to the library from inside your Flash Builder project. There is nothing you need to do on the ColdFusion server; it is already configured and ready to work with the AIR Object Relational Mapping (ORM) feature.

After creating a new Flex project in Flash Builder, simply add the `cfair.swc` library to your project.

1. In the Project view, right-click your project and choose Properties from the menu.
2. Go to the Flex Compiler screen and select the Library tab at the top of the screen.
3. At the right of the Library tab, click the Add Swc button and choose the `cfair.swc` file that ships with ColdFusion 9. This can be found under your CFIDE folder: `<ColdFusion Install Location>/CFIDE/scripts/AIR/cfair.swc`.

Now your Flex project will know about the new classes that are required to use the Flex offline AIR libraries.

Building the ColdFusion Service CFC

The AIR ORM feature knows how to manage the data and the calls back and forth to the server using only two specific methods in your CFC service: `fetch` and `sync`. You might be asking yourself: How can there only be two? With an application that modifies a single object, you can perform four operations on the object: you can load an existing object, create a new object, update an existing object, or delete an object. One operation reads data, and three operations modify data. We can group these four operations into the two methods, `fetch` and `sync`, greatly simplifying the client-side logic.

Letting the server know what needs to be updated, `fetch` will take care of pulling data out of your database and return it to the Flash application. The `sync` method will take care of modifying the data: updating, creating, and deleting. The `sync` method also checks for conflicts between the data sent to the server and the data that the server knows about.

For instance, if two clients, userA and userB, both load a piece of data and both try to save it, the first one to save the item, userA, will not have a problem. However, when userB tries to save the data, the `sync` method needs to check to see if someone else, in this case userA, changed it first. If the data has been changed, that is a conflict, and the data can't be saved automatically or else changes from userA might be lost. When a conflict like this is detected, you should not save the data but rather return a `Conflict` object (`CFIDE.AIR.Conflict.cfc`) to the client. This alerts the user that the data is out of date and that it needs to be checked and the error fixed before the user tries to save the data again.

NOTE

In the client libraries, when a conflict event is caught, you also have the option to override the local changes with the changes from the server. You can use the ActionScript `.keepServerObject()` function to do this automatically without alerting the user, or you can let the user decide.

The `fetch` Method

The purpose of the `fetch` method is to return data to the client. This data can come from any of the resources ColdFusion can use; however, usually this is data from a database.

This method can be named anything you want. However, by convention it is called `fetch`. If you want to use a different method name, you can set the name in the method when you call the server from Flash.

In the example in this chapter, we are using the new Hibernate ORM feature to quickly and easily load our data. We do this with the `EntityLoad()` method, telling ColdFusion to return all of the actors from the database as an array of `ACTORS.cfc` instances. ColdFusion will then convert these `ACTORS` instances to Flash ActionScript `ACTORS` objects on their way to your client-side code.

➜ For more information about the new Hibernate ORM feature, see Chapter 38, "Working with ORM."

```
<cffunction name="fetch" access="remote">
  <cfset results = EntityLoad ("ACTORS")>
  <cfreturn results/>
</cffunction>
```

The sync Method

The sync method is responsible for modifying your data. Unlike fetch, this method must be named sync. The reason for this is that ColdFusion has a class called SyncManager that implements the ISyncManager interface. This interface does not include the fetch method, but it does define the sync method. The SyncManager class is what the AIR libraries invoke, and after this object has done what it needs to do, it will call the sync method in your CFC.

This method can also work with multiple objects at once: if a user makes multiple changes while offline, when the application comes back online and connects to the ColdFusion server, AIR will send all of the updates in one request.

TIP

In general, you shouldn't place all of the code to insert, update, and delete an object in this one method. Instead, that logic should be in smaller, specialized methods, and the sync method should work like a controller, calling the correct method depending on the action required.

Since we are using the Hibernate ORM feature, we can call the Hibernate methods directly to update, create, and delete the objects, instead of needing to create specialized methods ourselves.

Here's how this method works: The first argument that is passed to the sync method is an array of type string called OPERATIONS. This array can have one of three values: INSERT, UPDATE, or DELETE. With this argument, you can create a simple if/else or switch statement to control the logic you need to invoke as you are working with each of the items that have been passed in to be saved.

The other two arguments for the sync method are clientObjects, which denotes the objects you've modified, and originalObjects, which denotes the objects before they were modified. By including both arguments, you can figure out if there is a conflict with the server before you save the data.

Let's look at a simple example of a sync method in its most basic form.

First, we define the method and the arguments:

```
<cffunction name="sync" access="remote">
  <cfargument name="operations" type="array" required="true">
  <cfargument name="clientobjects" type="array" required="true">
  <cfargument name="originalobjects" type="array" required="false">
```

Next, we create an array to hold any Conflict objects that we need to send back to the Flash application:

```
<cfset var conflicts = ArrayNew(1)>
<cfset var conflictcount = 1>
```

Then we create a loop to make sure we synchronize all of the objects that need to be synchronized:

```
<cfloop index="i" from="1" to="#ArrayLen( operations )#">
  <cfset operation = operations[i]>
  <cfset clientobject = clientobjects[i]>
  <cfset originalobject = originalobjects[i]>
```

And here is our if/else statement to determine what action is needed to synchronize this object:

```
        <cfif operation eq "INSERT" and !isSimpleValue(clientobject)>
          <!--- createObject(clientObject) --->
        <cfelseif operation eq "UPDATE" and !isSimpleValue(clientobject)>
           <!--- updateObject(clientObject) --->
        <cfelseif operation eq "DELETE">
           <!--- deleteObject(originalObject) --->
        </cfif>

      </cfloop>
```

And last, we return any objects that are in conflict:

```
      <cfreturn conflicts>
    </cffunction>
```

The next step in building the sync method is to add a check for conflicts. To do this, we need to load the object that does exist on the server, and then we need to compare it with the originalObject argument. You can see the full method in the ows/33/example1/components/ActorService.cfc file.

First we load the server object, if the operation is UPDATE or DELETE:

```
    <cfelseif listfindnocase("UPDATE,DELETE", operation) neq 0 >
        <cfif not isSimpleValue(originalobject)>
            <cfset serverobject = EntityLoadByPK("ACTORS",originalobject.GETACTORID())>
```

If the object has already been deleted, return a conflict; someone else deleted it first:

```
            <cfif not isdefined('serverobject') >
                    <cflog text="CONFLICT::SERVER OBJECT NOT FOUND, RECORD MAY BE DELETED
    ALREADY">
                     <cfset conflict = CreateObject("component","CFIDE.AIR.conflict")>
                     <cfset conflict.clientobject = clientobject>
                     <cfset conflict.originalobject = originalobject>
                     <cfset conflict.operation = operation>
                     <cfset conflicts[conflictcount++] = conflict>
                     <cfcontinue>
            </cfif>
        </cfif>
```

Detecting Conflict

The next step is to run the new ObjectEquals() function to compare the value of the properties between the original object sent back from Flash and the object that was loaded from the database. If ObjectEquals() returns false, you should create a new Conflict object to return.

```
    <cfset isNotConflict = ObjectEquals(originalobject, serverobject)>

    <cfif isNotConflict>
      <cfif operation eq "UPDATE">
        <cflog text="update object">
        <cfset obj = ORMGetSession().merge(clientobject)>
        <cfset EntitySave(obj)>
      <cfelseif operation eq "DELETE">
        <cflog text="delete object">
        <cfset obj = ORMGetSession().merge(originalobject)>
        <cfset EntityDelete(obj)>
```

```
  </cfif>
<cfelse><!----Conflict--->
  <cflog text = "is a conflict">
  <cfset conflict = CreateObject("component","CFIDE.AIR.conflict")>
  <cfset conflict.serverobject = serverobject>
  <cfset conflict.clientobject = clientobject>
  <cfset conflict.originalobject = originalobject>
  <cfset conflict.operation = operation>
  <cfset conflicts[conflictcount++] = conflict>
  <cfcontinue>
</cfif>
</cfif>
```

Building the Value Objects

AIR data management and synchronization work with what are called value objects. Instead of just sending simple values (like strings and numbers), Flash Remoting can send object instances back and forth between Flash and ColdFusion, and when it does, it converts the objects back and forth between ActionScript classes and ColdFusion CFC—so your ColdFusion CFC can return a CFC, and when it gets to Flash, it will be the matching ActionScript class. And this feature works both ways.

Creating the ColdFusion Value Object

To make a ColdFusion CFC a value object, you need to do two things.

First, you need to define the alias for the CFC. This is the fully qualified path that ColdFusion can use to create an instance of the CFC, and it's the string that will be mapped in our Action-Script class:

```
<cfcomponent output="false" alias="ows.33.example5.components.Actors"
```

Next, you need to define the `<cfproperty>` tags for all of the properties that you want to transfer back and forth. The Flash gateway will transfer only properties that are defined by `<cfproperty>` tags, and because ActionScript is a strongly typed object language and case sensitive and Cold-Fusion is not, the gateway will also reset the case of the properties and cast them into the type that is defined in the `<cfproperty>` tags. Listing 34.1 shows the code.

Listing 34.1 `Actors.CFC`

```
<cfcomponent output="false" alias="ows.33.example5.components.Actors"
persistent="true" entityname="ACTORS" table="ACTORS">
    <cfproperty name="ACTORID" type="numeric" default="0"  generator="increment">
    <cfproperty name="NAMEFIRST" type="string" default="">
    <cfproperty name="NAMELAST" type="string" default="">
    <cfproperty name="AGE" type="numeric" default="0">
    <cfproperty name="NAMEFIRSTREAL" type="string" default="">
    <cfproperty name="NAMELASTREAL" type="string" default="">
    <cfproperty name="AGEREAL" type="numeric" default="0">
    <cfproperty name="ISEGOMANIAC" type="numeric" default="0">
    <cfproperty name="ISTOTALBABE" type="numeric" default="0">
    <cfproperty name="GENDER" type="string" default="">

</cfcomponent>
```

Creating the ActionScript Value Object

The ActionScript object is very similar to the ColdFusion CFC. It needs to have exactly the same properties as the CFC. Remember that it needs to match the property name case, spelling, and data type. Listing 34.2 shows the code.

Listing 34.2 `Actors.as`

```
package model
{
    import mx.utils.StringUtil;

    [RemoteClass(alias="ows.33.example5.components.Actors")]
    [Bindable]
    [Entity]
    public class Actors
    {
        [Id]
        public var ACTORID:Number;
        public var NAMEFIRST:String;
        public var NAMELAST:String;
        public var AGE:Number;
        public var NAMEFIRSTREAL:String;
        public var NAMELASTREAL:String;
        public var AGEREAL:Number;
        public var ISEGOMANIAC:Number;
        public var ISTOTALBABE:Number;
        public var GENDER:String;
    }
}
```

The `Actors` class also has three ActionScript metadata tags that need to be set:

```
[RemoteClass(alias="ows.33.example5.components.Actors")]
[Bindable]
[Entity]
```

The `[RemoteClass]` tag needs to have `alias="` set to match the `alias` attribute set in the `<cfcomponent>` tag.

You also need to mark the class `[Bindable]` so the UI knows when data has changed.

The third metadata flag, `[Entity]`, is specific to the ColdFusion AIR libraries. This metadata will tell the AIR libraries to generate the SQLite tables, queries, and logic to manage instances of these objects.

Initializing syncManager

The ColdFusion AIR libraries work through a special class called the `syncManager`. This class is central to way the library implements its data persistence and synchronization.

When the application starts, you need to create an instance of `syncManager`: one per database. You should manage this instance and pass it to any component that needs to interact with the data.

NOTE

Why only one? syncManager takes care of all the database queries to the local SQLite database. If you create more then one instance of syncManager with a connection to the same database, you may get database errors when two queries try to run at the same time.

I recommend invoking the init() method in the preinitialize event handler, instead of in the usual creationComplete handler. Why? Initialization of syncManager doesn't depend on or reference any part of the UI, so there is no reason to wait for the whole application to load and finish rendering just to start loading the data.

```
<mx:VBox
    preinitialize="init()"
xmlns:mx="http://www.adobe.com/2006/mxml">
```

Here is the init() method that we will use to start the ColdFusion AIR support:

```
public function init():void
{
    syncmanager = new SyncManager();
```

Define the IP address and port of the ColdFusion instance that this application will connect to:

```
    syncmanager.cfServer = "127.0.0.1";
    syncmanager.cfPort = 8300;
```

Define the CFC that contains your sync method. Remember this is the CFC that implements the ISyncManager interface for this application.

```
    syncmanager.syncCFC = "ows.34.example1.components.ActorService";

    // Specify a user-defined CF destination, if not specified, default
    // destination 'ColdFusion' will be used
    syncmanager.destination = 'ColdFusion'
```

Even though syncManager creates a database structure that matches your objects and executes any queries that are needed to work, it doesn't define the database that it should use. Instead, the AIR libraries let you define this so that you can control where the database is stored on the user's disk and so you can also use it for your purposes outside the AIR libraries. For example, if you need to run a search query against the objects in the database instead of creating a second connection to the database, risking deadlock errors or race conditions, you can share the connection with the AIR libraries and use the same database:

```
    var dbFile:File = File.userDirectory.resolvePath("example5.db");
```

Open the database connection and create an active session for the database:

```
    var sessiontoken:SessionToken = syncmanager.openSession(dbFile, 999);
```

Add an event listener for any conflicts sent back from your ColdFusion server:

```
    syncmanager.addEventListener(ConflictEvent.CONFLICT, conflictHandler);
```

Add an event listener for the connect events, so you will know if there is a problem connecting to the ColdFusion server; if so, you can have your application work in offline mode:

```
        sessiontoken.addResponder(new mx.rpc.Responder(connectSuccess, connectFault));

    }
```

Loading Data

Now that you have your CFC service and a connection to ColdFusion server, all you need to do is call the `fetch` method of `syncManager`. The `fetch` method takes one argument: the name of the `fetch` method in your CFC. Remember that unlike the CFC `sync` method, which must be named `sync`, the `fetch` method can have any name you want: `fetch`, `list`, `getall`, or whatever. If you don't define a CFC method name, the method name will default to `fetch`.

```
// fetch the data.
var token:AsyncToken = syncmanager.fetch("fetch");
```

The second part of calling the server is to define the `result` and `fault` methods so you can get the data returned from the server or handle any exceptions thrown by ColdFusion.

In Flex, these two methods are defined in what is called an `IResponder` class. In this example, we are using the built-in `Responder` object, which takes two methods as arguments: the local `result` and `fault` methods. However, when you start getting lots of server calls in one MXML file, all of these result and fault handlers can become confusing. In that case, you may want to create your own ActionScript class that implements `IResponder` and include the `result` and `fault` methods in the class. If you've seen the Cairngorm commands framework for Flex, you may recognize that this is how the Cairngorm commands work.

```
//Specify the methods to handle the fetch results.
token.addResponder(new mx.rpc.Responder(fetchSuccess, fetchFault));
```

NOTE

A `Responder` class is a class that implements the `IResponder` interface, which declares two methods: `result` and `fault`. By using classes with these two methods, you ensure that Flex always knows which method should be invoked when data is returned. You also make your work easier. If you look at older network classes in Flash (such as `URLLoader` and `NetConnection`), you will see that you need to implement lots of events for all of the possible errors and actions. Using the `IResponder` interface in the new network libraries helps standardize the handling of network requests.

Once you get the data back from ColdFusion, you need to set the local property to which your UI is binding. In this example, `results` is the property that the data grid displays.

You also need to tell `syncManager` that you have new data and that it needs to update its local cache; if this is the first time the data has been returned, it will add the data to the local cache (SQLite database), or if the cache already has a copy of the object, it will update its local copy of the object:

```
public function fetchSuccess(event:ResultEvent):void
{
    results = new ArrayCollection(event.result as Array);
    syncmanager.getCurrentSession().saveCache(results);
}
```

What happens when the AIR application is offline? Remember that earlier we called our CFC `fetch` method through `syncManager`:

```
syncmanager.fetch("fetch");
```

Because the application went through `syncManager`, if the application is offline, the AIR libraries will automatically return the data from the database instead of calling the server.

Editing and Saving Data

When you edit an object with the AIR libraries, you use the same UI you used in Chapter 32 with Flash Remoting. The first thing you need to do is open the edit form as a pop-up:

```
        private function doEditActor(event:Event):void
{
  // get the selected row item that we want to edit.
  var selectedGridItem:Actors = actorsGrid.selectedItem as Actors;

  var popup:EditActor = new EditActor();
  popup.syncManager = this.syncmanager;
  popup.title = "Edit: " +StringUtil.trim(selectedGridItem.NAMEFIRST) +" "
+StringUtil.trim(selectedGridItem.NAMELAST);
  popup.actor = selectedGridItem;
  popup.width = 300;
  popup.height = 250;
 Cpopup.addEventListener("close", refresh, false, 0, true);


  PopUpManager.addPopUp( popup, this, true );
  PopUpManager.centerPopUp(popup);
}
```

For applications that use `syncManager`, be sure to pass in a reference to `syncManager` instead of initializing a new `syncManager` for the edit form:

```
popup.syncManager = this.syncmanager;
```

You also need to pass in a reference to the item the user has chosen to edit from the data grid:

```
popup.actor = selectedGridItem;
```

Once a user has used the `EditActor` component to edit the `this.actor` property, the user needs to call a `save` method. In this example, the `save` method does three things.

First it needs to get `currentSession` from `syncManager`. Then it needs to update the local version of the object with new edits. This updating does not update the object on the server; it updates only the local copy. Dividing the operation to update the local copy and the call to update the server into two server calls allows a user of the application to create, edit, and delete multiple objects and then send them all to the server in one request. For instance, a user working offline on an airplane could make multiple changes; then when the user returns home or to the office and is back online, the user can synchronize all of the changes on the server.

Your next step is add a Responder object so you will know when the local update has completed successfully and to handle any errors that may occur:

```
private function doSave():void
{
  var session:Session = syncManager.getCurrentSession();
  var saveToken:SessionToken = session.update(this.actor);
  saveToken.addResponder( new mx.rpc.Responder(doSaveResultHandler,
doSaveFaultHandler) );
}
```

After the object has been successfully saved in the local cache, you will update your local actor with the item returned from the cache, just to make sure you are always working on the correct copy of the object, though in most applications, these will be the same object. And since this save method is now complete, your edit component will take care of closing itself with PopUpManager.

```
private function doSaveResultHandler(event:SessionResultEvent):void
{
  this.actor = event.result as Actors;
  // save successful, close this popup.
  PopUpManager.removePopUp(this);
}
```

Synchronizing Data with the Server

To complete the process of editing an object, saving it locally, and then saving it on the server, you need to call a method on syncManager called commit. This method tells syncManager to send to the server all of the changes to all of the objects for which it has detected a change—if the application is online, that is.

The ActorList component includes a button that the user has to click to synchronize the local objects with the server. However, this task could just as easily be something you implement automatically in the code. For instance, when the pop-up closes, you could call commit automatically:

```
<mx:Button
  label="commit to server"
  click="commitChanges()"/>

public function commitChanges():void
{
  syncmanager.getCurrentSession().commit();
}
```

Invoking the commit method, with no arguments, will send all of the objects with changes to your "sync" method of your CFC service.

Managing Conflicts

When you call commit, your ColdFusion sync method may return an array of Conflict objects. These are special objects that include the operation that was attempted; INSERT, UPDATE, or DELETE. The Conflict object also includes the modified object, the original object that you started with, and the current object on the server. By including all three versions of the object, you are able to compare the properties to identify the conflict and respond accordingly.

When you receive `Conflict` objects, you have two options: to overwrite your copy with the copy on the server, or to keep your copy for more editing.

To overwrite your local changes with the object on the server, you need to tell `syncManager` to keep the server changes. When you do this, `syncManager` will update the local cache, overriding any local changes. To implement this approach, you use two methods. The `keepServerObjects` method lets you keep a single server object; this method is useful when you are looping over all of the conflicts and deciding whether you should keep the server or the client version on a case-by-case basis. The second method is `keepAllServerObjects`; this method lets you pass in the full array of conflicts and accept all of them at once.

For this example, you will keep all the server objects:

```
var token:SessionToken = syncmanager.getCurrentSession().keepAllServerObjects(event.
result as ArrayCollection);
```

You will also register a `Result` and also a `Fault` event listener so you can handle any exceptions that occur:

```
token.addResponder(new mx.rpc.Responder(conflictSuccess, conflictFault));
```

If you want to keep your local changes, there is no method like `keepServerObject` to execute. Instead, you need to prompt the user to edit the object again to fix the conflict. Then, after the conflicts are fixed, try to commit the changes to the server again.

CHAPTER 34

Creating Presentations

IN THIS CHAPTER

Presentations are a part of our lives. If you've sat through one Microsoft PowerPoint presentation, you've sat through a hundred. While these presentations may not always be exciting, they can be an effective way to present information for educational, commercial, or even entertainment purposes. ColdFusion makes it easy to create and work with presentations. These presentations need not be static, boring affairs but can be fully dynamic. Along with creating presentations (in either Connect or PowerPoint form), you can work with existing PowerPoint presentations.

Presenting `<cfpresentation>`

ColdFusion has three tags to work with presentations. The first and most important tag is the `<cfpresentation>` tag. All presentations begin and end with `<cfpresentation>`. Table 34.1 lists the main attributes of the tag.

Table 34.1 Main `<cfpresentation>` Attributes

ATTRIBUTE	FUNCTION
`title`	Specifies the title of the presentation.
`autoplay`	Determines whether the presentation starts automatically. The default value is `true`.
`control`	Specifies the type of control to use in the presentation. Valid values are `normal` and `brief`. The default is `normal`.
`controlLocation`	Indicates the location of the controls. Valid values are `left` and `right`. The default is `right`.
`destination`	Specifies a full path to store the resulting PowerPoint, HTML, or Connect presentation. Required when format is `html`. Use a directory, not a filename.
`directory`	Specifies the directory in which to store the presentation. This attribute is optional; if it is not specified, the presentation will play in the browser.

Table 34.1 (continued)

ATTRIBUTE	FUNCTION
`format`	Specifies the format of the presentation. Can be `html` for HTML presentations or `ppt` for PowerPoint.
`initialTab`	Indicates the selected tab in the control area. The valid values are `outline`, `search`, and `notes`. The default is `outline`.
`loop`	Specifies whether the presentation should loop. The default value is `false`.
`overwrite`	If the directory option is used, specifies whether the files should be overwritten. The default value is `yes`.
`showNotes`, `showOutline`, `showSearch`	Determines whether the Notes, Outline, and Search tabs are visible.

By itself, the `<cfpresentation>` tag can't do much. To complete the presentation, you need to add slides. As you can probably guess, this is done with `<cfpresentationslide>`. Slides can be made with HTML or ColdFusion or using an external source such as an Adobe Flash SWF file or even a remote URL. You can also embed a PowerPoint presentation, using all or some of the slides. You can also bind MP3 audio tracks to slides to provide narration or background music to the slide. Table 34.2 lists the main attributes for `<cfpresentationslide>`.

Table 34.2 Main `<cfpresentationslide>` Attributes

ATTRIBUTE	FUNCTION
`advance`	Allows you to override the `autoPlay` setting of `<cfpresentation>`. Valid values are `auto`, `never`, and `click`. If set to `auto`, the slide will automatically advance to the next slide. This will be the default if `autoPlay` is set to `true`. If set to `never`, the slide will not advance unless the user clicks the Advance button. If set to `click`, the entire slide becomes clickable, and clicking will advance the slide.
`audio`	Specifies the path to an MP3 file; cannot be used with `video`.
`duration`	Specifies the duration of the slide. If an MP3 file is used, the duration of the slide will default to the length of the MP3 file.
`notes`	Specifies notes to include with a slide.
`presenter`	Specifies the presenter associated with a slide; relates to the `<cfpresenter>` tag that will be discussed later.
`scale`	If HTML content is used for the slide, determines how much the content is scaled to fit into the presentation. Valid values are 0 to 1.
`slides`	Used when importing PowerPoint files. If specified, the value is either a range or list of slides to use from the PowerPoint presentation.
`src`	Specifies the source of the slide; used only if content is not provided in the `<cfpresentationslide>` slide. This attribute can point to content at either an absolute or relative path. This content can be an HTML file, a PowerPoint presentation, or a SWF file. A remote URL can also be used. If a SWF file is used, it must be served by a ColdFusion system.
`title`	Specifies the title of the slide.
`video`	Specifies a video to use for the presenter for the slide; cannot be used with `audio`. The video must be a SWF or FLV file and must be local to the file system.

Now that we've covered the basic attributes of the <cfpresentation> and <cfpresentationslide> tags, let's look at a simple example in Listing 34.1.

Listing 34.1 example1.cfm—Basic Presentation

```
<!---
Name:        example1.cfm
Author:      Raymond Camden (ray@camdenfamily.com)
Description: First presentation
--->

<cfpresentation title="First Presentation"
            autoPlay="false">

   <cfpresentationslide title="Welcome to CFPRESENTATION"
                   notes="These are some notes.">
<h1>Welcome to CFPRESENTATION</h1>

<p>
This is content for the first slide. I can include HTML
and it will be rendered by the presentation.
</p>
   </cfpresentationslide>

   <cfpresentationslide title="Sales Figures"
          notes="These are some notes for slide two.">
<h1>Sales Figures</h1>

<p>
Some fake data.
</p>

<p>
<table width="100%" border="1">
<tr>
   <th>Product</th>
   <th>Price</th>
</tr>
<tr>
   <td>Apples</td><td>$0.99</td>
</tr>
<tr>
   <td>Bananas</td><td>$1.99</td>
</tr>
<tr>
   <td>Nukes</td><td>$2.99</td>
</tr>
</table>
</p>
   </cfpresentationslide>
</cfpresentation>
```

Listing 34.1 is a simple presentation. It contains two slides, both of which contain simple, static text. You can see the result in Figure 34.1.

Now let's take a look at a truly dynamic presentation. Orange Whip Studios produces quite a few films. What if the company wants to create a presentation that shows its body of work? Listing 34.2

creates a simple portfolio. What's nice is that whenever a film is added to the database, the portfolio is automatically updated.

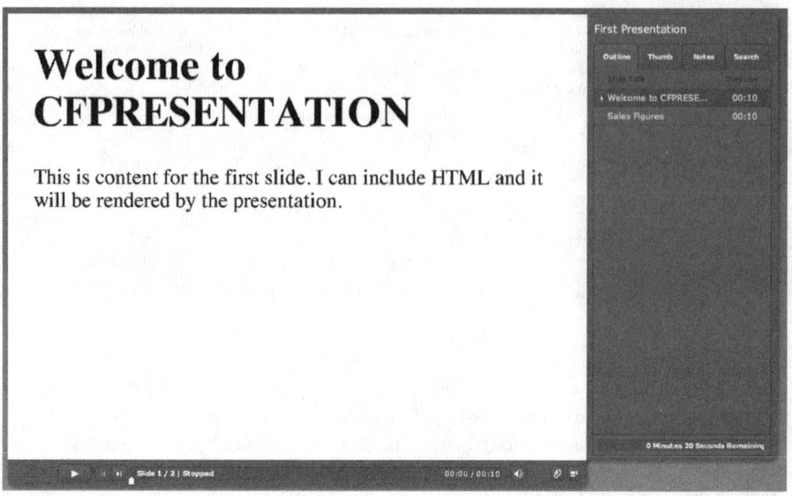

Figure 34.1

Simple presentation.

NOTE

Be sure to copy the `Application.cfc` file from the zip file containing all the chapter code. The `Application.cfc` file defines the default data source for the examples in this chapter.

Listing 34.2 `example2.cfm`—Dynamic Presentation

```
<!---
Name:        example2.cfm
Author:      Raymond Camden (ray@camdenfamily.com)
Description: Dynamic presentation
--->

<cfquery name="getMovies">
select   f.movietitle, f.pitchtext, f.amountbudgeted,
      f.summary, f.imagename, f.dateintheaters,
      r.rating
from  films f, filmsratings r
where f.ratingid = r.ratingid
</cfquery>

<cfpresentation title="Orange Whip Studios - Films"
            autoPlay="false">
   <cfpresentationslide
      title="Welcome to Orange Whip Studios"
         >
<h1>Welcome to Orange Whip Studios</h1>

<p>
Here is the latest gallery of our films.
</p>
   </cfpresentationslide>
```

Listing 34.2 (continued)

```
        <cfloop query="getMovies">
           <cfpresentationslide title="#movietitle#">

    <cfoutput>
    <h2>#movietitle#</h2>

    <p>
    <cfif len(trim(imagename))>
    <img src="../images/#imagename#" align="right">
    </cfif>
    <b>Rating:</b> #rating#<br />
    <b>Budget:</b> #dollarFormat(amountbudgeted)#<br />
    <b>Date:</b>
    #dateFormat(dateintheaters,"mmmm d, yyyy")#<br />
    <b>Pitch:</b> #pitchtext#
    </p>

    <p>
    <b>Summary:</b> #summary#
    </p>
    </cfoutput>

           </cfpresentationslide>

        </cfloop>

    </cfpresentation>
```

Listing 34.2 begins with a query that gets information about the films from the Orange Whip Studios database. Normally this query should be in a ColdFusion Component, but it is included here for simplicity. The presentation begins with an introduction slide. After that, the query is used to generate dynamic slides. Each slide contains information about the movie, including an optional image. The code could be expanded even further to show directors, actors, and the budget, but the code as it is now gives a nice overview of the films. Figure 34.2 shows the presentation.

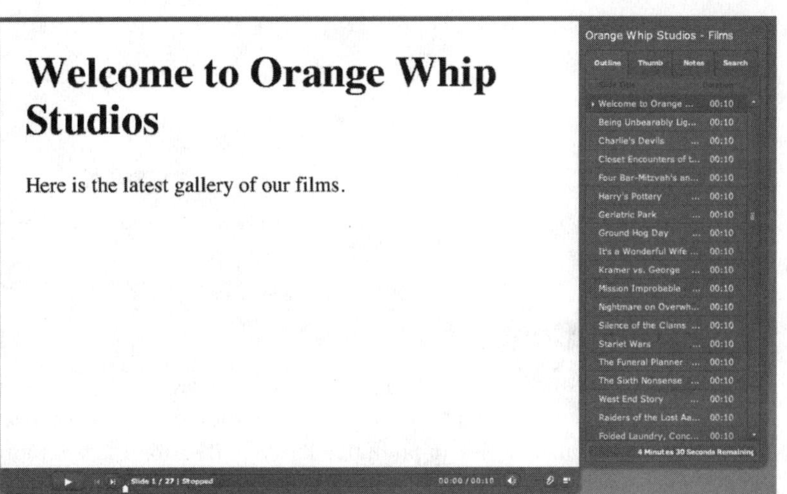

Figure 34.2

Dynamic presentation.

Setting Play and Control Options

Now that you've created a few presentations, let's discuss how to manipulate the way that the presentation plays and is controlled. Table 34.1 listed the attributes of `<cfpresentation>` that allow this sort of customization. Listing 34.3 is a modified version of Listing 34.2. This time the presentation is being built for a kiosk where no one will be there to click the Next button. The presentation needs to run by itself, without human intervention. Because so little change was needed, the listing shows only the changed `<cfpresentation>` tag.

Listing 34.3 `example3.cfm`—Dynamic Presentation (Autoplay)

```
<cfpresentation title="Orange Whip Studios - Films"
            autoPlay="true" loop="true"
            control="brief">
```

The first change was to set `autoPlay="true"`. This starts the presentation and makes it move through the slides by itself. Next, `loop="true"` ensures that the presentation will play forever. Last, `control="brief"` minimizes the controls. We can't remove the controls completely, but this setting makes them take up less space. Figure 34.3 shows the slimmer control scheme, at the bottom right.

Figure 34.3

A presentation that plays automatically.

Welcome to Orange Whip Studios

Here is the latest gallery of our films.

Embedding Content

Not all content for a presentation must be embedded directly in the presentation. Multiple options exist for providing content from outside the ColdFusion page. The `<cfpresentationslide>` tag supports a `src` attribute. This can point to a local ColdFusion file, a remote URL, or a local SWF file. Listing 34.4 shows a simple example of how to embed resources in presentations.

Listing 34.4 example4.cfm—Embedding Content in Slides

```
<!---
Name:        example4.cfm
Author:      Raymond Camden (ray@camdenfamily.com)
Description: Presentation with external content
--->

<cfpresentation title="Embedding Stuff!" showNotes="false"
            showSearch="false">

   <cfpresentationslide title="A Flash Slide"
         src="SimpleSearchMovie.swf" />

   <cfpresentationslide title="A CFM Slide"
         src="slide.cfm" />

   <cfpresentationslide title="An external URL"
         src="http://127.0.0.1/ows/34/slide2.cfm" />

</cfpresentation>
```

The presentation in Listing 34.4 contains three slides. The first slide points to a SWF file in the same directory. The second slide points to a CFM file. The third slide uses a full URL, but points to another file in the same directory. If you run this code on your own server, be sure to modify the URL to match the location for your machine, including the port number. As another example of how to customize the layout, the Notes and Search tabs were turned off. Be sure to copy `SimpleSearchMovie.swf`, `slide.cfm`, and `slide2.cfm` from the zip file. They are not shown here because they simply provide content for the presentation.

NOTE

Both `<cfpresentation>` and `<cfpresentationslide>` provide attributes to support the requesting of information via a proxy server or HTTP authorization. See the ColdFusion documentation language reference for more information.

Styling Your Presentation

Although the default presentation display looks pretty nice, you may want to tweak the layout and add your own style. Table 34.3 lists the attributes related to styling presentations.

Table 34.3 `<cfpresentation>` and `<cfpresentationslide>` Design Attributes

ATTRIBUTE	FUNCTION
`backgroundColor`	Sets the background color for the presentation. The setting can be a hex color or named color. The default is `#727971`. Used in `<cfpresentation>`.
`glowColor`	Sets the color used for the "glow" around buttons. The setting can be a hex color or named color. Used in `<cfpresentation>`.
`lightColor`	Sets the color used for light and shadow effects. The setting can be a hex color or named color. Used in `<cfpresentation>`.

Table 34.3 (continued)

ATTRIBUTE	FUNCTION
`primaryColor`	Sets the main color for the presentation. The setting can be a hex color or named color. Used in `<cfpresentation>`.
`shadowColor`	Sets the color used for shadow effects. The setting can be a hex color or named color. Used in `<cfpresentation>`.
`textColor`	Sets the color used for text. The setting can be a hex color or named color. Used in `<cfpresentation>`.
`marginTop`, `marginLeft`, `marginRight`, `marginBottom`	Sets the margin in pixels for a slide. The default is 0. Used in `<cfpresentationslide>`.

Listing 34.5 shows a rather ugly example of style customization.

Listing 34.5 `example5.cfm`—A "Stylish" Presentation

```
<!---
Name:        example5.cfm
Author:      Raymond Camden (ray@camdenfamily.com)
Description: Presentation with style
--->

<cfpresentation title="Designed Presentation"
            autoPlay="false" backGroundColor="green"
            glowColor="red" lightColor="pink"
            primaryColor="black" shadowColor="gray"
            textColor="blue">

   <cfpresentationslide title="Small Margins"
            marginleft="50" marginRight="50"
            marginTop="200" marginBottom="200"
   >
<h1>This is why I don't design</h1>

<p>
See how bad these colors go together? This is why I
don't do design work.
</p>
   </cfpresentationslide>

</cfpresentation>
```

As you can see, this presentation makes use of every design option listed in Table 34.3. The design choices aren't great, but this is something any decent designer can correct. Figure 34.4 shows why the author of this chapter isn't allowed to design.

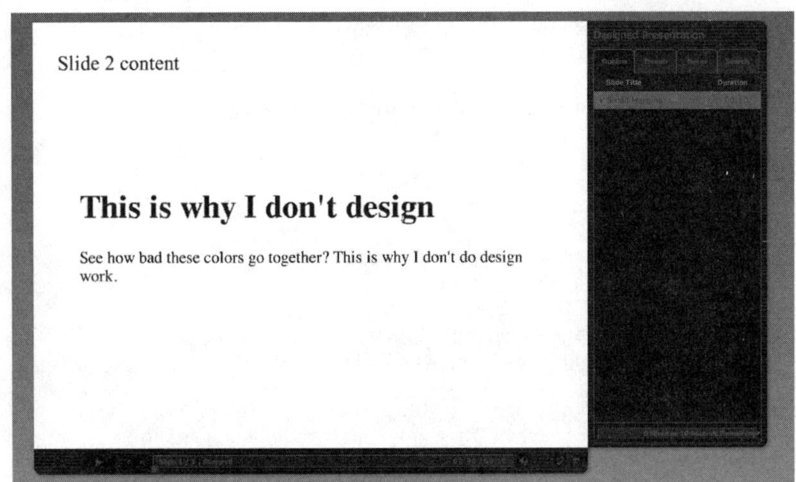

Figure 34.4

A presentation with(out) flair.

Adding Presenters

What would a presentation be without a presenter? ColdFusion presentations can have one or more presenters associated with them, with any presenter assigned to any particular slide (but no more than one presenter per slide). To add a presenter to a presentation, simply use the `<cfpresenter>` tag. Table 34.4 lists the attributes of `<cfpresenter>`.

Table 34.4 `<cfpresenter>` Attributes

ATTRIBUTE	FUNCTION
`biography`	Specifies an optional biography of the presenter.
`email`	Specifies the email address of the presenter. If used, a Contact button is added to the control panel of the presentation.
`image`	Specifies a picture of the presenter. The image must be a JPEG file and set relative to the CFM page creating the presentation. If a video is used with the slide, the video takes the place of the picture.
`name`	Specifies the name of the presenter. This name will also be used to identify the presenter to slides.
`logo`	Specifies the logo for the presenter's company or organization. The logo must be a JPEG file and set relative to the CFM page creating the presentation.
`title`	Specifies the presenter's title, such as "Director of Marketing."

Listing 34.6 creates a presentation that makes use of the presenter feature.

Listing 34.6 `example6.cfm`—Adding Presenters

```
<!---
Name:        example6.cfm
Author:      Raymond Camden (ray@camdenfamily.com)
Description: Presentation with presentors
--->

<cfpresentation title="Presenting Presentors!">

  <cfpresenter name="Raymond Camden"
         email="ray@camdenfamily.com"
         title="ColdFusion Jedi Master"
         image="ray.jpg" logo="logo.jpg"
         biography="Raymond likes ColdFusion">

  <cfpresenter name="Boring Guy" title="Nothing Important"
         biography="This guy hasn't done anything.">

   <cfpresentationslide title="Slide 1"
        presenter="Raymond Camden">
   <p>
   This is slide one. It is associated with
   Ray.
   </p>
   </cfpresentationslide>

   <cfpresentationslide title="Slide 2"
        presenter="Boring Guy">
   <p>
   This is slide two. It is associated with
   Boring Guy.
   </p>
   </cfpresentationslide>

   <cfpresentationslide title="Slide 3"
         presenter="Raymond Camden">
   <p>
   This is slide three. It is associated with
   Ray again.
   </p>
   </cfpresentationslide>

</cfpresentation>
```

The presentation in Listing 34.6 has two presenters. The first uses all the available options and is named Raymond Camden. The second is a presenter named Boring Guy. Then three slides are created. The first and third slides use Raymond Camden as the presenter. Be careful to ensure that the name exactly matches that in the `<cfpresenter>` tag. The second slide uses the Boring Guy presenter. The result is shown in Figure 34.5.

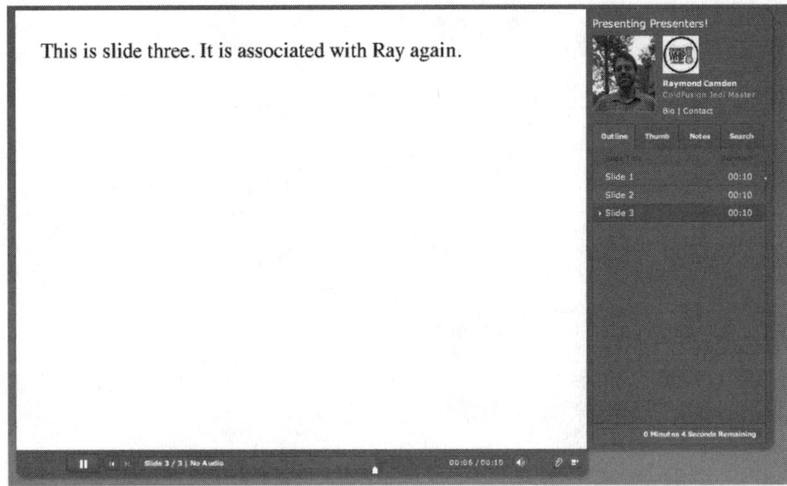

Figure 34.5

A presentation with a presenter.

Saving Your Presentation

So far, all presentations created in the listings were immediately displayed in the browser when requested. Although this process happens pretty quickly, you may want to store and save the presentation for use later. The `<cfpresentation>` tag supports an attribute named `directory`. If you use this attribute, the result of the presentation will be stored in the folder you specify. Listing 34.7 is a modified version of Listing 34.1. This time a `directory` attribute is provided.

Listing 34.7 `example7.cfm`—Saving Presentations

```
<!---
Name:        example7.cfm
Author:      Raymond Camden (ray@camdenfamily.com)
Description: First presentation
--->

<cfset directory = expandPath("./stored")>
<cfif not directoryExists(directory)>
   <cfdirectory action="create" directory="#directory#">
</cfif>

<cfpresentation title="First Presentation"
            autoPlay="false" directory="./stored" overwrite="true">

   <cfpresentationslide title="Welcome to CFPRESENTATION"
            notes="These are some notes.">
<h1>Welcome to CFPRESENTATION</h1>

<p>
This is content for the first slide. I can include HTML
and it will be rendered by the presentation.
</p>
```

Listing 34.7 (continued)

```
    </cfpresentationslide>

    <cfpresentationslide title="Sales Figures"
            notes="These are some notes for slide two.">
  <h1>Sales Figures</h1>

  <p>
  Some fake data.
  </p>

  <p>
  <table width="100%" border="1">
  <tr>
    <th>Product</th>
    <th>Price</th>
  </tr>
  <tr>
    <td>Apples</td><td>$0.99</td>
  </tr>
  <tr>
    <td>Bananas</td><td>$1.99</td>
  </tr>
  <tr>
    <td>Nukes</td><td>$2.99</td>
  </tr>
  </table>
  </p>
    </cfpresentationslide>
  </cfpresentation>
  <p>
  All done!
  </p>
```

The code begins by checking for the existence of a relative directory named `"stored"`. If this directory doesn't exist, it is created. Next the `<cfpresentation>` tag is passed the `directory` attribute. Note the `overwrite` attribute. This is specified so that ColdFusion will not throw an error if the template is run more than once. The "All done!" message is printed at the bottom of the file. When ColdFusion is asked to store the presentation, it won't actually display it. The `index.htm` file from the stored directory can now be opened directly in your browser either via HTTP (for example, `http://localhost:800/ows/34/stored/`) or via File > Open. The folder could be shipped on a CD or even emailed (if zipped, of course) to someone.

Converting from PowerPoint

ColdFusion 9 dramatically improves the power of `<cfpresentation>` by allowing it to work with Microsoft PowerPoint presentations. Not only can you convert PowerPoint files, but you can also convert presentations into HTML files. Along with converting PowerPoint files wholesale, you can specify specific slides to be imported and mix and match dynamic ColdFusion-generated slides with static PowerPoint content. Listing 34.8 shows a simple example.

Listing 34.8 example8.cfm—PowerPoint Support

```
<!---
Name:        example8.cfm
Author:      Raymond Camden (ray@camdenfamily.com)
Description: PowerPoint support
--->

<cfpresentation title="PowerPoint Presentation"
                autoPlay="false">

    <cfpresentationslide src="#expandPath('./my.ppt')#" />

</cfpresentation>
```

Pretty simple, right? Listing 34.8 demonstrates that it takes only three lines of code to convert an existing PowerPoint file (in this case, `my.ppt`) into a Flash-based presentation.

As stated earlier, you can also mix and match PowerPoint and ColdFusion-based slides (or SWF files, remote URLs, and so on). Listing 34.9 is a slightly enhanced example.

Listing 34.9 example9.cfm—PowerPoint Support

```
<!---
Name:        example9.cfm
Author:      Raymond Camden (ray@camdenfamily.com)
Description: PowerPoint support
--->

<cfpresentation title="PowerPoint Presentation"
                autoPlay="false">

    <cfpresenter name="Raymond Camden"
    email="ray@camdenfamily.com"
    title="ColdFusion Jedi Master"
    image="ray.jpg" logo="logo.jpg"
    biography="Raymond likes ColdFusion">

    <cfpresentationslide title="Welcome to Not-PowerPoint">
    <cfoutput>
    <h1>PowerPoint Support</h1>

    <p>
    One of the many new, and cool, features of ColdFusion 9. By the way,
    here is a bit of randomness just for the heck of it: #randRange(1,1000)#
    </p>
    </cfoutput>
    </cfpresentationslide>

    <cfpresentationslide src="#expandPath('./my.ppt')#" slides="2"
    presenter="Raymond Camden" />

</cfpresentation>
```

Listing 34.9 builds on the previous example. This time, however, we've mixed an inline slide defined with HTML and ColdFusion with a PowerPoint presentation. Also note the `slides="2"` argument. This tells ColdFusion to import only the second slide from the PowerPoint file.

Let's now look at a final example. While the Flash-based presentations we've worked with look pretty nice, you may want to support a simpler version of the presentation built with HTML instead. Listing 34.10 demonstrates how simple the process for doing this is.

Listing 34.10 `example10.cfm`—HTML Presentation

```
<!---
Name:        example10.cfm
Author:      Raymond Camden (ray@camdenfamily.com)
Description: PowerPoint support
--->

<cfset htmlversion = expandPath("./htmlversion")>
<cfif not directoryExists(htmlversion)>
    <cfdirectory action="create" directory="#htmlversion#">
</cfif>

<cfpresentation title="PowerPoint Presentation" overwrite="true"
               autoPlay="false" directory="#htmlversion#" format="html">

    <cfpresenter name="Raymond Camden"
    email="ray@camdenfamily.com"
    title="ColdFusion Jedi Master"
    image="ray.jpg" logo="logo.jpg"
    biography="Raymond likes ColdFusion">

    <cfpresentationslide title="Welcome to Not-PowerPoint">
    <cfoutput>
    <h1>PowerPoint Support</h1>

    <p>
    One of the many new, and cool, features of ColdFusion 9. By the way,
    here is a bit of randomness just for the heck of it: #randRange(1,1000)#
    </p>
    </cfoutput>
    </cfpresentationslide>

    <cfpresentationslide src="#expandPath('./my.ppt')#" slides="2"
    presenter="Raymond Camden" />

</cfpresentation>

<p>
Done.
</p>
```

Much as in Listing 34.7, we begin by checking for, and possibly creating, a folder within our current directory. Our subfolder in this example is named `htmlversion`.

We then added three arguments to the `<cfpresentation>` tag in Listing 34.9. The first argument, `overwrite="true"`, allows us to run the code as many times as we want without ColdFusion's having to consider about the existing files that may be there. The second addition, the `directory` attribute, uses the path we created earlier, `htmlversion`. The third argument is the `format="html"` attribute. That's it. ColdFusion has no problem working with the native slide and the PowerPoint presentation and converting everything to an HTML-based presentation that can be shared with others.

CHAPTER 35

Full-Text Searching

IN THIS CHAPTER

Getting to Know Solr

By now you're convinced that ColdFusion is the greatest package on the planet for publishing database data to the Web—but you haven't yet learned how to create that most popular of Web-based applications, the search engine. The success of Yahoo!, Google, and other search engines has made the concept of a Web-based search tool nearly as ubiquitous on the Internet as the word "ubiquitous" itself. An intelligent search tool is a must-have for an increasing number of sites. This chapter shows how to integrate the Solr search technology into your ColdFusion applications.

ColdFusion includes Solr search technology, which can be used in ColdFusion applications. This technology includes

- An engine for indexing and searching large amounts of textual and binary data
- A programming interface for searching the indexes

The Solr search engine excels at finding words in large chunks of unstructured text, such as the documents human beings tend to write. As a developer, you tell it what to search—and what to search for—and it will faithfully try to find it.

Solr can search a variety of files in a variety of languages, and it does all the fancy stuff you'd expect from a sophisticated search engine, such as handling `AND`, `OR`, wildcards, and so on. If you've ever used the search interface provided by Lexis-Nexis, you can expect the same type of functionality from your own applications that use Solr.

Conceptually, the Solr layer you will learn about in this chapter is similar to the data source/SQL layer we covered earlier in the book. The main difference is that while data sources and SQL excel at accessing neat rows and columns of information in structured database tables, Solr excels at accessing messy chunks of text strewn about in various folders on your hard drives.

Much of Solr's inner workings are thoughtfully hidden from ColdFusion developers. In a nutshell, here's how you integrate text searching into your ColdFusion applications. First you index your textual data with the ColdFusion administrator or the `<cfindex>` tag. Then you build a search form for users. Then you build an *action* template that employs the `<cfsearch>` tag and formats the search results.

NOTE

Solr is an open source project managed by the Apache Foundation. It is a server layer wrapper for the Lucene project, which is really the core search technology. You can find more information online at http://lucene.apache.org/solr/.

NOTE

While ColdFusion still supports, and ships with, the Verity search engine, Verity is deprecated and no longer recommended for new projects. You can migrate your Verity collections to Solr using a tool in the ColdFusion Administrator. Also note that almost everything described in this chapter apples to Verity collections as well.

Searching for Different Types of Files with Solr

ColdFusion's Solr functionality supports most popular file types, including native files such as documents produced with many of the Microsoft Office applications. This feature provides great flexibility when it comes to making files searchable via a Web browser.

For instance, in an intranet situation, employees can continue to use the word-processing and spreadsheet applications they use every day. All they have to do is save the documents in a folder tree that is indexed in a Solr collection. With just a few lines of code, you can turn those documents into a fully searchable company library. Solr can index Office documents, MP3s, PDFs, and other binary formats. For a complete list, see the official documentation.

NOTE

Different file types can be freely mixed and matched in a Solr collection. Don't worry about keeping the HTML and Word files in separate folders or collections. Store them wherever you want.

Creating a Search Tool for Your Documents

Let's say that Orange Whip Studios' Human Resources Department wants to make the company's personnel policies available online so employees can see what they are allowed to do (and not do) at any time. These policies are published internally and are not accessible to a large number of employees.

The documents are saved as various Word, plain-text, and Excel files. Collect all the documents into one folder on your Web server's local drive; explore what is necessary to make these documents searchable and retrievable from a Web browser using ColdFusion's Solr functionality as the back end. It's really pretty simple.

Understanding Collections

Solr's search functionality centers around a concept of a collection. A Solr *collection* is a mass of documents you want Solr to keep track of and make searchable. (Note that a collection also can consist of a query result set, which is explored later in this chapter.)

After Solr has been told which documents belong to a collection, it can index the documents and compile metadata about them for its own use. This index enables it to search through your documents quickly, without actually parsing through them line by line at run time. Conceptually, the key to Solr's strength is its capability to invest a certain amount of time up front in indexing and compiling information about your documents. You get the payoff on that investment when your users run their searches. Solr has already studied the documents and can therefore return information about them very quickly.

Again, you might find it useful to think of Solr collections as being the full-text search equivalent of data sources. Just as you need to set up a data source before you can use `<cfquery>` to retrieve data with SQL, you need to set up a collection before you can get started with Verity. As with setting up a new data source, you go to the ColdFusion Administrator to set up a new collection.

Creating a New Collection

Here are the steps needed to create the Solr collection for the Human Resources documents:

1. Go to the ColdFusion Administrator and click the ColdFusion Collections link in the Data & Services section, as shown in Figure 35.1. This screen lists all collections and contains a form used to create new collections.

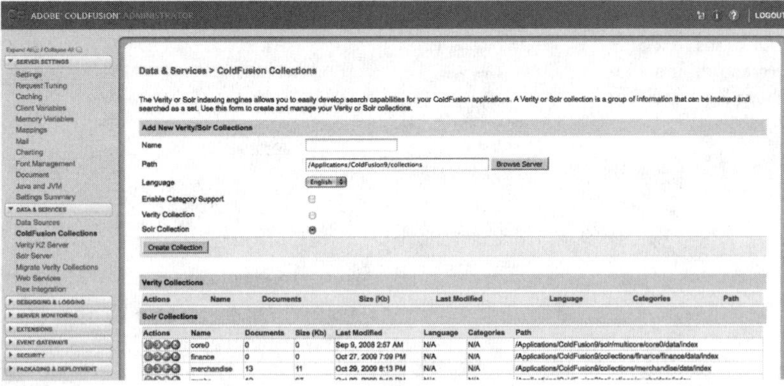

Figure 35.1

Solr collections must be created to use ColdFusion's full-text searching functionality.

2. Name the new collection `owshr` (as in "Orange Whip Studios HR").

3. You can change the path if you want the collection to be stored in a location other than the default (`/collections` under the ColdFusion root), but you should generally not do so unless you have a specific reason not to (such as drive space or file-permissions issues).

NOTE

The path you fill in when creating a new collection is simply where Solr's internal data about your documents will be kept. This is not the path to where the actual documents are.

4. Solr can perform intelligent searching if it knows the language that content is in. Select the primary language from the drop-down list.

5. Click the Create Collection button. After a moment, your new collection will appear in the list of collections (along with any other existing collections).

Indexing the Collection

Creating the collection simply results in the creation of the basic Solr infrastructure that will be used for the collection. You must *index* the collection in order to make the collection searchable.

Indexing is simple and can be done via the ColdFusion Administrator or through the `<cfindex>` tag. Let's start by indexing a collection through the ColdFusion Administrator.

Indexing Your Files with the ColdFusion Administrator

Locate the newly created collection in the ColdFusion Collections list, and click the Index icon (the leftmost icon) for the collection to be indexed (or just click on the collection name). This displays the Index Collection page (seen in Figure 35.2). The form is used to specify the text content that is to be made searchable.

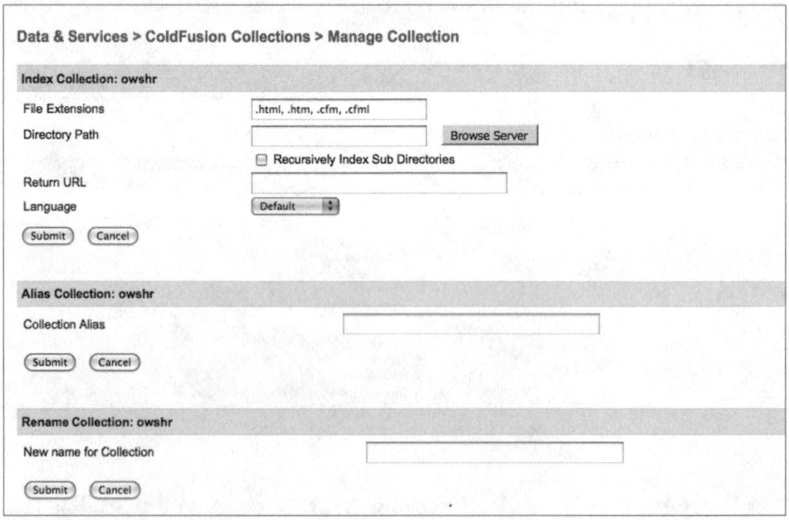

Figure 35.2

The Index Collection page is used to add items to a Solr collection, indexing them for searching.

Data & Services > ColdFusion Collections > Manage Collection

Index Collection: owshr

File Extensions .html, .htm, .cfm, .cfml

Directory Path Browse Server

Recursively Index Sub Directories

Return URL

Language Default

Submit Cancel

Alias Collection: owshr

Collection Alias

Submit Cancel

Rename Collection: owshr

New name for Collection

Submit Cancel

You must now tell ColdFusion what to index:

1. Enter the file extensions (comma delimited) as follows: `.html, .htm, .doc, .txt, .xls`
2. The Directory Path field specifies the location on the server's disk where the data to be made searchable is located. Copy the chapter's code from the Zip file downloaded from the Web site. Within that folder (named `35`) is a folder named `HR`. Under that folder is a folder named `Docs`. Enter that path in the Directory Path field.
3. Select Recursively Index Sub Directories (so that content in child folders is indexed too).
4. The Return URL field specifies the URL that will be used to return any content if the user searches for it. It is the path the Web server uses to find the content. Enter `http://localhost:80/ows/35/hr/docs/`or the appropriate URL for your server.

At this point, click the Submit button to index the content. When indexing is complete, you'll be returned to the ColdFusion Collections list page and the message "Collection `owshr` Indexed" will be displayed at the top.

You now know one way to index your documents. This method is handy for the following situations:

- When the documents change infrequently, or not on a fixed or predictable schedule
- When the documents live outside your ColdFusion application, such as in a folder full of Word files that employees might save and edit without your application knowing about it
- For testing and development
- With less complicated in-house applications

But other situations are likely to require the programmatic approach:

- When the documents are always changing
- When it's critical that new documents become searchable right away
- When it's important that your application be as self-tuning as possible—such as when you are working as an outside consultant
- With more complicated applications

Let's see how the programmatic approach is used.

Indexing Your Files with the `<cfindex>` Tag

You've learned how to index a collection using the ColdFusion Administrator, but that approach isn't always good enough. Sometimes you'll need a ColdFusion application to do the indexing itself, programmatically.

The `<cfindex>` tag cues Solr to wake up and index (or re-index) the files in the folder you specify. This is the second step in the overall process of making a Solr application come alive. (The first step is creating the collection in the ColdFusion Administrator; the third is actually searching the collection with the `<cfsearch>` tag, which we will cover shortly.)

The template in Listing 35.1 uses the `<cfindex>` tag to index the content of the `HR/Docs` subdirectory. This content consists of some Microsoft Word and Excel documents as well as some text and HTML files.

Listing 35.1 `indexing.cfm`—Indexing the `owshr` Collection

```
<!---
Module:         indexing.cfm
Author:         Leon Chalnick & Ben Forta
Function:       Indexes HTML, Text, Word and Excel
                          content for owshr collection.
--->

Indexing documents ...<br>

<!--- Index the owshr collection --->
<cfindex collection="owshr"
         action="refresh"
         type="path"
         key="#getDirectoryFromPath(getCurrentTemplatePath())#/hr/docs/"
         extensions=".htm, .html, .txt, .doc, .xls"
         recurse="yes"
         urlpath="http://localhost/ows/35/hr/docs">

Done!
```

The `<cfindex>` tag tells Solr to index your actual documents, and the `<cfindex>` tag's various parameters give Solr the particulars about what you want it to do. Take a look at each of the parameters:

- `collection` tells Solr which collection to use.
- `action` tells Solr you're interested in refreshing any data currently in the collection with new information. Other values are possible for `action` other than `refresh`, and are discussed in the section "Maintaining Collections," later in this chapter.
- `type` tells Solr you're interested in adding documents from a directory path on your Web server. You'll learn about another possible value for `type` later, when the topic of using Solr to index database data rather than document files is covered. Refer to the section "Indexing Your Table Data: Solr to the Rescue," later in this chapter.
- `key` tells Solr from which directory path to add documents. This parameter must evaluate to the complete file system path to the actual documents you want to index.
- `extensions` tells Solr which documents in the specified folder should be indexed. This parameter is useful if you want only certain types of documents to become searchable.
- `recurse` tells Solr whether you want it to index files in subfolders of the folder you specified with the `KEY` parameter. Possible values are `YES` and `NO`. You would usually specify `YES`.

- `urlpath` tells Solr to maintain URLs for each document as it indexes, by appending the file name to the value you supply with this parameter. If `recurse="YES"` and the file is in a subfolder, the folder name is appended as well. As long as the value you supply here is the URL version of the value you supplied for `KEY`, Solr automatically records the correct URL for each file as it indexes. You will see this in action later when you use the `#URL#` column returned by the `<cfsearch>` tag. This is discussed later in the "Search Results Page" section. Be sure to edit this line to match your Web server information.

That's about all there is to indexing document files. Now all you have to do is ensure that the code in Listing 35.1 runs whenever new documents are saved to the `ows/35/HR/Docs` folder.

Creating a Search Interface

Now that you've created the `owshr` collection and you've learned both techniques for indexing it, you can start putting together the ColdFusion templates to make your documents searchable. You'll see that the code you use to do this is similar in concept to the examples in Chapter 12, "ColdFusion Forms," in *Adobe ColdFusion 9 Web Application Construction Kit, Volume 1: Getting Started.*

Building the search interface involves constructing two pages. You need a simple search form page for users to enter their search criteria. This form's action template will actually conduct the search using `<cfsearch>`, and it can also display the search results.

The Search Form Page

Roll up your sleeves because we're writing more code: it's time to build a search form. Refer to Listing 35.2.

Listing 35.2 `searchform.cfm`—The Search Form Page

```
<!---
Name:          searchform.cfm
Author:        Leon Chalnick & Ben Forta
Description:   Presents a simple form for specifying
search criteria and number of rows to display
--->

<h2>Personnel Policy Documents</h2>
<p>
<strong>Search Form</strong>
</p>
<!--- Create search form --->
<form action="searchresults.cfm" method="post">

Keywords: <input type="text" name="criteria" size="30"><br/>
<input type="submit" value="Search">

</form>
```

The Search Results Page

This form submits these two pieces of information to the `searchresults.cfm` template, which contains the code that actually runs the Verity search and displays the results of the search to the user.

Take a look at that template now. As Listing 35.3 shows, it contains only one ColdFusion tag that you're not familiar with yet—the `<cfsearch>` tag.

Listing 35.3 `searchresults.cfm`—The Search Results Page

```
<!---
Name:           searchresults.cfm
Author:         Leon Chalnick & Ben Forta
Description:    Runs CFSEARCH and displays results.
--->

<!--- Run the search against the HRDocs collection --->
<cfsearch name="getResults"
          collection="owshr"
          criteria="#form.criteria#">

<!--- Display results --->
<h2>Personnel Policy Documents</h2>

<cfoutput>
Search Results: <strong>#form.criteria#</strong>
</cfoutput>

<p>

<!--- no files found for specified criteria? --->
<cfif getResults.RecordCount is 0>

   <strong>No files found for specified criteria</strong>

<cfelse>

 <!--- Found a match --->
 <table cellspacing=0 cellpadding=2>

  <!--- Display results --->
  <cfoutput query="getResults">
   <!--- alternate line background color --->
   <cfset bgcolor = currentRow mod 2?"ffffff":"ffffcf">
   <tr bgcolor="#bgcolor#" valign="top">
    <!--- current row number --->
    <td>#currentRow#</td>
    <td>
     <!--- Display title if there is one, else name --->
     <cfif Trim(Title) IS "">
      <cfset display=getFileFromPath(Key)>
     <cfelse>
      <cfset display=title>
     </cfif>
     <!--- Now display it --->
     <a href="#GetResults.url#">#display#</a> (#score#)
     <br>
```

Listing 35.3 (continued)

```
        <small>#summary#</small>
      </td>
    </tr>
  </cfoutput>
 </table>

</cfif>

</body>
</html>
```

Clearly, the focus of this template is the `<cfsearch>` tag near the top. The `<cfsearch>` tag tells Solr to actually run a search: take the search criteria that the user supplies and try to find documents that match.

Do you recall that Solr searches are similar to data source/SQL queries? With that similarity in mind, it's worth noting that the `<cfsearch>` tag acts a lot like the `<cfquery>` tag when you're dealing with database tables.

Take a look at the specific parameters you're supplying to the `<cfsearch>` tag in Listing 35.3. As you do so, keep in mind that most of these parameters look like the ones you'd supply to a `<cfquery>` tag.

Here are the parameters for `<cfsearch>`, as used in Listing 35.3:

- `name` gives the search a name. Whatever results are found by Solr are available (for your use as a developer) as a query that has the name you supply here. You can use the search results in `<cfoutput>` tags and in any of the other ways you normally use query results.
- `collection` tells Solr in which collection to search for documents. In this case, we are using the just-created `owshr` collection.
- `criteria` is probably the most important parameter here. This is what you're actually asking Solr to look for. You're simply passing to this parameter whatever the user types in the search form.

After the `<cfsearch>` is executed, the rest of Listing 35.3 displays the results to the user (as seen in Figure 35.3 for keyword `hire`). Here is the main thing to keep in mind: Now that the `<cfsearch>` has found its results, you treat it just as if it were a `<cfquery>` named `getResults`.

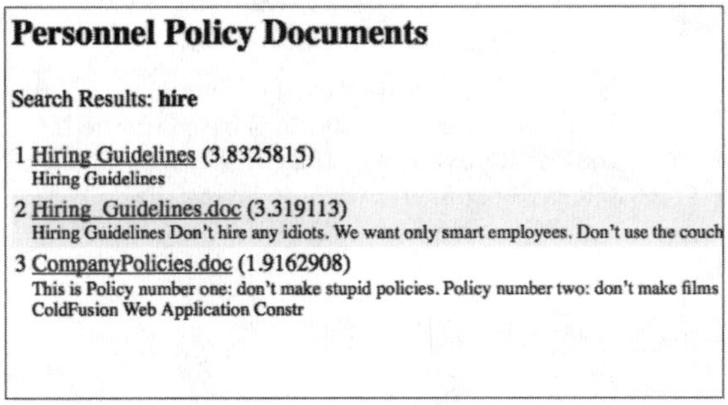

Figure 35.3

Results returned from a Solr search contain a score that can be used to determine how close a match each result is to the criteria. Note that your results may differ.

Personnel Policy Documents
Search Results: hire
1 Hiring Guidelines (3.8325815)
Hiring Guidelines
2 Hiring_Guidelines.doc (3.319113)
Hiring Guidelines Don't hire any idiots. We want only smart employees. Don't use the couch
3 CompanyPolicies.doc (1.9162908)
This is Policy number one: don't make stupid policies. Policy number two: don't make films
ColdFusion Web Application Constr

First, a `<cfif>` tag performs the now-familiar check to ensure that the built-in `RecordCount` variable is not `0` (which would mean Solr didn't find any results).

Provided there are results to display, your code moves into the large `<cfelse>` block that encompasses the remainder of the template. `<table>`, `<tr>`, and `<td>` tags are used to establish an HTML table in which to display the results, with headers.

Most of the important stuff happens in the large `<cfoutput>` block that follows. The `query="getResults"` parameter in the `<cfoutput>` tag causes this code to be executed once for each row in the search results, where each row represents a document found. Within the `<cfoutput>` block, special columns named `key`, `title`, `score`, and `context` are being used. Unlike results returned by a `<cfquery>`—where you've specified which columns your results will contain by including them in the `SELECT` part of your SQL statement—results returned by Solr searches always contain the same, predefined column names, which are shown in Table 35.1.

Table 35.1 Columns Returned by Verity Searches

COLUMN	CONTAINS
AUTHOR	Author information (if it can be obtained from Microsoft Office and Adobe PDF files).
CATEGORY	A list of categories that this document is associated with.
CATEGORYTREE	A hierarchical category tree.
CONTEXT	An excerpt of the matched text with the match highlighted in bold.
CUSTOMn	The value of a custom field you specify when you populate the collection. See the section "Indexing Additional Columns with Custom Fields."
KEY	The document's file name.
RANK	The relative ranking in the search results.
RECORDSSEARCHED	The number of records Solr searched. In other words, the number of records in the collection(s)
SCORE	A numerical value that signifies the strength of the match.
SIZE	The number of bytes in the found document.
SUMMARY	Summary as generated when indexed.
TITLE	The title of the document, if Solr is capable of determining what the title is. For example, if the file is an HTML document, Solr obtains the title from the `<title>` tags in the document's `<head>` section. Solr might not provide a title for other types of documents.
TYPE	The MIME type of the document.
URL	The URL that can be used to obtain the file from your Web server. The information in this column is based on the information you supplied to the `<cfindex>` tag with its `urlpath` parameter. If you didn't specify a `URLPATH` parameter when indexing the collection, this column is blank.

Refining Your Search

Often, typing a few keywords isn't enough to find the documents you want. Solr provides a way refine your search, by applying operators. For example, you may want to require that multiple words appear in a document, or perhaps to find documents that *don't* have a word. Solr supports these searches by supporting the special words `AND`, `OR`, and `NOT` in your search terms.

Performing `AND` and `NOT` Searches

If you want to refine your search a little, you can use special search operators in your search criteria to get more specific. Only the most common search operators are discussed at this point. Many others are available for your use.

By default, a search for multiple words, such as `"Jedi Master"`, will be an `OR` search. In other words, documents with either word will be matched. To perform an `AND` search and require all words appear, simply place the `AND` keyword between the terms: `"Jedi AND Master"`.

If you want to remove documents from the results that contain a keyword, use the `NOT` keyword. To find documents that contain `"Jedi"` but not `"Sith"`, you could use this search: `"Jedi NOT Sith"`.

Using Wildcards

Solr provides a few wildcards you can use in your searches, so you can find documents based on incomplete search words or phrases. The wildcards should look familiar to you if you've used the `LIKE` operator with SQL queries, as discussed in Chapter 7, "SQL Data Manipulation," in Volume 1. Table 35.2 summarizes the use of wildcard operators.

Table 35.2 Two Most Common Wildcards

WILDCARD	PURPOSE
*	Similar to the `%` wildcard in SQL, `*` stands in for any number of characters (including 0). A search for `Fu*` would find `Fusion`, `Fugazi`, and `Fuchsia`.
?	Just as in SQL, `?` stands in for any single character. More precise—and thus generally less helpful—than the `*` wildcard. A search for `?ar?et` would find both `Carpet` and `Target`, but not `Learjet`.

Indexing SQL Data

You've seen how easy it is to use ColdFusion's Solr functionality to index all sorts of files on your system. What if you want to index and search information in your database files? ColdFusion enables you to build a Solr index from data in your database as if the data were a bunch of document files.

In this section you will see how Solr lets you neatly get around the limitations that make SQL less than ideal for true text-based searching. By the time you're finished, you'll have a good understanding of when you should unleash Solr's rich search capabilities on your database data and when you're better off leaving things to SQL instead.

Searching Without Solr

You don't need to use Solr to make your database searchable, but it can make implementing a search interface much easier and help your users find what they want more easily. Look at what you'd need to do to search your data using the tools you already know: `<cfquery>` and SQL.

Say you want to set up a little search tool to enable your users to search the OWS database's `Merchandise` table. You want the user to be able to type a word or two into a form field and click Search to get the matching item.

The code in Listing 35.4 is a simple search form. The form is displayed in a browser.

Listing 35.4 `merchandisesearch_form1.cfm`—Merchandise Search Form

```
<!---
Name:          merchandisesearch_form1.cfm
Author:        Leon Chalnick & Ben Forta
Description:   Presents simple search form for searching
               for merchandise
--->

<!--- Create a search form --->
<h2>Please enter keywords to search for.</h2>

<form action="merchandisesearch_action1.cfm"
      method="post">
Keywords: <input type="text" name="criteria">
<br>
<input type="submit" value="Search">
</form>
```

The code in Listing 35.5 performs a simple search, then displays the results from the `Merchandise` table. Note that the `LIKE` keyword is used along with the `%` wildcard to search any part of the description.

Listing 35.5 `merchandisesearch_action1.cfm`—Searching the Inventory

```
<!---
Name:          merchandisesearch_action1.cfm
Author:        Leon Chalnick & Ben Forta
Description:   Takes criteria from and
               searches against Merchandise
               Description field in db.
--->

<!--- Execute SQL query to do the searching --->
<cfquery name="GetResults" datasource="ows">
  SELECT MerchID, MerchDescription
  FROM Merchandise
  WHERE MerchDescription LIKE
  <cfqueryparam cfsqltype="cf_sql_varchar" value="%#form.criteria#%">
```

Listing 35.5 (continued)

```
</cfquery>

<cfoutput>
<h2>
#GetResults.RecordCount# Merchandise record(s) found for
"#FORM.Criteria#".
</h2>
</cfoutput>

<!--- loop through each row outputting the description --->
<ul>
<cfoutput query="getresults">
  <li>#MerchDescription#
</cfoutput>
</ul>
```

This would work fine as long as your application required only simple searching. If the user entered `poster` for the search criteria, SQL's `LIKE` operator would faithfully find all the merchandise that had the word `poster` somewhere in the description.

But what if the user entered something such as `West End Tee`? No records would be found because no records have those exact words in them (although one merchandise item does have the phrase `West End Story Tee`). That's a limitation your users probably won't find acceptable.

You could simply check for each word in the search string, so that if a user enters `West End Story Tee` you generate a SQL statement that would end up looking like this:

```
SELECT MerchID, MerchDescription
FROM Merchandise
WHERE MerchDescription LIKE '%West%'
 AND MerchDescription LIKE '%End%'
 AND MerchDescription LIKE '%Story%'
 AND MerchDescription LIKE '%Tee%'
```

That would work in this example, but you could end up with completely inappropriate results, too. And as the amount of data to search grows, so does the likelihood that you'll miss matches and return mismatches.

Indexing Your Table Data: Solr to the Rescue

ColdFusion's Solr functionality provides an easy-to-implement solution that addresses this problem. You create a custom Solr collection filled with documents that aren't really documents at all. Each document is actually just a record from your database tables.

It works like this: You write a `<cfquery>` that retrieves the data you want to make searchable. You pass this data to a `<cfindex>` tag, which indexes the data as if it were documents. Additionally, you tell Solr which column from the query should be considered a document "file name," which column should be considered a document "title," and which column(s) should be considered a document's "body."

To try this out, create a new collection named `Merchandise` (using the ColdFusion Administrator). But don't add anything to the index. Instead, you'll populate this new collection with data from the `Merchandise` database table.

Take a look at the code in Listing 35.6. Notice that the `<cfindex>` tag looks similar to Listing 36.1, in which you indexed your document files. The central differences here are the fact that you're setting `type` to `custom` instead of `path` and that you're referring to column names from a `<cfquery>`.

Listing 35.6 `indexdata1.cfm`—Index a Collection with Database Data

```
<!---
Module:          indexdata1.cfm
Author:          Leon Chalnick & Ben Forta
Function:        Refreshes the Merchandise collection by
                 indexing a query result.
--->

<!--- Feedback --->
Getting data ...<br>

<!--- Retrieve all merchandise to be searched --->
<cfquery name="getresults" datasource="ows">
 select merchid, merchname, merchdescription
 from merchandise
</cfquery>

<!--- Feedback --->
Indexing data ...<br>

<!--- Build 'custom' index on query result above --->
<cfindex action="refresh"
        collection="merchandise"
        key="merchid"
        type="custom"
        title="merchname"
        query="getresults"
        body="merchdescription">

<!--- Feedback --->
Done!
```

The `<cfquery>` part is very simple—just get the basic information about the books. (Obviously, if you only want certain books to be indexed, a `WHERE` clause could be added to the `<cfquery>`'s SQL statement.) Next comes a `<cfindex>` tag, which looks a lot like the `<cfindex>` tag you used earlier to index your normal document files.

This time around, though, you specify a few new parameters that are necessary when indexing a database table instead of normal documents:

- `action="refresh"` tells Solr that you're supplying new data.
- `type="custom"` says that you're dealing with table data, rather than document files.
- `query="GetResults"` specifies from which `<cfquery>` to get the data.
- `key, title, body` specify which query columns should be treated like which parts of a document.

That's really about all there is to it. After the indexdata1.cfm template is executed, you should be able to search the Merchandise collection in much the same way as you searched the owshr collection previously.

The code in Listing 35.7 searches through the newly indexed Merchandise collection, based on whatever criteria the user types in the search form. Except for the introduction of the <cfsearch> tag, this code is virtually unchanged from Listing 35.5; the results are displayed to the user.

Listing 35.7 merchandisesearch_action2.cfm—Searching and Displaying Records

```
<!---
Name:           merchandisesearch_action2.cfm
Author:         Leon Chalnick & Ben Forta
--->

<!--- Perform a Solr search --->
<cfsearch collection="Merchandise"
          name="GetResults"
          criteria="#form.Criteria#">

<cfoutput>
<h2>
#GetResults.RecordCount# Merchandise record(s) found for
"#FORM.Criteria#".
</h2>
</cfoutput>

<!--- loop through each row outputting the description --->
<ul>
<cfoutput query="getresults">
  <li>#Title#
</cfoutput>
</ul>
```

As you can see, exposing your database data to Solr was easy. You really didn't have to do much work at all. But the user will notice a tremendous difference: All of Solr's searching niceties are suddenly available. You can find merchandise_form2.cfm in the Zip file downloaded from the Web site.

Displaying a Summary for Each Record

In addition to the score and title, Solr also provides a summary for each record in the search results. The summary is automatically generated based on the information you specified for the body when you indexed the collection with the <cfindex> tag. The summary helps the user to eyeball which documents they are interested in.

To display the summary to the user, refer to it in your ColdFusion templates in the same way you refer to the key, score, or title. An example of this is shown in Listing 35.8. Figure 35.4 shows what the search results will look like to the user. To test Listing 35.8, copy merchandisesearch_form3.cfm from the Zip file or edit the original form to post to this new action file.

Figure 35.4

Returned summary data is useful for presenting a short snippet of matched content.

1 Merchandise record(s) found for "shirt".

T-Shirt
Score: 4
T-Shirt Be the talk of the town with a West End Story Tee

Listing 35.8 `merchandisesearch_action3.cfm`—Include a Summary for Each Document

```
<!---
Name:          merchandisesearch_action3.cfm
Author:        Leon Chalnick & Ben Forta
--->

<!--- Perform a Solr search --->
<cfsearch collection="Merchandise"
          name="GetResults"
          criteria="#form.Criteria#">

<cfoutput>
<h2>
#GetResults.RecordCount# Merchandise record(s) found for
"#form.Criteria#".
</h2>
</cfoutput>

<!--- Use definition list to disply Solr output
 score, title and summary from each item found. --->
<dl>
<cfoutput query="GetResults">
<strong>#Title#</strong>
 <dt><emp>Score: #numberFormat(Score)#</emp>
 <dd><small>#Summary#</small></dd>
</cfoutput>
</dl>

</body>
</html>
```

Don't expect Solr summaries to always show the parts of the document that contain the search keywords; that's not how Solr summarization works. Solr selects each record's summary at the time the collection is indexed, and it's always the same for any given record, regardless of the search criteria that found it. The summary doesn't necessarily contain the keywords that were used as the search criteria.

Displaying Context for Each Record

The summary returned from a search reflects a specific portion of the document, but you may want to provide context related to the matched data. For example, if the match for a search was within one part of the document, you might want to highlight that passage of text in the result. Solr and the `<cfindex>` tag support this capability with the `contextPassages` attribute. This is a numeric argument that specifies the number of passages, or sentences, that should be returned.

(You can use the `contextBytes` attribute instead if you want to specify a number of bytes.) This specification will add a new column to the result, called `context`. What's interesting about this column is that Solr automatically highlights the matched term within the text. It does this using the `<b>` and `</b>` HTML tags, but you can override this behavior with the `contextHighlightBegin` and `contextHighlightEnd` attributes. Listing 35.9 demonstrates how the context can be displayed with the results.

Listing 35.9 `merchandisesearch_action_context.cfm`—Including Context for Each Document

```
<!---
Name:          merchandisesearch_action_context.cfm
Author:        Raymond Camden
--->

<!--- Perform a Solr search --->
<cfsearch collection="Merchandise"
          name="GetResults"
          criteria="#form.Criteria#"
             contextPassages="1"
             contextHighlightBegin="<em>"
             contextHighlightEnd="</em>">

<cfoutput>
<h2>
#GetResults.RecordCount# Merchandise record(s) found for
"#form.Criteria#".
</h2>
</cfoutput>

<!--- Use definition list to display Solr output
 score, title, summary, and context from each item found. --->
<dl>
<cfoutput query="GetResults">
 <strong>#Title#</strong>
 <dt><emp>Score: #numberFormat(Score)#</emp>
 <dd>
 <small>#Summary#</small><br/>
 <small>#context#</small>
 </dd>
</cfoutput>
</dl>

</body>
</html>
```

Note that the `<cfsearch>` tag has three new attributes added: `contextPassages`, `contextHighlight Begin`, and `contextHighlightEnd`. By specifying 1 for `contextPassages`, we are asking Solr to return one passage, or sentence, with the result. The two highlight-related attributes simply tell Solr to use the `<em>` tag pair to mark matches in the context. Finally, we added context to the output.

Indexing Multiple Query Columns as the Body

In Listing 35.6 you indexed the `Merchandise` collection with the results from a query. In that listing, you declared that the `MerchDescription` column from the `Merchandise` table should be considered the body of each book record (by setting the body parameter of the <cfindex> tag to "MerchDescription").

By default, when your application runs a Solr search, only the Body part of each record is actually searched for matching words. The information in the Title part of the record isn't searched.

There are two ways to make the title searchable. One is to specify the title in the criteria parameter, using relational operators and the substring operator. See the section "Indexing Additional Columns with Custom Fields."

An easier way is to go back to your <cfindex> tag and supply the information you're giving to the title parameter to the body parameter as well. The body parameter can take a comma-separated list of column names ("MerchName,MerchDescription"), rather than only one column name ("MerchDescription"). The searchable part of each record in your database is composed of the MerchName of the item, followed by the MerchDescription of the item.

There's no need to stop there. You can put a bunch of column names in the body parameter, as shown in Listing 35.10. For each row returned by the query, ColdFusion concatenates the Merch-Description and MerchName columns and presents them to Solr as the body of each document. The result is that all textual information about the merchandise description and name is now part of your collection and instantly searchable. You don't have to change a thing about the code in any of your search templates.

Listing 35.10 indexdata2.cfm—Supply Columns to the body Attribute

```
<!---
Module:         indexdata2.cfm
Author:         Leon Chalnick & Ben Forta
--->

<!--- Feedback --->
Getting data ...<br>

<!--- Retrieve all merchandise to be searched --->
<cfquery name="getresults" datasource="ows">
 select merchid, merchname, merchdescription
 from merchandise
</cfquery>

<!--- Feedback --->
Indexing data ...<br>

<!--- Build 'custom' index on query result above --->
<cfindex action="refresh"
         collection="merchandise"
         key="merchid"
         type="custom"
         title="merchname"
         query="getresults"
         body="merchname,merchdescription">

<!--- Feedback --->
Done!
```

It's important to note that when you supply several columns to the `body` parameter, Solr doesn't maintain the information in separate columns, fields, or anything else. The underlying table's structure isn't preserved; all the information is pressed together into one big, searchable mass. Don't expect to be able to refer to a `#MerchName#` variable, for instance, in the same way you can refer to the `#Title#` and `#Score#` variables after a `<cfsearch>` is executed.

That might or might not feel like a limitation, depending on the nature of the applications you're building. In a way, it's just the flip side of Solr's concentrating on text in a natural-language kind of way, rather than being obsessed with columns the way SQL is.

However, ColdFusion and Solr do enable you to store a limited amount of information in a more database-like way, using something called *custom fields.*

Indexing Additional Columns with Custom Fields

ColdFusion lets you index up to four additional fields when you're indexing database data. The fields—`custom1`, `custom2`, `custom3`, and `custom4`—are treated like the `Title` field you've already worked with. These custom fields come in handy when you have precise, code-style data that you want to keep associated with each record.

In Listing 35.11, you adjust the code from Listing 35.6 to fill the `custom1` field with your `FilmID`. Conceptually, it's as if Solr were making a little note on each document that it makes from the rows of your query. The `custom1` note is the `FilmID`. This example doesn't use the `custom2`, `3`, or `4` attributes, but they are used exactly the same way as `custom1`.

Listing 35.11 `indexdata3.cfm`—Adding Custom Fields to a Collection

```
<!---
Module:        indexdata3.cfm
Author:        Leon Chalnick & Ben Forta
--->

<!--- Feedback --->
Getting data ...<br>

<!--- Retrieve all merchandise to be searched --->
<cfquery name="getresults" datasource="ows">
 select merchid, merchname,
        merchdescription, filmid
 from merchandise
</cfquery>

<!--- Feedback --->
Indexing data ...<br>

<!--- Build 'custom' index on query result above --->
<cfindex action="refresh"
         collection="merchandise"
         key="merchid"
         type="custom"
         title="merchname"
         query="getresults"
```

Listing 35.11 (continued)

```
          body="merchname,merchdescription"
          custom1="filmid">

<!--- Feedback --->
Done!
```

Now that Solr knows the `FilmID` for each record in the collection, you can easily create a more sophisticated search tool that lets users select films along with their search words, similar to Listing 35.12.

Listing 35.12 `merchandisesearch_form4.cfm`—Search Form with User Interface

```
<!---
Name:          merchandisesearch_form4.cfm
Author:        Leon Chalnick & Ben Forta
--->

<!--- Get the movie titles for drop down list --->
<cfquery name="GetFilms" datasource="ows">
 SELECT FilmID, MovieTitle
 FROM Films
</cfquery>

<!--- Create a search form --->
<html>
<head>
   <title>Merchandise Search</title>
</head>

<body>

<h2>Please enter keywords to search for.</h2>

<cfform action="merchandisesearch_action4.cfm">
Keywords: <cfinput type="text" name="criteria">
<br>
Movie: <cfselect name="FilmID"
                query="GetFilms"
                value="FilmID"
                display="MovieTitle"
                queryPosition="below">
        <option />
       </cfselect>
<br>
<cfinput type="submit"
        name="sbmt"
        value="Search">
</cfform>

</body>
</html>
```

Now you just need to teach the receiving template how to deal with the user's entries for the `FilmID` field. To specify the additional criteria, use Solr's field operator, which you use here for the first time.

NOTE

The field operator, a colon, searches specific document fields–rather than the body–and finds only exact matches. Document fields you can use include `CUSTOM1`, `CUSTOM2`, `CUSTOM3`, `CUSTOM4`, `TITLE`, and `KEY`, all of which correspond to the values you supply to the `<cfindex>` tag when you index the data.

Listing 35.13 demonstrates the use of the field search operator. At the top of the template, you use some `<cfif>`, `<cfelse>`, and `<cfelseif>` tags to decide what you're going to ask Solr to look for. If the user specifies a specific film (using the `<select>` list, `FilmID`), you will ignore the keywords. If the `FilmID` is blank, search for the keywords that the user entered—but be sure the user specified either keywords or a film.

Depending on which field the user might have left blank, the `TheCriteria` variable will have slightly different values. The `TheCriteria` variable is then supplied to the `<cfsearch>` tag in its `criteria` parameter.

Listing 35.13 `merchandisesearch_action4.cfm`—Field Search Operator

```
<!---
Name:          merchandisesearch_action4.cfm
Author:        Leon Chalnick & Ben Forta
--->

<!--- Setup search criteria.
      Can be either merchandise for a specific film
      or search against merchandise name & desc --->
<cfparam name="FORM.FilmID" default="">
<cfif FORM.FilmID NEQ "">
 <!--- FilmID is specified --->
 <cfset theCriteria = "custom1:#form.filmid#">
 <!--- Get the movie titles for drop down list --->
 <cfquery name="GetFilms" datasource="ows">
 SELECT FilmID, MovieTitle
 FROM Films
 where filmid = <cfqueryparam cfsqltype="cf_sql_integer" value="#form.filmid#">
 </cfquery>

 <cfset search = "Items for film #getFilms.movietitle#">
<cfelse>
 <!--- Use text --->
 <cfset TheCriteria = "#Form.Criteria#">
 <cfset search = TheCriteria>
</cfif>


<!--- Perform a Solr search --->
<cfsearch collection="Merchandise"
          name="GetResults"
          criteria="#TheCriteria#">

<!--- Display the query results --->
<cfoutput>
<h2>
#GetResults.RecordCount# Merchandise record(s) found for:
#htmlEditFormat(search)#
</h2>
```

Listing 35.13 (continued)

```
</cfoutput>

<!--- Use definition list to display Verity output
 score, title and summary from each item found. --->
<dl>
<cfoutput query="GetResults">
 <strong>#Title#</strong>
 <dt><emp>Score: #numberFormat(Score)#</emp>
 <dd><small>#Summary#</small></dd>
</cfoutput>
</dl>
```

As you can see in Listing 35.13, the variable `TheCriteria` refers to the field containing `FilmID` by using the `Custom1` variable.

Understanding Solr and Your Table's Key Values

When you're indexing table data, it's important to understand that Solr doesn't think of the concept of a key in the same way your database tables do. A database will (typically, and if set up correctly) throw an error if you try to have multiple records with the same primary key. Solr will not throw an error if you insert multiple records with the same key. Rather, it will store only the last-entered item. You need to ensure that your key values are always unique.

Searching on More Than One Collection

To specify more than one Solr collection in a `<cfsearch>` tag, just specify all the collection names for the `collection` parameter and separate them with commas. All the collections are searched for matching documents.

Improving Search Results

So far, we've seen the power of Solr's indexing and search capabilities, including its basic searching and use of operators. But Solr provides other ways to improve your search. The first option we will look at is suggestions. As you can probably guess, suggestions are tips Solr provides to improve your search. These are typically based on misspellings. So a search for "Cmden," for example, may create a suggestion for "Camden" if Solr recognizes that the search was similar to something that exists in the index. Creating suggestions requires a bit more work on Solr's part, so the feature is enabled only when you ask for it. Listing 35.14 demonstrates a simple example of how suggestions can be used.

Listing 35.14 `action_suggestions.CFM`—Using Suggestions

```
<!---
Name:          action_suggestions.cfm
Author:        Raymond Camden
--->

<cfsearch collection="owshr"
```

Listing 35.14 (continued)

```
            name="GetResults"
            criteria="#form.criteria#"
            suggestions="always"
            status="result">

<!--- Display the query results --->
<cfoutput>
<h2>
#GetResults.RecordCount# record(s) found for:
#htmlEditFormat(form.criteria)#
</h2>
</cfoutput>

<cfif len(trim(result.suggestedquery))>
<cfoutput>
<p>
Maybe next time try #trim(result.suggestedquery)#?
</p>
</cfoutput>
</cfif>

<dl>
<cfoutput query="GetResults">
 <strong>#Title#</strong>
 <dt><emp>Score: #numberFormat(Score)#</emp>
 <dd><small>#Summary#</small></dd>
</cfoutput>
</dl>
```

Two important changes were added to the `<cfsearch>` tag. First, we asked it to always provide suggestions. Other valid values are `never` (which is the default) or a number. If a number is specified, Solr will provide suggestions only if the number of results is less than the number passed. To actually work with suggestions, a `status` attribute was added as well. This returns a structure of data about the search, including information about how many records were searched and how long the search took. It also returns a key named `suggestedquery`. Later in Listing 35.14, we check to see if any value was returned. (Notice that a trim is used. Unfortunately, Solr appears to return a single space character at the end of the search. Trimming the result cleans this input.) If a value was passed, a message is output letting the user know a good alternative to try. To see an example of this process, copy `form_suggestions.cfm` from the book's code Zip file and try searching for "nmber".

The next option to consider is categories. Categories provide a way to organize your index into relevant buckets. Solr supports both category trees and category values. Think of a category tree as simply a group. For example, you may have a category tree called "American Sports" and one called "European Sports." These represent two top-level categorizations. Below each of these you may want to use a category named "Football." By combining a category and category tree value, you can assign one document in your index to American Sports/Football and another to European Sports/Football. As anyone outside of the United States will tell you, there is a huge difference in the two types of football.

How you define your category tree and categories is completely up to you. You can also choose to use only one or the other. Listing 35.15 demonstrates one possible use of categories.

Listing 35.15 `index_category.cfm`—Using Categories

```
<!---
Module:         index_category.cfm
Author:         Raymond Camden
--->

<!--- Feedback --->
Getting data ...<br>

<!--- Retrieve all merchandise to be searched --->
<cfquery name="getresults" datasource="ows">
 select merchid, merchname, merchdescription, merchprice
 from merchandise
</cfquery>

<!--- Add a column for our category --->
<cfset queryAddColumn(getresults,"level","varchar",arrayNew(1))>

<!--- set the value based on price --->
<cfloop query="getresults">
    <cfif merchprice gte 100>
       <cfset querySetCell(getresults, "level", "pricey", currentrow)>
    <cfelse>
       <cfset querySetCell(getresults, "level", "cheap", currentrow)>
    </cfif>
</cfloop>

<!--- Feedback --->
Indexing data ...<br>

<!--- Build 'custom' index on query result above --->
<cfindex action="refresh"
         collection="merchandise"
         key="merchid"
         type="custom"
         title="merchname"
         query="getresults"
         body="merchname,merchdescription"
            category="level">

<!--- Feedback --->
Done!
```

Listing 35.15 is a modified version of the earlier `indexdata1.cfm` file. Previously, we simply passed that query as is to the `<cfindex>` tag. We could do that, if there were something within the database table that represented a category. In our case, though, there isn't. Therefore, we manually create a new column called `level`. This column will represent the price level of the product. We loop over the initial query, and for each product, we set either a `"pricey"` or `"cheap"` value for the `level` column. Last, the `<cfindex>` tag is told to use the `level` column for the category field.

Now that our index contains information with categories, how do we use it? Listing 35.16 demonstrates an example of searching with categories.

Listing 35.16 `search_category.cfm`—Using Categories

```
<!---
Module:         search_category.cfm
Author:         Raymond Camden
--->

<cfparam name="form.criteria" default="">
<cfparam name="form.category" default="">

<cfcollection action="categoryList" collection="merchandise"
              name="data">

<form action="search_category.cfm" method="post">
    <cfoutput>
    Keywords: <input type="text" name="criteria"
    value="#form.criteria#"><br/>
    </cfoutput>
    Filter by Category:
    <select name="category">
    <option value="" <cfif form.category is "">selected</cfif>>-</option>
    <cfloop item="category" collection="#data.categories#">
       <cfoutput>
       <option value="#category#"
       <cfif form.category is category>selected</cfif>>#category#</option>
       </cfoutput>
    </cfloop>
    </select><br/>
    <input type="submit" value="Search">
</form>

<cfif len(trim(form.criteria))>
    <cfsearch collection="merchandise" criteria="#form.criteria#"
              category="#form.category#" name="getResults">

    <cfoutput>
    <h2>
    #getResults.RecordCount# Merchandise record(s) found for
    "#form.Criteria#"<cfif len(form.category)>
    within the #form.category# category</cfif>.
    </h2>
    </cfoutput>

    <dl>
    <cfoutput query="getResults">
     <strong>#Title#</strong>
     <dt><emp>Score: #numberFormat(Score)#</emp>
     <dd>
     <small>#Summary#</small><br/>
     </dd>
    </cfoutput>
    </dl>

</cfif>
```

We're going to cheat here a little and introduce `<cfcollection>` a bit early. This tag is discussed more fully in the next section. One feature of this tag that is useful in particular for categories is the `categoryList` action. This action will scan an index and return a structure of data that contains a list of categories and category tree values. It will even tell you how many documents are tagged with each category or category tree. Listing 35.16 makes use of this action to create a drop-down form field displaying all the categories. Later in the file, the category value is passed to the `<cfsearch>` tag. If this tag is blank, it will be ignored. If the user picks a value, the results will be filtered to items that are within that category.

Maintaining Collections

In some situations, you might be able to simply create a Solr collection, index it, and forget about it. If the documents or data that make up the collection never change, you're in luck—you get to skip this whole section of the chapter.

It's likely, though, that you'll have to refresh that data at some point. Even when you don't have to refresh it, you might want to get it to run more quickly.

Repopulating Your Solr Collection

Whenever the original documents change from what they were when you indexed them, your collection will be a little bit out of sync with reality. The search results will be based on Solr's knowledge of the documents back when you did your indexing. If a document or database record has since been edited so that it no longer has certain words in it, it might be found in error if someone types in a search for those words. If the document is deleted altogether, Solr will still find it in its own records, which means your application might show a bad link that leads nowhere.

In a perfect world, Solr would dynamically watch your document folders and data tables and immediately reflect any changes, additions, or deletions in your collections. Unfortunately, the world isn't perfect, and this stuff doesn't happen automatically for you. The good news is that fixing it is no major chore.

If You Index Your Collections Interactively

As you recall, there are two ways of indexing a Solr collection: interactively with the ColdFusion Administrator or programmatically with the `<cfindex>` tag. If you did it interactively, there's not much I need to tell you; just go back to the Solr page in the Administrator and click the Purge button for your collection. Click the Index button, and do the same thing you did the first time. This should bring your collection up to date.

NOTE

You'd do the same basic thing if the location of the documents had changed.

If You Index Your Collections Programmatically

If you indexed the collection using `<cfindex>`—and you used `action="refresh"` in the `<cfindex>` tag, as seen previously—you should be able to bring your collection up to date simply by running the indexing template again.

TIP

You might consider scheduling this refresh template to be executed automatically at the end of each week, during off-peak hours. The indexing process can be resource intensive. It is therefore best to schedule this type of activity during off-peak hours.

Instead of `action="refresh"`, you can use `action="update"` in your `<cfindex>` tag. This updates information on documents already indexed but without deleting information on documents that no longer exist. You also can use `action="purge"` to completely remove all data from the collection. The `action="refresh"` previously recommended is really the same thing as a `purge` followed by an `update`.

Deleting and Repopulating Specific Records

If your application is aware of the moment that a document or table record is deleted or edited, you might want to update the Solr collection right then, so your collection stays in sync with the actual information. Clearly, you don't have to repopulate the entire collection just because one record has changed. ColdFusion and Solr address this by enabling you to delete items from a collection via the key value.

The following code snippet deletes the Solr record for a specific key value:

```
<!--- Delete a record from the Solr collection --->
<cfindex action="delete"
         collection="Merchandise"
         key="#Form.MerchID#">
```

To update a single row use the data index techniques seen previously, but use `<cfquery>` to *only* retrieve the row to be updated. So long as `action="refresh"` is being used (instead of `action="update"`) only that row will be updated, and all other Solr data will be left as is.

Administering Collections with `<cfcollection>`

The `<cfcollection>` tag enables you to administer collections programmatically in your own templates, as an alternative to using the ColdFusion Administrator. If you want your application to be capable of creating, deleting, and maintaining a collection on its own, the `<cfcollection>` tag is here to help.

This section will be of special interest if you are developing prebuilt applications that other people will deploy on their servers without your help, or if you are presented with a project in which you want to completely remove any need for anyone to interact with the ColdFusion Administrator interface. For example, you could use `<cfcollection>` in a template that acted as a setup script, creating the various files, database tables, and Solr collections your application needs to operate.

Optimizing a Solr Collection

After a Solr collection gets hit many times, performance can start to degrade. Depending on your application, this might never become a problem. If you notice your Solr searches becoming slower over time, you might want to try optimizing your collection. Optimizing your collection is similar conceptually to running Disk Defragmenter on a Windows machine.

Two ways to optimize a collection are available: You can use the ColdFusion Administrator or create a ColdFusion template that uses the `<cfcollection>` tag to optimize the collection programmatically.

To optimize a collection with the ColdFusion Administrator, locate the collection in the ColdFusion Collections page and click the Optimize button. Solr whirs around for a minute or two as the collection is optimized. Because optimization can take some time—especially with large collections—you should optimize a collection during off-peak hours if possible.

To optimize a collection with the `<cfcollection>` tag, just include the tag in a simple ColdFusion template. The tag must include an `action="optimize"` parameter, and the collection name must be provided in the `collection` parameter. For instance, the code in Listing 35.17 can be used to optimize the `owshr` collection created earlier in this chapter.

NOTE

You might find that you want to optimize your collections on a regular basis. You could schedule the template shown in Listing 35.17 to be automatically run once a week, for example, by using the ColdFusion scheduler.

Listing 35.17 `optimize.cfm`—Optimizing a Collection

```
<!---
Module:          Optimize.cfm
Author:          Leon Chalnick & Ben Forta
--->

<!--- feedback --->
Performing optimization ...<br>

<!--- optimize the verity collection --->
<cfcollection action="optimize"
              collection="owshr">

<!--- feedback --->
Done!
```

Deleting a Collection

To delete a collection altogether, use the `<cfcollection>` tag with `action="delete"`. Again, you could use the basic code shown in Listing 35.17 by simply changing the `action` to `delete`. After the collection has been deleted, ColdFusion displays an error message if a `<cfsearch>` tag that uses that collection name is encountered. The collection name will no longer appear in the ColdFusion Administrator, and Solr's index files will be removed from your server's hard drive. Note that only

Solr's internal index files will be deleted, not the actual documents that had been made searchable by the collection.

TIP

Alternatively, you could use the Delete button on the Solr Collections page of the ColdFusion Administrator to delete the collection.

Creating a Collection Programmatically

The `<cfcollection>` tag can also be used to create a collection from scratch. Basically, you supply the same information to the tag as you would normally supply to the ColdFusion Administrator when creating a new collection there. Provide a name for the new collection in the tag's `name` parameter, and provide the path for the new collection's internal index files with the `path` parameter.

Listing 35.18 demonstrates how to use `<cfcollection>` to create a new collection called `MoreHRDocs`.

Listing 35.18 `create.cfm`—Creating a Collection

```
<!---
Module:        create.cfm
Author:        Leon Chalnick & Ben Forta
Function:      Create a new collection.
--->


<!--- feedback --->
Creating collection ...<br>

<!--- Create the new verity collection --->
<cfcollection action="create"
              collection="finance"
              engine="solr"
              path="#server.coldfusion.rootdir#/collections/finance"
>

<!--- feedback --->
Done!
```

NOTE

Remember that the newly created collection can't be searched yet, because no information has been indexed. You still need to use the `<cfindex>` tag–after the `<cfcollection>` tag–to index documents or data from your database tables, as discussed earlier in this chapter.

You can't use the name of an existing local collection. Note the use of the `engine` attribute. This attribute tells ColdFusion to work specifically with a Solr collection. If this attribute is left off, ColdFusion will attempt to create a Verity collection. This process will work only on Microsoft Windows machines, however, and since Verity is deprecated, you should be sure to supply the `engine` attribute.

CHAPTER 36

Event Scheduling

IN THIS CHAPTER

ColdFusion Event Scheduling Concepts

The automated scheduling of activities is a part of everyday life. We schedule automatic monthly mortgage payments from our bank accounts, the recording of various television shows with our DVRs, notifications from our handheld devices and many other activities. By scheduling these events to occur in an automated fashion, we free up other resources to focus on issues that require our explicit interaction. It simply makes our lives easier knowing that the scheduled activity is going to get done without requiring our attention or time.

Of course, when we develop computerized systems to replace or enhance manual processes, we often want to schedule events to occur on a regular basis with the very same goals in mind. ColdFusion provides its own event scheduling mechanism that enables us to invoke one-time or recurring events. Through ColdFusion's scheduling mechanisms, you are able to invoke a specific ColdFusion template at a specific time. Because that template can be used to do just about anything that ColdFusion can do, this becomes a very powerful tool for the ColdFusion developer.

Here are some ideas for scheduled events:

- **Content management:** You can schedule the generation of PDFs or static HTML pages from content that is stored in a database. This technique is commonly used in content management systems to improve site performance.
- **Automated email applications:** You can schedule a process to check a POP3 server for email and respond to it automatically with various prescribed messages or actions. This frees up the site administrator from a tedious task.
- **Synchronization:** Synchronize data between multiple data sources and LDAP directories based on business rules.

ColdFusion provides two mechanisms for executing automated events, or *scheduled tasks*:

- The Scheduled Tasks page in the ColdFusion Administrator
- The `<cfschedule>` tag

The functionality provided by the Add/Edit Scheduled Task page and the `<cfschedule>` tag is essentially the same. Both enable you to create, update, run, and delete tasks. However, you should be aware of a few distinctions:

- If you want to see a list of all the scheduled tasks on your server, you must use the Scheduled Tasks page in the ColdFusion Administrator.
- The Add/Edit Scheduled Task page is simply an HTML form. You create or modify a task in the form, so it's a bit easier to work with than writing code.
- The `<cfschedule>` tag can be used without access to the ColdFusion Administrator.

It's important to recognize that when ColdFusion runs a scheduled task, it's run as if someone requested the URL (template) specified in the task. If you need a specific user to run that task (perhaps based on security concerns), you can specify the username and password. If output is to be generated by the task (perhaps for debugging purposes) you can specify that the output is to be published and then specify the file to which the output will be written.

➜ These concepts will be discussed in more detail in the section "Creating, Modifying, and Deleting Scheduled Tasks" later in this chapter.

Also note that ColdFusion logs the execution (start, completion, and errors) of scheduled tasks in the `scheduler.log` file.

ColdFusion Scheduling Versus Other Kinds of Scheduling

As you may already know, there are other ways to schedule automated tasks in computerized systems:

- Most advanced operating systems, such as Windows, Unix, and Linux, provide their own mechanism for scheduling tasks. In Windows you have `taskschd.msc` and the `AT` command (and there are some other GUI utilities that work with `AT` as well).
- Many powerful database products, such as Microsoft SQL Server and Oracle, come with their own scheduling capabilities as well.

ColdFusion's scheduling capability is limited to requesting URLs through HTTP. With this in mind, there are situations in which one of the other approaches is more appropriate. For example, if you needed your database to dump some of its data in an XML format to a file every night, you could use a ColdFusion template and a scheduled task to do this, but the database's native exporting tools and scheduling mechanism (assuming it had one) would probably be more appropriate.

Using ColdFusion's task scheduler has a couple of important benefits that are not necessarily provided by other scheduling approaches:

- The output from the specified URL can be saved to a file.
- The ColdFusion scheduler writes log entries each time a scheduled task is executed—and this log can be valuable in debugging.
- It can come in extremely handy if your application is hosted by an ISP that has limited your ability to run command-line programs or create scheduled tasks using their database server. In this situation, consider using ColdFusion's event scheduling capabilities. Even if the ISP doesn't provide you access to the ColdFusion Administrator, you can use the `<cfschedule>` tag to run your task.

Creating, Modifying, and Deleting Scheduled Tasks

You can use either the ColdFusion Administrator or the `<cfschedule>` tag to create, modify, run and delete scheduled tasks. Your server's administrator may have decided to prevent developers from accessing the ColdFusion Administrator. If you don't have access, you can still get the job done programmatically using the `<cfschedule>` tag. If you do have access to the ColdFusion Administrator, you'll find this method preferable under most circumstances.

➜ See Chapter 25, "ColdFusion Server Configuration," for a description of the ColdFusion Administrator usage.

Administering Scheduled Tasks

The ColdFusion Administrator can be used to list, create, modify, delete, run, and log the execution of scheduled events or tasks. Newly scheduled events are immediately recognized and will run as soon as they are scheduled to do so.

Scheduled Task Logging

You have the option of configuring the ColdFusion Administrator to log the execution of scheduled tasks. This setting is made at the bottom of the Logging Settings page.

NOTE

Even if you don't enable logging of scheduled tasks, scheduled tasks that you manually execute will be logged.

Whenever a scheduled task is executed, an entry is written to the file `scheduler.log` in the Logs directory (below the directory in which ColdFusion is installed). (See Chapter 17, "Debugging and Troubleshooting," in *Adobe ColdFusion 9 Web Application Construction Kit, Volume 1: Getting Started*, for more information on ColdFusion's logging capabilities.) You can review the entries in this log through the Log Files pages in the ColdFusion Administrator. The log file itself is a simple quote and comma-delimited text file.

The data presented in the log file is summarized in Table 36.1.

Table 36.1 Interpreting the `scheduler.log` File

VALUE	DESCRIPTION
"Information"	Severity; in this case, simply informational
"scheduler-0"	Thread ID
"11/15/09"	Date of task execution
"23:30:01"	Time of task execution
null value	Application name. This is null in the scheduler log. It does not reflect the name of your ColdFusion application.
[Update Index] Executing at Tues...	This message indicates the name of the scheduled task that is being referenced in this log entry.

As you browse through the `scheduler.log` file, you'll note that ColdFusion makes one entry when the event is executed. If it's a recurring event, you'll see another to indicate the rescheduling of the event's execution.

NOTE

The log does not provide information regarding the success or failure of whatever underlying function is being provided by the task that you're scheduling. Techniques for this kind of analysis are presented later in this chapter, in the section "Scheduling Application Examples."

Creating Scheduled Tasks with the ColdFusion Administrator

The ColdFusion Administrator's Scheduled Tasks page provides a listing of all scheduled tasks. This listing is where you start when you want to create, modify, delete, and run those tasks.

Click the Schedule New Task button to create a new task. Doing so opens the Add/Edit Scheduled Task Form. Each field is explained in the following sections.

Task Name

This is the name that you want to give this task. It will appear in the list on the Scheduled Tasks page.

Duration

These two fields are used to define a period of days over which the task will run. You must specify a `Start Date`. The `End Date` is optional and is only needed if you do not want a repeated task to run indefinitely.

Frequency

This part of the form enables you to specify the time frame in which the scheduled task operates. The time frame for execution can be

- A one-time event

- A recurring event that occurs once a day, once a week, or once a month
- A recurring event that occurs throughout the day

In any case you must at least enter a valid start time. When you are defining a task that must recur throughout the day, you must specify how often it recurs by entering hours, minutes, or seconds (or a combination). You cannot run tasks more frequently than once per minute.

Select the appropriate radio button and enter the time at which the task should run (or start running, in the `Daily every` section). If you are scheduling a task that occurs more than once a day, also enter the appropriate interval and if you like, enter an end time (after which the task will not be run again, until you reach the start time the following day).

NOTE

You can enter times in either 12- or 24-hour formats (i.e., 2:30:00 PM and 14:30:00 mean the same thing and either will work).

TIP

It's important to recognize that each scheduled task that the URL requests from our server adds to your server's overall workload and can affect performance. Think carefully about the frequency with which each scheduled task must occur because you don't want to make your server do a lot of unnecessary work.

URL

This is the URL that you want ColdFusion to request, i.e., the task to be executed. You can run URLs using only HTTP; you can't use HTTPS, FTP, or other protocols.

Username and Password

If the URL you are requesting is protected by the Web server's security mechanisms, you may need to authenticate with a valid username and password in order for the request to go through. Enter these values in these two fields.

NOTE

The only authentication that can be passed is basic clear text. If the server administrator has employed something more secure or proprietary, ColdFusion may not be able to authenticate when it executes this task. You can verify whether this is the case by saving the output of the URL request to a file. This technique is described in the section "Publish and File" later in this chapter.

Timeout (Seconds)

If you are requesting a URL that is complex or may take a while to complete, you may need to tell ColdFusion to give this request a longer timeout.

NOTE

ColdFusion's default request timeout duration is set on the Settings page in the ColdFusion Administrator.

➜ See Chapter 25 for a description of this setting.

In this situation, you can enter a longer time period, in seconds.

Proxy Server (and Port)

If your ColdFusion server goes through a proxy server to reach to the URL you're requesting, enter the proxy server and port information in these to fields.

Publish and File

If you want the output from the task to be saved to a file, select this check box and enter the pathname of the file in the File field (e.g., `c:tempoutput.htm`).

TIP

This feature is useful for debugging the execution of your task. If your task is something that doesn't really produce output for publishing (like HTML), you may still want to use this feature to write a date and time stamp or some other debugging information to a file to give you an indication of what happened with your process.

Resolve URL

If you are requesting a URL from an external site but you need to be able to use its internal references (perhaps you're requesting a URL from an external Web site that you plan on publishing on your server), you should check this box to resolve the URLs that are used within the page you're requesting.

TIP

When you're done creating a task, be sure to use the Submit button at the bottom of the form to save the new task.

Running, Modifying, and Deleting Scheduled Tasks

The Scheduled Tasks page in the ColdFusion Administrator lists all of the scheduled tasks in your ColdFusion server. There are four icons at the left of each entry. The first icon is for running the task, the second is for pausing the task, the third is for modifying the task, and the fourth is for deleting the task.

Running Scheduled Tasks

To run the task now, click the leftmost icon with the "!". This ad hoc method of executing a scheduled task is most helpful when you're getting your task set up and debugging the process.

TIP

If you configured the task to publish its output to a file, you can open that file after running the task to see what happened. If the URL you entered was incorrect or there was some other problem requesting it, you should have enough valuable information in the saved output to debug the situation.

Pausing a Scheduled Task

ColdFusion 9 has the capability to easily, temporarily cease the execution of a scheduled task. Simply click the pause icon. Your request to pause the task is submitted to the ColdFusion Administrator, which will report back that the task has been paused. The task will not run again until you've resumed it, by clicking the second icon again. And when you do, the icon will change back to its earlier appearance.

Modifying Scheduled Tasks

The third icon at the left of the task list (in the Scheduled Tasks page in the ColdFusion Administrator) is used to modify the configuration of that task. You can also just click on the task's name in the list. Clicking either the icon or the task name loads the Add/Edit Scheduled Task page.

The fields all work just as they did when you created the task. Make whatever changes are required and save the task using the Submit button at the bottom of the form.

NOTE

The act of saving a scheduled task like this creates its own entry in the `scheduler.log` file. This entry indicates that the task is being activated.

Deleting Scheduled Tasks

When you determine that you no longer need to keep a scheduled task, you can delete it by clicking the rightmost icon (of the four) in the Scheduled Tasks list. Having no-longer-scheduled tasks in the list doesn't hurt anything, but if there are a lot that are no longer running, it may make sense to delete some of them to make the list easier to read.

When you click the delete icon, you'll be prompted to confirm that you do indeed want to delete the task. Assuming you do, click the OK button; the task is removed from the list and the list is refreshed.

Creating, Modifying, and Deleting Tasks Using <CFSCHEDULE>

As explained earlier in the section "ColdFusion Event Scheduling Concepts," you can use either the ColdFusion Administrator or the `<cfschedule>` tag to manage scheduled tasks. You've already learned how to employ this functionality using the ColdFusion Administrator. This section demonstrates the use of `<cfschedule>` to accomplish the same things.

The `<cfschedule>` tag is commonly used when your server administrator has configured the ColdFusion Administrator so that you don't have access to the Scheduled Tasks list. When you can't use the ColdFusion Administrator's form-based interface, the `<cfschedule>` tag comes in very handy.

NOTE

You actually could build a form-based interface to the `<cfschedule>` tag. You could start by copying the HTML code from the ColdFusion Administrator and saving it somewhere that allows users access. You'd then have to build a template to validate the user's input. Assuming the input was good, you'd feed it to the `<cfschedule>` tag. Using this approach, the ColdFusion Administrator would remain protected and users would still have an easy-to-use, form-based interface for creating scheduled tasks.

Creating a Scheduled Task with <cfschedule>

Table 36.2 lists and describes the <cfschedule> tag attributes. Note that items marked with an asterisk (*) are required only under certain circumstances. The specific cases are noted in the description of the attribute.

Table 36.2 <cfschedule> Tag Attributes

ATTRIBUTE	REQUIRED	DESCRIPTION
`Task`	Yes	A descriptive name for the task.
`Action`	Yes	`Delete`, `Update`, `Pause`, `Resume`, or `Run`. Specifies which action is required of the task scheduler with respect to the named task. Note that `Update` produces a new task if the named task doesn't already exist. If the named task does exist, using `Update` will overwrite that task. `Run` executes the task now and `Delete` deletes it now.
`Operation`	Yes*	The type of operation to be performed but can be set only to `Httprequest`. Required only if the `Action` attribute is `Update`.
`Startdate`	Yes*	The date on which you want the scheduled event to begin. This attribute is required when the `Action` attribute is `Update`.
`Starttime`	Yes*	The time at which you want the scheduled event to begin executing. This attribute is required when the `Action` attribute is `Update`. Provide a complete time value in 12- or 24-hour format.
`URL`	Yes*	The URL to be requested when the task is executed. Required when the `Action` attribute is set to `Update`. It must start with `http://` and indicate the complete URL; relative addresses won't work. You can include a port in the URL (if you're using one other than 80, the default) or you can use the `PORT` attribute to specify the port (but don't do both).
`interval`	Yes*	The interval at which the scheduled task is to be executed. Valid values are `Once`, `Daily`, `Weekly`, `Monthly`, or a time interval in seconds (an integer value). This is required only when the `Action` attribute is set to `Update`. Use seconds to specify intervals that recur throughout the day (e.g., every hour = 3600).
`Publish`	No	Indicates whether the results of the URL request are to be saved to a file. Valid values are `Yes` and `No`.
`Path`	Yes*	The path, ending with a space " ", where the file specified in the `FILE` attribute is to be created. This is required only if `Publish` is set to `Yes`.
`File`	Yes*	The file name for the results of the scheduled task. This is required only when the `PUBLISH` attribute is set to `Yes`.
`Enddate`	No	The date on which the scheduled task should stop being executed.
`Endtime`	No	The time at which the scheduled task should stop being executed. You can use either 12- or 24-hour time formats.
`Requesttimeout`	No	The request timeout period (in seconds) that should be used for this request.

Table 36.2 (continued)

ATTRIBUTE	REQUIRED	DESCRIPTION
`Resolveurl`	No	Indicates whether you want the internal URLs (in the content of the requested URL) to be resolved so that they work when this page is loaded from a server other than the original server. Defaults to `No`.
`Username`	No	The username to use to authenticate when requesting a protected URL.
`Password`	No	The password to use to authenticate when requesting a protected URL.
`Proxyserver`	No	The hostname or IP address of a proxy server. This is required only if your ColdFusion server needs to use a proxy server to reach the requested URL.
`Proxyport`	No	The port used by your proxy server. It is used only if your proxy server works on a port other than 80.
`Port`	No	The port to be used by your server when executing this task. Defaults to 80. If you include the port in your URL, don't include a `Port` attribute.

When you're using `<cfschedule>` to create scheduled events, you set the `Action` attribute to `Update`. Suppose you wanted to create a scheduled task that involves updating the Solr index of your site. First you'd write the ColdFusion template that would update the Solr index. In this simple example, let's assume that this template is called `collection_update.cfm` and is located in a directory off the Web server's root named `/ows/36/`. The task it creates will be named `Update collection`. You want to keep the Solr collection up to date so you want this task to run nightly. Because you don't want it to run when there's a lot of traffic on your server, you want it to run every day at 09:00 a.m. See the `<cfschedule>` tag that you could use for this task in Listing 36.1.

Listing 36.1 `OWS_Solr_Update.cfm`—Using `<cfschedule>` to Create a New Scheduled Task

```
<!---
Name:          Schedule_Create_Solr_UPDATE.cfm
Author:        Matt Tatam
Description:   Schedules the OWS_Solr_Update.cfm at 9:00 am
--->
<cfschedule
action="UPDATE"
task="Update OWS Solr Collection"
operation="HTTPRequest"
url="http://localhost:8500/ows/36/OWS_Solr_Update.cfm"
startdate="13/11/2009"
startTime="09:00 am"
interval="Daily" />
```

After executing this code and opening the ColdFusion Administrator, you can see the resulting scheduled task displayed in the form.

As you can see in Listing 36.1, you do not have to write a lot of code to create a recurring task. Let's review what each attribute does.

- `Action="Update"`. Tells ColdFusion to update an existing task with the name specified in the `TASK` attribute. If that task does not exist, ColdFusion will create a new one.
- `Task="Update collection"`. Tells ColdFusion the name of the task to update (or create, as in our case).
- `Operation="HTTPRequest"`. Tells ColdFusion that this request is to be made through HTTP (this is the only way that requests currently can be made).
- `URL="http://localhost:8500/OWS/36/collection_update.cfm"`. Indicates the URL to be requested.
- `Startdate="13/11/2009"`. Indicates the date on which the task is to be first executed.
- `Starttime="09:00 am"`. Indicates the time at which the task is to begin running.
- `Interval="Daily"`. Indicates the time interval at which this event is to recur.

A more detailed example will be provided later in this chapter.

Modifying, Deleting, and Running Scheduled Tasks with the `<cfschedule>` Tag

Modifying scheduled tasks through use of `<cfschedule>` works virtually the same way as creating a scheduled task with `<cfschedule>`. The previous section provided a simple example of its usage for creating a scheduled task.

Suppose after updating the Solr collection nightly for a month, it became apparent that you don't need to update the collection more than once a week. The following code would make this modification (see Listing 36.2).

Listing 36.2 `Schedule_OWS_Update_Solr_UPDATE.cfm`—This Code Modifies an Existing Task

```
<!---
Name:           Schedule_OWS_Update_Solr_UPDATE.cfm
Author:         Matt Tatam
Description:    Schedules the OWS_Solr_Update.cfm at 01:00 am
--->
<cfschedule
action="UPDATE"
task="Update OWS Solr Collection"
operation="HTTPRequest"
url="http://localhost:8500/ows/36/OWS_Solr_Update.cfm"
startdate="13/11/2009"
startTime="01:00 am"
interval="Daily" />
```

Deleting a scheduled task with `<cfschedule>` is simply a question of setting the `ACTION` to `Delete` and naming the task:

```
<cfschedule Action="Delete" Task="Update OWS Solr Collection">
```

To execute a scheduled task immediately, use this code:

```
<cfschedule Action="Run" Task="Update OWS Solr Collection">
```

You can programmatically pause execution of a task like this:

```
<cfschedule Action="Pause" Task="Update OWS Solr Collection">
```

After pausing, you'll need to resume execution before you can do anything else with the task:

```
<cfschedule Action="Resume" Task="Update OWS Solr Collection">
```

Scheduling Application Examples

You're now ready to put your new understanding of ColdFusion's scheduling capabilities to use. First, you'll create a scheduled task for a POP3 application (List Unsubscriber) presented in Chapter 20, "Interacting with Email," in Volume 1. Then you'll build two simple scheduling applications. The first application sends email out on a regular basis.

Creating a Scheduled Task for a POP3 Application

First, please quickly review the POP3 application developed in Chapter 20. This application checks a POP3 email account and looks for incoming messages to the `mailings@orangewhipstudios.com` account in which the subject includes the word *remove*. When a message like this is found, the template identifies the sender in the Contacts table and sets the value of `MailingList` field to 0, flagging it as an account that should not have promotional email sent to it.

When you run this template, it will operate on the messages it finds in the `mailings@orangewhipstudios.com` account. But running this template only once is of limited usefulness. Moreover, you don't want to rely on a person to remember to execute this task from time to time. The ColdFusion task scheduler is ideally suited for this application.

Note that people may unsubscribe throughout the day. And yet, OWS staff may continue to send spam—ahem, make that "promotional email"—throughout the day. So we want to find a schedule that minimizes the opportunity for someone to unsubscribe and then wind up with three new emails from OWS. At the same time, we don't want to bog down ColdFusion by running this script every minute. Once an hour seems like a good compromise.

Listing 36.3 creates a scheduled task to run the `ListUnsubscriber.cfm` template from Chapter 20.

Listing 36.3 `ListUnsubscribe_Task.cfm`—Create a Scheduled Task

```
<!---
Name:         ListUnsubscribe_Task.cfm
Author:       Leon Chalnick, Matt Tatam
Description:  Creates a scheduled task to
```

Listing 36.3 (continued)

```
                 Run ListUnsubscriber.cfm
                 once per hour starting at
                 2:00:00 AM on 13 November 2009.
--->
<cfschedule
  task="Mailing list unsubscriber"
  action="UPDATE"
  operation="HTTPRequest"
  url="http://localhost:8500/ows/20/ListUnsubscriber.cfm"
  interval="3600"
  startdate="13/11/2009"
  starttime="02:00:00 AM"
>
```

This task will begin running at 2:00 A.M. each night and will run on the hour.

Building an Automatic Promotional Email Application

Let's assume that OWS's marketing department wants to capitalize on the large media blitz under way to support the new releases. It wants to send out promotional emails to local memorabilia dealers once a week that list the current merchandise available at the online store. To make matters tougher, the marketing department wants the email to be waiting in the dealers' in-boxes when they first check their email each Monday morning.

Therefore, you must build a ColdFusion scheduling application that has two parts:

- A page that queries the database for the current merchandise available, displays the results in an HTML table, and sends the email page to the dealer group email alias.
- A scheduled task page that sends the promotional email once each week on Monday morning.

Building the Email Application

The email application consists of two parts: the query that collects the data and the `<cfmail>` tag that sends it. See Listing 36.4 for this part of the application.

Listing 36.4 `Promo_Email.cfm`—The Email Application

```
<!---
Name:          Promo_Email.cfm
Author:        David Golden, Leon Chalnick
Description:   Queries database and generates email
--->

<!--- Get all merchandise info from database --->
<cfquery name="GetMerchInfo" datasource="OWS">
   SELECT MerchName, MerchDescription, MerchPrice
   FROM Merchandise
   ORDER BY FilmID
</cfquery>
<!--- Produce the email --->
```

Listing 36.4 (continued)

```
<cfmail to="dealers@ows.com" from="store@ows.com"
 subject="Merchandise Currently Available"
 server="mail.ows.com" type="HTML"
 >
<!DOCTYPE HTML PUBLIC "-//W3C//DTD HTML 4.0 Transitional//EN">
<html>
<head>
   <title>Available Merchandise From OWS Online Store</title>
</head>
<body>
<p>Greetings from Orange Whip Studios!</p>

<p>Here is a list of merchandise currently
available from the online store at Orange Whip
Studios. To order any of these items, go to
<a href="http://www.ows.com/store/">http://www.ows.com/store/</a>.
</p>

<!--- Display merchandise from query --->
<table border="1">
<tr>
   <th>Item name</th>
   <th>Description</th>
   <th>Price</th>
</tr>
<cfloop query="GetMerchInfo">
<cfoutput>
   <tr>
      <td>#MerchName#</td>
      <td>#MerchDescription#</td>
      <td>#DollarFormat(MerchPrice)#</td>
   </tr>
</cfoutput>
</cfloop>
</table>
</body>
</html>
</cfmail>
```

The `<cfquery>` tag selects all the merchandise in the database. The `<cfmail>` tag sends the mail to an email list of dealers. Notice the use of the `TYPE` attribute in the `<cfmail>` tag. By setting it to `HTML`, you are able to send nicely formatted email.

NOTE

Another way you could send this listing would be as an attached PDF file. To do this, you would separate the production of the PDF merchandise listing from the sending of the email. You could create a separate scheduled task to run this new page and save its output to a PDF file using `<cfreport>`. Another scheduled task would then be executed to send the mail and you would use the `<cfmailparam>` tag to attach the new PDF listing output created by the first new scheduled task.

The `<cfloop>` within the `<cfmail>` is used to output the query results in the body of the message.

Scheduling the Task

The second part of this application requires scheduling the task. In this sample application, you'll use your knowledge of the ColdFusion Administrator Scheduled Tasks page to accomplish this.

In the ColdFusion Administrator, click on Scheduled Tasks and view the Scheduled Tasks list (note that the list may contain different scheduled tasks on your ColdFusion sever). Click the Schedule New Task Button and open the Add/Edit Scheduled Task form. Complete the form.

Scheduling Updates to a Solr Collection

OWS wants Web site visitors to be able to do full-text searches of their Web site's content. A Solr collection was created to these ends (see Chapter 35, "Full-Text Searching," for more information about collections). In a nutshell, a Solr collection is a searchable index of one or more documents that you build in ColdFusion (either through the ColdFusion Administrator or through the `<cfcollection>` tag). You can then search these documents for words or phrases using the `<cfsearch>` tag.

As the content of OWS's site changes from time to time, it is important to update the Solr collection to reflect these changes. It has been determined that this should take place nightly at 11:30 P.M. As with most scheduled tasks, there are two parts to the solution. You must create the code to be run by the scheduled task and you must create the task itself.

Updating the Solr Collection

You can programmatically update a Solr collection through ColdFusion with the `<cfindex>` tag. The collection of the OWS site is created in Chapter 39, "Using Regular Expressions." Here, we're simply going to produce a template to update it. See Listing 36.5 for the code that updates the Solr collection.

Listing 36.5 `OWS_Solr_Update.cfm`—Updating the OWS Solr Collection

```
<!---
Name:          OWS_Solr_Update.cfm
Author:        Matt Tatam
Description:   Indexes a Solr Collection
--->
<cfindex collection="ows_Solr_collection" action ="update" type="Path"
Key="C:\ColdFusion9\wwwroot\ows" >
<!--- creates debugging display --->
<cfoutput>
OWS Solr Collection last Updated: #DateFormat(now())# #TimeFormat(now(), "h:mm:ss
tt")#
</cfoutput>
```

Note that a little bit of text is being output at the bottom of Listing 36.5. In the next section, you'll create a `<cfschedule>` tag to create the task. You'll configure this scheduled task so that the output is saved to a file. This debugging comment will be written to the specified file each time the task is executed.

Creating the Scheduled Task with <cfschedule>

Rather than create this task through the ColdFusion Administrator as you did in the previous example, this time you'll create it through code. See Listing 36.6. The task must be scheduled to run each night at 11:30 P.M. It must also save its output to a file named ows_Solr_update_output.htm in a folder named c:temp.

Listing 36.6 Sched_Solr_Update.cfm—Invoking OWS_Solr_Update.cfm

```
<!---
Name:           Schedule_OWS_Solr_UPDATE.cfm
Author:         Matt Tatam
Description:    Schedules the OWS_Solr_Update.cfm at 11:30 PM
--->
<cfschedule
action="UPDATE"
task="Update OWS Solr Collection"
operation="HTTPRequest"
url="http://localhost:8500/ows/36/OWS_Solr_Update.cfm"
startdate="13/11/2009"
startTime="11:30 PM"
interval="Daily"
file="ows_Solr_update_output.htm"  />
```

When you run this template through your browser, it instructs ColdFusion to create this scheduled task.

NOTE

When the this task is run, it won't work unless you have already created the OWS Solr collection and have a directory named c:temp.

When this scheduled task does actually run, it will create the output file, SolrUpdate_out.txt, in the c:temp folder.

PART 8

Advanced ColdFusion Development

CHAPTER 37

Using Stored Procedures

IN THIS CHAPTER

Most server-based database systems—SQL Server, Oracle, and MySQL—support *stored procedures*. A stored procedure is a chunk of SQL code that's given a name and stored as a part of your database, along with your actual data tables. After the stored procedure has been created, you can invoke it in your ColdFusion templates using the `<cfstoredproc>` tag.

NOTE

The use of stored procedures in database applications is a relatively advanced topic. It's not rocket science, but you will be more comfortable working with stored procedures if you are familiar with the SQL concepts introduced in the previous chapter or have a specific reason for using stored procedures in a particular ColdFusion application.

NOTE

At the time of this writing, stored procedures are supported by most server-based database systems (such as SQL Server, Oracle, and MySQL) but are not generally supported by file-based databases (such as Access). If you don't plan on using a server-based database system, you can skip this chapter without missing out on anything essential.

Why Use Stored Procedures?

Stored procedures provide a way to consolidate any number of SQL statements—such as `SELECT`, `INSERT`, `UPDATE`, and so on—into a little package that encapsulates a complete operation to be carried out in your application.

For instance, consider Orange Whip Studio's online store. When a customer places an order, the application needs to verify that the customer's account is in good standing and then carry out `INSERT` statements to the `MerchandiseOrders` and `MerchandiseOrdersItems` tables to record the actual order. In the future, the application might be expanded to first ensure that the selected merchandise is in stock. If not, the application would need to display some type of "Sorry, out of stock" message for the user, and it might need to update another table somewhere else to indicate that the merchandise needs to be reordered from the supplier.

This type of complex, causally related set of checks and record keeping is often referred to as a *business rule* or *business process*. Using the techniques you've learned so far in this book, you already know that you could accomplish the steps with several `<cfquery>` tags and some conditional processing using `<cfif>` and `<cfelse>` tags.

In this chapter, you will see that you could wrap up all the database-related actions required to place an order into a single stored procedure called, say, `PlaceOrder`, thus encapsulating the entire business process into one smart routine your ColdFusion templates need only refer to.

This shifts the responsibility for ensuring that the steps are followed properly away from your ColdFusion code, and hands it to the database server itself. This shift generally requires a little bit of extra work on your part up front but offers some real advantages later.

Calling Stored Procedures from ColdFusion Templates

Now that you have an idea about what kinds of things stored procedures can be used for, this is a good time to see how to integrate them into your ColdFusion templates. For the moment, assume that several stored procedures have already been created and are ready for use within your ColdFusion application. Maybe you put the stored procedures together yourself, or maybe they were created by another developer or by the database administrator, the DBA.

Two Ways to Execute Stored Procedures

There are two ways to execute a stored procedure from your ColdFusion templates. You can use the `<cfstoredproc>` tag, which is obviously designed specifically for stored procedures, or you can use the `<cfquery>` tag that you already know and love.

With the `<cfstoredproc>` Tag

The `<cfstoredproc>` tag is the formal, recommended way to call stored procedures. You can pass input parameters to the stored procedure, collect return codes and output parameters passed back by the procedure, and use any record sets (queries) the procedure returns. The `<cfstoredproc>` tag should also result in the fastest performance.

With the `<cfquery>` Tag

As an alternative to `<cfstoredproc>`, you can execute stored procedures via ordinary `<cfquery>` tags. Unfortunately, this method has two big disadvantages:

- You can't capture any output parameters or result codes returned by the procedure (only query-style output). You'll learn what these items are later in this chapter, in the section "Stored Procedures That Take Parameters and Return Status Codes."
- If the procedure returns multiple record sets, you can capture only one of them for use in your ColdFusion code. See the section "Calling Procedures with `<cfquery>` Instead of `<cfstoredproc>`" later in this chapter.

Using the <cfstoredproc> Tag

To call an existing stored procedure from a ColdFusion template, you refer to the procedure by name using the `<cfstoredproc>` tag. The `<cfstoredproc>` tag is similar to the `<cfquery>` tag in that it knows how to interact with data sources you've defined in the ColdFusion Administrator. However, rather than accepting ad hoc SQL query statements (such as `SELECT` and `DELETE`), `<cfstoredproc>` is very structured, optimized specifically for dealing with stored procedures.

The `<cfstoredproc>` tag takes a number of relatively simple parameters, as listed in Table 37.1.

Table 37.1 Important `<cfstoredproc>` Attributes

ATTRIBUTE	PURPOSE
`procedure`	The name of the stored procedure you want to execute. You usually can just provide the procedure name directly, as in `procedure="MyProcedure"`. Depending on the database system you are using, however, you might need to qualify the procedure name further using dot notation.
`datasource`	The appropriate data source name. Just like the `datasource` attribute for `<cfquery>`, this can be the name of any data source listed in the ColdFusion Administrator.
`returnCode`	Optional. `Yes` or `No`. This attribute determines whether ColdFusion should capture the status code (sometimes called the return code or return value) reported by the stored procedure after it executes. If you set this attribute to `Yes`, the status code will be available to you in a special variable called `CFSTOREDPROC.StatusCode` unless specified as something else with the `result` attribute. See "Stored Procedures That Take Parameters and Return Status Codes," later in this chapter.
`result`	Optional. By default, the status code value returned when `returnCode` is set to Yes will be available in a variable called `CFSTOREDPROC`. The result attribute lets you specify another variable name to create.

NOTE

The `<cfstoredproc>` tag also supports `username`, `password`, `cachedWithin`, `cachedAfter`, `blockfactor`, and `debug` attributes. All these attributes work similarly to the corresponding attributes of the `<cfquery>` tag.

For simple stored procedures, you can just use its `procedure` and `datasource` attributes. When the template is executed in a Web browser, the stored procedure executes on the database server, accomplishing whatever it was designed to accomplish as it goes.

For instance, suppose you have access to stored procedure called `PerformInventoryMaintenance`. It has been explained to you that this stored procedure performs some type of internal maintenance on the data in the `Merchandise` table, and that people need a way to execute the procedure via the company intranet. Listing 37.1 shows a ColdFusion template called `InventoryMaintenanceRun.cfm`, which does exactly that.

NOTE

The code listings in this chapter refer to a data source called `owsSqlServer` to indicate a copy of the `ows` sample database sitting on a Microsoft SQL Server database, and a data source called `owsMySQL` to indicate a version of the database sitting on a MySQL server. The examples in this chapter are for illustration purposes of the ColdFusion tags used to interact with stored procedures.

Listing 37.1 `InventoryMaintenanceRun.cfm`—Calling a Stored Procedure with `<cfstoredproc>`

```
<!---
 Filename: InventoryMaintenanceRun.cfm
 Author:  Nate Weiss (NMW)
 Purpose: Demonstrates use of the <cfstoredproc> tag
--->

<html>
<head><title>Inventory Maintenance</title></head>
<body>
<h2>Inventory Maintenance</h2>

<!--- If the submit button was not just pressed, display form --->
<cfif not isDefined("form.executeNow")>

  <!--- Provide button to start stored procedure --->
  <cfform action="#cgi.script_name#" method="post">
  <cfinput type="submit" name="executeNow"
          value="Perform Inventory Maintenance">
  </cfform>

<!--- If the user just clicked the submit button --->
<cfelse>

  <p>Executing stored procedure...</p>
  <!--- Go ahead and execute the stored procedure --->
  <cfstoredproc procedure="PerformInventoryMaintenance"
                datasource="owsSqlServer">
  <p>Done executing stored procedure!</p>

</cfif>
</body>
</html>
```

As you can see, the code to execute the stored procedure is extremely simple. You'll see in a moment how to use stored procedures that receive input and respond by providing output back to you. This particular stored procedure doesn't require any information to be provided to it, so the only things you must specify are the `procedure` and `datasource` parameters.

The `procedure` parameter tells ColdFusion what the name of the stored procedure is. The `datasource` parameter works just like it does for the `<cfquery>` tag; it must be the name of the appropriate data source as defined in the ColdFusion Administrator.

NOTE

Listing 37.1 uses a simple piece of `<cfif>` logic that tests to see whether a form parameter called `executeNow` exists. Assuming that it does not exist, the template puts a simple form–with a single submit button–on the page. Because the submit button is named `executeNow`, the `<cfif>` logic executes the second part of the template when the form is submitted; the second part contains the `<cfstoredproc>` tag that executes the stored procedure. The template is put together this way so you can see the form code and the form-processing code in one listing. See Chapter 12, "ColdFusion Forms," in *Adobe ColdFusion 9 Web Application Construction Kit Volume 1: Getting Started*, for further discussion of this type of single-template technique.

When the `InventoryMaintenanceRun.cfm` template from Listing 37.1 is first brought up in a Web browser, it displays a simple form. When the Perform Inventory Maintenance button is clicked, the procedure is executed and a simple message is displayed to the user to indicate that the work has been done.

Stored Procedures That Return Record Sets

Stored procedures also can return record sets to your ColdFusion templates. As far as your ColdFusion code is concerned, record sets are just like query results. They contain columns and rows of data—usually from one or more of the database's tables—that you can then use the same way you would use rows of data fetched by a `<cfquery>` tag.

For instance, consider a stored procedure called `FetchRatingsList` that returns rating information straight from the `FilmsRatings` table in the `owsSqlServer` database. This stored procedure sends back its information as a record set, just as if you had performed a simple `SELECT` type of query with a `<cfquery>` tag.

The person who created the stored procedure has told you that that the record set will contain two columns, `RatingID` and `Rating`, which correspond to the columns of the `FilmsRatings` table. In other words, executing this particular stored procedure is similar to running an ordinary `SELECT * FROM FilmsRating` query (you'll see more complex examples shortly).

The `<cfprocresult>` Tag

To use a record set returned by a stored procedure, you must use the `<cfprocresult>` tag, which tells ColdFusion to capture the record set as the stored procedure is executed. The `<cfprocresult>` tag takes just a few attributes and is easy to use.

Table 37.2 lists the attributes supported by `<cfprocresult>`. Most of the time, you will need to use only the `name` attribute.

Table 37.2 `<cfprocresult>` Tag Attributes

ATTRIBUTE	PURPOSE
`name`	A name for the record set. The record set will become available as a query object with whatever name you specify; the query object can be used just like any other (like the results of a `<cfquery>` or `<cfpop>` tag).
`resultSet`	An optional number that indicates which record set you are referring to. This attribute is important only for stored procedures that return several record sets. Defaults to `1`. See the section "Multiple Record Sets Are Fully Supported" later in this chapter.
`maxRows`	Optional; similar to the `maxRows` attribute of the `<cfquery>` tag. The maximum number of rows ColdFusion should retrieve from the database server as the stored procedure executes. If not provided, ColdFusion defaults to -1, which is the same as all rows.

NOTE

Because a record set captured from a stored procedure is made available to your ColdFusion templates as an ordinary CFML query object, the query object has the same `RecordCount`, `ColumnList`, and `CurrentRow` properties that the result of a normal `<cfquery>` tag would. You can use these to find out how much data the record set contains.

NOTE

The `<cfprocresult>` tag must be used between opening and closing `<cfstoredproc>` tags, as shown in the next section, in Listing 37.2.

Using `<cfprocresult>`

The `FilmEntry1.cfm` template in Listing 37.2 shows how to retrieve and use a record set returned from a stored procedure. As you can see, a `<cfstoredproc>` tag is used to refer to the stored procedure itself. Then the `<cfprocresult>` tag is used to capture the record set returned by the procedure.

NOTE

Remember, it's assumed that you have created a version of the Orange Whip Studios sample database for SQL Server (or whatever database server you are using), and that the database is accessible via the data source named `owsSqlServer`.

NOTE

In addition, for this template to work, you must have created the `FetchRatingsList` stored procedure.

Listing 37.2 `FilmEntry1.cfm`—Retrieving a Record Set from a Stored Procedure

```
<!---
 Filename: FilmEntry1.cfm
 Author:  Nate Weiss (NMW)
 Purpose: Demonstrates use of the <CFSTOREDPROC> tag
--->

<!--- Get list of ratings from database --->
<cfstoredproc procedure="FetchRatingsList" datasource="owsSqlServer">
 <cfprocresult name="getRatings">
</cfstoredproc>

<html>
<head><title>Film Entry Form</title></head>
<body>
<h2>Film Entry Form</h2>

<!--- Data entry form --->
<cfform action="#CGI.script_name#" method="post" preserveData="Yes">

 <!--- Text entry field for film title --->
 <p><b>Title for New Film:</b><br>
 <cfinput name="movieTitle" size="50" maxlength="50" required="yes"
  message="Please don't leave the film's title blank."><br>

<!--- Text entry field for pitch text --->
```

Listing 37.2 (continued)

```
<p><b>Short Description / One-Liner:</b><br>
<cfinput name="pitchText" size="50" maxlength="100" required="Yes"
 message="Please don't leave the one-liner blank."><br>

<!--- Text entry field for expense description --->
<p><b>New Film Budget:</b><br>
<cfinput name="amountBudgeted" size="15" required="Yes"
 message="Please enter a valid number for the film's budget."
 validate="float"><br>

<!--- Drop-down list of ratings --->
<p><b>Rating:</b><br>
<cfselect name="ratingID" query="getRatings" value="RatingID" display="Rating"/>
<!--- Text areas for summary --->
<p><b>Summary:</b><br>
<cftextarea name="summary" cols="40" rows="3" wrap="soft"></cftextarea>

<!--- Submit button for form --->
<p><cfinput name="submit" type="submit" value="Submit New Film">
</cfform>

</body>
</html>
```

Because this listing specifies `name="getRatings"` in the `<cfprocresult>` tag, the rest of the template is free to refer to `getRatings` just like the results of a `<cfquery>`. Here, the `getRatings` query object is provided to a `<cfselect>` tag to populate a drop-down list.

Using `<cfprocresult>` with Oracle

With Oracle databases, stored procedures can't return record sets in the traditional sense. They can return record-set-like data, but they do so via something called a *reference cursor*. You'll see an example of how to create a stored procedure that returns a reference cursor later in this chapter, but you need to consult your Oracle documentation if you want to learn all the ins and outs about reference cursors and the various ways in which they can be used.

ColdFusion makes using the data returned by reference cursors in Oracle stored procedures easy. Basically, you just add a `<cfprocresult>` tag to capture the data from each reference cursor.

➜ You can see an example of this in the file `FilmEntry1Oracle.cfm`, in the Zip file you can download from the book's Web site.

Stored Procedures That Take Parameters and Return Status Codes

So far you've been working with stored procedures that always work the same exact way each time they are called. The `PerformInventoryMaintenance` and `FetchRatingsList` procedures used in the first two examples don't accept any input from the calling application (in this case, a ColdFusion template) to do their work.

Most stored procedures, however, take input parameters or output parameters and also can return status codes. Here's what each of these terms means:

- **Input parameters.** Values you supply by name when you execute a stored procedure, similar to providing parameters to a ColdFusion tag. The stored procedure can then use the values of the input parameters internally, similar to variables. The stored procedure can take as many input parameters as needed for the task at hand. Similar to attributes for a ColdFusion tag, some input parameters are required, and others are optional. To supply an input parameter to a stored procedure, you use the `<cfprocparam>` tag (see Table 37.3 in the next section).
- **Output parameters.** Values the procedure can pass back to ColdFusion or to whatever other program might call the stored procedure. Each output parameter has a name, and the stored procedure can return as many output parameters as necessary. To capture the value of an output parameter from a stored procedure, use the `<cfprocparam>` tag with `type="OUT"` (see Table 37.3 in the next section).
- **Status codes.** Values returned by a stored procedure after it executes. Each stored procedure can return only one status code. The code is usually used to indicate whether the stored procedure was capable of successfully carrying out its work. With most database systems, the status code must be numeric, and defaults to `0`. To capture a procedure's status code, use `returnCode="Yes"` in the `<cfstoredproc>` tag (refer to Table 37.1 earlier in this chapter).

For instance, consider a new stored procedure called `InsertFilm` that enables the user to add a new film to Orange Whip Studio's `Films` table. Whoever created the stored procedure set it up to require five input parameters called `@MovieTitle`, `@PitchText`, `@AmountBudgeted`, `@RatingID`, and `@Summary`, which supply information about the new film. The procedure uses these values to insert a new record into the `Films` table.

The procedure also has one output parameter called `@NewFilmID`, which passes the ID number of the newly inserted film record back to ColdFusion (or whatever program is executing the stored procedure).

NOTE

Stored procedure parameter names start with an @ sign with Microsoft SQL Server and Sybase databases. Other databases systems, such as Oracle, don't use the @ sign in this way.

In addition, the stored procedure has been designed to perform a few sanity checks before blindly recording the new film:

- First, it ensures that the film doesn't already exist in the `Films` table. If a film with the same title is already in the table, the procedure stops with a return value of `-1`.
- It ensures that the rating specified by the `@RatingID` parameter is valid. If the rating number does not exist in the `Ratings` table, the procedure stops with a return value of `-2`.

Provided both of the tests are okay, the procedure inserts a new row in the `Inventory` table using the values of the supplied parameters. Finally, it sends a return value of `1` to indicate success.

Providing Parameters with `<cfprocparam>`

ColdFusion makes supplying input and output parameters to a stored procedure easy, via the `<cfprocparam>` tag. Table 37.3 shows the attributes supported by the `<cfprocparam>` tag.

Table 37.3 `<cfproparam>` Tag Attributes

ATTRIBUTE	PURPOSE
`type`	`In`, `Out`, or `InOut`. Use `type="In"` (the default) to supply an input parameter to the stored procedure. Use `type="Out"` to capture the value of an output parameter. Use `typw="InOut"` if the parameter behaves as both an input and output parameter (such parameters are rather rare).
`value`	For input parameters only. The actual value you want to provide to the procedure.
`null`	For input parameters only. `Yes` or `No`. If `null="Yes"`, the `value` attribute is ignored; instead, a null value is supplied as the parameter's value.
`variable`	For output parameters only. A variable name you want ColdFusion to place the value of the output parameter into. For instance, if you provide `variable="InsertedFilmID"`, you can output the value using `#InsertedFilmID#` after the `<cfstoredproc>` tag executes.
`cfsqltype`	Required. The parameter's data type. Unlike ColdFusion variables, stored procedure parameters are strongly typed, so you have to specify whether the parameter expects a numeric, string, date, or other type of value. The list of data types that you can supply to this attribute is the same as for the `<cfqueryparam>` tag.
`maxLength`	Optional. The maximum length of the parameter's value.
`scale`	Optional. The number of significant decimal places for the parameter. Relevant only for numeric parameters.

NOTE

If you're using Oracle, don't include a `<cfprocparam>` tag for output parameters that return reference cursors. Use the `<cfprocresult>` tag to capture that type of output, as discussed in the previous section.

`FilmEntry2.cfm`, shown in Listing 37.3, builds on the previous version of the data entry template from Listing 37.3. It creates a simple form a user can use to fill in the title, description, budget, rating, and summary for a new book. The form collects the information from the user and posts it back to the same template, which executes the stored procedure, feeding the user's entries to the procedure's input parameters.

Listing 37.3 `FilmEntry2.cfm`—A Simple Form for Collecting Input Parameters

```
<!---
 Filename: FilmEntry2.cfm
 Author:   Nate Weiss (NMW)
 Purpose: Demonstrates use of stored procedures
--->
```

Listing 37.3 (continued)

```
<!--- Is the form being submitted? --->
<cfset wasFormSubmitted = isDefined("form.ratingID")>

<!--- Insert film into database when form is submitted --->
<cfif wasFormSubmitted>
 <cfstoredproc procedure="InsertFilm" datasource="owsSqlServer" returncode="Yes">
  <!--- Provide form values to the procedure's input parameters --->
  <cfprocparam type="In" maxlength="50" cfsqltype="CF_SQL_VARCHAR"
   value="#form.movieTitle#">
  <cfprocparam type="In" maxlength="100" cfsqltype="CF_SQL_VARCHAR"
   value="#form.pitchText#">
  <cfprocparam type="In" maxlength="100" cfsqltype="CF_SQL_MONEY"
   value="#form.amountBudgeted#"
   null="#yesNoFormat(form.amountBudgeted eq '')#">
  <cfprocparam type="In" maxlength="100" cfsqltype="CF_SQL_INTEGER"
   value="#form.ratingID#">
  <cfprocparam type="In" cfsqltype="CF_SQL_LONGVARCHAR" value="#form.summary#">
  <!--- Capture @NewFilmID output parameter --->
  <!--- Value will be available in CFML variable named #InsertedFilmID# --->
  <cfprocparam type="Out" cfsqltype="CF_SQL_INTEGER" variable="InsertedFilmID">
 </cfstoredproc>

 <!--- Remember the status code returned by the stored procedure --->
 <cfset insertStatus = CFSTOREDPROC.StatusCode>
</cfif>
<!--- Get list of ratings from database --->
<cfstoredproc procedure="FetchRatingsList" datasource="owsSqlServer">
 <cfprocresult name="getRatings">
</cfstoredproc>

<html>
<head><title>Film Entry Form</title></head>
<body>
<h2>Film Entry Form</h2>

<!--- Data entry form --->
<cfform action="#CGI.script_name#" method="post" preserveData="Yes">

 <!--- Text entry field for film title --->
 <p><b>Title for New Film:</b><br>
 <cfinput name="movieTitle" size="50" maxlength="50" required="Yes"
  message="Please don't leave the film's title blank."><br>

 <!--- Text entry field for pitch text --->
 <p><b>Short Description / One-Liner:</b><br>
 <cfinput name="pitchText" size="50" maxlength="100" required="Yes"
  message="Please don't leave the one-liner blank."><br>

 <!--- Text entry field for expense description --->
 <p><b>New Film Budget:</b><br>
 <cfinput name="amountBudgeted" size="15" required="No"
  message="Only numbers may be provided for the film's budget."
  validate="float"> (leave blank if unknown)<br>

 <!--- Drop-down list of ratings --->
 <p><b>Rating:</b><br>
```

Listing 37.3 (continued)

```
<cfselect name="ratingID" query="getRatings" value="RatingID" display="Rating"/>

<!--- Text areas for summary --->
<p><b>Summary:</b><br>
<cftextarea name="summary" cols="40" rows="3" wrap="soft"></cftextarea>

<!--- Submit button for form --->
<p><cfinput type="submit" name="submit" value="Submit New Film">
</cfform>

<!--- If we executed the stored procedure --->
<cfif wasFormSubmitted>
 <!--- Display message based on status code reported by stored procedure --->
 <cfswitch expression="#insertStatus#">
  <!--- If the stored procedure returned a "success" status --->
  <cfcase value="1">
   <cfoutput>
    <p>Film "#FORM.movieTitle#" was inserted as Film ID #insertedFilmID#.<br>
   </cfoutput>
  </cfcase>
  <!--- If the status code was -1 --->
  <cfcase value="-1">
   <cfoutput>
    <p>Film "#Form.MovieTitle#" already exists in the database.<br>
   </cfoutput>
  </cfcase>
  <!--- If the status code was -2 --->
  <cfcase value="-2">
   <p>An invalid rating was provided.<br>
  </cfcase>
  <!--- If any other status code was returned --->
  <cfdefaultcase>
   <p>The procedure returned an unknown status code.<br>
  </cfdefaultcase>
 </cfswitch>
</cfif>

</body>
</html>
```

When the form is submitted, the `<cfif>` block at the top of the template is executed, which executes the `InsertFilm` stored procedure via the `<cfstoredproc>` tag. Within the `<cfstoredproc>` tag, six `<cfprocparam>` tags are used. The first five provide values for the `@MovieTitle`, `@PitchText`, and other input parameters. The last `<cfprocparam>` captures the value of the output parameter called `@NewFilmID`.

Note that the `cfsqltype` for each of the parameters has been set to the correct value for the type of information being passed. Also, the `null` attribute is used for the fifth `<cfprocparam>`, so that the film's budget will be recorded as a null value if the user leaves the budget blank on the form. After the procedure executes, the status code reported by the procedure is placed into the `insertStatus` variable.

At the bottom of the template, a `<cfswitch>` block is used to output a message to the user depending on the status code reported by the stored procedure. If the procedure returns a value of `1`, a success message is displayed, along with the new film's `FilmID` number—which was captured by the first `<cfprocparam>` tag at the top of the template. If the procedure returns some other status code, it is assumed that something went wrong, so the status code is shown to the user.

Ordinal Versus Named Parameter Positioning

When you use the `<cfprocparam>` tag to provide parameters to a stored procedure, you need to provide the `<cfprocparam>` tags in the correct order. That is, the first `<cfprocparam>` tag needs to correspond to the first parameter in the stored procedure's definition on the database server, the second `<cfprocparam>` tag needs to correspond to the second parameter, and so on. This is called *ordinal positioning*, meaning that the order of parameters is significant. ColdFusion does not support named parameters.

Parameter Data Types

As you saw in Listing 37.3, when you provide parameters to a stored procedure with the `<cfprocparam>` tag, you must specify the data type of the parameter, as defined by whoever created the procedure. ColdFusion requires that you provide the data type for each parameter you refer to in your templates, so it doesn't have to determine the data type itself on the fly each time the template runs. That would require a number of extra steps for ColdFusion, which in turn would slow your application.

It's important to specify the correct data type for each parameter. If you use the wrong data type, you might run into problems. The data type you provide for `CFSQLTYPE` in a `<cfprocparam>` tag must be one of ColdFusion's SQL data types. These data types are based on the data types defined by the ODBC standard—one of them will map to each of the database-specific data types used when your stored procedure was created.

For instance, if you have a stored procedure sitting on a Microsoft SQL Server that takes a parameter of SQL Server data type `int`, you should specify the `CF_SQL_INTEGER` data type in the corresponding `<cfprocparam>` tag.

Multiple Record Sets Are Fully Supported

Some stored procedures return more than one record set. For instance, consider a stored procedure called `FetchFilmInfo`. You are told that the procedure accepts one input parameter called `@FilmID`, and the procedure responds by returning five record sets of information related to the specified film. The first record set contains information about the film record itself; the second returns related records from the `Expenses` table; the third returns related records from the `Actors` table; the fourth returns related records from `Directors`; and the fifth returns information from the `Merchandise` table.

As you can see in Listing 37.4, the key to receiving more than one record set from a stored procedure is to include one `<cfprocresult>` tag for each record set, specifying `resultset="1"` for the first record set, `resultset="2"` for the second, and so on.

Listing 37.4 `ShowFilmExpenses.cfm`—Dealing with Multiple Record Sets

```
<!---
 Filename: ShowFilmExpenses.cfm
 Author:  Nate Weiss (NMW)
 Purpose: Demonstrates use of stored procedures
--->

<!--- Execute stored procedure to fetch film information --->
<cfstoredproc procedure="FetchFilmInfo" datasource="owsSqlServer">
  <!--- Provide the FilmID parameter --->
  <cfprocparam type="In" cfsqltype="CF_SQL_INTEGER" value="#url.filmID#">
  <!--- Film information --->
  <cfprocresult name="getFilm" resultset="1">
  <!--- Expense information --->
  <cfprocresult name="getExpenses" resultset="2">
  <!--- Actor information --->
  <cfprocresult name="getActors" resultset="3">
  <!--- Director information --->
  <cfprocresult name="getDirectors" resultset="4">
  <!--- Director information --->
  <cfprocresult name="getMerch" resultset="5">
</cfstoredproc>

<!--- Get subtotals from the recordsets returned by stored procedure --->
<cfset expenseSum = arraySum(listToArray(valueList(getExpenses.ExpenseAmount)))>
<cfset actorSum  = arraySum(listToArray(valueList(GetActors.Salary)))>
<cfset directorSum = arraySum(listToArray(valueList(GetDirectors.Salary)))>
<cfset merchSum  = arraySum(listToArray(valueList(GetMerch.TotalSales)))>
<!--- Add up all expenses --->
<cfset totalExpenses = expenseSum + actorSum + directorSum - merchSum>
<!--- Determine how much money is left in the budget --->
<cfset leftInBudget = getFilm.AmountBudgeted - totalExpenses>

<html>
<head><title>Film Expenses</title></head>
<body>
<!--- Company logo and page title --->
<img src="../images/logo_b.gif" width="73" height="73" align="absmiddle">
<font size="+2"><b>Film Expenses</b></font><br clear="all">

<cfoutput>
 <!--- Show film title--->
 <p><b>Film:</b> #getFilm.MovieTitle#<br>
 <!--- Film budget, expense total, and amount left in budget --->
 <p><b>Budget:</b> #lsCurrencyFormat(getFilm.AmountBudgeted)#<br>
 <b>Expenses:</b> #lsCurrencyFormat(totalExpenses)#<br>
 <b>Currently:</b> #lsCurrencyFormat(leftInBudget)#
 <!--- Are we currently over or under budget? --->
 #iif(leftInBudget lt 0, "'over budget'", "'under budget'")#<br>
 <!--- Output information about actors --->
 <p><b>Actors:</b>
 <cfloop query="getActors">
  <li>#NameFirst# #NameLast# (Salary: #lsCurrencyFormat(Salary)#)
 </cfloop>
 <!--- Output information about directors --->
 <p><b>Directors:</b>
 <cfloop query="getDirectors">
```

Listing 37.4 (continued)

```
  <li>#FirstName# #LastName# (Salary: #lsCurrencyFormat(Salary)#)
 </cfloop>
 <!--- Output information about expenses --->
 <p><b>Other Expenses:</b>
 <cfloop query="GetExpenses">
  <li>#Description# (#lsCurrencyFormat(ExpenseAmount)#)
 </cfloop>
 <!--- Output information about merchandise --->
 <p><b>Income from merchandise:</b>
 <cfloop query="getMerch">
  <li>#MerchName# (Sales: #lsCurrencyFormat(TotalSales)#)
 </cfloop>
</cfoutput>
</body>
</html>
```

After the `<cfstoredproc>` tag, the ColdFusion template is free to refer to the five record sets named in the `<cfprocresult>` tags as if they were the results of five separate `<cfquery>`-type queries. But because only one communication between ColdFusion and the database server needed to take place, you can expect performance to be faster using the single stored procedure.

NOTE

Your template doesn't have to handle or receive all the record sets a stored procedure spits out. For instance, if you weren't interested in the second record set from the `FetchFilmInfo` procedure, you could leave out the second `<cfprocresult>` tag. Neither ColdFusion nor your database server will mind.

If you're using Oracle, then `resultset="1"` refers to the first output parameter of type `REF CURSOR`, `resultset="2"` refers to the second such parameter, and so on. So if you had a procedure called `owsWeb.FetchFilmInfo` on your Oracle server that exposed five reference cursors (such as the five record sets returned by SQL Server used in the previous listing), hardly anything needs to change. You would simply use the same `<cfprocresult>` tags to capture the data from the reference cursors. An example of this can be found in the file `ShowFilmExpensesOracle.cfm`, available in the Zip file you can download from the book's Web site.

Calling Procedures with `<cfquery>` Instead of `<cfstoredproc>`

The `<cfstoredproc>` and related tags were added back in ColdFusion 4. Before that, the only way to call a stored procedure from a ColdFusion template was to use special procedure-calling syntax in a normal `cfquery` tag, where you would normally provide a SQL statement. You can still call stored procedures this way, and you actually might prefer to do so in some situations.

When you execute a stored procedure with `<cfquery>`, ColdFusion treats the response from the database server the way it would treat the response from an ordinary `SELECT` query. In fact, ColdFusion doesn't even realize that it's executing a stored procedure exactly; it's just passing on what it assumes to be a valid SQL statement and hopes to get some rows of table-style data in return.

The fact that ColdFusion is treating the stored procedure the same way it treats a `<select>` statement brings with it several important limitations:

- ColdFusion can't directly access the return code generated by the stored procedure.

- ColdFusion can't directly access any output parameters generated by the stored procedure.
- If the stored procedure returns more than one record set, only one of the record sets will be captured by ColdFusion and be available for your use in your templates. Details about this limitation will vary between types of database servers. With some database servers, only the first record set will be available for your use; with others, only the last will be available. The point is that stored procedures that return multiple record sets are not fully supported when using `cfquery`.

However, using `<cfquery>` also has an important advantage over `<cfstoredproc>`:

- With `<cfquery>`, you can pass a stored procedure's parameters by name, instead of only by position. For details, see "Using Your Database's Native Syntax" in this section.

Using the ODBC/JDBC `CALL` Command

With most types of database systems (including SQL Server and Oracle), you can use the `CALL` command defined by the ODBC standard to execute a stored procedure. Listing 37.5 demonstrates how the `FetchRatingsList` stored procedure can be called using this method.

Note that this template is almost exactly the same as the `FilmEntry1.cfm` template shown in Listing 37.2. The only change is that `<cfquery>` is being used instead of `<cfstoredproc>`. When this template is brought up in a browser, it should display its results exactly the same way.

Listing 37.5 `FilmEntry1a.cfm`—Calling a Stored Procedure

```
<!---
 Filename: FilmEntry1a.cfm
 Author:  Nate Weiss (NMW)
 Purpose: Demonstrates use of stored procedures
--->

<!--- Get list of ratings from database --->
<cfquery name="getRatings" datasource="owsSqlServer">
 {  CALL FetchRatingsList }
</cfquery>

<html>
<head><title>Film Entry Form</title></head>
<body>
<h2>Film Entry Form</h2>

<!--- Data entry form --->
<cfform action="#cgi.script_name#" method="post" preservedata="Yes">
 <!--- Text entry field for film title --->
 <p><b>Title for New Film:</b><br>
 <cfinput name="movieTitle" size="50" maxlength="50" required="Yes"
  message="Please don't leave the film's title blank."><br>
 <!--- Text entry field for pitch text --->
 <p><b>Short Description / One-Liner:</b><br>
 <cfinput name="pitchText" size="50" maxlength="100" required="Yes"
```

Listing 37.5 (continued)

```
      message="Please don't leave the one-liner blank."><br>

     <!--- Text entry field for expense description --->
     <p><b>New Film Budget:</b><br>
     <cfinput name="amountBudgeted" size="15" required="Yes"
      message="Please enter a valid number for the film's budget."
      validate="float"><br>

     <!--- Drop-down list of ratings --->
     <p><b>Rating:</b><br>
     <cfselect name="ratingID" query="getRatings" value="RatingID" display="Rating"/>
     <!--- Text areas for summary --->
     <p><b>Summary:</b><br>
     <cftextarea name="summary" cols="40" rows="3" wrap="soft"></cftextarea>

     <!--- Submit button for form --->
     <p><cfinput type="submit" name="submit" value="Submit New Film">
    </cfform>

    </body>
    </html>
```

As you can see in Listing 37.5, the syntax for using the `CALL` command is simply the word `CALL` and then the procedure name. The entire command is surrounded by a set of curly braces, which indicate that the command must be interpreted by JDBC before it gets sent on to the database server.

Input parameters can be supplied in parentheses after the procedure name, separated by commas. If no input parameters exist for the procedure, leave the parentheses off. Because you aren't referring to them by name, input parameters must be supplied in the proper order (as defined by the creator of the stored procedure). If an input parameter is of a character type (such as `char`, `varchar`, or `text`), enclose the parameter's value in single quotation marks. For instance, to call the `InsertFilm` stored procedure from Listing 37.3, you could replace the `<cfstoredproc>` block in that template with the following snippet (see `FilmEntry2a.cfm` from the Zip file to see this snippet in a complete template):

```
<cfquery datasource="owsSqlServer">
 {  CALL InsertFilm (
  '#FORM.movieTitle#',
  '#FORM.pitchText#',
   #FORM.amountBudgeted#,
   #FORM.ratingID#,
  '#FORM.summary#') }
</cfquery>
```

But remember that ColdFusion isn't aware of the return code or output parameters returned by the procedure, so the code in the rest of the listing would fail. You would need to have the stored procedure rewritten so that the information provided by the return code or output parameters instead get returned as a record set.

Using Your Database's Native Syntax

In addition to using the `CALL` command, most database drivers also let you use whatever native syntax you would use normally with that database system. All the same limitations (regarding return codes, output parameters, and so on) listed at the beginning of this section apply.

The native syntax to use varies according to the database server you're using; consult your database server documentation for details. Just as an example, if you were using Microsoft SQL Server, you could replace the `<cfquery>` shown in Listing 37.5 with the following code; the results would be the same:

```
<cfquery name="getRatings" datasource="owsSqlServer">
  EXEC FetchRatingsList
</cfquery>
```

One advantage of using the native syntax over the `CALL` syntax is that you may be able to refer to the input parameters by name, which leads to cleaner and more readable code. So if you were using Microsoft SQL Server, the `InsertFilm` procedure could be called with the following code (your database server documentation has specific details):

```
<cfquery datasource="owsSqlServer">
 EXEC InsertFilm
  @MovieTitle = '#form.movieTitle#',
  @PitchText = '#form.pitchText#',
  @AmountBudgeted = #form.amountBudgeted#,
  @RatingID = #form.ratingID#,
  @Summary = '#form.summary#'
</cfquery>
```

Depending on your database server, you might be able to add more code to the `<cfquery>` tag to be able to capture the status code and output parameters from the stored procedure. Again, just as an example, if you were using Microsoft SQL Server, you would be able to use something similar to the following:

```
<cfquery datasource="owsSqlServer" name="ExecProc">
 -- Declare T-SQL variables to hold values returned by stored procedure
 DECLARE @StatusCode INT, @NewFilmID INT
 -- Execute the stored procedure, assigning values to T-SQL variables
 EXEC @StatusCode = InsertFilm
  @MovieTitle = '#form.movieTitle#',
  @PitchText = '#form.pitchText#',
  @AmountBudgeted = #form.amountBudgeted#,
  @RatingID = #form.ratingID#,
  @Summary = '#form.summary#',
  @NewFilmID = @NewFilmID OUTPUT
 -- Select the T-SQL variables as a one-row recordset
 SELECT @StatusCode AS StatusCode, @NewFilmID AS NewFilmID
</cfquery>
```

You then could refer to `ExecProc.StatusCode` and `ExecProc.NewFilmID` in your CFML template code. The `FilmEntry2b.cfm` template may be found in the downloaded Zip file for this chapter and is a revised version of Listing 37.3 that uses this `<cfquery>` snippet instead of `<cfstoredproc>` to execute the `InsertFilm` stored procedure.

NOTE

You will need to consult your database documentation for more information about how to use this type of syntax. In general, it's really best to use `<cfstoredproc>` instead of `<cfquery>` if the stored procedure you want to use generates important status codes or output parameters.

CHAPTER 38
Working with ORM

IN THIS CHAPTER

Welcome to ORM

By now, you've written many ColdFusion templates, and it's a good bet that many of them make use of databases. One of ColdFusion's earliest reasons for success was how simple it made working with databases. ColdFusion 9 kicks this up a notch, making it even *easier* to develop database-backed Web sites and applications.

ColdFusion 9 introduces the concept of a built-in ORM framework. ORM—which stands for object relational model—provides a way to abstract away the database portion of your application. We tend to think of our applications in terms of objects. So a shopping cart is a "thing" and our products are more "things." These things, or objects, have properties and things we can do with them. ColdFusion Components (CFCs) go a long way toward letting us treat an application as a collection of objects.

Unfortunately, at some point we need to take these abstract objects and actually make them persist in a database. Our fancy objects have to be converted into vanilla SQL statements. While this isn't too difficult (again, ColdFusion makes database operations rather simple), it does take a lot of time. Writing a `SELECT` statement may be simple, but after you've written a few hundred of them, the process can get a bit old.

An ORM framework, like the one included in ColdFusion, allows us to work with the objects as they are and not worry about the database. We describe our objects in such a way that the framework can figure out how to store (persist) the object in a table. A good ORM framework can even handle the mundane tasks of manipulating database tables. So, for example, what happens when you decide to add the new property `nickname` to your application users? Before you add any code to work with this new property you have to open your database editing tool of choice, find the database, find the table, and then, finally, edit the table. ORM can actually do all of this for you. Even better, if you decide later that `nickname` was a stupid idea, you can get rid of it and let ORM handle cleaning up the table for you.

Here's another example. Have you ever worked with a database that had questionable naming rules? We all have. Imagine a user table with column names like so: `fstnme,lstnme,uname,pswd`. You can probably guess what those columns are, but the names certainly don't lend themselves to readability. With ORM, we can define our model with nice names and simply create a pointer to the obscure column names in the database.

Altogether, ORM provides an *incredible* rapid application development—or RAD—platform that will forever change your ColdFusion development.

NOTE

All the CFC listings in this chapter use tags. Are tags required for ORM? Heck no! Since many users will be new to both script-based tags and ORM, I decided to make this chapter as simple and accessible as possible. If you prefer script-based tags, use them. Nothing about ORM in ColdFusion 9 will require you to use one over the other.

ColdFusion and Hibernate

If an ORM framework sounds like a big deal, it is. Adobe didn't build ORM from scratch, however. ColdFusion 9 makes use of the Hibernate framework. Hibernate is an open source framework developed primarily for Java (although a .NET version also exists). ColdFusion ships with the Hibernate framework and has wrappers for its functionality. (Note that not everything found within Hibernate is available directly via ColdFusion tags and functions; the ColdFusion team focused on providing hooks to the most critical, most often needed parts. What you can't do directly using a native built-in tag or function is available via hooks to the engine that ColdFusion provides.) Hibernate is a *very* large framework and is extremely powerful. This chapter discusses the basics of working with ORM and ColdFusion, but it doesn't cover everything. For further information, you can visit the Hibernate Web site at http://www.hibernate.org. You can also find numerous books that focus just on Hibernate. One book in particular, *Java Persistence with Hibernate* by Christian Bauer and Gavin King, is highly recommended for folks who want to get really deep into the framework.

Getting Started with ORM

We'll start with the first steps to add ORM to a ColdFusion application. Hibernate is an extremely high-performing framework, but that does mean that more is happening than in a typical application. Because of this, ORM support is disabled in an application by default. To use ORM, you need to explicitly turn it on. This is done with two new additions to the `THIS` scope in your `Application.cfc` file. Listing 38.1 demonstrates an example of this feature.

Listing 38.1 `app1/Application.CFC`—Enabling ORM

```
<cfcomponent>

    <cfset this.name = "ows38_app1">
    <cfset this.datasource = "ows">
    <cfset this.ormenabled = true>

</cfcomponent>
```

This Application.cfc file is fairly trivial. Normally you would see much more (event handlers, more settings, and so on), but this is the bare minimum required code to *enable* ORM for an application. We stress the word *enable* here as this code only turns the feature on; ORM doesn't actually do anything yet.

As stated earlier, two values are required. The first is the data source, which sets the data source that will be used for all database operations using the ORM framework. Note that this sets a default for all other database operations as well. If for some reason you decide that ORM is simply too RAD for you, you can still use the this.datasource value as a quick way to set a default data source for your entire application. The second option, this.ormenabled, simply toggles the support for ORM in the application.

There is a third setting you can use in the THIS scope if you choose. The this.ormsettings value is a structure that passes additional configuration information to the ORM framework. This information allows you to tweak the behavior of the application. If, for example, you want the ORM framework to be able to edit and drop tables and columns from your database, you can enable it to do so—an extremely time-saving option early on during development, though you certainly don't want it turned on while running in a production environment. Other options include caching settings, and logging.

So now that we've enabled ORM for the application, how do we actually *use* it? When we work with ORM, we will be working with objects instead of database tables. These objects will be created with CFCs. For the most part, these CFCs are much like the components you've created in the past. However, we will use a special flag within the CFC file to alert ColdFusion and Hibernate that they should be persisted to the database. That flag is simply the persistent attribute.

Working with Persistent CFCs

When an application that has ORM enabled is started, it scans for persistent CFCs. This scan includes all the folders and files under the Application.cfc file. You can override this behavior if you wish. As mentioned earlier, you can create a special ormsettings structure that helps define the way that ORM is used in your application. One value you can supply is cfclocation. This is a relative path to a folder containing the persistent CFCs for your application. For our examples here, we will use the default behavior: letting ColdFusion simply scan everything.

The first step when creating a persistent CFC is to decide what the name of the file will be. This is an important decision. By default, the ORM framework assumes that a persistent component named foo will point to a table in your database table named foo. In cases where the table name is obscure or just not to your liking, you can override this default by supplying a table attribute to your component.

The next step in creating a persistent CFC is to add the persistent attribute to the component tag. Here's an example:

```
<component persistent="true">
</component>
```

If this code were in a file named art.cfc, it would represent a table named art in your database. What if the table had an odd name, perhaps art_Records? You could use art.cfc as a file name and simply supply the table attribute to let ColdFusion and Hibernate know the table to which the CFC will map:

```
<component persistent="true" table="art_Records">
</component>
```

Working with Properties

So far, we've simply created an empty component with the persistent flag. That isn't quite enough. We also need to define which properties make up our component. These properties will map to column names in the database table. To define them, we will use the <cfproperty> tag. This tag has existed for as long as CFCs have, but for the most part, people haven't used it. The tag's primary function was to help with Web services and Flash Remoting, but with ColdFusion 9 and ORM, it has a new function. Each cfproperty tag in our component helps define the object and its relationship to the database table.

Our persistent CFCs will use three basic types of properties. The first is the property that defines the primary key for our object. Every persistent CFC must have one of these.

The second type of property defines simple columns. You can imagine a table of people containing columns for names, ages, genders, and so on. These would all be defined with column type properties.

The third type of property defines relationships. As we know, many tables have relationships with other tables. A database table of works of art may be related to a table of artists that created the art. A table of users may be related to a table of groups, with multiple users and multiple groups and multiple links between them. This third type of property will help us define those relationships and provide a much cleaner way of handling them from within our ColdFusion application.

We could also use a fourth type of property, which we won't be discussing in this chapter. That property deals with versioning and helps handle cases in which multiple people may be working with the same record.

Now that we've talked about the properties that make up a persistent component, it's time for an example. Listing 38.2 defines a persistent component for the Directors table in the OWS database. Be sure to copy the Application.cfc file from the Zip file downloaded from the book's Web site. It isn't shown in the listing here as it is the same (except for the application name) as in the previous listing.

Listing 38.2 app2/director.cfc—Persistent CFC

```
<cfcomponent persistent="true" table="directors">

    <cfproperty name="directorid" fieldType="id" generator="increment">
    <cfproperty name="firstname" ormtype="string">
    <cfproperty name="lastname" ormtype="string">

</cfcomponent>
```

Listing 38.2 contains a few elements that we haven't discussed in detail yet, but by just reading the code you can probably make a good guess as to what each line does. We begin with the `cfcomponent` tag. We use the `persistent="true"` flag to warn ColdFusion that this is a component that maps to a table. The OWS database uses plural names for its tables. While that may be fine in the database, for our code we want to work with single `director` instances. Since we named the file `director`, we had to include the `table` attribute to let Hibernate know which table this file matches.

Next examine the three `cfproperty` tags. The first maps to the primary key for the table. The second two map to the first and last names of the director. The `cfproperty` tag is a critical tag when working with ORM. It has numerous new attributes specifically meant to help define the relationship between our objects and the tables in the database. Table 38.1 defines the most critical of those attributes, which also are the most common ones you will use. For a complete list, consult the documentation.

Table 38.1 Common `cfproperty` Arguments and Values

NAME	DESCRIPTION
`fieldtype`	Defines the role that the property plays in the object. Possible values are `column` (default), `id` (used for primary keys), `version` (used for versioning), `timestamp` (used to apply a timestamp automatically), `collection` (used for collections of value), and one of the relationship types. Relationships will be described later in the chapter.
`default`	Defines a default value for the property.
`name`	Specifies the name of the property. If the `column` argument isn't used, then ColdFusion and Hibernate will map this value to the database column of the same name.
`column`	Specifies the database column that maps to this property.
`type`	Specifies a ColdFusion data type for the property.
`ormtype`	Specifies a generic data type for the property. Possible values are `string`, `character`, `char`, `short`, `integer`, `int`, `long`, `big_decimal`, `float`, `double`, `Boolean`, `yes_no`, `true_false`, `text`, `date`, `timestamp`, `binary`, `serializable`, `blob`, and `clob`. Each of these types then gets mapped to a specific type in the database.
`persistent`	Specifies whether the property represents a value that gets persisted to the database. This value defaults to `true`.

Note that there are more argument values you can use for the `cfproperty` tag. Some allow much greater precision and detail in the database mappings. But in general, you will use the arguments in Table 38.1.

Now let's talk a bit more about primary keys. Every persistent component must have one primary key. Without it, Hibernate wouldn't know how to uniquely load one particular row of data. As stated earlier, you use a `fieldtype` value of `id` when defining the primary key in your component. The other important argument is `generator`. This tells Hibernate what kind of primary key is associated with your database table.

The possible values for the `generator` argument are `increment`, `identity`, `sequence`, `native`, `assigned`, `foreign`, `seqhilo`, `uuid`, `guid`, `select`, and `sequence-identity`. That's a pretty long list so we will focus on identity, sequence, and native. You use identity for databases that can generate a unique key for you: specifically, those that handle auto-incrementing. You use sequence for databases that support generated sequences for the primary key, with Oracle being a prime example. The preferred option for most developers, though, is native. This argument tells Hibernate to look at the database and figure out which database is best.

The OWS database that accompanies this book uses the Apache Derby database. The simplest option for that database and for our example code is increment. However, this option is safe to use only when Hibernate is the only application working with the data. In our simple examples, this choicě is satisfactory, but you will most likely want to use native for production applications.

Working with Entities

In the Hibernate world, persistent objects are referred as entities, and as you will see, many of the functions we discuss later use entity in their names. If this seems unusual to you, in your mind just substitute "CFC" whenever you see "entity."

So we have defined one persistent CFC (director.cfc in Listing 38.2); now how do we actually start creating content from it?

Hibernate and ColdFusion provide support for all the basic create, read, update, and delete (CRUD) functions you've come to know and love in Web development. If you've written any Web application that works with a database, then you are familiar with the code behind those terms. If you've written *many* Web applications, then you are also probably aware that most CRUD code is boilerplate, repetitive, and frankly pretty darn boring. Hibernate makes this boring code much simpler. Let's take a look at how CRUD is implemented in ColdFusion 9 and Hibernate.

Creating a New Entity

You can create an entity a several ways, but when talking about ORM, it makes sense to discuss the entityNew() function. The entityNew() function takes one argument: the name of the entity. This will match the name of the CFC created that defines the entity. Listing 38.3 demonstrates an example of this.

Listing 38.3 app2/create.cfm—Create a Persistent CFC

```
<!---
Module:         create.cfm
Author:         Raymond Camden
Function:       Create a new director entity.
--->

<cfset d = entityNew("director")>
<cfdump var="#d#" label="New Director">
```

A whole two lines of code there gives you a hint about how much work ORM is going to be saving us later. The first line simply creates an instance of the director entity, named d. The second line dumps this result. If you look at this dump in Figure 38.1, you will notice something odd. Quite a few functions exist even though we didn't actually write any methods for the component.

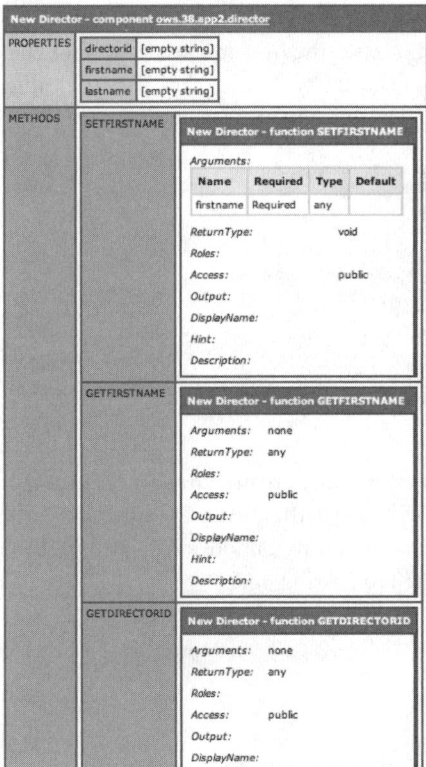

Figure 38.1
The dump of the `director` entity.

What's with all those functions? You may notice that they match the property values. For each `cfproperty` tag in the CFC, there is a `set` function and a `get` function. This matching is performed automatically for all persistent CFC. (Although if you want, you can disable this feature for a particular property.) This feature allows us to easily set values for each of the various properties. Listing 38.4 demonstrates an example of this.

Listing 38.4 `app2/create2.cfm`—Create (and Modify) a Persistent CFC

```
<!---
Module:        create2.cfm
Author:        Raymond Camden
Function:      Create a new director entity and modify it.
--->

<cfset d = entityNew("director")>
<cfdump var="#d#" label="New Director">

<cfset d.setFirstName("Raymond")>
<cfset d.setLastName("Vader")>

<cfdump var="#d#" label="Modified Director">
```

Listing 38.4 builds on the previous example. As before, a new `director` entity is created. Then we use the automatic method generation to set the first and last names for the director. Figure 38.2 shows the result of the two dumps of the entity. Notice that after the values have been modified, we see the entity correctly populated with a first and last name.

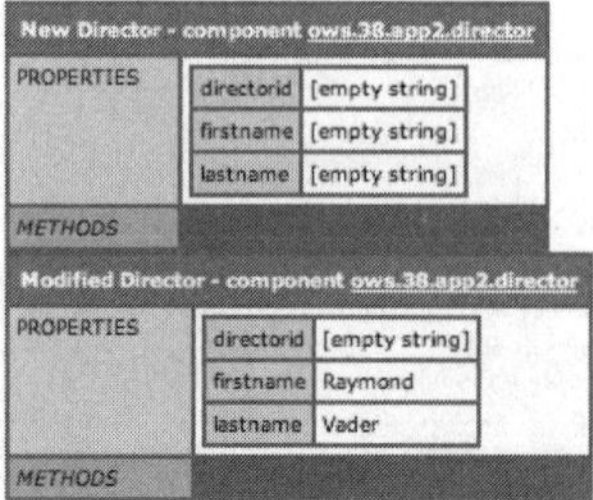

Figure 38.2

The director has a name!

Now you may be wondering: Have we actually created `director` entities? If you use a database tool to look at the `Directors` table, you will notice that no new records have been created. Why not? The `entityNew` function creates an empty entity but doesn't persist it. To do that, you must use the `entitySave` function, as demonstrated in Listing 38.5.

Listing 38.5 `app2/save.cfm`—Create (and Save) a Persistent CFC

```
<!---
Module:          save.cfm
Author:          Raymond Camden
Function:        Create a new director entity and save it
--->

<cfset d = entityNew("director")>

<cfset d.setFirstName("Raymond")>
<cfset d.setLastName("Vader")>

<cfdump var="#d#" label="Modified Director">

<cfset entitySave(d)>

<cfdump var="#d#" label="Director entity after it was saved.">
```

As before, the listing begins by creating a new entity based on the `director` component. The first name and last name values are set, and then the entire entity is dumped. Next we use the new `entitySave()` function mentioned before. Finally, we dump the entity again. Figure 38.3 shows something interesting: after the save, an ID value exists.

So let's be clear about what just happened here. When you used the `entitySave()` function, Hibernate took over the persistence of the entity. It took care of knowing what database you were using, what table the `director` component maps to, and which columns map to the properties. It then took all that knowledge and created the SQL code to persist the information in the database.

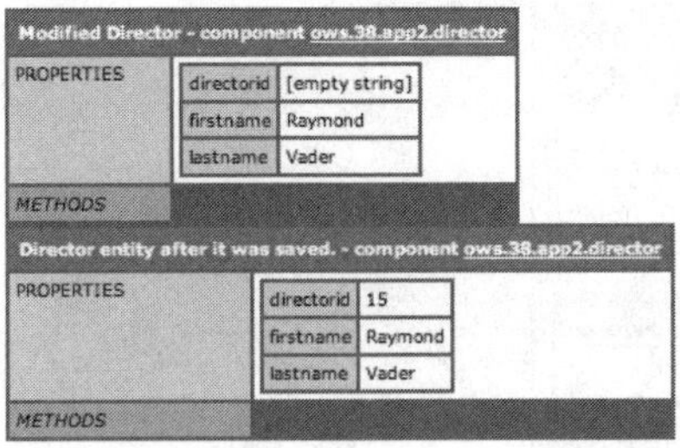

Figure 38.3
The director has an ID value now.

If your eyes are beginning to glisten with joy at the thought of not having to write SQL again, you aren't alone. Just wait though; things get even better.

Reading Entities

Time to move on to the next part of the CRUD puzzle: *R* for "read." ColdFusion and Hibernate provide several ways to read data. Some methods are more suited for returning multiple objects, and others are more suited for getting a unique object; one method is more suited for searching and will be discussed later in the chapter.

Let's begin by looking at one of the more powerful ways to read data: `entityLoad()`. The `entityLoad` function can return any number of objects, and it can perform sorting as well as filtering. In many ways, it is a Swiss Army knife of data fetching. Listing 38.6 shows the simplest possible example.

Listing 38.6 `app2/list1.cfm`—Director List

```
<!---
Module:         list1.cfm
Author:         Raymond Camden
Function:       List all directors
--->

<cfset directors = entityLoad("director")>
<cfdump var="#directors#">
```

Listing 38.6 demonstrates the absolute simplest use of `entityLoad()` possible. We pass in the name of the entity and ... well, that's it! This function returns an array of objects representing every single director in the database. Figure 38.4 shows the result of the dump.

Most likely you won't want to use a plain data dump in a production application. Remember that every persistent CFC comes with `get` and `set` functions automatically defined. To make our listing a bit prettier, we can modify it as shown in Listing 38.7.

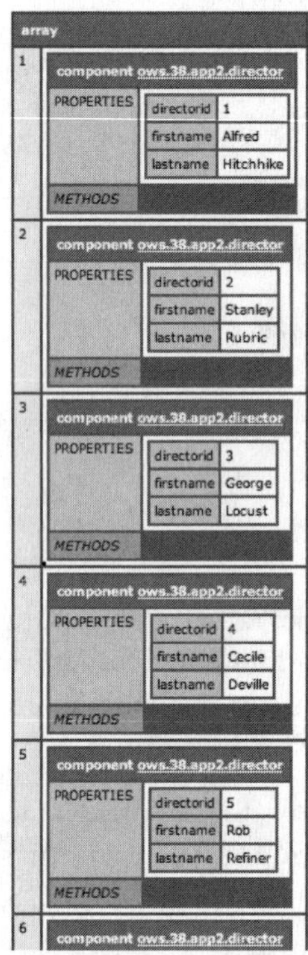

Figure 38.4

Results of the `entityLoad()` function.

Listing 38.7 `app2/list2.cfm`—Nicer-Looking Director List

```
<!---
Module:          list2.cfm
Author:          Raymond Camden
Function:        List all directors (nicely!)
--->

<cfset directors = entityLoad("director")>
<cfloop index="director" array="#directors#">
   <cfoutput>
   #director.getLastName()#, #director.getFirstName()#<br/>
   </cfoutput>
</cfloop>
```

The only real difference between Listings 38.7 and 38.6 is the way we display the data. In Listing 38.7, we use the array of `director` entities. We loop over each `director` entity and run the `getLastName()` and `getFirstName()` methods. This may be repetitive, but remember: we never wrote code for those methods, nor did we write a lick of SQL. Look at how much we are accomplishing for *very* little work!

Now let's look at another example. If you want to load one particular entity, you can pass a second argument to `entityLoad()` that represents the primary key. Listing 38.8 demonstrates two examples of this approach.

Listing 38.8 `app2/listonedirector.cfm`—Get One Director

```
<!---
Module:         listonedirector.cfm
Author:         Raymond Camden
Function:       Create a new director and get it.
--->

<cfset d = entityNew("director")>
<cfset d.setFirstName("Scott")>
<cfset d.setLastName("Stroz")>
<cfset entitySave(d)>

<cfset idtoload = entityLoad("director",d.getDirectorId())>
<cfdump var="#idtoload#">

<cfset idtoload2 = entityLoad("director",d.getDirectorId(),true)>
<cfdump var="#idtoload2#">
```

The listing begins by creating an entity for a new director, Scott Stroz. This `director` entity is saved with the `entitySave()` function. Then we use `entityLoad()` to get the `director` entity. Note we use the `getDirectorId()` method to get the ID of the `director` entity we just loaded. In case you are wondering, yes, this is kind of ridiculous. Normally you wouldn't reload an entity that you already have (and Hibernate is smart enough to recognize this for you). However, this code does demonstrate the syntax.

The second `entityLoad()` uses a third argument. This third argument tells Hibernate that we are getting one and only one object. What does this do? Well, normally `entityLoad()` returns an array of objects. If you know you only want to get one, you can tell Hibernate this, and you will get the object by itself, not in an array, as shown in Figure 38.5.

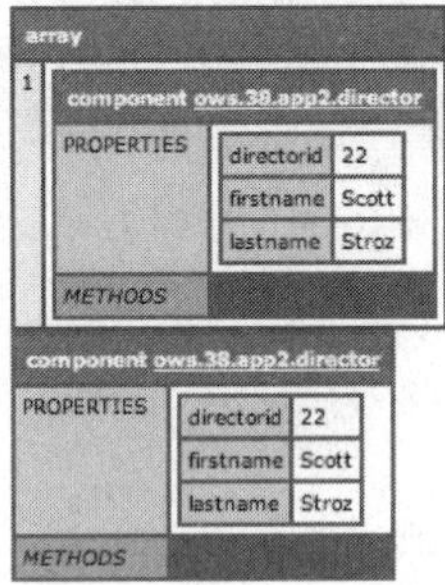

Figure 38.5
Results of the `entityLoad()` function: retrieving one object.

TIP

To save you some keystrokes, ColdFusion also comes with an `EntityLoadByPk` function. This function takes the name of an entity and the ID value of the record to load. Typically, you use this function when you know you are loading one particular object. Later examples will make use of this function.

Let's now move to another type of `entityLoad()` example: a filter. In the previous listing, the second argument was a primary key. If you pass a structure as the second argument, Hibernate treats this as a filter structure. By that we mean you can pass any number of keys that match fields in the component and specific values. Hibernate will return only entities that have fields that match the value you pass.

NOTE

The `entityLoad()` filter returns an *exact* match. You can't, for example, ask for records that have a numerical value less than some other value, nor can you find people with a last name *like* some search string. We will see examples of how to handle such matches later.

Listing 38.9 demonstrates this functionality.

Listing 38.9 `app2/list3.cfm`—Get the Vaders!

```
<!---
Module:          list3.cfm
Author:          Raymond Camden
Function:        Find all the Vaders!
--->

<cfset vaderpeeps = entityLoad("director", {lastname='Vader'})>
<cfdump var="#vaderpeeps#">
```

Once again we have a *very* short file here. This time `entityLoad()` has been passed a structure as the second argument. We can pass in any key that matches a property of a `director` entity. That means `directorid`, `firstname`, and `lastname` would all be valid here. Listing 38.9 specifies `lastname`. The value is `Vader`, which should match a few entries based on earlier examples.

We've seen a few ways to get entries; now let's look at how to provide a default sort. This is where things may get a bit confusing. All in all, `entityLoad()` can take up to four arguments. The meaning of each argument depends on how many you pass and their values. If you want to sort the results of `entityLoad()`, then you will pass a sort string as the third argument. However, the second argument must be a filter structure. What if you don't want to filter? Simple—pass an empty structure, as shown in Listing 38.10.

Listing 38.10 `app2/list4.cfm`—List and Sort Directors

```
<!---
Module:          list4.cfm
Author:          Raymond Camden
Function:        List and sort!
--->

<!--- sort by last name --->
<cfset sortedDirectors = entityLoad("director", {}, "lastname asc")>

<cfloop index="director" array="#sortedDirectors#">
    <cfoutput>
    #director.getLastName()#, #director.getFirstName()#<br/>
    </cfoutput>
</cfloop>
```

Listing 38.10 is almost exactly like Listing 38.7. The only difference is that in Listing 38.10, we pass an empty filter and sort string to `entityLoad()`. The sort string looks much like a typical

SQL-style sort. We provide both a field to sort by and an order. As in SQL, we can combine these with other columns. For example, `"lastname asc, firstname desc"` would first sort by last names in ascending order and then by first names in descending order. The rest of the code simply lists the data.

Updating Entities

We've discussed how to create and read entities. Now it's time to move on to updating. In the old days of SQL, we typically handled creation versus updating by using a simple `<cfif>` block. If the data was new, we performed an insert operation; if the data was old, we performed an update. Hibernate makes this process ridiculously simple. In fact, you don't have to anything. If you merely *change* an entity that already exists, Hibernate will handle all the details of persisting your changes in the database for you. Sure, you can still use `entitySave()` if you want, but you don't need to. Listing 38.11 demonstrates a simple example of this.

Listing 38.11 `app2/update.cfm`—An Update Example

```
<!---
Module:         update.cfm
Author:         Raymond Camden
Function:       Create a new director entity and save it
--->

<cfset d = entityNew("director")>

<cfset d.setFirstName("Raymond")>
<cfset d.setLastName("Vader")>

<cfset entitySave(d)>

<cfdump var="#d#" label="Director entity after it was saved.">

<cfset d.setFirstName("Todd")>
<cfset d.setLastName("Sharp")>

<cfdump var="#d#" label="Director entity after it was updated.">
```

Listing 38.11 is a modified form of Listing 38.5. We create a `director` entity, set some basic values, and then save. Then, after the dump, we modify the entity. This is a fairly unrealistic example, but it does demonstrate that nothing special needed to be done to perform an update versus a create operation. Figure 38.6 shows the results of the dumps.

Figure 38.6

Results of saving and then updating an object.

NOTE

Remember how we said that Hibernate was really smart? Well, it is smart enough to recognize in Listing 38.11 that there was no need to save the data with the initial values. In reality, it performed only one update. We will discuss this further later in the chapter. Just be aware that Hibernate goes out of its way to be as high performing as possible, even when we code in a less-than-optimal manner.

Deleting Entities

We are now ready for the final CRUD process: deletion. As you can probably guess, deletions are just as easy to perform as the other operations. To delete an object, you first have to get it. After you have the entity, you simply pass it to the `entityDelete()` function, as Listing 38.12 shows.

Listing 38.12 `app2/delete.cfm`—A Deletion Example

```
<!---
Module:         delete.cfm
Author:         Raymond Camden
Function:       Creates and then deletes a director
--->

<cfif not structKeyExists(url, "id")>

    <cfset d = entityNew("director")>

    <cfset d.setFirstName("Doomed")>
    <cfset d.setLastName("Man")>

    <cfset entitySave(d)>

    <cfdump var="#d#" label="Director entity after it was saved.">

    <cfoutput>
    <a href="delete.cfm?id=#d.getDirectorId()#">Delete me!</a>
    </cfoutput>

<cfelse>

    <cfset toDie = entityLoadByPk("director", url.id)>
    <cfset entityDelete(toDie)>

    <p>
    Entity Deleted!
    </p>

</cfif>
```

This listing is a bit more complex then earlier examples because we need to provide a way for the user to see the data that will be deleted before we actually delete it. Therefore, this file is run twice. When it is first loaded, it creates a new `director` entity and creates a link back to itself with the ID of the newly created entity. When the page is reloaded, the actual delete operation is performed, using `entityDelete`. All in all, the process is trivial. The most complex part of this script was what we did to make it more obvious to the reader.

Something that makes Hibernate even cooler is that it can also handle cascading deletions. For example, if you want to delete a blog entry that has related categories, Hibernate will handle removal of any entries in a join table that links entries and categories. How about comments for a blog entry? You can have Hibernate delete those as well. You don't have to use Hibernate for these tasks, of course, but if you want to do less cleanup and let Hibernate handle the work, you can.

Putting It Together

So far we've discussed how to create simple entities, or persistent components. We haven't discussed relationships yet, but we have covered the full CRUD process (create, read, update, and delete). Before going further, let's look at a full example. The following two code listings (found in the `38/app3` folder) allow you to edit `director` entities. You can create new `director` entities, edit existing ones, and perform deletions. Before using this application, be sure to also copy the `Application.cfc` file from the Zip file downloaded for this book.

Listing 38.13 is the first part of the application. It handles the listing and deletion of `director` entities.

Listing 38.13 `app3/index.cfm`—List and Delete Directors

```
<!---
Module:         index.cfm
Author:         Raymond Camden
Function:       List directors so you can add/edit/delete.
--->

<cfif structKeyExists(url, "delete")>
    <cfset directorToDie = entityLoadByPk("director", url.delete)>
    <cfset entityDelete(directorToDie)>
</cfif>

<cfset directors = entityLoad("director", {},  "lastname asc, firstname asc")>

<h2>Directors</h2>

<table border="1">
    <cfloop index="d" array="#directors#">
    <cfoutput>
    <tr>
        <td><a href="edit.cfm?id=#d.getDirectorId()#">#d.getLastName()#,
#d.getFirstName()#</a></td>
        <td><a href="index.cfm?delete=#d.getDirectorId()#">Delete</a></td>
    </tr>
    </cfoutput>
    </cfloop>
</table>

<a href="edit.cfm">Add New Director</a>
```

The code begins by checking for a delete attempt. If the `url` variable `delete` exists, it must be the ID of a `director` entity to delete. The `director` entity is loaded and then deleted. The next part simply grabs all the `director` entities and sorts on the names. Below this is a basic table. Each director is listed with an `edit` and `delete` link. The final piece is a link to the edit page, which allows us to add new directors.

Now let's take a look at Listing 38.14: the edit template.

Listing 38.14 `app3/edit.cfm`—Edit Directors

```
<!---
Module:         edit.cfm
Author:         Raymond Camden
Function:       Performs basic editing.
--->

<cfset errors = []>

<cfparam name="url.id" default="0">
<cfif url.id neq 0>
    <cfset director = entityLoadByPk("director", url.id)>
    <cfparam name="form.firstname" default="#director.getFirstName()#">
    <cfparam name="form.lastname" default="#director.getLastName()#">
<cfelse>
    <cfset director = entityNew("director")>
    <cfparam name="form.firstname" default="">
    <cfparam name="form.lastname" default="">
</cfif>

<cfif structKeyExists(form, "submit")>
    <cfif not len(trim(form.firstname))>
        <cfset arrayAppend(errors, "Include a first name.")>
    </cfif>
    <cfif not len(trim(form.lastname))>
        <cfset arrayAppend(errors, "Include a last name.")>
    </cfif>

    <cfif not arrayLen(errors)>
        <cfset director.setFirstName(trim(form.firstname))>
        <cfset director.setLastName(trim(form.lastname))>
        <cfset entitySave(director)>
        <cflocation url="index.cfm" addToken="false">
    </cfif>

</cfif>

<h2>Edit Director</h2>

<cfif arrayLen(errors)>
    <p>
    <b>Please fix these errors:<br/>
    <ul>
    <cfloop index="e" array="#errors#">
    <cfoutput>
    <li>#e#</li>
    </cfoutput>
    </cfloop>
    </ul>
    </b>
```

Listing 38.14 (continued)

```
    </p>
</cfif>

<cfoutput>
<form action="edit.cfm?id=#url.id#" method="post">
First Name: <input type="text" name="firstname" value="#form.firstname#"><br/>
Last Name: <input type="text" name="lastname" value="#form.lastname#"><br/>
<input type="submit" name="submit" value="Save">
</form>
</cfoutput>
```

This document is a fairly typical self-posting form. It begins by creating default form field values. If `url` values for `id` were passed, these values comes from `director` entities. If values were not passed, the field values default to nothing. If the form is submitted, we perform basic validation (the fields for the first and last names must have *something* in them). If these tests succeed, then we use an `entitySave` function to persist the data. Below all of this is the actual form itself. Since our `director` entity is so simple (two fields), there isn't a lot going on here.

Now that the application is ready (again, be sure to copy the `Application.cfc` file), test it. You may notice something odd when you perform a deletion. Before going further, be sure you try this yourself: Create a new `director` entity and save it. On the list of directors, click the `delete` link. Notice that the director is still there! To make matters more confusing, if you reload the page, the director is gone. So what the heck is happening here?

Hibernate and Sessions

So far we haven't discussed much about what Hibernate is doing with our data behind the scenes. We know that Hibernate is writing a lot of SQL for us, and that's great because it means less work for us. But it's also important to have some understanding of exactly *how* and *when* Hibernate writes SQL. Consider a simple example. Suppose I create a new `director` entity named `Scott Stroz`. I save that entity. Now in the same template, I change the name to `Jeanne Boudreaux`. I save the `director` entity again. So what do you think happened here?

Well, first off, Hibernate was smart enough to say, "Listen, I know you asked me to save the director Scott Stroz, but I know that you saved the name as Jeanne Boudreaux. Why should I bother writing two SQL statements when I know I only need one?" Let's consider a real-world example. Imagine you are at a restaurant and order a salad. (Hard to believe, but some people order salads as an entrée.) As the waiter is walking away, you quickly come to your senses and yell to the waiter to change your order to a hamburger. Now technically you asked for two different things, but really it's one order. The waiter knows to ignore the first request and simply get the hamburger.

Hibernate refers to all of this as a session. *It is very important that you do not confuse this session with the ColdFusion session.* It may make more sense if you mentally replace "Hibernate session" with "Hibernate request." Hibernate's session (again, a request) is a collection of all the requests made to the database: edits, deletions, requests, and so on. Hibernate will do everything possible to minimize the number of requests it makes to the database. If possible, it will wait until all the requests are made and then simply run them at the end. That's *exactly* what went wrong with our example application. Consider: We asked Hibernate to perform a deletion and to return a list of directors. The list of directors was returned before the delete operation actually took place. That's why on a second (or later) reload, the list is correct.

So how can we fix our application? Well, one way would be to use `<cflocation>` after the delete operation—something like this:

```
<cfif structKeyExists(url, "delete")>
    <cfset directorToDie = entityLoadByPk("director", url.delete)>
    <cfset entityDelete(directorToDie)>
    <cflocation url="index.cfm" addToken="false">
</cfif>
```

This will fix the problem since `<cflocation>` will end the request and then tell Hibernate to go ahead and finish its work. It also has the benefit of removing the `delete` variable from the query string. This works, but let's look at a more specific fix.

The new `ormFlush()` function tells Hibernate to flush, or "catch up," the requests made so far. With this function added after the delete operation, the list operation performed later in the listing will return the correct values. Here is the correct code block:

```
<cfif structKeyExists(url, "delete")>
    <cfset directorToDie = entityLoadByPk("director", url.delete)>
    <cfset entityDelete(directorToDie)>
    <cfset ormFlush()>
</cfif>
```

You can find this corrected code in the Zip file as `index2.cfm`. Copy this file over the existing `index.cfm` file, and everything should work as expected.

Working with Relationships

When we began the discussion of persistent entities, we mentioned that the `cfproperty` tag is critical to defining how an entity is used in ColdFusion and how Hibernate persists the data in the database. We mentioned that there are three main types of properties: primary keys, columns, and relationship definers. Relationships are a way to create connections between entities. Hibernate has four types of relationships:

- **One to many.** In a one-to-many relationship, a single entity is related to multiple other entities. A person has multiple jobs on a resume. A building has many floors.
- **Many to one.** In a many-to-one relationship, multiple entities are related to one other entity. Multiple pets belong to an owner. Multiple books rest on a shelf.
- **Many to many.** In a many-to-many relationship, many entities are related to multiple other items. Consider blog entries and categories. Typically, a blog entry belongs to multiple categories. Therefore, you can say both that entries have multiple categories, and categories have multiple entries. These types of relationships are normally

handled with a join table. You will see how easy Hibernate makes creating this type of relationship.

- **One to one.** One-to-one relationships are less common than the other types. In a one-to-one relationship, there is exactly one entity related to one other entity. For example, a user entity may relate exclusively to a profile entity.

Working with each of these relationships means making use of the `cfproperty` tag in a specific manner. Using these relationships will also add methods to our component. If you remember, we were given `get` and `set` methods to easily read and write information to an entity. Relationships expand on this with additional methods. We will look at examples of all these types of relationships and ways that you can use them in your own applications.

One-to-Many and Many-to-One Relationships

In our first example, we will look at both the one-to-many relationship and many-to-one relationship. As you can guess, these two are intimately related. It is common for an entity with a one-to-many relationship to be connected to an entity that has a many-to-one relationship back to it.

Our application is going to create an entity for films. Films have several properties, such as the movie title and date released. They also have expenses. Each (one) film is related to (many) expenses. On the flip side, (many) expenses are related to a (one) film. Let's look at how we can define these relationships with persistent components. (To make this example work, be sure to copy the `Application.cfc` file in the `38/app4` folder from the Zip file you downloaded for this book.) Listing 38.15 defines our `film` entity.

Listing 38.15 `app4/film.cfc?film` Entity

```
<cfcomponent persistent="true" table="films">

    <cfproperty name="id" column="filmid" fieldType="id" generator="increment">
    <cfproperty name="title" column="movietitle" ormtype="string">
    <cfproperty name="pitch" column="pitchtext" ormtype="string">
    <cfproperty name="budget" column="amountbudgeted" ormtype="float">
    <cfproperty name="summary" ormtype="text">
    <cfproperty name="image" column="imagename" ormtype="string">
    <cfproperty name="releasedate" column="dateintheaters" ormtype="date">

    <cfproperty name="expenses" fieldType="one-to-many" cfc="expense"
fkcolumn="filmid" inverse="true">

</cfcomponent>
```

A couple of things are going on here that you should be aware of. First note that, as with the `director` entity before, we named our file differently than the database table. Because of this, we have to specify the table in the `cfcomponent` tag. For purely personal, ascetic reasons, I also renamed the columns. Note that each property (except `summary` and `expenses`) has a `column` attribute. Because Hibernate can create an alias between the name you want and the column name, we don't have to be stuck with what could be considered poor naming practices. Obviously, this is a decision you may not agree with, but the point is that you don't have to be a slave to the database's naming scheme.

In general, everything is simple, but note the final `cfproperty`: `expenses`. Because this is not a simple column, we have to specify the field type. In this case, the value is one to many. We then need to provide Hibernate with additional information. First we tell it which other entity will be linked to this property. Next we tell Hibernate which column in the `expenses` table links back to the `film` entity.

The final property, `inverse`, simply tells Hibernate which entity will be managing the relationship. For now, don't be too concerned with this, but note that in a pair of CFCs linked by one-to-many and many-to-one relationships, you will use `inverse="true"` on the one-to-many side as we have here with the `film` entity. In this case, the value is `filmid`.

So far, so good. Now let's look at the `expense` entity, in Listing 38.16.

Listing 38.16 `app4/expense.cfc`—expense Entity

```
<cfcomponent persistent="true" table="expenses">

    <cfproperty name="id" column="expenseid" fieldType="id" generator="increment">
    <cfproperty name="amount" column="expenseamount" ormtype="float">
    <cfproperty name="description" ormtype="text">
    <cfproperty name="date" column="expensedate" ormtype="date">

    <cfproperty name="film" fieldtype="many-to-one" cfc="film" fkcolumn="filmid">

</cfcomponent>
```

This component is a bit simpler. The entity consists of one primary key and three simple columns. The last property is `many-to-one`. This creates the inverse of the relationship that `film` defined. In the many-to-one relationship, the `fkcolumn` attribute refers to the column in the *current* table, in this case `expenses`.

Now let's look at how this relationship is exposed in your ColdFusion code, in Listing 38.17.

Listing 38.17 `app4/index.cfm`—Film and Expense List

```
<!---
Module:         index.cfm
Author:         Raymond Camden
Function:       Film/Expense report
--->

<cfset films = entityLoad("film", {}, "title asc")>

<h1>Film Report</h1>

<table border="1">
    <tr>
        <th>Film</th><th>Release</th><th>Expenses</th>
    </tr>
```

Listing 38.17 (continued)

```
        <cfloop index="film" array="#films#">
        <cfoutput>
        <tr>
           <td>#film.getTitle()#<br/><i>#film.getPitch()#</i></td>
           <td>#dateFormat(film.getReleaseDate())#</td>
           <td>
           <cfset expenses = film.getExpenses()>
           <cfloop index="expense" array="#expenses#">
              #expense.getDescription()# (#dollarFormat(expense.getAmount())#)<br/>
           </cfloop>
           </td>
        </tr>
        </cfoutput>
        </cfloop>
    </table>
```

Listing 38.17 is a simple film report. It begins by grabbing a sorted list of films. That part isn't new. The report contains the title, pitch, and expenses. For the most part, the method calls, such as `getReleaseDate()`, are like those you've seen before. But `getExpenses()` is different. This call returns an array of values: in our example, each expense related to the film. Think about how you would accomplish this before ORM. You would need to write one SQL call to get your film data and a second call to get a list of expenses. With ColdFusion 9 and ORM, we simply work with one `film` object. Figure 38.7 shows a sample report.

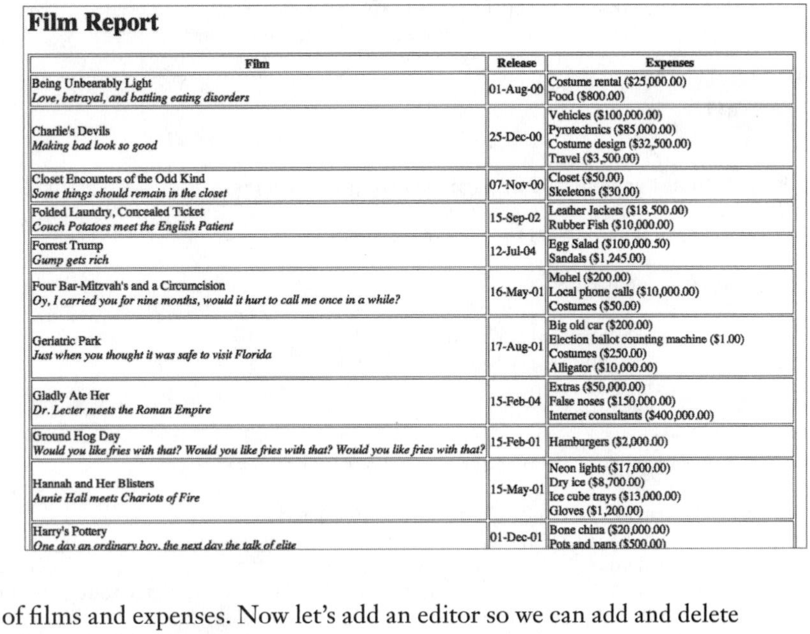

Figure 38.7

Film Report showing embedded expenses.

Film Report

Film	Release	Expenses
Being Unbearably Light *Love, betrayal, and battling eating disorders*	01-Aug-00	Costume rental ($25,000.00) Food ($800.00)
Charlie's Devils *Making bad look so good*	25-Dec-00	Vehicles ($100,000.00) Pyrotechnics ($85,000.00) Costume design ($32,500.00) Travel ($3,500.00)
Closet Encounters of the Odd Kind *Some things should remain in the closet*	07-Nov-00	Closet ($50.00) Skeletons ($30.00)
Folded Laundry, Concealed Ticket *Couch Potatoes meet the English Patient*	15-Sep-02	Leather Jackets ($18,500.00) Rubber Fish ($10,000.00)
Forrest Trump *Gump gets rich*	12-Jul-04	Egg Salad ($100,000.50) Sandals ($1,245.00)
Four Bar-Mitzvah's and a Circumcision *Oy, I carried you for nine months, would it hurt to call me once in a while?*	16-May-01	Mohel ($200.00) Local phone calls ($10,000.00) Costumes ($50.00)
Geriatric Park *Just when you thought it was safe to visit Florida*	17-Aug-01	Big old car ($200.00) Election ballot counting machine ($1.00) Costumes ($250.00) Alligator ($10,000.00)
Gladly Ate Her *Dr. Lecter meets the Roman Empire*	15-Feb-04	Extras ($50,000.00) False noses ($150,000.00) Internet consultants ($400,000.00)
Ground Hog Day *Would you like fries with that? Would you like fries with that? Would you like fries with that?*	15-Feb-01	Hamburgers ($2,000.00)
Hannah and Her Blisters *Annie Hall meets Chariots of Fire*	15-May-01	Neon lights ($17,000.00) Dry ice ($8,700.00) Ice cube trays ($13,000.00) Gloves ($1,200.00)
Harry's Pottery *One day an ordinary boy, the next day the talk of elite*	01-Dec-01	Bone china ($20,000.00) Pots and pans ($500.00)

We have a simple list of films and expenses. Now let's add an editor so we can add and delete expenses for a film, as shown in Listing 38.18.

NOTE

This template uses a `url` variable, `filmid`, passed to it. If you copy `ows/38/app4/index2.cfm` from the CD, you will see a modified version of Listing 38.17 that links to the expense editor.

Listing 38.18 `app4/expense_edit.cfm`—Expense Editor

```
<!---
Module:         expense_edit.cfm
Author:         Raymond Camden
Function:       Allows for expense editing (use with index2.cfm)
--->

<cfset film = entityLoadByPk("film", url.filmid)>

<cfif structKeyExists(form, "addexpense")>
    <cfif len(form.description) and isNumeric(form.amount)>
        <cfset expense = entityNew("expense")>
        <cfset expense.setDescription(form.description)>
        <cfset expense.setAmount(form.amount)>
        <cfset expense.setDate(now())>
        <cfset expense.setFilm(film)>
        <cfset entitySave(expense)>
        <cfset film.addExpenses(expense)>
        <cfset entitySave(film)>
    </cfif>
</cfif>
<cfif structKeyExists(url, "delete")>
    <cfset expense = entityLoadByPk("expense", url.delete)>
    <cfset entityDelete(expense)>
    <cfset ormFlush()>
</cfif>

<cfoutput>
<h1>Edit Expenses for Film: #film.getTitle()#</h1>

<cfset expenses = film.getExpenses()>

<table border="1">
    <tr>
        <th>Description</th>
        <th>Amount</th>
        <th>Date</th>
        <td> </td>
    </tr>
    <cfloop index="expense" array="#expenses#">
    <tr>
       <td>#expense.getDescription()#</td>
       <td>#dollarFormat(expense.getAmount())#</td>
       <td>#dateFormat(expense.getDate())#</td>
       <td><a href="expense_edit.cfm?filmid=#url.filmid#&delete=#expense.
getId()#">Delete</a></td>
    </tr>
    </cfloop>
</table>
```

Listing 38.18 (continued)

```
<h2>Add New Expense</h2>

<form action="#cgi.script_name#?filmid=#url.filmid#" method="post">
Description: <input type="text" name="description" maxlength="100"><br/>
Amount: <input type="text" name="amount" maxlength="10" size="10"><br/>
<input type="submit" name="addexpense" value="Add">
</form>

</cfoutput>
```

We have a lot going on here, so let's tackle it slowly. Like most self-posting forms, a lot of logic resides on top of the template, and that's the most critical part of this code listing anyway, so it's not such a big deal.

The template allows the addition and deletion of expenses. The two `<cfif>` blocks on top refer to both of those actions. The first block handles additions. Notice that we create a new `expense` entity. This is then populated with the description and amount. The date is set to `now`. (A better form would allow for dates to be specified as well.)

What is different about this entity is that it belongs to a film. To specify that, we use the `setFilm()` method. Since this is a bidirectional relationship (films have expenses, and expenses have a film), we also add the expense to the film. Both entities are persisted.

The `delete` method is simpler. First we load the expense, then we pass it to `entityDelete()`, and then we perform a flush. This process ensures that the expense report later shows the right data.

Many-to-Many Relationship

As the name implies, in a many-to-many relationship, we are saying that multiple entities relate to multiple other entities. Blog entries and categories provide an example. A blog typically has multiple entries. A blog also has multiple categories. One individual entry can be in multiple categories. This type of relationship is typically set up with a join table, which is a table that links one record of data (blog entry) to another (category). Normally working with these types of relationships is a bit of a chore. You have to ensure that any change is correctly persisted in the join table. ColdFusion 9 and ORM make the job much simpler.

At Orange Whip Studios, each film can have multiple directors and almost always has multiple actors: two perfect examples of many-to-many relationships. Listing 38.19 is the new version of our `film` entity.

Listing 38.19 `app5/film.cfc`—`film` Entity

```
<cfcomponent persistent="true" table="films">

    <cfproperty name="id" column="filmid" fieldType="id" generator="increment">
    <cfproperty name="title" column="movietitle" ormtype="string">
    <cfproperty name="pitch" column="pitchtext" ormtype="string">
    <cfproperty name="budget" column="amountbudgeted" ormtype="float">
    <cfproperty name="summary" ormtype="text">
    <cfproperty name="image" column="imagename" ormtype="string">
```

Listing 38.19 (continued)

```
    <cfproperty name="releasedate" column="dateintheaters" ormtype="date">

    <cfproperty name="expenses" fieldType="one-to-many" cfc="expense"
fkcolumn="filmid" inverse="true">

    <cfproperty name="actors" fieldType="many-to-many" cfc="actor"
    linktable="filmsactors" fkcolumn="filmid" inversejoincolumn="actorid"
singularname="actor">

    <cfproperty name="directors" fieldType="many-to-many" cfc="director"
    linktable="filmsdirectors" fkcolumn="filmid" inversejoincolumn="directorid"
singularname="director">

</cfcomponent>
```

The first set of `cfproperty` tags are no different than in the previous version. But look at the last two properties: `actors` and `directors`. As with `expenses`, we have to tell ORM that this is a special type of property: a many-to-many property. For each property we then provide detail about the relationship. First, we specify that both are related to a particular CFC. Second, we specify the link table that stores the records that link both sides. Third, we define a foreign key column; this is the column in the link table that refers to the film. The fourth argument, `inversejoincolumn`, is the column that refers to the entity we are linked to. Last, we specify the `singularname` argument, which is an optional setting; when ColdFusion 9 generates utility methods for our relationship, we can provide a clue about how to name methods that work with single instances. So going back to our blog example, defining `category` as the singular of `categories` allows us to create nicer method names (as you will see later).

The `director` CFC was defined earlier and won't change (be sure to copy it, and all the rest of the files, from the Zip file), but the `actor` CFC is new. Listing 38.20 shows it.

Listing 38.20 `app5/actor.cfc`?`actor` Entity

```
<cfcomponent persistent="true" table="actors">

    <cfproperty name="actorid" fieldType="id" generator="increment">
    <cfproperty name="firstname" column="namefirst" ormtype="string">
    <cfproperty name="lastname" column="namelast" ormtype="string">
    <cfproperty name="age" ormtype="integer">

</cfcomponent>
```

For the most part, there isn't anything new here, but here's something really nice: For some reason, the database table for `actors` prefers `namefirst` instead of `firstname` as for `directors`. That doesn't make sense. We can fix this problem here by using a proper name and simply telling Hibernate what the real column is. Can you imagine how frustrating this application would be without this change? Every time you worked with an actor or director, you would have to remember which style to use.

NOTE

The `actors` table in the OWS database includes a few other columns as well. To keep things simple, most of the entities in this chapter reference only a few of the columns. You can add the missing columns if you want or simply ignore them.

Now that we've defined our components (again, remember to copy all the files from the Zip file), we can update the earlier report to add actors and directors, as shown in Listing 38.21.

Listing 38.21 `app5/index.cfm`—Film Report Including Actors, Directors, and Expenses

```
<!---
Module:        index.cfm
Author:        Raymond Camden
Function:      Film report
--->

<cfset films = entityLoad("film", {}, "title asc")>

<h1>Film Report</h1>

<table border="1">
    <tr>
       <th>Film</th><th>Release</th><th>Directors</th><th>Actors</th><th>Expenses</
th>
    </tr>
    <cfloop index="film" array="#films#">
    <cfoutput>
    <tr>
       <td><a href="edit.cfm?filmid=#film.getId()#">#film.getTitle()#</a><br/>
       <i>#film.getPitch()#</i></td>
       <td>#dateFormat(film.getReleaseDate())#</td>
       <td>
       <cfset directors = film.getDirectors()>
       <cfloop index="director" array="#directors#">
           #director.getFirstName()# #director.getLastName()#<br/>
       </cfloop>
       </td>
       <td>
       <cfset actors = film.getActors()>
       <cfloop index="actor" array="#actors#">
           #actor.getFirstName()# #actor.getLastName()#<br/>
       </cfloop>
       </td>
       <td>
       <cfset expenses = film.getExpenses()>
       <cfloop index="expense" array="#expenses#">
           #expense.getDescription()# (#dollarFormat(expense.getAmount())#)<br/>
       </cfloop>
       </td>
    </tr>
    </cfoutput>
    </cfloop>
</table>
```

The main differences between this listing and Listing 38.17 are in the two new columns. However, notice that we display actors and directors much like expenses. In both cases, we can have multiple sets of related data, but the API is the same, whether we use `getExpenses()`or `getActors()` or `getDirectors()`.

Now let's look at an editor for our film data. Listing 38.22 is a somewhat complex listing, but it will make sense shortly.

Listing 38.22 `app5/edit.cfm`—Film Editor for Actors, Directors, and Expenses

```
<!---
Module:         expense_edit.cfm
Author:         Raymond Camden
Function:       Allows for expense editing (use with index2.cfm)
--->

<cfset film = entityLoadByPk("film", url.filmid)>

<!--- Used to remember which tab was selected --->
<cfset tab = "actors">

<!--- Handles add/deletes for expenses --->
<cfif structKeyExists(form, "addexpense")>
    <cfif len(form.description) and isNumeric(form.amount)>
        <cfset expense = entityNew("expense")>
        <cfset expense.setDescription(form.description)>
        <cfset expense.setAmount(form.amount)>
        <cfset expense.setDate(now())>
        <cfset expense.setFilm(film)>
        <cfset entitySave(expense)>
        <cfset film.addExpenses(expense)>
        <cfset entitySave(film)>
    </cfif>
    <cfset tab = "expenses">
</cfif>
<cfif structKeyExists(url, "deleteexpense")>
    <cfset expense = entityLoadByPk("expense", url.deleteexpense)>
    <cfset entityDelete(expense)>
    <cfset ormFlush()>
    <cfset tab = "expenses">
</cfif>

<!--- Handles updates for actors --->
<cfif structKeyExists(form, "selectactors")>
    <!--- value is a multi select control, could be null --->
    <cfparam name="form.actors" default="">

    <!--- first remove the actors --->
    <cfset actors = film.getActors()>
    <cfloop index="x" from="#arrayLen(actors)#" to="1" step="-1">
       <cfset film.removeActor(actors[x])>
    </cfloop>
    <!--- now add them - form.actors is a list of IDs --->
    <cfloop index="actorid" list="#form.actors#">
       <cfset actor = entityLoadByPk("actor", actorid)>
       <cfset film.addActor(actor)>
    </cfloop>
    <cfset ormFlush()>
    <cfset tab = "actors">
</cfif>
```

Listing 38.22 (continued)

```
<!--- Handles updates for directors --->
<cfif structKeyExists(form, "selectdirectors")>
   <!--- value is a multi select control, could be null --->
   <cfparam name="form.directors" default="">

   <!--- first remove the directors --->
   <cfset directors = film.getDirectors()>
   <cfloop index="x" from="#arrayLen(directors)#" to="1" step="-1">
      <cfset film.removeDirector(directors[x])>
   </cfloop>
   <!--- now add them - form.actors is a list of IDs --->
   <cfloop index="directorid" list="#form.directors#">
      <cfset director = entityLoadByPk("director", directorid)>
      <cfset film.addDirector(director)>
   </cfloop>
   <cfset ormFlush()>
   <cfset tab = "directors">
</cfif>

<cfoutput>
<h1>Edit Film: #film.getTitle()#</h1>
</cfoutput>

<cflayout type="tab">

   <cflayoutarea title="Actors" selected="#tab is 'actors'#">

   <cfset allActors = entityLoad("actor",{},  "lastname asc")>

   <cfoutput>
   <form action="#cgi.script_name#?filmid=#url.filmid#" method="post">
   <select name="actors" multiple size="20">
   <cfloop index="actor" array="#allActors#">
      <option value="#actor.getActorId()#" <cfif film.hasActor(actor)>selected</
cfif>>
      #actor.getLastName()#, #actor.getFirstName()#</option>
   </cfloop>
   </select><br/>
   <input type="submit" name="selectactors" value="Select Actors">
   </form>
   </cfoutput>

   </cflayoutarea>

   <cflayoutarea title="Directors" selected="#tab is 'directors'#">

   <cfset allDirectors = entityLoad("director",{},  "lastname asc")>

   <cfoutput>
   <form action="#cgi.script_name#?filmid=#url.filmid#" method="post">
   <select name="directors" multiple size="20">
   <cfloop index="director" array="#allDirectors#">
      <option value="#director.getDirectorId()#" <cfif film.
hasDirector(director)>selected</cfif>>
      #director.getLastName()#, #director.getFirstName()#</option>
   </cfloop>
   </select><br/>
```

Listing 38.22 (continued)

```
        <input type="submit" name="selectdirectors" value="Select Directors">
        </form>
        </cfoutput>

        </cflayoutarea>

        <cflayoutarea title="Expenses" selected="#tab is 'expenses'#">

        <cfset expenses = film.getExpenses()>

        <cfoutput>
        <table border="1">
            <tr>
                <th>Description</th>
                <th>Amount</th>
                <th>Date</th>
                <td> </td>
            </tr>
            <cfloop index="expense" array="#expenses#">
            <tr>
               <td>#expense.getDescription()#</td>
               <td>#dollarFormat(expense.getAmount())#</td>
               <td>#dateFormat(expense.getDate())#</td>
               <td><a href="edit.cfm?filmid=#url.filmid#&deleteexpense=#expense.
    getId()#">Delete</a></td>
            </tr>
            </cfloop>
        </table>

        <h2>Add New Expense</h2>

        <form action="#cgi.script_name#?filmid=#url.filmid#" method="post">
        Description: <input type="text" name="description" maxlength="100"><br/>
        Amount: <input type="text" name="amount" maxlength="10" size="10"><br/>
        <input type="submit" name="addexpense" value="Add">
        </form>
        </cfoutput>

        </cflayoutarea>

    </cflayout>
```

Wow, that's a lot. Before going any further, take a look at Figure 38.8. This is a screen shot of the application created in Listing 38.22.

As you can see in Figure 38.8, the code creates a tab-based interface, separating the actor, director, and expense editing onto different tabs. This interface is created using the `<cflayout>` tag (see Chapter 30, "Advanced ColdFusion-Powered Ajax"). Since the expense editing code hasn't changed, we won't discuss it. Also, the actor and director code is exactly same (except for the names of course), so we will focus on the actor code for now. As with the previous version of this code (Listing 38.18), the form performs all its handling at the top and then displays the current data at the bottom. Therefore, let's start by looking at the first `<cflayoutarea>` block.

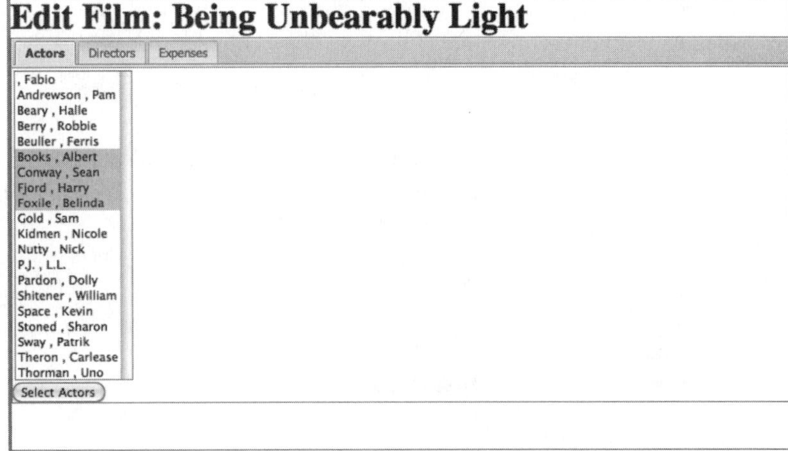

Figure 38.8

The film editor uses tabs to separate multiple editing functions.

Our form is simple. We want to use a simple HTML select box with the `multiple` option. We get all the actors using the `entityLoad()` function. Once we have that, it is a simple matter to loop over them. However, notice how we handle selection of the options. We use the `hasActor()` method on the `film` entity. This was generated for us by ColdFusion based on the fact that the relationship can point to multiple actors. The `hasActor()` method will return `true` if the actor is associated in that relationship. Think about the amount of SQL and other code you would normally have to write to handle this. With ORM, it's done for you.

Moving back to the top of the script, the logic to handle the saving of `actor` entities begins on line 34. To make the logic of removing existing `actor` entities and adding new ones easier, we simply remove *all* the `actor` instances. Because this is an array, we step through it backward. That ensures that removing an item doesn't create a bad step through the array. After removing all the `actor` entities, we then loop through the selected `actor` entities and add them one at a time.

And that's it. Completely. Not a line of SQL in sight! And as noted earlier, the logic for editing directors is exactly the same, so there is no need to go into detail for those blocks.

One-to-One Relationship

The final type of relationship, one to one, is a bit less common than the others. It defines a relationship in which exactly one row in one database table maps to exactly one row in another database table. Normally, such related data is kept in the same table, but you can imagine splitting up fields if a table becomes too large. Also, a table may have a set of fields that has grown complex enough to merit its own storage even though it is intimately related to other fields. While you might not run into one-to-one relationships often, when you do, ColdFusion and ORM handle them well and allow you to define entities that make use of such relations.

For our example, we will be creating a completely new table in the database. By default, ColdFusion and Hibernate will *not* change the structure of your database. That is very much a good thing. But there are certainly times when automatic database updating can be handy, such as when you're developing a new site. We will be adding an entity called `taxinfo` that represents tax-related information as it relates to people. This won't be a complete tax profile, but simply a few additional properties. We will group these properties within our `taxinfo` entity and create a one-to-one relationship with our contacts.

Our first listing will be the `Application.cfc` file. We haven't displayed this file for our previous listings as they didn't include anything terribly crucial. In this case, though, we've made some important changes, as you can see in Listing 38.23.

Listing 38.23 `app6/Application.cfc`—Application File

```
<cfcomponent>

    <cfset this.name = "ows38_app6">
    <cfset this.datasource = "ows">
    <cfset this.ormenabled = true>

    <cfset this.ormsettings = { dbcreate="update", dialect="Derby" }>

</cfcomponent>
```

The `name`, `datasource`, and `ormEnabled` settings are not new. The `ormsettings` structure is critical, though. First, note the `dbcreate` key. By setting it to `update`, we've told ColdFusion and Hibernate that they have permission to make changes to our database. This will be required so a table can be created for our new entity, `taxIifo`.

The second setting, `dialect`, tells Hibernate what type of database is being used. We don't always need this value, but in this case it helps Hibernate by providing some more information about the data.

Now let's look at the first of our entities, `contact.cfc`, in Listing 38.24.

Listing 38.24 `app6/contact.cfc`—`contact` Entity

```
<cfcomponent persistent="true" table="contacts">

    <cfproperty name="contactid" fieldType="id" generator="increment"
type="numeric">
    <cfproperty name="firstname" ormtype="string">
    <cfproperty name="lastname" ormtype="string">
    <cfproperty name="email" ormtype="string">

    <cfproperty name="taxinfo" fieldtype="one-to-one" cfc="taxinfo"
mappedBy="contact">

</cfcomponent>
```

Listing 38.24 contains our `contact` entity, which for the most part isn't new, but take note of the last property for `taxinfo`. We've defined our `fieldtype` as one to one. The CFC attribute obviously refers to the component that will represent the other side of the relationship. The `mappedBy` attribute tells Hibernate that `contact` (the current entity) is the "master" of the relationship. This means the actual link that connects the two components will be defined in the `TaxInfo` component. Listing 38.25 shows this component.

Listing 38.25 `app6/taxinfo.cfc`?TaxInfo Entity

```
<cfcomponent persistent="true">

    <cfproperty name="taxinfoid" fieldType="id" generator="increment"
type="numeric">
    <cfproperty name="ssn" ormtype="string">
    <cfproperty name="legaluscitizen" ormtype="boolean">
    <cfproperty name="numberofdependants" ormtype="integer">
    <cfproperty name="contact" fieldtype="one-to-one" cfc="contact"
fkcolumn="contactid">

</cfcomponent>
```

As before, we will focus only on what's new: in this case, the final `cfproperty`. For the most part, it is similar to its opposite in `contact.cfc`, but notice the final attribute. The `fkcolumn` attribute here refers to the fact that the `taxinfo` table will have a `contactid` column that links to the contacts table.

Now that we've defined our entities, let's look at a simple editor. Listing 38.26 demonstrates an index page that provides links to edit our contacts.

Listing 38.26 `app6/index.cfm`—Contact List

```
<cfset contacts = entityLoad("contact", {}, "lastname,firstname")>

<h2>Contacts</h2>

<table border="1" width="100%">
    <tr>
        <th>Name</th><th>Email</th><td></td>
    </tr>
    <cfloop index="contact" array="#contacts#">
    <cfoutput>
    <tr>
       <td>#contact.getLastName()#, #contact.getFirstName()#</td>
       <td><a href="mailto:#contact.getEmail()#">#contact.getEmail()#</a></td>
       <td><a href="edit.cfm?id=#contact.getContactId()#">Edit</a></td>
    </tr>
    </cfoutput>
    </cfloop>
</table>
```

For the most part, this listing follows the same flow we've seen in the earlier examples. We grab a list of contacts and display the list in a table. Each row contains an edit link, which links to the code in Listing 38.27.

Listing 38.27 `app6/edit.cfm`—Contact Editor

```
<cfparam name="url.id" default="">

<cfset contact = entityLoadByPk("contact", url.id)>
<cfparam name="form.firstname" default="#contact.getFirstName()#">
<cfparam name="form.lastname" default="#contact.getLastName()#">
<cfparam name="form.email" default="#contact.getEmail()#">
```

Listing 38.27 (continued)

```
<!--- Handle contacts w/o tax info --->
<cfif contact.hasTaxInfo()>
    <cfset taxInfo = contact.getTaxInfo()>
    <cfparam name="form.ssn" default="#taxInfo.getSSN()#">
    <cfparam name="form.legaluscitizen" default="#taxInfo.getLegalUSCitizen()#">
    <cfparam name="form.numberofdependants" default="#taxInfo.
getNumberOfDependants()#">
<cfelse>
    <cfset taxInfo = entityNew("taxInfo")>
    <cfparam name="form.ssn" default="">
    <cfparam name="form.legaluscitizen" default="">
    <cfparam name="form.numberofdependants" default="">
</cfif>

<cfif structKeyExists(form, "save")>
    <!--- update contact --->
    <cfset contact.setFirstName(form.firstname)>
    <cfset contact.setLastName(form.lastname)>
    <cfset contact.setEmail(form.email)>

    <!--- update taxinfo --->
    <cfset taxInfo.setSSN(form.ssn)>
    <cfset taxInfo.setLegalUSCitizen(form.legaluscitizen)>
    <cfset taxInfo.setNumberOfDependants(val(form.numberofdependants))>
    <cfset taxInfo.setContact(contact)>
    <cfset entitySave(taxInfo)>

    <cfset contact.setTaxInfo(taxInfo)>
    <cfset entitySave(contact)>

    <cflocation url="index.cfm" addToken="false">
</cfif>


<cfoutput>
<form action="edit.cfm?id=#url.id#" method="post">

<h2>Edit Contact - Personal Info</h2>

<table>
    <tr>
        <td>First Name:</td>
        <td><input type="text" name="firstname" value="#form.firstname#"></td>
    </tr>
    <tr>
        <td>Last Name:</td>
        <td><input type="text" name="lastname" value="#form.lastname#"></td>
    </tr>
    <tr>
        <td>Email:</td>
        <td><input type="text" name="email" value="#form.email#"></td>
    </tr>

</table>
```

Listing 38.27 (continued)

```
<h2>Edit Contact - Tax Info</h2>

<table>

    <tr>
        <td>SSN:</td>
        <td><input type="text" name="ssn" value="#form.ssn#" maxlength="10"
size="10"></td>
    </tr>
    <tr>
       <td>Legal US Citizen?</td>
       <td>
       <select name="legaluscitizen">
       <option value="yes"
       <cfif form.legaluscitizen is "" or form.legaluscitizen is true>selected</
cfif>>Yes</option>
       <option value="no"
       <cfif form.legaluscitizen neq "" and  not form.legaluscitizen>selected</
cfif>>No</option>
       </select>
       </td>
    </tr>
    <tr>
        <td>Number of Dependants:</td>
        <td><input type="text" name="numberofdependants" value="#form.
numberofdependants#" maxlength="2" size="2"></td>
    </tr>

</table>

<input type="submit" name="save" value="Save">

</form>
</cfoutput>
```

As before, the editor uses a top-level handler for both defaulting the data and handling the form submission. The actual form is at the bottom and for the most part isn't very interesting. It visually separates the tax information from the other contact fields, but that isn't strictly required. Make note of how we check to see if tax information for the contact exists:

```
<cfif contact.hasTaxInfo()>
```

If the contact has a related record in the `taxinfo` table, this line will return `true`, and we can then grab it using the `getTaxInfo()` method of the `contact` object. Skip down to the form processing, and notice that we work with two entities. First the `taxinfo` object (which will either be the existing related entity or a new one) is updated with the values from the form. This is then saved. To ensure that we properly link the `taxinfo` entity to `contact`, we run the following line:

```
<cfset contact.setTaxInfo(taxInfo)>
```

For existing contacts, this code won't do anything, but for a contact who never had a corresponding record, this code will ensure that the row in the `taxinfo` table is properly linked to the contact record.

Enhancing Your Entities

So far, all the entities we've worked on have been fairly simple. Each was made up of just properties. Some of these properties were a bit complex (relationships typically are), but for the most part, our components simply had properties and nothing more. However, we need not stop there. We can add any other method we want to these components. This is a great way to add functionality.

Consider the enhanced contact component defined in Listing 38.28.

Listing 38.28 app6/contact2.cfc—Enhanced Contact Entity

```
<cfcomponent persistent="true" table="contacts">

    <cfproperty name="contactid" fieldType="id" generator="increment" type="numeric">
    <cfproperty name="firstname" ormtype="string">
    <cfproperty name="lastname" ormtype="string">
    <cfproperty name="email" ormtype="string">

    <cfproperty name="taxinfo" fieldtype="one-to-one" cfc="taxinfo"
mappedBy="contact">

    <cffunction name="getName" returnType="string">
        <cfreturn trim(getLastName()) & ", " & trim(getFirstName())>
    </cffunction>

</cfcomponent>
```

The first portion of this listing is no different than Listing 38.24, but notice the new function at the end. The `getName()` method handles a simple need we have with names: presenting them in "last comma first" format. We also added a trim here since the database had some white space around the names. Typically formatting issues aren't handled in components, but that's a discussion for later. In the meantime, this is a practical enhancement to the component that will be very useful.

Before going further, either copy `contact2.cfc` over the existing `contact.cfc` file or simply copy in this function. To use this enhancement, we can update the original listing page. We can change the following:

```
<td>#contact.getLastName()#, #contact.getFirstName()#</td>
```

to this much simpler code:

```
<td>#contact.getName()#</td>
```

You can see an example of this in the `index2.cfm` file located in the Zip file you downloaded from the book's Web site. This is only a simple example, but it shows that our components can be much more than simple "table mirrors"; they can have additional functionality and features based on whatever your business needs require.

Searching with ORM

We've discussed how you can use ORM to load data without writing SQL. The `entityLoad()` function allows you to both load and sort data. It also allows filtering. What it does not provide, though, is a search capability. So while `entityLoad` can be used to find all entities with a particular value—for instance, `name="Raymond"`—it cannot search for people with a name *like* `"Raymond"`. For searches that require this type of functionality, we can use the `ormExecuteQuery` function. This function uses a powerful feature called Hibernate Query Language (HQL). As you can guess, this is a bit like SQL. Some HQL statements will look a *lot* like SQL in fact. But as you will see, we can do some very powerful things with HQL that would be much more difficult with SQL.

Listing 38.29 provides a trivial example.

Listing 38.29 `app7/search1.cfm`—First HQL Example

```
<!---
Module:          search1.cfm
Author:          Raymond Camden
Function:        Get all directors
--->

<cfset directors = ormExecuteQuery("from director")>

<cfdump var="#directors#">
```

NOTE

Be sure to copy the `Application.cfc` and `director.cfc` files from the Zip file. They aren't listed here as they aren't new material.

Listing 38.29 demonstrates the simplest HQL statement possible, specifically the `from director` argument passed to `ormExecuteQuery`. It looks like SQL, right? But where is the `select` portion? Remember that Hibernate already knows what columns exist in the database. Because of this, you don't really need to specify which columns you want, right? This example doesn't do any ordering or filtering, so by itself, the statement equates to `select * from director`. However, unlike a typical query, this will return entities. Figure 38.9 shows the result, an array of entities.

Figure 38.9

The result of searching for all directors.

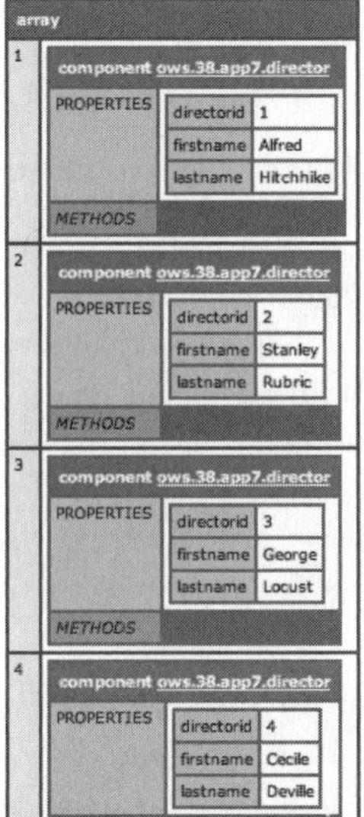

A search that doesn't actually search, isn't very useful. Listing 38.30 demonstrates how we can make this application dynamic.

Listing 38.30 `app7/search2.cfm`—Example of Searching with HQL

```
<!---
Module:         search2.cfm
Author:         Raymond Camden
Function:       Search directors
--->

<cfparam name="form.search" default="">

<cfoutput>
<form action="search2.cfm" method="post">
<input type="text" name="search" value="#form.search#">
<input type="submit" value="Search">
</form>
</cfoutput>

<cfif len(form.search)>
    <cfset directors =
    ormExecuteQuery("from director where
                    firstname like '%#form.search#%' or lastname like '%#form.
search#%'")>

    <cfdump var="#directors#">
</cfif>
```

Listing 38.30 demonstrates a simple search form. The form on top posts back to itself one field, `search`. If `form.search` contains a value, we perform the query. Notice that we've added a `where` clause. As in a typical SQL clause, we can add as many conditional statements as we want. In this case, we want to search against both the `firstname` and `lastname` fields.

NOTE

Derby is case sensitive for `like` searches.

When the application is executed, Hibernate will translate the HQL into a query that matches the table and columns in your database. If we had mapped `firstname` to some other column (`fstNme`, for example), our HQL would work just fine.

You may have noticed that HQL in the previous example included the dynamic portions directly within the string. You've probably read that this approach is a bad idea in typical queries, and that you should use the `<cfqueryparam>` tag used instead. The `<cfqueryparam>` tag helps provide security and gives a small performance boost to your dynamic queries. This feature is known as *bound parameters*. Does HQL support this? Absolutely. Listing 38.31 modifies our previous example to make use of bound parameters.

Listing 38.31 `app7/search3.cfm`—Using Bound Parameters

```
<!---
Module:        search3.cfm
Author:        Raymond Camden
Function:      Search directors
--->

<cfparam name="form.search" default="">

<cfoutput>
<form action="search3.cfm" method="post">
<input type="text" name="search" value="#form.search#">
<input type="submit" value="Search">
</form>
</cfoutput>

<cfif len(form.search)>
    <cfset term = "%" & form.search & "%">
    <cfset directors =
    ormExecuteQuery("from director where
                     firstname like ? or lastname like ?",
                     [term,term])>

    <cfdump var="#directors#">
</cfif>
```

The main difference between this listing and Listing 38.31 is the use of bound parameters. You can apply bound parameters in two ways in HQL. Listing 38.31 demonstrates one way, using question marks. Notice that the string has two question marks. These characters represent the bound parameters. To pass the actual values for those question marks, we use an array in the second parameter for `ormExecuteQuery()`. Our array must have one matching value for every question mark; therefore, we repeat the question mark twice.

The second way of applying bound parameters is demonstrated in Listing 38.32.

Listing 38.32 `app7/search4.cfm`—Using Bound Parameters (Again)

```
<!---
Module:        search4.cfm
Author:        Raymond Camden
Function:      Search directors
--->

<cfparam name="form.search" default="">

<cfoutput>
<form action="search4.cfm" method="post">
<input type="text" name="search" value="#form.search#">
<input type="submit" value="Search">
</form>
</cfoutput>

<cfif len(form.search)>
    <cfset term = "%" & form.search & "%">
```

Listing 38.32 (continued)

```
        <cfset directors =
        ormExecuteQuery("from director where
                        firstname like :name or lastname like :name",
                        {name=term})>

        <cfdump var="#directors#">
    </cfif>
```

Let's focus just on the changes in this listing compared to Listing 38.31. Notice that we've removed the question marks used to specify the locations of the bound parameters. We've replaced them with labels—in this case, both are `:name`. Using named parameters means we have a different way to pass the values: this time, as a structure. Because we are using a structure, we need to specify the value only once.

So which is better: question marks and positional markers or named parameters? As with most things, it depends. For a simple query, positional markers may be easier to use. But for a complex query, named parameters make more sense, and they are easier to work with than a large list of question marks.

Lazy Is Good!

Earlier in the chapter, we mentioned that Hibernate goes out of its way to perform as well as possible. Hibernate is smart enough, for example, to ignore you if you ask for the same object multiple times in the same request. It knows it already loaded the object once and that it doesn't need to go to the database again. Another example of this performance focus is in the way Hibernate fetches related data. We talked about relationships earlier and demonstrated how you can easily fetch related data using simple functions. This can, at times, lead to performance problems. Imagine a blog entry with a thousand comments. If you wanted to get the blog entry and didn't want the comments, does it make sense for Hibernate to fetch all that data? Of course not! This is why ColdFusion and Hibernate provide you with multiple options for configuring the way that data is fetched. The best option will always be the one that suits your business needs, and having a good awareness of what your options are will help you design the best applications.

Your persistent component properties can use the `lazy` attribute, which tells Hibernate how to behave with related objects. If `lazy` is set to `false`, Hibernate will retrieve *all* the related objects. In the example of a blog entry with comments, this setting would tell Hibernate to retrieve every comment when it gets the entry.

Another option is to use the `true` setting. In our blog entry and comments scenario, Hibernate will load the comments only if you specifically ask for them. So consider the following code example:

```
<cfset entry = entityLoadByPk("blogentry", 1)>
<cfoutput>#entry.getTitle()#</cfoutput>
```

The comments were never accessed, and therefore, were never loaded.

Add a third line:

```
<cfoutput>#arrayLen(entry.getComments())# Total Comments</cfoutput>
```

Now Hibernate will need to go back to the database to fetch the objects.

A third option is to use `lazy="extra"`. This is a rather interesting version of laziness. In this form, when comments are fetched, only a proxy version of the array of objects will be fetched. These proxy objects are lightweight (including just the primary key). Therefore, checking the size of the comments (using `arrayLen` as we did here) will be a much quicker process. If you loop through the comments and display values only for the first five, then Hibernate will only actually fetch those records. The rest will exist in their smaller, simpler proxy state.

There are further optimizations that you can apply to your persistent CFCs and Hibernate that extend beyond the scope of this book.

Digging Deeper into Hibernate

We cannot cover everything possible with ColdFusion 9 ORM and Hibernate, but fortunately there is a large community of Hibernate users outside the ColdFusion world, and you can find numerous resources, Web pages, and books that discuss Hibernate.

After you become more familiar with Hibernate, you may want access to the Java APIs beyond what ColdFusion provides. ColdFusion provides two functions for this purpose: `ormGetSession` and `ormGetSessionFactory`. Both of these functions return Java objects that enable lower-level Hibernate use and configuration.

CHAPTER 39

Using Regular Expressions

IN THIS CHAPTER

Introducing Regular Expressions

ColdFusion includes support for *regular expressions*. If you've worked at all with Perl, you probably know all about regular expressions because they are such a central part of Perl's string handling and manipulation capabilities, and generally walk hand in hand with the Perl language itself. As a rule, they aren't nearly as important to ColdFusion coders as they are to Perl coders, but regular expressions are still incredibly useful in ColdFusion development.

This chapter introduces you to regular expressions and explains how they can be used in ColdFusion applications.

What Are Regular Expressions?

Regular expressions are a way of looking for characters within chunks of text, using special wildcards to describe exactly what you're looking for. There are a lot of different wildcards you can use, from the simple `*` and `?` characters that you probably recognize from the DOS or Unix command line, to less common, more powerful wildcards that really only apply to regular expressions.

What Are Regular Expressions Similar To?

The analogy isn't perfect, but you can think of regular expressions as being kind of like `WHERE` statements in SQL, except that regular expressions are for querying plain text rather than database tables. Instead of specifying what records you want to find with a `WHERE` clause, you specify which characters you want to find using regular expressions.

Actually, the analogy works better if you think of regular expressions as being specifically analogous to a `SELECT` query that uses the `LIKE` keyword to search the database based on wildcards. You remember the `LIKE` keyword from SQL, don't you? It lets you select records using syntax such as

```
SELECT * FROM Films WHERE Summary LIKE '%color%'
```

As you probably know, the database would respond to this query with all films that contain the word `color` in the summary. The `%` characters are behaving as wildcards; you can think of each `%` as being shorthand for saying "any amount of text." So you are asking the database to return all records where `Summary` includes any amount of text, followed by the word `color`, followed by any amount of text. SQL also lets you use sets of characters as wildcards, like this:

```
SELECT * FROM Films WHERE Summary LIKE '%[Pp]ress [0-9]%'
```

To this second query, the database would respond with all films where the summary contains the phrase `Press 1` or `Press 2` (or `Press 3`, and so on), using either a lowercase or uppercase `P`.

Even if you're not familiar with these SQL wildcards, you can see the basic idea. The various wildcard characters are used to describe what you're looking for. Regular expressions are really no different conceptually, except that there are lots of wildcards instead of only a few.

NOTE

Regular expression purists may shudder at the way I'm using the term "wildcard" here. Bear with me. We'll get to the nitty-gritty later.

At the risk of belaboring this introduction, and as I hinted in the first paragraph, you can also think of regular expressions as similar to the `*` and `?` wildcards that you use on the command line to find files. Again, as you probably know, MS-DOS and Windows command prompt lets you use commands like this:

```
c:\>dir P*.txt
```

This command finds all files in the current directory that start with `P` and that have a `.txt` extension. The `*` wildcard does the same thing here as the `%` wildcard does in SQL: It stands in for the idea of *any number of characters*.

So, you're already familiar with a couple of regular expression–like ways of using wildcards to find information. Now you just need to learn the specific wildcards you can use with regular expressions, and how to use them in your ColdFusion applications. That's what the rest of this chapter is all about.

What Are Regular Expressions Used For?

Within the context of ColdFusion applications, regular expressions are generally used for these purposes:

- **Pattern searching.** Regular expressions can be used as a kind of search utility that finds one or more *exact* occurrences of a pattern. By *pattern*, I mean a word, number, entire phrase, or any combination of characters, both printable and not. A match is successful when one or more occurrences of the pattern exist. You might use pattern searching to find all telephone numbers in a given paragraph of text, or all hyperlinks in a chunk of HTML.

- **Pattern testing.** Testing a pattern is a form of data validation, and an excellent one at that. The regular expression in this context is the rule, or set of rules, that your data conforms to in order to pass the test. You might use pattern testing to validate a user's form entries.

- **Pattern removal.** Pattern removal ensures data integrity by allowing you to search and remove unwanted or hazardous patterns within a block of text. Any string that causes complications within your application is hazardous. You might use pattern removal to remove all curse words, email addresses, or telephone numbers from a chunk of text, leaving the rest of the text alone.
- **Pattern replacement.** Functioning as a search-and-replace mechanism, pattern replacement allows you to find one or more occurrences of a pattern within a block of text and then replace it with a new pattern, parts of the original pattern, or a mixture of both. You might use pattern replacement to surround all email addresses in a block of text with a `mailto:` hyperlink so the user can click the address to send a message.

You'll see regular expressions being used for each of these purposes in this chapter's example listings.

What Do Regular Expressions Look Like?

Just so you can get a quick sense of what they look like, I'll show you some regular expressions now. Unless you've used regular expressions before, don't expect to understand these examples at this point. I'm showing them to you now just so you'll get an idea of how powerful the various wildcards are.

This regular expression matches the abbreviation CFML (each letter can be in upper- or lowercase, and each letter may or may not have a period after it):

```
[Cc]\.?[Ff]\.?[Mm]\.?[Ll]\.?
```

This regular expression matches any HTML tag (or, for that matter, a CFML, XML, or any other type of angle-bracketed tag):

```
<.*?>
```

This regular expression provides one way of matching an email address:

```
([\w._]+)\@([\w_]+(\.[\w_]+)+)
```

Do Regular Expressions Differ Among Languages?

Yes. There are many tools and programming languages that provide regular expression functionality of one sort or another. Perl, JavaScript, grep/egrep, POSIX, and ColdFusion are just a few; there are plenty more. Over the years, some of the tools and languages have added their own extensions or improvements. Most of the basic regular expression wildcards will work in any of these tools, but other wildcards might work in Tool A but not in Tool B, or might have a slightly different meaning in Tool C. People often refer to the various levels of compatibility as "flavors" (the Perl flavor, the POSIX flavor, and so on).

You can think of these tweaks and flavors as resembling the various changes and improvements that have been made over the years to SQL, to the point where queries written for Access, Oracle, and Sybase databases might look considerably different (especially if the queries are doing something complicated). But that doesn't change the fact that they are all based on the same basic syntax; if you've learned one, you've basically learned them all.

NOTE

The term *regular expression* gets a bit tedious to read over and over again, so I will often use the term RegEx instead. It's a customary way to shorten the term.

RegEx Support in ColdFusion

Now that you have an idea of what regular expressions are, you need to understand what kind of support ColdFusion provides for them. The basic facts are these:

- The syntax you can use in your regular expressions (that is, the wildcards and such) is nearly identical to the syntax supported in Perl.
- In ColdFusion, you use functions like `reFind()`, `reMatch()`, and `reReplace()` to perform a RegEx operation. This is in contrast to the way regular expressions are invoked in Perl or JavaScript, which allow you to sprinkle them throughout your code almost as if the expressions were ordinary strings.

Where Can You Use Regular Expressions?

You still haven't learned how to construct these strange-looking regular expression things, but assuming you have one of them already (such as the `<.*?>` or `([\w._]+)\@([\w_]+(\.[\w_]+)+)` expressions that I mentioned earlier), you might be wondering where you can use them. In Perl, you tell the engine that a string should be interpreted as a regular expression by delimiting it with `/` characters, optionally adding additional "switches" to control options such as case sensitivity. That wouldn't work so well in CFML, due to its tag-based nature. Instead, you use the special set of RegEx functions, listed in Table 39.1.

Table 39.1 ColdFusion's RegEx Functions

FUNCTION	DESCRIPTION
`reFind()`	Attempts to find a match for a regular expression within a block of text. This function is similar conceptually to the normal `find()` function, except that the string you're looking for can include regular expression wildcards.
`reFindNoCase()`	Same as `reFind()`, except that the matching ignores capitalization.
`reMatch()`	Attempts to find as many matches in a string as possible. All matches are returned in an array.
`reMatchNoCase()`	Same as `reMatchNoCase()`, except that the matching ignores capitalization.
`reReplace()`	Finds matches within a block of text, replacing the matches with whatever replacement string you specify. You can use special characters in the replacement string to pull off all sorts of fancy replacement tricks.
`reReplaceNoCase()`	Same as `reReplace()`, except performing the matching without respect to capitalization.

Using Regular Expressions in ColdFusion

The next two portions of this chapter will teach you about two concepts:

- How to use CFML's RegEx functions (`reFind()` and the others listed in Table 39.1) to actually perform regular expression operations within your ColdFusion pages
- How to craft the regular expression for a particular task, using the various RegEx wildcards available to you

This is a kind of chicken-and-egg scenario for me. How can I explain how to incorporate regular expressions like `([\w._]+)\@([\w_]+(\.[\w_]+)+)` in your CFML code if you don't yet understand what all those wildcards mean? On the other hand, wouldn't it be pretty boring to learn about all the wildcards before knowing how to put them to use?

To put it another way, it's hard for me to guess what kind of learner you are, or how much you already know about regular expressions. If you don't know anything at all about them, you might want to learn about the various wildcards first. If you've already used them in other tools, you probably just want to know how to use them in ColdFusion. So feel free to skip ahead to the "Crafting Your Own Regular Expressions" section if you don't like looking at all these wildcards without understanding what they mean.

Finding Matches with `reFind()`

Assuming you have already crafted the wildcard-laden RegEx criteria you want, you can use the `reFind()` function to tell ColdFusion to search a chunk of text with the criteria, like this:

```
reFind(regex, string [, start] [, returnSubExpressions] )
```

Table 39.2 describes each of the `reFind()` arguments.

Table 39.2 `reFind()` Function Syntax

ARGUMENT	DESCRIPTION
`regex`	Required. The regular expression that describes the text that you want to find.
`string`	Required. The text that you want to search.
`start`	Optional. The starting position for the search. The default is `1`.
`returnSubExpressions`	Optional. A Boolean value indicating whether you want to obtain information about the position and length of the actual text that was found by the various portions of the regular expression. The default is False. You will learn more about this topic in the section "Getting the Matched Text Using `returnSubExpressions`" later in this chapter.

The `reFind()` function returns one of two things, depending on whether the `returnSubExpressions` argument is True or False:

- Assuming that `returnSubExpressions` is False (the default), the function returns the character position of the text that's found (that is, the first substring that matches the search criteria). If no match is found in the text, the function returns 0 (zero). This behavior is consistent with the ordinary, non-RegEx `find()` function.

- If `returnSubExpressions` is True, the function returns a CFML structure composed of two arrays called `pos` and `len`. These arrays contain the position and length of the first substring that matches the search criteria. The first value in the arrays (that is, `pos[1]` and `len[1]`) correspond to the match as a whole. The remaining values in the arrays correspond to any subexpressions defined by the regular expression.

The bit about the subexpressions might be confusing at this point, since you haven't learned what subexpressions actually are. Don't worry about it for the moment. Just think of the subexpressions argument as something you should set to True if you need to get the actual text that was found.

A Simple Example

For the moment, accept it on faith that the following regular expression will find a sensibly formed Internet email address (such as `nate@nateweiss.com` or `nate@nateweiss.co.uk`):

```
([\w._]+)\@([\w_]+(\.[\w_]+)+)
```

Listing 39.1 shows how to use this regular expression to find an email address within a chunk of text.

Listing 39.1 `RegExFindEmail1.cfm`—A Simple Regular Expression Example

```
<!---
 Filename: RegExFindEmail1.cfm
 Author: Nate Weiss (NMW)
 Purpose: Demonstrates basic use of reFind()
--->

<!--- The text to search --->
<cfset text = "My email address is nate@nateweiss.com. Write to me anytime.">

<!--- Attempt to find a match --->
<cfset foundPos = reFind("([\w._]+)@([\w_]+(\.[\w_]+)+)", text)>

<!--- Display the result --->
<cfif foundPos gt 0>
 <cfoutput>
 <p>A match was found at position #foundPos#.</p>
 </cfoutput>
<cfelse>
 <p>No matches were found.</p>
</cfif>
```

If you visit this page with your browser, the character position of the email address is displayed. If you change the `text` variable so that it no longer contains an Internet-style email address, the listing displays "No matches were found."

Ignoring Capitalization with `reFindNoCase()`

Internet email addresses aren't generally considered to be case-sensitive, so you might want to tell ColdFusion to perform the match without respect to case. To do so, use `reFindNoCase()` instead of `reFind()`. Both functions take the same arguments and are used in exactly the same way, so there's no need to provide a separate example listing for `reFindNoCase()`.

In short, anywhere you see `reFind()` in this chapter, you could use `reFindNoCase()` instead, and vice versa. Just use the one that's appropriate for the task at hand. Also, note that it is possible to use case-insensitive regular expressions, making `reFindNoCase()` unnecessary.

Getting the Matched Text Using the Found Position

Sometimes you just want to find out whether a match exists within a chunk of text. In such a case, you would use the `reFind()` function as it was used in Listing 39.1.

You can also use that form of `reFind()` if the nature of the RegEx is such that the actual match will always have the same length. For instance, if you were searching specifically for a U.S. telephone number in the form (999)999-9999 (where each of the 9s represents a number), you could use the following regular expression:

```
\([0-9]{3}\)[0-9]{3}-[0-9]{4}
```

Because the length of a matched phone number will always be the same due to the nature of phone numbers, it's a simple matter to extract the actual phone number that was found. You use ColdFusion's built-in `mid()` function, feeding it the position returned by the `reFind()` function as the start position, and the number `13` as the length. For an example, see as `RegExFindPhone1.cfm` in the Zip file downloaded from the book's Web site.

Getting the Matched Text Using `returnSubExpressions`

If you want to adjust the email address example in Listing 39.1 so that it displays the actual email address found, the task is a bit more complicated because not all email addresses are the same length. What would you supply to the third argument of the `mid()` function? You can't use a constant number, as described earlier. Clearly, you need some way of telling `reFind()` to return the length, in addition to the position, of the match.

This is when the `returnSubExpressions` argument comes into play. If you set this argument to True when you use `reFind()`, the function will return a structure that contains the position and length of the match. (The structure also includes the position and length that correspond to any subexpressions in the structure, but don't worry about that right now.)

Listing 39.2 shows how to use this parameter of the `reFind()` function. It uses the first element in `pos` and `len` arrays to determine the position and length of the matched text and then displays the match (Figure 39.1).

Figure 39.1

It's easy to display a matched substring, even if its length will vary at run time.

A match was found at position 21.

The actual match is: nate@nateweiss.com

Listing 39.2 `RegExFindEmail2.cfm`—Using the `returnSubExpressions` Argument of `reFind()`

```
<!---
 Filename: RegExFindEmail2.cfm
 Author: Nate Weiss (NMW)
 Purpose: Demonstrates basic use of reFind()
--->

<!--- The text to search --->
<cfset text = "My email address is nate@nateweiss.com. Write to me anytime.">

<!--- Attempt to find a match --->
<cfset matchStruct = reFind("([\w._]+)\@([\w_]+(\.[\w_]+)+)", text, 1, True)>

<!--- Display the result --->
<cfif matchStruct.pos[1] gt 0>
 <cfset foundString = mid(text, matchStruct.pos[1], matchStruct.len[1])>

 <cfoutput>
 <p>A match was found at position #matchStruct.pos[1]#.</p>
 <p>The actual match is: #foundString#</p>
 </cfoutput>
<cfelse>
 <p>No matches were found.</p>
</cfif>
```

Working with Subexpressions

As exhibited by the last example, the first values in the `pos` and `len` arrays correspond to the position and length of the match found by the `reFind()` function. Those values (`pos[1]` and `len[1]`) will always exist. So why are `pos` and `len` implemented as arrays if the first value in each is the only interesting value? What other information do they hold?

The answer is this: If your regular expression contains any *subexpressions*, there will be an additional value in the `pos` and `len` arrays that corresponds to the actual text matched by the subexpression. If your regular expression has two subexpressions, `pos[2]` and `len[2]` are the position and length of the first subexpression's match, and `pos[3]` and `len[3]` are the position and length for the second subexpression.

So, what's a subexpression? When you are using regular expressions to solve specific problems (such as finding email addresses or phone numbers in a chunk of text), you are often looking for several different patterns of text, one after another. That is, the nature of the problem is often such that the regular expression is made up of several *parts* ("look for this, followed by that"), where all of the parts must be found in order for the whole regular expression to be satisfied. If you place parentheses around each of the parts, the parts become subexpressions.

Subexpressions do two things:

- They make the overall RegEx criteria more flexible, because you can use many regular expression wildcards on each subexpression. This capability allows you to say that some subexpressions must be found while others are optional, or that a particular subexpression can be repeated multiple times, and so on. To put it another way, the parentheses allow you to work with the enclosed characters or wildcards as an isolated group. This isn't so different conceptually from the way parentheses work in `<cfif>` statements or SQL criteria.
- The match for each subexpression is included in the `len` and `pos` arrays, so you can easily find out what specific text was actually matched by each part of your RegEx criteria. You get position and length information not only for the match as a whole, but for each of its constituent parts.

TIP

If you don't want a particular set of parentheses, or subexpressions, to be included in the `len` and `pos` arrays (that is, if you are only interested in the grouping properties of the parentheses and not in their returning-the-match properties), you can put a `?:` right after the opening parenthesis. See Table 39.11 near the end of this chapter for details.

In real-world use, most regular expressions contain subexpressions—it's the nature of the beast. In fact, each of the regular expressions in the example listings shown so far has included subexpressions because the problems they are trying to solve (finding email addresses and phone numbers) require that they look for strings that consist of a few different parts.

Take a look at the regular expression used in Listing 39.2, which matches email addresses:

```
([\w._]+)@([\w_]+(\.[\w_]+)+)
```

I know you haven't learned what all the wildcards mean yet; for now, just concentrate on the parentheses. It may help you to keep in mind that the plain-English meaning of each of the `[\w_]+` sequences is "match one or more letters, numbers, or underscores."

By concentrating on the parentheses, you can easily recognize the three subexpressions in this RegEx. The first is at the beginning and matches the portion of the email address up to the `@` sign. The second subexpression begins after the `@` sign and continues to the end of the RegEx; it matches the "domain name" portion of the email address. Within this second subexpression is a third one, which says that the domain name portion of the email address can contain any number of subparts (but at least one), where each subpart is made up of a dot and some letters (such as `.com` or `.uk`).

Now look at the RegEx described earlier for matching phone numbers:

```
(\([0-9]{3}\))([0-9]{3}-[0-9]{4})
```

This one has two subexpressions. You might have thought it has three because there appear to be three sets of parentheses. But the parentheses characters that are preceded by backslash characters don't count, because the backslash is a special escape character that tells the RegEx engine to treat the next character literally. Here, the backslashes tell ColdFusion to look for actual parentheses in the text, rather than treating those parentheses as delimiters for subexpressions.

So the phone number example includes just two subexpressions. The first subexpression starts at the very beginning and ends just after the `\)` characters and it matches the area code portion of the phone number. The second subexpression contains the remainder of the phone number (three numbers followed by a hyphen, then four more numbers). See Listing 39.3.

Listing 39.3 `RegExFindEmail3.cfm`—Getting the Matched Text for Each Subexpression

```
<!---
 Filename: RegExFindEmail3.cfm
 Author: Nate Weiss (NMW)
 Purpose: Demonstrates basic use of reFind()
--->

<!--- The text to search --->
<cfset text = "My email address is nate@nateweiss.com. Write to me anytime.">

<!--- Attempt to find a match --->
<cfset matchStruct = reFind("([\w._]+)@([\w_]+(\.[\w_]+)+)", text, 1, True)>

<!--- Display the result --->
<cfif matchStruct.pos[1] gt 0>

 <!--- The first elements of the arrays represent the overall match --->
 <cfset foundString = mid(text, matchStruct.pos[1], matchStruct.len[1])>
 <!--- The subsequent elements represent each of the subexpressions --->
 <cfset userNamePart = mid(text, matchStruct.pos[2], matchStruct.len[2])>
 <cfset domainPart = mid(text, matchStruct.pos[3], matchStruct.len[3])>
 <cfset suffixPart = mid(text, matchStruct.pos[4], matchStruct.len[4])>

 <cfoutput>
 <p>A match was found at position #matchStruct.pos[1]#.<br>
 The actual email address is: <b>#foundString#</b><br>
 The username part of the address is: #userNamePart#<br>
 The domain part of the address is: #domainPart#<br>
 The suffix part of the address is: #suffixPart#<br>
 </p>
 </cfoutput>
<cfelse>
 <p>No matches were found.</p>
</cfif>
```

This listing is similar to the preceding one (Listing 39.2), except that instead of working with only the first values in the `pos` and `len` arrays, Listing 39.3 also works with the second, third, and fourth values. It displays the username, domain name, and domain suffix portions of the match, respectively.

TIP

If you need to know the number of subexpressions in a RegEx, you can use `arrayLen()` with either the `pos` or `len` array and then subtract 1 from the result (because the first values of the array is for the match as a whole). In Listing 39.3, you could output the value of `arrayLen(MatchStruct.pos)-1` to find the number of subexpressions in the email RegEx (the answer would be 3).

Working with Multiple Matches

So far, this chapter's listings have shown you how to find the first match in a given chunk of text. Often, that's all you need to do. There are times, however, when you might need to match multiple phone numbers, email addresses, or something else.

The `reFind()` and `reFindNoCase()` functions don't specifically provide any means to find multiple matches at once, but you can use the `start` argument mentioned in Table 39.2 to achieve the same result. This is a manual process that is now much easier with `reMatch()` and `reMatchAll()`. For an example of the manual process, see `RegExFindEmail4.cfm` in the Zip file downloaded from the book's Web site. Listing 39.4 demonstrates how much easier this process is.

Listing 39.4 `RegExFindEmail5.cfm`—Finding Multiple Matches with a `reMatch()` Call

```
<!--- The Text to Search --->
<cfsavecontent variable="text">
Here is text with names and email address.
Ray's email is ray@camdenfamily.com,
Todd's email address is todd@cfsilence.com.
Lastly, Luke Skywalker's email address is luke@newalliance.gov.
</cfsavecontent>

<!--- Find all matches. --->
<cfset matches = reMatch("([\w._]+)@([\w_]+(\.[\w_]+)+)", text)>

<cfoutput>
<p>
There were #arrayLen(matches)# matches.
</p>

<p>
Matches:<br />
</cfoutput>

<cfloop index="match" array="#matches#">
    <cfoutput>#match#<br /></cfoutput>
</cfloop>
```

NOTE

The template begins by creating a variable from a block of text using the `cfsavecontent` tag. This is a handy way to quickly create a large block of text as a variable. Next, the `reMatch()` function is called using the email RegEx against the text variable. The size of the resultant array is then displayed along with a list of all the matches.

Replacing Text using `reReplace()`

As you learned from Table 39.1, ColdFusion provides `reReplace()` and `reReplaceNoCase()` functions in addition to the functions you've seen so far.

The `reReplace()` and `reReplaceNoCase()` functions each take three required arguments and one optional argument, as follows:

```
reReplace(string, regex, substring [, scope ])
```

The meaning of each argument is explained in Table 39.3.

Table 39.3 `reReplace()` Function Syntax

ARGUMENT	DESCRIPTION
`String`	Required. The string in which you want to find matches.
`Regex`	Required. The regular expression criteria you want to use to find matches.
`Substring`	Required. The string that you want each match to be replaced with. You can use backreferences in the string to include pieces of the original match in the replacement.
`Scope`	Optional. The default is `ONE`, which means that only the first match is replaced. You can also set this argument to `ALL`, which will cause all matches to be replaced.

The function returns the altered version of the string (the original string is not modified). Think of it as being like the `replace()` function on steroids, since the text you're looking for can be expressed using RegEx wildcards instead of a literal substring.

NOTE

The syntax for both `reReplace()` and `reReplaceNoCase()` is the same. Anywhere you see one, you could use the other. Just use the function that's appropriate for the task, depending on how you want the replacement operation to behave in regard to capitalization. Again, though, do not forget that you can actually do case-insensitive regular-expression matching, so you need not ever use `reReplaceNoCase()`.

Using `reReplace` to Filter Posted Content

The next few examples will implement an editable home page for the fictitious Orange Whip Studios company. The basic idea is for the application to maintain a text message in the `APPLICATION` scope; this message appears on the home page. An edit link allows the user to type a new message in a simple form (Figure 39.2). When the form is submitted, the new message is displayed on the home page from that point forward (Figure 39.3). Listing 39.5 shows the simple logic for this example.

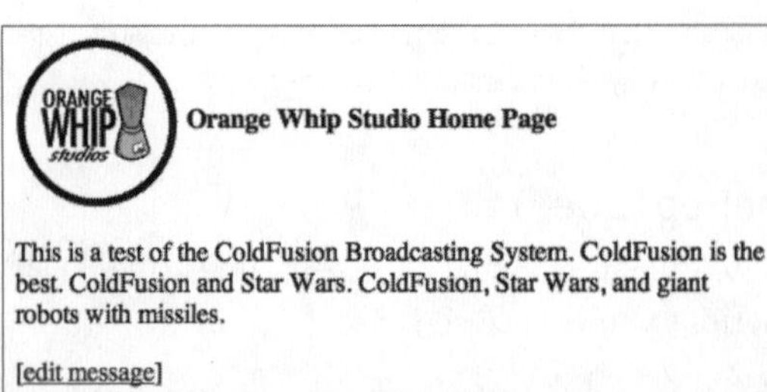

Figure 39.2

Users can edit the home page message with this simple form.

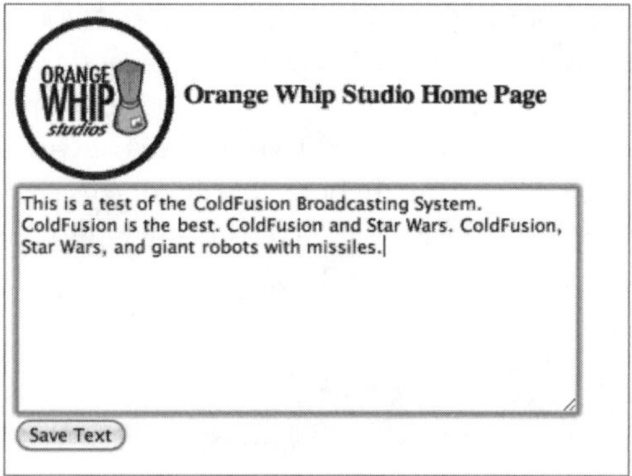

Figure 39.3
The message on the home page.

Listing 39.5 `EditableHomePage1.cfm`—Removing Text Based on a Regular Expression

```
<!---
 Filename: EditableHomePage1.cfm
 Author: Nate Weiss (NMW)
 Purpose: Example of altering text with regular expressions
--->

<!--- Enable application variables --->
<cfapplication name="OrangeWhipIntranet">

<!--- Declare the HomePage variables and give them initial values --->
<cfparam name="application.homePage" default="#structNew()#">
<cfparam name="application.homePage.messageAsPosted" type="string" default="">
<cfparam name="application.homePage.messageToDisplay" type="string" default="">

<!--- If the user is submitting an edited message --->
<cfif isDefined("form.messageText")>

 <!--- First of all, remove all tags from the posted message --->
 <cfset messageWithoutTags = reReplace(form.messageText,
 "<.*?>", <!--- (matches tags) --->
 "", <!--- (replace with empty string) --->
 "ALL")>

 <!--- Save the "before" version of the new message --->
 <cfset application.homePage.messageAsPosted = messageWithoutTags>

 <!---
 (other code will be added here in following examples)
 --->

 <!--- Save the "after" version of the new message --->
 <cfset application.homePage.messageToDisplay = messageWithoutTags>
</cfif>

<!--- This include file takes care of dispaying the actual page --->
<!--- (including the message) or the form for editing the message --->
<cfinclude template="EditableHomePageDisplay.cfm">
```

At the top of this listing, three application variables called `homepage`, `homePage.messageAsPosted`, and `HomePage.messageToDisplay` are established. If the user is currently posting a new message, the `<cfif>` block executes. This block is responsible for saving the edited message. Inside the `<cfif>` block, the `reReplace()` function is used to find all HTML (or XML, CFML, or any other type of tag) and replace the tags with an empty string. In other words, all tags are removed from the user's message in order to prevent users from entering HTML that might look bad or generally mess things up.

NOTE

Once again, you have to take it on faith that the `<.*?>` regular expression used in this example is an appropriate one to use for removing tags from a chunk of text. For details, see the section "Crafting Your Own Regular Expressions" in this chapter.

Once the tags have been removed, the resulting text is saved to the `homePage.messageAsPosted` and `homePage.messageToDisplay` variables, which will be displayed by the next listing. For now, the two variables will always hold the same value, but you will see a few different versions of this listing that save slightly different values in each.

Finally, a `<cfinclude>` tag is used to include the `EditableHomePageDisplay.cfm` template, shown in Listing 39.6. This code is responsible for displaying the message on the home page (as shown in Figure 39.2) or displaying the edit form (as shown in Figure 39.3) if the user clicks the edit link.

Listing 39.6 `EditableHomePageDisplay.cfm`—Form and Display Portion of Editable Home Page

```
<!---
 Filename: EditableHomePageDisplay.cfm
 Author: Nate Weiss (NMW)
 Please Note Included by the EditableHomePage.cfm examples
--->


<html>
<head><title>Orange Whip Studios Home Page</title></head>
<body>
<cfoutput>
 <!--- Orange Whip Studios logo and page title --->
 <img src="../images/logo_c.gif" width="101" height="101" alt="" align="absmiddle">
 <b>Orange Whip Studio Home Page</b><br clear="all">

 <!--- Assuming that the user is not trying to edit the page --->
 <cfif not isDefined("url.edit")>

   <!--- Display the home page message --->
   <p>#paragraphFormat(application.homePage.messageToDisplay)#

   <!--- Provide a link to edit the message --->
   <p>[<a href="#cgi.script_name#?edit=Yes">edit message</a>]</p>

 <!--- If the user wants to edit the page --->
 <cfelse>

   <!--- Simple form to edit the home page message --->
   <form action="#cgi.script_name#" method="post">
```

Listing 39.6 (continued)

```
      <!--- Text area for typing the new message --->
      <textarea
      name="messageText"
      cols="60"
      rows="10">#htmlEditFormat(application.homePage.messageAsPosted)#</textarea><br>

      <!--- Submit button to save the message --->
      <input
      type="submit"
      value="Save Text">
      </form>

   </cfif>
  </cfoutput>

  </body>
  </html>
```

There is nothing particularly interesting about this listing. It's a simple file that either displays the home page or an edit form, as appropriate. Note that the `homePage.messageToDisplay` is what is normally displayed on the home page, whereas `homePage.messageAsPosted` is what appears in the edit form. Right now, these two values are always the same, but subsequent versions of Listing 38.5 will change that.

Clearly, you aren't limited to only removing the tags; you can replace them with any string you want. If you wanted the user to get a visual cue about the removal of any tags from the message, you could change the third argument of the `reReplace()` function so that the tags are replaced with a message such as `[tags removed]`. And in the next section, you'll learn how to use the RegEx backreference wildcard so that the actual match can be incorporated into the replacement string dynamically.

Altering Text with Backreferences

Listing 39.5 showed you how to use `reReplace()` to replace any matches for a regular expression with a replacement string (in that example, the replacement was an empty string). Using a simple replacement string is fine when you want to remove matches from a chunk of text, or to replace all matches with the same replacement string.

But what if you want the replacements to be more flexible, so that the replaced text is based somehow on the actual match? The `reReplace()` function supports *backreferences*, which allow you to do just that. A backreference is a special RegEx wildcard that can be used in the replacement string to represent the actual value of a subexpression. Backreferences are commonly used to alter or reformat the substrings matched by a regular expression.

In ColdFusion, you include backreferences in your replacement strings using `\1`, `\2`, `\3`, and so on, where the number after the backslash indicates the number of a subexpression. If your replacement string contains a `\1`, the actual value matched by the first subexpression (that is, the first parenthesized part of the RegEx) will appear in place of the `\1`. If the replacement includes `\2`, the result will have the value of the second subexpression in place of the `\2`, and so on.

TIP

Think of backreferences as a special kind of variable. For each actual match, these special variables are filled with the values of each subexpression that contributed to the match. The replacement is then made using the values of the special variables. The process is repeated for each match.

The next example listing is a new version of the earlier code (Listing 39.5) for tweaking the home page message submitted by users. This version uses backreferences to make two additional changes to the message posted by the user:

- "Malformed" phone numbers are rearranged so that the area code appears in parentheses, in the form `(999)999-9999`. If the user enters a phone number as `800/555-1212` or `800 555 1212`, it will be rearranged to read `(800)555-1212`.
- Any email addresses in the text will be surrounded by "mailto" hyperlinks that activate the user's email client when clicked. If `bfoxile@orangewhipstudios.com` is found in the text, it will be changed to an `<a>` link that includes an `href="mailto:bfoxile@orangewhipstudios.com"` attribute.

The user can type a message that contains phone numbers and email addresses; the home page will display a version of the message that has been altered in a reasonably intelligent and consistent fashion. Listing 39.7 shows the code for this new version of the home page example.

Listing 39.7 `EditableHomePage2.cfm`—Using Backreferences to Make Intelligent Alterations

```
<!---
 Filename: EditableHomePage2.cfm
 Author: Nate Weiss (NMW)
 Purpose: Example of altering text with regular expressions
--->

<!--- Enable application variables --->
<cfapplication name="OrangeWhipIntranet">

<!--- Declare the HomePage variables and give them initial values --->
<cfparam name="application.homePage" default="#structNew()#">
<cfparam name="application.homePage.messageAsPosted" type="string" default="">
<cfparam name="application.homePage.messageToDisplay" type="string" default="">

<!--- If the user is submitting an edited message --->
<cfif isDefined("form.messageText")>

 <!--- First of all, remove all tags from the posted message --->
 <cfset form.messageText = reReplace(form.messageText,
 "<[^>]*>", <!--- (matches tags) --->
 "", <!--- (replace with empty string) --->
 "ALL")>

 <!--- Save the "before" version of the new message --->
 <cfset application.homePage.messageAsPosted = form.messageText>

 <!--- Format any lazily-typed phone numbers in (999)999-999 format --->
 <cfset form.MessageText = reReplaceNoCase(form.messageText,
 "([0-9]{3})[-/ ]([0-9]{3})[- ]([0-9]{4})", <!--- (matches phone) --->
```

Listing 39.7 (continued)

```
"(\1)\2-\3", <!--- (phone format) --->
"ALL")>

<!--- Surround all email addresses with "mailto" links --->
<cfset form.messageText = reReplaceNoCase(form.messageText,
"(([\w._]+)@([\w_]+(\.[\w_]+)+))", <!--- (matches email addresses) --->
"<a href=mailto:\1>\1</a>", <!--- (email address in link) --->
"ALL")>

<!--- Save the "after" version of the new message --->
<cfset application.homePage.messageToDisplay = form.messageText>
</cfif>

<!--- This include file takes care of dispaying the actual page --->
<!--- (including the message) or the form for editing the message --->
<cfinclude template="EditableHomePageDisplay.cfm">
```

Much of this listing is unchanged from the version in Listing 39.5. The difference is the addition of the second and third uses of `reReplace()` (the first `reReplace()` was in the previous version).

The second `reReplace()` is the one that reformats the phone numbers. This function contains three parenthesized subexpressions (which correspond to the area code, exchange, and last four digits of the phone number, respectively). Therefore, the `\1` in the replacement string will contain the area code when an actual match is encountered, the `\2` will contain the exchange portion of the phone number, and so on.

The final `reReplace()` does something similar except for email addresses. This replacement is interested in working only with the match as a whole, so an additional set of parentheses have been added around the entire regular expression, so that the entire RegEx is considered a subexpression. Therefore, the entire match will appear in place of the `\1` in the replacement string when this code executes. This is different from the behavior of `reFind` and `reFindNoCase` where `returnSubExpressions` is true. These functions will return the entire match automatically. An alternative is to omit the extra set of parentheses and refer to each part of the email address separately in the replacement string, like so:

```
<!--- Surround all email addresses with "mailto" links --->
<cfset FORM.messageText = reReplaceNoCase( FORM.messageText,
"([\w._]+)@([\w_]+(\.[\w_]+)+)", <!--- (matches email addresses) --->
"<a href=mailto:\1\@2\3>\1\@2\3</a>", <!--- (email address in link) --->
"ALL")>
```

NOTE

In Perl, you use `$1`, `$2`, and so on, rather than `\1` and `\2`, because the `$` is special to Perl.

NOTE

You can also use backreferences in the regular expression itself, often to match repeating patterns. For details, see the "Metacharacters 303: Backreferences Redux" section near the end of this chapter.

Some Convenient RegEx UDFs

The listings for this chapter include a file called `RegExFunctions.cfm`, which creates several user-defined functions (UDFs) that might come in handy when you're working with regular expressions. To use the library, simply `<cfinclude>` it in your own templates. Table 39.4 lists the functions included in this simple UDF library.

Table 39.4 Functions in UDF Library `RegExFunctions.cfm`

FUNCTION	DESCRIPTION
`reFindString()`	Performs a regular expression match and returns the matched string. Returns an empty string if no match is found. This is a shortcut for using the `pos[1]` and `len[1]` values as shown in Listing 39.3.
`adjustNewlinesToLinefeeds()`	Replaces any CRLF or CR sequences in a chunk of text with LF characters. This is handy when using multiline mode with `(?m)`. Accepts just one argument, `str`, as shown in the section "Understanding Multiline Mode" later in this chapter.

Using a RegEx Testing Page

Sometimes it's a lot easier to craft a regular expression if you have an interactive environment to play with. The example listings for this chapter include a convenient regular expression "tester" page for creating or troubleshooting your regular expressions. You can also use this tester page to work through some of the RegEx syntax examples in the next section of this chapter, "Crafting Your Own Regular Expressions."

To use the page, follow these steps:

1. Visit the `RegExTester.cfm` page with your browser. Be sure to copy the file from the Zip file downloaded at the book's Web site.
2. Enter your regular expression. If you want case to be considered, check the Case Sensitive option.
3. Enter the text you want to search or get the text from a Web page on your server or elsewhere on the Internet, and provide the URL (including the `http://` part) in the field provided. To get the text from a file on your computer, use the Browse button to select the file to upload.
4. Click the Match Now button to display the matches.

TIP

If you need to jog your memory on a particular metacharacter, you can click the Help link to bring up the RegEx portion of the ColdFusion documentation.

Crafting Your Own Regular Expressions

Up to this point, this chapter has introduced you to the `reFind()`, `reMatch()` and `reReplace()` functions (and their case-insensitive counterparts). Along the way, you learned about a number of RegEx concepts, such as subexpressions and backreferences. You've also seen some decent examples of actual RegEx criteria syntax (that is, the various wildcards you can use in regular expressions)—but you haven't been formally introduced to what each of the wildcards does.

The remainder of this chapter will focus on the regular expressions themselves.

Understanding Literals and Metacharacters

Every regular expression you write includes two types of characters: *literals* and *metacharacters*.

Literals, or *literal characters*, are normal text characters that represent themselves literally. In other words, literals are all the characters in a RegEx that aren't wildcards of one form or another. In the email RegEx that's been used several times in this chapter (see Listing 39.1), the only literal character is the `@` sign. If your search involves the word *dog*, your RegEx will likely contain the literal `d`, `o`, and `g` characters.

Metacharacters are the various special characters (what I've been calling *wildcards* up to this point) that have special meaning to the regular expression engine. You've already seen a few of the most common metacharacters, such as the `[`, `]`, `{`, `}`, and `+` characters. You'll learn about all the rest in the pages to come.

NOTE

Up to this point, I've been using the term wildcard as an approximate synonym for metacharacter. Wildcard is less technical and perhaps a bit less precise, but it rolls off the tongue a lot more easily and is more intuitively understood. I imagine you've understood what I've meant by wildcard all along, whereas metacharacter might have slipped us up a bit. I'll continue to use wildcard during the less formal parts of the remaining discussion.

Including Metacharacters Literally

Sometimes, you need to include one of the metacharacters as a literal. To do so, you escape the metacharacter by preceding it with a backslash. You saw this demonstrated in Listing 39.2, where the sequences `\(` and `\)` were used to denote literal parentheses characters (that is, parentheses that should actually be searched for, rather than having their usual special meaning of indicating a subexpression).

NOTE

If you need to search for a literal backslash, escape the backslash with another backslash. Just use two backslashes together, as in `\\`.

NOTE

Remember that the backslash serves another purpose, too: indicating a backreference. For details, see the earlier section "Altering Text with Backreferences."

Introducing the Cast of Metacharacters

The RegEx implementation in ColdFusion supports a lot of metacharacters, which can be broken into the conceptual groups shown in Table 39.5.

Table 39.5 Metacharacter Types

TYPE	DESCRIPTION
Character classes	Character classes define a set of characters that will match. They are defined with square brackets: `[aeiou]` matches any single vowel; `[0-9]` matches any single number, and `[^0-9]` matches any single character except numbers. There are also special shortcuts for often-used sets of characters, such as `\w` or for any letter or number, or `\s` for any white-space character. Finally, there's the dot character (.), which matches any character at all.
Quantifiers	These metacharacters allow you to specify how many times a certain item can appear to still be considered a match. Quantifiers include `?` for optional matches, `+` for one or more matches, and `*` for any number of matches (including none). There are also the *interval quantifiers*: `{num}` for `num` number of matches; `{num,max}` for `num` to `max` number of matches; and `{num,}` for `num` or more matches.
Alternation	You can establish OR conditions in your regular expressions with the `|` character. Parentheses constrain how far the `|` reaches, so `(you|we)` matches `you` or `we`.
String anchors	String anchors let you specify that a match must occur at a particular location in a chunk of text. Anchors include ^ for matches at the beginning of the text (or line) and `$` for matches at the end. There are also the `\A` and `\Z` anchors, which are similar, except do not work in multiline mode.
Escape sequences	Escape sequences are mostly for matching certain unprintable characters; for example, `\t` to match tabs or `\n` to match newlines.
Modifiers	Modifiers allow you to turn on different types of RegEx behavior for use in special cases. Modifiers include `(?m)` for line-by-line matching and `(?=)` for lookahead matching.

The next few sections present a kind of crash course in metacharacters. I've titled these sections Metacharacters 101, Metacharacters 102, and so on. By the end of this little course, you'll have a pretty good understanding of regular expression syntax. Aren't you glad you didn't actually have a course like this in school?

Metacharacters 101: Character Classes

Of all of the metacharacters available in regular expressions, character classes are probably the most important. Character classes are a way of specifying a set of characters, any one of which can be considered a match. You can specify your own classes or use any number of predefined classes supported by RegEx.

Specifying Character Classes with `[ ]`

You can specify any set of characters as a character class with the square bracket characters `[` and `]`. The class `[aeiouAEIOU]` will match any vowel; `[12345]` will match a 1, 2, 3, 4, or 5 character. For instance, perhaps your last name is Andersen and people often misspell it as Anderson or forget to capitalize the first letter. You could find any of the various spellings using `[Aa]nders[eo]n` as the regular expression.

The hyphen character has special meaning when it is between a set of square brackets: It indicates a range of acceptable characters. For instance, `[1-5]` is easier to type than `[12345]` and will still match a 1, 2, 3, 4, or 5 character. Very common character classes are `[A-Za-z]` for matching any letter, and `[0-9]` for matching any single number character. If your company uses an ID number composed of two letters followed by a dash and then three numbers, you could use this as the regular expression:

```
[A-Z][A-Z]-[0-9][0-9][0-9]
```

As you'll learn in Metacharacters 102, you could use quantifiers as an easier way of specifying the part consisting of three numbers at the end.

Negating a Character Class with `^`

If the square bracket contents for a character class start with a caret character, the character class is negated, meaning that the class will match any character that isn't in the class. For example, `[^A-Za-z0-9]` matches anything other than a number or letter, and `[^aeiouAEIOU]` matches anything other than a vowel.

NOTE

Keep in mind that there are lots of characters other than letters and numbers, including unprintable characters such as tabs and newlines. So, while you may think at first glance that `[^aeiouAEIOU]` would simply match all consonants, that's not all it will match. It will also match unprintable characters, and all other characters, too, including punctuation characters (commas, periods, and the like).

Common Character Classes

Because certain character classes are called for frequently (such as `[A-Za-z]` for matching any letter, and `[0-9]` for matching any digit), ColdFusion supports a number of shortcuts for the most commonly needed character classes. Different regular expression tools support slightly different ways of specifying these shortcuts, but most adhere to the shortcuts supported by Perl or by POSIX. ColdFusion's RegEx implementation supports both. The Perl shortcuts, in particular, are really easy to type.

Table 39.6 shows common character classes you might need to use in your regular expressions, with the Perl-style and POSIX-style shortcuts for each. The Normal column shows how to write the character class using the normal square bracket syntax. The Perl Shortcut and POSIX Shortcut columns show the shortcuts for each class; for some of the classes, there is a POSIX shortcut but no corresponding Perl shortcut, in which case the Perl Shortcut column is left blank. A few shortcuts shown at the bottom of the table would be virtually impossible to type using the manual `[ ]` syntax, so the Normal column is left blank.

Table 39.6 Common Character Classes and Their Shortcuts

NORMAL	PERL	POSIX SHORTCUT	MATCHES SHORTCUT
`[A-Z]`		`[[:upper:]]`	Any uppercase letter
`[a-z]`		`[[:lower:]]`	Any lowercase letter
`[A-Za-z]`		`[[:alpha:]]`	Any letter, regardless of case
`[0-9]`	`\d`	`[[:digit:]]`	Any number character (digit)
`[^0-9]`	`\D`	`[^[:digit:]]`	Any character other than a number
`[0-9A-Za-z]`	`\w`	`[[:alnum:]]`	Any letter or number character
`[^0-9A-Za-z]`	`\W`	`[^[:alnum:]]`	Any character other than a number or letter
`[ \t]`		`[[:blank:]]`	A space or a tab
`[ \t\n\r\f]`	`\s`	`[[:space:]]`	Any white-space character, which means any spaces, tabs, or any of the end-of-line indicators (newlines, form feeds, and carriage returns)
`[^ \t\n\r\f]`	`\S`	`[[:graph:]]`	Any non-white-space character
	. (dot)		Any character at all; it's important to understand that in ColdFusion, the dot character always matches newlines, which is not always the case with Perl

NOTE

As noted in Table 39.6, ColdFusion's dot metacharacter always matches any character, including newlines. In other words, the behavior is consistent with Perl behavior when Perl's `/s` switch is in effect.

In the preceding section, we discussed a regular expression for matching an ID number that comprised two letters, a dash, and three numbers. The RegEx looked like this:

```
[A-Z][A-Z]-[0-9][0-9][0-9]
```

You can use Perl-style shortcuts to make the RegEx easier to type and look at, like this:

```
[A-Z][A-Z]-\d\d\d
```

Or, you can use POSIX-style shortcuts, like so:

```
[[:upper:]][[:upper:]]-[[:digit:]][[:digit:]][[:digit:]]
```

Feel free to mix and match the two types of shortcuts, like so:

```
[[:upper:]][[:upper:]]-\n\n
```

NOTE

The POSIX shortcuts can be negated with the ^ character, as shown in the POSIX Column for the `[^0-9]` class in Table 39.6.

NOTE

You might be wondering why you would use `[[:upper:]]` instead of `[A-Z]`, because it doesn't seem to be much of a shortcut at all (there's actually more to type). The main benefit is that the POSIX shortcuts attempt to understand uppercase and lower-case letters for each language, whereas something like `[A-Z]` will work only for English and other roman-style character sets.

Metacharacters 102: Quantifiers

As you learned in Table 39.5, *quantifiers* allow you to specify how many times certain parts of a RegEx can match for the overall regular expression to be considered a match. You will learn about the many quantifiers in detail as we work through the Metacharacters section.

Regardless of which quantifier you're using, you always place it right after the item that you want to affect. That item might be a single character, a character class, or the set of parentheses that sets off a subexpression. If character classes are the foundation of what regular expressions are about, quantifiers give the technology its muscle; without them, it would be hard to solve anything but simple problems with RegEx.

Table 39.7 lists the quantifier metacharacters available for your use.

Table 39.7 RegEx Quantifiers

QUANTIFIER	DESCRIPTION
`?`	Means that the preceding item is optional. In more technical terms, `?` matches the preceding item zero or one times. The preceding item might be a single character, a character class, or a subexpression.
`+`	Means that the preceding item appears at least once; that is, `+` matches the preceding item one or more times. Again, the preceding item might be a single character, a character class, or a subexpression.
`*`	Means that the preceding item is optional, but also may appear any number of times. Conceptually, it's like combining `?` and `+`. That is, it matches the preceding item zero or more times.
`{num}`	Matches the preceding item exactly `num` times; for instance, either `[0-9]{3}` or `\d{3}` will match three numbers (digits).
`{num,max}`	Matches the preceding item between `num` and `max` times. So, if you were looking for all words between 5 and 10 letters in length, you could use `[A-Za-z]{5,10}` or `[[:alpha:]]{5,10}`.
`{num,}`	Matches the preceding item at least `num` times, without a maximum, so `[A-Za-z]{10,}` could be used to find long words (longer than 10 letters). If you think about it, the `+` character (earlier in this table) could be considered a shortcut for `{1,}`.

Using Quantifiers

Let's look at a few examples of using character classes and quantifiers. Say you need to create a regular expression that will match a U.S. ZIP code. Let's start off with the simple five-digit version of a ZIP code. Using the character class skills you learned in Metacharacters 101, you know you could use this:

```
[0-9][0-9][0-9][0-9][0-9]
```

or this:

```
\d\d\d\d\d
```

You can use the `{num}` quantifier from Table 39.7 to avoid having to type a separate class for each digit, like so:

```
[0-9]{5}
```

or like so:

```
\d{5}
```

Now let's say you want to match the nine-digit version of a ZIP code. Just add another class and quantifier sequence, like so:

```
\d{5}-\d{4}
```

Making Certain Portions Be Optional with ?

Okay, what if you wanted to accept either five- or nine-digit ZIP codes? You can use the `?` quantifier to say that the second portion of the code is optional, as in the following:

```
\d{5}(-\d{5})?
```

Note that the `?` quantifier respects parentheses, so in this example everything within the parentheses is modified by the `?`.

Including One or More Matches with +

Another cool quantifier is the `+` metacharacter. Because it matches one or more times, `+` is essential for matching substrings that will vary in length. That turns out to describe the majority of regular expression problems, so you'll be using `+` a lot.

The following matches any number of digits:

```
[0-9]+
```

Like `?` and all the other quantifiers, the `+` character respects parentheses. When it follows a parenthesized group, `+` matches the entire group one or more times. You can also nest these sets of parentheses within one another, an approach that forms the basis of the email address RegEx you have seen throughout this chapter:

```
[\w._]+@[\w_]+(\.[\w_]+)+
```

That looks complex at first, but it's not so bad if you concentrate on each portion separately. The first portion is in charge of matching the username part of the email address (the part before the `@` sign). I came up with `[\w._]+` for this part, which matches any number of letters, numbers, dots, or underscores. After the `@` sign, the next portion is `[\w_]+`, which is almost the same except that it doesn't match dots. Next comes a parenthesized group. Inside the parentheses, the expression reads \.[\w_]+, which means a dot, then any number of letters, numbers, or underscores. The fact that there's a + after the parentheses means that this pattern (a dot, then other stuff) can be repeated any number of times.

In plain English, then, the expression reads "any number of normal characters, then an @ sign, then any number of groups, where the groups each have dots at the beginning," which is a fair description of a validly formed email address.

NOTE

Some of the examples in this chapter add a few additional sets of parentheses to this regular expression so that it contains subexpressions for each part of the email address. Those parentheses don't have anything to do with the + sign, and don't affect which addresses actually match. They just make it possible to capture each portion of the match separately.

Matching Any Number of Matches with *

The * metacharacter is similar to + in that it will match one, two, or any other number of whatever preceded it. The difference is that it will also match zero times: It matches even if the preceding item isn't present at all. I like to think of this quantifier as meaning "any amount of the preceding, but let it be optional."

For instance, it could be used to find <b> (boldface) tags in a chunk of HTML:

```
<b>.*</b>
```

In plain English, this means to match a <b>, then any amount of anything, then </b>. This seems sensible enough. If you try it against this text:

```
The <b>Bear</b> walked alone
```

you will find that the <b>Bear</b> part is what matches, which is what you would expect. However, if you try it against this text:

```
The <b>Bear</b> and the <b>Fox</b> walked hand in hand.
```

it will match the <b>Bear</b> and the <b>Fox</b> part of the text. That is, the RegEx engine finds the first <b>, then matches everything up to the last </b>. What's going on? Although it might seem counterintuitive at first, it's important to understand that the .* part *really does* mean "any number of any characters." There's nothing in the </b>.*</b> expression that says that the .* part isn't supposed to match the characters in the </b> part. It's an important concept that is crucial to understand when crafting regular expressions.

By default, regular expressions are "greedy," which means that the processor is always willing to return the least rigorous interpretation of your RegEx as possible. Or, to put it another way, the engine will always assume that you want the longest possible match. The ColdFusion documentation refers to this as *maximal matching*, but most regular expression references call it *greedy matching*.

One way to fix the boldface-text example is to replace the .* with [^<]*, like so:

```
<b>[^<]*</b>
```

See the difference? In plain English, this now means "match <b>, then match any number of anything that isn't a <, then match </b>."

When used against the previous text sample, this version of the RegEx will correctly match <b>Bear</b> and <b>Fox</b>, making it a pretty good solution to the problem. However, it will fail if the text contains any < characters between the <b> and </b>, like this:

```
The <b><i>Bear</i></b> and the <b>Fox</b> walked hand in hand.
```

Using this text, the <b>[^<]*</b> expression will only match <b>Fox</b>. Bummer. All is not lost, though. You can tell the RegEx engine not to use greedy matching, which brings us to our next topic.

Using Minimal Matching (Non-Greedy) Quantifiers

As you have seen, the fact that regular expressions will match the longest possible substring by default, maximal matching (greedy matching) can sometimes be a problem. In such situations, you can use slightly different quantifiers to tell the RegEx engine to match the shortest possible substring instead. The ColdFusion documentation refers to this as *minimal matching* (as opposed to maximal matching), but most RegEx texts call it *non-greedy matching.*

There is a non-greedy version of each of the quantifiers shown in Table 39.8. To indicate that you want to use the non-greedy version, follow the quantifier with a ? character, as shown in Table 39.8.

Using your newfound knowledge of non-greedy quantifiers, the boldfaced-text problem becomes easy to solve:

```
<b>(.*?)</b>
```

Table 39.8 Minimal Matching (Non-Greedy) Quantifiers

QUANTIFIER	DESCRIPTION
??	Non-greedy version of ?, which means that the preceding item is optional. The difference in the non-greedy version is that the RegEx engine will first try to match based on the item's absence. In other words, the item will only be included in the match if it is not possible to get a match without the item.
+?	Non-greedy version of +, which means that the preceding item will match at least once, but as few times as possible.
*?	Non-greedy version of *, which means that the preceding item can appear any number of times (including none at all), but the shortest possible string will always be found.
{num,max}?	Non-greedy version of {num,max}, which means that the preceding item will match between num and max times, but as few times as actually possible.
{num,}?	Non-greedy version of {num,}, which means that the preceding item will match at least num times, but as few times as actually possible.

If you wanted to ensure that there was at least one character between the <b> and </b> tags, you could use the non-greedy version of + instead of *, like so:

```
<b>(.+?)</b>
```

This expression will match all bold text, but not empty `<b></b>` tags.

Metacharacters 201: Alternation

Sometimes you might need to find matches that contain one string or pattern, or another string or pattern. That is, sometimes you need the conceptual equivalent of what would be called an "or" in normal programming languages, or the `OR` part of a SQL query.

To perform "or" matches with regular expressions, use the `|` character (usually called the *pipe* character). Each pipe represents the idea of "or." Just as in normal programming, the `|` character's effect can be constrained with parentheses, so `Number (1|2)` is different from `Number 1|2`. The first would match the string `Number 1` or `Number 2`, whereas the second would match `Number 1` or just the number `2`.

The following RegEx would match the phrase My Red Fox, My Brown Fox, or My Beige Fox. It would also match My 1 Fox, My 2 Foxes, My 3 Foxes, or any other number of foxes:

```
My ((Red|Brown|Beige|1) Fox|[0-9]+Foxes)\b
```

Metacharacters 202: Word Boundaries

Often, you will need to write regular expressions that are aware of word boundaries. ColdFusion supports the Perl-style `\b` and `\B` boundary sequences, as described in Table 39.9.

Table 39.9 Perl-Style Boundary Sequences

SEQUENCE	MEANING
`\b`	Matches what can generally be described in plain English as a *word boundary*. Technically, a boundary is defined as the transition between an alphanumeric character and a nonalphanumeric character.
`\B`	The opposite of `\b`, matching any character that is not a word boundary. Generally less useful than `\b` in most scenarios.

The `\b` boundary sequence is particularly handy for making sure that your regular expression matches only whole words. For instance, the regular expression `\b[Cc]at\b` would match cat or Cat, but not Cats, Catsup, or Scat.

Metacharacters 203: String Anchors

String anchors are conceptually similar to boundary sequences (see the preceding section), because they are another way of making sure that your regular expression doesn't find undesired "partial matches." Whereas boundaries are about making sure the match "bumps up" against the beginning or end of a word, string anchors are about making sure the match "bumps up" against the beginning or end of the entire chunk of text being searched.

The RegEx string anchors are listed in Table 39.10.

Table 39.10 String Anchors

ANCHOR	DESCRIPTION
`^`	Matches the beginning the chunk of text being searched. Or, in multiline mode, matches the beginning of a line (multiline mode is discussed next).
`$`	Matches the end of the text being searched. Or, in multiline mode, matches the end of a line.
`\A`	Always matches the beginning of the chunk of text being searched, regardless of whether multiline mode is being used.
`\Z`	Always matches the end of the text being searched, regardless of multiline mode.

For instance, perhaps you have a form field called `ZipFieldPlus4`, which you want to validate to make sure it contains a properly formatted U.S. postal ZIP code (the nine-digit "+4" variety). If you didn't know about string anchors, you might decide to use `\d{5}-\d{4}` as the regular expression, like so:

```
<cfif reFind("\d{5}-\d{4}", form.zipCodePlus4)>
 Okay
<cfelse>
 Not Valid
</cfif>
```

This regular expression seems to do the job. It displays "Okay" if the user enters something like `01201-9809`, and "Not Valid" if the user enters `01201-98` or just `01201`.

However, it will also display "Okay" if the user types `Foo 01201-9809` or `01201-9809Bar`, because there is nothing about the regular expression that says the ZIP code must be the *only* thing the user enters. The solution is to anchor the regular expression to the beginning and end of the string using `^` and `$`, like so:

```
<cfif reFind("^\d{5}-\d{4}$", FORM.zipCodePlus4)>
 Okay
<cfelse>
 Not Valid
</cfif>
```

Alternatively, you could use the `\A` and `\Z` sequences, like so:

```
<cfif reFind("\A\d{5}-\d{4}\Z", FORM.zipCodePlus4)>
 Okay
<cfelse>
 Not Valid
</cfif>
```

These two snippets will perform the same way, because `^` is synonymous with `\A` (and `$` is synonymous with `\Z`) unless the regular expression uses multiline mode.

Understanding Multiline Mode

If you start your regular expression with the special sequence `(?m)`, the regular expression is processed in what the ColdFusion and Perl engines call *multiline mode*. Multiline mode means that the

^ and $ characters match the beginning and end of a line within the chunk of text being searched, rather than the beginning and end of the entire chunk of text.

Let's say you were going to search the following chunk of text:

```
1 frog a leaping
2 foxes jumping
100 programs crashing
5 golden rings
```

The following regular expression would get only the first line; because multiline mode is not in effect, ^ will match only the very beginning of the text:

```
^\d+[[:print:]]+
```

This one matches all four lines; because multimode is on, ^ matches the beginning of a line:

```
(?m)^\d+[[:print:]]+
```

This next one matches the first three lines (because they all end with `ing`), but not the last line:

```
(?m)^\d+[[:print:]]+ing$
```

All this said, it is very important to understand what the definition of a line is for the purposes of multiline mode processing. When you use `(?m)` with ColdFusion, each linefeed character (that's ASCII character 10) is considered to start a new line; this is the Unix method of indicating new lines. Carriage return characters (ASCII code 13) are not considered the start of new lines, which means that

- Multimode processing won't work correctly with chunks of text that originate on Macintosh computers, because the text might contain only carriage return characters and no linefeeds.
- Chunks of text that originate on Windows/MS-DOS machines probably contain CRLF sequences (a carriage return followed by a linefeed), to separate the lines. As far as RegEx multimode processing is concerned, a carriage return character sits at the very end of every line, which means that the $ will not work properly because it matches only linefeeds, not carriage returns.
- Chunks of text that originate on Unix machines will work fine (but if the chunks of text are coming from the public, it's unlikely that they are using Unix browsers).

Therefore, if you are going to use multiline mode, I recommend that you use ColdFusion's normal `replace()` method to massage the chunk of text that you're going to search. First, replace each CRLF with a linefeed (that should take care of the Windows text), and then replace any remaining carriage returns with linefeeds (to deal with the Mac text). Assuming that the chunk of text you will be searching is in a string variable called `str`, the following two lines will do the job:

```
<cfset str = reReplace(str, Chr(13)&Chr(10), Chr(10), "ALL")>
<cfset str = reReplace(str, Chr(13), Chr(10), "ALL")>
```

Another option would be to use the `adjustNewlinesToLinefeeds()` function included in the `RegExFunctions.cfm` UDF library, like so:

```
<cfset str = adjustNewlinesToLinefeeds(str)>
```

Metacharacters 301: Match Modifiers

Perl 5 introduced a number of special modifiers that begin with the sequence (?, as listed in Table 39.11. Most of these modifiers are discussed elsewhere in this chapter, as indicated.

Table 39.11 Match Modifiers Supported in ColdFusion

MODIFIER	DESCRIPTION
(?x)	Allows you to write the rest of the expression with indentation, white space, and comments. A nice alternative to writing a very complex expression all on one long line (see example after this table).
(?m)	Tells the engine to use multiline mode for purposes of matching ^ and $ (discussed in the preceding section, "Understanding Multiline Mode").
(?i)	Tells the engine to perform case-insensitive matches, regardless of whether you are using `reFind()` or `reFindNoCase()`—or, for that matter, `reReplace()` versus `reReplaceNoCase()`.
?:	Used at the beginning of a set of parentheses, tells the engine not to consider the value as a subexpression. That is, (?:) means that the parentheses will not add an item to the `len` and `pos` arrays. The parentheses still behave normally in all other respects (for instance, a quantifier after a set of the parentheses still applies to everything within the set).
?=	Used at the beginning of a set of parentheses, tells the engine to match whatever is inside the parentheses using positive lookahead. This means you want to make sure that the pattern exists but that you don't need it to be part of the actual match.
?!	Used at the beginning of a set of parentheses, tells the engine to match whatever is inside the parentheses using negative lookahead, which means that you want to make sure that the pattern does not exist.

NOTE

The ColdFusion documentation implies that you can use only `(?x)` or `(?m)` or `(?i)` at the very beginning of a regular expression. Actually, you can use them anywhere in the expression, but they always affect the whole expression, ignoring parentheses. There is no way to say that you only want part of the expression to be affected by `(?i)`, for instance. This is consistent with Perl's behavior. Just the same, I recommend putting these match modifiers at the beginning of the expression, because that's the documented usage.

As an example of using the (?x) modifier, consider the simple phone number RegEx that has been used elsewhere in this chapter. When used in a `reFind()`, it can look a bit unwieldy and somewhat inscrutable:

```
<cfset match = reFind("(\([0-9]{3}\))([0-9]{3}-[0-9]{4})", text, 1, true)>
```

Using (?x), you can spread the regular expression over as many lines as you want, using whatever indention you want. You can also use the # sign to add comments, like this:

```
<cfset match = reFind("(?x)

 ( ## (begin capturing area code with subexpression)
 \([0-9]{3}\) ## Area Code portion, surrounded by literal parentheses
 ) ## (end capturing of area code)
```

```
    ( ## (begin capturing actual phone number)
    [0-9]{3} ## "Exchange" portion of phone number,
    - ## then a hyphen,
    [0-9]{4} ## then the last four digits of phone number
    ) ## (end capturing of phone number)

", text, 1, True)>
```

Anything from a ## to the end of the line is considered to be a comment.

NOTE

Actually, the RegEx comment indicator is a single #, not ##, but because # has special meaning to ColdFusion, you need to use two pound signs together in order to get the # character into the RegEx string. This is the case anytime you need to embed # within a quoted string in CFML.

TIP

If you need to match a space character while using `(?x)`, escape the space character by typing a \ followed by a space. That tells the processor to consider the space as an actual part of the match criteria, rather than part of the indention and other decorative white space.

Metacharacters 302: Lookahead Matching

As noted in Table 39.11, you can use the positive lookahead modifier at the beginning of any parenthesized set of items. Positive lookahead means that you want to test that a pattern exists, but without it actually being considered part of the match. For instance, consider the following regular expression:

```
\bBelinda (?=Foxile)
```

This expression will match `Belinda` in a chunk of text, but only if it is followed by `Foxile`. `Belinda` followed by `Carlisle` will not match.

Negative lookahead, conversely, means that you want to test that a pattern does not exist. Conceptually, it's kind of like being able to say "this but not that." The following expression will match any `Belinda`, as long as it's not `Belinda Carlisle`:

```
\bBelinda (?!Carlisle)
```

Here's another example of using lookahead. Say you are using a simple regular expression such as the following to match telephone numbers in the form (999)999-9999:

```
(\([0-9]{3}\))([0-9]{3}-[0-9]{4})
```

The following variation adds negative lookahead to match only the phone numbers that are not in the 212 area code:

```
(\((?!212)[0-9]{3}\))([0-9]{3}-[0-9]{4})
```

This last variation adds negative lookahead together with backreferences in the regular expression to match only the phone numbers that are not in the 212 area code, but where the phrase `(new listing)` appears after the number:

```
(\((?!212)[0-9]{3}\))([0-9]{3}-[0-9]{4})\s+(?=\(new listing\))
```

NOTE

ColdFusion does not support look-behind processing (Perl's `(?<=)` and `(?<!)` sequences).

Metacharacters 303: Backreferences Redux

Earlier in this chapter, used backreferences such as `\1` and `\2` in the replacement string when using `REReplace()`, which allowed you to perform far more intelligent replacements than when using static replacement strings. You can also use backreferences in the regular expression itself: Each backreference is like a variable that holds the value of the corresponding subexpression. Let's look at our telephone number RegEx again. Here's the normal version of the expression:

```
(\([0-9]{3}\))([0-9]{3}-[0-9]{4})
```

The following variation matches only the phone numbers with the same last four digits:

```
(\([0-9]{3}\))([0-9]{3}-(\d)\3\3\3)
```

This variation adds negative lookahead (discussed in the preceding section) to match only phone numbers in which the last four digits are not the same:

```
(\([0-9]{3}\))([0-9]{3}-(?!(\d)\3\3\3))
```

Metacharacters 304: Escape Sequences

ColdFusion supports the use of normal Perl escape sequences in regular expressions, as shown in Table 39.12. Previously, you needed to add these special characters to your RegEx string using the `Chr()` function. You can still do so, but these escape sequences are more standard and easier to type and read.

Table 39.12 RegEx Escape Sequences

ESCAPE SEQUENCE	DESCRIPTION
`\n`	Newline.
`\t`	Tab.
`\f`	Form feed.
`\r`	Carriage return.
`\x00`	Allows you to specify any character, using a two-digit hexadecimal number. For instance, the ASCII code for an exclamation point is 33 using normal (decimal) numbers; this is 21 in hexadecimal, so you could use `\x21` to specify an exclamation point in a RegEx. (Clearly, there would be more point to this if it were a character that's not on your keyboard, but you get the idea.)
`\000`	Allows you to specify any character using a three-digit octal character. The octal version of 33 is 41, so you can also use `\041` to specify an exclamation point.

Note that these escape sequences can be used in character classes, so `[\x00-xC8]` would match any of the first 200 characters in the character set (`C8` is hexadecimal for what we humans call 200).

CHAPTER 40

ColdFusion Scripting

IN THIS CHAPTER

Have you ever heard someone complain about ColdFusion that they didn't like that "you have to code in tags"? The very good news is that times have changed for scripting in ColdFusion 9.

Some may know that there's long been a feature called `<cfscript>`, which allows writing CFML in a more script-like way. The truth is that it offered just a tiny subset of CFML functionality.

ColdFusion 9 has dramatically changed the landscape for those who prefer to write or read code using scripting. Many more things (nearly anything) can now be done in scripting. In this chapter, you'll explore both what's long been possible and, more important, what's new.

A New Era in CFML Scripting

When originally created, the CFML language was designed as a tag-based language because its goal was to make it easier to be understood by HTML developers, who were familiar with the concept of tags in creating HTML dynamically. Building HTML pages was the stock in trade for ColdFusion in its early years.

Times Have Changed

Of course, the Web and ColdFusion have both evolved tremendously since then. Many more CFML developers have worked with other programming languages such as Java, PHP, and C# or with client application languages such as JavaScript and ActionScript. These all follow a more traditional script-based (rather than tag-based) design.

It's also now possible for CFML to be used to create applications that have nothing to do with HTML (such as generating JSON, XML, Web Services, and more). ColdFusion Components (CFCs) can even declare (at the component or method level) that they will create no output at all.

For many developers, being forced to use tags has added a needless burden to development. For others, it may well have hampered the adoption (or retention) of CFML as a language they want to use.

Again, previous releases of ColdFusion did enable some script-based development, by way of the `<cfscript>` tag, and it provided for a limited subset of the CFML language that could be used within that tag. The vast majority of tags had no script-based equivalent, however, so `<cfscript>` was not commonly used by most developers, and the feature really hadn't evolved much in several years.

Now CFML Has Changed

ColdFusion 9 marks a dramatic change in CFML scripting. Many more formerly tag-based operations can be scripted, such that some CFML templates can now be written in `<cfscript>` only. Indeed, it's now possible to create a CFC entirely in `<cfscript>`: You don't need to use the `<cfscript>` tag at all. You'll see an example of that later in this chapter.

To be clear, though, if you like tags, you can continue to use them. The newly enhanced `<cfscript>` support merely gives developers new options and greater freedom in coding styles. Broader support for scripting may well improve ColdFusion's credibility and appeal in the wider Web development community.

In the following sections, I'll discuss ColdFusion scripting fundamentals, cover various scripting enhancements in ColdFusion 9, map tags to their script equivalents, discuss scripting with respect to ColdFusion components and user-defined functions, discuss error handling in scripts, and finish with various traps to resolve and avoid.

What Is `<cfscript>`?

ColdFusion scripting allows you to write portions of your templates with script-based syntax, which is often more concise and straightforward than ColdFusion's traditional tag-based syntax.

Scripting syntax is very similar to JavaScript syntax with a couple exceptions that I'll discuss soon.

Listing 40.1 shows an example of some simple assignments first in tags and then in their `<cfscript>` counterparts. Try running Listing 40.1, and you'll see that each version does the same thing.

Listing 40.1 `SimpleScriptExample.cfm`—A Simple Example of ColdFusion Scripting

```
<!--- Author: Charlie Arehart -- carehart.org
      A simple demonstration of assignment using tags and then scripting--->

<!--- Tag-based assignment --->
<cfset person=structnew()>
<cfset person.fname="Bob">
<cfset person.name="Smith">
<cfset person.children=arraynew(1)>
<cfset person.children[1]="Sally">
<cfset person.children[2]="Jimmy">
<cfdump var="#person#">

<cfscript>
```

Listing 40.1 (continued)

```
    // script-based assignment
    person={fname="Bob",lname="Smith",children=["Sally","Jimmy"]};
    writedump(person);
</cfscript>
```

Both segments produce the same output. For many, the scripted section is more readable and intuitive than the tag-based section. You'll notice I also used a new function available in ColdFusion 9, `writedump()`. This is one of several new functions in ColdFusion 9 designed specifically to bring more tag-based functionality to scripting, as you'll see later.

Actually, I cheated in the scripting: I used a way of creating structures and arrays in a single statement (using the braces and brackets, `{}`and `[]`, respectively) that is in fact not unique to scripting. It could have been used in the first `<cfset>`, as of ColdFusion 8. (Implicit array and structure creation is discussed in Chapter 8, "The Basics of CFML," in *Adobe ColdFusion 9 Web Application Construction Kit, Volume 1: Getting Started*.) But this helps to drive home the point that CFML can now be written in a far more compact way and with scripting that is familiar to many.

Listing 40.2 demonstrates this more clearly. It shows first a (commented-out) tag-based index loop and then its `<cfscript>` counterpart. Again, each version would produce the same output.

Listing 40.2 `LoopScriptExample.cfm`—An Example of Looping in ColdFusion Scripting

```
<!--- Author: Adam Phillip Churvis -- ProductivityEnhancement.com --->
<!--- Edited by: Charlie Arehart, carehart.org --->
<!--- Indexed For loop  --->

<!--- Tag-based --->
<cfset colorCodes = ["Red,Orange,Yellow"]>
<cfloop index="i" from="1" to="#ArrayLen(colorCodes)#">
  <cfoutput><p>#colorCodes[i]#</p></cfoutput>
</cfloop>

<cfscript>
   // Script-based
   colorCodes = ["Red,Orange,Yellow"];
   for(i=1; i <= ArrayLen(colorCodes); i=i+1) {
     WriteOutput("<p>" & colorCodes[i] & "</p>");
   }
</cfscript>
```

For those from scripting backgrounds, the scripted loop is more readable because it uses familiar constructs from other script-based languages (such as `//` for comments, bracketed `for` blocks, and not a single `#`). Although this sort of syntax may be foreign to longtime ColdFusion developers, its similarity to other languages will make other developers more comfortable.

Some may notice that I use `<=` for the conditional comparison (as opposed to the older `LTE` form, which may be more familiar to taggers) and `++` for incrementing a variable. These are not actually unique to scripting, because they can be used in tags, too, as of ColdFusion 8. They will certainly be more familiar to script programmers.

TIP

For those programmers familiar with ternary operators, ColdFusion 9 has introduced them for expressions used both within script and within tags. A simplistic example of this is as follows:

```
<cfset c = (a GT b)? a : b >
```

where, if a is greater than b, then c is assigned the value of a; otherwise, c is assigned the value of b.

Differences Between <cfscript> and JavaScript

Some will notice that <cfscript> looks a lot like JavaScript, another scripting language, but note that ColdFusion scripting is executed entirely on the server side. JavaScript is executed entirely in the user's browser.

There are other differences as well. First, ColdFusion is absolutely fanatical about requiring that all statements be terminated with a semicolon, where JavaScript is more relaxed about that. Second, there is no Document Object Model (DOM) for ColdFusion scripting to access or manipulate, because ColdFusion has no representation of the client page, or "document."

TIP

Unlike JavaScript, <cfscript> does not allow you to escape quotes with the backslash character (\).

Implementing <cfscript>

As you have seen in the prior code examples, to use ColdFusion scripting in your templates, place a <cfscript></cfscript> tag pair in a template, and then write ColdFusion scripting statements in the body of the tag. You can intersperse <cfscript> blocks with blocks of tag-based CFML throughout a ColdFusion template. The converse is not true, though: You cannot put tags anywhere inside a <cfscript> block.

Scripting code can, however, use any CFML functions and can of course access any CFML variables.

TIP

You should avoid defining <cfscript> blocks with a single line of code, such as

```
<cfscript>
   ArrayPrepend(myarray, "New First Element");
</cfscript>
```

It would be more succinct in that example to create just a single tag:

```
<cfset  ArrayPrepend(myarray, "New First Element)">
```

You'll see many more examples of using <cfscript> throughout this chapter, but let's take a brief detour and discuss a rather unusual new aspect of using scripting in ColdFusion 9: the ability to create a CFC entirely in script.

Implementing CFCs in Script

As of ColdFusion 9, you can even create a CFC that is entirely script-based. It does not require either `<cfscript>` or `<cfcomponent>` but is instead wrapped in a `component` statement. Listing 40.3 shows an example of this.

Listing 40.3 `ScriptedCFC.cfc`—A Scripted CFC

```
// Author: Charlie Arehart -- carehart.org
// This is a demonstration of a CFC written entirely in CFSCRIPT

component  displayname="scriptedCFC" hint="I am a scripted CFC" output="false"
{
   property name="AProperty" type="string" hint="I am a property" default="test";

   public string function GetData( string fname="Bob" ) description="I return data"
output="false"
   {
      //note that if you create any local variables, use var!
      var somevariable="somevalue";
      return "Hi #arguments.fname#";
   }
}
```

You could of course invoke this CFC just like any other, whether using `<cfinvoke>`, `<cfobject>`, `createObject()`, or the `new` operator introduced in ColdFusion 9. An example template that calls this CFC (in various ways) is provided in the listings as `InvokeScriptedCFC.cfm`.

NOTE

You may be wondering, "If we can create CFC files as all script, why not CFM files?" The problem is that, unlike CFC files, CFM pages are designed inherently such that any text on the page not surrounded in a tag will be assumed to be passed as output of the page. So, without at least the `<cfscript>` tags, the script code would simply be ignored and sent out to the caller as plain text.

As for the function definition in Listing 40.3, you may notice things like the specification of a datatype for the function (what it must return), which arguments it accepts and their data types, and so on. These are things now possible with function definition as of ColdFusion 9.

ColdFusion 9 also lifts the restriction on using the `var` keyword. You can now use it anywhere within a function. It need not be in the first statement at the top of the function.

Although creating methods is a large part of creating CFCs, it's worth noting that you can also create functions within script to use simply as user-defined functions. Therefore, this chapter offers more information on defining functions below, in the "Defining Functions in Script" section.

Even so, there are still more details and features about creating CFCs in script, including new ways to use JavaDoc-style comments to assist with declaring metadata about the CFC, how properties now auto-generate getters and setters (what some refer to as implicit getters and setters), and more. Those are discussed in Chapter 24, "Creating Advanced ColdFusion Components."

Finally, you can also see the ColdFusion documentation *Developing Adobe ColdFusion 9 Applications*; refer to the "Defining Components and Functions in CFScript" section of the "Extending ColdFusion Pages with CFML Scripting" chapter.

Replacing Tags with Script

The `<cfscript>` tag already offered many alternatives to tag-based CFML, but with ColdFusion 9 you can replace even more tag-based CFML with scripting (although it's important to note that Adobe has implemented some tags as statements, some as functions, and some as CFCs).

Unfortunately, the ColdFusion documentation (currently) does not distinguish between statement and function equivalents (referring to them both as just *CFScript equivalents*), while confusingly referring to the CFC equivalents as *script functions* (and listing them separately).

Table 40.1 tries to resolve that by mapping tags to their available script-based equivalents, indicating which are statements, which are functions, and which are CFCs. It also shows all the equivalents in a single table. As indicated by the footnotes after the table, some statements and functions are implemented in such a way that they can take arguments comprised of multiple lines of code, which will be explained soon.

NOTE

ColdFusion 9 Updater 1, also known as 9.0.1, adds some new functionality related to scripting. For instance, it adds a few new tag-equivalent CFCs, which are also noted with a footnote after Table 40.1.

Table 40.1 Tags and Their Script Equivalents

TAG	STATEMENT EQUIVALENT	FUNCTION EQUIVALENT	CFC (OR "FUNCTION") EQUIVALENT
`<cfabort>`	`abort`[1]		
`<cfbreak>`	`break`[0]		
`<cfcase>`	`case`[3]		
`<cfcatch>`		`catch()`[3]	
`<cfcomponent>`		`component()`[3]	
`<cfcontinue>`	`continue`[0]		
`<cfdefaultcase>`	`default`[3]		
`<cfdirectory>`		See `directory*()` functions	
`<cfdbinfo>`			`dbinfo`[4]
`<cfdump>`		`writedump()`[1]	
`<cfelse>`, `<cfelseif>`	`else`[3], `elseif`[3]		
`<cfexit>`	`exit`[1]		
`<cffeed>`			`feed`[4]

Table 40.1 (continued)

TAG	STATEMENT EQUIVALENT	FUNCTION EQUIVALENT	CFC (OR "FUNCTION") EQUIVALENT
<cffile>		See file*() functions	
<cffinally>	finally[3]		
<cfftp>			ftp
<cffunction>		function()[2,3]	
<cfhttp>			http
<cfimage>		See image*() functions	
<cfimap>			imap[4]
<cfif>	if[3]		
<cfimport>	import[1]		
<cfinclude>	include[1]		
<cfinterface>	interface[3]		
<cfldap>			ldap[4]
<cflocation>		location()[1,2]	
<cflock>	lock[3]		
<cflog>		writelog()[2]	
<cfloop>	for[3], do[3]		
<cfmail>			mail
<cfobject>	new[1]	createobject()[2]	
<cfoutput>		writeoutput()[1]	
<cfparam>	param[2]		
<cfpdf>			pdf
<cfpop>			pop[4]
<cfprocessingdirective>	pageencoding[1] (must appear on first line inside of component definition)		
<cfproperty>	property[2]		
<cfquery>			query
<cfrethrow>	rethrow[0]		
<cfreturn>	return[1]		
<cfsavecontent>	cfsavecontent[3]		
<cfset>	*assignment expression*		
<cfswitch>		switch()[3]	
<cfstoredproc> / <cfstoredprocresult>			storedproc / storedprocresult

Table 40.1 (continued)

TAG	STATEMENT EQUIVALENT	FUNCTION EQUIVALENT	CFC (OR "FUNCTION") EQUIVALENT
`<cfthread>`	`thread`[2,3]		
`<cfthrow>`		`throw()`[2]	
`<cftrace>`		`trace()`[2]	
`<cftransaction>`		`transaction()`[2,3]	
`<cftry>`	`try`[3]		

[0] Indicates statement takes (or can take) no arguments
[1] Indicates statement or function takes (or can take) one unnamed arguments
[2] Indicates statement or function takes (or can take) multiple arguments
[3] Indicates statement or function takes (or can take) multi-line arguments
[4] Indicates CFC added in 9.0.1

There doesn't always seem to be a clear reason why a tag would be implemented either as a statement or as a function. As the saying goes, "It is what it is." You just have to deal with it.

To help you better understand the difference between these types (statement, function, and CFC), the following sections look at some examples of using each type.

NOTE

Many tags still have no scripting alternative. It is possible, of course, to call upon any tag by way of calling a function or CFC from within script, where that called function or CFC has been written to use whatever tags you desire, giving you full access to all of CFML.

Using Script Statements

Most tags have equivalent *statements* in scripting, which will seem very familiar to those with experience in other scripting languages. For traditional tag-based CFML developers, the differences are minor, except for a few cases. This section introduces you to how to use script equivalents that are implemented as statements.

Just as some tags take no attributes, so also do their corresponding script statements take no arguments (such as `break` or `continue`). Other statements can take only one argument, which either must be provided (such as `include`) or is optional (such as `exit`). Still others can (and generally do) wrap several lines of code that follow (such as `for`, `if`, and so on), whose nested lines you indicate using braces.

Examples of a few of each type of statement follow. In each example shown, you'll see first the tag-based equivalent and then the script-based equivalent. This is not an exhaustive list showing examples for every script statement. The goal is just to help you become familiar with the alternative types and how to implement them.

Statements with No Arguments

The following are examples of some script-based tag equivalents implemented as statements that take no arguments because their corresponding tags also take no arguments.

break

```
<cfbreak>
break;
```

Other statements like this are `continue` and `rethrow`.

Statements That Take One Unnamed Argument

The following are examples of some statements that take only one, unnamed argument.

`include` Processing

```
<cfinclude template="templatename.ext">

include "templatename.ext";
```

The argument values in statements like these would accept whatever are valid values for the one attribute supported by the tags (`template` in the case of the `include` statement). It seems that the engineers decided that if there was only one attribute, there was no need to make you name it (and indeed, you cannot).

Other examples like this are `abort`, `exit`, `import`, and `return`. Note that in the case of `abort`, `exit`, and `return`, even the one argument is optional.

CAUTION

If while working with the `import` statement, you get an error (when trying to instantiate a CFC) reporting "Could not find the ColdFusion Component or Interface," the problem may have to do not just with the current setting for your `import` but possibly with a previous value for it. For more on that, see the "Common Problems and Solutions" section later in this chapter.

Statements That Take Multiple Arguments

The following is an example of some statements that take multiple arguments.

Page Parameter Setting

```
<cfparam name="somevar" default="someval" type="sometype">

param name="somevar" default="someval" type="sometype";
```

Other statements that take multiple arguments are `property` and `thread`.

Statements That Take Multi-line Arguments

The following are some examples of the kind of script statements that can take an argument that encompasses multiple lines of code, just like their tag-based equivalents (such as `<cflock>`, `<cfsavecontent>`, and so on).

Note that in script you use braces (the `{` and `}` characters) to open and close a line. Some may refer to these statements as "having a body," referring to the code enclosed within the braces.

NOTE

Whether the braces should start on the line that opens the statement or on the next line, where/how they should be indented is a personal choice. ColdFusion imposes no requirements.

Lock Processing

```
<cflock scope="scope" type="type" timeout="nn">
       [CFML to be locked (another variant for lock uses Name attr)]
</cflock>

lock scope="scope" type="type" timeout="nn" {
       [script to be locked (another variant for lock uses Name attr)]
}
```

Other statements like this are `interface`, `savecontent`, `thread`, and `try/finally`. (There are still others, such as `if`, `else`, `for`, and `do`, that are more traditional scripting statements used for flow of control. These are covered in the next section.)

Before leaving the subject of statements that can take multi-line arguments, let's take a look at a somewhat unusual one, `savecontent`. You may know that if you want to evaluate a variable whose result would go (along with the rest of the content) into the saved content variable, you must use a `<cfoutput>`. In the case of `savecontent`, however, the following is correct.

`savecontent` Processing

```
<cfsavecontent variable="somevar">
       [CFML/HTML to build content to save to somevar]
       <!--- note that to render variables requires cfoutput --->
</cfsavecontent>
<cfdump var="#somevar#">

savecontent variable="somevar" {
       [CFML script to build content to save to somevar]
       // note that to render variables requires writeoutput
}

writedump(somevar);
```

NOTE

In the previous examples, it would be permitted to split the multiple arguments over multiple lines, rather than list them all on one line, if you prefer.

You may notice in the previous examples that these multi-line examples also happen to take an argument (sometimes multiple). I thought it was more helpful to discuss them here as multi-line statements.

Some Common Multi-line Programming Statements

Beyond the statements with multi-line arguments discussed above, there are many other multi-line scripting statements that, although familiar to those with scripting experience from other languages, may be quite new and different for those new to scripting.

I've provided below several examples of such common programming functionality that you may want to implement in scripting code, particularly for different kinds of loops. Again, I don't provide the details for every possible statement. See the ColdFusion documentation on scripting for more details.

As you consider these examples, note that there are sometimes ways that the multi-line scripting statements work that are a bit different from their tag-based equivalents. See, for example, the `do-while` loop (for which there is no exact tag equivalent) and `switch-case` and `try-catch` in script, where in each case some of the statements are in a slightly different order as compared to their corresponding tag equivalents.

Also, one more potential concern when working with multi-line script statements is the possibility that you may encounter some mistakes while getting used to them (whether actual errors or possibly logic errors) if you use the braces inappropriately. For more on that, see the "Common Problems and Solutions" section later in this chapter.

Now let's look at the examples of some common multi-line statements.

`if-elseif-else`

```
<cfif condition1>
  [logic]
<cfelseif condition2>
  [logic]
<cfelse>
  [logic]
</cfif>

if(condition1) {
  [logic];
} else if(condition2) {
  [logic];
} else {
  [logic];
}
```

`switch-case`

```
<cfswitch expression="">
  <cfcase value="value1">
    [logic]
  </cfcase>
  <cfcase value="value2">
    [logic]
  </cfcase>
  <cfdefaultcase>
    [logic]
  </cfdefaultcase>
</cfswitch>

switch(expression) {
  case "value1":
    [logic];
    break;
  case "value2":
```

```
      [logic];
      break;
    default:
      [logic];
  }
```

`for` Loops

```
<cfloop index="i" from="1" to="10">
  [logic]
</cfloop>

for(i=1; i <= 10; i++) {
  [logic];
}
```

`while` Loops

```
<cfloop condition="#expression#">
  [logic];
</cfloop>

while(expression) {
  [logic];
}
```

`do-while` Loops

```
do {
  [logic];
} while(expression);

(No tag-based equivalent)
```

`for-in` (Collection/Structure) Loops

```
<cfloop collection="#structure#" item="key">
  [logic]
</cfloop>

for(key in structure) {
  [logic];
}
```

Note that ColdFusion 9.0.1 has added support for using the `var` keyword in such `for-in` constructs:

```
for(var key in structure) {
  [logic];
}
```

Array Loops

```
<cfloop array="#array#" index="i">
  [logic]
</cfloop>

for(i=1; i <= ArrayLen(array); i++) {
  [logic]
}
```

Note that ColdFusion 9.0.1 has added support for looping over arrays with a `for-in` construct (the `new` option to use the `var` keyword applies as well):

```
for (var item in array){
       writeoutput(item);
}
```

List Loops

```
<cfloop list="#list#" index="listelem">
  <cfoutput>#listelem#</cfoutput><br>
</cfloop>

for(i=1; i <= ListLen(list); i++) {
  writeoutput(listgetat(list,i)&'<br>');
}
```

Query Loops

```
<cfloop query="queryName">
  <cfoutput>#queryname.columname#<br></cfoutput>
</cfloop>

for(i=1;i <=queryname.recordcount;i++) {
   writeoutput(queryname.columnname[i] & '<br>');
}
```

While I'm discussing loop processing, note that both script-based loops can be interrupted programmatically, using either `continue` or `break`. `continue` tells ColdFusion to skip to the beginning of the next loop iteration, while `break` exits the current loop or case statement.

I'll conclude this section with some examples of additional common multi-line scripting statements: those for `try-catch` processing.

`try-catch` Handling

```
try {
  [logic];
}
catch(Expression exception) {
  [logic];
}
catch(Any exception) {
  [logic];
}
finally {
  [logic]
}

<cftry>
  [logic]
  <cfcatch type="Expression">
    [logic];
  </cfcatch>
  <cfcatch type="Any">
    [logic];
```

```
  </cfcatch>
  <cffinally>
    [logic]
  </cffinally>
</cftry>
```

Actually, you may have noticed that although the `try` statement is a multi-line statement, it is used with `catch`, which is in fact a function. There's actually a good bit more that I can explain about error handling in scripting, both in terms of what you pass to that `catch` function, as well as how to implement throw and rethrow processing. These are all covered in the "Exception Handling in Script" section later in this chapter.

Unusual Statements

Finally, I should mention two kinds of statements that don't really fit into the above categories ("no arguments," "with arguments," and "multi-line").

First is variable assignment, which has no real statement. You simply define an expression that equates to what would have been the attribute-value pair of a `<cfset>` tag.

Variable Assignment

```
<cfset myVariable = "Value">
<cfset var myVariable = "Value">
<cfset session.myVariable = "Value">

myVariable = "Value";
var myVariable = "Value";
session.myvariable = "value";
```

And then there are comments. With tags, there's just one tag for comments regardless of whether it takes up one or more lines. In scripting, however, there are two different ways to indicate comments, either on a single line or over (potentially) multiple lines.

Comments

```
<!--- single or
        multi-line comment --- >

//single line example
/*multi-line
  example */
```

Using Script Functions

Although to this point I've focused on statement-based scripting, Table 40.1 did show several instances of tags that are implemented instead as functions. A couple of examples will help show how to implement them. Again, we won't show examples of all the function-based script equivalents.

NOTE

If you have jumped to this section of the chapter without reading the introduction to this section, the ColdFusion documentation also uses the term *script functions* to refer instead to what are CFC-based script equivalents. Those are discussed in the "Using Script Functions (CFCs)" section later in this chapter.

Single-Argument Functions

Just as with traditional CFML functions (whether in tags or in script), there are some script functions that take one argument (which can be unnamed) and others that can take several.

Let's look first at those that take one unnamed argument.

`writeoutput`

```
<cfoutput>#somevar#</cfoutput>
```

```
Writeoutput(somevar);
```

Even though `<cfoutput>` can accept multiple attributes, they don't apply to its script equivalent.

The other tags with script equivalents that can work with just one argument are `location()` and `writedump()`. These statements can actually take multiple arguments, but you provide just the one that's at the heart of its process (the URL for `location()` or the variable for `writedump()`).

`location` **Processing**

```
<cflocation url="someurl">
```

```
location("someurl");
```

Multiple-Argument Functions

Many of the functions take multiple arguments, such as `createobject()`, `location()`, `throw()`, `trace()`, and `writelog()`. And some of these, such as `function()`and `transaction()`, also accept an argument with multiple statements (have a body). I discussed statements that have a body previously, and the issues discussed there apply to them as well.

Moving on, some functions let you pass multiple arguments and let you do it either as name-value pairs or as positional arguments, such as the following:

`location` **Processing**

```
<cflocation url="someurl">
<cflocation url="someurl" addtoken="false">
```

```
location(url="someurl");
location(url="someurl",addtoken="false");
location("someurl","false");
```

I haven't found any documentation clarifying what the positional arguments would be, so you may discover them by trial and error.

In the case of functions that accept multiple arguments, you can also generally use `attribute collection` if the tag supports it. Here's an example using `location`:

`location` **Processing with** `attributecollection`

```
parms=structnew();
parms.url="someurl";
parms.addtoken="true";
location(attributecollection=parms);
```

Using Script Functions (CFCs)

The last kind of script equivalents shown in Table 40.1 are those implemented as CFCs. Actually, they're CFCs, so you will create an instance of the CFC and then call methods within the CFC, many of which equate to the corresponding attributes or returned variables that are more typically used with tags.

The difference (needing to call a method to do the equivalent of setting a tag attribute) may seem a little verbose to some tastes (which is ironic, given the argument by some against tags), but the value of being able to script all or part of a template is compelling enough to some that it may be a reasonable trade-off.

Examples of Scripting `<cfquery>` and `<cfhttp>`

I'll show a couple examples of calling such a tag-equivalent CFC, first by showing how to do the equivalent of a `<cfquery>` tag in script. Then I'll discuss some details about working with them. See Listing 40.4, which includes comments.

Listing 40.4 `cfhttpEquivalentExample.cfm`—Scripting `<cfhttp>`

```
<cfscript>
   /* Author: Charlie Arehart -- carehart.org
      Performs the equivalent of CFHTTP against google.com*/

    httpService = createobject("component","http");

      // see the chapter for other ways to initialize the CFC

    httpService.setUrl("http://www.google.com");

      /* set ResolveURL="true", just as with CFHTTP, so that any
      images or other paths returned in the html are set to be
      relative to the server from which the URL's' been requested
      */

      httpService.setResolveURL("true");
    result = httpService.send().getPrefix();

      // output result just like as with cfhttp.filecontent

      writeoutput(result.filecontent);
</cfscript>
```

Next is a little more elaborate example that does a <cfquery> tag in script. See Listing 40.5, which includes comments, and which I will expand on after the code.

Listing 40.5 QueryExample.cfm—Scripting <cfquery>

```
<cfscript>
   /* Author: Charlie Arehart -- carehart.org
      Performs the equivalent of CFQUERY against the Actors table */

   queryService = new query();
   // See chapter for other alternatives to initialize the CFC

   queryService.setDatasource("ows");
   queryService.setName("GetActors");
   // See chapter for other alternatives to set properties

   // Can add the equivalent of more attributes, such as CachedWithin

   queryService.setcachedwithin(CreateTimeSpan(0, 6, 0, 0));

   // You can also add the equivalent of cfqueryparams, using addParam

   /* the first example uses a name-value pair to provide an age=40 value
      for the :age indication in the SQL statement */

   queryService.addParam(name="age",value="40",cfsqltype="numeric");

   /* the second example uses an unnamed parameter for the first ?
      indicator in the SQL statement, providing the value 'M' for
         the gender column in the where clause */

   queryService.addParam(value="M",cfsqltype="cf_sql_varchar");

   result = queryService.execute(
      sql="SELECT namefirst, namelast, age, gender
         FROM Actors WHERE age >= :age and gender = ?
         ORDER BY namelast, namefirst ");

   GetActors = result.getResult();

   // getPrefix() returns query resultset metadata,
   // including the query parameters (as sqlparameters)

   metaInfo = result.getPrefix();

   writeoutput("<h4>Found #metaInfo.recordcount# records for actors
      with age>='#metainfo.sqlparameters[1]#' and
         gender='#metainfo.sqlparameters[2]#</h4>");

   // you can loop over the query by treating each row as an array element

   for(i=1;i <=GetActors.recordcount;i++) {
      writeoutput(getactors.namefirst[i] & getactors.namelast[i]
      & '<br>');
   }
```

Listing 40.5 (continued)

```
    writedump(GetActors);

    // note that while the GetActors dump does not show
    // recordcount, you can use it

    writedump(metaInfo);

    // and while the GetActors dump does show sqlparameters,
    // you can't use it and must use the output of getPrefix
</cfscript>
```

Although it's beyond the scope of this chapter to detail each such CFC-based script equivalent, the listings above do show some real examples of doing first a `<cfhttp>` and then a `<cfquery>` in script. They serve as models of how you can expect to be able to execute other "tags as CFCs."

For more details on each of the CFC-based tag equivalents, see *Adobe ColdFusion 9 CFML Reference*, particularly the "Script Functions Implemented as CFCs" chapter.

CAUTION

If you get an error reporting "Could not find the ColdFusion Component or Interface," the problem is likely that someone has removed a needed (default) custom tag path definition from the ColdFusion Administrator. For more on that, see the "Common Problems and Solutions" section later in this chapter.

Still, there are a few points that apply to working with any of the several CFC-based tag equivalents.

Flexibility in Splitting Long Lines

Take a look at the `execute` and `writeoutput` methods in the previous listing. Did you notice that I was able to freely split long strings (whether SQL statements or output strings) across multiple lines, as I passed those in as arguments to methods? That's helpful if you prefer to have really long lines. (And it's technically not limited to script within CFCs. It's just that this was the first example that usefully demonstrated that.)

Flexibility and Choices in Initializing CFCs

Some may also have noticed that I showed how to use the `new` operator in instantiating the CFC. That's not unique to scripting (it could be used in a `<cfset>`, for instance, and is new as of ColdFusion 9), and it can be used to instantiate any CFC at all. It will be especially familiar to those coming from a scripting background, so I have shown it here as an example.

But there are actually several ways you can instantiate and initialize one of these CFCs. For instance, the older `createobject` function would work:

```
queryservice=createobject("component","query");
```

But going back to the `new` operator, note that you also could have created the CFC and set its properties in one statement, as follows:

```
queryService = new query(datasource="ows",name="GetActors");
```

And some will know that you can use an `init` method with `createobject` (see the ColdFusion documentation on `createobject` for more information). The `init` method can be used with the `new` operator as well:

```
queryService = new query().init(datasource="ows",name="GetActors");
```

Further, note that even if you chose for some reason not to use the properties in the initialization, you could simply pass several at once (rather than the individual ones I showed), as follows:

```
queryService.setAttributes(datasource="ows",name="GetActors");
```

Where Are These Tag-Equivalent CFCs Located?

Before leaving the subject of tags as CFCs, some may wonder just where these tag-equivalent CFCs are located within the ColdFusion installation directory. You can find them here: `cf_root\CustomTags\com\adobe\coldfusion`.

CAUTION

These script-equivalent CFCs are (currently) offered in plain text, so you can examine them further to understand how they work and perhaps identify capabilities that may not yet be fully documented. Of course, you shouldn't edit them, or you risk breaking their functionality for you and any other user on your ColdFusion server.

NOTE

The CFCs each extend the `base.cfc` located there, which really just calls the tags as tags.

This directory (within `[coldfusion]CustomTags`) is identified and stored within ColdFusion's configuration at the installation of ColdFusion 9, with the custom tag location path being placed in the ColdFusion Administrator configuration. As mentioned already, if that default custom tag path is removed, then calling these tag-equivalent CFCs will fail. See the "Common Problems and Solutions" section for more information.

Defining Functions in Script

To define a function using script, you declare your function just as you would in JavaScript, using the `function` keyword. You saw an example of that in Listing 40.3.

Functions can be defined within a CFML template, in which case they're referred to as *user-defined functions* (or UDFs or just *functions*), and they're callable from within that template or a template that includes it. Or functions can be defined within a ColdFusion Component, in which case they're generally referred to as *methods*.

For more information on creating user-defined functions, see Chapter 22, "Building User-Defined Functions," in Volume 1.

This section discusses just a few points you should know about creating functions in script (and in general), especially with respect to changes in ColdFusion 9.

Making Variables Private to the Function

I mentioned earlier in this chapter that code in script can access any valid ColdFusion variables. When it comes to defining functions, though, some languages operate whereby any variables you create in a function are not exposed to the calling program (unless specifically returned or unless you permit access by the caller). In ColdFusion, however, variables created in a function are available to callers unless you specifically prevent that.

That's where the `var` keyword comes into play. Listing 40.3 showed an example of prefixing the first reference to a variable with the `var` keyword. That tells ColdFusion that you intend that the value of that variable should not be available outside the current function/method.

Again, as discussed in that section, with ColdFusion 9 you can now use the `var` keyword at any point in the function when you are defining a new variable. Another new feature in ColdFusion 9 is the `local` scope, which provides yet another way to provide easy access to working with variables in the function `LOCAL` (or `VAR`) scope. The `LOCAL` scope is discussed further in Chapter 22.

Improved Support for Function Typing

As in JavaScript, functions can also accept arguments and return values.

Although it's long been possible to create user-defined functions in script, and also using the `<cffunction>` tag, a problem in scripting was that you couldn't indicate any metadata about the incoming arguments or returned data. They were presumed to be of type `any`, because the function definition in scripting was only partially implemented. Only with `<cffunction>` and `<cfargument>` could you specify such metadata about the function.

Now in ColdFusion 9, as you saw earlier in Listing 40.3, it's finally possible to declare the return type, the package type, and other metadata about the function. This becomes especially valuable (indeed vital) for creating CFCs entirely in script.

Again, Listing 40.3 showed an example of creating a function within a CFC (a *method*), including the new options to define the return type, input argument types, and other information. Briefly, the key information is provided in the first line defining the function:

```
public string function GetData( string fname="Bob" ) description="I return data"
output="false"
```

Again, for more information on creating user-defined functions in general, see Chapter 22. See also the *Developing ColdFusion 9 Applications* documentation, particularly the "Writing and Calling User-Defined Functions" chapter.

Finally, no discussion of user-defined functions would be complete without referring you to `http://cflib.org`, a Web site that contains hundreds of useful UDFs and libraries of UDFs available for free download and use. It even has an area (`http://cflib.org/library/CFMLLib`) devoted to creating still more UDF versions of CFML tags (though there's some overlap with new features added in ColdFusion 9). Do yourself a favor and head over there now for a quick tour of what they offer.

Exception Handling in Script

CFML error handling in general is covered in Chapter 44, "Error Handling," online. If you're already familiar with implementing structured exception handling in your CFML code, then you're also familiar with using `<cftry>-<cfcatch>` constructs and the various types of errors that can be handled by specifying type attributes in your `<cfcatch>` blocks.

Fortunately, ColdFusion scripting provides an equivalent with `try-catch`. Listing 44.6 demonstrates a comparison of tag-based and script-based `try-catch` handling. When you run Listing 40.6, note that it tries to open a file named `test.txt`, which has been provided in the sample source code. Try changing the `filename` variable value to `test2.txt` (which does not exist), and notice the types of exceptions that are thrown, caught, and handled.

Listing 40.6 `ExceptionHandling.cfm`—Handling Exceptions in ColdFusion Script

```
<!--- Author: Charlie Arehart -- carehart.org --->
<!--- Exception handling --->

<cfset filename="test.txt">
<!--- Tag-based --->
<cftry>
  <cfset result = FileOpen(expandpath(filename))>
  <p>It worked!</p>

  <cfcatch type="Expression">
    <p>An Expression exception was thrown.</p>
       <cfoutput>#cfcatch.message#</cfoutput>
    <!--- could use cfmail, cfquery, or other tags --->  </cfcatch>
  <cfcatch type="Security">
    <p>A Security exception was thrown.</p>
       <cfoutput>#cfcatch.message#</cfoutput>
    <!--- could use cfmail, cfquery, or other tags --->
    <!--- note use of optional rethrow below, to pass the error
         to the next higher error handler, if any --->
    <cfrethrow>
</cfcatch>
</cftry>

<cfscript>
  // Script-based
  try {
    result = FileOpen(expandpath(filename));
    WriteOutput("<p>It worked!</p>");
  }
  catch(Expression exceptionVariable) {
    WriteOutput("<p>An Expression exception was thrown.</p>
      <p>#exceptionVariable.message#</p>");
    // could use mail, query, or other script-based tag equivalents  }
  catch(Security exceptionVariable) {

    WriteOutput("<p>An Expression exception was thrown.</p>
      <p>#exceptionVariable.message#</p>");
    // could use mail, query, or other script-based tag equivalents
    /* note use of optional rethrow below, to pass the error
      to the next higher error handler, if any */
```

Listing 40.6 (continued)

```
        rethrow;
    }
</cfscript>
```

There are a couple differences between `try-catch` in `<cfscript>` and the tag-based equivalents. First, note that the tag-based `<cfcatch>` is placed within a `<cftry>`, whereas a script-based `catch` is placed after a `try`. Second, note that with `<cfcatch>`, there's an available, predefined `CATCH` scope holding details of the error, whereas with the `catch` statement, you instead name a variable to hold those details.

I've also shown the optional extra error-handling features to do a *rethrow*—to throw the error, once caught, to a higher-level error-handling mechanism, if any. If there's no higher-order error-handling mechanism, it just causes the error to appear on the screen as if you hadn't caught it in the first place. The real reason I'm showing it, of course, is to point out that there is (as of Cold-Fusion 9) an available `rethrow` statement.

Note as well that, unlike in past versions of ColdFusion, you can execute more operations within the error handling (as anywhere in script) than you could in the past, such as tag-based equivalents to `<cfmail>`, `<cflog>`, `<cfquery>`, and so on, as discussed earlier in this chapter.

You could also *throw* a custom exception of your own design, again to be handled by a higher-level error handler, using `<cfthrow>` in the tag example or `throw` as is now also available in script, as well the new `<cffinally>` tag or its script-based equivalent, `finally`. I leave it as an exercise for the reader to explore those alternative error-handling features in the ColdFusion documentation.

Common Problems and Solutions

Even with the removal of many incompatibilities in script-based operators (as compared to JavaScript and other languages), there are some challenges as you switch between using tag- and script-based coding. This section contains some general issues and then some details on more particular ones.

To resolve some common errors that may occur as you move to scripting, follow these simple guidelines:

- Make sure each statement ends with a semicolon (;).
- For every opening `(` and `{`, make sure there is a corresponding closing `)` and `}`.
- Check for closing tag `>` symbols when converting tag-based code to script. It's easy to forget to remove the `>` symbol at the end of each tag, which you need to replace with a semicolon (;).
- Make sure your scripts don't contain any ColdFusion tags, because `<cfscript>` doesn't allow them.

A Note About the {} Symbols

As you've seen in the script examples so far, `<cfscript>` uses `{}` to create blocks of script code that the `if` or `else` part of an `if-else` statement should execute. Actually, the use of `{}` is optional if either the `if` or `else` keyword is handling only one line of code. If you leave the brackets out, however, things can get confusing should you need to add lines to your code later. For that reason, including these symbols in your script code is a good habit, even when they aren't explicitly needed.

The following code is an example of when you need to use `{}`. By itself, this code throws an error:

```
<cfscript>
  a = 1;
  if(a == 1)
   b = 1;
   b = 2;
  else
   b = 3;
</cfscript>

<cfoutput>#b#</cfoutput>
```

By definition, this code should set the value of `2` to the variable `b`, but it doesn't do that because the second expression, `b = 2`, isn't evaluated. To make this code behave correctly, you must insert `{}` around clauses that contain two or more expressions:

```
<cfscript>
  a = 1;
  if(a == 1) {
   b = 1;
   b = 2;
  } else {
   b = 3;
  }
</cfscript>

<cfoutput>#b#</cfoutput>
```

Now the code works as it should and returns `2` as the value held in the variable `b`.

"Could Not Find the ColdFusion Component or Interface"

The error "Could not find the ColdFusion Component or Interface" means that a CFC you're trying to instantiate cannot be found in the normal range of places that ColdFusion searches for CFCs when you try to instantiate them; these locations include the current directory relative to the caller, the Web root, and any directories defined in the ColdFusion Administrator for custom tag paths or mappings.

Although this problem can happen to any CFML developer for a number of reasons, there are two particular times this error may occur that relate directly to features discussed in this chapter.

When Executing CFC-Based Tag Equivalents

The first situation I'll discuss for that error is when you're trying to execute one of the several CFC-based tag equivalents, like the `http.cfc` or `query.cfc` examples above in Listings 40.4 and 40.5.

If you get this error in that case, the problem is very likely that someone (with access to your ColdFusion Administrator interface) has removed a needed custom tag path definition, which would have been placed there by default at installation.

See the Extensions > Custom Tag Paths page. There must be a custom tag path there pointing to the location of the `CustomTags` directory within your ColdFusion installation.

On a Standard or Server installation, that directory would be the *[cf9]*`\CustomTags` directory, such as `C:\ColdFusion9\CustomTags`. On a multi-server installation, that might be something like `C:\JRun4\servers\cfusion\cfusion-ear\cfusion-war\WEB-INF\cfusion\CustomTags`.

When Executing CFC-Based Tag Equivalents

The second situation I'll discuss for that error is when you're using (or have used) the new `import` (or `cfimport path` equivalent). An unusual problem related to this is that although technically they impact only the path on which they're executed, they have an unusual behavior in that once they've been executed and a CFC has been found based on that imported path, ColdFusion will continue to use that path for that instantiated CFC even if you remove the `import` statement/tag from the page.

That behavior will be very unexpected by most developers and could lead to subtle bugs or the aforementioned error (if you move a CFC out of the directory where the page had previously found it).

Fortunately, there's a simple solution, but it relies on a new feature in ColdFusion 9, so it may not be obvious. The ColdFusion 9 Administrator interface offers a new Clear Component Cache Now button (in addition to the long-existing Clear Template Cache Now). Clicking that button should resolve this issue.

If the problem remains, try restarting ColdFusion. If that doesn't solve it, then you may be suffering from the original intended purpose of this error: ColdFusion simply can't find your CFC in the normal locations it looks.

CHAPTER 41

Working with XML

IN THIS CHAPTER

Extensible Markup Language (XML) files have become a common means of sharing and exchanging data between systems and applications, as well as between servers and browsers. In contrast to more traditional data exchange formats such as CSV and other flat-file formats, XML files describe data and organize it in a tag-based structure.

In ColdFusion, you may be interested in reading or writing XML files. These can take the form of flat text files, content generated in a Web page or Web service, data shared via an RSS feed (see Chapter 60, "Working with Feeds," in *Adobe ColdFusion 9 Web Application Construction Kit, Volume 3: Advanced Application Development*), and so on. Various CFML features also work with XML, including `<CFPDF>`, `<CFREPORT>`, and `<CFWDDX>`.

This chapter gives you a practical description of how XML is used in ColdFusion. We will cover just the basics of reading, writing, and returning XML, XML schemas, XML namespaces, and other XML concepts; an exhaustive discussion of the subject and all uses of XML in CFML would require a book of its own.

XML Document Structure

Listing 41.1 is an XML document that describes a company's employees.

Listing 41.1 `Company.xml`—An XML Document

```
<?xml version="1.0" ?>
<company name="ABC MegaCorp, Inc." location="NY">
  <comments>A very big company that does many different things.</comments>
  <employee ssn="123-45-6789">
    <first-name>Ed</first-name>
      <last-name>Johnson</last-name>
      <department>Human Resources</department>
      <children>
        <child name="Sean" />
```

Listing 41.1 (continued)

```
      <child name="Polly" />
    </children>
  </employee>
  <employee ssn="541-29-8376">
    <first-name>Maria</first-name>
    <last-name>Smith</last-name>
    <department>Accounting</department>
    <children>
      <child name="Sandra" />
    </children>
  </employee>
  <employee ssn="568-73-1924">
    <first-name>Eric</first-name>
    <last-name>Masters</last-name>
    <department>Accounting</department>
  </employee>
</company>
```

Let's break down the composition of this document.

The first line is called an *XML declaration*. This tells an XML parser that the ensuing content is intended to be properly formed XML that conforms to version 1.0 of the XML specification. Though this declaration is not required in all XML documents, it's a good habit to always put it at the top of the document.

The second line is the opening tag for this document's *root element*. Every XML document must have one and only one element at the root of its hierarchy, and in this case the root element is `company`.

The `company` element contains a `comments` element that describes the company. Between the opening and closing tags of the `company` element are `employee` elements for each of the company's employees. The `employee` element contains an `ssn` attribute as well as `first-name`, `last-name`, and `department` elements, plus an optional `children` element to describe the employee's children.

While an XML document may seem similar to an HTML document, the structure of an XML document is more formal. XML is case sensitive (so `<a>` and `<A>` are two different tags), whereas HTML is not (so `<a>` and `<A>` are equivalent). XML also requires that all attribute values be surrounded with double quotes. In HTML, we could write `location=CA`, but XML requires that we write `location="CA"` instead.

Probably the biggest problem people have with XML concerns the requirement for closing tags. In an XML document, every tag must be closed. Even if the tag has no content (such as the `child` elements in Listing 41.1), you must close the tag; if you don't, the XML parser that processes the document will throw an error. In the case of the `<child>` tags in Listing 41.1, we used a special shorthand closing syntax: `<child name="Sandra" />` is equivalent to `<child name="Sandra"></child>`.

One last note: The following characters are illegal in attribute values and element content and must be escaped using their equivalent entity escape codes:

- Ampersand (&): `&`
- Greater-than sign (>): `>`

- Less-than sign (<): `<`
- Double quote ("): `"`

Fortunately, CFML includes an `XMLFormat` function to help with this challenge. That and entity references will be discussed in more detail later in the chapter.

Following the example and guidelines outlined in this section ensures that an XML document is *well formed*, meaning that it follows the standard rules of XML document structure. Any XML parser should be able to read a well-formed document.

Elements and Their Attributes

In Listing 41.1, notice that the description of data about each employee was provided as a nested XML element, such as `<first-name>`. You may have wondered why such information wasn't offered in attributes of the `<employee>` element, as with the `ssn` attribute. XML design is flexible about when to use elements to store data and when to use attributes. For instance, this portion of Listing 41.1:

```
<employee ssn="568-73-1924">
  <first-name>Eric</first-name>
  <last-name>Masters</last-name>
  <department>Accounting</department>
</employee>
```

could also have been represented like this:

```
<employee ssn="568-73-1924" first-name="Eric" last-name="Masters"
department="Accounting" />
```

Some people like using elements; others prefer attributes. Different groups claim that one method is inherently superior to the other, but this is not really true. The decision as to whether to use an attribute or a child element in any given circumstance is one that should be made according to the developer's opinion of what will work for that situation.

Most important, the choice of the XML format rests with whomever creates the XML file (or specifies how XML files are to be created). If you're reading someone else's XML or creating XML to be read by someone else's process, you have no choice but to process the XML according to that defined format. If you're creating an XML file to let others read it and there's no defined format, you're free to decide how to format the XML.

In making your decision, here a few rules to keep in mind:

- All attributes of a single element must have unique names.
- Attributes cannot contain embedded tags. If something has a substructure of its own, it must be represented as an element.
- Child elements are often more difficult to handle in code than are attributes. This is because accessing an element's content means using a property, whereas accessing an attribute can be done directly.

Naming Conventions

There seem to be as many "standard" XML naming conventions as there are XML developers. Some people would name my `first-name` element from Listing 41.1 `FirstName`; others would name it `first_name`; yet others would name it `fn`. All of these are valid names, but `first-name` may be the simplest and easiest for most people to understand.

There is no one standard naming convention. Rather, the naming convention is the one created by whomever defined the XML file format you're reading from or writing to; if you're creating the XML file format, use the format that is most comfortable for you and the other developers on your team. The conventions presented here are merely guidelines.

- Make all element and attribute names lowercase, because XML is case sensitive. On most platforms, if you have a `first-name` element and you look for an element named `First-Name`, the application will not find the element you're looking for. Because different people have different capitalization rules, it's best to eliminate the issue entirely and use lowercase for all names.
- Use hyphens to separate multiple words in an element or attribute name. Some teams use underscores, but I avoid them because it's often difficult to see an underscore when code is underlined or outlined in an IDE. Hyphens are always easy to see.
- Don't abbreviate element names unless you absolutely must. XML is known for being a very verbose format. Because of this, developers often abbreviate the names of elements, using `fn`, for instance, instead of the more verbose `first-name`. However, `fn` does not describe what the element does, whereas `first-name` describes it perfectly. Remember that XML was invented to make data understandable by both machines and humans.

Reading and Creating XML Documents

In this section, we'll look at three ways to work with XML documents, whether you're reading them from a file or URL using `XMLParse()` or creating them within CFML using `<CFXML>` or `XMLNew()`.

If you want to make the XML you obtain from a file or Web page easy to read and manipulate, you can convert it to a ColdFusion-specific *XML object*, using the `XMLParse()` function. The XML as found in a file or Web page is just a string of text. If you *parse* it, ColdFusion then lets you access the information in the XML file much like a collection of structures and arrays.

Reading an XML File Using `XmlParse()`

To parse an XML document stored somewhere on disk, use `XmlParse()`, as demonstrated in Listing 41.2. You can also name a file or a Web page URL from which to obtain the XML content to be parsed. Let's look at the processes for each.

Listing 41.2 `ParseXML.cfm`—Parsing an XML Document on Disk

```
<cfset xmlObject = XmlParse("company.xml","yes")>

<cfdump var="#xmlObject#">
```

Figure 41.1 shows the output of `xmlObject` in the browser. You could have replaced the filename with a URL, to retrieve an XML string from a Web page. An example is `http://www.adobe.com/crossdomain.xml`. The `"Yes"` is the value of the `caseSensitive` argument to `XmlParse()`, which makes the created object case sensitive.

That was pretty painless, wasn't it?

By parsing the file's contents with the `XmlParse()` function, we converted the XML document (a string of XML) into a variable called `xmlObject`, which is an object that ColdFusion recognizes as a set of employees, rather than just as a string of text.

CAUTION

The two terms *XML document* and *XML object* are not interchangeable, although some people use them that way. In this book, *XML document* refers to a string of XML-encoded text, and XML object refers to a complex variable that ColdFusion can manipulate directly.

Figure 41.1

A ColdFusion XML object as displayed by `<cfdump>`.

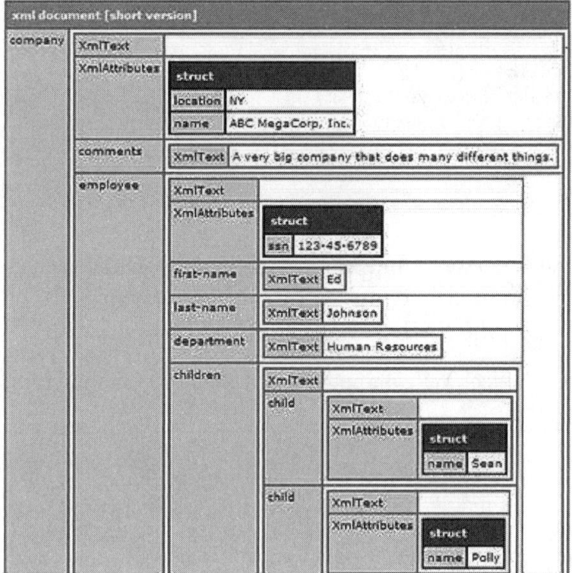

Creating XML Documents Using CFXML

Sometimes, rather than reading an XML document, you will want to create one from within CFML. For example, you may want to do this to query a database and convert its results to XML. That XML could be written to the browser or returned as a CFC method result, as will be shown later in this section, or it can simply be saved to a file, as shown in Listing 41.3.

Listing 41.3 `XMLFromADatabase.cfm`—Creating an XML Document from Database Content

```
<cfquery name="employeesQuery" datasource="Chapter41_DSN">
SELECT SSN, FirstName, LastName, Department
FROM Employee
</cfquery>

<cfxml variable="xmlObject" casesensitive="yes">
<company>
  <cfoutput query="employeesQuery">
  <employee ssn="#XmlFormat(SSN)#">
    <first-name>#XmlFormat(FirstName)#</first-name>
    <last-name>#XmlFormat(LastName)#</last-name>
    <department>#XmlFormat(Department)#</department>
  </employee>
  </cfoutput>
</company>
</cfxml>

<cffile action="WRITE"
    file="#ExpandPath('EmployeeXML.xml')#"
    output="#ToString(xmlObject)#">
```

NOTE

To set up `Chapter41_DSN`, see the `Readme.txt` file in the `Chapter41` folder in the downloadable code for this book.

Listing 41.3 queries the database to find employee information and then creates an XML object and writes the XML object to disk. Using `ToString()` converts an XML object back into an XML document (text string), and the XML document is then written to disk.

Running Listing 41.3 produces a file named `EmployeeXML.xml`, as shown in Listing 41.4.

Listing 41.4 `EmployeeXML.xml`—XML Generated from a Database

```
<?xml version="1.0" encoding="UTF-8"?>
<company>

  <employee ssn="123-45-6789">
    <first-name>Ed</first-name>
    <last-name>Johnson</last-name>
    <department>Human Resources</department>
  </employee>

  <employee ssn="541-29-8376">
    <first-name>Maria</first-name>
    <last-name>Smith</last-name>
    <department>Accounting</department>
```

Listing 41.4 (continued)

```
</employee>

  <employee ssn="568-73-1924">
    <first-name>Eric</first-name>
    <last-name>Masters</last-name>
    <department>Accounting</department>
  </employee>

</company>
```

The <cfxml> call creates the same kind of XML object that is created by XmlParse(), with the difference being that XmlParse() creates an XML object based on an XML document.

TIP

You may have noticed the caseSensitive attribute in the <cfxml> call earlier. By default, ColdFusion is not case sensitive in its XML handling. However, because other platforms may be case sensitive, you should make sure that your XML documents are case sensitive as well.

Notice the use of XmlFormat(). Anytime you place data in an XML document, you should use XmlFormat(), which replaces special or high-ASCII characters with their entity reference equivalents (see the section "Entity References" later in this chapter for more information).

You may ask why we should bother to use <CFXML>, since you end up outputting the XML as a string, and it's true that you could just as well have created the XML and written it to a file without using <CFXML>. The advantage is that <CFXML>will ensure that the XML is well formed. If it's not well formed, you'll receive an error during processing of the <CFXML> tag.

You could also have changed the code to write the XML to a browser (to be retrieved by anyone requesting the page in a browser), by replacing the <CFFILE> in Listing 41.3 with <CFOUTPUT>, or more particularly,

```
<cfsetting showdebugoutput="No">

<cfcontent type="text/xml">

<cfoutput>#ToString(xmlObject)#</cfoutput>
```

Note the use of <CFCONTENT> to tell the browser to expect a plain text XML file (rather than the default text or HTML file), and the use of <cfsetting> to turn off ColdFusion's debugging feature (which is also HTML). An example is provided in the online files as XMLFromADatabaseToBrowser.cfm.

You could also create and return XML in this way within a CFC method or user-defined function using <CFFUNCTION>, by specifying its ReturnType="xml" option and returning the XML. This code could either be used to return data to another CFML template invoking the CFC, or to an application (perhaps on a remote server) calling the CFC as a Web service.

If you return the raw xmlObject, it can only be read by another ColdFusion server calling the Web service (such as when returning a query result set). If you use ToString() as shown here, it will return just XML as text. See the examples provided online as XMLFromADatabaseInCFC.cfc and invoke_xml_method.cfm.

Creating XML Documents Using XmlNew()

While <cfxml> provides a way to quickly create an XML document within CFML, there is another way—one that is often more flexible because you can take very granular control over the content of the document. Listing 41.5 shows the XmlNew() and XmlElemNew() functions in action.

Listing 41.5 XmlNew.cfm—Using XmlNew() and XmlElemNew() to Dynamically Create an XML Object

```
<cfscript>
  xmlObject = XmlNew("Yes");
  xmlObject["company"] = XmlElemNew(xmlObject, "company");

  employeeNode1 = XmlElemNew(xmlObject, "employee");
  employeeNode1.xmlAttributes["ssn"] = "123-45-6789";
  employeeNode1["first-name"] = XmlElemNew(xmlObject, "first-name");
  employeeNode1["first-name"].xmlText = "Ed";
  employeeNode1["last-name"] = XmlElemNew(xmlObject, "last-name");
  employeeNode1["last-name"].xmlText = "Johnson";
  employeeNode1["department"] = XmlElemNew(xmlObject, "department");
  employeeNode1["department"].xmlText = "Human Resources";

  employeeNode2 = XmlElemNew(xmlObject, "employee");
  employeeNode2.xmlAttributes["ssn"] = "541-29-8376";
  employeeNode2["first-name"] = XmlElemNew(xmlObject, "first-name");
  employeeNode2["first-name"].xmlText = "Maria";
  employeeNode2["last-name"] = XmlElemNew(xmlObject, "last-name");
  employeeNode2["last-name"].xmlText = "Smith";
  employeeNode2["department"] = XmlElemNew(xmlObject, "department");
  employeeNode2["department"].xmlText = "Accounting";

  employeeNode3 = XmlElemNew(xmlObject, "employee");
  employeeNode3.xmlAttributes["ssn"] = "568-73-1924";
  employeeNode3["first-name"] = XmlElemNew(xmlObject, "first-name");
  employeeNode3["first-name"].xmlText = "Eric";
  employeeNode3["last-name"] = XmlElemNew(xmlObject, "last-name");
  employeeNode3["last-name"].xmlText = "Masters";
  employeeNode3["department"] = XmlElemNew(xmlObject, "department");
  employeeNode3["department"].xmlText = "Accounting";

  ArrayAppend(xmlObject["company"].xmlChildren, employeeNode1);
  ArrayAppend(xmlObject["company"].xmlChildren, employeeNode2);
  ArrayAppend(xmlObject["company"].xmlChildren, employeeNode3);
</cfscript>

<cfdump var="#xmlObject#">
```

The XML object created by Listing 41.5 is exactly the same as the one created by the <CFXML> tag in Listing 41.3.

When dynamically creating XML documents as we've done in this example, we first use XmlNew() to create a new XML object (the "Yes" is the value of the caseSensitive argument to XmlNew(), which makes the XML object case sensitive):

```
xmlObject = XmlNew("Yes");
```

Then we create elements inside this object using `XmlElemNew()`:

```
xmlObject["company"] = XmlElemNew(xmlObject, "company");
employeeNode1 = XmlElemNew(xmlObject, "employee");
employeeNode1["first-name"] = XmlElemNew(xmlObject, "first-name");
```

We then use `ArrayAppend()` to place the employee nodes in the company's child node array:

```
ArrayAppend(xmlObject["company"].xmlChildren, employeeNode1);
```

This method of assembling nodes and then using array operations to connect all the nodes together is a common one. Its chief benefit is making code more readable and modular. Otherwise, we'd be using code like this to set the first name:

```
xmlObject["company"]["employee"][1]["first-name"] = XmlElemNew(xmlObject, "first-name");
xmlObject["company"]["employee"][1]["first-name"].xmlText = "Ed";
```

While the preceding example does not use `XMLFormat()`, we could and should, especially if we are creating the XML elements from variables rather than strings. The issue is that if the data being used to create the XML elements or content includes any special characters, it can cause an error. This issue is discussed further in the section "Using Special Characters in XML" later in this chapter.

Accessing XML Elements and Attributes

Whether we created an XML object using `XMLParse()`, `<CFXML>`, or `XMLNew()`, we now have an XML object in memory. If we wanted to explore or manipulate it, how would we access its elements and their properties? ColdFusion makes it easy for us by exposing the elements and attributes as if they were arrays and structures. For example, to access the second employee element, I'd use syntax like this:

```
xmlObject["company"]["employee"][2]
```

Notice the bracket notation, just as if I were accessing a set of nested structures with an array at the end. What if I wanted to access the second employee's first name? I'd extend the syntax like this:

```
xmlObject["company"]["employee"][2]["first-name"].xmlText
```

Notice the `xmlText` property at the end of the reference. If I had referred instead to just the `first-name` element, that expression would have returned an XML element object reference rather than a string. The `xmlText` contains the text stored in the element object itself.

What about attributes? Let's say I wanted to access the SSN of the third employee. I'd use similar syntax, like this:

```
xmlObject["company"]["employee"][3].xmlAttributes["ssn"]
```

Because attributes are always strings, attributes do not require that you put `xmlText` at the end of the reference.

TIP

When referencing element and attribute names, I always use bracket notation (`["company"]`) rather than dot notation (`.company`). I do this for two reasons. First, XML is case sensitive, and dot notation often has problems with mixed-case documents. Second, you cannot use dot notation with element names that contain hyphens, so for consistency's sake, I use bracket notation everywhere.

The form of XML notation we've been using so far, in which the element names are used like the names of arrays, is known as *short-form notation*:

```
xmlObject["company"]["employee"][2]
```

This is different from *long-form notation*, which would reference the second employee node as follows:

```
xmlObject.xmlRoot.xmlChildren[2]
```

Instead of using `company`, we use `xmlRoot` (because it is the document's *root node*), and instead of using `employee[2]`, we use `xmlChildren[2]` (because it is the second child of `xmlRoot`). There is no array reference after `xmlRoot` because, like all XML documents, this one has only one root element. The advantage to using long-form notation is that it doesn't matter what the name of each individual node is, because nodes are referenced using the `xmlChildren` array of the parent element. The disadvantage is that now you have to do more work to find out what node is being referenced.

The two different notation methods exist for an important reason. Long-form notation is like looking at text-based driving directions from a site like MapQuest: The instructions are very detailed, but they don't give any perspective on where you are at any given point. In contrast, short-form notation is like looking at a map: You can easily see where you are at any given time, but it's not always easy to find out how to get there.

You're not limited to using only one method at a time. You can combine both long-form and short-form notation, as I'm doing here:

```
xmlObject["company"].xmlChildren[2]["first-name"].xmlText
```

Instead of directly referencing the `employee` array, I'm using `xmlChildren`.

So far, the only element properties we've seen are `xmlText`, `xmlAttributes`, and `xmlChildren`. These properties are present for every node in a document, and they are, for the most part, the only properties you'll use in most of your code.

Table 41.1 lists the properties of every element in an XML object.

Table 41.1 XMLNode Properties

PROPERTY NAME	TYPE	DESCRIPTION
`xmlName`	String	The name of the element. If the element has a namespace prefix, `xmlName` contains the fully qualified name. (See the later section "XML Namespaces" for more information.)
`xmlNsPrefix`	String	The element's namespace prefix. If the element does not have a namespace, `xmlNsPrefix` is blank.
`xmlNsURI`	String	The element's namespace URI. If the element does not have a namespace, `xmlNsURI` is blank.
`xmlText`	String	The text between the element's opening and closing tags (not counting text inside of any child elements).

Table 41.1 (continued)

PROPERTY NAME	TYPE	DESCRIPTION
xmlCData	String	Any CDATA content between the element's opening and closing tags (not counting CDATA sections inside of any child elements). See the section on "CDATA Sections" later in this chapter for more details.
xmlComment	String	A single value containing the text of all the comments inside the element (not counting comments inside of any child elements).
xmlAttributes	Structure	A structure containing a key for each of the element's attributes.
xmlChildren	Array of XML elements	An array containing an entry for each of the element's child elements.
xmlParent	XML element	A reference to the element's parent element.
xmlNodes	Array of XML nodes	An array containing an entry for each child *node* of the element (not including attribute nodes). This is very rarely used.

Using Array and Structure Functions

Table 41.1 shows that `xmlChildren` is an array, and `xmlAttributes` is a structure. This means we can use ColdFusion's native structure and array functions to modify XML objects. If we wanted to delete the third employee node from the document, for instance, we'd use `ArrayDeleteAt()`:

```
ArrayDeleteAt(xmlObject["company"].xmlChildren, 3)
```

Similarly, to find out how many attributes a particular element has, we'd use `StructCount()`:

```
StructCount(xmlObject["company"]["employee"][1].xmlAttributes)
```

Developing Applications, which is part of the ColdFusion documentation set, shows which array and structure functions can be used with XML objects and when.

Using Special Characters in XML

The previous examples of XML creation have been simple enough, but there are some special considerations that you should keep in mind when creating XML. We showed the use of `XMLFormat()` earlier, in Listing 41.3. Let's now look at why you should use this function.

One of the frustrations developers encounter is trying to use special characters inside an otherwise well-formed XML document. For example, let's say we want to embed some text with an ampersand inside of a document:

```
<company name="Baker & Associates" location="CA">
  ...
</company>
```

XML parsers would not be able to process that document because the ampersand is a special character. This section shows you two different ways to deal with this problem: entity references and `CDATA` sections.

Entity References

If you've ever used a sequence such as ` ` or `&` within HTML or another markup language, then you've used *entity references*. Entity references are a way to encode special characters so that they can be used within an XML document without affecting parsers' abilities to read them. Here's an example:

```
<company name="Baker &amp; Associates" location="CA">
  ...
</company>
```

An entity reference begins with an ampersand and ends with a semicolon. Following are some of the entity references you may have seen in HTML:

```
  (nonbreaking space)
&amp; (ampersand)
&iexcl; (inverted exclamation mark)
&Uuml; (capital U with umlaut)
```

Whenever a browser sees one of these entity references, the browser knows to display the corresponding character instead.

There are approximately 250 references defined in HTML. In XML, however, there are only five:

```
&amp; (ampersand)
&lt; (less-than sign)
&gt; (greater-than sign)
&quot; (double-quote)
&apos; (single-quote)
```

Any special characters outside of this set (specifically, high-ASCII characters above ASCII 127) must be encoded using a *character reference*, which looks like one of these two examples:

```
 
 
```

Both of these examples represent a nonbreaking space, ASCII 160. The `&#` introduces a decimal number, and `&#x` introduces a hexadecimal (base 16) number.

Fortunately, you may not need to remember all these rules, if you remember instead to use `XmlFormat()` whenever you put data into an XML document, as shown in Listing 41.3. The `XmlFormat()` automatically handles special characters by replacing them with their appropriate entity and character references before putting them into the document.

CDATA Sections

`XmlFormat()` is well suited for special characters that may occur in isolated areas of your XML document, but what if you have a section of your document that represents HTML markup with lots of special characters, or tags that don't parse correctly because they're not well formed?

In situations like these, `XmlFormat()` can go from being a blessing to being a curse—as a result of all the escaping that's done to the stored text. A good alternative is to use a CDATA section as shown in Listing 41.6.

Listing 41.6 `Namespaces.xml`—A Portion of Listing 41.1, Using `CDATA` Rather Than Regular Text

```
<company name="ABC MegaCorp, Inc." location="NY">
  <comments>
    <![CDATA[
      <P>A very large company with 4 divisions:
      <UL>
        <LI>Financial Services
        <LI>Baby Food
        <LI>Large Vehicles
        <LI>Fashion Consultation
      </UL>
    ]]>
  </comments>
  <employee ssn="123-45-6789">
    ...
  </employee>
  <employee ssn="541-29-8376">
    ...
  </employee>
</company>
```

The content inside the `CDATA` section is unparsed, so it can contain any characters—even the special characters that are normally unusable in XML content. The only restriction is that you cannot use the sequence `]]>` except to end the `CDATA` block.

To use `CDATA` within ColdFusion, use a node's `xmlCData` property rather than its `xmlText` property. The content you place into `xmlCData` is automatically placed into a `CDATA` section within the document, whereas content inside of `xmlText` is encoded and not put inside of a `CDATA` section:

```
<cfset myXmlNode.xmlCData = "<P>This is content I do not want to escape">
```

`CDATA` sections are also ideal for long passages of text with many special characters, because escaped characters can take up anywhere from three to eight times as much space as their unescaped counterparts. The disadvantage to using a `CDATA` section is slightly more complex code.

From this point forward we will not use any more `CDATA` sections in order to keep the focus on new topics.

XML Namespaces

Whether reading or creating XML, inexperienced programmers often overlook XML's ability to partition a single document into multiple sections or to represent multiple concepts in a single document by using *namespaces*. These collections of tag and attribute names are bound together using prefixes, and kept separate from tags and attributes in other namespaces.

In Listing 41.7, the single company document in Listing 41.1 is extended by adding starting salary information and putting directory information in its own namespace.

Listing 41.7 `ExtendedCompany.xml`—The <company> Entry with Starting Salary Information Added

```
<company
  xmlns:directory="http://www.mycompany.com/directory"
  xmlns:salary="http://www.mycompany.com/salary">
  <directory:employee ssn="123-45-6789">
    <directory:first-name>Ed</directory:first-name>
    <directory:last-name>Johnson</directory:last-name>
    <directory:department>Human Resources</directory:department>
  </directory:employee>
  <directory:employee ssn="541-29-8376">
    <directory:first-name>Maria</directory:first-name>
    <directory:last-name>Smith</directory:last-name>
    <directory:department>Accounting</directory:department>
  </directory:employee>
  <directory:employee ssn="568-73-1924">
    <directory:first-name>Eric</directory:first-name>
    <directory:last-name>Masters</directory:last-name>
    <directory:department>Accounting</directory:department>
  </directory:employee>
  <salary:starting-salaries>
    <salary:low>32000</salary:low>
    <salary:avg>56000</salary:avg>
    <salary:high>78000</salary:high>
  </salary:starting-salaries>
</company>
```

Namespaces are also important to XML schemas, as you will see later. In essence, namespaces separate parts of an XML document that serve distinct functionality.

In Listing 41.7, we declare two namespaces: one for elements concerning a company's directory entry, and another for the company's starting salary information. As a result, while I'm storing only one document, that document can store two different kinds of information together, with two completely separate schemas.

Another benefit of namespaces has to do with portability. Listing 41.8 shows another XML document with the same information as in Listing 41.7, but using different namespace prefixes.

Listing 41.8 `ExtendedCompany2.xml`—Another XML Document with Different Namespace Prefixes

```
<company
  xmlns:dir="http://www.mycompany.com/directory"
  xmlns:sal="http://www.mycompany.com/salary">
  <dir:employee ssn="123-45-6789">
    <dir:first-name>Ed</dir:first-name>
    <dir:last-name>Johnson</dir:last-name>
    <dir:department>Human Resources</dir:department>
  </dir:employee>
  <dir:employee ssn="541-29-8376">
    <dir:first-name>Maria</dir:first-name>
    <dir:last-name>Smith</dir:last-name>
    <dir:department>Accounting</dir:department>
  </dir:employee>
  <dir:employee ssn="568-73-1924">
    <dir:first-name>Eric</dir:first-name>
    <dir:last-name>Masters</dir:last-name>
```

Listing 41.8 (continued)

```
        <dir:department>Accounting</dir:department>
      </dir:employee>
      <sal:starting-salaries>
        <sal:low>32000</sal:low>
        <sal:avg>56000</sal:avg>
        <sal:high>78000</sal:high>
      </sal:starting-salaries>
    </company>
```

Listings 41.7 and 41.8 are the exact same document, even though the namespace prefixes are different. What makes the namespaces unique is not the prefix before the name, but rather the URI (Uniform Resource Identifier) to which you bind the prefix. (In Listings 41.7 and 41.8, the URIs were `http://www.mycompany.com/directory` and `http://www.mycompany.com/salary`.) When two different documents bind two distinct prefixes to the same URI, then those two prefixes represent the same namespace.

NOTE

The difference between a URI and a URL is very small. A URL (Uniform Resource Locator) is always a Web address. A URI is a more general term for any unique identifier used to identify something. A URL is a type of URI.

The URIs used in the `xmlns` attributes in Listings 41.7 and 41.8 do not have to point to anything in particular. Parsers will not retrieve anything from the URI specified at that address. The namespace URI is merely a unique identifier for that namespace that keeps one namespace separate from another. That said, it's usually a good idea to use the namespace URI to point to one of two things:

- *Your company's home page.* In cases where multiple companies use XML to transfer and store information in a single document, the namespace URI can be a way to self-document the relationship of nodes to companies.
- *A Web address at your company that gives information about the schema.* This is a way of linking your XML file directly to its documentation. Although parsers will not use the document at this address, someone who reads the file and wants to know what's going on will be able to visit the URL and find out. (The W3C does this.)

The Default Namespace

Most developers are surprised to learn that even if no namespaces are declared in their document, they are still using a namespace. Even Listing 41.1 had a namespace. The only difference between the namespace in Listing 41.1 and the ones in Listing 41.7 is that the namespaces in Listing 41.7 are explicitly declared.

A namespace without a prefix is called a *default namespace.* Any tags that are not part of an explicitly declared namespace are part of this default namespace. To bind the default namespace to a URI, use the following syntax:

```
<element xmlns="http://www.mycompany.com" />
```

When to Use Namespaces

Namespaces are not always useful, but here are some situations when you *should* consider using a namespace:

- *When you are writing a solution to communicate between companies (or even divisions within a company).* Separating namespaces lets each company or division define its own functionality and own rules for interaction.
- *When you are using XML to control the behavior of a modular application.* Separating functionality into discrete namespaces lets you change parts of the application without affecting others, especially when a schema change is involved. Usually you will want to use one namespace per module.

This list is not exhaustive; it is only meant to give you an idea of some of the situations in which namespaces are useful.

Because the rest of the chapter focuses on schemas, we will be making heavy use of namespaces. In the next chapter, you will also get a real-world idea of how namespaces make XSLT possible.

Validating XML

Any XML parser will tell you whether your XML document is well formed (that is, whether all tags are closed and nothing is improperly nested). But just because a document is well formed does not mean it adheres to the structure your business logic expects.

To know that your XML document is not only well formed but also valid in accordance with your business rules, you must *validate* the document. Validating an XML document ensures that tags are nested in their proper hierarchy (so that something that's supposed to be a child is not actually a parent); that there are no extraneous attributes; and that all required elements and attributes are present.

NOTE

While this section discusses validation in this sense, you may be looking for functions in CFML to help you test other aspects of XML. See *CFML Reference* in the ColdFusion documentation for more on `IsXML`, `IsXMLDoc`, `IsXMLRoot`, `IsXMLElem`, `IsXMLNode`, and `IsXMLAttribute`.

There are two major methods for validating XML: the older DTD (Document Type Definition) standard, and the newer and more flexible XML Schema standard. XML Schema is a more capable standard that is widely accepted.

NOTE

Some other validation standards have come and gone. Chief among them are XDR (XML Data-Reduced), which was Microsoft's attempt at a proprietary schema language, and Relax NG, yet another attempt at defining an XML syntax for creating schemas. However, XML Schema will most likely be the XML validation standard for some time, thanks to its flexibility, wide-ranging support, and status as a W3C recommendation.

DTDs

DTDs (Document Type Definitions) are a holdover from the days of SGML. The DTD describes the elements and attributes available in a document, how they can be nested, and which ones are required and which are optional. But its lack of support for namespaces and inheritance, as well as its somewhat confusing syntax, make the DTD too limited for most programmers' needs.

With this in mind, the remainder of this chapter covers XML validation using the XML Schema standard, which does everything DTDs can do and more.

XML Schemas

An *XML schema* is the definition of the required structure of an XML document. By defining a schema, we can then use it to validate that a given XML document is not only well formed but follows the format defined in the schema. For demonstration purposes, Listing 41.9 shows a simplified version of the original single-company XML shown in Listing 41.1.

Listing 41.9 `SimpleCompany.xml`—A Simpler XML Document

```
<?xml version="1.0" ?>
<company>
  <employee ssn="123-45-6789">
    <first-name>Ed</first-name>
    <last-name>Johnson</last-name>
    <department>Human Resources</department>
  </employee>
  <employee ssn="541-29-8376">
    <first-name>Maria</first-name>
    <last-name>Smith</last-name>
    <department>Accounting</department>
  </employee>
  <employee ssn="568-73-1924">
    <first-name>Eric</first-name>
    <last-name>Masters</last-name>
    <department>Accounting</department>
  </employee>
</company>
```

Listing 41.10 shows a schema definition for the document. The remainder of this section explains its components, and the next section shows how to use that schema file to validate a given XML document.

Listing 41.10 `CompanyDirectory.xsd`—An XML Schema Document

```
<xsd:schema xmlns:xsd="http://www.w3.org/2001/XMLSchema">
  <xsd:element name="company" type="CompanyType" />

  <xsd:complexType name="CompanyType">
    <xsd:sequence>
      <xsd:element name="employee" type="EmployeeType" minOccurs="0"
maxOccurs="unbounded" />
    </xsd:sequence>
  </xsd:complexType>
```

Listing 41.10 (continued)

```
    <xsd:complexType name="EmployeeType">
      <xsd:sequence>
        <xsd:element name="first-name" type="xsd:string" />
        <xsd:element name="last-name" type="xsd:string" />
        <xsd:element name="department" type="xsd:string" />
      </xsd:sequence>
      <xsd:attribute name="ssn" type="SSNType" />
    </xsd:complexType>

    <xsd:simpleType name="SSNType">
      <xsd:restriction base="xsd:string">
        <xsd:pattern value="\d{3}-\d{2}-\d{4}" />
        <xsd:length value="11" />
      </xsd:restriction>
    </xsd:simpleType>
  </xsd:schema>
```

This schema defines a top-level `company` element and its lower-level `employee` elements. For more information on the XML schema language and how to build schemas, see "More XML Resources" at the end of this chapter.

Validating XML in ColdFusion

Validating XML in ColdFusion is a simple process, assuming you've already written the appropriate schema or DTD. Both `XmlParse()` and the new function `XmlValidate()` provide the capability to target a schema and validate a document's contents.

`XMLParse()` also offers an optional third argument to name a validator (an XSD file). Going back to Listing 41.2, the first line could be changed to use the validator in Listing 41.10:

```
<cfset xmlObject = XmlParse('Company.xml', true,"CompanyDirectory.xsd")>
```

This code would attempt to validate the XML in `company.xml` against the XSD file in Listing 41.10, but it would fail because the XSD file is defined for the simpler XML file specified in Listing 41.9.

More important, using validation in `XMLParse()` has a drawback in that if and when an error occurs, the tag will fail and your ColdFusion page will receive an error unless you have handled the failure using `CFTRY` or `CFCATCH`. The advantage of `XMLValidate()` is discussed in the next section.

Validating by Using `XmlValidate()`

Use of `XMLValidate()` offers greater control over error handling and also provides additional information in the result structure returned from the function. `XmlValidate()` takes two arguments, as shown in Listing 41.11.

Listing 41.11 `ValidateXML.cfm`—Using `XmlValidate()` to Validate a Document

```
<cfset xmlObject = XmlParse('Company.xml', true)>

<cfset errorStruct = XmlValidate(xmlObject, "CompanyDirectory.xsd")>

<cfdump var="#errorStruct#">
```

The first argument is a reference to the XML document that needs validating, and the second argument is a reference to the schema document against which the XML document must be validated. Note that each argument can take a number of inputs:

- Both arguments can take a string representation of the XML markup.
- Both arguments can take a filename.
- Both arguments can take a URL.
- The first argument (the XML document) can also take a parsed XML object.

`XmlValidate()` returns a structure describing whether validation succeeded, as well as any errors that may have occurred during validation. Most often you will use `errorStruct.status`, which is `YES` or `NO`, depending on whether validation was successful, to determine whether or not to continue processing the document. (The other keys in the structure are usually only helpful during debugging.)

Note that by passing in the schema object to `XmlValidate()`, you can dynamically control the schema against which a given document is validated, as shown in the next section.

Embedding Schema Information within a Document

You will most often pass a schema to the `XmlValidate()` function in order to control how a document is validated, but it is sometimes necessary to embed a reference to the schema within the document itself. This is done by using syntax like this:

```
<company xmlns:xsi="http://www.w3.org/2001/XMLSchema-instance"
     xsi:noNamespaceSchemaLocation="CompanyDirectory.xsd">
  <employee ssn="123-45-6789">
    <first-name>Ed</first-name>
    <last-name>Johnson</last-name>
    <department>Human Resources</department>
  </employee>
  <employee ssn="541-29-8376">
    <first-name>Maria</first-name>
    <last-name>Smith</last-name>
    <department>Accounting</department>
  </employee>
  <employee ssn="568-73-1924">
    <first-name>Eric</first-name>
    <last-name>Masters</last-name>
    <department>Accounting</department>
  </employee>
</company>
```

This syntax example points the parser to the schema at Listing 41.10.

Note that this method is far from foolproof, because when the calling program validates this document using the provided schema, there is no guarantee that the schema is actually the correct one. The person who created the XML file could very well point the URL anywhere and still have a valid document at that location.

To make use of a schema location provided within the source document, you would call `XmlValidate()` without a second argument, like this:

```
XmlValidate(xmlObject);
```

This tells ColdFusion to use the embedded schema location.

You can also use this form of embedded schema with `XMLParse()`, by leaving off the third argument (don't name a validator). But note that the URL offered in the XML file's `xsi:noNamespaceSchemaLocation` argument (as shown earlier) must be a complete URL. It cannot be a filename only, as with `XmlValidate()`.

More XML Resources

This chapter has touched on many of the most important topics in the world of XML. But there is a wealth of additional information available elsewhere. Here is a list of sites that should prove valuable to you in learning more about XML.

- `http://www.w3c.org` is the site for the World Wide Web Consortium and has information about XML standards. The articles here tend to be dry and wordy, but they are full of excellent information.
- `http://www.w3schools.com/xml/` is a site offering basic, advanced, and other tutorials and examples for working with XML. The parent site is dedicated to offering free tutorials about Web standard technologies.
- `http://www.zvon.org` is an indispensable site for learning about the world of XML and its various satellite technologies. There is a substantial amount of information here, and the site has excellent tutorials for people just starting out.
- `http://msdn.microsoft.com/en-us/library/ms256177.aspx` is the MSDN main reference page for XML standards. It has an excellent XML schema reference, as well as information on namespaces and DTDs. (MSDN is the Web site of the Microsoft Developer Network.)

CHAPTER 42

Manipulating XML with XSLT and XPath

IN THIS CHAPTER

As you saw in the previous chapter, XML is a way to structure data hierarchically using elements and attributes, much like a relational database structures data using tables and columns. Ultimately, XML is just a different way of structuring and storing data.

This also means that you will eventually want to start pulling data out of the XML structure and formatting it for use within your application. This could mean searching an XML document to find a node or set of nodes (using XPath), or it could mean transforming the XML into another format using a style sheet (using XSLT). Both of these technologies are discussed in this chapter.

Understanding XPath

XPath is a simple query language for XML that mimics standard directory access syntax. For example, if I had a company directory and wanted to access the third company node, I could use syntax like this:

```
/companies/company[3]
```

XPath syntax has the advantage of being both more understandable and more portable than a platform-specific notation, such as the ColdFusion variable syntax described in the preceding chapter. In addition, because XPath was created for searching documents, it tends to be more flexible than a platform-specific method.

XPath is to XML as URLs are to the Internet. Where a URL is a patternistic way to search for resources online, XPath is a language used to search for nodes within an XML document.

Example: A CD Collection

Listing 42.1 is an XML document describing a few of the CDs in my collection. This CD collection will be the input XML document for all of the examples in this chapter.

Listing 42.1 `CDCollection.xml`—The XML Document Used for This Chapter

```
<?xml version="1.0" ?>
<cdcollection>
  <artist id="1" name="Air">
    <genre>Electronic</genre>
    <cd id="1" name="10,000 Hz Legend" rating="3">
      <recommend cd="2" />
    </cd>
    <cd id="2" name="Talkie Walkie" rating="4">
      <recommend cd="1" />
      <recommend cd="6" />
    </cd>
  </artist>
  <artist id="2" name="Kylie Minogue">
    <genre>Dance</genre>
    <cd id="3" name="Fever" rating="3">
      <recommend cd="4" />
    </cd>
    <cd id="4" name="Body Language" rating="4">
      <recommend cd="5" />
    </cd>
    <recommend artist="3" />
  </artist>
  <artist id="3" name="Dannii Minogue">
    <genre>Dance</genre>
    <genre>Electronic</genre>
    <cd id="5" name="Neon Nights" rating="5">
      <recommend cd="4" />
    </cd>
    <cd id="6" name="You Won't Forget About Me EP" rating="5">
      <recommend cd="5" />
    </cd>
    <recommend artist="2" />
  </artist>
  <artist id="4" name="Brooklyn Funk Essentials">
    <genre>Funk</genre>
    <genre>Dance</genre>
    <genre>Spoken Word</genre>
    <cd id="7" name="Cool &amp; Steady &amp; Easy" rating="5">
      <recommend cd="4" />
      <recommend cd="5" />
    </cd>
    <recommend artist="1" />
    <recommend artist="5" />
  </artist>
  <artist id="5" name="Felix Da Housecat">
    <genre>Electronica</genre>
    <genre>Dance</genre>
    <genre>Retro</genre>
    <cd id="8" name="A Bugged Out Mix" rating="3">
      <recommend cd="4" />
      <recommend cd="6" />
      <recommend cd="9" />
    </cd>
    <cd id="9" name="Kittenz and Thee Glitz" rating="5" />
    <cd id="10" name="Devin Dazzle &amp; The Neon Fever" rating="5">
      <recommend cd="9" />
```

Listing 42.1 (CONTINUED)

```
      </cd>
      <recommend artist="2" />
      <recommend artist="4" />
    </artist>
  </cdcollection>
```

The collection is broken down by artist, each of whom can have one or more genres, one or more CDs, and one or more recommendations for other artists. Each CD can have one or more recommendations for other CDs. By the end of the chapter we will have turned this XML structure into an HTML listing that displays all this information in a user-friendly format.

XPath Syntax

The syntax of an XPath search expression is based on the same syntax as file paths in Unix or Windows, with the addition of features that allow the developer to restrict the returned node set based on some criteria. For example, to find all `cd` nodes with a `rating` higher than 3, I would use syntax like this:

```
/cdcollection/artist/cd[@rating > 3]
```

In essence, I am using typical directory hierarchy syntax to *select* nodes, then using typical array/ structure syntax to *restrict* nodes. When I run the XPath search against my document, I will get back an array containing all the nodes that match the expression.

Selections Using / and //

Much like you *select* columns from a table in an SQL statement, you *select* nodes from an XML document in an XPath expression. For instance, in this syntax:

```
/cdcollection
```

we're selecting the `cdcollection` element directly underneath the root node of the document.

If we wanted to select children of `cdcollection`, we'd extend the previous selection with another one:

```
/cdcollection/artist
```

And so forth until we've drilled down to the level of the XML hierarchy for which we're looking.

It is possible to shorten certain XPath expressions. For instance, this expression:

```
/cdcollection/artist/cd
```

could also be written as

```
//cd
```

The two expressions will return the same results; however, they do not mean the same thing. The first expression specifies that we want to retrieve the `cd` nodes at that *exact* position in the hierarchy, whereas the second specifies that we want to retrieve *all* `cd` nodes anywhere in the hierarchy. In effect, `//` means "search the entire document."

While // is certainly more convenient in some cases, its use can present some problems. First, because it is not doing any kind of restriction by document structure, the XPath engine must visit every node in the document to find all the possible matches. This makes searches using // much slower in most cases.

Second, consider this expression:

```
/cdcollection/artist/recommend
```

Shortening that expression to:

```
//recommend
```

returns not only those `recommend` nodes underneath an `artist` node, but the `recommend` nodes found under any `cd` nodes as well. In order to return the same data as the original expression, we'd have to use syntax like this:

```
//artist/recommend
```

But again, using the // instead of giving a fully qualified path will make the search take longer, especially on large documents.

Restrictions Using []

Now, let's say that we have an XPath expression like this:

```
/cdcollection/artist/cd
```

That would select all the `cd` nodes at that position in the hierarchy (regardless of which artist element where they were contained). But what if I only wanted to select the `cd` nodes underneath the first `artist` node? I would use a *restriction* like

```
/cdcollection/artist[1]/cd
```

much as I would if I were accessing an array element in ColdFusion. Let's walk through the expression as it stands right now.

1. XPath selects the `cdcollection` node underneath the root.
2. XPath then selects all of the `artist` nodes underneath the node that's been found so far.
3. Then XPath applies the restriction `[1]` to the currently selected set, meaning to take only the first `artist` node it finds.
4. Finally, XPath selects all the `cd` child nodes of the currently selected `artist` node.

There are other restriction formats. For instance, if I wanted to find only those CD nodes with a rating higher than 3, I would use syntax like this:

```
/cdcollection/artist/cd[@rating > 3]
```

The `@` symbol is XPath shorthand for "attribute," so whenever you are referencing an attribute name in XPath, just remember to prefix it with `@`.

Restrictions can contain further selections, as in this expression that retrieves all artist nodes containing at least one CD with a rating higher than 3:

```
/cdcollection/artist[cd/@rating > 3]
```

Notice that the selection inside of the square brackets did not start with / or //. This means that the selection starts from the *context node*, meaning the node immediately outside the square brackets.

What if you were searching for artists in a particular genre? (Remember that genre is an element rather than an attribute like rating.) Restrictions by element value look similar to restrictions by attribute value:

```
/cdcollection/artist[genre = 'Electronica']
```

That expression would return all `artist` elements containing at least one `genre` element with a value of `Electronica`.

It is also possible to combine expressions using Boolean operators. If I wanted to find all artist nodes in the `Electronica` genre that also have at least one CD with a rating higher than 3, I could use syntax like this:

```
/cdcollection/artist[genre = 'Electronica' and cd/@rating > 3]
```

If I wanted to find artists who were either in the `Electronica` genre *or* had a CD rated higher than 3, I could use an `or` search like this:

```
/cdcollection/artist[genre = 'Electronica' or cd/@rating > 3]
```

There is also a negation operator; if I wanted to find artists in the `Electronica` genre but who do *not* have any CDs rated higher than 3, I could use syntax like this:

```
/cdcollection/artist[genre = 'Electronica' and not(cd/@rating > 3)]
```

Using `XmlSearch()` to Retrieve an Array of Nodes

Given the CD collection shown in Listing 42.1, how would I find all of the artist recommendation nodes? I could use ColdFusion to loop through the artist nodes, and then find each artist's recommendation nodes; or I could use `XmlSearch()` to run an XPath search, as in Listing 42.2.

Listing 42.2 `FindArtistRecommendations.cfm`—Using XPath to Search the CD Collection

```
<cffile action="READ"
  file="#ExpandPath('CDCollection.xml')#"
  variable="xmlDocument">

<cfset xmlObject = XmlParse(xmlDocument)>
<cfset results = XmlSearch(xmlObject, "/cdcollection/artist/recommend")>

<cfdump var="#results#">
```

The ColdFusion function `XmlSearch()` takes the XPath string (in this case `/cdcollection/artist/recommend`) and returns an array of XML elements, as shown in Figure 42.1.

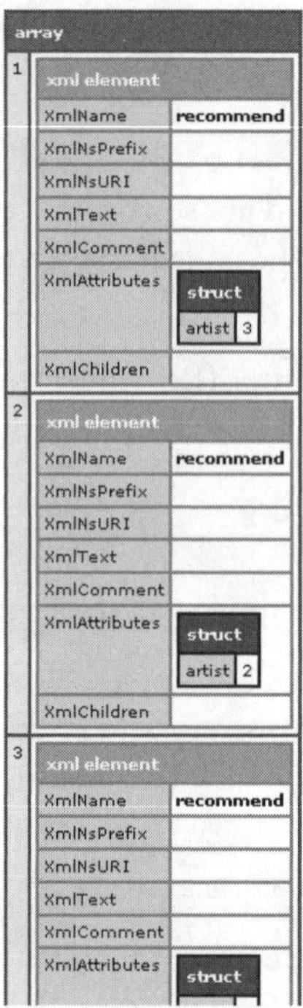

Figure 42.1
The result of an XPath search using `XmlSearch()`.

Each element in the array represents one of the elements found by the XPath search.

Your knowledge of XPath can also be used with the ColdFusion tag, `CFSPRYDATASET`, which through its optional `XPATH` attribute allows you to extract data when processing XML data. For more information, see the Adobe *CFML Reference* manual.

There's much more you can learn about XPath. If you want to delve further, see "More XPath and XSLT Resources" at the end of this chapter.

Transforming XML into Content by Using XSLT

CFML is an excellent tool for transforming content from a relational database into HTML, XML, or almost any form of content markup due to its native support for looping over a query set. However, this is less so when the source data is XML itself. . ColdFusion can certainly loop over data in an XML object, and can search for data using `XmlSearch()`, but there is a much better solution for transforming XML into other forms of content.

Extensible Stylesheet Language for Transformations (XSLT) was created by the W3C in 1998 as a way to easily define a transformation from an XML document to some other content format. Using XSLT, I could transform a document like Listing 42.1 into the HTML table shown in Figure 42.2 using a simple stylesheet.

Figure 42.2
HTML table.

Artist/CD Name	Rating (for CDs)	Recommendations
Air Electronic		
10,000 Hz Legend	Like It	• Talkie Walkie
Talkie Walkie	Love It	• 10,000 Hz Legend • You Won't Forget About Me EP
Kylie Minogue Dance		• Dannii Minogue
Fever	Like It	• Body Language
Body Language	Love It	• Neon Nights
Dannii Minogue Dance, Electronic		• Kylie Minogue
Neon Nights	Favorite!	• Body Language
You Won't Forget About Me EP	Favorite!	• Neon Nights
Brooklyn Funk Essentials New Artist! Funk, Dance, Spoken Word		• Air • Felix Da Housecat
Cool & Steady & Easy	Favorite!	• Body Language • Neon Nights
Felix Da Housecat Electronica, Dance, Retro		• Kylie Minogue • Brooklyn Funk Essentials
A Bugged Out Mix	Like It	• Body Language • You Won't Forget About Me EP • Kittenz and Thee Glitz
Kittenz and Thee Glitz	Favorite!	
Devin Dazzle & The Neon Fever	Favorite!	• Kittenz and Thee Glitz

We will build the stylesheet that creates this table throughout the chapter. If you want to take a look at the stylesheet that created Figure 42.2, look at Listing 42.11 near the end of the chapter.

Creating a Basic Transformation

Before we can build a complex listing of artists, CDs, ratings, and recommendations, let's start with a simple nested bulleted list of artists and CDs. The list will display each artist's name in bold, followed by a bulleted list of the artist's genres and a separate list of the artist's CDs. Listing 42.3 shows an XSL stylesheet that gives us this information.

Listing 42.3 `BasicTransformation.xsl`—An XSLT Stylesheet to Create a Listing of Artists and CDs

```
<xsl:transform
  version="1.0"
  xmlns:xsl="http://www.w3.org/1999/XSL/Transform">
```

Listing 42.3 (CONTINUED)

```
   <xsl:output omit-xml-declaration="yes" />

   <xsl:template match="/cdcollection">
     <ul>
       <xsl:apply-templates />
     </ul>
   </xsl:template>

   <xsl:template match="/cdcollection/artist">
     <li>
       <b><xsl:value-of select="@name" /></b>
       <br />

       Genre:
       <ul>
         <xsl:apply-templates select="genre" />
       </ul>

       CDs:
       <ul>
         <xsl:apply-templates select="cd" />
       </ul>
     </li>
   </xsl:template>

   <xsl:template match="/cdcollection/artist/genre">
     <li><xsl:value-of select="." /></li>
   </xsl:template>

   <xsl:template match="/cdcollection/artist/cd">
     <li><xsl:value-of select="@name" /></li>
   </xsl:template>

 </xsl:transform>
```

Running that transformation (see "Performing the Transformation by Using `XmlTransform()`" later in the chapter) produces the HTML in Listing 42.4.

Listing 42.4 `ArtistsAndCDs.htm`—A Simple Listing of Artists and CDs

```
<ul>
  <li>
    <b>Air</b><br/>
    Genre:
    <ul>
      <li>Electronic</li>
    </ul>
    CDs:
    <ul>
      <li>10,000 Hz Legend</li>
      <li>Talkie Walkie</li>
    </ul>
  </li>
  <li>
    <b>Kylie Minogue</b><br/>
```

Listing 42.4 (continued)

```
      Genre:
      <ul>
        <li>Dance</li>
      </ul>
      CDs:
      <ul>
        <li>Fever</li>
        <li>Body Language</li>
      </ul>
    </li>
    <li>
      <b>Dannii Minogue</b><br/>
      Genre:
      <ul>
        <li>Dance</li>
        <li>Electronic</li>
      </ul>
      CDs:
      <ul>
        <li>Neon Nights</li>
        <li>You Won't Forget About Me EP</li>
      </ul>
    </li>
    <li>
      <b>Brooklyn Funk Essentials</b><br/>
      Genre:
      <ul>
        <li>Funk</li>
        <li>Dance</li>
        <li>Spoken Word</li>
      </ul>
      CDs:
      <ul>
        <li>Cool &amp; Steady &amp; Easy</li>
      </ul>
    </li>
    <li>
      <b>Felix Da Housecat</b><br/>
      Genre:
      <ul>
        <li>Electronica</li>
        <li>Dance</li>
        <li>Retro</li>
      </ul>
      CDs:
      <ul>
        <li>A Bugged Out Mix</li>
        <li>Kittenz and Thee Glitz</li>
        <li>Devin Dazzle &amp; The Neon Fever</li>
      </ul>
    </li>
  </ul>
```

Don't be overwhelmed by the stylesheet. It may seem completely foreign, so let's break it down bit by bit.

<xsl:transform>

XSL stylesheets are well-formed XML documents that use a specific set of tags to tell the XSL processor how to run the transformation. All transformation stylesheets use <xsl:transform> as their root element. (You may sometimes see <xsl:stylesheet> used instead of <xsl:transform>; they are interchangeable in most cases.)

The version attribute of <xsl:transform> specifies the version of the XSL standard that will be used to process the stylesheet, and the xmlns:xsl attribute identifies the namespace that contains the XSL tags. By and large, the transformations you create will always use the same values for these attributes as you see in Listing 42.3.

<xsl:output>

The first tag inside <xsl:transform> in Listing 42.3 is an <xsl:output> tag, which in this case tells the XSL processor not to output the XML declaration in the resulting HTML. If this <xsl:output> were not present, the resulting HTML file would have as its first line

```
<?xml version="1.0" encoding="UTF-8"?>
```

which is not valid in an HTML document. There are nine other attributes of <xsl:output> that let you specify other behaviors of the output engine; these are summarized in Table 42.1.

By far the most commonly used attribute of <xsl:output> is omit-xml-declaration.

<xsl:template> and <xsl:apply-templates>

After specifying the output rules for the stylesheet by using <xsl:output>, we can now define the templates used to create the output content by using <xsl:template>.

There are four templates in this stylesheet, corresponding to the four elements we want to process. This is not to say that there will always be a one-to-one correspondence between templates and elements; in fact, there are usually only a few templates in a stylesheet compared to the number of elements present. In this first example, however, we want to keep things simple.

Here is the first <xsl:template> template:

```
<xsl:template match="/cdcollection">
  <ul>
    <xsl:apply-templates />
  </ul>
</xsl:template>
```

The first line of the template is the opening <xsl:template> tag, containing a single match attribute. match tells the XSL processor which nodes in the source document this template processes; in this case, this template handles cdcollection nodes located immediately under the document root.

Inside the template is a <ul> element with an <xsl:apply-templates> tag in between its opening and closing tag. <xsl:apply-templates> tells the XSL processor to start looping through the children of the current cdcollection node and to start applying XSL templates to each one.

One of the hardest things for beginning XSL programmers to grasp is exactly how an XSL processor uses the stylesheet. The conception that many have is that the stylesheet tells the processor in which order to process nodes in the XML document. However, the reverse is true. The XSL processor loops over nodes in the XML document, and for each one, attempts to find a template in the stylesheet that matches the current node. Once it finds the template, it calls the template almost as if the template were a function. It's more of an event-driven model than a procedural one.

<xsl:value-of>

So once the XSL processor sees the `<xsl:apply-templates>` in the `/cdcollection` template, the processor loops over all the children of the `cdcollection` node. When it sees that the child node is an `artist` node, it looks for a template that matches and finds this one:

```
<xsl:template match="/cdcollection/artist">
  <li>
    <b><xsl:value-of select="@name" /></b>
    <br />

    Genre:
    <ul>
      <xsl:apply-templates select="genre" />
    </ul>

    CDs:
    <ul>
      <xsl:apply-templates select="cd" />
    </ul>
  </li>
</xsl:template>
```

For each artist node, the XSL processor outputs an opening `<li>` tag, then puts out the artist's name in bold by using `<xsl:value-of>`, which is another XSL tag. Its select attribute takes an XPath expression and outputs the returned value, which in this case is the name of the current artist.

<xsl:apply-templates> Revisited

After outputting the name of the artist by using `<xsl:value-of>`, the artist template generates the lists of genres and CDs for the artist. Unlike the previous use of `<xsl:apply-templates>`, we are no longer indiscriminately looping over all child nodes. Rather, we are using the select attribute of `<xsl:apply-templates>` to selectively loop over only certain children (`select` works the same way for both `<xsl:value-of>` and `<xsl:apply-templates>`; in both cases `select` specifies an XPath expression that works from the current node).

<xsl:value-of>

That covers elements within three of the four templates shown in Listing 42.3. The only thing remaining to be explained is `<xsl:value-of>` in the `genre` template:

```
<xsl:value-of select="." />
```

The period is an XPath expression meaning "current node." Getting the value of the current node returns the content between the opening and closing tags; thus, `<xsl:value-of>` means to output whatever the current genre is.

Performing the Transformation by Using `XmlTransform()`

An XSL stylesheet by itself does nothing. In order to transform the input XML according to the stylesheet, you must use ColdFusion to run the transformation as shown in Listing 42.5.

Listing 42.5 `TransformArtistAndCDList.cfm`—Transforming XML Content Using XSL

```
<cffile action="READ"
  file="#ExpandPath('CDCollection.xml')#"
  variable="xmlDocument">

<cfset transformedContent = XmlTransform(xmlDocument, "BasicTransformation.xsl")>

<cffile action="WRITE"
  file="#ExpandPath('ArtistsAndCDs.htm')#"
  output="#transformedContent#">

Finished transforming content!
```

The `XmlTransform()` function applies the specified stylesheet to the passed-in XML document and returns the generated output as a string. In Listing 42.5 we are writing it to a file, but you could just as easily output it to the screen, return it from a CFC method call, or use it in some other way.

The XSL file argument can be either a relative or absolute file path. It can also be an XSL stylesheet stored in a string or a URL to a file, where valid protocol identifiers include `http`, `https`, `ftp`, and `file`.

Ignoring Nodes in the Hierarchy

So far we've been able to completely ignore the recommend nodes in the XML document by simply never including them in the select attributes that retrieve sets of nodes. But what if we wanted to skip elements in the document hierarchy (for instance, what if we wanted to show a list of CDs without showing artists at all)? Listing 42.6 shows a stylesheet that does just that.

Listing 42.6 `CDList.xsl`—A Stylesheet That Bypasses Artist Information

```
<xsl:transform
  version="1.0"
  xmlns:xsl="http://www.w3.org/1999/XSL/Transform">

  <xsl:output omit-xml-declaration="yes" />

  <xsl:template match="/cdcollection">
    <ul>
      <xsl:apply-templates select="//cd" />
    </ul>
  </xsl:template>

  <xsl:template match="/cdcollection/artist/cd">
    <li><xsl:value-of select="@name" /></li>
  </xsl:template>

</xsl:transform>
```

All we have to do is create a template for the root node, then use XPath to find all `cd` nodes in the file and output each one using the separately defined template.

NOTE

Why did we create a match for the root node of the file? One of the lesser-known caveats of XSL development is that if you don't include a root node, the XSL processor will output the value of every element it comes across until it finds the first match. This means that you run the risk of having errant text pop up if you don't always include a match for the root node.

Creating a More Complex Transformation

So now that we've created a few simple transformations, let's tackle the complex listing seen at the beginning of the chapter.

`<xsl:if>`

Although XSL is not a programming language in the traditional sense, it does have some of the standard flow control constructs present in other languages. The first of these is `<xsl:if>`, as demonstrated in Listing 42.7.

Listing 42.7 `IfInATransformation.xsl`—Using `<xsl:if>`

```
<xsl:transform
  version="1.0"
  xmlns:xsl="http://www.w3.org/1999/XSL/Transform">

  <xsl:output omit-xml-declaration="yes" />

  <xsl:template match="/cdcollection">
    <style>
      td {
        vertical-align: top;
      }
    </style>

    <table cellspacing="0">
      <tr>
        <th>Artist/CD Name</th>
      </tr>
      <xsl:apply-templates />
    </table>
  </xsl:template>

  <xsl:template match="/cdcollection/artist">
    <tr>
      <td>
        <b><xsl:value-of select="@name" /></b>
        <xsl:if test="count(cd) = 1">
          <br /><span style="color: red;">New Artist!</span>
        </xsl:if>
      </td>
    </tr>
    <xsl:apply-templates select="cd" />
    <tr>
```

Listing 42.7 (CONTINUED)

```
      <td><hr /></td>
    </tr>
  </xsl:template>

  <xsl:template match="/cdcollection/artist/cd">
    <tr>
      <td><xsl:value-of select="@name" /></td>
    </tr>
  </xsl:template>

</xsl:transform>
```

In Listing 42.7, we use `<xsl:if>` to output a block of text that says "New Artist" if the artist only has one CD in the collection. `count()` is an XPath function that counts the number of nodes that match the given expression.

It is worth noting that XSL does not have an else construct like `CFELSE` or the `else` keyword in other languages. One alternative is to use syntax like this:

```
<xsl:if test="count(cd) = 1">
  ... code goes here ...
</xsl:if>
<xsl:if test="not(count(cd) = 1)">
  ... other code goes here ...
</xsl:if>
```

The alternative is to use `<xsl:choose>` and `<xsl:otherwise>` as described in the next section.

`<xsl:choose>`, `<xsl:when>`, and `<xsl:otherwise>`

The second XSL flow control construct is almost like the equivalent of `CFSWITCH`. In Listing 42.8, we use `<xsl:choose>`, `<xsl:when>`, and `<xsl:otherwise>` to convert the numeric rating into a user-friendly text string.

Listing 42.8 `ChooseInATransformation.xsl`—Using `<xsl:choose>`

```
<xsl:transform
  version="1.0"
  xmlns:xsl="http://www.w3.org/1999/XSL/Transform">

  <xsl:output omit-xml-declaration="yes" />

  <xsl:template match="/cdcollection">
    <style>
      td {
        vertical-align: top;
      }
    </style>

    <table cellspacing="0">
      <tr>
        <th>Artist/CD Name</th>
        <th>Rating (for CDs)</th>
      </tr>
      <xsl:apply-templates />
```

Listing 42.8 (CONTINUED)

```
    </table>
  </xsl:template>

  <xsl:template match="/cdcollection/artist">
    <tr>
      <td colspan="2">
        <b><xsl:value-of select="@name" /></b>
        <xsl:if test="count(cd) = 1">
          <br /><span style="color: red;">New Artist!</span>
        </xsl:if>
      </td>
    </tr>
    <xsl:apply-templates select="/cdcollection/artist/cd" />
    <tr>
      <td colspan="2"><hr /></td>
    </tr>
  </xsl:template>

  <xsl:template match="cd">
    <tr>
      <td><xsl:value-of select="@name" /></td>
      <td>
        <xsl:choose>
          <xsl:when test="@rating = 1">It's OK</xsl:when>
          <xsl:when test="@rating = 2">Decent</xsl:when>
          <xsl:when test="@rating = 3">Like It</xsl:when>
          <xsl:when test="@rating = 4">Love It</xsl:when>
          <xsl:when test="@rating = 5">Favorite!</xsl:when>
          <xsl:otherwise>Unknown</xsl:otherwise>
        </xsl:choose>
      </td>
    </tr>
  </xsl:template>

</xsl:transform>
```

The major difference between `<xsl:choose>` and switch constructs in other languages is that XSL evaluates each condition separately—for instance, a set of `elseif` statements—making `<xsl:choose>` more flexible (but also slower) than switch constructs in other languages.

`<xsl:for-each>` and `<xsl:text>`

The last of the flow control constructs in XSL is the loop construct, `<xsl:for-each>`. Where `<xsl:apply-templates>` tells the XSL processor to loop over child nodes and find a matching template for each one, `<xsl:for-each>` gives a specific action to be taken for each node.

In Listing 42.9, I am using `<xsl:for-each>` to put out the list of genres in which each artist performs.

Listing 42.9 `LoopInATransformation.xsl`—Using `<xsl:for-each>`

```
<xsl:transform
  version="1.0"
  xmlns:xsl="http://www.w3.org/1999/XSL/Transform">
```

Listing 42.9 (continued)

```
    <xsl:output omit-xml-declaration="yes" />

    <xsl:template match="/cdcollection">
      <style>
        td {
          vertical-align: top;
        }
      </style>

      <table cellspacing="0">
        <tr>
          <th>Artist/CD Name</th>
          <th>Rating (for CDs)</th>
        </tr>
        <xsl:apply-templates />
      </table>
    </xsl:template>

    <xsl:template match="/cdcollection/artist">
      <tr>
        <td colspan="2">
          <b><xsl:value-of select="@name" /></b><br />
          <xsl:if test="count(cd) = 1">
            <span style="color: red;">New Artist!</span><br />
          </xsl:if>
          <xsl:for-each select="genre">
            <xsl:value-of select="." />
            <xsl:if test="position() &lt; last()">
              <xsl:text>, </xsl:text>
            </xsl:if>
          </xsl:for-each>
        </td>
      </tr>
      <xsl:apply-templates select="cd" />
      <tr>
        <td colspan="2"><hr /></td>
      </tr>
    </xsl:template>

    <xsl:template match="/cdcollection/artist/cd">
      <tr>
        <td><xsl:value-of select="@name" /></td>
        <td>
          <xsl:choose>
            <xsl:when test="@rating = 1">It's OK</xsl:when>
            <xsl:when test="@rating = 2">Decent</xsl:when>
            <xsl:when test="@rating = 3">Like It</xsl:when>
            <xsl:when test="@rating = 4">Love It</xsl:when>
            <xsl:when test="@rating = 5">Favorite!</xsl:when>
            <xsl:otherwise>Unknown</xsl:otherwise>
          </xsl:choose>
        </td>
      </tr>
    </xsl:template>

  </xsl:transform>
```

There are several new concepts in the <xsl:for-each> loop above, so let's break it down line by line.

The first line is the <xsl:for-each> loop, and the `select` attribute works exactly like the `select` attribute of <xsl:apply-templates>.

You're familiar with <xsl:value-of> by now, but there's something peculiar about the <xsl:if> test. What we're doing is putting out a comma only if the current node is not the last genre in the selected set. `position()` and `last()` are XPath functions that return the position of the current node and last node in the current set, respectively.

However, the `<` seems out of place. In any other language, we would just say:

```
position() < last()
```

But remember that an XSL stylesheet is just another XML document. That means it must be well formed, so special characters must be escaped. As such, we must replace the < with `<`.

Finally, let's turn our attention to the <xsl:text> element. Unfortunately, XSL can be very sloppy with whitespace, but there are times when we want to include literal whitespace or other text within a stylesheet, and embedding text within an <xsl:text> does just that.

<xsl:element> and <xsl:attribute>

Now that we've covered flow control in XSL, it's time for one of the most difficult concepts for many programmers to master. I want to surround the names of artists and CDs in my list with a link to another ColdFusion page, such that in the output stream I get markup like

```
<a href="ArtistDetail.cfm?id=1">10,000 Hz Legend</a>
```

Most developers' first instinct would be something like the following:

```
<xsl:template match="/cdcollection/artist">
  <a href="ArtistDetail.cfm?id=<xsl:value-of select="@id" />"><xsl:value-of select="@
name" /></a>
</xsl:template>
```

This is much like what would be done in ColdFusion, but it is not valid in XSL because the markup is not valid XML. It would seem that we are out of luck, but XSL provides the <xsl:element> and <xsl:attribute> tags to do just what we're trying to do, as shown in Listing 42.10.

Listing 42.10 `DynamicElements.xsl`—Using <xsl:element> to Create Dynamic HTML Elements

```
<xsl:transform
 version="1.0"
 xmlns:xsl="http://www.w3.org/1999/XSL/Transform">

 <xsl:output omit-xml-declaration="yes" />

 <xsl:template match="/cdcollection">
   <style>
     td {
       vertical-align: top;
     }
```

Listing 42.10 (CONTINUED)

```
    </style>

    <table cellspacing="0">
      <tr>
        <th>Artist/CD Name</th>
        <th>Rating (for CDs)</th>
      </tr>
      <xsl:apply-templates />
    </table>
  </xsl:template>

  <xsl:template match="/cdcollection/artist">
    <tr>
      <td colspan="2">
        <b>
          <xsl:element name="a">
            <xsl:attribute name="href">
              <xsl:text>ArtistDetail.cfm?id=</xsl:text>
              <xsl:value-of select="@id" />
            </xsl:attribute>
            <xsl:value-of select="@name" />
          </xsl:element>
        </b><br />
        <xsl:if test="count(cd) = 1">
          <span style="color: red;">New Artist!</span><br />
        </xsl:if>
        <xsl:for-each select="genre">
          <xsl:value-of select="." />
          <xsl:if test="position() &lt; last()">
            <xsl:text>, </xsl:text>
          </xsl:if>
        </xsl:for-each>
      </td>
    </tr>
    <xsl:apply-templates select="cd" />
    <tr>
      <td colspan="2"><hr /></td>
    </tr>
  </xsl:template>
  <xsl:template match="/cdcollection/artist/cd">
    <tr>
      <td>
        <xsl:element name="a">
          <xsl:attribute name="href">
            <xsl:text>CDDetail.cfm?id=</xsl:text>
            <xsl:value-of select="@id" />
          </xsl:attribute>
          <xsl:value-of select="@name" />
        </xsl:element>
      </td>
      <td>
        <xsl:choose>
          <xsl:when test="@rating = 1">It's OK</xsl:when>
          <xsl:when test="@rating = 2">Decent</xsl:when>
          <xsl:when test="@rating = 3">Like It</xsl:when>
          <xsl:when test="@rating = 4">Love It</xsl:when>
          <xsl:when test="@rating = 5">Favorite!</xsl:when>
```

Listing 42.10 (continued)

```
            <xsl:otherwise>Unknown</xsl:otherwise>
          </xsl:choose>
        </td>
      </tr>
    </xsl:template>

</xsl:transform>
```

Because the two sections containing `<xsl:element>` are so similar, let's just dissect the first one:

```
<xsl:element name="a">
  <xsl:attribute name="href">
    <xsl:text>ArtistDetail.cfm?id=</xsl:text>
    <xsl:value-of select="@id" />
  </xsl:attribute>
  <xsl:value-of select="@name" />
</xsl:element>
```

Here I am creating an `<a>` element with a single `href` attribute. I can break the attribute value across multiple lines because `<xsl:text>` ensures that the only whitespace in the attribute is what's inside of the `<xsl:text>` block.

Using Named Templates

Now we finally come to displaying artist and CD recommendations. Basically, we want to display the name of the recommended artists and/or CDs next to each artist and/or CD that has `recommend` nodes in the source document. This means that we need a way to look up an artist's or CD's name given its ID. In most languages, you'd create a function to do this work for you, but remember that XSL for the most part does not have the concept of a "function."

However, XSL does have templates. Until now, all of our templates have used the `match` attribute to specify that they be called automatically for certain nodes in the input XML document:

```
<xsl:template match="/cdcollection/artist/cd">
...
</xsl:template>
```

There is also, however, a name attribute used to specify that a given template is programmatically called from within another template:

```
<xsl:template name="MyTemplateName">
...
</xsl:template>
```

This second form of `<xsl:template>` can be called using the `<xsl:call-template>` tag:

```
<xsl:call-template name="MyTemplateName" />
```

The real beauty of named templates, however, is the ability to pass parameters. To define a parameter in the named template, you use the `<xsl:param>` tag:

```
<xsl:template name="MyTemplateName">
  <xsl:param name="MyParamName" />
  ...
</xsl:template>
```

And to pass the parameter in the template call, you use the `<xsl:with-param>` tag:

```
<xsl:call-template name="MyTemplateName">
  <xsl:with-param name="MyParamName" select="XPathExpression" />
</xsl:call-template>
```

So coming back to the main Artist/CD Listing transformation, Listing 42.11 shows the complete transformation with all the new features present.

Listing 42.11 `CompleteTransformation.xsl`—A Complete Listing of Artists, CDs, and Recommendations

```
<xsl:transform
  version="1.0"
  xmlns:xsl="http://www.w3.org/1999/XSL/Transform">

  <xsl:output omit-xml-declaration="yes" />

  <xsl:template match="/cdcollection">
    <style>
      td {
        vertical-align: top;
      }
    </style>

    <table cellspacing="0">
      <tr>
        <th>Artist/CD Name</th>
        <th>Rating (for CDs)</th>
        <th>Recommendations</th>
      </tr>
      <xsl:apply-templates />
    </table>
  </xsl:template>

  <xsl:template match="/cdcollection/artist">
    <tr>
      <td colspan="2">
        <b>
          <xsl:element name="a">
            <xsl:attribute name="href">
              <xsl:text>ArtistDetail.cfm?id=</xsl:text>
              <xsl:value-of select="@id" />
            </xsl:attribute>
            <xsl:value-of select="@name" />
          </xsl:element>
        </b><br />
        <xsl:if test="count(cd) = 1">
          <span style="color: red;">New Artist!</span><br />
        </xsl:if>
        <xsl:for-each select="genre">
          <xsl:value-of select="." />
          <xsl:if test="position() &lt; last()">
            <xsl:text>, </xsl:text>
          </xsl:if>
        </xsl:for-each>
      </td>
```

Listing 42.11 (continued)

```
        <td>
          <xsl:if test="count(recommend)">
            <ul>
              <xsl:for-each select="recommend">
                <li>
                  <xsl:call-template name="FindArtistName">
                    <xsl:with-param name="id" select="@artist" />
                  </xsl:call-template>
                </li>
              </xsl:for-each>
            </ul>
          </xsl:if>
        </td>
      </tr>
      <xsl:apply-templates select="cd" />
      <tr>
        <td colspan="3"><hr /></td>
      </tr>
    </xsl:template>

    <xsl:template match="/cdcollection/artist/cd">
      <tr>
        <td>
          <xsl:element name="a">
            <xsl:attribute name="href">
              <xsl:text>CDDetail.cfm?id=</xsl:text>
              <xsl:value-of select="@id" />
            </xsl:attribute>
            <xsl:value-of select="@name" />
          </xsl:element>
        </td>
        <td>
          <xsl:choose>
            <xsl:when test="@rating = 1">It's OK</xsl:when>
            <xsl:when test="@rating = 2">Decent</xsl:when>
            <xsl:when test="@rating = 3">Like It</xsl:when>
            <xsl:when test="@rating = 4">Love It</xsl:when>
            <xsl:when test="@rating = 5">Favorite!</xsl:when>
            <xsl:otherwise>Unknown</xsl:otherwise>
          </xsl:choose>
        </td>
        <td>
          <xsl:if test="count(recommend)">
            <ul>
              <xsl:for-each select="recommend">
                <li>
                  <xsl:call-template name="FindCDName">
                    <xsl:with-param name="id" select="@cd" />
                  </xsl:call-template>
                </li>
              </xsl:for-each>
            </ul>
          </xsl:if>
        </td>
      </tr>
    </xsl:template>
```

Listing 42.11 (continued)

```
  <xsl:template name="FindArtistName">
    <xsl:param name="id" />

    <xsl:value-of select="//artist[@id = $id]/@name" />
  </xsl:template>

  <xsl:template name="FindCDName">
    <xsl:param name="id" />

    <xsl:value-of select="//cd[@id = $id]/@name" />
  </xsl:template>

</xsl:transform>
```

In the main templates for `cd` and `artist`, I loop over the `recommend` nodes (if they exist) using `<xsl:for-each>`, and for each one, I call the `FindArtistName` or `FindCDName` template, passing in the `artist` or `cd` attribute. Notice that inside the named templates, I reference the parameter value by using `$id`. `$` is an XPath prefix that means "parameter" or "variable."

Listing 42.12 shows the HTML markup generated by `CompleteTransformation.xsl`. To generate this file, run `TransformComplexList.cfm`, which is included in the sample code for this chapter. Note that I have cleaned up the markup to make it easier to read; this in no way affects the displayed content.

Listing 42.12 `CompleteArtistsAndCDs.htm`—The Output of the Final Transformation

```
<style>
  td {
    vertical-align: top;
  }
</style>

<table cellspacing="0">
<tr>
  <th>Artist/CD Name</th>
<th>Rating (for CDs)</th>
  <th>Recommendations</th>
</tr>
<tr>
  <td colspan="2">
    <b><a href="ArtistDetail.cfm?id=1">Air</a></b><br/>
    Electronic
  </td>
  <td/>
</tr>
<tr>
  <td><a href="CDDetail.cfm?id=1">10,000 Hz Legend</a></td>
  <td>Like It</td>
  <td>
    <ul>
      <li>Talkie Walkie</li>
    </ul>
  </td>
</tr>
```

Listing 42.12 (continued)

```
<tr>
  <td><a href="CDDetail.cfm?id=2">Talkie Walkie</a></td>
  <td>Love It</td>
  <td>
    <ul>
      <li>10,000 Hz Legend</li>
      <li>You Won't Forget About Me EP</li>
    </ul>
  </td>
</tr>
<tr><td colspan="3"><hr/></td></tr>
<tr>
  <td colspan="2">
    <b><a href="ArtistDetail.cfm?id=2">Kylie Minogue</a></b><br/>
    Dance
  </td>
  <td>
    <ul>
      <li>Dannii Minogue</li>
    </ul>
  </td>
</tr>
<tr>
  <td><a href="CDDetail.cfm?id=3">Fever</a></td>
  <td>Like It</td>
  <td>
    <ul>
      <li>Body Language</li>
    </ul>
  </td>
</tr>
<tr>
  <td><a href="CDDetail.cfm?id=4">Body Language</a></td>
  <td>Love It</td>
  <td>
    <ul>
      <li>Neon Nights</li>
    </ul>
  </td>
</tr>
<tr><td colspan="3"><hr/></td></tr>
<tr>
  <td colspan="2">
    <b><a href="ArtistDetail.cfm?id=3">Dannii Minogue</a></b><br/>
    Dance, Electronic
  </td>
  <td>
    <ul>
      <li>Kylie Minogue</li>
    </ul>
  </td>
</tr>
<tr>
  <td><a href="CDDetail.cfm?id=5">Neon Nights</a></td>
  <td>Favorite!</td>
  <td>
```

Listing 42.12 (continued)

```
        <ul>
          <li>Body Language</li>
        </ul>
      </td>
    </tr>
    <tr>
      <td><a href="CDDetail.cfm?id=6">You Won't Forget About Me EP</a></td>
      <td>Favorite!</td>
      <td>
        <ul>
          <li>Neon Nights</li>
        </ul>
      </td>
    </tr>
    <tr><td colspan="3"><hr/></td></tr>
    <tr>
      <td colspan="2">
        <b><a href="ArtistDetail.cfm?id=4">Brooklyn Funk Essentials</a></b><br/>
        <span style="color: red;">New Artist!</span><br/>
        Funk, Dance, Spoken Word
      </td>
      <td>
        <ul>
          <li>Air</li>
          <li>Felix Da Housecat</li>
        </ul>
      </td>
    </tr>
    <tr>
      <td><a href="CDDetail.cfm?id=7">Cool &amp; Steady &amp; Easy</a></td>
      <td>Favorite!</td>
      <td>
        <ul>
          <li>Body Language</li>
          <li>Neon Nights</li>
        </ul>
      </td>
    </tr>
    <tr><td colspan="3"><hr/></td></tr>
    <tr>
      <td colspan="2">
        <b><a href="ArtistDetail.cfm?id=5">Felix Da Housecat</a></b><br/>
        Electronica, Dance, Retro
      </td>
      <td>
        <ul>
          <li>Kylie Minogue</li>
          <li>Brooklyn Funk Essentials</li>
        </ul>
      </td>
    </tr>
    <tr>
      <td><a href="CDDetail.cfm?id=8">A Bugged Out Mix</a></td>
      <td>Like It</td>
      <td>
        <ul>
```

Listing 42.12 (continued)

```
        <li>Body Language</li>
        <li>You Won't Forget About Me EP</li>
        <li>Kittenz and Thee Glitz</li>
      </ul>
    </td>
  </tr>
  <tr>
    <td><a href="CDDetail.cfm?id=9">Kittenz and Thee Glitz</a></td>
    <td>Favorite!</td>
    <td/>
  </tr>
  <tr>
    <td><a href="CDDetail.cfm?id=10">Devin Dazzle &amp; The Neon Fever</a></td>
    <td>Favorite!</td>
    <td>
      <ul>
        <li>Kittenz and Thee Glitz</li>
      </ul>
    </td>
  </tr>
  <tr><td colspan="3"><hr/></td></tr>
  </table>
```

Take some time to compare Listings 42.11 and 42.12 to see how the XSL stylesheet generated the HTML markup. Also compare these listings to Figure 42.2 to see how it all fits together.

NOTE

You can also pass XSLT parameter values on the `XmlTransform()` function itself, using an optional third argument. In this way, you can name a structure created to hold keys whose names are mapped to the XSLT parameters in the XSL file. For more information, see the Adobe *CFML Reference* manual.

Note that ColdFusion XML forms, generating XForms-compliant XML, are normally formatted using an XSLT skin. You can use XML forms with skins that ColdFusion provides or use the knowledge you've learned in this chapter to customize them.

More XPath and XSLT Resources

This chapter only scratched the surface of the many things you can do with XSLT and XPath. For more information, check out these sites.

- `http://www.w3c.org/TR/xpath` is the W3C's working specification for XPath. This document is not for the faint of heart, but it is the definitive standard on XPath syntax and operation.
- `http://www.w3schools.com/xsl/` is a site offering basic and advanced topics as well as examples and references for working with XSL. The parent site is dedicated to offering free tutorials about Web standard technologies.
- `http://www.zvon.org/xxl/XPathTutorial/General/examples.html` is the XPath Tutorial at `www.zvon.org`. It's very much like an immersion course in XPath, so it's easy to feel lost at first, but there is some excellent information here.

- `http://www.w3.org/TR/xslt` is the W3C's working specification for XSLT. This document is a very scientific document and is not recommended for beginners. However, for those looking for a deep understanding of how XSLT works, this is just the place to go.
- `http://www.zvon.org/xxl/XSLTutorial/Output/index.html` is the XSLT tutorial at `www.zvon.org`. This is an excellent starting point for people who want an easy introduction to the world of practical XSLT.
- `http://www.zvon.org/xxl/XSLTreference/Output/index.html` is the XSLT/XPath reference at `www.zvon.org`. This is an indispensable tool for anyone developing XSLT stylesheets.

INDEX

D

E

Q

R

S

T